READINGS IN MANAGEMENT

MAX D. RICHARDS

Distinguished Professor of Management
The Roy E. Crummer
Graduate School of Business
Rollins College
Winter Park, Florida

Published by

G99

SOUTH-WESTERN PUBLISHING CO.

NCINNATI   WEST CHICAGO, IL   DALLAS   PELHAM MANOR, NY   LIVERMORE, CA

ISBN: 0-538-07990-8

Library of Congress Catalog Card Number: 85-71773

1 2 3 4 5 6 7 8 9 D 4 3 2 1 0 9 8 7 6

Printed in the United States of America

Preface

As with previous editions of this book, the problems of developing a new edition are challenging, yet they differ from those of previous versions. One is confronted with the question of whether a new development is fundamental, or a passing fancy, or a minor variant of an already existing framework. In the previous two editions, for example, conditional or situational theories of management were much in evidence, while today that type of development has subsided or at least has been encapsulated naturally into everyday management thinking. The Japanese management or quality circle ideas have, in fact, received quite a bit of attention as additions to or basic changes in our way of thinking about management. Thus papers from these and other new thrusts in management thought have been incorporated here.

Progress in management thought is, hopefully, represented in the new articles selected for this edition. At the same time, the stability in our thinking is reinforced by placement of these new papers within the familiar framework of the management functions of planning, organizing, directing, controlling, and staffing. And as in previous editions, the first section of the book is devoted to those fundamental ideas useful to the executive in the performance of a wide range of managerial functions.

The editorial comments are presented to place some particular articles and groups of articles into perspective and to explain the rationale for their inclusion here. Of course, some previous articles have been replaced by new ones. Many of these new articles could serve us well for a long period of time, and some have already stood the test of time. I have avoided replacing papers just for the sake of change. Some have been retained not only because of a lack of acceptable replacements but also because of their inherent ability to withstand attack from worthy challengers. Yet here, too, evolution is apparent: superior works have successfully attacked and superseded previous studies. These changes in the text also reflect the relative emphasis and deemphasis of certain broad areas of study in the totality of management thought.

Three persons deserve special recognition for their help and encouragement for this revision. First, Dean Martin Schatz very graciously encouraged the project and made available the resources and skills of the Crummer Graduate School of Business Administration of Rollins College. Professor R. William Millman of the Pennsylvania State University provided much assistance. As important has been the help of my wife, Ruth Sara Nixon Richards, as she dug through the libraries with me, copied, read manuscript and galleys, and kept me on the straight and narrow. I appreciate the help of these cohorts as well as the spirit of William A. Nielander, my original colleague in this journey into management thought. Each guides me, but the result is my own responsibility.

Max D. Richards
Winter Park, Florida

Contents

SECTION A FOUNDATIONS OF MANAGEMENT

CHAPTER 1   THE NATURE OF MANAGEMENT

Article   *Page*

1. The New Management Thinkers   3
   Modesto A. Maidique

2. Managerial Work: Analysis from Observation   13
   Henry Mintzberg

3. Theory Z: An Elaboration of Methodology and Findings.   30
   William G. Ouchi

   Bibliography   42

CHAPTER 2   VALUES AND SOCIAL ISSUES

4. Social Responsibility in Future Worlds.   45
   Derek C. Bok

5. The Four Faces of Social Responsibility   51
   Dan R. Dalton and *Richard A. Cosier*

6. The Challenge of the "New Breed"   64
   Stanley Peterfreund

   Bibliography   70

CHAPTER 3   SYSTEMS AND INFORMATION

7. The Parable of the Spindle.   73
   Elias H. Porter

8. A Framework for Management Information Systems   84
   G. Anthony Gorry and *Michael S. Scott Morton*

9. Communication and the Managerial Function: A Contingency
   Approach   100
   Richard C. Huseman and *Elmore R. Alexander III*

10. Listening Is Good Business   114
    Ralph G. Nichols

    Bibliography   129

CHAPTER 4   APPROACHES TO DECISIONS

11. A New Look at Managerial Decision Making   132
    Victor H. Vroom

12. The "Elite" Decision Makers: What Makes Them Tick?   149
    Charles H. Ford

13. Adaptors and Innovators—Why New Initiatives Get Blocked   159
       M.J. Kirton

14. Operational Techniques of Creative Thinking   171
       Charles S. Whiting

    Bibliography   182

CHAPTER 5   PERSPECTIVES ON DECISION MAKING

15. A Heretical View of Management Science   185
       Theodore Levitt

16. Treading Softly with Management Science   191
       Roger D. Eck

17. How Top Executives Think   199
       Kelly Costigan

    Bibliography   201

SECTION B   PLANNING

CHAPTER 6   GOALS AND PLANNING

18. Important Considerations in the Budgeting Process   205
       Steven D. Grossman and *Richard Lindhe*

19. Strategic Goals: Process and Politics   215
       James Brian Quinn

20. Criteria of Organizational Effectiveness   230
       Stanley E. Seashore

    Bibliography   236

CHAPTER 7   STRATEGY AND THE FUTURE

21. The Futility of Forecasting   238
       Reed Moyer

22. Playing by the Rules of the Corporate Strategy Game   251
       Walter Kiechel III

23. Socio-Political Forecasting: A New Dimension to Strategic
    Planning   257
       Ian H. Wilson

24. The Corporate Appraisal: Assessing Company Strengths and
    Weaknesses   269
       David E. Hussey

    Bibliography   281

SECTION C   CONTROLLING

CHAPTER 8   THE MEANING OF CONTROL

25. The Control Function of Management   285
       Kenneth A. Merchant

26.   The Poverty of Management Control Philosophy   302
        Geert Hofstede

      Bibliography   315

CHAPTER 9   MEASUREMENTS AND CONTROL

27.   The Meanings of Measurements   318
        Joseph W. Wilkinson

28.   A Technique for Measuring Management Productivity   325
        Frank Dewitt

29.   Implementing the Social Audit in an Organization   333
        Keith Davis and *Robert L. Blomstrom*

30.   Industrial Administration through the Eyes of an Investment
      Company.   340
        Erwin H. Schell

      Bibliography   347

SECTION D   DIRECTING

CHAPTER 10   MOTIVATION AND BEHAVIOR

31.   The Human Side of Enterprise   351
        Douglas Murray McGregor

32.   The Effective Use of Managerial Power   360
        Gary Yukl and *Tom Taber*

33.   That Urge to Achieve   367
        David C. McClelland

34.   Guidelines for Managing Motivation   376
        Curtis W. Cook

      Bibliography   385

CHAPTER 11   LEADERSHIP

35.   How to Choose a Leadership Pattern   388
        Robert Tannenbaum and *Warren H. Schmidt*

36.   Leadership in a Declining Work Ethic   400
        Ann Howard and *James A. Wilson*

37.   Leadership, Management, and the Seven Keys   420
        Craig M. Watson

      Bibliography   427

SECTION E   ORGANIZING

CHAPTER 12   ESTABLISHING STRUCTURE

38.   Designing the Innovating Organization.   431
        Jay R. Galbraith

39.   Teams Which Excel   455
        Patrick J. Sweeney and *Douglas M. Allen*

40. Organizing for Diversification.   462
     Jay W. Lorsch

41. Matrix Organization Designs   475
     Jay R. Galbraith

42. The Individualized Organization: Problems and Promise.   488
     Edward E. Lawler III

     Bibliography   499

CHAPTER 13   ORGANIZATION ANALYSIS AND CHANGE

43. Adaptation: A Key to Organizational Health.   502
     Thomas B. Lifson

44. Patterns of Organization Change.   510
     Larry E. Greiner

45. Organizational Structure: The Source of Low Productivity   524
     Gregory Hendrick

46. Managing the Internal Corporate Venturing Process   533
     Robert A. Burgelman

     Bibliography   553

SECTION F   STAFFING

CHAPTER 14   MANAGING MANAGERS

47. Manager, Manage Thyself!   558
     Sumer C. Aggarwal

48. Skills of an Effective Administrator.   566
     Robert L. Katz

49. Managing the Career Plateau   580
     Thomas P. Ference, James A.F. Stoner, and *E. Kirby Warren*

50. The Annual Performance Review Discussion—Making It
     Constructive.   592
     Herbert H. Meyer

     Bibliography   599

CHAPTER 15   DEVELOPING MANAGERS

51. Management Development as a Process of Influence   602
     Edgar H. Schein

52. How to Salvage Problem Executives   619
     Gail Gregg

53. Changing Supervisory and Managerial Behavior   627
     William C. Byham

     Bibliography   641

Section A
Foundations of Management

The organization of this book follows the logic of the management processes in which managers supposedly engage: planning and control, directing (or leading), organizing, and staffing. Significant articles are provided for each of these process areas in the later sections of the book. Section A, however, examines some ideas that cut across two or more of the managerial functions and thus can be appropriately studied as fundamentals rather than repeatedly reviewed in discussions of different functions.

Management is an applied activity in that basic knowledge of some sort is used in the solution of problems within organizations. For example, managers need to understand basic economics so that they may resolve the multitude of issues in which economic factors play a role. Indeed, economic consequences bear upon most organizational issues. Yet other basic sciences also are of relevance to managers, such as psychology, international trade, political science, and sociology. Some ideas that pervade the managerial processes deserve attention before the processes themselves are examined.

Thus, the first chapter examines the question of what management is all about, particularly some areas of most recent concern and interest. The second chapter examines how organizational behavior operates within value systems and social issues as well as how it enhances or constrains these systems. The following three chapters deal with information and the ways managers use information to make decisions within organizations. These decision techniques and creative acts are useful whether we are considering the planning function, the staffing function, or any other area of management that is our concern. Within this context, the ideas discussed in Section A are fundamental to the managerial processes described in the rest of the book. When managers lack a firm base of knowledge, the application of managerial processes suffers.

Chapter 1

The Nature
of Management

The purpose of this chapter is to develop a broad range of thinking that describes or prescribes different points of view toward management. In a fairly wide-ranging review of modern additions to management thought, Modesto Maidique examines everything from Japanese management to the 7S system of management developed at McKinsey and Company and described by Craig Watson in Chapter 11. While Maidique does not avoid a critical stance, the general tone of his judgements about the new management developments is favorable.

In the second article Mintzberg makes no judgements about what management theory should resemble except that the result should be developed from empirical research. He reports the now-famous technique he developed and the results he achieved. They constitute a line of thinking that must be considered in any analysis of management thought. Similarly, Ouchi developed his Theory Z type of management from a series of research studies. He describes the nature and evolution of these studies of a period that brought forth the conclusions constituting Theory Z.

While these three articles reveal some new and some old concepts in management theory, the emphasis is upon the newer ideas. This emphasis is not necessarily conclusive evidence of the superiority of the new management thinking over concepts developed over a long period. These articles do, however, address important conflicting views of management. It is unfortunate that all controversy cannot be addressed, let alone resolved. Hopefully, these introductory materials will provide a basis of consideration of management ideas in perspective.

1 • THE NEW MANAGEMENT THINKERS[1]

Modesto A. Maidique

The success of Japanese industrial products in domestic U.S. markets—coupled with declining American industrial competitiveness—has prompted management scholars to reconsider the principles that underpin conventional American management thought. This introspection has resulted in a massive attack on established management beliefs that could lead to a new management gospel.

THE DEATH OF CORPORATE STRATEGY

The debate began in earnest in 1980 with a forcefully written *Harvard Business Review* article by Robert Hayes and Bill Abernathy titled, "Managing Our Way to Economic Decline." In their controversial, award-winning article and elsewhere, they argued for a back-to-basics in American management. Corporate portfolio management, return on investment, the marketing concept, financial controls, "management by the numbers," pseudo-professional managers, and conglomerates all came under attack as false prophets that helped to create the illusion that managers could manage without "knowing their territory." Hayes and Abernathy declare, "The newest and best principles of management . . . despite their sophistication and widespread usefulness encourage a preference for (1) analytic detachment rather than the insight that comes from 'hands on experience,' and (2) short-term cost reduction rather than long-term technological competitiveness. It is this new managerial gospel, we feel, that has played a major role in undermining the vigor of the American industry."[2]

Much of Hayes and Abernathy's criticism focuses on individual analytical and strategic principles, but the concept of corporate strategy—the crown jewel of modern management[3]—remains intact. Now there are no more sacred cows, corporate strategy is also under siege.[4]

The attacks on the corporate strategy concept come from several directions. On the one hand, like many other business school management tools, corporate strategy helps in subtle ways to reinforce the concept of the manager as a grand thinker removed from the smell of battle, unaware—maybe even uncaring—about the basics of his operation. At the other extreme, the traditional corporate strategy framework is, at best, an incomplete abstraction on which to design a business.

---

[1] © 1983 by the Regents of the University of California. Reprinted from *California Management Review*, Vol. XXVI, No. 1, pp. 151 to 161 by permission of the Regents.

[2] R. Hayes and W. Abernathy, "Managing Our Way to Economic Decline," *Harvard Business Review* (July/August, 1980), pp. 67–77.

[3] K. Andrews, *The Concept of Corporate Strategy* (Homewood, Illinois: Dow Jones-Irwin, 1971; see also Richard D. Irwin, Inc., 1980).

[4] W. Kiechel, "Corporate Strategists Under Fire," *Fortune* (27 December 1982), pp. 32–39.

Corporate strategy is generally defined as a pragmatic set of plans and policies to reach one or more, usually financial, business objectives. Yet Tom Watson, Jr., the architect of the modern IBM, once wrote that it was not the choice of an optimal strategy but "faithful adherence to a sound set of beliefs," such as "respect for the individual," that was "the most important factor in corporate success."[5] Stanford's Richard Pascale and Harvard's Anthony Athos agree. They argue persuasively in their best-selling *The Art of Japanese Management* that the bond produced by shared values is "probably the most under-publicized 'secret weapon' of great companies."[6]

The power of purpose, values, and symbolism in securing organizational commitment is as old as organizations themselves. Confucius once pointed out that it was on "observance of ritual" that the administration of a state depends.[7] A half century ago, Chester Barnard, who has been a wellspring of inspiration for modern management thinkers—including the recent wave of best selling writers—wrote that the principal responsibility of the executive leader was the "creation of moral codes for others" followed by the "process of inculcating points of view, fundamental attitudes, loyalties, to the organization."[8] A decade ago, Peter Drucker argued that the most important cause of business failure was inability to articulate the "basic concepts, values, policies, and beliefs" that give direction to the business, its managers and its employees.[9]

A different attack against conventional strategic thinking has been propounded by James Brian Quinn, who argues that there is a wide gap between the way real world managers *actually* develop strategy and current academic strategic planning paradigms. Strategies in successul enterprises, Quinn argues, do not emerge as fully integrated realities but "incrementally, as a series of partial, tentative, somewhat fragmented decisions and personal commitments."[10] To Robert Burgelman, the current debate on strategy can be partially rationalized by recognizing that there are in general not one but two fundamentally different strategic processes simultaneously going on in the firm. One is classic: it induces managers to make decisions within the framework of the current goals and policies. The second, a messier one, mediates autonomous, pathfinding proposals that may significantly modify the current strategic direction.[11]

[5] T. Watson, *A Business and its Beliefs: The Ideas That Helped Build IBM* (McGraw-Hill Book Co., 1963), p. 5.

[6] R. Pascale and A. Athos, *The Art of Japanese Management: Applications for American Executives* (New York: Warner Books, 1981), p. 307.

[7] A. Waley, Trans., *The Analects of Confucius* (New York: Vintage Books, 1938), p. 161.

[8] C. Barnard, *The Functions of the Executive* (Cambridge , Mass. 1968), p. 279.

[9] P. Drucker, *Management: Tasks, Responsibilities, Practices* (New York: Harper & Row 1974), pp. 75–77,

[10] J. Quinn, *Strategies for Change: Logical Incrementalism* (Homewood, Illinois: Richard D. Irwin, Inc. 1980), p. 204.

Richard Pascale goes further. He encourages managers to "defy strategic concepts" altogether and to shed the grand strategy addiction that pervades American management circles. "Our strategy fetish," Pascale declares, "is a cultural peculiarity. We get off on strategy like the French get off on good food or romance."[12]

Pascale and Athos argue against the over-intellectualization of strategy and reliance on "big brain" strategic coups. "Careful scrutiny reveals that despite the exalted status of 'strategy' in the lexicon of American management, few great successes stem from one bold-stroke strategic thrust. More often, they result from one half-good idea that is improved upon incrementally. These improvements are invariably the result of a lot of 'little people' paying attention to the product, the customer, and the marketplace."[13] Corporate strategy (the Japanese don't even use the phrase) really evolves as iterative, incremental, experimental adjustments to the dynamics of opportunity. Success, in Pascale's view, does not lie as much in concept as in the skill to effectively coordinate and integrate the talents of a myriad of workers and specialists. To teach otherwise is "pedagogical deceit."[14]

On the other hand, the concept of corporate strategy, neo-corporate strategists might argue, encompasses both business basics as well as philosophical beliefs. And in a sense, they will be right. But, as theoreticians elaborated the concept of corporate strategy and taught it to generations of students, it became a more sterile way to view a business.

The same is true of contemporary economics. As classical economic theory was refined by neo-classical economists in an attempt to make it more quantitative, the subtlety, intricacy, and potential of technology disappeared to be replaced by equilibrium equations that were easier to formalize and manipulate. According to Lester Thurow, "The economics of the textbooks and of the graduate schools . . . is moving towards narrower and narrower interpretations. The mathematical sophistication intensifies as an understanding of the real world diminishes."[15] Similarly, making corporate strategy a universally applicable abstraction required that it be pruned of its technological specificity, prompting Wick Skinner, in desperation, to write a classic article title, "Manufacturing—the Missing Link in Corporate Strategy."[16]

---

[11] R. Burgelman, "A Model of the Interaction of Strategic Behavior, Corporate Context and the Concept of Strategy," *The Academy of Management Review,* vol. 8, No. 1 (January 1983), pp. 61–70.

[12] R. Pascale, "Out Curious Addiction to Corporate Grand Strategy," *Fortune* (25 Jan. 1982), pp. 115–16.

[13] Pascale and Athos, op. cit., p. 306.

[14] Pascale, op. cit., pp. 116–17.

[15] L. Thurow, *Dangerous Currents: The State of Economics* (New York: Random House, 1983), p. 236.

[16] W. Skinner, "Manufacturing—Missing Link in Corporate Strategy," *Harvard Business Review* (May/June 1969), p. 136. See also W. Skinner, *Manufacturing in the Corporate Strategy* (New York: John Wiley & Sons, Inc., 1978).

TOWARDS A NEW MANAGEMENT GOSPEL

What comes after corporate strategy? Management thinking is in a state of turmoil. Managers are questioning the value of an MBA and academics are asking themselves what MBA's should learn. As if this confusion weren't enough, economists, policy makers, and industry experts are simultaneously attempting to devise a new framework of analysis to deal with declining U.S. industrial competitiveness. Thus, the 1980s are certainly fertile ground for new approaches to both management and economic thinking, and, indeed, new recipes are coming from all sides.

To Bill Abernathy and his *Industrial Renaissance* coauthors, "The central challenge today is to master both the work of production and the competitively significant developments of process/product technology."[17] This challenge can only be met, according to these authors, by an American industrial renaissance, the outlines of which can already be seen in certain major U.S. industrial plants in which manufacturing is receiving new attention and workers are being given the opportunity to participate in improving production technology and equipment. To Robert Reich at the Kennedy School of Government at Harvard, the answer to our industrial malaise is also improved teamwork and cooperation. To Reich, cooperation makes an enterprise more capable of adapting quickly to the manufacture of the specialized, high-quality, technology-driven products that will be necessary for U.S. success in international markets. Furthermore, America is no longer a frontier economy, thus the ideology of individual daring is outdated. "America's economic future depends less on lonely geniuses and backyard inventors than on versatile organizations."[18] What is needed now is government prioritization of industries, the "industrial policy," that some of the industrial nations, notably Japan, have already implemented. Curiously, for someone who is trying to dispel "frontier mentality," Reich chose the title, *The Next American Frontier,* as the title to his book. In *A Business Plan for America,* Givertz and Kotkin make the opposing argument. To them, America was built, and still continues to be built, on the shoulders of its entrepreneurs. They point out that in instance after instance new entrepreneurial concerns are rising from the rubble of America's sunset industries and that in the last two decades it is small business that has created the lion's share of net new jobs.[19]

There would appear to be considerably less divergence of opinion amongst the ranks of the new management thinkers. Several of the new prescriptions have been shaped in collaboration and some use the same

---

[17] W. Abernathy, K. Clark, and A. Kantrow, *Industrial Renaissance: Producing a Competitive Future for America* (New York: Basic Books, Inc., 1983), p. 119.

[18] R. Reich, *The Next American Frontier* (New York: Times Books, 1983), p. 279.

[19] D. Givertz and J. Kotkin, *A Business Plan for America* (Forthcoming, New York: G.P. Putnam's Sons, 1984), Chapter 1.

empirical data as a base.[20] All of them have been influenced by the reality of the Japanese economic miracle. Not surprisingly there is a high level of consistency in the new wave of management thinking.

First, every book in the recent wave of bestselling books on business management—*Theory Z, The Art of Japanese Management, The One-Minute Manager,*[21] and *In Search of Excellence*—is about people—how to motivate, communicate, inspire, and lead—not about strategy. In *Theory Z,* Ouchi explains that what he learned from his comparison of Japanese and American firms can be simply stated: "involved workers are the key to productivity."[22] The key lessons of *Theory Z* are that people oriented factors—trust, subtlety, and intimacy—are the fundamental determinants of organizational productivity.

Not surprisingly, Pascale and Athos reach similar conclusions. They argue that we need to learn a great deal from the Japanese about how to better manage ambiguity, uncertainty, and interdependence in organizations. But, most importantly, they present a new framework for business management, developed in collaboration with their colleagues at McKinsey, that attempts to fuse together much of the new thinking.

To be sure, much of the McKinsey-Pascale-Athos proposed 7S framework (strategy, structure, systems, staff, style, skills, and superordinate goals) is really the old gospel sliced with a different knife. What is perhaps most significant in their book, however, is their concept of superordinate goals, "the significant meanings or guiding concepts that an organization imbues in its members."[23] In a strict sense, however, even this 'S' is more

---

[20] Indeed, to the outsider, as a group they might appear highly incestuous. Much of the research behind Ouchi's comparative study of American and Japanese management was done at Stanford University in conjunction with Pascale. Pascale in turn worked with Athos and with Peters and Waterman on the McKinsey study of managerial excellence. The 7S framework (see also reference 22) was developed by a team that included Peters, Waterman. Pascale and Athos and others at McKinsey. See W. Ouchi, *Theory Z: How American Business Can Meet the Japanese Challenge* (Reading, Mass.: Addison-Wesley, 1981); R. Pascale and A. Athos, *The Art of Japanese Management: Applications for American Executives* (New York: Warner Books, 1981); and T. Peters and R. Waterman, *In Search of Excellence: Lessons from America's Best-Run Companies* (New York: Harper & Row, 1982). The authors of *Corporate Cultures* (one of the authors is a principal at McKinsey) refer to Peters as the "intellectual and spiritual godfather" of their book. Pascale, Peters, Ouchi, Waterman, and Abernathy have all taught at Stanford University, and Hayes is a Stanford Ph.D.; while Athos, Abernathy, Deal, and Hayes are currently professors at Harvard University. See T. Deal and A. Kennedy, *Corporate Cultures: The Rites and Rituals of Corporate Life* (Reading, Mass.: Addison-Wesley, 1982).

[21] K. Blanchard and S. Johnson, *The One-Minute Manager* (New York: William Morrow and Company, Inc., 1982).

[22] W. Ouchi, *Theory Z: How American Business Can Meet the Japanese Challenge* (Reading, Mass.: Addison-Wesley, 1982), p. 4.

[23] Pascale and Athos, op. cit., p. 125. For the original articulation of the 7S framework, which has been copyrighted by McKinsey and Co., Inc., see R. Waterman, Jr., T. Peters, and J. R. Phillips, "Structure is not Organization," *Business Horizons* (June 1980), pp. 14–26.

a question of emphasis rather than a departure from the conventional gospel. In his influential neo-corporate strategy book, *Competitive Strategy,* which applies the modern industrial organization economics framework to business policy, Michael Porter argues that corporate self-analysis is usually conducted in terms of what the corporation has done (strategy). A complete analysis, however, should include what it can do (its skills, its capabilities and its weaknesses), what it assumes about itself and its environment (assumptions), and what it *believes about itself* (beliefs).[24]

The McKinsey-Pascale-Athos framework, however, does much more than create a new laundry list of analytical variables. It persuasively crystallizes a new set of priorities that expands conventional notions of managing the firm. Pascale and Athos also highlight the importance of style and of the skill set of key personnel, but their principal contribution is in reminding us that institutions work better, and get more commitment from their members, if their goals are perceived as more significant than simply making a commercial profit. This is an old idea, but it is argued more clearly and convincingly by Pascale and Athos than by any of the new—or old—management thinkers.

What the new framework does not do is to address Hayes and Abernathy's concern with managements that have drifted away from understanding their firm's business, "their territory," and, in particular, their manufacturing and R&D technology. Hayes and Abernathy argue that a company's operations organization usually commands over 80 percent of the capital and human resources of the firm and, thus, should be a focus of managerial involvement, an argument parallel to that Wick Skinner has been championing since the early 70s. Yet nowhere in the McKinsey-Pascale-Athos framework is technology singled out as deserving of special attention.

Shortly after *The Art of Japanese Management* began to fade from national attention, Tom Peters and Robert H. Waterman published *In Search of Excellence, Lessons from America's Best-Run Companies.* Soon it became the most widely read management book of the 80s. With sales approaching the half-million mark, *In Search of Excellence* may become *the* management book of the decade.

Notwithstanding its extraordinary commercial success, *In Search of Excellence* has come under heavy criticism from American academicians. In contrast to the methodically argued *Theory Z* and the persuasively and tightly written *The Art of Japanese Management, In Search of Excellence* often comes across as a potpourri of loosely interconnected, and often redundant, vignettes in search of a framework. Like much early research,

---

[24] Porter's real contribution, however, is applying the framework of microeconomics to managerial industry analysis. Porter's framework expands industry analysis beyond the usual focus on competitors (rivals) to include the bargaining power of buyers and suppliers, the threat of new entrants and substitutes, and the overall structure and state of development of the industry. See M. Porter, *Competitive Strategy: Techniques for Analyzing Industries and Competitors* (New York: The Free Press, 1980), pp. 47–74.

the book is based on interviews with only "highly regarded," large American companies (43 companies, typically $1 billion in sales or more). The flip side, the underachieving companies, was not studied as a control group. The authors relied on their "insight into underachievement"[25] with respect to these firms. But who is to say that the underachievers don't follow at least some of the same practices? The book is also plagued by unsubstantiated generalizations, factual errors,[26] incomplete footnoting, and a wide range in the quality of evidence used to support the principal arguments. For instance, notwithstanding the thousands of management books that use specific, concrete examples from real companies, Peters and Waterman argue in their introduction that "field data is too often overlooked in books on management," a generalization sure to enrage hundreds and perhaps thousands of case book writers.[27] Never was a book on management so successful and yet so vulnerable to academic criticism. Indeed, *In Search of Excellence* is an open target for academic nitpickers. But it works.

It works for three principal reasons. First, its tenor is positive. It appeals to American pride. It says Americans—at least some Americans—do know how to manage. The secret Japanese potion is available at the corner drugstore, not just in Kyoto. This message is just what the doctor ordered for a nation which is questioning its ability to compete in an economically restructured world. Secondly, its message is simple, easy to comprehend, and delivered in an informal, conversational style—and most importantly, it makes sense. It has face validity for the practicing manager. Succinctly put, the excellent companies succeed not because they are brilliant, but because they are brilliant on the basics—hard work, quick action, keeping things simple, sticking to what they know best, customer interaction, respect for employees, and giving meaning to their mission. Finally, and perhaps most importantly, unlike most books on management, *In Search of Excellence* is written in an enthusiastic, almost evangelistic style that for most managers is a welcome respite from the colorless prose of academic texts. Peters and Waterman talks about "love" for the product, about being motivated by "simple—even beautiful—values," about the "fun" of managing and working.[28] In the process, they engage the reader in the same way that they were engaged by their subjects. Referring to one of the excellent companies, they write, "We ourselves tried to remain sober, not to become fans. But it proved impossible."[29] As I underlined some of the superb lines in the book, made annotations on many of its pages (occasionally expressing strong disagreement), I understood what Peters and Waterman meant.

[25] Peters and Waterman, op. cit., p. 13.
[26] "Hugely successful" Apple Computer's sales in 1981 are given as "approaching $750M in 1981." The company's sales that year were $334M. See Peters and Waterman, ibid., p. 286. According to a letter from one of the authors (Waterman) many of the errors, including this one, have been corrected in the last printing. R. Waterman, Letter, July 21, 1983.
[27] Peters and Waterman, ibid., p. 26.
[28] Peters and Waterman, ibid., p. 37.
[29] Peters and Waterman, ibid., p. 246.

THE REVIVAL MESSAGE

But, despite its magnetic appeal, *In Search of Excellence* is not an instant panacea for those who seek managerial excellence. It seems that the things that make the excellent organizations great—that is, the large companies that illustrate the people-oriented thesis of *Theory Z, The Art of Japanese Management,* and *In Search of Excellence*—take a long time to develop. A. Lawrence Lowell, when president of Harvard University, once responded to the question, "What does it take to make a university great?" by declaring crisply, "Three hundred years." The second essential incredient of organizational excellence is executive leadership, preferably of the durable and continuous type. Peters and Waterman explain:

> How did these companies get the way they are? Is it always a case of a strong leader at the helm? We must admit that our bias at the beginning was to discount the role of leadership heavily, if for no other reason than that everybody's answer to what's wrong (or right) with whatever organization is its leader. Our strong belief was that the excellent companies had gotten to be the way they are because of a unique set of cultural attributes that distinguish them from the rest, and if we understood those attributes well enough, we could do more than just mutter "leadership" in response to questions like "Why is J&J so good?" Unfortunately, what we found was that associated with almost every excellent company was a strong leader (or two) who seemed to have had a lot to do with making the company excellent in the first place. Many of these companies— for instance, IBM, P&G, Emerson, J&J, and Dana seem to have taken on their basic character under the tutelage of a very special person. Moreover, they did it at a fairly early stage of their development.[30]

To this list one could add HP, 3M, DEC, McDonald's, Mars, Tandem, Wal-Mart, Delta, J. C. Penney, Marriott, Wang, Disney Productions, Eastman-Kodak, Intel, and a host of others. In virtually all of the excellent companies, a leader (or two) laid down the basic value set during a long turn at the helm. "Organizations," as Abraham Zaleznik has explained, "bear the imprint of men who lead and work in them and do not evolve simply as depersonalized structures."[31]

Thus, the search for success then boils down to two alternatives: (1) if you already have a leader, then recommend that he read the new management books; they may give him some good ideas; and (2) if you don't, find a leader with vision, and in ten or twenty years he or she may build you an excellent company which people will write management books about.[32]

Indeed, much of the new management gospel is a revival message. The importance of leadership, closeness with customers and employees, and technology are all lessons American businessmen once knew well. Indeed, many still do. As Goethe once wrote, "All the clever thoughts have long since been thought. What matters is to think them anew."[33] Chester Barnard,

---

[30] Peters and Waterman, ibid., p. 26.

[31] A Zaleznik, *Human Dilemmas of Leadership* (New York: Harper & Row, 1966), p. 222.

[32] W. Kiechel, "Wanted: Corporate Leaders," *Fortune* (30 May 1983), pp. 135–40.

[33] J. W. Goethe, *Goethe's World View,* presented in his *Reflections and Maxims,* translated by Heinz Norden (Frederic Ungar Publishing Co., 1963), p. 129.

for instance, wrote fifty years ago that the customers should be viewed as an integral part of the organizational system.[34, 35] Once there were no business schools, even the owner's son worked his way up through the ranks; steelmen were steelmen, and railroad men were railroad men, and it was generally accepted that it was great (even heroic) men who gave life to great institutions. The new principles of management seemed to challenge this experience. Now, however, the utopia of the headless business guided to success by bright strategists is dead. As Zaleznik points out, "History seems to show that no sooner do we feel secure in the Promised Land (or whatever we would like to call utopias), than the bureaucratic solution seems to come unstuck. A new crisis emerges and we wait expectantly for the reappearance of the hero."[36]

For the quarter century following the Second World War, there was little need for heroes in the U.S. America had emerged from the war as the dominant economic, political, industrial, and military power in the world—the basis of the Pax Americana. It was during this epoch that management scholars concentrated on the development of new strategic tools of analysis that would liberate us once and for all from the "great man hypothesis." It was during these years that Galbraith and his followers pronounced entrepreneurs and daring inventors a dying breed.[37] "The entrepreneur no longer exists as a person in the mature industrial enterprise . . . the entrepreneur [has been replaced] as the directing force of the enterprise, with management."[38]

But American dominance was short-lived. The second half of the 20th Century was punctuated by a series of crises which gradually eroded American influence and self-confidence—the Soviet A-bomb, the Sputnik, the ill-fated Vietnam War, the twin oil shocks (OPEC and Iran), and Watergate. Now the focus is on the Great American Management-Productivity Crisis. This most recent crisis, spurred in large part by the rapid rise of the Europeans and the Japanese as vigorous competitors, has intensified the need for managerial leadership in industrial America. A response to these changed circumstances is in part what the new wave of management thinking is about.

THE NEW CHALLENGE TO ACADEMIA

As the U.S. completes a painful transition from world dominance to a leadership role in a competitive world, American scholars face a formidable challenge to integrate the lessons of the past with complex new realities.

---

[34] H. Simon, *Administrative Behavior: A Study of Decision-Making Processes in Administrative Organizations* (New York: The Free Press, 1976), p. 16.

[35] Barnard, op. cit., p. 71.

[36] Zaleznik, op. cit., p. 224.

[37] G. Gilder, *Wealth and Poverty* (New York: Basic Books, 1981), p. 74.

[38] J. K. Galbraith, *The New Industrial State* (New York: Mentor Books, 1967, 1971), p. 84.

In summary, what is needed now is a revitalized synthesis of (1) the potency of MacGregor Burns's "transforming" leadership; [39] (2) Andrew's core concept of corporate strategy; (3) Barnard, Peters and Waterman's organizational closeness to customers and employees; (4) the inspiring shared values of Watson, Pascale and Athos; and (5) Hayes, Abernathy, and Skinner's down-to-earth concern for hands-on attention to *technology* as a central link underpinning the entire business framework. In these areas, the new management thinkers led the way for others to follow.

This new challenge to American business scholars and managers has been brought into clear focus by observing and contrasting our practices and philosophies with those of managers in other countries, particularly the Japanese. On the other hand, simply copying the Japanese at what they excel in—"the art of adapting, adjusting, fitting . . . sifting, and excluding" as Kurt Singer has pointed out in *Mirror, Sword and Jewel*—is not enough, or perhaps not even appropriate. [40,41]

American management needs to intensively continue its process of self-renewal and its search for new frameworks of analysis while keeping in mind what de Tocqueville once pointed out is the true source of American economic strength, "a clear, free, original and inventive power of mind." [42] Though this statement was written a century and a half ago, the airplane, plastics, the transistor, the integrated circuit, color television, microprocessors, genetic engineering, and personal computers—not to mention hula hoops—have borne out de Tocqueville's insight.

[39] J. MacGregor Burns, *Leadership* (New York: Harper & Row, 1978).

[40] K. Singer, *Mirror, Sword and Jewel, The Geometry of Japanese Life* (Tokyo: Kodansha International, 1973), p. 98

[41] B. Briggs, "The Dangerous Folly Called Theory Z," *Fortune,* (17 May 1982), pp. 41–53.

[42] A. de Tocqueville, *Democracy in America* (New York: Mentor Books, 1956).

2 • MANAGERIAL WORK: ANALYSIS FROM OBSERVATION[1]

Henry Mintzberg[2]

What do managers do? Ask this question and you will likely be told that managers plan, organize, coordinate, and control. Since Henri Fayol, Reference [9], page 30, first proposed these words in 1916, they have dominated the vocabulary of management. (See, for example, [8], [12], [17].) How valuable are they in describing managerial work? Consider one morning's work of the president of a large organization:

> As he enters his office at 8:23, the manager's secretary motions for him to pick up the telephone. "Jerry, there was a bad fire in the plant last night, about $30,000 damage. We should be back in operation by Wednesday. Thought you should know."
>
> At 8:45, a Mr. Jamison is ushered into the manager's office. They discuss Mr. Jamison's retirement plans and his cottage in New Hampshire. Then the manager presents a plaque to him commemorating his thirty-two years with the organization.
>
> Mail processing follows: An innocent-looking letter, signed by a Detroit lawyer, reads: "A group of us in Detroit has decided not to buy any of your products because you used that anti-flag, anti-American pinko, Bill Lindell, upon your Thursday night TV show." The manager dictates a restrained reply.
>
> The 10:00 meeting is scheduled by a professional staffer. He claims that his superior, a high-ranking vice-president of the organization, mistreats his staff, and that if the man is not fired, they will all walk out. As soon as the meeting ends, the manager rearranges his schedule to investigate the claim and to react to this crisis.

Which of these activities may be called planning, and which may be called organizing, coordinating, and controlling? Indeed, what do words such as *coordinating* and *planning* mean in the context of real activity? In fact, these four words do not describe the actual work of managers at all; they describe certain vague objectives of managerial work. ". . . they are just ways of indicating what we need to explain." [1, p. 537]

Other approaches to the study of managerial work have developed, one dealing with managerial decision-making and policy-making processes, another with the manager's interpersonal activities. (See, for example, [2] and [10].) And some empirical researchers, using the "diary" method, have studied, what might be called, managerial "media"—by what means, with whom, how long, and where managers spend their time.[3] But in no part of this literature is the actual content of managerial work systematically and

---

[1] From *Management Science,* Vol. 18, No. 2 (October, 1971), pp. B97-B110. Reprinted by permission of the Institute of Management Science and Henry Mintzberg.
[2] Henry Mintzberg, Professor of Management, McGill University, Montreal, Quebec.
[3] Carlson [6] carried out the classic study just after World War II. He asked nine Swedish managing directors to record on diary pads details of each activity in which they engaged. His method was used by a group of other researchers, many of them working in the United Kingdom. (See References [4], [5], [15], [25], page 30.)

meaningfully described. [4] Thus, the question posed at the start—what do managers do?—remains essentially unanswered in the literature of management.

This is indeed an odd situation. We claim to teach management in schools of both business and public administration; we undertake major research programs in management; we find a growing segment of the management science community concerned with the problems of senior management. Most of these people—the planners, information and control theorists, systems analysts, etc.—are attempting to analyze and change working habits that they themselves do not understand. Thus, at a conference called at M.I.T. to assess the impact of the computer on the manager, and attended by a number of America's foremost management scientists, a participant found it necessary to comment after lengthy discussion [20, p. 198]:

> I'd like to return to an earlier point. It seems to me that until we get into the question of what the top manager does or what the functions are that define the top management job, we're not going to get out of the kind of difficulty that keeps cropping up. What I'm really doing is leading up to my earlier question which no one really answered. And that is: Is it possible to arrive at a specification of what constitutes the job of a top manager?

His question was not answered.

RESEARCH STUDY ON MANAGERIAL WORK

In late 1966, I began research on this question, seeking to replace Fayol's words by a set that would more accurately describe what managers do. In essence, I sought to develop by the process of induction a statement of managerial work that would have empirical validity. Using a method called "structured observation", I observed for one-week periods the chief executives of five medium to large organizations (a consulting firm, a school system, a technology firm, a consumer goods manufacturer, and a hospital).

Structured as well as unstructured (i.e., anecdotal) data were collected in three records. In the *chronology record,* activity patterns throughout the working day were recorded. In the *mail record,* for each of 890 pieces of mail processed during the five weeks, were recorded its purpose, format and sender, the attention it received and the action it elicited. And, recorded in the *contact record,* for each of 368 verbal interactions, were the purpose, the medium (telephone call, scheduled or unscheduled meeting, tour), the participants, the form of initiation, and the location. It should be noted that all categorizing was done during and after observation so as to ensure that the categories reflected only the work under observation. [19] contains a fuller description of this methodology and a tabulation of the results of the study.

---

[4] One major project, involving numerous publications, took place at Ohio State University and spanned three decades. Some of the vocabulary used followed Fayol. The results have generated little interest in this area. (See, for example, [13].)

Two sets of conclusions are presented below. The first deals with certain characteristics of managerial work, as they appeared from analysis of the numerical data (e.g., How much time is spent with peers? What is the average duration of meetings? What proportion of contacts are initiated by the manager himself?). The second describes the basic content of managerial work in terms of ten roles. This description derives from an analysis of the data on the recorded *purpose* of each contact and piece of mail.

The liberty is taken of referring to these findings as descriptive of managerial, as opposed to chief executive, work. This is done because many of the findings are supported by studies of other types of managers. Specifically, most of the conclusions on work characteristics are to be found in the combined results of a group of studies of foremen [11], [6]; middle managers [4], [5], [15], [25]; and chief executives [6]. And although there is little useful material on managerial roles, three studies do provide some evidence of the applicability of the role set. Most important, Sayles' empirical study of production managers [24] suggests that at least five of the ten roles are performed at the lower end of the managerial hierarchy. And some further evidence is provided by comments in Whyte's study of leadership in a street gang [26] and Neustadt's study of three United States presidents [21]. (Reference is made to these findings where appropriate.) Thus, although most of the illustrations are drawn from my study of chief executives, there is some justification in asking the reader to consider when he sees the terms *manager* and his *organization* not only *presidents* and their *companies,* but also *foremen* and their *shops, directors* and their *branches, vice-presidents* and their *divisions.* The term *manager* shall be used with reference to all those people in charge of formal organizations or their subunits.

SOME CHARACTERISTICS OF MANAGERIAL WORK

Six sets of characteristics of managerial work derive from analysis of the data of this study. Each has a significant bearing on the manager's ability to administer a complex organization.

Characteristic 1. The Manager Performs a Great Quantity of Work at an Unrelenting Pace.

Despite a semblance of normal working hours, in truth managerial work appears to be very taxing. The five men in this study processed an average of thirty-six pieces of mail each day, participated in eight meetings (half of which were scheduled), engaged in five telephone calls, and took one tour. In his study of foremen, Guest [11] found that the number of activities per day averaged 583, with no real break in the pace.

Free time appears to be very rare. If by chance a manager has caught up with the mail, satisfied the callers, dealt with all the disturbances, and avoided scheduled meetings, a subordinate will likely show up to usurp the available time. It seems that the manager cannot expect to have much time for leisurely reflection during office hours. During "off" hours, our chief executives spent much time on work-related reading. High-level managers appear to be able to escape neither from an environment which recognizes the power and status of their positions nor from their own minds which have been trained to search continually for new information.

Characteristic 2. Managerial Activity Is Characterized by Variety, Fragmentation, and Brevity.

There seems to be no pattern to managerial activity. Rather, variety and fragmentation appear to be characteristic, as successive activities deal with issues that differ greatly both in type and in content. In effect the manager must be prepared to shift moods quickly and frequently.

A typical chief executive day may begin with a telephone call from a director who asks a favor (a "status request"); then a subordinate calls to tell of a strike at one of the facilities (fast movement of information, termed *instant communication*); this is followed by a relaxed scheduled event at which the manager speaks to a group of visiting dignitaries (ceremony); the manager returns to find a message from a major customer who is demanding the renegotiation of a contract (pressure); and so on. Throughout the day, the managers of our study encountered this great variety of activity. Most surprisingly, the significant activities were interspersed with the trivial in no particular pattern.

Furthermore, these managerial activities were characterized by their brevity. Half of all the activities studied lasted less than nine minutes and only 10 percent exceeded one hour's duration. Guest's foremen averaged 48 seconds per activity, and Carlson [6] stressed that his chief executives were unable to work without frequent interruption.

In my own study of chief executives, I felt that the managers demonstrated a preference for tasks of short duration and encouraged interruption. Perhaps the manager becomes accustomed to variety, or perhaps the flow of "instant communication" cannot be delayed. A more plausible explanation might be that the manager becomes conditioned by his workload. He develops a sensitive appreciation for the opportunity cost of his own time. Also, he is aware of the ever present assortment of obligations associated with his job—accumulations of mail that cannot be delayed, the callers that must be attended to, the meetings that require his participation. In other words, no matter what he is doing, the manager is plagued by what he must do and what he might do. Thus, the manager is forced to treat issues in an abrupt and superficial way.

Characteristic 3. Managers Prefer Issues That Are Current, Specific, and Ad Hoc.

Ad hoc operating reports received more attention that did routine ones; current, uncertain information—gossip, speculation, heresay—which flows quickly was preferred to historical, certain information; "instant communication" received first consideration; few contacts were held on a routine or "clocked" basis; almost all contacts concerned well-defined issues. The managerial environment is clearly one of stimulus-response. It breeds, not reflective planners, but adaptable information manipulators who prefer the live, concrete situation, men who demonstrate a marked action-orientation.

Characteristic 4. The Manager Sits Between His Organization and a Network of Contacts.

In virtually every empirical study of managerial time allocation, it was reported that managers spent a surprisingly large amount of time in horizontal or lateral (nonline) communication. It is clear from this study and from that of Sayles [24] that the manager is surrounded by a diverse and complex web of contacts which serves as his self-designed external information system. Included in this web can be clients, associates and suppliers, outside staff experts, peers (managers of related or similar organizations), trade organizations, government officials, independents (those with no relevant organizational affiliation), and directors or superiors. (Among these, directors in this study and superiors in other studies did *not* stand out as particularly active individuals.)

The managers in this study received far more information than they emitted, much of it coming from contacts, and more from subordinates who acted as filters. Figuratively, the manager appears as the neck of an hourglass, sifting information into his own organization from its environment.

Characteristic 5. The Manager Demonstrates a Strong Preference for the Verbal Media.

The manager has five media at his command—mail (documented), telephone (purely verbal), unscheduled meeting (informal face-to-face), scheduled meeting (formal face-to-face), and tour (observational). Along with all the other empirical studies of work characteristics, I found a strong predominance of verbal forms of communication.

Mail. By all indications, managers dislike the documented form of communication. In this study, they gave cursory attention to such items as operating reports and periodicals. It was estimated that only 13 percent of the input mail was of specific and immediate use to the managers. Much of the rest dealt with formalities and provided general reference data. The managers studied initiated very little mail, only 25 pieces in the 5 weeks. The rest of the outgoing mail was sent in reaction to mail received—a reply to a request, an acknowledgment, some information forwarded to a part of the organization. The managers appeared to dislike this form of communication, perhaps because the mail is a relatively slow and tedious medium.

Telephone and Unscheduled Meetings. The less formal means of verbal communication—the telephone, a purely verbal form, and the unscheduled meeting, a face-to-face form—were used frequently (two-thirds of the contacts in the study) but for brief encounters (average duration of six and twelve minutes respectively). They were used primarily to deliver requests and to transmit pressing information to those outsiders and subordinates who had informal relationships with the manager.

Scheduled Meetings. These tended to be of long duration, averaging sixty-eight minutes in this study, and absorbing over half the managers' time. Such meetings provided the managers with their main opportunities to interact with large groups and to leave the confines of their own offices. Scheduled meetings were used when the participants were unfamiliar to the manager (e.g., students who requested that he speak at a university), when a large quantity of information had to be transmitted (e.g., presentation of a report), when ceremony had to take place, and when complex strategy-making or negotiation had to be undertaken. An important feature of the scheduled meeting was the incidental, but by no means irrelevant, information that flowed at the start and end of such meetings.

Tours. Although the walking tour would appear to be a powerful tool for gaining information in an informal way, in this study tours accounted for only three percent of the managers' time.

In general, it can be concluded that the manager uses each medium for particular purposes. Nevertheless, where possible, he appears to gravitate to verbal media since these provide greater flexibility, require less effort, and bring faster response. It should be noted here that the manager does not leave the telephone or the meeting to get back to work. Rather, communication is his work, and these media are his tools. The operating work of the organization—producing a product, doing research, purchasing a part— appears to be undertaken infrequently by the senior manager. The manager's productive output must be measured in terms of information, a great part of which is transmitted verbally.

Characteristic 6. Despite the Preponderance of Obligations, the Manager Appears to Be Able to Control His Own Affairs.

Carlson suggested in his study of Swedish chief executives that these men were puppets, with little control over their own affairs. A cursory examination of our data indicates that this is true. Our managers were responsible for the initiation of only 32 percent of their verbal contacts and a smaller proportion of their mail. Activities were also classified as to the nature of the managers' participation, and the active ones were outnumbered by the passive ones (e.g., making requests versus receiving requests). On the surface, the manager is indeed a puppet, answering requests in the mail, returning telephone calls, attending meetings initiated by others, yielding to subordinates' requests for time, reacting to crises.

However, such a view is misleading. There is evidence that the senior manager can exert control over his own affairs in two significant ways: (1) It is he who defines many of his own long-term commitments, by developing appropriate information channels which later feed him information, by initiating projects which later demand his time, by joining committees or outside boards which provide contacts in return for his services, and so on. (2) The manager can exploit situations that appear as obligations. He can lobby at ceremonial speeches; he can impose his values on his organization when his authorization is requested; he can motivate his subordinates whenever he interacts with them; he can use the crisis situation as an opportunity to innovate.

Perhaps these are two points that help distinguish successful and unsuccessful managers. All managers appear to be puppets. Some decide who will pull the strings and how, and they then take advantage of each move that they are forced to make. Others, unable to exploit this high-tension environment, are swallowed up by this most demanding of jobs.

THE MANAGER'S WORK ROLES

In describing the essential content of managerial work, one should aim to model managerial activity, that is, to describe it as a set of programs. But an undertaking as complex as this must be preceded by the development of a useful typological description of managerial work. In other words, we must first understand the distinct components of managerial work. At the present time we do not.

In this study, 890 pieces of mail and 368 verbal contacts were categorized as to purpose. The incoming mail was found to carry acknowledgments, requests and solicitations of various kinds, reference data, news, analytical reports, reports on events and on operations, advice on various situations, and statements of problems, pressures, and ideas. In reacting to mail, the managers acknowledged some, replied to the requests (e.g., by sending information), and forwarded much to subordinates (usually for their information). Verbal contacts involved a variety of purposes. In 15% of them activities were scheduled, in 6% ceremonial events took place, and a few involved external board work. About 34% involved requests of various kinds, some insignificant, some for information, some for authorization of proposed actions. Another 36% essentially involved the flow of information to and from the manager, while the remainder dealt specifically with issues of strategy and with negotiations. (For details, see [19].)

In this study, each piece of mail and verbal contact categorized in this way was subjected to one question: Why did the manager do this? The answers were collected and grouped and regrouped in various ways (over the course of three years) until a typology emerged that was felt to be satisfactory. While an example, presented below, will partially explain this process to the reader, it must be remembered that (in the words of Bronowski [3, p. 62]): "Every induction is a speculation and it guesses at a unity which the facts present but do not strictly imply."

Consider the following sequence of two episodes: A chief executive attends a meeting of an external board on which he sits. Upon his return to his organization, he immediately goes to the office of a subordinate, tells of a conversation he had with a fellow board member, and concludes with the statement: "It looks like we shall get the contract."

The purposes of these two contacts are clear—to attend an external board meeting and to give current information (instant communication) to a subordinate. But why did the manager attend the meeting? Indeed, why does he belong on the board? And why did he give this particular information to his subordinate?

Basing analysis on this incident, one can argue as follows: The manager belongs on the board in part so that he can be exposed to special information which is of use to his organization. The subordinate needs the information but has not the status which would give him access to it. The chief executive does. Board memberships bring chief executives in contact with one another for the purpose of trading information.

Two aspects of managerial work emerge from this brief analysis. The manager serves in a *liaison* capacity because of the status of his office, and what he learns here enables him to act as *disseminator* of information to his organization. We refer to these as *roles*—organized sets of behaviors belonging to identifiable offices or positions [23]. Ten roles were chosen to capture all the activities observed during this study.

All activities were found to involve one or more of three basic behaviors —interpersonal contact, the processing of information, and the making of decisions. As a result, our ten roles are divided into three corresponding groups. Three roles—labelled *figurehead, liaison,* and *leader*—deal with behavior that is essentially interpersonal in nature. Three others—*nerve center, disseminator,* and *spokesman*—deal with information-processing activities performed by the manager. And the remaining four—*entrepreneur, disturbance handler, resource allocator,* and *negotiator*—cover the decision-making activities of the manager. We describe each of these roles in turn, asking the reader to note that they form a *gestalt,* a unified whole whose parts cannot be considered in isolation.

The Interpersonal Roles

Three roles relate to the manager's behavior that focuses on interpersonal contact. These roles derive directly from the authority and status associated with holding managerial office.

Figurehead. As legal authority in his organization, the manager is a symbol, obliged to perform a number of duties. He must preside at ceremonial events, sign legal documents, receive visitors, make himself available to many of those who feel, in the words of one of the men studied, "that the only way to get something done is to get to the top." There is evidence that this role applies at other levels as well. Davis [7, pp. 43-44] cites the case of the field sales manager who must deal with those customers who believe that their accounts deserve his attention.

Leader. Leadership is the most widely recognized of managerial roles. It describes the manager's relationship with his subordinates—his attempts to motivate them and his development of the milieu in which they work. Leadership actions pervade all activity—in contrast to most roles, it is possible to designate only a few activities as dealing exclusively with leadership (these mostly related to staffing duties). Each time a manager encourages a subordinate, or meddles in his affairs, or replies to one of his requests, he is playing the *leader* role. Subordinates seek out and react to these leadership clues, and, as a result, they impart significant power to the manager.

Liaison. As noted earlier, the empirical studies have emphasized the importance of lateral or horizontal communication in the work of managers at all levels. It is clear from our study that this is explained largely in terms of the *liaison* role. The manager establishes his network of contacts essentially to bring information and favors to his organization. As Sayles notes in his study of production supervisors [24, p. 258], "The one enduring objective [of the manager] is the effort to build and maintain a predictable, reciprocating system of relationships. . . ."

Making use of his status, the manager interacts with a variety of peers and other people outside his organization. He provides time, information, and favors in return for the same from others. Foremen deal with staff groups and other foremen; chief executives join boards of directors and maintain extensive networks of individual relationships. Neustadt notes this behavior in analyzing the work of President Roosevelt [21, p. 150]:

> His personal sources were the product of a sociability and curiosity that reached back to the other Roosevelt's time. He had an enormous acquaintance in various phases of national life and at various levels of government; he also had his wife and her variety of contacts. He extended his acquaintanceships abroad; in the war years Winston Churchill, among others, became a "personal source." Roosevelt quite deliberately exploited these relationships and mixed them up to widen his own range of information. He changed his sources as his interests changed, but no one who had ever interested him was quite forgotten or immune to sudden use.

The Informational Roles

A second set of managerial activities relates primarily to the processing of information. Together they suggest three significant managerial roles: one describing the manager as a focal point for a certain kind of organizational information, the other two describing relatively simple transmission of this information.

Nerve Center. There is indication, both from this study and from those by Neustadt and Whyte, that the manager serves as the focal point in his organization for the movement of nonroutine information. Homans, who analyzed Whyte's study, draws the following conclusions [26, p. 187]:

> Since interaction flowed toward [the leaders], they were better informed about the problems and desires of group members than were any of the followers and therefore better able to decide on an appropriate course of action. Since they were in close touch with other gang leaders, they were also better informed than their followers about conditions in Cornerville at large. Moreover, in their positions at the focus of the chains of interaction, they were better able than any follower to pass on to the group decisions that had been reached.

The term *nerve center* is chosen to encompass those many activities in which the manager receives information.

Within his own organization, the manager has legal authority that formally connects him—and only him—to *every* member. Hence, the manager emerges as *nerve center* of internal information. He may not know as much about any one function as the subordinate who specializes in it, but he comes to know more about his total organization than any other member. He is the information generalist. Furthermore, because of the manager's status and its manifestation in the *liaison* role, the manager gains unique access to a variety of knowledgeable outsiders including peers who are themselves *nerve centers* of their own organizations. Hence, the manager emerges as his organization's *nerve center* of external information as well.

As noted earlier, the manager's nerve center information is of a special kind. He appears to find it most important to get his information quickly and informally. As a result, he will not hesitate to bypass formal information channels to get it, and he is prepared to deal with a large amount of gossip, hearsay, and opinion which has not yet become substantiated fact.

Disseminator. Much of the manager's information must be transmitted to subordinates. Some of this is of a *factual* nature, received from outside the organization or from other subordinates. And some is of a *value* nature. Here, the manager acts as the mechanism by which organizational influencers (owners, governments, employee groups, the general public, etc., or simply the "boss") make their preferences known to the organization. It is the manager's duty to integrate these value positions, and to express general organizational preferences as a guide to decisions made by subordinates. One of the men studied commented: "One of the principal functions of this position is to integrate the hospital interests with the public interests." Papandreou describes this duty in a paper published in 1952, referring to management as the "peak coordinator" [22].

Spokesman. In his *spokesman* role, the manager is obliged to transmit his information to outsiders. He informs influencers and other interested parties about his organization's performance, its policies, and its plans. Furthermore, he is expected to serve outside his organization as an expert in its industry. Hospital administrators are expected to spend some time serving outside as public experts on health, and corporation presidents, perhaps as chamber of commerce executives.

The Decisional Roles

The manager's legal authority requires that he assume responsibility for all of his organization's important actions. The *nerve center* role suggests that only he can fully understand complex decisions, particularly those involving difficult value tradeoffs. As a result, the manager emerges as the key figure in the making and interrelating of all significant decisions in his organization, a process that can be referred to as *strategy making*. Four roles describe the manager's control over the strategy-making system in his organization.

Entrepreneur. The *entrepreneur* role describes the manager as initiator and designer of much of the controlled change in his organization. The manager looks for opportunities and potential problems which may cause him to initiate action. Action takes the form of *improvement projects*—the marketing of a new product, the strengthening of a weak department, the purchasing of new equipment, the reorganization of formal structure, and so on.

The manager can involve himself in each improvement project in one of three ways: (1) He may *delegate* all responsibility for its design and approval, implicitly retaining the right to replace that subordinate who takes charge of it. (2) He may delegate the design work to a subordinate, but retain the right to *approve* it before implementation. (3) He may actively *supervise* the design work himself.

Improvement projects exhibit a number of interesting characteristics. They appear to involve a number of subdecisions, consciously sequenced over long periods of time and separated by delays of various kinds. Furthermore, the manager appears to supervise a great many of these at any one time—perhaps fifty to one hundred in the case of chief executives. In fact, in his handling of improvement projects, the manager may be likened to a juggler. At any one point, he maintains a number of balls in the air. Periodically one comes down, receives a short burst of energy, and goes up again. Meanwhile, an inventory of new balls waits on the sidelines and, at random intervals, old balls are discarded and new ones added. Both Lindblom [2] and Marples [18] touch on these aspects of strategy making, the former stressing the disjointed and incremental nature of the decisions, and the latter depicting the sequential episodes in terms of a stranded rope made up of fibers of different lengths each of which surfaces periodically.

Disturbance Handler. While the *entrepreneur* role focuses on voluntary change, the *disturbance handler* role deals with corrections which the manager is forced to make. We may describe this role as follows: The organization consists basically of specialist operating programs. From time to time, it experiences a stimulus that cannot be handled routinely, either because an operating program has broken down or because the stimulus is new and it is not clear which operating program should handle it. These situations constitute disturbances. As generalist, the manager is obliged to assume responsibility for dealing with the stimulus. Thus, the handling of disturbances is an essential duty of the manager.

There is clear evidence for this role both in our study of chief executives and in Sayles' study of production supervisors [24, p. 162]:

> The achievement of this stability, which is the manager's objective, is a never-to-be-attained ideal. He is like a symphony orchestra conductor, endeavoring to maintain a melodious performance in which contributions of the various instruments are coordinated and sequenced, patterned and paced, while the orchestra members are having various personal difficulties, stagehands are moving music stands, alternating excessive heat and cold are creating audience and instrument problems, and the sponsor of the concert is insisting on irrational changes in the program.

Sayles goes further to point out the very important balance that the manager must maintain between change and stability. To Sayles, the manager seeks "a dynamic type of stability" (p. 162). Most disturbances elicit short-term adjustments which bring back equilibrium; persistent ones require the introduction of long-term structural change.

Resource Allocator. The manager maintains ultimate authority over his organization's strategy-making system by controlling the allocation of its resources. By deciding who will get what (and who will do what), the manager directs the course of his organization. He does this in three ways:

(1) *In scheduling his own time,* the manager allocates his most precious resource and thereby determines organizational priorities. Issues that receive low priority do not reach the *nerve center* of the organization and are blocked for want of resources.

(2) In designing the organizational structure and in carrying out many improvement projects, the manager *programs the work of his subordinates.* In other words, he allocates their time by deciding what will be done and who will do it.

(3) Most significantly, the manager maintains control over resource allocation by the requirement that he *authorize all significant decisions* before they are implemented. By retaining this power, the manager ensures that different decisions are interrelated—that conflicts are avoided, that resource constraints are respected, and that decisions complement one another.

Decisions appear to be authorized in one of two ways. Where the costs and benefits of a proposal can be quantified, where it is competing for specified resources with other known proposals, and where it can wait for a certain time of year, approval for a proposal is sought in the context of a formal *budgeting* procedure. But these conditions are most often not met— timing may be crucial, nonmonetary costs may predominate, and so on. In these cases, approval is sought in terms of an *ad hoc request for authorization.* Subordinate and manager meet (perhaps informally) to discuss one proposal alone.

Authorization choices are enormously complex ones for the manager. A myriad of factors must be considered (resource constraints, influencer preferences, consistency with other decisions, feasibility, payoff, timing, subordinate feelings, etc.). But the fact that the manager is authorizing the decision rather than supervising its design suggests that he has little time to give to it. To alleviate this difficulty, it appears that managers use special kinds of *models* and *plans* in their decision-making. These exist only in their minds and are loose, but they serve to guide behavior. Models may answer questions such as, "Does this proposal make sense in terms of the trends that I see in tariff legislation?" or "Will the EDP department be able to get along with marketing on this?" Plans exist in the sense that, on questioning, managers reveal images (in terms of proposed improvement projects) of where they would like their organizations to go: "Well, once I get these foreign operations fully developed, I would like to begin to look into a reorganization," said one subject of this study.

Negotiator. The final role describes the manager as participant in negotiation activity. To some students of the management process [8, p. 343], this is not truly part of the job of managing. But such distinctions are arbitrary. Negotiation is an integral part of managerial work, as this study notes for chief executives and as that of Sayles made very clear for production supervisors [24, p. 131]: "Sophisticated managers place great stress on negotiations as a way of life. They negotiate with groups who are setting standards for their work, who are performing support activity for them, and to whom they wish to 'sell' their services."

The manager must participate in important negotiation sessions because he is his organization's legal authority, its *spokesman* and its *resource allocator*. Negotiation is resource trading in real time. If the resource commitments are to be large, the legal authority must be present.

These ten roles suggest that the manager of an organization bears a great burden of responsibility. He must oversee his organization's status system; he must serve as a crucial informational link between it and its environment; he must interpret and reflect its basic values; he must maintain the stability of its operations; and he must adapt it in a controlled and balanced way to a changing environment.

MANAGEMENT AS A PROFESSION AND AS A SCIENCE

Is management a profession? To the extent that different managers perform one set of basic roles, management satisfies one criterion for becoming a profession. But a profession must require, in the words of the Random House Dictionary, "knowledge of some department of learning or science." Which of the ten roles now requires specialized learning? Indeed, what school of business or public administration teaches its students how to disseminate information, allocate resources, perform as figurehead, make contacts, or handle disturbances? We simply know very little about teaching these things. The reason is that we have never tried to document and describe in a meaningful way the procedures (or programs) that managers use.

The evidence of this research suggests that there is as yet no science in managerial work—that managers do not work according to procedures that have been prescribed by scientific analysis. Indeed, except for his use of the telephone, the airplane, and the dictating machine, it would appear that the manager of today is indistinguishable from his predecessors. He may seek different information, but he gets much of it in the same way—from word-of-mouth. He may make decisions dealing with modern technology but he uses the same intuitive (that is, nonexplicit) procedures in making them. Even the computer, which has had such a great impact on other organizational work, has apparently done little to alter the working methods of the general manager.

How do we develop a scientific base to understand the work of the manager? The description of roles is a first and necessary step. But tighter forms of research are necessary. Specifically, we must attempt to model managerial work—to describe it as a system of programs. First, it will be necessary to decide what programs managers actually use. Among a great number of programs in the manager's repertoire, we might expect to find a time scheduling program, an information disseminating program, and a disturbance-handling program. Then, researchers will have to devote a considerable amount of effort to studying and accurately describing the content of each of these programs—the information and heuristics used. Finally, it will be necessary to describe the interrelationships among all of these programs so that they may be combined into an integrated descriptive model of managerial work.

When the management scientist begins to understand the programs that managers use, he can begin to design meaningful systems and provide help for the manager. He may ask: Which managerial activities can be fully reprogrammed (i.e., automated)? Which cannot be reprogrammed because they require human responses? Which can be partially reprogrammed to operate in a man-machine system? Perhaps scheduling, information collecting, and resource allocating activities lend themselves to varying degrees of reprogramming. Management will emerge as a science to the extent that such efforts are successful.

IMPROVING THE MANAGER'S EFFECTIVENESS

Fayol's fifty-year-old description of managerial work is no longer of use to us. And we shall not disentangle the complexity of managerial work if we insist on viewing the manager simply as a decision-maker or simply as a motivator of subordinates. In fact, we are unlikely to overestimate the complexity of the manager's work, and we shall make little headway if we take overly simple or narrow points of view in our research.

A major problem faces today's manager. Despite the growing size of modern organizations and the growing complexity of their problems (particularly those in the public sector), the manager can expect little help. He must design his own information system, and he must take full charge of his organization's strategy-making system. Furthermore, the manager faces what might be called the *dilemma of delegation*. He has unique access to much important information but he lacks a formal means of disseminating it. As much of it is verbal, he cannot spread it around in an efficient manner. How can he delegate a task with confidence when he has neither the time nor the means to send the necessary information along with it?

Thus, the manager is usually forced to carry a great burden of responsibility in his organization. As organizations become increasingly large and complex, this burden increases. Unfortunately, the man cannot significantly increase his available time or significantly improve his abilities to manage. Hence, in the large, complex bureaucracy, the top manager's time assumes an enormous opportunity cost and he faces the real danger of becoming a major obstruction in the flow of decisions and information.

Because of this, as we have seen, managerial work assumes a number of distinctive characteristics. The quantity of work is great; the pace is unrelenting; there is great variety, fragmentation, and brevity in the work activities; the manager must concentrate on issues that are current, specific, and ad hoc, and to do so, he finds that he must rely on verbal forms of communications. Yet it is on this man that the burden lies for designing and operating strategy-making and information processing systems that are to solve his organization's (and society's) problems.

The manager can do something to alleviate these problems. He can learn more about his own roles in his organization, and he can use this information to schedule his time in a more efficient manner. He can recognize that only he has much of the information needed by his organization. Then, he can seek to find better means of disseminating it into the organization. Finally, he can turn to the skills of his management scientists to help reduce his workload and to improve his ability to make decisions.

The management scientist can learn to help the manager to the extent he can develop an understanding of the manager's work and the manager's information. To date, strategic planners, operations researchers, and information system designers have provided little help for the senior manager. They simply have had no framework available by which to understand the work of the men who employed them, and they have had poor access to the information which has never been documented. It is folly to believe that a man with poor access to the organization's true *nerve center* can design a formal management information system. Similarly, how can the long-range planner, a man usually uninformed about many of the *current* events that take place in and around his organization, design meaningful strategic plans? For good reason, the literature documents many manager complaints of naïve planning and many planner complaints of disinterested managers. In my view, our lack of understanding of managerial work has been the greatest block to the progress of management science.

The ultimate solution to the problem—to the overburdened manager seeking meaningful help—must derive from research. We must observe, describe, and understand the real work of managing; then and only then shall we significantly improve it.

REFERENCES FOR ARTICLE

1. BRAYBROOKE, DAVID. "The Mystery of Executive Success Re-examined." *Administrative Science Quarterly.* Vol. 8 (1964), pp. 533-560.

2. ————— and LINDBLOM, CHARLES E. *A Strategy of Decision.* New York: The Free Press, 1963.

3. BROWNOWSKI, J. "The Creative Process." *Scientific American.* Vol. 199 (September, 1958), pp. 59-65.

4. BURNS, TOM. "The Directions of Activity and Communication in a Departmental Executive Group." *Human Relations.* Vol. 7 (1954), pp. 73-97.

5. ————— "Management in Action." Operational Research Quarterly. Vol. 8 (1957), pp. 45-60.

6. CARLSON, SUNE. *Executive Behavior.* Stockholm: Strömbergs, 1951.

7. DAVIS, ROBERT T. *Performance and Development of Field Sales Managers.* Division of Research, Graduate School of Business Administration, Harvard University, Boston, 1957.

8. DRUCKER, PETER F. *The Practice of Management.* New York: Harper & Row, Publishers, 1954.

9. FAYOL, HENRI. *Administration industrielle et générale.* Paris: Dunods, 1950 (first published 1916).

10. GIBB, CECIL A. "Leadership." *The Handbook of Social Psychology.* Edited by Gardner Lindzey and Elliot A. Aronson. Vol. 4, 2d ed., Chapter 31. Reading, Mass.: Addison-Wesley Co., Inc., 1969.

11. GUEST, ROBERT H. "Of Time and the Foreman." *Personnel.* Vol. 32 (1955-56) pp. 478-486.

12. GULICK, LUTHER H. "Notes on the Theory of Organization." *Papers on the Science of Administration.* Edited by Luther Gulick and Lyndall Urwick. New York: Columbia University Press, 1937.

13. HEMPHILL, JOHN K. *Dimensions of Executive Positions.* Bureau of Business Research Monograph No. 98. Ohio State University, Columbus, 1960.

14. HOMANS, GEORGE C. *The Human Group.* New York: Harcourt Brace Jovanovich, Inc., 1950.

15. HORNE, J. H. and LUPTON, TOM. "The Work Activities of Middle Managers—An Exploratory Study." *The Journal of Management Studies.* Vol. 2 (February, 1965), pp. 14-33.

16. KELLY, JOE. "The Study of Executive Behavior by Activity Sampling." *Human Relations.* Vol. 17 (August, 1964), pp. 277-287.

17. MACKENZIE, R. ALEX. "The Management Process in 3D." *Harvard Business Review* (November-December, 1969), pp. 80-87.

18. MARPLES, D. L. "Studies of Managers—A Fresh Start?" *The Journal of Management Studies.* Vol. 4 (October, 1967), pp. 282-299.

19. MINTZBERG, HENRY. "Structured Observation as a Method to Study Managerial Work." The Journal of Management Studies. Vol. 7 (February, 1970), pp. 87-104.

20. MYERS, CHARLES A. (ed.). *The Impact of Computers on Management.* Cambridge, Mass.: The M.I.T. Press, 1967.

21. NEUSTADT, RICHARD E. *Presidential Power: The Politics of Leadership.* New York: The New American Library, 1964.

22. PAPANDREOU, ANDREAS G. "Some Basic Problems in the Theory of the Firm." *A Survey of Contemporary Economics.* Edited by Bernard F. Haley, Vol. II, pp. 183-219. Homewood, Ill.: Richard D. Irwin, Inc., 1952.

23. SARBIN, T. R. and ALLEN, V. L. "Role Theory." *The Handbook of Social Psychology.* Edited by Gardner Lindzey and Elliot A. Aronson. Vol. I, 2d ed., pp. 488-567. Reading, Mass.: Addison-Wesley Co., Inc., 1968.

24. SAYLES, LEONARD R. *Managerial Behavior: Administration in Complex Enterprises.* New York: McGraw-Hill, Inc., 1964.

25. STEWART, ROSEMARY. *Managers and Their Jobs.* London: Macmillan, Inc., 1967.

26. WHYTE, WILLIAM F. *Street Corner Society.* 2d ed. Chicago: University of Chicago Press, 1955.

3 • THEORY Z: AN ELABORATION OF METHODOLOGY AND FINDINGS[1]

William G. Ouchi[2]

In the book, *Theory Z* [7], the managerial style of a U.S. electronics company referred to as Company Z is compared to that of the typical Japanese company. Many similarities between Japanese companies and Company Z are also noted. Theory Z is really a typology which describes the visible features of such companies. In this article, the research on Company Z will be described, and then the features of Theory Z will be described in a conceptual manner which ties them together in an integrated theoretical focus.

COMPANY Z RESEARCHED

The research on Company Z took place in several stages. The first stage involved a study of 78 retail department store companies in the eastern half of the United States [6]. The objective of this study was to identify precisely the basis on which the performance of salesclerks, merchandise managers, and operating personnel was measured in the retail industry. The premise was that if individual performance can be clearly measured in any organizational setting, it must be in the retail business where quantitative measures are common. For example, an operations department may be evaluated by the number of hours it takes to move a rack of dresses from the rail yard to the racks in the store; a salesperson may be evaluated according to total sales volume less returns and exchanges; and a merchandise manager may be evaluated by the average gross margin, "markdowns" (discounted goods), and number of times the inventory is "turned over" each period.

Despite the apparent ease with which individual performance can be measured in department stores, however, the study indicated that the more profitable companies relied less upon such measures than did the less profitable companies [9]. In the less profitable companies, there was generally a straightforward application of the official or "bureaucratic" measures of individual performance in setting wages and promotions. In the more profitable companies, the managers within stores and departments tended to rely more upon their own subjective sense of how well employees were doing. The reason for this subjective evaluation in the face of so many quantitative

[1] From *Journal of Contemporary Business*, Vol. 11, No. 2, pp. 27-41. Reprinted by permission of the *Journal of Contemporary Business*.
[2] William G. Ouchi, Professor of Management, Graduate School of Management, University of California, Los Angeles.

measures was that the quantitative measures, no matter how complete, were never complete enough. For example, although the salesclerk can be evaluated according to sales volume, it is also important that each salesperson take accurate stock counts so that out-of-stocks will not occur, that they help to train new salespeople, and that they offer special forms of assistance to customers in order to keep them coming back. None of these important elements of performance can be audited at a reasonable cost through any quantitative means. The only method by which to monitor these more subtle activities is through an understanding by the manager and the employee of what the company expects of each, coupled with a flexible and subjective evaluation by the manager.

The companies which seemed to most successfully apply this subtle form of evaluation had some characteristics in common. First, they were characterized by a high level of trust between managers and employees. Employees will typically permit a manager to employ subjective and idiosyncratic (nonuniversal) criteria of evaluation only if they trust the manager and share with the manager a common set of objectives. If the manager cannot be trusted, then he or she may apply capricious or unfair criteria in order to promote some employees over others. Without mutual trust, therefore, local and subjective evaluation is not possible.

Second, these successful companies were characterized by having longer-than-average tenure among their employees. Only with long-term employees is it possible to develop a mutually consistent understanding of store policy, and only with long association is it possible for the two parties to develop an understanding of one another's goals which ultimately leads to the development of trust.

Third, the successful companies tended to have a distinctive focused culture in which employees and customers alike could readily identify. The consequence is that employees know what to expect of one another due to their common view of how the company should be run, and customers may effectively become an active part of the managerial system. In a store which projects a well-known and distinctive array of services and goods, a customer may challenge an employee who seeks to cut corners, avoid work, or otherwise deviate from that well-known standard. In a company which has no such distinctive culture, a customer who receives substandard service may think that such service is normal for the store and thus one important element of control is lost.

This study demonstrated that, even in a setting in which individual performance is apparently simple to measure, no complete means of bureaucratic measurement and control are feasible. Instead, the existence of a distinctive culture and of trusting relationships is all important. This surprising result led me to ask whether there was a more systematic way to study the importance of subtlety and culture in management. By reputation, it seemed that Japanese companies manifested these characteristics in strong form, which led to the next stage of research.

JAPANESE AND U.S. COMPANIES COMPARED

The second stage of research involved a comparison of Japanese with American companies in several industries [4]. This study, unlike the department store study, did not involve the use of questionnaires but rather rested on interviews with managers in both the United States and Japan, and on an extensive review of the research done by others in this area. This study led to the descriptions which are fully presented in the book *Theory Z,* and which will be reviewed briefly in this paper. In general, this interview study confirmed what others had found: Japanese companies, by comparison with U.S. companies, rely to a great extent upon subtle and local evaluations of performance. These evaluations are embedded in a typically distinctive corporate culture which is widely accepted among employees of all ranks, and is supported by an atmosphere of trust growing in part out of the long association provided by the common Japanese practice of lifetime employment. It has been long known, particularly since Abegglen's notable work, that Japanese companies have characteristics that differ sharply from common Western management approaches [1]. It has furthermore been assumed by both managers and academics that these differences are culturally specific, that the approach that succeeds in Japan has no application in the United States and vice versa. However, I was approached by several American managers who asserted that this interpretation is grossly incorrect. They claimed that their companies, indigenous U.S. firms, had always had characteristics that were typically thought to be Japanese. They further asserted that their companies had never heard of ''Japanese Managment'' and were instead unique creations that had been built by strong-willed U.S. founders operating in their own distinctive ways.

Surprised by this revelation, I gathered a research team of students and interviewed managers from several U.S. industries, asking whether they could identify any U.S. companies which had these ''Japanese Management'' characteristics. These respondents could not only think of examples, but several of them mentioned the same companies. This convergence of opinion implied that indeed there might be some universal form of management which is commonplace in Japan, rare in the United States today, but capable of succeeding in both environments. In order to pursue this possibility in a systematic way, the next stage of research was designed.

Company A vs. Company Z

The first problem was to locate a firm that was indigenously American, but that had the ''Japanese Management'' features which I had by then labeled ''Type Z.'' One category of electronics firms was selected from 1,000 of the largest U.S. industrial firms. This category listed 22 such companies. A brief questionnaire was designed and sent to the top three operating officers of each of the 22 companies as well as to trade association officers, trade magazine editors, and 50 randomly selected securities analysts. The questionnaire, which alphabetically listed the 22 companies, was sent to these individuals and each respondent was asked to indicate which, if any, of the companies corresponded to a one-paragraph description of "Company A" (the bureaucratic organization) and which, if any, matched a one-paragraph description of "Company Z." The two paragraphs were written so that each company could be viewed in a positive light. A separate study which included three samples of managers demonstrated that each of the one-paragraph descriptions of Company A and of Company Z sounded equally attractive. This screening survey was used to identify one company that was most nearly a pure example of Type A organization and another that was most nearly a pure example of Type Z organization [8]. The two firms agreed to participate in the research, a process which took four years.

Questionnaires were ultimately administered to more than 1,200 employees and their spouses in the two companies. These questionnaires permitted us to statistically compare the similarity or difference between the companies with respect to expectation of lifetime employment, frequency of decision by consensus, commitment to a distinctive philosophy of management, and the other characteristics which distinguish a Theory Z company from a Theory A company [3].

Some scholars have suggested that a Theory Z company appeals only to individuals who have high needs for security and low needs for achievement, so that it can never be a general management form in the United States. In order to test this hypothesis, a subsidiary study was conducted. Census maps were obtained for the Standard Labor Area, or job market, in which each company did most of its new employee recruitment. Residential blocks were randomly selected from these maps, and then dwelling units were randomly selected from each block. A separate questionnaire was designed, using standard test items which measure an individual's underlying strength of needs for affiliation, for achievement, and for independence. Questionnaires were then handed out door-to-door by the research team who asked residents for cooperation in the study. The mean scores for this random sample clearly demonstrated that neither Company A nor Company Z attracted unusual employees: the employees hired at Company A and Company Z did not differ from the labor pool at large in their needs for affiliation, for achievement, or for individuality.

Companies A and Z also operated plants in South America. Alfred M. Jaeger, a doctoral student, spent six months studying these two plants [2]. The original employee questionnaire was translated into Latin American languages and administered to employees in these plants, and Jaeger also studied several aspects of the relationship between headquarters and these overseas plants. In brief, he found that Company A had a very distant and narrow relationship with its South American employees. The plant manager was one of very few employees in the plant who spoke English; he reported monthly operating results, and he had little other contact with company headquarters.

The Company Z plant in South America, by comparison, had a broad range of frequent contact with headquarters. The Company Z culture had been transplanted virtually intact to South America: most of the local employees either spoke English or were enrolled in English-language courses; new managers hired or promoted were ordinarily sent to headquarters for a period of several months of training and acculturation to the Company Z culture; and the plant had a record of frequent visitors from headquarters. Indeed, I was struck by the physical similarity of the plant to the company's headquarters plants: the placement of people was the same, the design of the building and color schemes were the same. and arrangement of the visitor entrance was nearly identical with any other plant of Company Z. Jaeger had initially hypothesized that the Company Z culture would not successfully transfer to South America, but he found that employee commitment and loyalty were high, turnover was low, and the culture of the firm seemed to be firmly and successfully in place in this distant land.

Another doctoral student, Margaret Davis, undertook home interviews with several families of Company Z and Company A employees. These interviews were part of a larger study that she was conducting on the relationship between work and family life, particularly with respect to the allocation of time and potential conflicting demands on a husband or wife who holds a full-time job. Davis reported no notable differences between employees of the two companies with respect to time conflicts between work and home life.

A third doctoral student, Alan Wilkins, undertook a novel study of the role of storytelling as a means of sustaining the subtleties of the culture in Company Z [11]. Wilkens interviewed several randomly-selected employees in Company A and in Company Z. He asked the respondents to tell him any stories that were related to their work. He tape recorded the interviews, and then prepared complete transcripts of each. These he painstakingly submitted to a form of content analysis known as script analysis, breaking each interview into discrete elements or parts of stories. These parts were then analyzed statistically. The analysis demonstrated that employees at Company A told relatively few stories each, that only one story was told in common (it was a negative story concerning a mass layoff a few years ago), and that there was no evidence of a commonly held set of values or beliefs about the company. At Company Z, by contrast, each employee told several stories, many stories were widely known and told, and virtually all of the stories had a meaning that attributed positive features to the company. Wilkins concluded that at Company Z, the subtleties of the culture are in part communicated to new employees through these stories.

Further research on this topic by Joanne Martin, Alan Wilkins, Melanie Powers, and others has gone on in a laboratory setting [5]. This research involved dividing subjects into two groups. One group was given a report containing tables of numbers relating to a business problem. The second group was given the same information, except that the information was not in the form of tables but in the form of a story about what had happened in the company. Subjects were then asked how much they could remember of the reports they had read and whether they believed the reports. The result was that information communicated in stories was both better remembered and more completely believed. Thus, Wilkins' interpretation of the role of stories in organizational life was supported.

Another doctoral student, Jerry B. Johnson, performed a detailed statistical analysis of the questionnaires that had been administered in the main study. In particular, he tested several theories of employee commitment or loyalty in order to see, for example, whether commitment is most strongly affected by the age of the employee, sex, profession, education, or some other factor. While Johnson discovered several interesting and important determinants of commitment, none was as important as the management philosophy of Company Z. Knowing that the company was committed to giving maximum freedom and influence to all employees, that it was committed to secure jobs, and that it was honest and high-performing outweighed all other factors in creating strong feelings of loyalty and commitment.

On the basis of this research, Theory Z was developed. The empirical research supports the position that Company Z is identified by the following seven organizational characteristics:

- long-term employment,
- slow evaluation and promotion,
- nonspecialized career paths,
- consensus decision-making,
- collective responsibility,
- distinctive management philosophy, and
- wholistic relations.

Originally, I had hypothesized that Company Z would not differ from Company A in its orientation to individual rather than collective responsibility. Because of the strongly held belief that individuals in the United States are, in fact, and should be held personally responsible for outcomes and performance, I believed that no difference would appear between the companies. Indeed, an analysis of the first wave of data, collected through questionnaires from the officers of the two companies, showed no difference. However, subsequent analysis of the data from employees at all levels of the two companies revealed a large and significant difference, with Company Z employees expressing a more collective sense of responsibility than Company A employees. Thus, although the people at the top of the two companies have the same orientation toward individual responsibility for operating results, the middle managers, professionals, and operators at lower levels of Company Z have a more collective orientation than do their counterparts at Company A. On all seven organizational characteristics, Company Z differs significantly from Company A.

We have, therefore, a typology composed of seven elements, with the two companies differing significantly on all seven. We have successfully identified seven organizational characteristics which discriminate between these two types of organization, but in this study it was not possible to determine which of these seven is more important, or whether all are equally important. Anyone interested either in making practical use of these findings or in extending this research would certainly gain by knowing, or at least having an educated guess at, which of these is more important and which less important.

Theoretical Interpretation

The empirical evidence demonstrates that different organizational types can exist in the United States, but until a much more complex and extensive research program is mounted, we cannot empirically determine which of the seven organizational characteristics is determinative and which derivative. It becomes, therefore, a theoretical task to attempt to construct a satisfactory explanation of this matter. To begin, let me take a simple position derived from a view first taken several decades ago by the economist Von Hayek and more recently crystallized by another economist, Oliver Williamson [12].

In every organization, no matter how large, all employees, no matter how humble their tasks, possess some specialized information about how best to do their jobs. No one else knows what employees know about the details of their particular jobs. Therefore, an organization can achieve full efficiency only by granting all employees the freedom and autonomy to make their own decisions about how their work is to be done, but that freedom can be misused. Employees are capable of abusing that freedom to cut corners, loaf, or otherwise cheat customers, coworkers, the owners of the company, and the public-at-large. Thus, no management will grant such freedom to employees unless they have good reason to trust them. To trust another is to know that congruent objectives are shared. Unless management knows that workers share congruent goals with respect to serving customers, owners, other employees, and the public-at-large, management would be guilty of gross negligence in granting such freedom.

For their part, workers have the ability to restrict the freedom of managers to assign work, to call for overtime, to promote, hire, fire, and otherwise conduct the affairs of the firm. When workers do not trust management, they typically form collective bargaining units through which they can effectively restrain the freedom and the flexibility of management. Of course, a management so restrained cannot operate in a manner that is fully efficient. Thus, without trust, managers and workers will constrain one another's freedom, and productivity will decline as a result.

One assumption necessary for the following argument to proceed is that no one will trust an individual or an institution whose motives are not understood. *If you are ignorant of my motives, you will mistrust me because it is possible that my goals may be reached only by keeping you from reaching your goals.* Without an understanding of motives, therefore, there cannot be trust. When motives are not fully understood, trust can still exist: if you know that you have at least some influence over my actions and you generally believe that we share congruent goals, then you are likely to be willing to grant me a great amount of freedom, expecting no treachery but being able to protect yourself if treachery occurs. Finally, we can observe that unless individuals have intimate access to one another, understanding and trust cannot develop, nor is influence possible. It is, therefore, necessarily the case that there must be access, understanding, and influence if there is to be trust. Without trust, there can be no freedom; without freedom, there cannot be high productivity.

The central characteristic of Company Z is that it maximizes the freedom of each individual employee. That may be, at first, a counter-intuitive observation. On first look, one thinks of Company Z as a highly constrained setting in which people tell similar stories, hold similar beliefs, and behave in similar ways. Certainly, most Westerners react to Japanese firms with some fear of their apparent regimentation, wearing of uniforms, and morning exercises. To some, such organizations appear to embody deindividuation and loss of personal freedom. This was my initial reaction as well, and I at first was cynical of the emphasis Company Z executives placed on commitment to the freedom and individuality of each employee. Indeed, they said, they regarded employees as independent contractors, capable of reaching their own decisions and acting independently. As part of the main study, we measured the level of autonomy and personal initiative that was permissible and typical in the two companies. We found that employees at Company Z, much to our surprise, reported higher feelings of freedom, autonomy, and ability to take individual initiative. I had interpreted the homogeneity in Company Z to be indicative of deindividuation, but the empirical evidence caused me to look elsewhere.

A great part of the apparent homogeneity in Company Z is a lack of differentiation between the top management and the rest of the organization. At Company A, executives carry themselves with an air of certainty that suggests superiority; they clearly set themselves apart from other managers in their dress, speech, size, and location of their offices, and in many ways that are familiar. At Company Z, however, executives take pains to dress casually and to behave with some humility; a naive outsider could not easily separate executives from middle managers at Company Z. In many Japanese companies as well, the executives will come to work dressed in the same company uniform that is worn by hourly employees. Engineers will be located in the middle of the production area rather than in separate quarters, so that production workers will have ready access to them, and vice versa.

A few weeks ago, I met with the American and the Japanese managers who run the U.S. operations of a large Japanese electronics company. They were discussing the importance, to the Japanese, of understanding coworkers' motives as a necessary precondition for trust. The American top manager agreed that this was indeed important and remarked to his Japanese counterpart that he felt they had developed a good understanding of one another's goals. "Well, yes," replied the Japanese, "but if we were both Japanese and had worked together for the same six-month period, then by now I would know the names and ages of your children, the hobbies that your wife enjoys, all about your childhood, youth, and college years, and several other things that have shaped you and your goals. In fact, I know none of these things about you. Our relationship has not become that close.''

An apparent and a real homogeneity exists among executives, managers, professionals, and workers in the Japanese management style along with an intimacy of personal relationships that produces close understanding. In both cases, the underlying purpose of the social style is the same; it produces ready access between people, and from this access can develop understanding, mutual influence, and trust. From trust comes freedom and from freedom, productivity. When the company president comes to work in overalls, he is not expecting the hourly worker to believe that they are identical in influence. He is, however, reminding both the worker and himself, as well as any middle-management onlookers, that the distances between people need not be great and must not be allowed to become great. If social distance increases, then understanding, access, and mutual influence will diminish and trust will evaporate.

At Company Z, a typical plant manager is expected to engage in the ritual of the monthly beer bust: he joins the factory workers once a month for a beer or two and engages in three-legged sack races, water-balloon throwing, and other activities that subject him to the kind of mild humiliation that makes him human and narrows the social distance, thus allowing trust to develop. None of us is foolish enough to say to our subordinates, ''I am the boss. You will therefore keep your distance!'' Few of us, however, can resist the temptation to allow social distance to develop through the unspoken but equally clear signals of how we dress, speak, ornament, and otherwise comport ourselves with subordinates. Social distance does keep people away; it buffers us from the petty problems and the real criticisms of our subordinates.

If we restrict our interactions with subordinates to that narrow range of activities that takes place in the plant or office, then we can sustain the fiction that we are in every way superior, because we are, in fact, entirely superior within that artificially narrow pattern of life. However, if we dine with our subordinates, if we drink with them, if we play softball, golf, or volleyball with them, then we will inevitably create some settings in which those who are superior at work become, if only for a moment, subordinate because we cannot hit the ball as far, run as fast, drink as much, nor sing as beautifully. The clear signal that we accept the basic equality of our subordinates provides an atmosphere in which access, understanding, and mutual influence can develop, and that clear signal cannot be given at work, because at work there is always the clear, if unspoken, overlay of hierarchy.

Theory Z in a New Light

Each of the seven elements of Theory Z can contribute to an atmosphere of trust. Each provides some measure of access, understanding, or mutual influence. Each contributes in some way to the capacity of the organization to maximize the freedom of employees, so that they can make full use of their skills and abilities to perform their tasks more efficiently.

The expectation of lifetime employment has a great effect even on the newest and the youngest of employees. With the expectation of spending an entire career with the same set of coworkers, each person knows that, in the end, their acts (good and bad), their selfishness, and their generosity, will be known and either will be rewarded or punished. Over the course of a lifetime, no significant act or omission can be concealed. Since each employee knows that others have little incentive to cheat, betray, or mislead, trust can be more completely developed. Over a lifetime career, there is the possibility of serial justice. Acts of generosity or of perversity committed five years ago can, in the end be justly compensated.

If evaluation and promotion proceed slowly, then young people learn that there is no advantage in undertaking projects that are highly visible in preference to those that are, in fact, more valuable to the firm's success. To do so is in effect to steal from the company in order to advance one's career, but such attempted theft cannot succeed if the period before promotion is long.

When career paths are relatively nonspecialized, then the incentives of employees are transformed in an important way. An employee who has worked 15 years in Company Z and has moved from one division to another, from manufacturing to engineering, or from production to materials control to accounting, has gained a great deal of knowledge, much of which is of use only at Company Z and at no other company. The specialist who has remained always in computer programming can take 100 percent of his or her skill and "sell" it to another employer, thus losing no value in changing companies, but such is not the case for a nonspecialist. Thus, the veteran workers of Company Z have an incentive to remain there as time passes, because they are not as valuable to any other company and thus cannot earn equivalent salaries elsewhere. The advantage, however, does not lie exclusively with the employer. The veteran employee of Company Z is capable of executing forms of coordination and of completing tasks that no outsider of comparable years could manage. Thus, veteran employees have a higher value to Company Z than do other engineers or salespersons of the same age, and the company has an incentive to pay them a higher wage. The firm has an incentive to keep the employee, and the employee has an incentive to stay. Thus, lifetime employment is greatly strengthened in an entirely voluntary manner. The career wanderings of the nonspecialists equip them with the language, the contacts, and the incentives to be cooperative and open with those who represent other functions and divisions, thus further developing access, understanding, and the possibility of mutual influence.

Consensus decision-making is perhaps the most direct form of mutual influence, particularly when the process includes both superiors and subordinates. In many cases, the symbolic value of a decision thus made may outweigh the actual value derived from a more creative or more rapidly implemented decision per se. Participative decision-making has long been widely recognized by students of management as an important and direct form of mutual influence in organizations, and it does not require further elaboration here.

Collective responsibility is a matter of some complexity. To say that an organization like Company Z is characterized by a sense of collective responsibility is not to say that individualism is absent. Rather, individuals feel strongly responsible for their own performance, but recognize that they share only a partial responsibility for acts that occur in a team. An anthropologist visiting the University of California at Los Angeles recently interviewed both American and Japanese managers employed by Japanese companies in the United States. She found that the American managers tended to feel individually responsible for the acts of each of their subordinates, while Japanese managers rarely felt so. To an American manager, it appears that the subordinate is seen as an extension of himself, as though the subordinate has no identity separate or autonomous from the thoughts, intentions, and actions of the superior. To the Japanese manager, however, it seems clear that each decision is the joint product of several people, and, thus, it would be inappropriate to assign responsibility to any one person entirely, least of all to the superior. In Japanese companies, individual competition for promotion is typically quite intense. Individual evaluations do occur, and individuals do make decisions. However, most of these judgments of individuals occur only after several years have passed, by which time it is typically simple to identify those individuals who have performed very well or poorly time after time, and project after project. Because the evaluations tend to occur only after several years, individuals have no need to arrive at attributions of individual achievement in the short-run, and thus the truly interdependent nature of work and of credit can be recognized in the short-run. An outsider who inspects any single decision or task in Company Z or in a Japanese firm will find that the attributions of responsibility tend to be collective, but a longer time view of those same organizations will show that clear-cut evaluations on an individual basis are made in the long-run.

The distinctive philosophy of management is typically a statement of values, or ends held by the managers of the firm, and of the beliefs they hold about how best to achieve those ends. Those explicitly stated values and beliefs are open to ready scrutiny by employees, stockholders, customers, and the public-at-large. In any organization in which participation is voluntary, therefore, the open and explicit statement of values and beliefs will cause the organization to adopt a philosophy that meets the goals of all parties, including managers, employees, owners, customers, and the public-at-large. Of course, should any organization adopt a position that is sharply at odds with broader social values or with the goals of any particular group, it will lose their support. An organization may choose not to state its values and beliefs openly, thus making public scrutiny more difficult, but without scrutiny it cannot expect to gain the trust of the various parties and thus must operate at a handicap.

It appears that there is a sort of self-regulation inherent in Company Z. Because it is open about its purposes, the company admits external scrutiny of those purposes. It is, therefore, under consistent environmental pressure to adopt purposes that are acceptable to the larger social and economic environment. On the other hand, having passed the test of external scrutiny, Company Z manifestly possesses goals that are acceptable to and perhaps even admired by its many publics, and thus it more readily acquires their trust and their active cooperation in pursuing its ends.

The central importance of a wholistic network of personal relationships has been discussed at length above. In Company Z, because employees interact with one another and with people of different hierarchical levels and different functions and divisions, the social distance between subgroups is lessened. This greater intimacy provides access that encourages the development of understanding and creates the possibility of mutual influence. With these comes trust, and with trust, freedom, full use of individual ability, and productivity in both social and economic life.

Not one of the seven characteristics of Theory Z alone is definitive. Rather, they comprise a complex of characteristics which together produce an atmosphere conducive to a high level of teamwork. We could just as easily produce a step-by-step analysis of Company A, showing how, in each instance, the characteristics of that organizational type will hinder the development of trust, freedom, and high productivity. If the expectation is for short-term employment, then the incentive to lie and cheat in order to advance one's career is greater, and, knowing this, each employee will be less trusting of others. If promotion is rapid and careers highly specialized, then the incentives to be uncooperative and selfish are heightened. If decisions are typically made individually, then the understanding of decisions and of their underlying motives is clouded and the basis for trust is further undermined. If a purely individual view of achievement is held, then it will be necessary to construct bureaucratic measures of individual, short-run performance. These measures, no matter how specific, can never fully capture the subtleties of teamwork and of cooperation that are the essence of organizational life, but will instead create even more direct incentives for selfish individual efforts. Without a publicly visible philosophy of management, the purposes of the organization remain unknown and, therefore, somewhat suspect to the prudent person. Without a wholistic range of human interaction, it is possible that interaction among individuals will be limited to a hierarchical mode defined by corporate rank, and in that case access, understanding, and mutual influence are attenuated, and trust can hardly develop in a robust manner.

CONCLUSION

In every organization, no matter how large, all employees, no matter how humble their tasks, possess some specialized information about how best to do their jobs. Theory Z describes the managerial conditions under which an atmosphere of trust will develop, within which each person can be free to make use of specialized knowledge, pursuing ends that are publicly known and acceptable. It is under this condition that efficiency and productivity can be realized.

REFERENCES FOR ARTICLE

1. ABEGGLEN, JAMES C. *The Japanese Factory: Aspects of Its Social Organization.* Glencoe, IL: The Free Press (1958).
2. JAEGER, ALFRED M. "An Investigation of Organization Culture in a Multinational Context." Unpublished doctoral dissertation, Graduate School of Business, Stanford University (1979).
3. JOHNSON, JERRY B. "The Generalized Reinforcement of Organizational Attachment." Unpublished doctoral dissertation, Graduate School of Business, Stanford University (1981).
4. JOHNSON, RICHARD T., and WILLIAM G. OUCHI. "Made in America: (Under Japanese Management)." *Harvard Business Review* (September/October 1974), pp. 61-69.
5. MARTIN, JOANNE, and MELANIE POWERS, "Scepticism and the True Believer: The Effects of Case and/or Base Rate Information on Belief and Commitment." Working paper, Graduate School of Business, Stanford University (May 1980).
6. OUCHI, WILLIAM G. "A Novel Approach to Organization Control." Unpublished doctoral dissertation, University of Chicago (1972).
7. _____. *Theory Z: How American Business Can Meet the Japanese Challenge.* Reading, MA: Addison-Wesley (1981).
8. OUCHI, WILLIAM G., and JERRY B. JOHNSON. "Types of Organizational Control and Their Relationship to Emotional Well Being." *Administrative Science Quarterly,* Vol. 23, No. 2 (June 1978), pp. 293-317.
9. OUCHI, WILLIAM G., and MARY ANN MAGUIRE. "Organizational Control: Two Functions." *Administrative Science Quarterly,* Vol. 20, No. 4 (December 1975), pp. 559-569.
10. WILKINS, ALAN L., and JOANNE MARTIN. "Organizational Legends." Working paper. Graduate School of Business, Stanford University (1981).
11. WILKINS, ALAN L. "Organizational Stories as an Expression of Management Philosophy." Unpublished doctoral dissertation, Graduate School of Business. Stanford University (1978).
12. WILLIAMSON, OLIVER E. *Markets and Hierarchies: Analysis and Antitrust Implications.* NY: The Free Press (1975).

BIBLIOGRAPHY, CHAPTER 1

Boddweyn, J. "Management: The Trees, the Forest and the Landscape." *Management International Review,* Vol. 7 (1967), pp. 131-135.
Drucker, Peter F. *Management: Tasks, Responsibilities, Practices.* New York: Harper & Row, Publishers Inc. 1974.
_____ .*The Practice of Management.* New York: Harper & Row, Publishers, Inc., 1954. Chapter 29.

Dubin, Robert. "Management: Meanings, Methods, and Moxie." *Academy of Management Review*, Vol. 7, No. 3 (1982), pp. 372-379.

Fottler, Myron D. "Is Management Really Generic?" *Academy of Management Review*, Vo. 6, No. 1 (1981), pp. 1-12.

House, Robert J. "Scientific Investigation in Management." *Management International Review*, Vol. 10 (1970), pp. 139-150.

Hurni, Melvin. "Characteristics of Management Science." *Management Technology* (December, 1960), pp. 37-46.

Isenberg, Daniel. "How Senior Managers Think." *Harvard Business Review*, Vol. 62, No. 6 (November-December, 1984), pp. 80-90.

Koontz, Harold. "The Management Theory Jungle Revisited." *Academy of Management Review*, Vol. 5, No. 2 (1980), pp. 175-187.

Koprowski, Eugene J. "Exploring the Meaning of 'Good' Management." *Academy of Management Review*, Vol. 6, No. 3 (1981), pp. 459-467.

Longenecker, Justin G., and C. D. Pringle. "The Illusion of Contingency Theory as a General Theory." *Academy of Management Review*, Vol. 3, No. 3 (July, 1978), pp. 679-683.

Luthans, Fred, and T. I. Stewart. "A General Contingency Theory of Management." *Academy of Management Review*, Vol. 2, No. 2 (April, 1977), pp. 181-195.

Maidique, Modesto A., and Robert H. Hayes. "The Art of High-Technology Management." *Sloan Management Review*, Vol. 25, No. 2, pp. 17-28.

Mintzberg, Henry. "Power and Organization Life Cycles." *Academy of Management Review*, Vol. 9, No. 2 (1984), pp. 207-224.

Pfeffer, Jeffrey. "Beyond Management and the Worker: The Institutional Function of Management." *Academy of Management Review*, Vol. 1, No. 2 (April, 1976), pp. 36-46.

Smiddy, Harold F., and L. Naum. "Evolution of a 'Science of Managing' in America." *Management Science* (October, 1954), pp. 1-31.

Sullivan, Jeremiah J. "A Critique of Theory Z." *Academy of Management Review*, Vol. 8, No. 1 (1983), pp. 132-142.

Tannenbaum, R. "The Manager Concept: A Rational Synthesis." *Journal of Business*, Vol. 22, No. 4 (October, 1949), pp. 229-240.

Tilles, Seymour. "The Manager's Job: A Systems Approach." *Harvard Business Review*, Vol. 41, No. 1 (January-February, 1963), pp. 73-81.

Walton, C. "Management as a Drama of the Mind." Beta Gamma Sigma *Invited Essay* (September, 1976).

Weiss, Andrew. "Simple Truth of Japanese Manufacturing." *Harvard Business Review*, Vol. 62, No. 4 (1984), pp. 119-125.

Welsh, John A., and J. F. White. "Recognizing and Dealing with the Entrepreneur." *Advanced Management Journal* (Summer, 1978), pp. 21-31.

Whitsett, D. A. "Making Sense of Management Theories." *Personnel*, Vol. 52, No. 3, pp. 44-52.

Wooton, Leland M. "The Mixed Blessings of Contingency Management." *Academy of Management Review*, Vol. 2, No. 3 (July, 1977), pp. 431-440.

Yoder, Dale, *et al.* "Managers' Theories of Management." *Academy of Management Journal*, Vol. 6, No. 3 (September, 1963), pp. 204-211.

Zalenik, Abraham. "Managers and Leaders: Are they Different?" *Harvard Business Review*, Vol. 55, No. 3 (May-June, 1977), pp. 67-78.

Chapter 2

Values and
Social Issues

The purpose of this chapter is to examine how social issues and the concepts of social responsibility interweave with management ideas and practice. What are the interrelationships that exert their mutual influences upon individuals and groups in our society? In the first article, Bok raises serious questions as to whether the professions are devoted to the broad social purposes to which their activities pertain or only to the narrow special parochial interests of the professionals themselves.

Dalton and Cosier then examine the legal dimensions and responsibilities of corporate and managerial behaviors. While we may have predispositions of the social value of a particular managerial activity, Dalton and Cosier show that judgements of the responsibility of any action are open to a great deal of uncertainty. These are not necessarily black-and-white or open-and-shut judgements; rather, they are subject to interpretations about which persons of good judgement could disagree.

In the final article Peterfreund shows how changes in the value systems of individuals over time have affected perceptions of social responsibility. That is, the value set upon which we base our actions and behavior does not comprise immutable and unchanging ideas. What employees believe and are willing to base their actions upon has evolved over time. As such changes evolve, those individuals with unchanging values and interpretation of the application of these values may well clash with associates who have modified their ideas. An appreciation of differences in beliefs appears useful, but tolerance of differences and consideration of changes may be paramount in effective management of the "transformed" work force.

4 • SOCIAL RESPONSIBILITY IN FUTURE WORLDS[1]

Derek C. Bok[2]

PROFESSIONAL STUDY

If the past is any guide, more than 90 percent of you will eventually find yourselves studying law, business, or medicine or enrolling in some other kind of graduate or professional school. The training you receive will open the door to a vocation of your choice. But what sort of experience will you find there? What will it do for you? And what kinds of dangers should you be on guard to avoid?

Many people have a slightly distorted view of what a good professional training can achieve. Some feel that it stocks the mind with a vast supply of specialized knowledge—about legal rules and procedures, about corporate organization and behavior, or about the human body and how it functions. Others think that professional training gives students a set of special tools and advanced techniques with which to pry open problems impervious to the lay mind. Both these notions are partly true, but both are incomplete. A good professional education does convey a lot of special knowledge and a grasp of sophisticated technique but it incorporates them into something greater and more important—an instinctive ability to recognize the characteristic problems of the profession and to break them down into manageable parts that can be thought through systematically. The normal way to develop this ability is to subject students to a period of total immersion in which almost all their time is spent in studying, going to class and living and talking and arguing about the problems of the profession with other students like themselves.

Such training brings great benefits to those who pursue it diligently. Not only can you receive the proper credentials of your calling; you gain a power of analysis not available to people outside your profession. That power in turn opens up opportunities to render great service to others, to achieve the satisfactions of good craftsmanship, to find an identity to define your role in life, not to mention gaining your economic security and material rewards.

Along with all these benefits, however, come certain dangers. As Richard Wilbur once remarked, the genie is powerful because we have pressed him into a bottle. The pressures imposed by a good professional education can be a transforming experience. But few transformations occur without

[1] Based on the Baccaulaureate Speech by President Derek C. Bok at the Commencement Ceremony of Harvard University, Cambridge, Mass., June 1982. First appeared in *Computers and People*, September-October, 1982. Reprinted by permission of Derek C. Bok.
[2] Derek C. Bok, President, Harvard University, Cambridge, Mass.

the risk of losing something of value along the way. In graduate education, the risk you run is of acquiring a somewhat distorted perspective, a set of values that seem slightly askew, a cast of mind that evidences what the French describe as "deformation professionelle".

THE DEFORMATION OF PROFESSIONALISM

And what, precisely, are these deformations? One of them surely is a tendency to grow less concerned about society's problems and more preoccupied with the special predicament of your client. It is the client, after all, to whom you will owe your loyalty and it is the client who pays the fee. Most of all, it is the client's problem that has immediacy and concreteness. What are the distant issues of national health insurance or neighborhood clinics compared with the urgent details of a swelling tumor, a baby's cleft palate, or a damaged heart? How long can you be distracted by the injustices of our penal system or the wasteful delays of our trial courts in the presence of a corporate client facing a union election, a company take-over, or an antitrust decree?

TENDENCY TO WITHDRAW FROM SUFFERING

As you address the problems of your clients, it is also tempting to conceive of their predicament in terms that are more and more intellectual and less and less human. All professional schools tend to turn human situations into problems that can be picked apart and analyzed rationally. Professional life often supports this view of the world. Most of you who enter law or business will offer your services to banks, manufacturing companies, or retail stores—and it is easy to perceive these organizations as hollow abstractions rather than communities of living people. In medicine, the process of abstraction is even more understandable and compelling. As every study of medical education reveals, few students have feelings tough enough to cope with the terrifying immediacy of death and disease. Many tend to withdraw from the suffering and abnormalities of their patients and begin to conceive of them less as frightened, vulnerable human beings and more as a puzzling deficiency in red blood cells, an unusual kidney malfunction, an odd lesion in the lower intestine. Reinforcing these pressures is the image of success that society has imposed on all of our professions, the image of the emotionless practitioner—cool, detached, objective, and totally in control.

Still another tendency in graduate or professional school is to become so steeped in its special methods of analysis that one ignores other ways of apprehending human experience. Each of these schools arouses an immediate insecurity in its students and a corresponding desire to prove themselves by mastering the technical apparatus of the profession. As you grow more and more adept in these techniques, it is only natural that you be tempted to press these methods on problems where they do not fit. Business school students may cease to wonder about how to work with other human beings and begin to think about the efficient management of human resources. Law students may seize their yellow pads and jot down all the arguments for and against marrying their high school sweethearts. Psychiatrists often see every conceivable human situation as a product of repressed sexual desires.

The quirks I have described may strike you as quaint, but they can have serious effects, not only as your personal and family life, but on your careers as well.

HUMAN DIMENSIONS

I mentioned that most professional schools tend to emphasize the intellectual aspects of practice and to set aside the personal, the emotional, the deeply human dimensions of their calling. The bias is understandable, since formal learning is much more suited to dealing with intellectual and analytic problems than with the more intuitive and psychological aspects of experience. And yet, if you begin to accept this view of the world, you may lose many of the greatest rewards of professional life by failing to perceive much of the human interest and drama that arise in every professional practice. Not only can your work grow colorless and dull; you may accomplish less as well. After all, solutions to most legal disputes and most corporate problems cannot be found through analysis alone but depend on being aware of the feelings, the motives, the needs and aspirations of all the human beings involved. The same is even true in more technical fields such as medicine. How can anyone expect to cope effectively with human health by scientific methods alone when one-third of all patients fail to take the drugs their doctors have prescribed, when half of all illness results from drinking, smoking, and other personal habits; when one-third to a half of all cases in general medicine practice have a strong psychosomatic base.

GREAT SOCIAL CONTRIBUTIONS

Apart from the effects on your careers, the deformations I have described can also have consequences for the professions themselves. For example, if you come to regard the problems of your clients as an intellectual challenge and not as an intensely human predicament, you are likely to move toward certain kinds of careers where the intellectual demands seem greatest— toward the sophisticated specialties in medicine; toward corporate legal practice; toward finance, planning, or consulting in business. While there is nothing inherently wrong with these lines of work, they are not necessarily the fields in which the greatest social contributions lie. For the next generation at least, our health care system will probably need able practitioners in primary care and family medicine more than specialists in cardiology or neurosurgery. As attorneys, you may serve society better as public interest lawyers and neighborhood practitioners, or dare I say it—by not becoming lawyers at all, than you will by being fresh recruits for corporate tax, securities regulation, and antitrust litigation. The economy, with its lagging productivity, may benefit more from production managers than from investment analysts, corporate planners, or roving consultants.

ETHICAL DILEMMAS

Another byproduct of professional training is that the constant emphasis on solving problems through conventional modes of analysis may cause young professionals to ignore the ethical dilemmas of their practice. Alas, you are not likely to detect much serious attention to ethics in the professional school you enter. And that is a serious deficiency at a time when every profession bristles with moral dilemmas and the public trust in professionals has everywhere declined. As a "New York Times" article recently concluded: "If medical education does not come to grips with the ethical as well as the technical problems in the field, society may soon discover that modern medicine has given a relatively small number of men and women enormous power—which they have not been adequately trained to wield." Exactly the same could be said of all the other major professions as well.

There is a final danger to consider that may be even more important. I have already observed that students in professional schools grow more and more preoccupied with the needs and problems of the clients they serve and less and less concerned with the impact of their profession on the larger society. That would be a problem in any era. It is a particularly serious problem today.

SOCIETY'S CONCERNS

I cannot remember a time when society's concerns about the professions have seemed more distant from the daily preoccupations of our professional schools and the body of practitioners they serve. In medicine, for example, the public is not greatly troubled by the technical quality of service that doctors offer their patients. What does concern the public is how medical services can be organized to extend adequate care to all segments of society; how to contain medical costs so that they cease to rise at much faster rates than those of other goods and services; and how to address the great moral dilemmas of euthanasia, abortion, and artificial insemination. What troubles thinking people most about our legal system is not that lawyers are poorly trained but that we rely too much on law and litigation in most of our institutions while failing to insure that poor people have proper access to basic legal services at prices they can afford. In business, our principal concern is how our corporations can work more effectively with government to increase productivity and address social problems and how business can be kept accountable to the public interest in an age when markets do not provide a perfect discipline and government regulation is often inefficient and ineffective.

FAILURE OF GOVERNMENT REGULATION

These are not problems that receive much attention in our professional schools today despite their high priority in the public mind. And that is a serious matter, for there is one thing that we have surely learned from the failures of government regulation over the years. If we wish our professions to serve the public better, we must enlist the active cooperation of professionals themselves. Without their help, little of lasting value can occur.

The problems I have described are not your problems now, but they will be your problems very soon. I hope that you will address them boldly and never regard yourselves as human clay to be molded and shaped by your professional school experience. There was a time when I could not have brought myself to utter this last remark: it would have seemed too obvious and banal. But I was startled to find in my last years as a faculty member that many students had managed to persuade themselves that the Law School was "programming them" for lucrative corporate practice and co-opting them from careers fighting for noble causes or serving the needy. Such attitudes are not merely far-fetched; they are extremely dangerous, for they offer easy rationalizations to avoid responsibility for what you make of your lives. Professional schools graduate every kind of practitioner serving every conceivable segment of society. They give you tools with which to work. But the ends and values to which you direct your talents are yours and yours alone to decide, and professional maturity begins with that realization.

FRESH FIELDS AND PASTURES NEW

In making these decisions, you begin with a strong defense against narrowing tendencies of professional training, for you would not have been admitted to Harvard College had you not been interested in a broad range of human and social questions, and four years here should have helped to cement that foundation. In one respect, however, I fear that your Harvard experience may not have served you well. By gaining admission here you prevailed in a remarkably stiff competition. By working hard to win acceptance by a professional school, you have continued to run in a demanding race. Fresh opportunities lie before you to compete for the best residencies, the best law firms, the best positions in the best corporations. These competitions are excellent motivation devices that call on powerful human instincts.

A LIFE THAT ENGAGES ALL OF YOUR INTERESTS

But it is a characteristic of competitions that one must play by other people's rules and compete for prizes that other people have chosen. And that is a poor preparation for later life, especially if you mean to live an independent existence and resist the deformations I have tried to describe.

To guard against these dangers, I hope that you will pause now and then to free your minds from your immediate problems and ambitions and imagine how your lives will seem to you at the end of your careers. If you can somehow manage the feat of looking back upon your future lives, I suspect that you will begin to feel less concerned with whether you succeed by narrow professional standards. Instead, I suspect that you will hope more and more for a life that continuously engages all of your interests and absorbs all of your energies. And as you think further. I suspect you will come to realize that no life can engage you fully unless it is open to the feelings of everyone around you and that no career can absorb your energies for very long unless it allows you to contribute generously to the welfare of others. If these be your sentiments, I hope that you will guard them well so that you can make a life that is worthy of your talents and equal to this brave beginning. Congratulations to you all. You deserve the very best. I feel sure that you will find it.

5 • THE FOUR FACES OF SOCIAL RESPONSIBILITY[1]

Dan R. Dalton[2]
Richard A. Cosier[3]

Imagine that your company is considering introducing a new plastic container to the market. Your company considers itself to be socially responsible; therefore, an extensive impact assessment program is undertaken. One of your environmentally-minded employees suggests that people might light the containers and then cook their meals over the fire. Although the idea sounds bizarre, you don't want to take any chances, so for over a month you cook hamburgers over a fire made from your plastic bottles. Rats are fed this hamburger, then carefully monitored for negative side effects. Tests indicate that these rats suffer no ill effects.

Of course you also perform an extensive series of tests involving energy usage, disposal, and recycling opportunities. Then you invite the public to carefully scheduled hearings across the country in order to encourage consumer inputs. Finally, you market the new product and land a major soft drink company as a customer.

Sound as if your company has fulfilled its responsibilities and forestalled any possible objections? In the mid-1970s Monsanto went through this very process in developing Cycle-Safe bottles and spent more than $47 million to market the product. But in 1977 the FDA banned the bottle because, when stored at 120 degrees for an extended period of time, molecules strayed from the plastic into the contents. Rats, fed with doses that were equivalent to consuming thousands of quarts of soft drink over a human lifetime, developed an above-normal number of tumors.

Monsanto felt that they were providing a product that did something for society—a plastic bottle that could be recycled. But social responsibility is unavoidably a matter of degree and interpretation. Forces outside of the business are liable to interpret a product to be socially unacceptable, even when the company has undertaken an extensive impact analysis.

A precise evaluation of what is socially responsible is difficult to establish and of course, many definitions have been suggested. Joseph McGuire, in *Business and Society,* provided a persuasive focus when he stated that the corporation "must act 'justly' as a proper citizen should." Large corporations have, not only legal obligations, but also certain responsibilities to society which extend beyond the parameters set by law. As the Monsanto case illustrates, the line between legality and responsibility is sometimes very fine.

[1] From *Business Horizons,* Vol. 25, No. 3 (May-June, 1982), pp. 19—27. Reprinted by permission of *Business Horizons.*
[2] Dan R. Dalton, Assistant Professor, Indiana University Graduate School of Business.
[3] Richard A. Cosier, Associate Professor, Indiana University Graduate School of Business.

Peter Drucker offers a useful way to distinguish between behaviors in organizations; the first is what an organization does *to* society, the other what an organization can do *for* society. This suggests that organizations can be evaluated on at least two dimensions with respect to their performance as ''citizens'': legality and responsibility. The accompanying Table illustrates the various combinations of legality and responsibility which may characterize an organization's performance.

These combinations are the *four faces of social responsibility*. Each cell of the table represents a strategy which could be adopted by an organization. It is unfortunate, but we think true, that no matter which strategy is chosen, the corporation is subject to some criticism.

THE FOUR FACES OF SOCIAL RESPONSIBILITY

	Illegal	Legal
Irresponsible	A	C
Responsible	B	D

ILLEGAL AND IRRESPONSIBLE

In modern society, this strategy, if not fatal, is certainly extremely high risk. In an age of social consciousness, it is difficult to imagine an organization that would regularly engage in illegal and irresponsible behavior. What, for example, would be the consequences of an organization's blatantly refusing to employ certain minority groups or deliberately and knowingly using a carcinogenic preservative in foodstuff? Besides the fact that such behavior is patently illegal, it is offensive and irresponsible.

There are, however, instances of illegal and irresponsible corporate conduct which are not so easily condemned.

YOU CAN HARDLY BLAME THEM

Most of us have value systems. They vary, to be sure, from individual to individual and from corporation to corporation. They do, however, have common elements: they are tempered by temptation, consequence, and risk. Sometimes when faced with high temptation, low consequence, and low risk, our value systems are not the constraining force they could be. This may be the human condition and insufficient justification for the excesses which often accompany individual and corporate decision making. Nonetheless, an appreciation of these factors often makes those decisions entirely understandable.

Suppose that the state in which you live invokes a regulation that all motor vehicles operated on a public thoroughfare must be equipped with an "X" type pollution-control device. This law, for the sake of discussion, is retroactive. All automobiles registered in the state must be refitted with such a device, which cost $500. All automobiles are subject to periodic inspection to assure compliance with the law. Assume that the maximum fine (consequence) for violating this statute is $50. Assume, furthermore, that there is one chance in one hundred that you will be inspected and found in violation. The analytical question is simply stated: Would you have the device installed? If you do, it will cost $500. If you do not, the cost will be $500 plus a $50 fine, but only *if* you are caught. Many, if not most, of us surely would not install the device. Strictly speaking, our behavior is both illegal and irresponsible. Our failure to comply exacerbates a societal problem—namely, polluting the air. Our reluctance under the described circumstances, however, is understandable: temptation along with low consequence and low risk.

Compare this situation with that of a large organization faced with the decision to install pollution abatement equipment in one of its plants. Suppose, in this case, the total cost of the installation is $500,000; the maximum fine for noncompliance is $10,000; the chance of being caught is one in one hundred. We ask the same question: Would you comply? We have actually been charitable with the balance of costs and probabilities in this example. The Occupational Safety and Health Administration (OSHA), which was given the charter for establishing and enforcing occupational safety and health standards, has a limited number of inspectors and approximately five million organizations subject to its mandate. It has been estimated that an organization could plan on being inspected about every seventy-seven years, or approximately as often as you could expect to see Halley's comet.[4] Furthermore, $10,000 is a very large fine by OSHA standards. The fundamental point, of course, is that the temptation to ignore the law ($500,000) is large, the fine ($10,000) low, and the risk (once every seventy-seven years) very small. You cannot be surprised when an organization does not comply any more than you would be surprised that the individual with the polluting car did not comply.

It can be argued that the organization has the greater responsibility. Certainly, a polluting smokestack is more visible, literally and figuratively, than an automobile's exhaust. However, we daresay that the marginal pol-

⁴ "Why Nobody Wants to Listen to OSHA," *Business Week*, June 14, 1976: 76, from Randall S. Schuler, *Personnel and Human Resource Management* (St. Paul: West Publishing Company, 1981).

lution attributable to automobiles far exceeds that of smokestacks in most (if not all) regions. Illegal? Yes. Irresponsible? Yes. Understandable?

Whether or not the behavior is "understandable," the result, at a minimum, is bad publicity. The observation that a corporation is likely to be criticized for operating in that "Illegal/Irresponsible" area is obvious. There has, however, been testimony and documentation that the weight of potential litigations in a classic cost/benefit analysis is far less than the cost of recalling or correcting the alleged deficiencies. While we have suggested that behavior in this area is high risk, there is precious little evidence that it is suicidal.

ILLEGAL/RESPONSIBLE

Being in this cell raises very interesting issues. Monsanto found itself in this cell in the Cycle-Safe incident. The FDA ruled their product "illegal," even though Monsanto felt socially responsible. Many times however, organizations find themselves in this area because of jurisdictional disputes. Suppose that prior to the Civil Rights Act of 1964 and attendant legislation, an organization chose to embark on a program to employ women in equal capacities as male employees. At the time, this would have been forward-looking and extremely responsible corporate behavior. Unfortunately, much of the behavior involved in implementing that strategy would have been unquestionably illegal. During that period, "protective legislation" was very common. This legislation, designed to "protect" women, restricted working hours, overtime, the amount of weight that could be lifted, and types of jobs (bartending, for example) available to women. These and similar matters were eventually adjudicated largely at the federal court level.

Grover Starling cites an interesting jurisdictional paradox. It seems that the Federal Meat Inspection Service ordered an Armour meat-packing plant to create an aperture in a conveyor line so that inspectors could remove samples for testing. Accordingly, the company did so. The Occupational Safety and Health Administration soon arrived and demanded that the aperture be closed. It seems that an aperture on that line constituted a safety hazard. Predictably, each agency threatened to close down the plant if it refused to comply with its orders.[5] This example demonstrates how an organization could be operating in a fundamentally desirable manner (safely) and yet run afoul of legislation at some level. An organization might adopt a program to train underprivileged children, for example, and find itself in violation of a minimum wage law.

One potential strategy for dealing with problems in this cell is challenging the law. Laws can be, and are regularly, deliberately violated for no other reason than to challenge their application. You cannot get a hearing in a state or federal court on a "what if" basis. In order to get a hearing, someone must be in jeopardy. A classic example is the famous Gideon vs.

[5] Grover Starling, *The Changing Environment of Business* (Boston: Kent Publishing Company, 1980).

Wainwright case where the Supreme Court ruled that a suspect has the right to counsel and that the state must provide such counsel if the accused could not afford it. This case could not have been decided without an issue—a man convicted without benefit of counsel. Gideon had to be in jeopardy. Courts do not rule on hypothetical cases.

The public is often critical of the corporate use of the courts. It is true that the courts, aside from their jurisprudential charter, are often used as a delay mechanism. There are, for example, legendary antitrust cases which have been in the courts for years. The courts have ruled against the acquisition, but organizations, through a series of legal maneuvers, have managed to stall the actual separations. In the meantime, presumably, the benefits of the acquisition continue to accrue. Interestingly, everyone's "pursuit of justice" is someone else's "delay." Even in Gideon vs. Wainwright, we have little doubt that the prosecuting attorney's office saw the several appeals as both a nuisance and a delay.

Again, organizations can find themselves in a dilemma. An organization in the "Illegal/Responsible" cell faces a paradox. It is likely to be criticized whether it lives within the law or, potentially, challenges it.

IRRESPONSIBLE/LEGAL

Historically, there have been astonishing excesses in this area. Some of them would have been laughable if they had not been so serious. For example, prior to the Pure Food and Drug Act, the advertising for a diet pill promised that a person taking this pill could eat virtually anything at any time and still lose weight. Too good to be true? Actually, the claim was quite true; the product lived up to its billing with frightening efficacy. It seems that the primary active ingredient in this "diet supplement" was tapeworm larvae. These larvae would develop in the intestinal tract and, of course, be well fed; the pill taker would in time, quite literally, starve to death.

In another case, which can only be described as amazing, an "anti-alcoholic elixir" was guaranteed to prevent the person who received the "potion" from drinking to excess. It was *very* effective. The product contained such a large dose of codeine that the people taking it became essentially comatose. The good news, of course, is that they certainly did not drink very much. And at the time, this product was not illegal.

There are more current examples with which we are family familiar— black lung disease in miners and asbestos poisoning, among others. Certainly, it was not always illegal to have miners working in mines without sufficient safety equipment to forestall black lung; nor was it illegal to have employees regularly working with asbestos without adequate protection. It can be argued that these consequences were not anticipated and that these situations were not deliberately socially irresponsible. It is, however, less persuasive to make that argument with respect to the ages and extended working hours of children in our industrial past.

But enough of the past. Do major organizations continue to engage in behaviors which, while not illegal, may be completely irresponsible? Among several examples that come to mind, one is, we think, appropriate for discussion but likely to be highly contentious—the manufacture and distribution of cigarettes. Obviously, cigarette manufacturing is not illegal. Is it irresponsible?

We noted earlier that knowledge of the effects of certain drugs may have been lacking in the past. We mentioned codeine-based elixirs. There are others. Some compounds contained as much as three grams of cocaine per base ounce. One asthma reliever was nearly pure cocaine. Even so, perhaps their effects were little understood and little harm was thought to have been done. Can the same be said of tobacco industry? Is there anyone who is not aware of the harmful effects of smoking? True, there are warning labels which imply that the purchaser knows what he or she is taking. But how many people would endorse the use of codeine or cocaine or any other harmful substance, even with an appropriate warning label. Comparing apples and oranges? Perhaps, but fifty years from now, writers may talk about the manufacture of tobacco products and use terms such as "astonishing," "amazing," and "laughable" as we have to describe other legal, but irresponsible, behaviors.

Certainly, issues other than health are contained in this category. Suppose an organization is faced with more demand for its product than it can meet. Naturally, the organization does not care to encourage competition and would prefer to meet the demand itself if possible. Unfortunately, their plants are already operating twenty-four hours per day, seven days a week. There is simply no further capacity. Management decides to build a new plant, which can be completed in no less than four years.

In the meantime, it is discovered that an existing, abandoned plant can be acquired and refitted in six months. Now, this plant will not be efficient, and will be only marginally profitable at best. It will, however, serve to meet the escalating demand until such time as the new plant is ready for full operation, some four years hence.

Juryrigging this abandoned plant, however, involves several problems. Foremost among them is the fact that the community does not have the infrastructure to serve the plant and the expected influx of employees. School systems will have to be expanded; housing will have to be built; recreational services improved. For the sake of this discussion, suppose that the temporary plant will employ 1,200 persons. It would be reasonable to estimate that this would mean the addition of 3,000 to 3,500 persons in the community. But, remember, this plant will be closed as soon as the new plant in another location is operational.

What is your decision? Do you authorize the refitting of this temporary plant? Certainly, if you notify the community that the plant is temporary, you will pay certain costs. The community would be understandably unlikely to make permanent improvements. Local banks would be somewhat less than enthusiastic about financing building projects, home mortgages, or consumer loans of any description. The simple solution is obvious—don't tell.

The point is that to deliberately use this plant as a stop-gap measure knowing full well that it will be temporary is not illegal. We are aware of no legislation which would prevent this action. There remain, however, some obvious social ramifications of this strategy. The ultimate closing of this plant is likely to reduce this community to a ghost town; there will be widespread unemployment; property values will fall precipitously; the tax base will be destroyed.

Once again, operating in this area is subject to criticism, underscoring our earlier point that being a "law-abiding" corporate citizen is not nearly enough; while organizations may not violate a single law, they may not be socially responsible. What of gambling casinos dealing, not only in games of chance but also offering endless free liquor and decolletage? How about the manufacturers of handguns? Automobiles with questionable, if not lethal, fuel systems? Can a society hold organizations to a standard higher than that demanded by law?

LEGAL/RESPONSIBLE

It would seem that we have finally arrived at a strategy for which an organization cannot be criticized. An organization in this sector is a law-abiding corporate citizen and engages in behaviors which exceed those required by law—voluntary socially oriented action. Alas, even this proactive strategy is subject to four severe criticisms.

• Such behavior amounts to a unilateral, involuntary redistribution of assets;

• These actions lead to inequitable, regressive redistribution of assets;

• An organization engaging in these behaviors clearly exceeds its province; and

• Social responsibility is entirely too expensive and rarely subjected to cost/benefit analysis.

INVOLUNTARY REDISTRIBUTION

Probably the chief spokesperson of this position is Nobel laureate and economist, Milton Friedman. He points out that today, unlike one hundred years ago, managers do not "own" the business. They are employees, nothing more and nothing less. As such their primary responsibility is to the owner—the stockholder. Their relationship is essentially a fiduciary one. Friedman argues that the primary charter of the manager, therefore, is to conduct the business in accordance with the wishes of the employer, given that these wishes are within the limits embodied in the law and ethical custom. Any social actions beyond that amount to an involuntary redistribution of assets. To the extent that these actions reduce dividends, stockholders suffer; to the extent that these actions raise prices, consumers suffer;

to the extent that such actions reduce potential wages and benefits, employees suffer. Should any or all of these interested parties care to make philanthropic contributions to fund socially desirable projects, they may do so. Without their consent, however, such redistributions are clearly unilateral and involuntary.

INEQUITABLE, REGRESSIVE REDISTRIBUTIONS

This tendency can be referred to as a reverse Robin Hood effect.[6] Mr. Hood and his band of merry men stole from the rich and gave to the poor, but many programs under the loose rubric of social responsibility have not followed this redistribution pattern. In fact, it can be argued that many programs actually rob the poor to serve the rich. Obviously, the more wealthy persons are, the more regressive this social responsibility "tax."

Many projects which are not commercially feasible are supported by the largest of organizations under the banner of social responsibility. Opera and dance companies, for example, may be subsidized by corporate contributions. Public television is heavily financed by corporate sponsors. The reason that these subsidiaries are essential to the operation of these programs is that public demand for these products is altogether insufficient to defray their costs. Presumably, the money to finance these ventures comes from somewhere in the organizational coffers. Consumers, employees, and others "contribute," as we previously noted, to the availability of these funds.

Who, however, is the primary beneficiary of these subsidized programs? For the most part, it seems fair to suggest that those who regularly attend ballets, operas, dance companies, live theatre, symphonies, and watch similar programming on public television are relatively more affluent. It would appear that real income is transferred from the poorer to the richer in this exercise of social responsibility.

EXCEEDING PROVINCE

One, if not the foremost, justification for government involvement in private affairs is market failure. When the market cannot provide, for whatever reasons, that which the public demands, then government is (or should be) enfranchised to supply or finance that product or service. National defense, health and safety, and welfare are a few of the services which the private sector is unable to supply. It may be that libraries, museums, parks and recreation, operas, symphonies, and support for other performing arts are in this category as well. The objection which is central here is that it is not the province of private organizations to decide which of these projects should be funded and to what extent. Such support should not be a function of the predilections of corporate officials; this is the charter of government.

---

[6] Discussion based largely on Dean Carson, "Companies as Heroes?" . . . New York Times, 1977.

The issue clearly goes beyond fighting over who is going to play with what toys. In theory, public officials are subject to review by the citizenry. If the public does not approve of the manner in which funds are being prioritized for social concerns, they may petition their various legislatures. Failing in this, they may not support the reelection of the appropriate public officials. The public, on the other hand, does not vote or in any other manner approve or endorse highly ranking officers of corporations. By what right should corporations decide what is "good" and what is "right." It may well be that a given corporate image of righteousness is somewhat different from your own.

The potential for corporate influence in this "public" area is enormous. Theodore Levitt, while (we hope) overstating the case somewhat, presents a clear view of the potential of business statesmanship:

"Proliferating employee welfare programs, its serpentine involvement in community, government, charitable, and educational affairs, its prodigious currying of political and public favor through hundreds of peripheral preoccupations, all these well-intended but insidious contrivances are greasing the rails for our collective descent into a social order that would be as repugnant to the corporations themselves as to their critics. The danger is that all things will turn the corporation into a twentieth-centruy equivalent of the medieval Church. The corporation would eventually invest itself with all-embracing duties, obligations, and finally powers—ministering to the whole man and molding him and society in the image of the corporation's narrow ambitions and its essentially unsocial needs."[7]

A grim scenario, to be sure. The fundamental point remains. Critics argue that any of these voluntary socially responsible behaviors simply exceed the province of the corporation.

EXPENSE OF SOCIAL RESPONSIBILITY

A final objection to the general issue of social responsibility, whether mandated by regulation or voluntarily pursued by organizations, is that it is oppressively expensive. The necessity to comply with ever-stricter environmental standards, for example, has literally forced the closing of hundreds of industrial locations across the country. Furthermore, it has been argued that these regulations have seriously affected domestic industry's ability to compete in international markets.

No one would argue that expense alone is sufficient to discard programs of environmental protection, employee safety, consumer protection, or a host of other socially responsive concerns. However, it can be argued that these programs should be subjected to a cost/benefit analysis. Quite often, this is not done. An automobile, for example, could be manufactured so soundly that driver deaths in accidents could be practically eliminated on

[7] Theodore Levitt, "The Dangers of Social Responsibility," *Harvard Business Review*, 1958:44.

our highways. But at what cost? We do not intend to address the question of what a human life is worth. Obviously, its value is incalculable. The fact remains that we live in a finite world; resources are limited. When we choose to make expenditures in one area, we necessarily restrict or eliminate expenditures in another. At what point do safety programs become overly paternalistic? At some time, employees, for example, must bear a certain responsibility for their own safety. The same can be said for those who operate motor vehicles on public byways.

While this principle seems clear, it is often not considered. What expense is justifiable to renovate and refit public buildings to render them essentially fireproof? Or, if not fireproof, at least such that the loss of human life by fire is remote. The hard fact is that very few people die each year in fires in multi-storied buildings. Who is going to pay for such judicious safety? And for the benefit of how many?

The same approach can be pursued with respect to airliner safety. Fortunately very few people lose their lives each year in commercial airplanes. There is no doubt that airplanes could be manufactured so that they would be even safer in accidents. Again, at what cost? We do not wish to appear insensitive; the loss of a human life is a tragedy, especially if it could have been prevented. "Safety at any cost," however, is simply not viable in a society restricted by finite resources.

The objection regarding the expense of social responsibility is easily restated. Aside from its absolute expense, which can be formidable, critics argue that social responsibility is often not accompanied by sufficient benefits to justify its cost.

Once again, even while being both legal and responsible, an organization is likely to receive severe criticism.

We have suggested that every cell (Illegal/Irresponsible; Illegal/Responsible; Legal/Irresponsible; Legal/Responsible) is subject to criticism. Furthermore, the cell that your organization occupies may be determined by individuals outside of your firm—federal agencies or consumer groups, to name a few. It may be a classic expression of the aphorism, "You're damned if you do; you're damned if you don't." Inasmuch as all strategies are subject to criticism, where should the organization operate? Which is the optimum strategy?

We think there are three fundamental principles which should be considered by an organization with respect to choosing a strategy for social responsibility; *primum non nocere,* organizational accountability, and the double standard.

PRIMUM NON NOCERE

This notion was first explicated over 2,500 years ago in the Hippocractic oath. Freely translated, it means "Above all, knowingly do no harm." This would seem to be a sound principle for both legality and responsibility. Organizations should not engage in any behavior if they know that harm will be done as a result. This is not meant to be literally interpreted. Certainly, knowing that some individuals will injure themselves is insufficient to bar the manufacture and distribution of, for example, steak knives. This, like any principle, should be tempered with good sense.

ORGANIZATIONAL ACCOUNTABILITY

An organization should be responsible for its impacts, *to* or *for* society, whether they are intended or not. Ordinarily, in the course of providing a good or a service, costs are incurred. Presumably, the price of the product or service is, at least in part, a function of the costs of its manufacture or delivery. The difference between the cost and the price is profit—the *sine qua non* of private enterprise. This would be acceptable, except for one oversight—very often society underwrites portions of the cost. Historically, given that the production of energy through sulphurous coal leads to higher levels of air pollution, the costs of producing electricity have been artificially low. That pollution is a cost. Sooner or later, someone has to pay to clean it up. But who? The consumer did not have to pay a premium for the electricity to enter a "clean-up" fund. The power company made no such contribution.

Today, we could argue that cigarette manufacturing enterprises enjoy a certain cost reduction. The manufacturer and the smoker can be thought of as enjoying a subsidy. Arguably, the retail price of cigarettes does not approach that necessary to cover its total costs. Where, for instance, is the fund that will eventually be called upon to pay for the medical costs allegedly associated with smoking? The point is that someone should be accountable for these behaviors.

DOUBLE STANDARD

Traditionally, the concept of a "double standard" has had a negative connotation. In the area of social corporate responsibility, we think it is reasonable, even commendable. As we have continuously noted, there are no rules that apply to organizations about what, where, when, how much, and how often they can engage in behaviors *for* society, but a certain power-responsibility equation has been suggested.[8] Essentially, this equation argues that the social responsibility expected of an organization should be commensurate with the size of the social power it exercises. Large companies—AT&T, General Motors, Exxon, IBM, General Electric, DuPont—whose operations can literally dominate entire regions of the country have a greater responsibility than smaller organizations with less influence.

The larger an organization becomes, the more actual and potential influence it commands over society. Society, necessarily, takes a greater

[8] Y.N. Chang and Filemon Campo-Flores, *Business Policy and Strategy* (Santa Monica, California, Goodyear Publishing Company, 1980).

interest in the affairs of such organizations. Society has correspondingly less expectation of social responsibility from smaller organizations.

This is the nature of the double standard to which we have referred. While any double standard is somewhat unfair, it highlights an observation made by Drucker. He argues that the quest for social responsibility is not a result of hostility towards the business community. Rather the demand for social responsibility is, in large measure, the price of success. Success and influence may well lead to a greater responsibility to society. A double standard, to be sure, but perhaps a reasonable one.

SO WHICH STRATEGY?

We believe that organizations should adopt a strategy reflected in cell D—legal and responsible. Remember, however, that the classification of cell "D" will be determined by the public (or government acting "for" the public). Organizations have to anticipate, and in some cases, influence the public reaction—be proactive. However, a proactive stance involves some risk. As we noted earlier, critics abound regardless of the cell in the table occupied by the organization. A certain risk, nevertheless, is necessary for any business to succeed. Drucker rightly states that to try to eliminate risk in business is futile. Risk is inherent in the commitment of present resources to future expectations. The attempt to eliminate risk may result in the greatest risk of all—rigidity.

We would argue that merely being a law-abiding corporate citizen is something less than social responsibility. It may be that large organizations must "do something." Affirmative action is a compelling analogy. It is not enough not to discriminate. Organizations must "do something" proactively to further the goals of equal employment opportunity. Perhaps this is true for other issues of corporate social responsibility as well. There may be an expectation that organizations must "do something" to further benefit society beyond following its formal laws.

Basically, some action is better than no action. Throughout the course of history, inaction has never advanced mankind. In our view, errors of commission are far better than those of omission. If our ancestors had heeded the critics who were opposed to doing something, we might all still be drawing on cave walls. This issue is not entirely philosophical; there are important pragmatic considerations as well, as evidenced in the remarks of DuPont chairperson, Irving S. Shapiro:

"I think we're a means to an end, and while producing goods and providing jobs is our primary function, we can live successfully in a society if the hearts of its cities are decaying and its people can't make the whole system work. . . . It means that, just as you want libraries, and you want schools, and you want fire departments and police departments, you also want businesses to help do something about unsolved social problems."[9]

⁹ Irving, S. Shapiro, "Today's Executive: Private Steward and Public Servant," *Harvard Business Review,* 1978:101.

Occasionally, it is argued that true social responsibility does not exist. Organizations do not operate out of social responsibility—but good business. Many instances of activities which could be referred to as "responsible" are public relations strategies which are sound business; it pays to advertise. Truly philanthropic efforts occur without fanfare. Some argue that only when organizations anonymously contribute their executives and other resources to socially responsible programs do you have true responsiveness. Perhaps. But we choose not to define social responsibility as philanthropy. We have no objection to enlightened self-interest.

Assuming that society is not totally victimized by actions justified under the banner of social responsibility, then corporations, even pursuing their interests, present a win-win situation. If restoring land to its natural state after mining is *only* done because it is good business, fine. Society benefits. The same can be said for many, if not most, socially responsible behaviors by organizations. We are less concerned with *why* it is done than with the fact that it *is* done. We think it can be best done legally and responsibly.

6 • THE CHALLENGE OF THE "NEW BREED"[1]

Stanley Peterfreund[2]

There's a "new breed" of people in the American work force. The new breed *is* different. They are viewed as "a problem" by many people. They need not be. I think they're seen as a problem because management becomes frustrated after expending so much energy trying to "change them to be like us." The effort is misspent; they don't want to be like us. I suggest that management may have some changing to do—or at least meet the new breed half way. To explain why, let me try to communicate what we, in our research, find to be the difference between the "traditional" employee and these "maverick" people.

As perceived by many management and supervisory people, the new breed (whether they are white collar, blue collar, engineers, or artisans):

Challenge authority, don't follow orders.
Have no loyalty to their employer, no commitment to their company.
Are overly ambitious, impatient to get ahead.
Care only about money, are less dedicated (or "professional").
Don't care how they look.
Are arrogant and rebellious.

For their part, the new breed and some of the most astute management observers, view what's happening quite differently. As they see themselves, the new breed:

Have no patience for meaningless work; they are in revolt against the dum-dum jobs of the world.
Are committed to "doing their thing"; if they can't find satisfaction doing it in one place, they'll go somewhere else to do it.
Are better educated than generations gone by, more sophisticated. They ask questions—the right questions. This distresses many supervisory people.
Want to get ahead. Never have so many been so interested in continuing their self-development, or felt so strongly that it's sinful for talent to be under-utilized.
Have a broader span of interest in outside affairs, in the world around them. But they have no less interest, perhaps even more, in what's going on in the environment in which they work.
Come to work no less motivated than their predecessors, but are more likely to become demotivated by what they see and experience than any work group before them.

In short, *the new breed could be the most potent, most productive human resource ever available to business and industry.* But as long as there is a mismatch of perceptions—as long as their elders see them nega-

[1] From *Michigan Business Review,* Vol. 26, No. 1 (January, 1974), pp. 26–31. Reprinted by permission from the January, 1974, issue of the *University of Michigan Business Review* published by the Graduate School of Business Administration, The University of Michigan.
[2] Stanley Peterfreund, President, Stanley Peterfreund Associates, Inc., Englewood Cliffs, New Jersey.

tively—the risk is the phenomenon of self-fulfilling prophesy. But there's hope. In one new plant, full of new breed'ers, all of the signs were developing that a much older, traditional management team was on its way to widening the schisms brought about by the generation gap. The General Manager, aged 57, came in one day, a sheepish look on his face and reported: "Last night I told my wife I'd finally matured. She thought I'd flipped. But an amazing thing happened to me yesterday. I walked through my plant, and you know what? *I saw the faces through the beards.*"

Emerging Personnel Trends

Given these people changes, what manifestations should managers watch for? What trends?

a. *The Rise of Individualism; the Drive for Personal Identity and Recognition.* Basically, industry is seeing a manifestation of what's going on in the broader society in which it operates. As individuals gain confidence in themselves, they tend to lose confidence in their institutions. Especially those institutions that don't recognize what's going on and change accordingly.

In the days of peonage and servitude, orders were obeyed, authority was respected without questioning, survival was a strong motive. In an affluent society, experiencing this surge of individualism that denotes greater self-confidence and security in one's self than in the institution, the dependency on an employer for a job, on a union to speak for the worker, on the church for divine guidance, on someone else to tell a person what to do, is lessened.

In schools, this is expressed in terms of demands for individualized instruction. In consumerism, it's a reaction to dealing with computers or impersonal service. In industry, some persons are becoming progressively more upset when they feel they're being treated as "a number" rather than as an individual person. They're hungry for personal recognition; for a chance to develop their careers, at their own pace, consistent with their own abilities. They want to work in an environment in which they feel they don't have to bury their own identity.

My guess is that it's unlikely that massive plants of over 10,000 employees will ever be built again. One can already see trends in employee communication away from mass media to more personalized communication. All of this is part of a broader need—to manage individuals, not some abstract "employee body." The sooner companies recognize this and organize their personnel relations accordingly, the more hopeful the outlook will be for successful employee relations in the future.

b. *The Importance of the Work Itself.* Job enlargement, job involvement, job expansion have been around for a long time. Be prepared for a new surge of pressure in this area. GM at Lordstown was merely a signal. Rebellion against meaningless work will grow. Increasingly, people won't tolerate empty, vacant jobs. Twenty years ago, automation was viewed as a threat; today it's viewed as a relief. And indeed, ultimately, automating routine, repetitive tasks may be the best solution. Meanwhile, able managers will look for ways to give people whole jobs and greater responsibility. Where employers have done so, lower turnover, less absenteeism, and ultimately greater productivity have been the results. Here's one area where the employee's interest and the company's happily correspond. But, be aware, too, that as greater responsibility is assumed by rank and file employees, the job of the foreman, the first line supervisor, must change, too. New concepts of how to manage, how to supervise, will be needed, for the bull of the woods will be doomed.

c. *The Mobile Employee—Changing Loyalties.* Few college students today start on a given campus, spend four years there, and graduate from that school. They take a year off. They travel. They transfer to other colleges. They're on the move. For what reason, should it be expected that other high school graduates, merely because they are not fortunate to go to college, will be any less itchy during their early years of employment? Further, college graduates no longer choose their first employer as the place to make a lifetime career, but as a stepping stone. It's normal for young graduates to move at least once, before they even develop thoughts of career commitment.

Within a few decades, employees with 20 or 30 or 40 years of service in a single company will be rare. Managers have to adjust to new concepts of turnover; of employees coming and going with much greater frequency. This, in turn, means that new methods of orientation and training will be needed, to make new employees as productive as possible, as early as possible, so that there can be a maximum return during their tenure. It also means developing employees to be flexible and adaptable; there'll be far more need for backups and shifting people around.

d. *The Second Career.* A corollary of the above is the growing notion of at least two careers, not one. It appalls the new breed, in their early twenties, to look ahead to "doing the same thing" for 30 to 45 years. That may explain why there are growing numbers of managers and professionals, too, who leave secure positions in their 40's, and switch occupations completely. It may explain, too, why growing numbers of young people look to civil service occupations favorably, attracted by the concept of retiring in 20 to 25 years, with an income base that enables them to do "what they really want to do."

Industry must recognize this, compete with it. Again, new concepts of employment and benefits will be needed to respond to these trends. For instance, the concept of a national pension pool, rather than individual company plans, is being advocated with growing vigor. It seems inevitable that transferable retirement benefits will soon be a part of the scene. And new programs will be needed to handle the growing demand for continuing adult education and self-development opportunities, as people prepare for their new careers; look for greater utilization of tuition refund programs, and pressures to stretch them for courses that are not so directly related to the user's present occupation.

e. *Options—in Benefits, Jobs, Careers, Life Itself.* I've stressed the desire of people to be masters of their own destinies. To an employer, the implications affect personnel policies—permitting an individual to transfer, try new jobs, new pursuits, within a single company. But even more pressing, in planning personnel benefits, is the need to recognize that an era may be ending, where a single, set, uniform benefit program works effectively. Industry has so successfully impressed employees with the concept that benefits are part of their income, that these employees are now saying (with some justification), "If that's the case, we want the option to choose." A young person, buying a house or raising a family, feels he needs the benefit now—not at age 65, when he'll be getting Social Security payments, anyway. I think the concept of variable benefit programs, with individual options, will come fast—and in the near future.

f. *New Concepts of Work Days, Work Hours.* There's been substantial publicity, through the press and magazines, of "new approaches" to work weeks. It may take time, but today's concept of working eight hours a day, five days a week, is fading away. Thirty-five hours a week already is normal for white collar and professional work in many areas. Four-day weeks are appearing with more frequency; one of our clients is pioneering a three-day week (with 12-hour days). Other firms give employees the option of picking their own hours—starting earlier or later. Still others assign "a day's work" and the employee is free to go when finished. At least one of our clients has its primary shift work from 5 PM to midnight, because of the much greater availability of better workers to fit their needs during these hours. (The old "first shift" is now the smaller one.) The variations are infinite. The point is twofold:

(1) In almost all of these experiments, the employees are pleased and the results satisfying to the company; and
(2) Management must puncture the parameter of traditional thinking about work hours, and develop new concepts that best suit its operations.

g. *Equal Employment Opportunities/Affirmative Action.* In the last decade, remarkable progress has been made in the employment of minority group members. On a headcount basis, few would quarrel that numerically there's been progress—at least in entry level jobs. But now the Government is underscoring that affirmative action, in the sense of upward progression, is also mandatory, with compliance reviews built in to assure that minorities are more widely distributed, vertically, along the organization chart.

In addition, there is an even greater focus on Equal Employment Oppor-

tunity and Affirmative Action for women. Again, employers have no option
—they *must* identify, develop, and advance females and commit themselves
to a timetable to do so. Managers *must* drop the traditional concept of male
jobs and female jobs. They *must* recognize the principle of equality of opportunity, but be prepared to cope with the actuality that all persons are
not equal—for this is where the conflicts arise.

The likely effect of this could be chaos, unless the program is managed
effectively. *Equal* Employment Opportunity, for the next five to ten years
will become *Un*equal Employment Opportunity for white males. It's like
handicapping a horse race; the previous winners carry the most weight the
next time they race. And nowhere will the problem be more pronounced
than among those white male supervisors who must objectively recommend,
promote, and transfer people if Affirmative Action is to work, and who at
the same time find their own future prospects threatened by women and
minorities on the move.

How, Then, to Manage the New Breed

If one is looking for a magic formula, a panacea, it won't be found here.
Hopefully, the previous paragraphs have pointed out, at least implicitly,
some of the emerging trends for which management must prepare. Beyond
these are several others which merit explicit citation. Some may sound like
principles of sound management in any era; if traditionally they've been
desirable, today and tomorrow they become essential.

1. *Examine the Quality and Attractiveness of the Jobs.* Will they meet
the expectations of the new employee? To answer this question, the manager
must be alert to the trends in the field of education. The traditional approach
to academic education and vocational training is rapidly being replaced by
new concepts of career education. Looking ahead, new members of the work
force will be oriented to the world of work at a much earlier age, and will
be much more likely to emerge from their educational experience with
income-producing skills matched more closely to aptitudes and ability.
Management must be prepared to deal with people who will be more sophisticated from the day they report for work.

2. *Bury Biases! Take the Sexist Labels Off Jobs.* Whether by tradition,
or as a reflection of our culture, yesterday's labor force entered a job arena
with extremely rigid stereotypes of what was "man's work" and which
were "women's jobs." World War II upset some of these stereotypes, but
things soon returned to "normal." Today's personnel, under the impetus of
"women's lib" and with the added clout of government legislation and con-
formance reviews, are puncturing the barriers. Tomorrow's work force will
mature in a new societal and educational environment in which "the world
is *your* oyster, regardless of sex." Are employers ready?

3. *Communicate More Effectively*—certainly not just with the new breed, but most assuredly because of them. If, indeed, managers evolve jobs that contain more opportunity for freedom of action, give individual employees more responsibility, and afford the incumbents more challenge and interest, then it becomes essential that the employees be well informed just to do their jobs well. But beyond this, if management is at the edge of an era of organizational democratization, then it will be able to secure *effective* participation, and *significant* contributions only to the extent that it has a well informed constituency, armed with the information needed to make the greater desired involvement pay off for all parties concerned.

4. *Organizations Will Have to Sharpen their Management of Personnel Development,* moving toward "a plan for the man" concept. As noted above, the trend in education today is toward individualized instruction, with prescriptive direction. There will be no less need to acquaint individuals in an organization's employ, with the career path opportunities open to them, and to guide and counsel them in how best they can prepare themselves to move toward the goals they choose. Unless a firm's employees understand that their developmental goals can be achieved *within* the organization, the turnover and mobility pattern will only accelerate.

5. *Employers Will Have to Negotiate and Develop New Time Frames and Policies for Advancement.* To lean further on the analogy with individualized instruction, the essence of the more successful new approaches to education is to afford the individual an opportunity to learn and grow at his own rate of ability and comprehension. Yet, in many job situations, personnel policies are geared to time in grade, or length of service, or seniority. The rate of individual growth has always varied, whether in school or in the job. What is new is the need to begin recognizing this fact, especially in the policies and practices governing promotion and advancement.

6. *Devise Better Systems to Reward Individuals in More Direct Relationship to their Achievement.* Whether by money, status, or other forms of recognition, the new breed wants to know that someone cares, watches, and knows what each individual does, contributes, and accomplishes. While self-esteem is one of the greatest values of the new generation, it still requires reinforcement and recognition by others. And despite all the management theory to the contrary, nothing does this better than appropriate financial compensation. Rigid salary structures, classifications, or grades will have to be replaced by more flexible approaches. There will have to be a means of rewarding the star performers. People should be paid the most when they're worth the most, rewarded the most when they contribute the most. Consequently, compensation may fluctuate far more in the future—high rewards one year for outstanding performance, less pay another. The concept of programming pay in a linear (upward, only) fashion

may be on the way out. Any good salesman accepts variable income as the name of the game, today. Other occupations may accept this in the future, too. But don't overlook another form of compensation: time off. The new breed values time for its own pursuits. Time off, as a reward for greater productivity, may prove to be a potent incentive.

7. *Develop Better Standards of Performance.* At the very least, managers have to develop better guides to estimating the worth of white collar workers than now prevail. Blue collar workers already are the minority; yet most white collar personnel systems and practices have evolved from the blue collar world. The white collar workers are still the "after-thought" in many organizations.

There will be a need for new ways to measure white collar productivity, more attention to professionalizing white collar functions, new looks to the white collar environment (to offset the "bull pen philosophy," the long rows of desks, the "everybody out in the open" philosophy—so they can be watched, like school children, in their neat rows of desks).

8. *Finally, Management Has to Be Tougher.* More demanding. Raise its expectations. Assign missions which stretch its people more. Managers may have to negotiate goals with subordinates rather than set them unilaterally, though this should not be cause for despair: most experiments in participative goal setting have resulted in greater, not lesser targets. Once set, though, the key is to make people accountable for achieving their objectives.

Laxity, boredom, disinterest, poor motivational stimulus is what turns the new breed off. They're challenging management. The most effective response—and the greatest potential—lies in challenging the new breed more.

BIBLIOGRAPHY, CHAPTER 2

Ackerman, R. W. "How Companies Respond to Social Demands." *Harvard Business Review,* Vol. 51 (1973), pp. 88-98.

Alexander, Gordon J., and R. A. Buchholz. "Corporate Social Responsibility and Stock Market Performance." *Academy of Management Journal,* Vol. 21, No. 3 (September, 1978), pp. 479-486.

Armstrong, R. "The Passion That Rules Ralph Nader." *Fortune,* Vol. 83 (1971), p. 114.

Bell, D., *et al.* "Corporations and Conscience: The Issues." *Sloan Management Review,* Vol. 13, No. 1 (Fall, 1971), pp. 1-24.

Berger, Peter L. "New Attack on the Legitimacy of Business." *Harvard Business Review,* Vol. 59, No. 5 (1981), pp. 82-90.

Bok, Derek C. "A Flawed System." *Harvard Magazine,* Vol. 85, No. 5 (May-June, 1983), pp. 38-71.

Boulding, Kenneth E. "The Ethics of Rational Decision." *Management Science,* Vol. 12, No. 6 (February, 1966), pp. 161-169.

Bowman, E. H., and M. Haire. "A Strategic Posture Toward Corporate Social Responsibility." *California Management Review,* Vol. 18 (1975), pp. 49-58.

Burck, G. "The Hazards of Corporate Responsibility." *Fortune,* Vol. 87 (1973), p. 144.

Chrisman, James J., and Archie B. Carroll. "SMR Forum: Corporate Responsibility—Reconciling Economic and Social Goals." *Sloan Management Review,* Vol. 25, No. 2 (Winter, 1984), pp. 59-65.

Cochran, Phillip L., and Robert A. Wood. "Corporate Social Responsibility and Financial Performance." *Academy of Management Journal,* Vol. 27, No. 1 (March, 1984,), pp. 42-56.

Cressey, Donald R., and Charles A. Moore. "Managerial Values and Corporate Codes of Ethics." *California Management Review,* Vol. 25, No. 4 (Summer, 1983), pp. 53-77.

Keim, Gerald D. "Corporate Social Responsibility: An Assessment of the Enlightened Self-Interest Model." *Academy of Management Review,* Vol. 3, No. 1 (January, 1978), pp. 32-39.

Lodge, G. C. "Business and the Changing Society." *Harvard Business Review,* Vol. 52 (1974), pp. 59-76.

Maclagan, Patrick W. "The Concept of Responsibility: Some Implications for Organizational Behavior and Development." *Journal of Management Studies,* Vol. 20, No. 4 (1983), pp. 411-423.

Nash, Laura L. "Ethics Without the Sermon." *Harvard Business Review,* Vol. 59, No. 6 (1981), pp. 79-90.

Ohmann, O. A., " 'Skyhooks' With Special Implications for Monday through Friday." *Harvard Business Review,* Vol. 33, No. 3 (May-June, 1955), pp. 1-10.

Posher, Barry Z, and Warren H. Schmidt. "Values and the American Manager: An Update." *California Management Review,* Vol. 26, No. 3 (1983), pp. 202-216.

Robertson, W. "Those Daring Young Con Men of Equity Funding." *Fortune,* Vol. 88, No. 2 (August, 1973).

Rosow, Jerome M. "Changing Attitudes to Work and Life Styles." *Journal of Contemporary Business,* Vol. 8, No. 4, pp. 5-18.

Schein, Edgar H. "The Problem of Moral Education for the Business Manager." *Industrial Management Review,* Vol. 8, No. 1 (Fall, 1966).

Sethi, S., and D. Votaw. "Do We Need a New Corporate Response to a Changing Social Environment?" *California Management Review,* Vol. 12, No. 1 (Fall, 1969), pp. 17-31.

Sherwin, Douglas S. "The Ethical Roots of the Business System." *Harvard Business Review,* Vol. 63, No. 6 (1985), pp. 183-192.

Wuthnou, Robert. "The Moral Crisis in American Capitalism." *Harvard Business Review,* Vol. 60, No. 2 (1982), pp. 76-84.

Yankelovich, D. "Social Values." From the William Elliott Lectures, *Historical, Legal and Value Changes: Their Impact on Insurance.* University Park, PA: The College of Business Administration, The Pennsylvania State University, 1977.

Chapter 3

Systems and
Information

Communication and calculative technologies have made possible a realization (or at least a better understanding) of an information age in which data are automatically recorded and transcribed into relevant information and alternatives for human decisions. Such concepts for the generation and manipulation of data are increasingly employed in everyday life and, in particular, in the operations of economic organizations.

Despite sophisticated technology, Porter, in the first article, is able to show the various interpretations that can be made about the same information and the same phenomena. The development of data manipulation techniques will not necessarily deal successfully with these varying interpretations. The human element is needed to deal with the data within a context of the choices that need to be made in the organization. These varying needs can be anticipated to some extent and planned for in the design of the management information systems, as Gorry and Scott Morton show. They develop a framework within which the multiple requirements for information in the organization can be met, hopefully, within one grand design. They distinguish the information system design for alternate needs of the organization, however, showing the differing requirements of strategic planning information from data for short-run control of operations.

Huseman and Alexander extend the concept of matching data needs in the organization to systems design, particularly as the matching relates to communication. They relate how the design of a communication approach is contingent upon the needs for information.

In the final paper Nichols examines personal communication and how it influences organizational communication through listening. We can design the most sophisticated data collection and information processing system in the world, but if the channels of communication that are to receive and act upon that information are dulled or turned off, the prior efforts in design are in vain. The Nichols report is a classic message. Are we listening?

7 • THE PARABLE OF THE SPINDLE[1]

Elias H. Porter[2]

More and more we hear the word "systems" used in discussions of business problems. Research people are studying systems, experts are looking at organizations as systems, and a growing number of departments and companies have the word "systems" in their names.

Just what *is* a system in the business sense? What does it do? What good is it to management? To answer these questions I shall first use a parable from the restaurant industry. What, you may ask, can executives in manufacturing, retailing, or service systems learn from restaurant systems? I readily admit that if you envisage only menus, customers, waitresses, and cooks in a restaurant, you will find no transferable knowledge. But if you see (as I hope you will) inputs, rate variations, displays, feedback loops, memory devices, queuing, omissions, errors, chunking, approximating, channeling, and filtering in a restaurant system—then you should indeed find some practical value in my parable.

The implications of the parable will be discussed specifically in the second part of this article, after we have reduced it to a paradigm.

THE PARABLE

Once upon a time the president of a large chain of short-order restaurants attended a lecture on "Human Relations in Business and Industry." He attended the lecture in the hope he would learn something useful. His years of experience had led him to believe that if human relations problems ever plagued any business, then they certainly plagued the restaurant business.

The speaker discussed the many pressures which create human relations problems. He spoke of psychological pressures, sociological pressures, conflicts in values, conflicts in power structure, and so on. The president did not understand all that was said, but he did go home with one idea. If there were so many different sources of pressure, maybe it was expecting too much of his managers to think they would see them all, let alone cope with them all. The thought occurred to him that maybe he should bring in a team of consultants from several different academic disciplines and have each contribute his part to the solution of the human relations problems.

And so it came to pass that the president of the restaurant chain and his top-management staff met one morning with a sociologist, a psychologist, and an anthropologist. The president outlined the problem to the men of science and spoke of his hope that they might come up with an

[1] From *Harvard Business Review* (May-June, 1962), pp. 58-66. Reprinted by permission of the *Harvard Business Review*.
[2] Elias H. Porter, Research Director of Plans and Operations, System Development Corporation, Santa Monica, California, 1962.

interdisciplinary answer to the human relations problems. The personnel manager presented exit-interview findings which he interpreted as indicating that most people quit their restaurant jobs because of too much sense of pressure caused by the inefficiencies and ill tempers of co-workers.

This was the mission which the scientists were assigned: find out why the waitresses break down in tears; find out why the cooks walk off the job; find out why the managers get so upset that they summarily fire employees on the spot. Find out the cause of the problems, and find out what to do about them.

Later, in one of the plush conference rooms, the scientists sat down to plan their attack. It soon became clear that they might just as well be three blind men, and the problem might just as well be the proverbial elephant. Their training and experience had taught them to look at events in different ways. And so they decided that inasmuch as they couldn't speak each others' languages, they might as well pursue their tasks separately. Each went to a different city and began his observations in his own way.

The Sociologist

First to return was the sociologist. In his report to top management he said:

I think I have discovered something that is pretty fundamental. In one sense it is so obvious that it has probably been completely overlooked before. It is during the *rush hours* that your human relations problems arise. That is when the waitresses break out in tears. That is when the cooks grow temperamental and walk off the job. That is when your managers lose their tempers and dismiss employees summarily.

After elaborating on this theme and showing several charts with sloping lines and bar graphs to back up his assertions, he came to his diagnosis of the situation. "In brief, gentlemen," he stated, "you have a sociological problem on your hands." He walked to the blackboard and began to write. As he wrote, he spoke:

You have a stress pattern during the rush hours. There is stress between the customer and the waitress. . . .
There is stress between the waitress and the cook. . . .
And up here is the manager. There is stress between the waitress and the manager. . . .
And between the manager and the cook. . . .
And the manager is buffeted by complaints from the customer.
We can see one thing which, sociologically speaking, doesn't seem right. The manager has the highest status in the restaurant. The cook has the next highest status. The waitresses, however, are always "local hire" and have the lowest status. Of course, they have higher status than bus boys and dish washers but certainly lower status than the cook, and yet they give orders to the cook.
It doesn't seem right for a lower status person to give orders to a higher status person. We've got to find a way to break up the face-to-face relationship between the waitresses and the cook. We've got to fix it so that they don't

have to talk with one another. Now my idea is to put a "spindle" on the order counter. The "spindle," as I choose to call it, is a wheel on a shaft. The wheel has clips on it so the girls can simply put their orders on the wheel rather than calling out orders to the cook.

When the sociologist left the meeting, the president and his staff talked of what had been said. It made some sense. However, they decided to wait to hear from the other scientists before taking any action.

The Psychologist

Next to return from his studies was the psychologist. He reported to top management:

I think I have discovered something that is pretty fundamental. In one sense it is so obvious that it has probably been completely overlooked before. It is during the *rush hours* that your human relations problems arise. That is when the waitresses break out in tears. That is when the cooks grow temperamental and walk off the job. That is when your managers lose their tempers and dismiss employees summarily.

Then the psychologist sketched on the blackboard the identical pattern of stress between customer, waitress, cook, and management. But his interpretation was somewhat different:

Psychologically speaking we can see that the manager is the father figure, the cook is the son, and the waitress is the daughter. Now we know that in our culture you can't have daughters giving orders to the sons. It louses up their ego structure.

What we've got to do is to find a way to break up the face-to-face relationship between them. Now one idea I've thought up is to put what I call a "spindle" on the order counter. It's kind of a wheel on a shaft with little clips on it so that the waitresses can put their orders on it rather than calling out orders to the cook.

What the psychologist said made sense, too, in a way. Some of the staff favored the status-conflict interpretation while others thought the sex-conflict interpretation to be the right one; the president kept his own counsel.

The Anthropologist

The next scientist to report was the anthropologist. He reported to top management:

I think I have discovered something that is pretty fundamental. In one sense it is so obvious that it has probably been completely overlooked before. It is during the *rush hours* that your human relations problems arise. That is when the waitresses break out in tears. That is when the cooks grow temperamental and walk off the job. That is when your managers lose their tempers and dismiss employees summarily.

After elaborating for a few moments he came to his diagnosis of the situation. "In brief, gentlemen," he stated, "you have an anthropological problem on your hands." He walked to the blackboard and began to sketch. Once again there appeared the stress pattern between customer, waitress, cook, and management:

> We anthropologists know that man behaves according to his value systems. Now, the manager holds as a central value the continued growth and development of the restaurant organization. The cooks tend to share this central value system, for as the organization prospers, so do they. But the waitresses are a different story. The only reason most of them are working is to help supplement the family income. They couldn't care less whether the organization thrives or not as long as it's a decent place to work. Now, you can't have a noncentral value system giving orders to a central value system.
>
> What we've got to do is to find some way of breaking up the face-to-face contact between the waitresses and the cook. One way that has occurred to me is to place on the order counter an adaptation of the old-fashioned spindle. By having a wheel at the top of the shaft and putting clips every few inches apart, the waitresses can put their orders on the wheel and not have to call out orders to the cook. Here is a model of what I mean.

Triumph of the Spindle

When the anthropologist had left, there was much discussion of which scientist was right. The president finally spoke. "Gentlemen, it's clear that these men don't agree on the reason for conflict, but all have come up with the same basic idea about the spindle. Let's take a chance and try it out."

And it came to pass that the spindle was introduced throughout the chain of restaurants. It did more to reduce the human relations problems in the restaurant industry than any other other innovation of which the restaurant people knew. Soon it was copied. Like wild fire the spindle spread from coast to coast and from border to border.

So much for the parable. Let us now proceed to the paradigm.

THE PARADIGM

Each of the three scientists had a different problem: status conflict, sex rivalry, and value conflict. Maybe it was none of these but simply a problem in the division of work between men and machines and how they are related one to the other: a problem of system design. Let us explore this possibility by observing the functions which the spindle fulfills.

Functions Served

First of all, the spindle acts as a memory device for the cook. He no longer needs to remember all the orders given him by the waitresses. This makes his job easier and less "stressful"—especially during the rush hours.

Secondly, the spindle acts as a buffering device. It buffers the cook against a sudden, overwhelming load of orders. Ten waitresses can place their orders on the spindle almost simultaneously. The cook takes them off the spindle according to his work rate—not the input rate. This makes his job easier, more within reach of human capacity—especially during the rush hours.

Thirdly, the spindle acts as a queuing device—in two ways. It holds the order in a proper waiting line until the cook can get to them. When dependent on his memory only, the cook can get orders mixed up. It also does all the "standing in line" for the waitresses. They need never again stand in line to pass an order to the cook. This makes their jobs easier—especially during the rush hours.

Fourthly, the spindle permits a visual display of all the orders waiting to be filled. The cook can often see that several of the orders call for the same item. He can prepare four hamburgers in about the same time as he can prepare one. By reason of having "random access" to all the orders in the system at that point he is able to organize his work around several orders simultaneously with greater efficiency. This makes his job easier—especially during the rush hours.

To appreciate the fifth function which the spindle serves, we must go back to the procedures used before the advent of the spindle. In looking at these procedures we are going to examine them in "general system behavior theory" terms:

On the menu certain "information" exists in the physical form of printed words. The customer "transforms" this information into the physical form of spoken words. The information is once again transformed by the waitress. Now it exists in the physical form of written notes made by the waitress. Once again the information is transformed as the waitress converts her notes into spoken words directed to the cook. The cook transforms the information from the physical form of spoken words to the physical form of prepared food. We have an "information flow" which looks like this:

	Printed		Spoken		Written	Spoken		Prepared
Menu	Words	→ Customer	Words	→ Waitress	Notes	Words	→ Cook	Food →

Now every so often it happened that an error was made, and the customer didn't get what he ordered. Of course you and I would have been the first to admit that we had made an error, but not all cooks and waitresses have this admirable character trait. This is rather understandable since the waitress was trying to do things correctly and rapidly (she wanted all the tips she could get!), and when she was suddenly confronted with the fact that an error had been made, her first reaction was that the cook had goofed. The cook, on the other hand, was trying to do his best. He knew in his own heart that he had prepared just what she had told him to prepare. "It's the waitress' fault," was his thought.

So what did the cook and waitress learn? Did they learn to prevent a recurrence of the error? Indeed not! The waitress learned that the cook was a stupid so-and-so, and the cook learned that the waitress was a scatter-brained so-and-so. This kind of emotionalized learning situation and strainer-of-interpersonal-relations any organization can do without—especially during the rush hours.

Changes Effected

Consider now how the spindle changes all this. The waitress prepares the order slip and the cook works directly from it. If the waitress records the order incorrectly, it is obvious to her upon examining the order slip. Similarly, if the cook misreads the slip, an examination of the order slip makes it obvious to him. The fifth function of the spindle, then, is to provide "feedback" to both waitress and cook regarding errors. The spindle markedly alters the emotional relationship and redirects the learning process.

As errors are examined under conditions of feedback, new responses are engendered. The cook and waitress may find the present order slip to be hard to read, and they may request the manager to try out a different style of order slip. Now they are working together to solve the system's problems rather than working against each other and disregarding the system's problems. Maybe they find that abbreviations cause some random errors. For example, it might be that HB (Hamburger) and BB (Beefburger) get mixed up just a little too often, so the cook and waitress get together with the manager and change the name of Beefburger to Caravan Special on the menu because the new symbol (CS) will transmit itself through the system with much less ambiguity—especially during the rush hours.

HANDLING OVERLOAD

Had I been asked a few years ago to advise on human relations problems in the restaurant industry as a professional psychologist, my approach would have been limited to what I now call a "component" approach. My thinking would have been directed at the components in the system—in this case, the people involved. I would have explored such answers as incentive schemes, human relations training, selection procedures, and possibly some time-and-motion studies. My efforts would have been limited to attempts to *change the components to fit in with the system as designed no matter how poor the design might be.*

But now I would first concern myself with the "information" which must be "processed" by the system. My concern would be centered on the functions which would have to be performed by the system and how they might best be performed. I would concern myself especially with how the system is designed to handle conditions of information overload.

It is significant that in our parable the three scientists each discovered that the human relations problems arose mostly during the rush hours, in the period of "information overload." How a system responds to conditions of overload depends on how the system is designed. Let us look at how various design features permit the handling of conditions of overload in a number of different kinds of systems.

Increase in Channels

One of the most common adjustments that a system makes to an excess input load is to increase the number of "channels" for handling the information. Restaurants put more waitresses and cooks on the job to handle rush-hour loads. The Post Office hires extra help before Christmas. The telephone system has recently introduced automatic-switching equipment to handle heavy communication loads; when the load gets to a certain point, additional lines are automatically "cut in" to handle the additional calls. Even our fire departments increase "channels." If there is not enough equipment at the scene, more is called in. Department stores put on additional clerks to handle holiday crowds. Military commanders augment crews in anticipation of overload conditions. Extra communication lines may be called up. More troops are deployed.

Almost everywhere we look we see that systems are very commonly designed to increase or decrease the number of channels according to the load.

Waiting Lines

But there comes a time when just increasing the number of channels is not enough. Then we see another common adjustment process, that of "queuing" or forming a waiting line. There are few readers who have not had the experience of waiting in a restaurant to be seated. Other examples are common. Raw materials are stored awaiting production processes. Orders wait in queue until filled. Manufactured goods are stored on docks awaiting shipment. The stock market ticker tape falls behind.

We have already seen how the spindle makes it unnecessary for the waitresses to queue to give orders. And we are all familiar with the modern custom in most restaurants of having a hostess take our names and the size of our party. What happens when the hostess takes our names down on paper? For one, we do not have to go through the exasperating business of jostling to hold our position in line. Also, the "holding of proper position" is done by machine; that is, it is done by the list rather than by our elbows.

Use of Filtering

The hostess' list also illustrates the way in which a system can make still a third type of adjustment, that of "filtering." Because she jots down the size of the group, she can now selectively pull groups out of the queue according to the size of the table last vacated. Some readers will recall that many restaurants used to have all tables or booths of the same size and that everyone was seated in turn according to how long he had waited. It used to be infuriating for a party of four to see a single person being seated at a table for four while they continued to wait. The modern notion of accommodations of varying sizes, combined with the means of filtering, makes the use of floor space much more efficient and the waiting less lengthy. We can see filtering in other systems as well.

1. The Post Office handles registered mail before it handles other mail, delivers special delivery letters before other letters.

2. In the case of our other most important communication system, the telephone system, there is no other way for dial equipment to recognize an important call from an unimportant call; it cannot tell whether a doctor is dialing or the baby is playing. However, where long-distance calls must go through operators, there is a chance for filtering. For instance, in trying to place a call to a disaster area the operator may accept only those calls which are of an emergency nature.
3. Military systems assign priorities to messages so as to assure differential handling.
4. Orders may be sent to production facilities in bunches that make up a full workday rather than in a first-in-first-out pattern. Special orders may be marked for priority attention.

Variations of Omission

A system can be so designed as to permit "omissions," a simple rejection or nonacceptance of an input. The long-distance operator may refuse to accept a call as a means of preventing the lines from becoming overloaded. The dial system gives a busy signal and rejects the call. A manufacturing organization may reject an order it cannot fill within a certain time. A company may discontinue manufacture of one line temporarily in order to catch up on a more profitable line that is back-ordered.

As another example of how the design determines what adjustments the system can make, consider the way the short-order restaurant system design utilizes the omission process.

If waiting lines get too long, customers will turn away. That is not good for business, so restaurants often practice another kind of omission. On the menu you may find the words, "No substitutions." Instead of rejecting customers, the restaurants restrict the range of inputs they will accept in the way of orders. Thus time is saved in preparing the food, which in turn cuts down the waiting time in the queue.

The goal of most restaurants is to process as many customers per unit time as is possible. With a fixed profit margin per meal served, the more meals served, the more profit. But when people are in the queue, they are not spending money. One solution to this is the installation of a bar. This permits the customers to spend while waiting. It is a solution enjoyed by many customers as well as by management.

Chunking and Approximating

Another big timesaver in the restaurant system is the use of a fifth adjustment process, that of "chunking." Big chunks of information can be passed by predetermined arrangements. You may find a menu so printed that it asks you to order by number. The order may be presented to the cook as "4D" (No. 4 Dinner), for example. The cook already knows what makes up the dinner and does not need to be told each item with each order. Preplanning permits chunking, and chunking frees communication channels.

Somewhat akin to the chunking process is a sixth adjustment process, "approximating." To illustrate:

1. A business forecaster may not be able to make an exact count of future sales, but he may predict confidently that the sales will be small, moderate, or large.
2. An overburdened Post Office crew may do an initial sorting of mail as "local" or "out of town."
3. An airborne radar crew may report a "large formation" headed toward the coast.
4. An intelligence agency may get a report of "heightened" air activity in a given area.
5. An investment house may predict "increased" activity in a certain line of stocks.
6. Stock market reports state that industrials are "up" and utilities are "down."

Approximating thus means making a gross discrimination of the input rather than making a fine discrimination.

Trading Errors

A rather unusual adjustment process that a system can adopt to cope with overload is to accept an increase in the number of errors made. It is almost as if systems said to themselves, "It's better to make mistakes than not to deal with the input." For example, the sorting of mail is not checked during rush periods. Mail which is missent must be returned, but in a rush that risk is worth the cost; more mail gets sent where it is supposed to go even though there are more errors. Thus, quality control is given up for the sake of speed. On the other hand, some systems are so designed as to be insensitive to errors. The telephone system will permit you to dial as many wrong numbers as you are capable of dialing.

It is interesting to see in the restaurant system design a deliberate making of errors of one sort in order to prevent the making of errors of another sort during rush hours.

Picture yourself and a couple of friends dropping into a restaurant during the middle of an afternoon. You are the only customers there. The waitress takes your order. You ask for a hamburger with "everything on it." The next person asks for a hamburger but wants only lettuce and a slice of tomato on it. The third person asks for a hamburger but specifies relish and mayonnaise. The work load is low. There is time to individualize orders.

But during rush hours it would be too easy to make errors. Then the cook prepares only the meat and bun. The waitress goes to a table where there are bowls with lettuce leaves and tomato slices and little paper cups of relish and mayonnaise. On each plate she places a lettuce leaf, a tomato slice, a cup of relish, and a cup of mayonnaise. In most instances she will have brought something that the customer did not order, and in this sense she would have made an "error"; but she would have avoided the error of not bringing the customer something he *did* want.

Other examples of the same type are common. For instance, a sales department sends out brochures to everyone who inquires about a product so as not to miss someone who is really interested. Again, the Strategic

Air Command, as a central policy, uses this deliberate making of one type of "error" to avoid a possible error of more severe consequences. The commander may order the force launched under "positive control." It is better to have launched in error than to be caught on the ground and destroyed.

CONCLUSION

And so we see that there is a new frame of reference, a new point of view coming into use in approaching the problems of organizations. This new frame of reference looks at organizations as systems which (1) process information, transforming the information from one form into another, and (2) are or are not designed to cope with the conditions of overload that may be imposed on them. This new frame of reference is expressed as an interest in how the structure or design of an organization dynamically influences the operating characteristics and the capacities of the system to handle various conditions of information overload.

At the University of Michigan there are some 50 scientists whose primary interests lie in looking for similarities and differences in system behavior at all levels. They examine single cells, whole organs, individuals, groups, and societies for the manners in which these systems cope with their environments in common and in unique ways. They search the work of other scientists for clues to system behavior at one level that is followed at higher or lower orders of organization. As for the application of this "system frame of reference," one finds such organizations as System Development Corporation, the RAND Corporation, and the MITRE Corporation using it in approaching the complex problems of advanced military systems. Here is just a sampling of specific developments that bear close watching:

1. Because it is possible to view organizations as systems which process data in a continuous sequence of "information transformations" and which may make numerous types of adjustments at the points of transformation, a wholly new concept of training has arisen. In the past, training in business and industry as well as in the military was largely limited to training a man or men to do a given task in a certain way. Now training can be provided that teaches a man or men to adopt adjustment processes suited to the design of the system and the condition of overload. In other words, training for flexibility rather than rigidity is now possible. It should not be long before internal competition is replaced by internal cooperation as the main means of enhancing production.

2. Because it is possible to view a business or industry as an information processing system, it is possible to simulate the information flow on digital computers and, by controlling the adjustment processes at each point where the data are transformed, to learn what effects and costs would be involved in change. The manager will then be able to test his policies realistically on the computer before committing himself in action. A com-

puter program called SIMPAC (Simulating Package) has already been
developed at System Development Corporation for this purpose.

3. A digital computer program capable of "learning" has been developed.
   By analyzing how data can be sensed, compared with other data, and stored
   in the computer's "memory," scientists have been able to "teach" a prototype computer program to recognize letters of the alphabet, cartoon char-
   acters, and spoken words. One can look forward to the day when, opening
   a bank account, he will be asked to sign his name in a variety of situations—
   e.g., standing, sitting, bending over, and maybe even after a couple of
   martinis. The computer will learn to recognize his signature from these
   samples, and at the clearinghouse, after that, his account will be automatically debited and the payee's account automatically credited.

Ludwig von Bertalanffy, the father of general system theory, predicted
that general system theory would unify the sciences, thus making it possible
for a scientist trained in one area to talk in common terms with another
scientist trained in another area.[3] It also seems certain that business and
industry will soon profit from the application of the theory of how systems
behave.

[3] "General System Theory," *General Systems,* Volume I (Ann Arbor: Society for
General Systems Research, 1956), pp. 1-10.

8 · A FRAMEWORK FOR MANAGEMENT INFORMATION SYSTEMS[1]

G. Anthony Gorry[2]
Michael S. Scott Morton[3]

Introduction

A framework for viewing management information systems (MIS) is essential if an organization is to plan effectively and make sensible allocations of resources to information systems tasks. The use of computers in organizations has grown tremendously in the 1955 to 1971 period, but very few of the resulting systems have had a significant impact on the way in which management makes decisions. A framework which allows an organization to gain perspective on the field of information systems can be a powerful means of providing focus and improving the effectiveness of the systems efforts.

In many groups doing MIS work, this lack of perspective prevents a full appreciation of the variety of organizational uses for computers. Without a framework to guide management and systems planners, the system tends to serve the strongest manager or react to the greatest crisis. As a result, systems activities too often move from crisis to crisis, following no clear path and receiving only *ex post facto* justification. This tendency inflicts an unnecessary expense on the organization. Not only are costly computer resources wasted, but even more costly human resources are mismanaged. The cost of systems and programming personnel is generally twice that of the hardware involved in a typical project, and the ratio is growing larger as the cost of hardware drops and salaries rise.[4] Competent people are expensive. More importantly, they exist only in limited numbers. This limitation actively constrains the amount of systems development work that can be undertaken in a given organization, and so good resource allocation is critical.

Developments in two distinct areas within the last five years offer us the potential to develop altogether new ways of supporting decision processes. First, there has been considerable technological progress. The evolution of remote access to computers with short turnaround time and flexible user interfaces has been rapid. Powerful mini-computers are available at low cost and users can be linked to computer resources through inexpensive typewriter and graphical display devices. The second development has been a conceptual one. There is emerging an understanding of the potential role of information systems within organizations. We are add-

[1] From *Sloan Management Review*, Vol. 13, No. 1 (Fall, 1971), pp. 55-70. Reprinted by permission of the *Sloan Management Review*.
[2] G. Anthony Gorry, Professor, Massachusetts Institute of Technology.
[3] Michael S. Scott Morton, Professor, Massachusetts Institute of Technology.
[4] J. W. Taylor and N. J. Dean. "Managing to Manage the Computer," *Harvard Business Review*, Vol. 44, No. 5 (September-October, 1966), pp. 98-100.

ing to our knowledge of how human beings solve problems and of how to build models that capture aspects of the human decision-making processes.[5]

The progress in these areas has been dramatic. Entirely new kinds of planning and control systems can now be built—ones that dynamically involve the manager's judgments and support him with analysis, models, and flexible access to relevant information. But to realize this potential fully, given an organization's limited resources, there must be an appropriate framework within which to view management decision making and the required systems support. The purpose of this paper is to present a framework that helps us to understand the evolution of MIS activities within organizations and to recognize some of the potential problems and benefits resulting from our new technology. Thus, this framework is designed to be useful in planning for information systems activities within an organization and for distinguishing between the various model building activities, models, computer systems, and so forth which are used for supporting different kinds of decisions. It is by definition, a static picture, and is not designed to say anything about how information systems are built.

In the next section we shall consider some of the general advantages of developing a framework for information systems work. We shall then propose a specific framework which we have found to be useful in the analysis of MIS activities. We believe that this framework offers us a new way to characterize the progress made to date and offers us insight into the problems that have been encountered. Finally, we shall use this framework to analyze the types of resources that are required in the different decision areas and the ways in which these resources should be used.

Framework Development

The framework we develop here is one for managerial activities, not for information systems. It is a way of looking at decisions made in an organization. Information systems should exist only to support decisions, and hence we are looking for a characterization of organizational activity in terms of the type of decisions involved. For reasons which we make clear later, we believe that an understanding of managerial activity is a prerequisite for effective systems design and implementation. Most MIS groups become involved in system development and implementation without a prior analysis of the variety of managerial activities. This has, in our opinion, prevented them from developing a sufficiently broad definition of their purpose and has resulted in generally inefficient allocation of resources.

In attempting to understand the evolution and problems of management information systems, we have found the work of Robert Anthony and Herbert Simon particularly useful. *In Planning and Control Systems:*

[5] Scott Morton, M.S. *Management Decision Systems* (Boston: Harvard University Graduate School of Business Administration, 1971); and Soelberg, P.O., "Unprogrammed Decision Making," *Industrial Management Review,* Vol. 8, No. 2 (Spring, 1967), pp. 19-30.

A Framework for Analysis,[6] Anthony addresses the problem of developing a classification scheme that will allow management some perspective when dealing with planning and control systems. He develops a taxonomy for managerial activity consisting of three categories and argues that these categories represent activities sufficiently different in kind to require the development of different systems.

The first of Anthony's categories of managerial activity is *strategic planning:* "*Strategic planning* is the process of deciding on objectives of the organization, on changes in these objectives, on the resources used to attain these objectives, and on the policies that are to govern the acquisition, use, and disposition of these resources.[7] Certain things can be said about strategic planning generally. First, it focuses on the choice of objectives for the organization and on the activities and means required to achieve these objectives. As a result, a major problem in this area is predicting the future of the organization and its environment. Second, the strategic planning process typically involves a small number of high-level people who operate in a nonrepetitive and often very creative way. The complexity of the problems that arise and the nonroutine manner in which they are handled make it quite difficult to appraise the quality of this planning process.

The second category defined by Anthony is *management control:* " . . . the process by which managers assure that resources are obtained and used effectively and efficiently in the accomplishment of the organization's objectives."[8] He stresses three key aspects of this area. First, the activity involves interpersonal interaction. Second, it takes place within the context of the policies and objectives developed in the strategic planning process. Third, the paramount goal of management control is the assurance of effective and efficient performance.

Anthony's third category is *operational control,* by which means "the process of assuring that specific tasks are carried out effectively and efficiently."[9] The basic distinction between management control and operational control is concerned with tasks (such as manufacturing a specific part) whereas management control is most often concerned with people. There is much less judgment to be exercised in the operational control area because the tasks, goals, and resources have been carefully delineated through the management control activity.

We recognize, as does Anthony, that the boundaries between these three categories are often not clear. In spite of their limitations and uncertainties, however, we have found the categories useful in the analysis of information system activities. For example, if we consider the information requirements of these three activities, we can see that they are very different from one another. Further, this difference is not simply a matter of

    [6] Anthony, R. N. *Planning and Control Systems: A Framework for Analysis* (Boston: Harvard University Graduate School of Business Administration, 1965).
    [7] *Ibid.,* p. 24.
    [8] *Ibid.,* p. 27.
    [9] *Ibid.,* p. 69.

aggregation, but one of fundamental character of the information needed by managers in these areas.

Strategic planning is concerned with setting broad policies and goals for the organization. As a result, the relationship of the organization to its environment is a central matter of concern. Also, the nature of the activity is such that predictions about the future are particularly important. In general, then, we can say that the information needed by strategic planners is aggregate information, and obtained mainly from sources external to the organization itself. Both the scope and variety of the information are quite large, but the requirements for accuracy are not particular stringent. Finally, the nonroutine nature of the strategic planning process means that the demands for this information occur infrequently.

The information needs for the operational control area stand in sharp contrast to those of strategic planning. The task orientation of operational control requires information of a well-defined and narrow scope. This information is quite detailed and arises largely from sources within the organization. Very frequent use is made of this information, and it must therefore be accurate.

The information requirements for management control fall between the extremes for operational control and strategic planning. In addition, it is important to recognize that much of the information relevant to management control is obtained through the process of interpersonal interaction.

In Table 1 we have summarized these general observations about the categories of management activity. This summary is subject to the same limitations and uncertainties which are exhibited by the concepts of management control strategic planning, and operational control. Nonetheless,

TABLE 1

INFORMATION REQUIREMENTS BY DECISION CATEGORY

Characteristics of Information	Operational Control	Management Control	Strategic Planning
Source	Largely internal ⟶		External
Scope	Well defined, narrow ⟶		Very wide
Level of Aggregation	Detailed ⟶		Aggregate
Time Horizon	Historical ⟶		Future
Currency	Highly current ⟶		Quite old
Required Accuracy	High ⟶		Low
Frequency of Use	Very frequent ⟶		Infrequent

it does underscore our contention that because the activities themselves are different, the information requirements to support them are also different.

This summary of information requirements in Table 1 suggests the reason why many organizations have found it increasingly difficult to realize some of their long-range plans for information systems . Many of these plans are based on the "total systems approach." Some of the proponents of this approach advocate that systems throughout the organization be tightly linked, with the output of one becoming the direct input of another, and that the whole structure be built on the detailed data used or controlling operations.[10] In doing so, they are suggesting an approach to systems design that is at best uneconomic and at worst based on a serious misconception. The first major problem with this view is that it does not recognize the ongoing nature of systems development in the operational control area. There is little reason to believe that the systems work in any major organization will be complete within the foreseeable future. To say that management information systems activity must wait "until we get our operational control systems in hand" is to say that efforts to assist management with systems support will be deferred indefinitely.

The second and perhaps most serious problem with this total systems view is that it fails to represent properly the information needs of the management control and strategic planning activities. Neither of these areas *necessarily* needs information that is a mere aggregation of data from the operational control data base. In many cases, if such a link is needed, it is more cost effective to use sampling from this data base and other statistical techniques to develop the required information. In our opinion, it rarely makes sense to couple managers in the management control and strategic planning areas directly with the masses of detailed data required for operational control. Not only is direct coupling unnecessary, but it also can be an expensive and difficult technical problem.

For these reasons it is easy to understand why so many companies have had the following experience. Original plans for operational control systems were met with more or less difficulty, but as time passed it became increasingly apparent that the planned systems for higher management were not being developed on schedule, if at all. To make matters worse, the systems which were developed for senior management had relatively little impact on the way in which the managers made decisions. This last problem is a direct result of the failure to understand the basic information needs of the different activities.

We have tried to show in the above discussion how Anthony's classification of *managerial* activities is a useful one for people working in information systems design and implementation; we shall return later to consider in more detail some of the implications of his ideas.

In *The New Science of Management Decision,* Simon is concerned with the manner in which human beings solve problems regardless of their

---

[10] Becker, J. L. "Planning the Total Information System," A. D. Meacham and V. B. Thompson (eds.), *Total Systems,* (New York: American Data Processing, 1962), pp. 66-73.

position within an organization. His distinction between "programmed" and "nonprogrammed" decisions is a useful one:

"Decisions are programmed to the extent that they are repetitive and routine, to the extent that a definite procedure has been worked out for handling them so that they don't have to be treated *de novo* each time they occur. . . . Decisions are nonprogrammed to the extent that they are novel, unstructured, and consequential. There is no cut-and-dried method of handling the problem because it hasn't arisen before, or because its precise nature and structure are elusive or complex, or because it is so important that it deserves a custom-tailored treatment. . . . By nonprogrammed I mean a response where the system has no specific procedure to deal with situations like the one at hand, but must fall back on whatever *general* capacity it has for intelligent, adaptive, problem-oriented action.[11]

We shall use the terms "structured" and "unstructured" for programmed and nonprogrammed because they imply less dependence on the computer and more dependence on the basic character of the problem-solving activity in question. The procedures, the kinds of computation, and the types of information vary depending on the extent to which the problem in question is unstructured. The basis for these differences is that in the unstructured case the human decision maker must provide judgment and evaluation as well as insights into problem definition. In a very structured situation, much if not all of the decision making process can be automated. Later in this paper we shall argue that systems built to support structured decision making will be significantly different from those designed to assist managers in dealing with unstructured problems. Further, we shall show that these differences can be traced to the character of the models which are relevant to each of these problems and the way in which these models are developed.

This focus on decisions requires an understanding of the human decision making process. Research on human problem solving supports Simon's claim that all problem solving can be broken down into three categories:

"The first phase of the decision-making process—searching the environment for conditions calling for decision—I shall call *intelligence* activity (borrowing the military meaning of intelligence). The second phase—inventing, developing, and analyzing possible courses of action—I shall call *design* activity. The third phase—selecting a course of action from those available—I shall call *choice* activity. . . . Generally speaking, intelligence activity precedes design, and design activity precedes choice. The cycle of phases is, however, far more complex than the sequence suggests. Each phase in making a particular decision is itself a complex decision-making process. The design phase, for example, may call for new intelligence activities; problems at any given level generate subproblems that in turn

[11] Simon, H. A. *The New Science of Management Decision* (New York: Harper & Row, 1960), pp. 5-6.

have their intelligence, design and choice phases and so on. There are wheels within wheels. . . . Nevertheless, the three large phases are often clearly discernible as the organizational decision process unfolds. They are closely related to the stages in problem solving first described by John Dewey: 'What is the problem? What are the alternatives? Which alternative is best?' " [12]

A fully structured problem is one in which all three phases—intelligence, design, and choice—are structured. That is, we can specify algorithms, or decision rules, that will allow us to find the problem, design alternative solutions, and select the best solution. An example here might be the use of the classical economic order quantity (EOQ) formula on a straightforward inventory control problem. An unstructured problem is one in which none of the three phases is structured. Many job-shop scheduling problems are of this type.

In the ideas of Simon and Anthony, then, we have two different ways of looking at managerial activity within organizations. Anthony's categorization is based on the purpose of the management activity, whereas Simon's classification is based on the way in which the manager deals with the problems which confront him. The combination of these two views provide a useful framework within which to examine the purposes and problems of information systems activity. The essence of this combination is shown in Figure 1. The figure contains a class of decisions we have called "semistructured "—decisions with one or two of the intelligence, design, and choice phases unstructured..

Decisions above the dividing line in Figure 1 are largely structured, and we shall call the information systems that support them "Structured Decision Systems" (SDS). Decisions below the line are largely unstructured, and their supporting information systems are "Decision Support Systems" (DSS). The SDS area encompasses almost all of what *has* been called Management Information Systems (MIS) in the literature—an area that has had almost nothing to do with real managers or information but has been largely routine data processing. We exclude from consideration here all of the *information handling* activities in an organization. A large percentage of computer time in many organizations is spent on straightforward data handling with no decisions, however structured, involved. The payroll application, for example, is a data handling operation.

In Figure 1, we have listed some examples in each of the six cells. It should be stressed, however, that these cells are not well-defined categories. Although this may sometimes cause problems, the majority of important decisions can be classified into their appropriate cell without difficulty.

Decision Making Within the Framework

Planning and Resource Allocation Decisions. An immediate observation can be made about the framework we have presented. Almost all the

[12] *Ibid.*, pp. 2-3.

FIGURE 1

INFORMATION SYSTEMS: A FRAMEWORK

	Operational Control	Management Control	Strategic Planning
Structured	Accounts Receivable	Budget Analysis— Engineered Costs	Tanker Fleet Mix
	Order Entry	Short-Term Forecasting	Warehouse and Factory Location
	Inventory Control		
Semi-Structured	Production Scheduling	Variance Analysis — Overall Budget	Mergers and Acquisitions
	Cash Management	Budget Preparation	New Product Planning
Unstructured	PERT/COST Systems	Sales and Production	R & D Planning

so-called MIS activity has been directed at decisions in the structured half of the matrix (see Figure 1), specifically in the "operation control" cell. On the other hand, most of the areas of greatest concern to managers, areas where decisions have a significant effect on the company, are in the lower half of the matrix. That is, managers deal for the most part with unstructured decisions. This implies, of course, that computers and related systems which have so far been largely applied to the structured operational control area have not yet any real impact on management decision making. The areas of high potential do not lie in bigger and better systems of the kind most companies now use. To have all the effort concentrated in only one of the six cells suggests at the very least a severe imbalance.

A second point to be noted on the planning question is the evolutionary nature of the line separating structured from unstructured decisions. This line is moving down over time. As we improve our understanding of a particular decision, we can move it above the line and allow the system to take care of it, freeing the manager for other tasks. For example, in previous years the inventory reordering decision in most organizations was made by a well-paid member of middle management. It was a decision that involved a high degree of skill and could have a significant effect on the profits of the organization. Today this decision has moved from the unstructured operational control area to the structured. We have a set of decision rules (the EOQ formula) which on average do a better job for the standard items than most human decision makers. This movement of the line does not imply any replacement of managers since we are dealing with an almost infinite set of problems. For every one we solve, there are 10 more demanding our attention.

It is worth noting that the approach taken in building systems in the unstructured area hastens this movement of the line because it focuses our analytical attention on decisions and decision rules. We would therefore expect a continuing flow of decisions across the line, or at least into the "grey" semi-structured decision area.

Through the development of a model of a given problem solving process for a decision in one of the cells, we can establish the character of each of the three phases. To the extent that any of these phases can be structured, we can design direct systems support. For those aspects of the process which are unstructured (given our current understanding of the situation), we would call on the manager to provide the necessary analysis. Thus a problem might be broken down into a set of related subproblems, some of which are "solved" automatically by the system and the remainder by the user alone or with varying degrees of computational and display support. Regardless of the resulting division of labor, however, it is essential that a model of the decision process be constructed *prior* to the system design. It is only in this way that a good perspective on the potential application of systems support can be ascertained.

Structured/Unstructured Decisions. Information systems ought to be centered around the important decisions of the organization, many of which are relatively unstructured. It is therefore essential that models be built of the decision process involved. Model development is fundamental because it is a prerequisite for the analysis of the volume of information, and because it is the key to understanding which portions of the decision process can be supported or automated. Both the successes and failures in the current use of computers can be understood largely in terms of the difficulty of this model development.

Our discussion of Structured Decision Systems showed that the vast majority of the effort (and success) has been in the area of structured operational control where there is relatively little ambiguity as to the goals sought. For example, the typical inventory control problem can be precisely stated, and it is clear what the criterion is by which solutions are to be judged. Hence we have an easily understood optimization problem. This type of problem lends itself to the development of formal "scientific" models, such as those typical of operations research.

Another important characteristic of problems of this type is that they are to a large extent "organization independent." By this we mean that the essential aspects of the problem tend to be the same in many organizations, although the details may differ. This generality has two important effects. First, it encourages widespread interest and effort in the development of solutions to the problem. Second, it makes the adaptation of general models to the situation in a particular organizational setting relatively easy.

The situation with regard to areas of management decision making is quite different. To the extent that a given problem is semi-structured or unstructured, there is an absence of a routine procedure for dealing with it. There is also a tendency toward ambiguity in the problem definition because of the lack of formalization of any or all of the intelligence, design, or choice phases. Confusion may exist as to the appropriate criterion for evaluating solutions, or as to the means for generating trial solutions to the problems of this type as being unique to a given organization.

In general, then, we can say that the information systems problem in the structured operational control area is basically that of implementing a given general model in a certain organizational context. On the other hand, work in the unstructured areas is much more involved with model development and formalization. Furthermore, the source of models in the former case is apt to be the operations research or management science literature. In the latter case, the relevant models are most often the unverbalized models used by the managers of the organization. This suggests that the procedure for the development of systems, the types of systems, and the skills of the analysts involved may be quite different in the two areas.

Although the evolution of information systems activities in most organizations has led to the accumulation of a variety of technical skills, the impact of computers on the way in which top managers make decisions has been minimal. One major reason for this is that the support of these decision makers is not principally a technical problem. If it were, it would have been solved. Certainly there are technical problems associated with work in these problem areas, but the technology and the technological skills in most large organizations are more than sufficient. The missing ingredient, apart from the basic awareness of the problem, is the skill to elicit from management its view of the organization and its environment, and to formalize models of this view.

To improve the quality of decisions, a systems designer can seek to improve the quality of the information inputs or to change the decision process, or both. Because of the existence of a variety of optimization models for operational control problems, there is a tendency to emphasize improvement of the information inputs at the expense of improvement in the decision making process. Although this emphasis is appropriate for structured operational control problems, it can retard progress in developing support for unstructured problem solving. The difficulty with this view is that it tends to attribute low quality in management decision making to low quality information inputs. Hence, systems are designed to supply more current, more accurate, or more detailed information.

While improving the quality of information available to managers may improve the quality of their decisions, we do not believe that major advances will be realized in this way.[13] Most managers do not have great informational needs. Rather, they have need of new methods to understand and process the information they already available to them. Generally speaking, the models that they employ in dealing with this information are very primitive, and as a result, the range of responses that they can generate is very limited. For example, many managers employ simple historical models in their attempts to anticipate the future.[14] Further, these models are static in nature, although the processes they purport to represent are highly dynamic. In such a situation, there is much more to be gained by improving the information processing ability of managers in order that they may deal effectively with the information that they already have, than by adding to the reams of data confronting them, or by improving the quality of those data.[15]

If this view is correct, it suggests that the Decision Support Systems area is important and that these systems may best be built by people other than those currently involved in the operational control systems area. The requisite skills are those of the model building based on close interaction with management, structuring and formalizing the procedures employed by managers, and segregating those aspects of the decision process which can be automated. In addition, systems in this area must be able to assist the evolution of the manager's decision making ability through increasing his understanding of the environment. Hence, one important role of a DSS is educative. Even in areas in which we cannot structure the decision process, we can provide models of the environment from which the manager can develop insights into the relationship of his decisions to the goals he wishes to achieve.

In discussing models and their importance to systems in the DSS area, we should place special emphasis on the role which the manager assumes in the process of model building. To a large extent, he is the source upon which the analyst draws. That is, although a repertoire of "operations research" models may be very valuable for the analyst, his task is not simply to impose a model on the situation. These models may be the building blocks. The

[13] Ackoff, R. "Management Misinformation Systems," *Management Science*, Vol. 11, No. 4 (December, 1967), pp. B147-B156.

[14] Pounds, W. F. "The Process of Problem Finding," *Industrial Management Review*, Vol. 11, No. 1 (Fall, 1969), pp. 1-20.

[15] Gorry, G. A. "The Development of Managerial Models," *Sloan Management Review*, Vol. 12, No. 2 (Winter, 1971), pp. 1-16.

analyst must possess a certain empathy for the manager, and *vice versa* Whether the current systems designers in a given organization process this quality is a question worthy of consideration by management.

This approach in no way precludes normative statements about decision procedures. The emphasis on the development of descriptive models of managerial problem solving is only to ensure that the existing situation is well understood by both the analyst and the manager. Once this understanding has been attained, various approaches to improving the process can be explored. In fact, a major benefit of developing descriptive models of this type is the exposure of the decision making process to objective analysis.

In summary then, we have asserted that there are two sets of implications which flow from our use of this framework. The first set centers on an organization's planning and resource allocation decision in relation to information systems. The second flow from the distinction we have drawn between structured and unstructured types of decisions. The focus of our attention should be on the critical *decisions* in an organization and on explicit modeling of these decisions prior to the design of information systems support.

The second major point in relation to the structured/unstructured dimension that we have raised is that the kinds of implementation problems, the skills required by the managers and analysts, and the characteristics of the design process are different above and below the dashed line in Figure 1. In discussing these differences, we have tried to stress the fundamental shift in approach that is required if Decision Support Systems are to be built in a way that makes them effective in an organization. The approach and technology that have been used over the last 15 years to build information systems in the structured operational control area are often inappropriate in the case of Decision Support Systems.

Implications of the Framework

System Design Differences. The decision categories we have borrowed from Anthony have a set of implications distinct from those discussed in connection with the structured and unstructured areas. The first of these has to do with the systems design differences that follow from supporting decisions in the three areas.

As was seen earlier, information requirements differ sharply among the three areas. There are few occasions in which it makes sense to connect systems directly across boundaries. Aggregating the detailed accounting records (used in operational control) to provide a base for a five-year sales forecast (required for a strategic planning decision) is an expensive and unnecessary process. We can often sample, estimate, or otherwise obtain data for use in strategic planning without resorting to the operational control data base. This does imply that we should *never* use such a data base, but merely that it is not necessarily the best way of obtaining the information.

This point is also relevant in the collection and maintenance of data. Techniques appropriate for operational control, such as the use of on-line data collection terminals, are rarely justified for strategic planning systems. Similarly, elaborate environmental sampling methods may be critical for an operational control decision. In looking at each of the information characteristics in Table 1, it is apparent that quite different data bases will be required to support decisions in the three areas. Therefore, the first implication of the decision classification in our framework is that the "totally-integrated-management-information-systems" ideas so popular in the literature are a poor design concept. More particularly, the "integrated" or "company-wide" data base is a misleading notion, and even if it could be achieved would be exorbitantly expensive.

Information differences among the three decision areas also imply related differences in hardware and software requirements. On the one hand, strategic planning decisions require access to a data base which is used infrequently and may involve an interface with a variety of complex models. Operational control decisions, on the other hand, often require a larger data base with continuous updating and frequent access to current information.

Differences in Organizational Structure. A second distinction is in the organizational structure and the managerial and analyst skills which will be involved across the three areas. The managerial talents required, as well as the numbers and training of the managers involved, differ sharply for these categories. The process of deciding on key problems that might be worth supporting with a formal system is a much smaller, tighter process in the strategic planning area than in the operational control area. The decision to be supported is probably not a recurring one and will normally not involve changes in the procedures and structure employed by the remainder of the firm. Because it is a relatively isolated decision in both time and scope, it need not involve as many people. However, the process of defining the problem must be dominated by the managers involved if the right problem and hence the best model formulation are to be selected. Similarly, the implementation process must be tightly focused on the immediate problem. The skills required of the managers involved are analytical and reflective, rather than communicative and procedural. In the strategic planning case, the manager must supply both the problem definition and the key relationships that make up the model. This requires an ability to think logically and a familarity with models and computation. In the case of operational control, the particular solution and the models involved are much more the concern of the technical specialist. This is not to say that in unstructured operational control the manager's judgment will not be involved in the process of solving problems. However, his role in *building* that model can be much more passive than in the strategic area.

The decision process, the implementation process, and the level of analytical sophistication of the managers (as opposed to the staff) in strategic planning all differ quite markedly from their counterparts in operational control. The decision makers in operational control have a more constrained problem. They have often had several years in which to define the general nature of the problem and to consider solutions. In addition, to the extent that these managers have a technical background, they are more likely to be familiar with the analysis involved in solving structured and unstructured problems. In any event, the nature of the operational control problem, its size, and the frequency of the decision all combine to produce design and implementation problems of a different variety. The managers involved in any given problem tend to be from the decision area in question, be it strategic planning, management control, or operational control. As a result, their training, background, and style of decision making are often different. This means that the types of models to be used, the method of elucidating these from the managers, and the skills of the analysts will differ across these three areas.

As the types of skills possessed by the managers differ, so will the kinds of systems analysts who can operate effectively. We have already distinguished between analysts who can handle structured as opposed to unstructured model building. There is a similar distinction to be made between the kind of person who can work well with a small group of senior managers (on either a structured or unstructured problem) and the person who is able to communicate with the various production personnel on an unstructured job-shop scheduling problem, for example.

In problems in the strategic area, the analyst has to be able to communicate effectively with the few managers who have the basic knowledge required to define the problem and its major variables. The skills required to do this include background and experience which are wide enough to match those of the line executives involved. Good communication depends on a common understanding of the basic variables involved, and few analysts involved in current MIS activity have this skill.

A breadth of background implies a wide repertoire of models with which the analyst is familiar. In the operational control area, an analyst can usefully specialize to great depth in a particular, narrow problem area. The depth, and the resulting improvement in the final system, often pays off because of the frequency with which the decision is made. In the strategic area the coverage of potential problems is enormous and the frequency of a particular decision relatively low. The range of models with which the analyst is familiar may be of greater benefit than depth in any one type.

In addition to the managerial and analyst issues raised above, there is a further difference in the way the information systems group is organized. A group dealing only with operational control problems would be structured differently and perhaps report to a different organizational position than a group working in all three areas. It is not our purpose here to go into detail on the organizational issues, but the material above suggests that on strategic problems, a task force reporting to the user and virtually independent of the computer group may make sense. The important issues are problem definition and problem structure; the implementation and computer issues are relatively simple by comparison. In management control, the single user, although still dominant in his application, has problems of interfacing with other users. An organizational design that encourages cross functional (marketing, production, distribution, etc.) cooperation is probably desirable. In operational control, the organizational design should include the user as a major influence, but he will have to be balanced with operational systems experts, and the whole group can quite possibly stay within functional boundaries. These examples are merely illustrative of the kind of organizational differences involved. Each organization has to examine its current status and needs and make structural changes in light of them.

Model Differences. The third distinction flowing from the framework is among the types of models involved. Again looking at Table 1 and the information differences, it is clear that model requirements depend, for example, on the frequency of decisions in each area and their relative magnitude. A strategic decision to change the whole distribution system occurs rarely. It is significant in cost, perhaps hundreds of millions of dollars, and it therefore can support a complex model, but the model need not be efficient in any sense. An operational control decision, however, may be made frequently, perhaps daily. The impact of each decision is small but the cumulative impact can involve large sums of money. Models for the decision may have to be efficient in running time, have ready access to current data, and be structured so as to be easily changed. Emphasis has to be on simplicity of building, careful attention to modularity, and so forth.

The sources of models for operational control are numerous. There is a history of activity, the problems are often similar across organizations, and the literature is extensive. In strategic planning, and to a lesser extent management control, we are still in the early stages of development. Our models tend to be individual and have to come from the managers involved. It is a model creation process as opposed to the application of a model.

In summary then, we have outlined implications for the organization which follow from the three major decision categories in the framework. We have posed the issues in terms of operational control and strategic planning, and with every point we assume that management control lies somewhere in between the two. The three major implications we have discussed are the advisability of following the integrated data base path; the differences in managerial and analyst skills as well as the appropriate forms of organizational structure for building systems in the three areas; and differences in the types of models involved. Distinguishing among decision areas is clearly important if an organization is going to be successful in its use of information systems.

Summary

The information systems field absorbs a significant percentage of the resources of many organizations. Despite these expenditures, there is very little perspective on the field and the issues within it. As a result, there has been a tendency to make incremental improvements to existing systems. The framework we suggest for looking at decisions within an organization provides one perspective on the information systems issues. From this perspective, it becomes clear that our planning for information systems has resulted in a heavy concentration in the operational control area. In addition, there is a series of implications for the organization which flows from the distinction between the decision areas. Model structure and the implementation process differ sharply between the structured and unstructured areas. Data base concepts, types of analysts and managers, and organizational structure all differ along the Strategic Planning to Operational Control axis.

We believe that each organization must share *some* common framework among its members if it is to plan and make resource allocation decisions which result in effective use of information systems. We suggest that the framework that has been presented here is an appropriate place to start.

9 • COMMUNICATION AND THE MANAGERIAL FUNCTION: A CONTINGENCY APPROACH[1]

Richard C. Huseman
Elmore R. Alexander III

The importance of communication to organizational theory has long been recognized. As early as 1938 Chester Barnard (in *The Functions of the Executive*) stated that:

> . . . in an exhaustive theory of organization, communication would occupy a central place, because the structure, extensiveness, and scope of organizations are almost entirely determined by communication [p. 9].

Barnard specifically related communication to the managerial function when he noted that the first function of the executive is to "establish and maintain a system of communication" [p. 221].

More recently, Connolly has suggested that an appropriate conception of organizations is "in terms of complex, decision related communication networks" [1977, p. 205]. In addition, Farace, Monge, and Russell maintain that "the managerial dyad, linking hierarchical levels in an organization, has long been recognized as the basic unit of instruction, report, and performance appraisal" [1977, p. 8]. Inherent in the managerial dyad is communication between the manager and the managed.

The central role of face-to-face communication in the managerial function is also supported by numerous empirical studies of manager time allocation. For example, a study by Burns [1954] found that communication activity accounted for 80 percent of the middle manager's time. A later study of managers in a manufacturing company stated that 89 percent of the manager's time was spent in face-to-face communication (Lawler, Porter and Tennenbaum [1968]). More recently in a detailed analysis of how managers spend their time, Mintzberg [1973] revealed that 78 percent of a manager's time is spent in face-to-face communication. When one adds to that percentage the element of written communication, the conclusion reached is that for all practical purposes communication is the managerial function.

Having established the importance of communication to the managerial function, what can be said in terms of how the manager can communicate more effectively and thereby increase his managerial effectiveness? Traditionally approaches for improving communication effectiveness have not been tailored to specific organizational variables such as particular people, tasks, or uncertainty. Approaches to improving communication effectiveness have frequently been tied

---

[1]Richard C. Huseman and Archie B. Carroll, *Readings in Organizational Behavior: Dimensions of Management Actions* (Allyn & Bacon, Inc., 1979). Reprinted by permission of Allyn & Bacon, Inc.

to "fixed" models of communication. There has, however, been an increasing tendency for those who study organizational behavior to support the view that effective managerial behavior is situation specific. It is this approach, contingency theory, that enables one to deal more comfortably with a basic fact of life in large organizations: different units of the organization may operate best under different philosophies and different managerial approaches. It would also seem reasonable that contingency theory would promote the best configuration of communication strategies and procedures for specific situations in organizational life.

If contingency theory holds promise for managerial communication in organizations, important questions emerge; namely, how and on what variables is communication behavior contingent? The purpose of the remainder of this article is (1) to examine contingency views of organizational design as they relate to the manager's communication roles and (2) to develop a contingency model for managerial communication.

CONTINGENCY VIEWS OF ORGANIZATIONS AND THE MANAGER'S COMMUNICATION ROLES

As a communicator within his organization, the manager is primarily engaged in the activity of coordinating the work of his subordinates. Of the seven internal managerial roles suggested by Mintzberg [1973], for example, six involve communication for the purpose of coordination—monitor, disseminator, spokesman, disturbance handler, resource allocator, and negotiator. Several alternatives for handling these responsibilities are available. March and Simon [1958] made the classic distinction between coordination techniques when they suggested that organizations could be coordinated in two basic ways: by feedback and by plan. Coordination by plan is achieved by preestablished procedures and schedules, while coordination by feedback entails the interchange of information between superior and subordinate with a corresponding adjustment of either subordinate activity or superior expectations. We would suggest, however, that this dichotomous classification is not entirely sufficient for the modern organization. Rather there is a need to add a third category of coordination—coordination by lateral interaction. The distinction suggested here is that organizations not only utilize coordination by vertical interchange, as is implied by March and Simon's concept of feedback, but also establish coordination via lateral interaction (i.e., direct contact between individuals in different departments). As will be seen in subsequent sections, this distinction is becoming increasingly important for the modern manager.

The purpose of this section is to look at the writings of several organizational researchers to ascertain the implications of their positions as they relate to the nature of the manager's communicative roles. More specifically, we will be examining several contingency views of organizational design, seeking to understand how the demands on the manager as a communicator vary across different organizational environments. This analysis will center around the work of Galbraith and Perrow. In some respects the selection of any one or two writers from the wide range of articulations of contingency theory could be considered arbitrary. However, both of these writers present analyses based on attempts to integrate the work of numerous other theorists, and thus a reasonable claim for their appropriateness for our purposes (developing a contingency model of managerial communication) can be made. This is not to say that our analysis does not exclude many aspects of contingency theory as it is currently developed. However, the limits of space and time dictate these exclusions. Specifically, our analysis will attempt to highlight factors that affect the degree to which the three identified coordination techniques—plan, feedback, and lateral interaction—are appropriate in various organizational settings.

Perrow: Technology as a Basis for Comparing Organizations

Perrow [1967] views technology as the defining characteristic of organizations. In this sense technology is considered to be the "actions that an individual performs upon an object . . . in order to make some change in the object" [Perrow, 1967, p. 195]. Perrow operationalizes technology as a function of two factors—the number of exceptional cases encountered in the work and the search process that is undertaken by the individual when exceptions occur. Dichotomizing, he indicates that organizations may encounter few or many exceptions in accomplishing their work and that the search process when exceptions are encountered can treat either analyzable or unanalyzable problems. He labels the four combinations of these conditions of technology routine, engineered, craft, and nonroutine. Figure 1 summarizes his typology providing examples of both service and industrial organizations exhibiting the particular technologies.

Before proceeding further into a discussion of the implications of Perrow's typology for communication, it will be useful to note a similar typology developed by Shull (see Shull, Delbecq and Cummings [1970]; or Shull and Judd [1971]). Whereas Perrow's typology applies to interorganizational variations in technology, Shull's typology views intraorganizational variations. Shull considers technology to be a function of two factors similar to those of Perrow—task characteristics (repetitive versus nonrepetitive) and personal characteristics (technical versus professional). With the exception of the replacement of the label *nonroutine* with *heuristic,* their labels for the four dichotomized conditions of technology are the same. The importance of Shull's typology to our discussion is that his attention to intraorganizational variation allows us to extend any conclusions concerning interorganizational variation to differences within organizations as well.

Perrow views task-related interaction patterns or what we have referred to previously as the internal communication or coordination function as concerning two distinct areas: (1) technical control and support and (2) supervision.[2] Technical control and support involves such areas as accounting, quality control, and scheduling, normally considered to be staff activities or coordination. Supervi-

---

[2]Op. cit. pp. 194–208.

FIGURE 1

PERROW'S CONCEPT OF TECHNOLOGY[3]

	Electronics Manufacturing CRAFT Graduate Education	Research & Development Organization NONROUTINE Organizational Consulting Firm
Unanalyzable Problems		
Search		
Analyzable Problems	Assembly Line Operations ROUTINE Personnel Placement	Machine Operations ENGINEERED Data Processing Center

Few   Many

Exceptions

sion, on the other hand, relates to typical line supervision. Perrow notes that within routine technologies both types of coordination should utilize coordination by plan. Engineered technologies utilize supervision coordination by plan, but technical coordination should be by feedback. Craft technologies, on the other hand, should exhibit the exact reverse of engineered technologies—technical coordination by plan and supervisory coordination by feedback. In nonroutine technologies, both types of coordination should be of the feedback type.

Perrow notes further that while the routine technology resembles the "mechanistic" organization of the Burns and Stalker [1961] dichotomy the nonroutine technology resembles the "organic" organization. This is quite useful because Burns and Stalker were specific in outlining the types of communication that would be effective in the two types of organizations. With respect to the effective mechanistic organization, they indicated that interaction between incumbents tends to be vertical (between superiors and subordinates) and that this interaction contains primarily instructions and decisions issued by the superior (Burns and Stalker [1961, p. 75]). In effective organic organizations, communication tends to be lateral rather than vertical and resembles consultation as opposed to command (Burns and Stalker [1961, p. 76]). From the standpoint of our terminology, the

---

[3]Adapted from C. Perrow, "A Framework for the Comparative Analysis of Organizations," *American Sociological Review,* Vol. XXXII (1967), pp. 196, 198.

mechanistic organization utilizes coordination by plan whereas the organic organization utilizes coordination by lateral interaction. Thus, we can more precisely define the nature of communication in the nonroutine technology as resembling what we have called lateral interaction. Figure 2 summarizes this relationship.

Galbraith: An Information Processing View of Organizational Design

Galbraith [1971, 1973, 1974] views the question of the appropriateness of various organizational designs from an information-processing point of view. From his perspective, the task of organizational design is to coordinate across the various subtasks of the organization. However, since no manager can communicate with *all* subgroups (managers who try suffer from what is referred to as "information overload"), it is necessary to design mechanisms or communication patterns that will allow for the accomplishment of the necessary coordination. The appropriateness of various mechanisms depends on the degree of task uncertainty. As he puts it, "the greater the task uncertainty, the greater the amount of information that must be processed among decison makers during task execution in order to achieve a given level of performance" [1974, p. 28]. Thus, as task uncertainty increases, the manager must develop mechanisms to facilitate the processing of greater amounts of information without resulting in information overload.

It is useful at this point to consider what constitutes a certain or an uncertain task environment. In this respect Galbraith depends on the work of Lawrence and Lorsch [1967]. Lawrence and Lorsch measured task uncertainty by the rate of new product introduction. Thus, an industry such as the container industry in which no new products have been introduced in the past ten years exhibits a high degree of task certainty, whereas an industry such as the plastics industry in

FIGURE 2

THE RELATIONSHIP OF TECHNOLOGY AND COORDINATION
TECHNIQUE

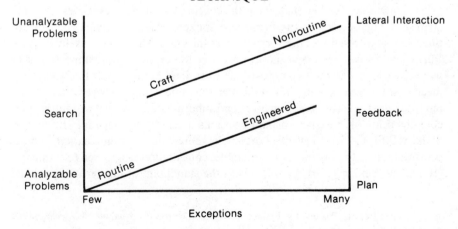

which 35 percent of its products have been introduced in the last ten years exhibits a high degree of task uncertainty. Uncertainty can thus be viewed as the degree to which organizational tasks are made unsure due to the changefulness of production activities. Although this is primarily related to industrial production, it seems certain that a similar dimension operates in service organizations.

Having indicated that information-processing demands vary as a function of task uncertainty and having defined task uncertainty, it is now appropriate to describe the hierarchy of communication patterns or design mechanisms that allow for the accomplishment of necessary coordination.

At the low end of the hierarchy where task uncertainty is low, coordination can be achieved through rules, organizational hierarchy, or goals. This is comparable to what we identified earlier as coordination by plan. In such a situation, organizational tasks are broken into various subtasks and the precise functioning and interrelationship of each is defined by rules, procedures, hierarchy, or goals. As one encounters increased levels of uncertainty, the demands on information processing increase correspondingly. Galbraith indicates that the organization faced with such increased demands has two options. The organization may either attempt to reduce the need for information processing or it must increase its capacity to process information. Since the former entails no new coordination or communication mechanisms, we will not concern ourselves with it. We will examine the two mechanisms that Galbraith indicates can be used to increase information processing capacity.

The appropriate response to intermediate demands on information processing is to create vertical information systems. Computerization and formalization of communication channels are two examples of vertical information systems. The concept at this point is to create mechanisms that will allow more information to be processed vertically (as is the case with feedback coordination) without encountering information overload. Such mechanisms will work to a point. However, as uncertainty increases, information demand eventually outstrips the vertical system's capacity. At this point, Galbraith suggests the creation of lateral relationships. This is effective in increasing information-processing capacity in that it moves decision-making down in the organization to a point where the information needed for decision-making is already present. This reduces the need for the formal organization to process as much information.

Figure 3 represents a summarization of Galbraith's position. As uncertainty increases, demands on organization information processing increase and the organization must move from coordination by plan to coordination by feedback and finally to coordination by lateral interaction.

TOWARD A CONTINGENCY MODEL OF MANAGERIAL COMMUNICATION

What we have attempted up to this point is to indicate the implications of two contingency models for the manager's role as a communicator. This role is seen as being primarily concerned with coordination of subordinate tasks. Three dis-

FIGURE 3

THE RELATIONSHIP OF UNCERTAINTY, INFORMATION
PROCESSING DEMANDS, AND COORDINATION TECHNIQUE

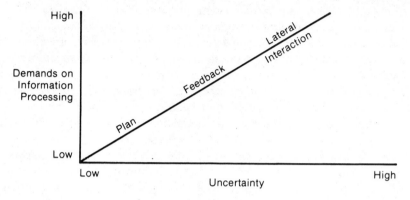

tinct mechanisms or communication patterns are available—plan, feedback, and lateral interaction. Two tasks remain in the development of a useful contingency model of managerial communication. First, we must attempt to integrate the position articulated by Galbraith with that articulated by Perrow; and, second, we must attempt to integrate this model with our knowledge from organizational communication research. The first task will be attempted in this section along with laying the groundwork for attempting the second in the following section.

It seems to these authors that Galbraith and Perrow are not talking about terribly dissimilar aspects of the organizational environment. What Galbraith views as uncertainty, Perrow seems to call technology and proceeds to divide up into notions of exceptions and search processes. In this respect, Perrow adds precision to the distinction articulated by Galbraith; however, Galbraith adds to our understanding by identifying the intervening variable of concern to this discussion—demands on information processing. Thus, it seems reasonable to suggest by way of synthesis that the appropriateness of particular communication patterns is a function of organizational technology. Additionally, through the link provided by Shull, we can state further that intraorganizational variations in the appropriateness of particular communication patterns are a function of subunit technology. By way of Galbraith's analysis, we expect that this relationship operates through technology's impact on demands on information technology. Thus, as technology moves from routine to nonroutine, the demands on information processing increase; and to remain effective coordination must move from a dependence on plans to feedback and finally to lateral interaction.

The question of how this relates to what we know from traditional organizational research remains to be answered. Although this question will be addressed in the main in the next section, a brief discussion is appropriate at this point. The link to be made is between coordination by plan, feedback, and lateral interaction and more traditional concepts of organizational communication. The claim to be made here is that coordination by plan is downward communication; feedback implies upward communication; and lateral communication implies horizontal and diagonal communication. If the reader recalls our initial distinctions of the three coordination mechanisms, the link to the three communication patterns above should be evident. Coordination by plan involves sending information (rules, regulations, schedules) down through the organizational hierarchy. Coordination by feedback, on the other hand, adds the solicitation of information from lower levels by higher levels within the hierarchy. Finally, lateral interaction engages individuals at varying organizational levels in the exchange of task-related information. Figure 4 integrates these traditional concepts of organizational communication into our previous model.

IMPLEMENTING A CONTINGENCY MODEL OF MANAGERIAL COMMUNICATION

At this juncture we will attempt to examine the implications of the contingency model of communication. Special attention will be given to attempting to integrate those implications with previous organizational communication research.

FIGURE 4

A CONTINGENCY MODEL OF MANAGERIAL COMMUNICATION

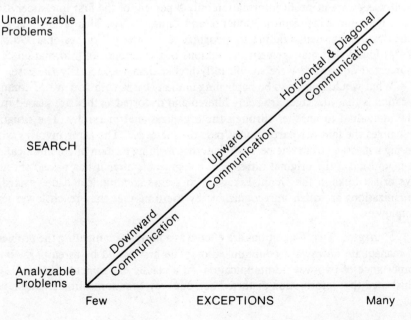

As is suggested in Figure 4, the manager's attention should move from one type of communication mode to another as the organizational environment (technology) changes. For example, the manager whose organization (or department) faces few exceptions in its work and whose problems are highly analyzable (e.g., routine assembly line operations) should concentrate on facilitating the downward flow of information. On the other hand, if the technology is nonroutine, the manager should focus his attention on horizontal and diagonal communication. This is not to argue that one type of communication should be the manager's sole concern, but rather that the particular type suggested represents the area where the manager can most profitably concentrate his attention. All three types of communication occur and deserve each manager's attention. However, the effectiveness of coordination will primarily depend on one type and that type should correspondingly receive more attention from the manager.

The remainder of this article will highlight how the manager can facilitate various types of communication within his organization or department. A section will be devoted to each of the three basic types of organizational communication. Problems associated with each type of communication will be identified and an attempt will be made to suggest strategies for dealing with the problems.

Downward Communication

Problems. The most persistent problem with downward communication that has been identified in the literature concerns the accuracy and adequacy of information reaching lower organizational levels. The magnitude of this problem was highlighted by an Opinion Research Corporation study which found in examining a large metal-producing firm that whereas 91 percent of top management was aware of profit information only 5 percent of the first line supervisors had such knowledge (Smith, Richetto, and Zima [1972]). This problem is magnified by management's failure to recognize its existence. For example, Odiorne [1954] found that management perceptions of the amount of information communicated downward were significantly higher than was actually the case.

What would appear to be happening in many cases with downward communication is that messages are being filtered and distorted as they are passed from one individual to another through the organizational hierarchy. The situation resembles the familiar party game "pass the message." The game involves whispering a message from one person to another forming a chain of communication. It is unusual if the original message is recognizable after it has passed through five or six links in the chain. Likewise, messages communicated downward in organizations are often unrecognizable by the time that they reach lower level employees.

Strategies. Two suggestions are offered as a means of mitigating the problems of inadequate downward communication. The first would be to emphasize the importance of two-way communication. In a classic experiment, Haney [1964] illustrated that information distorted in a one-way communication situation was accurately communicated when feedback between the communicator and the communicatee was allowed. Thus, a manager concerned with the accuracy of downward communication should develop methods of seeking feedback from subordinates to determine their understanding of his messages. Furthermore, he should attempt to ensure that his subordinates adopt a similar communication style in transmitting the messages on down through the hierarchy.

A second suggestion would be to note the importance of using multiple and coordinated communication media. At a minimum, the manager has both written and oral communication media at his disposal. Written media include not only memos and letters but also the in-house newspaper and the bulletin board. Several studies indicate that the most effective means of communicating information downward in organizations involves a combination of the various media in a coordinated fashion. This position has been confirmed experimentally by Dahle [1953] and from survey data by Level [1972]. Additionally, Davis's research on grapevine communication [1973] would suggest that even the corporate grapevine can be managed to serve as an effective communicative instrument of the manager. The important factor to keep in mind is that multiple and coordinated media approaches to downward communication will increase the likelihood that intended messages are received and understood by the maximum number of lower level employees.

Upward Communication

Problems. The problems of distortion and filtering identified as problems of downward communication are also present in upward communication. Additionally, these problems are exacerbated by status differences. The fact that superiors possess greater power and authority than their subordinates results in unique pressures that add further distortion to the serial transmission of information.

Huseman, Lahiff, and Wells [1974] identified several bases of distortion in and the lack of adequate upward communication. They suggest, for example, that, since individuals often feel that the relinquishment of sole possession of information decreases their power, there is a pressure to hoard information. The psychological costs of sharing information add to these pressures. Additionally, information-sharing norms within many organizations forestall adequate upward communication. Good examples of this are the manager who uses his higher status to communicate his separateness from his workers and the manager who listens to subordinate suggestions but never follows through on them. Rosen and Tesser [1970] have empirically tested the operation of one of these bases for problems with upward communication which they call the MUM effect. The MUM effect implies that, in an attempt to create as favorable an impression on their superiors as possible, subordinates filter out unpleasant messages so that only pleasant information passes upward through the organization. All these factors create distortions in the upward flow of information within organizations, which may have dangerous implications in terms of decisions made at higher levels in the organization.

Solutions. With slight alterations, the solutions suggested in the preceding section with regard to downward communication are applicable to problems of upward communication. While the manager cannot necessarily tap multiple media in obtaining messages from the lower levels of the organization, he can tap multiple information sources; that is, the effective manager will not rely on a single source of information but will seek out confirmation of important facts from several sources. Two-way communication is also useful in developing the type of climate that results in less filtering and distortion of upward-communicated messages. There is nothing that will be more effective in acquiring accurate and complete information than rewarding subordinates for such behavior. Two-way communication serves that end in that attention given through feedback communicates to the employee that he has been heard and appreciated. The manager must make sure, however, that organizational rewards reflect a recognition of the importance of communicating completely and accurately.

Several group techniques exist to facilitate the securing of information from lower levels of the organization. One of the most effective of these is the nominal group process. This process combines individual listing of suggestions in a group atmosphere in a manner designed to maximize creativity and to forestall closure. Subordinates are asked first to list their suggestions silently on a sheet of paper. After a period of time (approximately 15 minutes), individual suggestions are listed on flip charts or a blackboard in a round-robin fashion (first listing everyone's first suggestion, then everyone's second, and so on). Comments are not allowed during either of these first two steps. After everyone's suggestions have been listed, each person ranks the total list of ideas on the basis of quality. Low-ranking ideas are eliminated and the group begins discussion on the remaining ideas. If it is difficult to bring subordinates together, the delphi method can be used. The basic steps of the nominal group process are maintained; however, suggestions are exchanged through the mail. The delphi method can be especially useful to the large geographically diversified organization. Several recent publications explain the use of these two techniques in detail (Delbecq and Van de Ven [1975]; Huseman *et al.* [1974]).

Horizontal and Diagonal Communication

Problems. Managing horizontal and diagonal communication entails very different and perhaps more difficult problems than does either upward or downward communication. Classical theories of organization recognized neither the existence nor the importance of horizontal or diagonal communication, and it is only recently that much has been written about how they function within the organization. This lack of recognition has had a definite impact on the quality of nonvertical organizational communication. For example, Walton [1962] found that communicating horizontally is not rewarded within the typical organization. That this lack of rewards would decrease the amount of horizontal communication should be obvious; and Wickesberg [1968] goes further to suggest, as a result of a study he conducted, that the lack of official organizational sanction of nonvertical communications results in a decrease in the quality of the nonvertical communication that does exist. Thus, a prime problem of horizontal and diagonal communication is its quantity and quality.

A second problem is that of conflict. Any time that individuals from different departments within an organization interact there is a great potential for conflict. Such conflict may be perceptually based (caused by the development of different perceptions of relevant factors within the various departments) or goal-based (caused by the differing importance of various organizational goals within the various departments). Whatever its cause, conflict is an inevitable result of inter-departmental (nonvertical) interaction.

Strategies. An obvious solution to the problem of quality and quantity, although certainly not an easy one, is a restructuring of the organizational reward structure so that nonvertical communication is both sanctioned and rewarded. This may mean as little as managers becoming involved in establishing and promoting relationships between their subordinates and members of other departments. It may entail the allocation of additional organizational resources in the form of the establishment of interdepartmental committees and the hiring of liaison personnel. For the organization whose environment demands nonvertical interaction, however, such investments are essential to effective coordination.

Effective management of conflict is an extremely difficult task. Although we will not attempt to review the entirety of the conflict resolution research, two approaches deserve mention at this point. First, Lawrence and Lorsch [1967] suggest that managers who effectively manage interdepartmental conflict of the sort implied in the previous section exhibit use of a problem orientation. This implies that such managers avoid smoothing over differences or resolving the differences through the imposition of power, but rather confront the issues at hand and seek integrative solutions that attempt to meet both departments' needs. Second, in situations where perceptual differences are the prime source of disagreement, perception expansion training may improve the quality of interdepartmental interaction significantly. Huseman [1973] has described the format of such a training program. The program involves nominal grouping to identify departmental perceptions and then structured and controlled discussions between the two departments concerning the identified conflicting perceptions.

CONCLUSION

Our purpose in this article has been to examine communication and the managerial function. In brief, we have attempted to address the broad question of how the manager can communicate effectively and improve his managerial effectiveness. Our basic approach has been to suggest that contingency theory holds promise for managerial communication. Specifically, we have suggested a contingency model of managerial communication that identifies the major variables on which communication is contingent.

While we have identified major communication problem areas and have suggested strategies for coping with these problems, our major thrust has been to draw attention to the fact that managerial communication in organizations is situation specific. Or, to put it more simply: communication strategies that are appropriate for one situation may be inappropriate for the next. It is our conviction that a contingency approach to organizational communication enables the modern manager to identify communication strategies that will maximize managerial effectiveness.

REFERENCES FOR ARTICLE

1. BARNARD, C. *The Functions of the Executive.* Cambridge, Mass.: Harvard University Press, 1938.
2. BURNS, T. "The Directions of Activity and Communication in a Departmental Executive Group." *Human Relations,* Vol. VII (1954), pp. 73–97.
3. BURNS, T. and G. STALKER. *The Management of Innovation.* London: Tavistock, 1961.
4. CONNOLLY, T. "Information Processing and Decision Making in Organizations." *New Directions in Organizational Behavior,* edited by B. Straw and G. Salancik. Chicago: St. Clair Press, 1977, pp. 205–234.
5. DAHLE, T. "An Objective and Comparative Study of Five Methods of Transmitting Information to Business and Industrial Employees." Doctoral dissertation, Purdue University, 1953.
6. DAVIS, K. "The Care and Cultivation of the Corporate Grapevine." *Dun's Review,* Vol. CI (July, 1973), pp. 44–47.
7. DELBECQ, A. and A. VAN DE VEN. *A Guide to Nominal Group and Delphi Processes.* Glenview, Il.: Scott, Foresman & Company, 1974.
8. GALBRAITH, J. "Designing Matrix Organizations." *Business Horizons,* Vol. XIV (1971), pp. 29–40.
9. GALBRAITH, J. *Organization Design.* Reading, Mass.: Addison-Wesley Publishing Co., Inc., 1973.
10. GALBRAITH, J. "Organization Design: An Information Processing View." *Interfaces,* Vol. IV (1974), pp. 28–36.
11. HAGE, J., M. AIKEN, and C. MARRETT. "Organizational Structure and Communications." *American Sociological Review,* Vol. XXXVI (1971), pp. 860–871.
12. HANEY, W. "A Comparative Study of Unilateral and Bilateral Communication." *Academy of Management Journal,* Vol. VII (1964), pp. 128–136.
13. HUSEMAN, R. "Perception Expansion Training: An Approach to Conflict Reduction." A lecture to the International Communication Association Convention, Montreal, April 25–28, 1970.
14. HUSEMAN, R., J. LAHIFF, and R. WELLS. "Communication Thermoclines: Toward a Process of Identification." *Personnel Journal,* Vol. LIII (1974), pp. 124–135.
15. LAWLER, E., L. PORTER, and A. TENNENBAUM. "Managers' Attitudes Toward Interaction Episodes." *Journal of Applied Psychology,* Vol. LII (1968), pp. 432–439.
16. LAWRENCE, P. and J. LORSCH. *Organization and Environment.* Boston: Division of Research, Harvard Business School, 1967
17. LEVEL, D. "Communication Effectiveness: Method and Situation." *The Journal of Business Communication,* Vol. X (1972), pp. 19–25.
18. MARCH, J. and H. SIMON. *Organizations.* New York: Wiley, 1958.

19. MINTZBERG, H. *The Nature of Managerial Work.* New York City: Harper & Row, Publishers, Inc., 1973.
20. ODIORNE, G. "An Application of the Communication Audit." *Personnel Psychology,* Vol. VII (1954), pp. 235–243.
21. PERROW, C. "A Framework for the Comparative Analysis of Organizations." *American Sociological Review,* Vol. XXXII (1967), pp. 194–208.
22. ROSEN, S. and A. TESSER. "On Reluctance to Communicate Undesirable Information: The MUM Effect." *Sociometry,* Vol. XXXIII (1970), pp. 253–263.
23. SHULL, F., A. DELBECQ, and L. CUMMINGS. *Organizational Decision Making.* New York City: McGraw-Hill, Inc., 1970.
24. SHULL, F. and R. JUDD. "Matrix Organization and Control Systems." *Management International Review,* Vol. VI (1971), pp. 65–87.
25. SMITH, R., G. RICHETTO, and J. ZIMA. "Organizational Behavior: An Approach to Human Communication." *Readings in Interpersonal and Organizational Communication,* edited by R. Huseman, C. Logue, and D. Freshly. Boston: Holbrook Press, Inc., 1977, pp. 3–24.

10 • LISTENING IS GOOD BUSINESS[1]

Ralph G. Nichols[2]

In the year 1940, Dr. Harry Goldstein completed an important educational research project at Columbia University. Two very significant observations emerged from it. *One:* he discovered that it is perfectly possible for us to listen to speech—without any significant loss of comprehension—at three times the normal speaking rate. *Two:* he suggested that America may have overlooked a very important element in her educational system, that of refining our ability to listen.

Quite a few people read this study, and wondered about it; but not very many did anything about it. Shortly after that, however, Richard Hubbell, an important figure in the television industry, produced a new book. In it he declared without equivocation that 98 percent of all that a man learns in his lifetime he learns through his eyes or through his ears.

Hubbell's book threw a spotlight upon a long-neglected organ we own—our ears; and it threw into focus one of the most important educational researchers of our time. Dr. Paul Rankin of Ohio State University was determined to find out what proportion of our waking day we spend in verbal communication. He kept a careful log on 65 white-collar workers at 15-minute intervals for two months on end. Here is what he found:

> Seven out of every ten minutes that you and I are conscious, alive and awake we are communicating verbally in one of its forms; and that communication time is devoted 9 percent to writing, 16 percent to reading, 30 percent to speaking, and 45 percent to listening.

OUR UPSIDE-DOWN SCHOOLS

With respect to training in these communication skills, America has built her school system upside-down. Primary and secondary schools devote some 12 years to teaching a youngster how to write a sentence, in the hope that sometime he will be able to write a full paragraph, and then a complete report. Countless tax dollars and teacher hours of energy are spent in improving the least-used channel of communication.

For some inexplicable reason we chop off all reading improvement training at the end of the eighth grade. From that time on the reading we do is of an extensive, voluntary and general character. Then we moan because America averages out as a nation of eighth grade readers. In view of the eight years of training we receive at best, we shouldn't be shocked at that fact. However, a lot of tax dollars are devoted to improving this second least-used channel of communication.

[1] From *Management of Personnel Quarterly,* Vol. 1, No. 2 (Winter, 1962), pp. 2-9. Reprinted by permission of Ralph G. Nichols and The University of Michigan, Bureau of Industrial Relations.

[2] Ralph G. Nichols, Department of Rhetoric, University of Minnesota.

Then we come to something important quantitatively—speech itself. Thirty percent of our communication time is spent in it; yet speech training in America is largely an extra-curricular activity. In a typical school you will find an all-school play once or twice a year. There may be a debating team with a couple of lawyers' sons on it. There will be an orator, an extemporary speaker, and that is about the size of it. You will find it very difficult to discover a high school where even one semester of speech training is required of the students.

Then we come to listening. Forty-five percent of our communication time is spent in it. In 1948, when I first became concerned about this field, hardly anyone had considered refining his listening ability.

I asked my University for a sabbatical leave that year, and spent 12 months doing research, trying to identify the characteristics of a good and bad listener. First, I learned that nobody knew much about effective listening. Only one small girls' college in Missouri, Stephens College, was teaching listening. Only three experimental and scientific research reports in the field of listening comprehension had been published in 1948. By comparison, over 3,000 scientific studies had been published in the field of reading comprehension.

TEN YEARS MAKE A DIFFERENCE

By 1958 a very dramatic change had occurred. Most of our leading universities were teaching listening under that label. Today these schools are not only teaching listening—they are conducting graduate-level research in the field. Today scores of businesses and industries have instituted listening training programs for selected management personnel. Several departments of the Federal Government have followed suit.

A number of units of our military service have started listening training programs. Effective listening has practical application to current business practices. For example, there is a growing conviction that most salesmen talk too much and listen too little. There is a good deal of evidence accumulating to support this conviction.

TWO CENTRAL QUESTIONS

In view of this tremendous surge of interest in listening in just ten years' time, I should like to raise two questions and very closely pursue answers to them.

Question No. 1: Is efficient listening a problem in business and industrial management?

For our first bit of insight on this, I should like to revert to the classroom for just a moment, for the first person to produce important evidence on it was H. E. Jones, a professor at Columbia University. He was in charge of all the beginning psychology classes there, and he frequently lectured to a population of some 476 freshmen.

It seemed to him, when he gave comprehension tests on his lecture content, that the students weren't getting very much of what he was trying to say. He hit upon a novel idea for an experiment and, with the cooperation of 50 of his colleagues on the Columbia faculty, he proceeded with the study. Each professor agreed to prepare and deliver a ten-minute lecture on his own subject to Jones' students. Each one submitted his lecture excerpt to Jones ahead of time, and Jones painstakingly built an objective test over the contents. Half of the questions in each quiz demanded a recalling of facts, and the other half required the understanding of a principle or two imbedded in the lecture excerpt.

EFFICIENCY LEVEL—25 PERCENT

Professor No. 1 came in, gave his ten-minute lecture, disappeared, and the group was questioned on its content. No. 2 followed. At the end of the 50th presentation and the 50th quiz, Jones scored the papers and found that freshmen were able to respond correctly to only about 50 percent of the items in the test. Then came the shock. Two months later he reassembled the 476 freshmen and gave them the whole battery of tests a second time. This time they were able to respond correctly to only 25 percent of the items in the quizzes. Jones was forced to conclude, reluctantly, that without training, Columbia University freshmen operate at a 25 percent level of efficiency when they listen.

I couldn't believe it could be that bad. I decided to repeat the experiment at the University of Minnesota, and did so. I didn't let two months go by, for I was pretty certain that the curve of forgetting takes the downward swoop long before two months pass. I let two weeks pass, and got exactly the same statistics: 50 percent response in the immediate test situation; 25 percent after two weeks had passed. Several other universities have conducted the same experiment, and all have come up with similar statistics.

I think it is accurate and conservative to say that we operate at precisely a 25 percent level of efficiency when listening to a ten-minute talk. How do you like that? I know you are interested in efficiency. Some of us like to talk in terms of 90, 93, 95 or even 98 percent efficiency in the things we do—yet in the thing we do most frequently in all our lives (save possibly for breathing), we probably operate at about a 25 percent level of efficiency.

Is this important in business and industrial management? Let us consider some evidence that will be nearer to your heart.

EVIDENCE FROM INDUSTRY

A few years ago a young man went to a speech professor at a large state university and said that he would like to acquire a Ph.D. degree in the field of speech. My professional friend said, "Well, your credentials look good enough; but instead of doing a Ph.D. in the speech field, I would like you to do it in the field of listening. I have a project in mind. Take a notebook; go to this firm in New Orleans; and interview all the management

people you can get in to see during one week. Ask them these questions."
Then he gave the student a list of questions he was to ask of each manager.

The young man disappeared, and came back a week later. He had a little notebook full of testimony that he had acquired from these management people. The gist of it was that they worked for a tremendous organization, that they had a great future, that they felt they had one of the finest communications systems ever devised in any business or industry.

They said, "Our workers know what they are trying to do. They understand our program. We have the most loyal group of employees to be found anywhere. The morale in our outfit is tremendous. The future looks good."

"Okay," said my friend the speech professor. "Put on a pair of coveralls. Go down to that same firm and see Joe Walker, head of the company's trucking department. You are to work for him for one year. Every day, carry a notebook in your inside pocket, and whenever you hear the employees say anything about their management—write it down in your notebook."

Twelve months later the student came back with a great stack of notebooks. My friend spent several weeks pouring over the testimony in them, and when he got through announced that it was the most vicious, malicious, denunciatory attack of one group upon another he ever had seen.

Trying to find out what the employees really knew of their firm's policies, procedures, and philosophy, he concluded that the workers understood *less* than 25 percent of what their managers thought they understood.

I doubted this generalization and discussed my skepticism with Erle Savage, a senior partner of the Pidgeon Savage Lewis Corporation of Minneapolis, an advertising and communications firm. He looked at me when I told him about the study, and said, "Professor, don't be so skeptical. As a matter of fact, the picture is even worse than your friend reports it to you. My company has just made a very careful study of the communicative efficiency of 100 representative business and industrial managements. This chart shows the composite picture of what we discovered."

As you can see, there is a tremendous loss of information—37 percent —between the Board of Directors and the Vice-Presidential level. General supervisors got 56 percent of the information; plant managers 40 percent; and general foremen received only 30 percent of what had been transmitted downward to them. An average of only 20 percent of the communication sent downward through the five levels of management finally gets to the worker level in the 100 representative American companies.

Studies have dug deeper. What kind of person is the employee who understands only 20 percent of what his management thinks (and hopes) he understands? The 20 percent-informed individual is usually a negative-minded fellow. He believes that there are big fat managers up there at the top, exploiting him, hogging most of the profits and not giving a proper share to him. His first inclination may be to steal something in order to get even—and the easiest thing to steal in our economy is time. One can check in late and pretend he got there early. Or he can leave early and report he left late. It is always easy to slow down at the desk or on the assembly line

Dilution of information occurs as a result of improper Communications flow...

100%	63%	56%	40%	30%	20%
BOARD	VICE PRESIDENT	GENERAL SUPERVISOR	PLANT MANAGER	GENERAL FOREMAN	WORKER

Reproduced by Special Permission of Pidgeon Savage Lewis, Inc.

or wherever one is working. All this is costly business. If this doesn't satisfy him, a person can start stealing tools or equipment. People have been found carrying out a hammer or saw beneath overcoats as they walk out at night. One person was even caught with a nickel roll of toilet tissue under his jacket—trying to get even.

UPWARD COMMUNICATION

Communicative efficiency down through the levels of management is terribly poor, and we are only beginning to appreciate the enormity of the problem. But I am much more concerned about another kind of communication. I am much more excited about the efficiency or inefficiency of upward communication than of that which passes downward through the channels. Why? Because I hold the deep conviction that the efficiency of downward communication is going to be improved significantly only when top management better understands the attitudes, the opinions, the ideas and the suggestions of the people at the bottom of the whole structure.

What kind of efficiency do we have when the levels of management report upward? We have begun to collect a lot of evidence on that. A recent study made of 24 industrial plants reveals a very peculiar thing. In the early stages of their study the researchers recognized that ten distinct factors are probably the most important in the morale of any employee group. They asked managers to rate these ten morale factors in the order of their importance as they thought they were influencing the employee group.

The managers put these three factors in the bottom three ranks. Eight: full appreciation of work done. Nine: feeling "in" on things. Ten: sympathetic help on personal problems.

Then the researchers went to the employee group and asked them to rate the ten morale factors in the rank-order of their actual influence. They rated these factors as follows: First: full appreciation of work done. Two: feeling "in" on things. Three: sympathetic help on personal problems.

It is almost incredible that management could guess exactly wrong, putting the three most important factors in the three least important spots; but this kind of evidence emerges again and again when objective studies are made of how well management really understands the attitudes and opinions of the employee group.

ATTEMPTS TO IMPROVE

Knowing this, a number of forward-looking firms and businesses in America are making very serious attempts to do something about it. A lot of different techniques have been tried. The old one, of course, was to have the boss know everybody. Many a president took great pride in the fact that he knew everybody on his payroll. Many of them liked to spend half a day walking through the shop or plant, shaking hands with all the workers.

This didn't work badly as long as the number was small enough to make it possible. But soon our companies got too big; so then we tried different systems.

We have had labor-management meetings in which labor was supposed to "speak out." We have had elected representatives of labor meet with selected management people. Neither of these things worked very well. We have tried hiring a chaplain as a special counselor, with the open invitation to everyone in the whole organization to go and talk to the chaplain at any time. This method might have succeeded had not some malcontended employee started a rumor that the chaplain was a stool pigeon "planted" by the board of directors. Of course, the potential value of this technique was soon lost.

Labor reporters for the house publications have been tried. We have tried suggestion and complaint boxes, father confessors, opinion and attitude surveys; and even though each device probably has some merit to it, in every case it has a built-in weakness.

THE CENTRAL REMEDY

Their failing is that they *are* merely devices or techniques, and as such it seems to me they do not get at the head of the problem, which is sympathetic listening by one man to another. My feelings were pretty well restated in a study made by Loyola University researchers. They spent 18 months making this study. They were trying to find out what the attributes of a good manager really are. They finally came up with this generalization:

Of all the sources of information a manager has by which he can come to know and accurately size up the personalities of the people in his department, listening to the individual employee is the most important.

The most stereotyped report they got from worker after worker who like their superiors was this one: "I like my boss. He listens to me. I can talk to him."

Frank E. Fischer, managing director of the American Management Association's School of Management, summarizes the situation in one sentence. He says, "Efficient listening is of such critical importance to industry, that as research and methodology improve, I feel that training departments will have to offer courses in this field."

Granted that such a course is needed, how do you keep a listening training program alive in an industry? There is only one possible justification for keeping it alive, and that is if it is paying you money. If it is not paying off, get rid of it.

A few years ago a large firm located near Chicago was having a lot of trouble. They had been losing money in one particular plant for several months, and they tried a number of devices to get the plant operating productively again. Finally, hunting around for some new idea, they hired an outside psychologist to come in to teach all of their foremen how to listen. The psychologist got all the foreman into a room and essentially taught them how to grunt. He said, "When your men come in and complain to you about not having enough baths or not enough rest rooms or all of the other grievances they have, I want you to look sympathetic and say 'hummm' and nod affirmatively to them. Don't argue or talk back. Ask questions if you want to, such as 'Well, what did your wife say?' or 'Do all the boys think this way?' Throw out little questions like these, but you are never to debate with one of these fellows. And you must all practice until you can say 'hummm,' looking sympathetic while you're saying it." He coached these fellows for a couple of weeks and sent them back to their jobs.

As usual, streams of complainers made their way to the foremen's offices. To their surprise, instead of getting rude treatment, they found a man saying, 'Hmmm, is that so? Well, what did you do then, Joe?" Several of them acted as though they were bulls in a china shop, muttered a half-baked apology of some kind, and backed out. The result was that after three months had gone by some 90 percent of the grievances had disappeared, and the plant was making money again. The management of the plant was so sold on listening training that they decided if it was good for foremen, it would be just as well to have the plant managers learn how to listen too. They soon spread it through all of their levels of management.

I have pursued my first question long enough, is inefficient listening a problem in business and industrial management? I trust that perhaps you will concede it is.

Question No. 2: What can be done about it?

A few years ago I screened out the 100 worst listeners and the 100 best listeners I could identify in my University's freshman population. Standardized listening tests and lecture-comprehension tests were used, and we had two widely contrasting groups. These poor suffering 200 freshmen were then subjected to about 20 different kinds of objective tests and measures. I got scores on their reading, writing, speaking, mathematical and scientific aptitudes; six different types of personality inventories and each one filled out a lengthy questionnaire. In addition, I had a personal interview with each of the 200.

TEN BAD HABITS

When I got all done it seemed to me that ten things clearly differentiated a good listener from a bad one. I published an article about "The Ten Worst Listening Habits of the American People." Other universities read the article and repeated the study. Essentially, they came to the same conclusions. Thus, for whatever it is worth, I should like to enumerate and comment briefly on what seems to be the ten worst listening habits that afflict us. Why? Because listening training is largely the business of eliminating these bad listening habits, and replacing them with their counterpart skills.

1. Calling the Subject Uninteresting

Bad listening habit number one is to declare the subject uninteresting. The chairman announces a topic, or perhaps the bad listener reads it on the program and says to himself, "Gee, how dull can they get, anyhow? You'd think for the money they shell out they could get a decent speaker on a decent subject. This is such a dull topic that I think I'll worry about that secretary of mine. Am I going to keep her on another year, or am I going to sack her right now?" A lot of us store up these mental tangents to use in moments of boredom, and this is what the bad listener *always* does.

The good listener starts at the same point, but goes to a different conclusion. He says, "Gee, that sounds like a dull subject. I don't know what it has to do with me in my business. However, I'm trapped here, I can't get up and walk out. It would be terribly embarrassing and very conspicuous. Inasmuch as I am trapped, I guess I'll tune in on this guy to see if he has anything to say that I can use."

And the key to good listening in the first instance is that three-letter word—"use." The good listener is a sifter, a screener, a winnower, always hunting for something worthwhile or practical that he can store away in the back of his mind and put to work for him in the days or months ahead.

This is a selfish activity, but a very profitable one. We openly acknowledge the selfish character of it, and urge our trainees to become better listeners by hunting for the useful and practical. G. K. Chesterton put it beautifully many years ago in these words: "In all this world there is no such thing as an uninteresting subject. There are only uninterested people."

2. Criticizing the Delivery

Bad listening habit number two is criticizing the speaker's delivery. A bad listener does it almost every time. The speaker starts to talk, and the man thinks, "Gee, is that the best they can get? This man can't even talk. All he does is try to read from his notes. Hasn't anyone ever told him to look his listeners in the eye when he talks to them? I have never heard a voice as unpleasant as this fellow's. All he does is fidget, snort and cough. Nobody could get anything from such a character. I'll tune him out and worry about that sales pitch I have to make next week." And off he goes on a mental tangent.

The good listener moves in a different direction. He says, "I don't know when I have heard such an inept speaker. You'd think they would get a better man than that for what they pay him. But wait a minute! This guy knows something I don't know, or he wouldn't be up there. Inasmuch as I have paid tuition or a registration fee, I'll dig his message out of him if it kills me. I'll concentrate on his content and forget about the lack of smoothness in this character's delivery."

After an hour or two of concentrating on content, he doesn't even remember the eccentricities and the oddities of the speaker. He begins to get interested in the subject. Actually, the speaker does very little of the learning. If learning takes place, it is because of action inside the brain of the listener—the man out front.

Suppose that right now a janitor interrupted you, yelling in broken, profane English, "Get the hell out of here! The building is on fire!" You wouldn't lean backward and say, "Please, sir, will you not couch that admonition in better rhetoric?" You would rush pell-mell out of the room, as you know. That is my point. The message is ten times as important as the clothing in which it comes. Form has little to do with the significance of the communication taking place.

3. Getting Overstimulated

I feel like an authority on this one, for I have been overstimulated as long as I can remember. I get so excited about people and things that I just can't control myself. How does it work? A speaker starts to develop his topic. I am out in the audience, and before he talks three or four minutes he walks rough-shod on one of my pet biases or convictions. Immediately I want to throw up my hand and challenge him on the spot. If it is too formal a spot, I will sit there and gnash my teeth and figure out the meanest, dirtiest, most embarrassing question I can hurl at him. I have often sat for 30 minutes composing the most embarrassing question that could possibly be phrased for the speaker to answer. If that doesn't fit, I will sit and build a great rebuttal speech. Maybe I know of a little evidence that contradicts something he has presented, and I will plan my rebuttal effort.

All too often I have hurled my nasty question or great rebuttal at the speaker, only to find him looking at me in complete wonderment and saying "Nichols, didn't you hear when I went on to say that so-and-so was also true?'' I hadn't. My listening efficiency had dropped to a zero percent level because I had been overstimulated and excited about my contribution to come.

It happens all the time. And it is important! We now think it is so important that we put at the top of each blackboard in every classroom where we teach listening—and, by the way, we teach 25 percent of the incoming freshmen on my campus to be better listeners because we don't think many will get through college if we don't—this slogan: "Withhold Evaluation until Comprehension is Complete." It sounds kind of abstract and meaningless, but it isn't. In smaller words we might say, "Hear the man out before you judge him." Unless you fully comprehend his point, you are going to make a snap judgment of it, and at least half the time you are going to guess wrong.

4. Listening Only for Facts

Bad listening habit number four is listening only for facts. I know that you have great respect for facts. I have, too; but a curious thing exists about those facts. I personally asked the 100 worst listeners I could locate what they concentrated on in a listening situation. Ninety-seven of the 100 testified proudly that they "listened for the facts." The truth was that they got a few facts, garbled a shocking number, and completely lost the bulk of them.

I asked the 100 best listeners what they concentrated on in a listening situation, and a bit timidly and apologetically they testified in equal proportion, "When we listen we try to get the gist of it—the main idea."

The truth was that these idea listeners *had* recognized generalizations or principles, and had used them as connecting threads to give sense and system to the whole talk. Two days later they somehow appended more facts to these connecting threads than the bad listeners were able to catalogue and report.

We had to conclude that if one wants to be a good listener he should try to get the gist of the discourse—the main thread, the idea, the principle, the concept, the generalization. We should quit worrying about the facts. Facts can be retained only when they make sense, and they make sense only when they support a generalization of some kind.

5. Outlining Everything

Bad listening habit number five is trying to make an outline of everything. This is a curious business. We found that the 100 worst listeners thought that notetaking and outlining were synonymous. They knew only one way to take notes—to make an outline of the speech. There is nothing wrong with outlining if the speaker is following an outline pattern of organization. He should be, I would concede. However, between today and the day you and I die, probably not one-third of the speakers we hear are going to have organized their discourses carefully on an outline pattern or scheme—

and one of the most frustrating things in this world is to try to outline the un-outlinable.

The student who does it always comes out with a sheet of notebook paper that is a perfect and beautiful thing in terms of symmetry—all the margins and indentations perfectly ordered, the symbols all nicely subordinated; and there is meaningless jargon after each symbol. Two months later, when he tries to review his notes, they have no meaning whatsoever.

We asked the 100 best listeners what they did for notetaking and they said, "It all depends on the speaker. We listen for a while and do nothing. When we figure out if he is organized or not, we sometimes write little abstracts. We listen three or four minutes and write a one-sentence summary of what has been said. Sometimes we annotate the workbook or textbook as we listen. Sometimes we use the 'fact versus principle' technique."

I am fascinated about this last technique for I feel it is highly effective. They have two sheets of notebook paper side by side when they go in to hear a lecture. At the top of one sheet they write the word "facts," and at the top of the opposite sheet they write the word "principles." Then they sort of lean back thinking. "Produce, Mister, produce!" They merely list in vertical columns the facts or principles produced. The system calls for a minimum of writing. If the man is a phony and has no ideas, they have two blank sheets of paper. If he happens to be a producer (and some of them are), you will find him grinding out from 20 to 40 facts every time he gives a talk, with two or three very important principles on the other side. These are the best possible notes to have when we come to a period for review.

Our conclusion had to be that the good listener is a flexible character who has many systems of taking notes, and that he carefully picks out the best one for the type of speaker he hears.

6. Faking Attention

Bad listening habit number six is faking attention to the speaker. As a schoolteacher, for many years I felt I was going over big if I looked over the classroom and saw the bulk of my students with their chins in their hands looking up at me in this fashion. I was always pleased to see the girls in the first rows in this posture. I thought they were tuning me in.

We now know that the surest index to inattention in all this world is this posture on the part of the listener. Having paid the speaker the overt courtesy of appearing to tune him in, the listener feels conscience-free to take off on one of a thousand mental tangents, and that is precisely where he has gone. If you ever face an audience and, looking out across the room, see the bulk of your listeners in this pose, stop short in your talk and tell them to stand up and do calisthenics with you to get their blood circulating again.

Efficient listening is characterized by a quicker action of the heart, a faster circulation of blood, a small rise in body temperature. It is energy-burning and energy-consuming. It is dynamic and constructive.

7. Tolerating or Creating Distractions

Bad listening habit number seven is . . . so obviously clear that I will not elaborate on it.

8. Evading the Difficult

Bad listening habit number eight is much more important. This is avoiding difficult and technical presentations.

We asked our 100 worst listeners what they did in terms of listening to radio and television. We found that these 100 worst listeners were authorities on Bob Hope, Red Skelton and the Lone Ranger. Apparently they had spent their lives listening to these programs. Not one of those bad listeners had ever sat clear through the "Chicago Round Table," "Town Meeting of the Air," "Meet the Press," "Invitation to Learning," "See It Now," or "You Are There."

We asked the 100 best listeners, and they knew all about Bob Hope and Red Skelton, to be sure; but, voluntarily or otherwise, they had many times sat through some of these more difficult, technical and educational programs on radio and television.

Pursuing this aspect of good listening, we finally concluded that the one word in the dictionary that best describes the bad listener is the word "inexperienced." It is true he spends 45 percent of his communication day listening to something, but that something is always easy, recreational or narrative in character. He avoids, as though it were poison, anything tough, technical or expository in character.

Take a youngster who has never heard anything more difficult than Bob Hope and put him in an auditorium with 300 other freshmen; trot out the best professor of biochemistry on the faculty and let him start a lecture. The boy says, "Gee, what am I doin' here? What's he talkin' about?" He cancels that course and maybe heads into an economics class. It is just as rough over there. Inside of three months he washes out of school and is gone. He is inundated. For every two freshmen who come to our university and college campuses in America today, one washes out before the end of his sophomore year—and often before the end of his freshmen year.

At the other end of the curriculum, in most instances, for every one graduate to whom we can award a four-year degree there are two employers waiting to bid for his services. Fifty percent mortality on the intake! And we meet half of the demand on the outgo! I claim this is critical.

I am not sure how long we can stay in the world competition we are engaged in with this horrible loss of trained manpower. I get excited about it, perhaps overexcited. I actually feel that if we could get a little training grade by grade, ten minutes a week, in tough technical material, we would have a tremendous decrease of that 50 percent mortality at the college level. America needs more educated men and women to improve her economy and her culture.

9. Submitting to Emotional Words

Bad listening habit number nine is letting emotion-laden words throw us out of tune with the speaker.

This is a curious business; but it is a fact that a single word may have such an emotional load in it that it throws some listener or group of listeners right out of perspective.

When I was in college I was on the debate team, and my colleague was a Negro boy whose first name was Lionel. He was intelligent and an excellent speaker; and we did all right until we met a certain college away from home. Inadvertently in that debate one of the opposition said, "The niggers will be coming over." I happened to be looking at Lionel's black throat, saw the blood rush upward into his black face, and realized he was the next speaker in the debate, and he went out and made a tremendous ten-minute speech on the race problem in America. It was a great talk—but we were supposed to be debating the Philippine Island question. We lost that debate.

Word got around, and every debate tournament we entered we lost because the opposition soon learned that all they had to do to lick us was to drop the word "nigger" into the conversation and we would go berserk. To this day if anybody says that word in my hearing, I begin to erupt emotionally and am unable to think for three or four minutes.

I don't know what words throw you out of tune with a speaker, but I will warrant that a few of these may affect you. We have pinned down a number of them. We know that the word "mother-in-law" sometimes does it. The word "evolution" does it sometimes. "Automation" and "big business" are troublemakers. "Income tax," "landlord," "landlady," "Harry Truman," and "Sherman Adams" are all fighting words that have tended to disrupt listening efficiency for some people at some time or other. Last year I learned that department store personnel do not want to be called "clerks." Unfortunately I had used the word "clerks" in a talk, and I had five women approach me afterwards. They wished to be called "retail sales personnel."

One of the most important studies that could be made would be for some researcher to identify the 100 greatest word barriers to learning. I wish I knew what they were. If we knew what 100 words cause most of our difficulty as barriers to communication, we could consider them grade by grade; we could lay them out in the open, discuss them, rationalize them and get them behind us. How silly it is to let a simple word—merely a symbol of something—get us so excited as to disrupt our listening efficiency; yet this goes on all the time.

10. Wasting Through Power

I have left bad listening habit No. 10 until the last because I think it is by far the most important of all. It is wasting the differential between thought speed and speech speed.

On the average in America we talk 125 words per minute; but if you put a man up in front of an audience and get that degree of formality in the situation that always ensues when he starts speaking informatively or instructionally to a group seated before him, he slows down. In America we average 100 words per minute when we speak informatively to an audience. How fast do people out front listen? Or, to put it more accurately, how fast do listeners think in words per minute when they listen? We know from three different studies that you will never face an audience of any size at all that does not think at an easy cruising speed of 400 to 500 words per minute. The difference between speech speed and thought speed operates as a tremendous pitfall. It is a snare and a delusion. It is a breeder of false security, and a breeder of mental tangents.

MENTAL TANGENTS AT WORK

I believe I can give you fairly good insight as to what a male engineer thinks about when he is listening to a professor of engineering. Travel with me mentally, and imagine you are a group of senior engineering students about ready to graduate.

I am an old professor of engineering, and I walk in and glower at you at the beginning of your last class in your senior year, and I say, "Well, you think you're going to make it, eh? Some of you are going to get your sheepskins—but I'll tell you now that there are a few of you who aren't going to make it. We're going to flunk a couple of you. If you *do* make it, there is something you must remember as long as you live. The successful engineer is the man who appreciates the value and the worth of a slide rule! He is the man who never goes anywhere without one in his pocket or at his belt.

"Because a slide rule is the most important requirement for a successful career in engineering, I am going to spend this last class hour with you reviewing the mathematic computations possible when using it."

What do the students think about? One is thinking: "This old goat going over that again? I got that in physics when I was a junior in high school. They told me all about it again in my senior year, and again as a freshman and sophomore in college. How can a man stall that way and take taxpayers' money for a salary? Guess I'll worry about that soft tire on my Ford. I noticed the right rear was a little soft this morning. If that darned thing is flat when I get out of here, am I going to change it or let 'er sit until tomorrow, and get some help on it?"

He worries 50 seconds about the tire and then he checks in on the professor. The professor is now adding two digit figures on the slide rule. It is old stuff. Out goes the student worrying now about an approaching chemistry quiz. He spends 50 seconds on the chemistry quiz and ten seconds on the professor. In again, and out again. It wouldn't be so bad, if he always checked in for the ten!

Sooner or later this male engineering student gets to that inevitable tangent that occurs to every male at the college level. He begins to wonder which woman to call for a date Saturday night. "I wonder if I should call Susie. She's plump and jolly and I've had her out a lot of times and she's a lot of fun. She always makes candy that's so darned good!" He figures he could easily get a date with Susie—and then a thought strikes him. "I wonder if I could rate a date with Martha who came in from out of town. I don't know her last name, but gee, what a woman! That gal is tall, sinuous and glamorous. When she walks it's like watching a snake crawl. If I could rate a date with that creature, brother!" And this lad is off on a mental tangent from which there is no return!

The next thing he hears is the bell at the end of the hour.

As the bell rings he hears the old professor say, "Remember, when you take the cube root do it step by step, as a. . . ."

"Cube root? I never heard of it!" In absolute panic he grabs a friend going out the back door and he says, "How do you do cube root?" And the friend doesn't know either, for he has been out on a mental tangent too.

This is why we listen at an average efficiency level of 25 percent. It is because of the constant allurement of mental tangents. It seems to be almost impossible to keep our minds free from them.

What is the answer? It is obvious. If you can think four times faster than any man can talk to you, this should be a source of power; it should not be a weakness. As it operates without training it is a liability, but with training it can be converted into a tremendous asset.

MENTAL MANIPULATIONS

These activities, these mental manipulations, are three in number. Wherever you find listening training succeeding today, you will find them in the training program.

1. Anticipate Speaker's Next Point

Number one is to anticipate what the speaker is going to say next. One of the best things we can possibly do is to dash ahead of him mentally and try to guess what his next main point is likely to be. If we guess it is going to be point A and it turns out to be point A, learning is reinforced, nearly doubled; for that point comes twice into our brain centers instead of once.

If we guess wrong, what then? If we guess it is going to be point A and it turns out to be point Z, we can't help ourselves. We begin to compare Z with A, and wonder why he didn't make A his next point.

When we compare the thought we felt he was going to make with the one he actually produced, we begin to apply the oldest law of learning in the books—which is that we learn best by comparison and contrast. To anticipate—to "guess ahead," is the one wager in life we cannot lose. Whether we guess right or wrong, we win.

2. Identify Elements

Mental exercise number two is to identify the supporting elements the speaker uses in building his points. By and large, we use only three ways to build points. We explain the point, we get emotional and harangue the point, or we illustrate the point with a factual generalization following the illustration.

The sophisticated listener knows this. He spends a little of the differential between thought speed and speaking speed to identify what is being used as point-support material. This becomes very profitable in terms of listening efficiency.

3. Make Mental Summaries

Finally and most important, the good listener throws in periodic mental summaries as he listens. At the end of about three or four minutes, if the speaker draws a long breath or walks around the lectern, or takes a swallow of water, or if there is any pause at all, the sharp listener dashes clear back to the beginning of the discourse and makes a quick mental summary of what has been said up to the point of the break. We call these "dashes" mental recapitulations. There ought to be half a dozen or more in every lengthy talk we hear. They are the greatest dividend-payer in listening efficiency that we can possibly master and practice.

These periodic listening summaries are tremendous reinforcements of learning; and the beautiful thing about it is that we use to our own profit the ever-present differential between thought speed and speech speed.

A LOOK AHEAD

I would predict that within another five years or so no employer of white-collar personnel in America is going to sign up a young college or high school graduate without first inquiring about his listening index. If the young man asking you for a job says, "Well, my index is 17," I would advise you not to sign him up. We can no longer afford the luxury of a bad listener on our payrolls. One bad listener can cause more damage in the complex economy in which we operate than all your good listeners can compensate for. But if he says, "My listening index is 91," sign him up; for he is going to be a producer for you.

BIBLIOGRAPHY, CHAPTER 3

Aaker, David A. "Organizing a Strategic Information Scanning System." *California Management Review,* Vol. 25, No. 2 (January, 1983), pp. 76-83.
Alexander, Elmore R. III. "The Effect of Communication on Interpersonal Conflict." *Proceedings of Academy of Management Meetings* (August, 1976), pp. 403-407.

Alter, Steven L. "How Effective Managers Use Information Systems." *Harvard Business Review*, Vol. 54, No. 6 (November-December, 1976), pp. 97-104.

Bedeian, A.G. "A Historical Review of Efforts in the Area of Management Semantics." *Academy of Management Journal*, Vol. 17, No. 4 (March, 1974), pp. 101-114.

Benjamin, Robert I., *et al.* "Information Technology: A Strategic Opportunity." *Sloan Management Review* (Spring, 1984), pp. 3-10.

Berkeley, Edmund C. (ed.). "Idea Processing." *Computers and People* (July-August, 1982), p. 6.

Blair, David C. "The Management of Information: Basic Distinctions." *Sloan Management Review*, Vol. 26, No. 1 (1984), pp. 13-23.

Boulding, Kenneth E. "General Systems Theory—The Skeleton of Science." *Management Science* (April, 1956), pp. 197-208.

D'Aprix, Roger. "The Oldest (and Best) Way to Communicate with Employees." *Harvard Business Review*, Vol. 60, No. 5 (1982), pp. 30-32.

Gooding, J. "It's No Easy Trick to Be the Well-Informed Executive." *Fortune*, Vol. 87, No. 1 (January, 1973), pp. 85-89.

Hellriegel, D. and J. Slocum, "Integrating Systems Concepts and Organizational Strategy." *Business Horizons* (April, 1972), pp. 71-78.

Hill, Raymond E., and L. S. Baron. "Interpersonal Openness and Communication Effectiveness." *Proceedings of Academy of Management Meetings* (August, 1976), pp. 408-411.

Keller, Robert T., and Winford E. Holland. "Communicators and Innovators in Research and Development Organizations." *Academy of Management Journal*, Vol. 26, No. 4 (December, 1983), pp. 742-749.

Kozoll, Charles E. "Overcoming Communication Barriers." *Manage*, Vol. 30, No. 5 (November-December, 1978), pp. 14-16.

Magee, John F. "What Information Technology Has in Store for Managers." *Sloan Management Review*, Vol. 26, No. 2 (Winter, 1985), pp. 45-50.

Mayer, R. J. "Communications and Conflict in Organizations." *Human Resource Management*, Vol. 13, No. 4 (Winter, 1974), pp. 2-10.

McCaskey, Michael B. "The Hidden Messages Managers Send." *Harvard Business Review*, Vol. 57, No. 6 (November-December, 1979), pp. 135-148.

Murray, J. A. "Intelligence Systems of the MNCs." *Columbia Journal of World Business*, Vol. 7, No. 5 (September-October, 1972), pp. 63-71.

Nulty, Peter. "How Personal Computers Change Managers' Lives." *Fortune* (September 3, 1984), pp. 38-48.

Poole, Marshall Scott. "An Information-Task Approach to Organizational Communication." *Academy of Management Review*, Vol. 3, No. 3 (July, 1978), pp. 493-504.

Rowan, Roy. "Where Did That Rumor Come from?" *Fortune* (August 13, 1979), pp. 130-137.

Simon, Herbert A. "Information Can Be Managed." *Think*, Vol. 33, No. 3 (May-June, 1967), pp. 9-12.

Strassmann, Paul A. "Managing the Costs of Information." *Harvard Business Review*, Vol. 54, No. 5 (September-October, 1976), pp. 133-142.

"Teaching the Boss to Write," *Business Week* (October 25, 1976), pp. 56-58.

Watson, Kathleen M. "An Analysis of Communication Patterns: A Model for Discriminating Leader and Subordinate Roles." *Academy of Management Journal*, Vol. 25, No. 1 (March, 1982), pp. 107-120.

Chapter 4

Approaches to Decisions

Decision making pervades managerial activity. In fact, there are analysts who contend that it is the core of managerial activity. While the editor of this book has taken that position in the past, decision making in the framework of this book is considered as a fundamental managerial activity, but not the totality of the managerial experience. In fact, we can view a great deal of human experience within a decision-making context, but to do so would be to miss much of the emotional and spiritual aspects of life.

Organizations do not possess, perhaps, the degree of spiritual and emotive elements that individuals experience. Thus, decisions and choice are relatively more important for organizational life. Vroom examines the contingencies of choice that influence the type and content of decision: the degree to which information exists, the degree of problem structuring, the need for managerial commitment, the extent of subordinate motivation, and the level of existing conflict.

Another major difference between decision making within different parts of the organization can be noted by examination of choice at different levels. Ford's study of elite decision makers shows that top managers give greater attention to the ultimate and far-reaching impact that managerial decisions can have, whereas lower level managers are less cognizant of such concerns.

While a great deal of attention is given to analysis in decision making, another factor that is just as important is creativity, to which great leaders owe a great deal. Kirton shows the importance of innovators to the organization, the conflict between innovators and mere adaptors in the system, and the resulting impact upon the organization of the interactions between the two. Finally, Whiting goes a step further to illuminate how each of us can become more creative in our decisions as well as in our personal lives. If organizations are to renew themselves over time, the initiatives must be not only developed but also shepherded through the organization. We introduce these issues in this chapter and examine them in a different context in later sections of the book.

11 • A NEW LOOK AT MANAGERIAL DECISION MAKING[1]

Victor H. Vroom[2]

All managers are decision makers. Furthermore, their effectiveness as managers is largely reflected in their track record in making the right decisions. These right decisions in turn largely depend on whether or not the manager has utilized the right person or persons in the right ways in helping him solve the problem.

Our concern in this article is with decision making as a social process. We view the manager's task as determining how the problem is to be solved, not the solution to be adopted. Within that overall framework, we have attempted to answer two broad sets of questions: What decision-making processes should managers use to deal effectively with the problems they encounter in their jobs? What decision-making processes do they use in dealing with these problems and what considerations affect their decisions about how much to share their decision-making power with subordinates?

The reader will recognize the former as a normative or prescriptive question. A rational and analytic answer to it would constitute a normative model of decision making as a social process. The second question is descriptive, since it concerns how managers do, rather than should, behave.

Towards a Normal Model

About four years ago, Philip Yetton, then a graduate student at Carnegie-Mellon University, and I began a major research program in an attempt to answer these normative and descriptive questions.

We began with the normative question: What would be a rational way of deciding on the form and amount of participation in decision making that should be used in different situations? We were tired of debates over the relative merits of Theory X and Theory Y and of the truism that leadership depends upon the situation. We felt that it was time for the behavioral sciences to move beyond such generalities and to attempt to come to grips with the complexities of the phenomena with which they intended to deal.

Our aim was ambitious—to develop a set of ground rules for matching a manager's leadership behavior to the demands of the situation. It was critical that these ground rules be consistent with research evidence concerning the consequences of participation and that the model based on the rules be operational, so that any manager could see it to determine how he should act in any decision-making situation.

[1] From *Organizational Dynamics,* Vol. 1, No. 4 (Spring, 1972), pp. 66-80. Reprinted by permission of the publisher from *Organizational Dynamics* (Spring, 1972). Copyright 1972 by AMACOM, a division of American Management Associations. All rights reserved.
[2] Victor H. Vroom, Professor, Yale University.

Table 1 shows a set of alternative decision processes that we have employed in our research. Each process is represented by a symbol (e.g., AI, CI, GII) that will be used as a convenient method of referring to each process. The first letter in this symbol signifies the basic properties of the process (A stands for autocratic; C for consultative; and G for group). The Roman numerals that follow the first letter constitute variants on that process. Thus, AI represents the first variant on an autocratic process, and AII the second variant.

TABLE 1

TYPES OF MANAGEMENT DECISION STYLES

AI	You solve the problem or make the decision yourself, using information available to you at that time.
AII	You obtain the necessary information from your subordinate(s), then decide on the solution to the problem yourself. You may or may not tell your subordinates what the problem is in getting the information from them. The role played by your subordinates in making the decision is clearly one of providing the necessary information to you, rather than generating or evaluating alternative solutions.
CI	You share the problem with relevant subordinates individually, getting their ideas and suggestions without bringing them together as a group. Then *you* make the decision that may or may not reflect your subordinates' influence.
CII	You share the problem with your subordinates as a group, collectively obtaining their ideas and suggestions. Then *you* make the decision that may or may not reflect your subordinates' influence.
GII	You share a problem with your subordinates as a group. Together you generate and evaluate alternatives and attempt to reach agreement (consensus) on a solution. Your role is much like that of chairman. You do not try to influence the group to adopt *your* solution and you are willing to accept and implement any solution that has the support of the entire group.

(GI is omitted because it applies only to more comprehensive models outside the scope of this article.)

Conceptual and Empirical Basis of the Model

A model designed to regulate, in some rational way, choices among the decisions processes shown in Table 1 should be based on sound empirical evidence concerning the likely consequences of the styles. The more complete the empirical base of knowledge, the greater the certainty with which we can develop the model and the greater will be its usefulness. To aid in understanding the conceptual basis of the model, it is important to distinguish among three classes of outcomes that bear on the ultimate effectiveness of decisions. These are:

1) The quality or rationality of the decision.
2) The acceptance or commitment on the part of subordinates to execute the decision effectively.
3) The amount of time required to make the decision.

The effects of participation on each of these outcomes or consequences were summed up by the author in *The Handbook of Social Psychology* as follows:

> The results suggest that allocating problem solving and decision-making tasks to entire groups requires a greater investment of man hours but produces higher acceptance of decisions and a higher probability that the decision will be executed efficiently. Differences between these two methods in quality of decisions and in elapsed time are inconclusive and probably highly varia- ble . . . It would be naive to think that group decision making is always more "effective" than autocratic decision making, or vice versa; the relative effective- ness of these two extreme methods depends both on the weights attached to quality, acceptance and time variables and on differences in amounts of these outcomes resulting from these methods, neither of which is invariant from one situation to another. The critics and proponents of participative management would do well to direct their efforts toward identifying the properties of situa- tions in which different decision-making approaches are effective rather than wholesale condemnation or deification of one approach.

We have gone on from there to identify the properties of the situation or problem that will be the basic elements in the model. These problem attributes are of two types: 1) Those that specify the importance for a particular problem of quality and acceptance, and 2) those that, on the basis of available evidence, have a high probability of moderating the effects of participation on each of these outcomes. Table 2 shows the problem attributes used in the present form of the model. For each attribute a question is provided that might be used by a leader in diagnosing a particular problem prior to choosing his leadership style.

In phrasing the questions, we have held technical language to a mini- mum. Furthermore, we have phrased the questions in Yes-No form, trans- lating the continuous variables defined above into dichotomous variables. For example, instead of attempting to determine how important the de- cision quality is to the effectiveness of the decision (attribute A), the leader is asked in the first question to judge whether there is any quality component to the problem. Similarly, the difficult task of specifying exactly how much information the leader possesses that is relevant to the decision (attribute B) is reduced to a simple judgment by the leader concerning whether or not he has sufficient information to make a high quality decision.

We have found that managers can diagnose a situation quickly and accurately by answering this set of seven questions concerning it. But how can such responses generate a prescription concerning the most effective leadership style or decision process? What kind of normative model of participation in decision making can be built from this set of problem attributes?

Figure 1 shows one such model expressed in the form of a decision tree. It is the seventh version of such a model that we have developed over the last three years. The problem attributes, expressed in question form, are arranged along the top of the figure. To use the model for a particular de- cision-making situation, one starts at the left-hand side and works toward

TABLE 2

PROBLEM ATTRIBUTES USED IN THE MODEL

Problem Attributes	Diagnostic Questions
A. The importance of the quality of the decision.	Is there a quality requirement such that one solution is likely to be more rational than another?
B. The extent to which the leader possesses sufficient information/expertise to make a high-quality decision by himself.	Do I have sufficient information to make a high-quality decision?
C. The extent to which the problem is structured.	Is the problem structured?
D. The extent to which acceptance or commitment on the part of subordinates is critical to the effective implementation of the decision.	Is acceptance of decision by subordinates critical to effective implementation?
E. The prior probability that the leader's autocratic decision will receive acceptance by subordinates.	If you were to make the decision by yourself, is it reasonably certain that it would be accepted by your subordinates?
F. The extent to which subordinates are motivated to attain the organizational goals as represented in the objectives explicit in the statement of the problem.	Do subordinates share the organizational goals to be obtained in solving this problem?
G. The extent to which subordinates are likely to be in conflict over preferred solutions.	Is conflict among subordinates likely in preferred solutions?

the right asking oneself the question immediately above any box that is encountered. When a terminal node is reached, a number will be found designating the problem type and one of the decision-making processes appearing in Table 1. AI is prescribed for four problem types (1, 2, 4, and 5); AII is prescribed for two problem types (9 and 10); CI is prescribed for only one problem type (8); CII is prescribed for four problem types (7, 11, 13, and 14); and GII is prescribed for three problem types (3, 6, and 12). The relative frequency with which each of the five decision processes would be prescribed for any manager would, of course, depend on the distribution of problem types encountered in his decision making.

Rationale Underlying the Model. The decision processes specified for each problem type are not arbitrary. The model's behavior is governed by a set of principles intended to be consistent with existing evidence concerning the consequences of participation in decision making on organizational effectiveness.

There are two mechanisms underlying the behavior of the model. The first is a set of seven rules that serve to protect the quality and the acceptance of the decision by eliminating alternatives that risk one or the

FIGURE 1
Decision Model

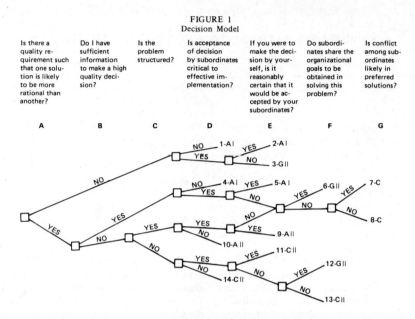

Is there a quality requirement such that one solution is likely to be more rational than another?	Do I have sufficient information to make a high quality decision?	Is the problem structured?	Is acceptance of decision by subordinates critical to effective implementation?	If you were to make the decision by yourself, is it reasonably certain that it would be accepted by your subordinates?	Do subordinates share the organizational goals to be obtained in solving this problem?	Is conflict among subordinates likely in preferred solutions?
A	B	C	D	E	F	G

other of these decision outcomes. Once the rules have been applied, a feasible set of decision processes is generated. The second mechanism is a principle for choosing among alternatives in the feasible set where more than one exists.

Let us examine the rules first, because they do much of the work of the model. As previously indicated, the rules are intended to protect both the quality and acceptance of the decision. In the form of the model shown, there are three rules that protect decision quality and four that protect acceptance.

1. *The Information Rule.* If the quality of the decision is important and if the leader does not possess enough information or expertise to solve the problem by himself, AI is eliminated from the feasible set. (Its use risks a low-quality decision.)

2. *The Goal Congruence Rule.* If the quality of the decision is important and if the subordinates do not share the organizational goals to be obtained in solving the problem, GII is eliminated from the feasible set. (Alternatives that eliminate the leader's final control over the decision reached may jeopardize the quality of the decision.)

3. *The Unstructured Problem Rule.* In decisions in which the quality of the decision is important, if the leader lacks the necessary information or expertise to solve the problem by himself, and if the problem is unstructured, i.e., he does not know exactly what information is needed and

where it is located, the method used must provide not only for him to collect the information but to do so in an efficient and effective manner. Methods that involve interaction among all subordinates with full knowledge of the problem are likely to be both more efficient and more likely to generate a high-quality solution to the problem. Under these conditions, AI, AII, and CI are eliminated from the feasible set. (AI does not provide for him to collect the necessary information, and AII and CI represent more cumbersome, less effective, and less efficient means of bringing the necessary information to bear on the solution of the problem than methods that do permit those with the necessary information to interact.)

4. *The Acceptance Rule.* If the acceptance of the decision by subordinates is critical to effective implementation, and if it is not certain that an autocratic decision made by the leader would receive that acceptance, AI and AII are eliminated from the feasible set. (Neither provides an opportunity for subordinates to participate in the decision and both risk the necessary acceptance.)

5. *The Conflict Rule.* If the acceptance of the decision is critical, and an autocratic decision is not certain to be accepted, and subordinates are likely to be in conflict or disagreement over the appropriate solution, AI, AII, and CI are eliminated from the feasible set. (The method used in solving the problem should enable those in disagreement to resolve their differences with full knowledge of the problem. Accordingly, under these conditions, AI, AII, and CI, which involve no interaction or only "one-on-one" relationships and therefore provide no opportunity for those in conflict to resolve their differences, are eliminated from the feasible set. Their use runs the risk of leaving some of the subordinates with less than the necessary commitment to the final decision.)

6. *The Fairness Rule.* If the quality of decision is unimportant and if acceptance is critical and not certain to result from an autocratic decision, AI, AII, CI, and CII are eliminated from the feasible set. (The method used should maximize the probability of acceptance as this is the only relevant consideration in determining the effectiveness of the decision. Under these circumstances, AI, AII, CI, and CII, which create less acceptance or commitment than GII, are eliminated from the feasible set. To use them is to run the risk of getting less than the needed acceptance of the decision.)

7. *The Acceptance Priority Rule.* If acceptance is critical, not assured by an autocratic decision, and if subordinates can be trusted, AI, AII, CI, and CII are eliminated from the feasible set. (Methods that provide equal partnership in the decision-making process can provide greater acceptance without risking decision quality. Use of any method other than GII results in an unnecessary risk that the decision will not be fully accepted or receive the necessary commitment on the part of subordinates.)

Once all seven rules have been applied to a given problem, we emerge with a feasible set of decision processes. The feasible set for each of the fourteen problem types is shown in Table 3. It can be seen that there are some problem types for which only one method remains in the feasible set, others for which two methods remain feasible, and still others for which five methods remain feasible.

TABLE 3

PROBLEM TYPES AND THE FEASIBLE SET
OF DECISION PROCESSES

Problem Type	Acceptable Methods
1.	AI, AII, CI, CII, GII
2.	AI, AII, CI, CII, GII
3.	GII
4.	AI, AII, CI, CII, GII*
5.	AI, AII, CI, CII, GII*
6.	GII
7.	CII
8.	CI, CII
9.	AII, CI, CII, GII*
10.	AII, CI, CII, GII*
11.	CII, GII*
12.	GII
13.	CII
14.	CII, GII*

* Within the feasible set only when the answer to question F is Yes.

When more than one method remains in the feasible set, there are a number of ways in which one might choose among them. The mechanism we have selected and the principle underlying the choices of the model in Figure 1 utilizes the number of man-hours used in solving the problem as the basis for choice. Given a set of methods with equal likelihood of meeting both quality and acceptance requirements for the decision, it chooses that method that requires the least investment in man-hours. On the basis of the empirical evidence summarized earlier, this is deemed to be the method furthest to the left within the feasible set. For example, since AI, AII, CI, CII, and GII are all feasible as in Problem Types 1 and 2, AI would be the method chosen.

To illustrate application of the model in actual administrative situations, we will analyze four cases with the help of the model. While we attempt to describe these cases as completely as is necessary to permit the reader to make the judgments required by the model, there may remain some room for subjectivity. The reader may wish after reading the case to analyze it himself using the model and then to compare his analysis with that of the author.

CASE I. You are a manufacturing manager in a large electronics plant. The company's management has recently installed new machines and put in a new simplified work system, but to the surprise of everyone, yourself included, the expected increase in productivity was not realized. In fact, production has begun to drop, quality has fallen off, and the number of employee separations has risen.

You do not believe that there is anything wrong with the machines. You have had reports from other companies that are using them and they confirm this opinion. You have also had representatives from the firm that built the machines go over them and they report that they are operating at peak efficiency.

You suspect that some parts of the new work system may be responsible for the change, but this view is not widely shared among your immediate subordinates who are four first-line supervisors, each in charge of a section, and your supply manager. The drop in production has been variously attributed to poor training of the operators, lack of an adequate system of financial incentives, and poor morale. Clearly, this is an issue about which there is considerable depth of feeling within individuals and potential disagreement among your subordinates.

This morning you received a phone call from your division manager. He had just received your production figures for the last six months and was calling to express his concern. He indicated that the problem was yours to solve in any way that you think best, but that he would like to know within a week what steps you plan to take.

You share your division manager's concern with the falling productivity and know that your men are also concerned. The problem is to decide what steps to take to rectify the situation.

> *Analysis*
> Questions—
>   A (Quality?) = Yes
>   B (Managers Information?) = No
>   C (Structured?) = No
>   D (Acceptance?) = Yes
>   E (Prior Probability of Acceptance?) = No
>   F (Goal Congruence?) = Yes
>   G (Conflict) = Yes
> Problem Type—12
> Feasible Set—GII
> Minimum Man-Hours Solution (from Figure 1)—GII
> Rule Violations—
>   AI violates rules 1, 3, 4, 5, 7
>   AII violates rules 3, 4, 5, 7
>   CI violates rules 3, 5, 7
>   CII violates rule 7

CASE II. You are general foreman in charge of a large gang laying an oil pipeline and have to estimate your expected rate of progress in order to schedule material deliveries to the next field site.

You know the nature of the terrain you will be traveling and have the historical data needed to compute the mean and variance in the rate of speed over that type of terrain. Given these two variables, it is a simple matter to calculate the earliest and latest times at which materials and support facilities will be needed at the next site. It is important that your estimate be reasonably accurate. Underestimates result in idle foremen and workers, and an overestimate results in tying up materials for a period of time before they are to be used.

Progress has been good and your five foremen and other members of the gang stand to receive substantial bonuses if the project is completed ahead of schedule.

> *Analysis*
> Questions—
>   A (Quality?) = Yes
>   B (Manager's Information?) = Yes
>   D (Acceptance?) = No
> Problem Type—4
> Feasible Set—AI, AII, CI, CII, GII
> Minimum Man-Hours Solution (from Figure 1)—AI
> Rule Violations—None

CASE III. You are supervising the work of 12 engineers. Their formal training and work experience are very similar, permitting you to use them interchangeably on projects. Yesterday, your manager informed you that a request had been received from an overseas affiliate for four engineers to go abroad on extended loan for a period of six to eight months. For a number of reasons, he argued and you agreed that this request should be met from your group.

All your engineers are capable of handling this assignment and, from the standpoint of present and future projects, there is no particular reason why anyone should be retained over any other. The problem is somewhat complicated by the fact that the overseas assignment is in what is generally regarded as an undesirable location.

> *Analysis*
> Questions—
>   A (Quality?) = No
>   D (Acceptance?) = Yes
>   E Prior Probability of Acceptance?) = No
>   G (Conflict?) = Yes
> Problem Type—3
> Feasible Set—GII
> Minimum Man-Hours Solution (from Figure 1)—GII
> Rule Violations—
>   AI and AII violate rules 4,5, and 6
>   CI violates rules 5 and 6
>   CII violates rule 6

CASE IV. You are on the division manager's staff and work on a wide variety of problems of both an administrative and technical nature. You have been given the assignment of developing a standard method to be used in each of the five plants in the division for manually reading equipment registers, recording the readings, and transmitting the scorings to a centralized information system.

Until now there has been a high error rate in the reading and/or transmittal of the data. Some locations have considerably higher error rates than others, and the methods used to record and transmit the data vary among plants. It is probable, therefore, that part of the error variance is a function of specific local conditions rather than anything else, and this will complicate the establishment of any system common to all plants. You have the information on error rates but no information on the local practices that generate these errors or on the local conditions that necessitate the different practices.

Everyone would benefit from an improvement in the quality of the data; it is used in a number of important decisions. Your contacts with the plants are through the quality-control supervisors who are responsible for collecting the data. They are a conscientious group committed to doing their jobs well, but are highly sensitive to interference on the part of higher management in their own operations. Any solution that does not receive the active support of the various plant supervisors is unlikely to reduce the error rate significantly.

> *Analysis*
> Questions—
>   A (Quality?) = Yes
>   B (Manager's Information?) = No
>   C (Structured?) = No
>   D (Acceptance?) = Yes
>   E (Prior Probability of Acceptance?) = No
>   F (Goal Congruence?) = Yes
> Problem Type—12
> Feasible Set—GII
> Minimum Man-Hours Solution (from Figure 1)—GII
> Rule Violations—
>   AI violates rules 1, 3, 4, and 7
>   AII violates rules 3, 4, and 7
>   CI violates rules 3 and 7
>   CII violates rule 7

Short Versus Long-Term Models

The model described above seeks to protect the quality of the decision and to expend the least number of man-hours in the process. Because it focuses on conditions surrounding the making and implementation of a particular decision rather than any long-term considerations, we can term it a short-term model.

It seems likely, however, that the leadership methods that may be optimal for short-term results may be different from those that would be optimal over a longer period of time. Consider a leader, for example, who has been uniformly pursuing an autocratic style (AI or AII) and, perhaps as a consequence, has subordinates who might be termed "yes men" (attribute E) but who also cannot be trusted to pursue organizational goals (attribute F), largely because the leader has never bothered to explain them.

It appears likely, however, that the manager who used more participative methods would, in time, change the status of these problem attributes so as to develop ultimately a more effective problem-solving system. A promising approach to the development of a long-term model is one that places less weight on man-hours as the basis for choice of method within the feasible set. Given a long-term orientation, one would be interested in the possibility of a trade-off between man-hours in problem solving and team development, both of which increase with participation. Viewed in these terms, the time-minimizing model places maximum relative weight on man-hours and no weight on development, and hence chooses the style farthest to the left within the feasible set. A model that places less weight on man-hours and more weight on development would, if these assumptions are correct, choose a style further to the right within the feasible set.

We recognize, of course, that the minimum man-hours solution suggested by the model is not always the best solution to every problem. A manager faced, for example, with the problem of handling any one of the four cases previously examined might well choose more time-consuming alternatives on the grounds that the greater time invested would be justified in developing his subordinates. Similar considerations exist in other decision-making situations. For this reason we have come to emphasize the feasible set of decision methods in our work with managers. Faced with considerations not included in the model, the manager should consider any alternative within the feasible set, and not opt automatically for the minimum man-hours solution.

As I am writing this, I have in front of me a "black box" that constitutes an electronic version of the normative model discussed on the preceding pages. (The author is indebted to Peter Fuss of Bell Telephone Laboratories for his interest in the model and his skill in developing the "black box.") The box, which is small enough to fit into the palm of one hand, has a set of seven switches, each appropriately labeled with the questions (A through G) used in Figure 1. A manager faced with a concrete problem or decision can "diagnose" that problem by setting each switch in either its "yes" or "no" position. Once the problem has been described, the manager depresses a button that illuminates at least one or as many as five lights, each of which denotes one of the decision processes (AI, AII, etc.). The lights that are illuminated constitute the feasible set of decision processes for the problem as shown in Table III. The lights not illuminated correspond to alternatives that violate one or more of the seven rules previously stated.

In this prototype version of the box, the lights are illuminated in decreasing order of brightness from left to right within the feasible set. The brightest light corresponds to the alternative shown in Figure 1. Thus, if both CII and GII were feasible alternatives, CII would be brighter than GII, since it requires fewer man-hours. However, a manager who was not under any undue time pressure and who wished to invest time in the development of his subordinates might select an alternative corresponding to one of the dimmer lights.

Toward a Descriptive Model of Leader Behavior

So far we have been concerned with the normative questions defined at the outset. But how do managers really behave? What considerations affect their decisions about how much to share their decision-making power with their subordinates? In what respects is their behavior different from or similar to that of the model? These questions are but a few of those that we attempted to answer in a large-scale research program aimed at gaining a greater understanding of the factors that influence managers in their choice of decision processes to fit the demands of the situation. This research program was financially supported by the McKinsey Foundation, General Electric Foundation, Smith Richardson Foundation, and the Office of Naval Research.

Two different research methods have been utilized in studying these factors. The first investigation utilized a method that we have come to term "recalled problems." Over 500 managers from 11 different countries representing a variety of firms were asked to provide a written description of a problem that they had recently had to solve. These varied in length from one paragraph to several pages and covered virtually every facet of managerial decision making. For each case, the manager was asked to indicate which of the decision processes shown in Table I they used to solve the problem. Finally, each manager was asked to answer the questions shown in Table II corresponding to the problem attributes used in the normative model.

The wealth of data, both qualitative and quantitative, served two purposes. Since each manager had diagnosed a situation that he had encountered in terms that are used in the normative model and had indicated the methods that he had used in dealing with it, it is possible to determine what differences, if any, there were between the model's behavior and his own behavior. Second, the written cases provided the basis for the construction of a standard set of cases used in later research to determine the factors that influence managers to share or retain their decision-making power. Each case depicted a manager faced with a problem to solve or decision to make. The cases spanned a wide range of managerial problems including production scheduling, quality control, portfolio management, personnel allocation, and research and development. In each case, a person could readily assume the role of the manager described and could indicate which of the decision processes he would use if he actually were faced with that situation.

In most of our research, a set of thirty cases has been used and the subjects have been several thousand managers who were participants in management development programs in the United States and abroad. Cases were selected systematically. We desired cases that could not only be coded unambiguously in the terms used in the normative model but that would also permit the assessment of the effects of each of the problem attributes used in the model on the person's behavior. The solution was to select cases in accordance with an experimental design so that they varied in terms of the seven attributes used in the model and variation in each attribute was independent of each other attribute. Several such standardized sets of cases have been developed, and over a thousand managers have now been studied using this approach.

To summarize everything we learned in the course of this research is well beyond the scope of this paper, but it is possible to discuss some of the highlights. Since the results obtained from the two research methods—recalled and standardized problems—are consistent, we can present the major results independent of the method used.

Perhaps the most striking finding is the weakening of the widespread view that participativeness is a general trait that individual managers exhibit in different amounts. To be sure, there were differences *among* managers in their general tendencies to utilize participative methods as opposed to autocratic ones. On the standardized problems, these differences accounted for about 10 percent of the total variance in the decision processes observed. These differences in behavior between managers, however, were small in comparison with differences *within* managers. On the standardized problems, no manager indicated that he would use the same decision process on all problems or decisions, and most used all five methods under some circumstances.

Some of this variance in behavior within managers can be attributed to widely shared tendencies to respond to some situations by sharing power and others by retaining it. It makes more sense to talk about participative and autocratic situations than it does to talk about participative and autocratic managers. In fact, on the standardized problems, the variance in behavior across problems or cases is about three times as large as the variance across managers!

What are the characteristics of an autocratic as opposed to a participative situation? An answer to this question would constitute a partial descriptive model of this aspect of the decision-making process and has been our goal in much of the research that we have conducted. From our observations of behavior on both recalled problems and on standardized problems, it is clear that the decision-making process employed by a typical manager is influenced by a large number of factors, many of which also show up in the normative model. Following are several conclusions substantiated by the results on both recalled and standardized problems: Managers use decision processes providing less opportunity for participation (1) when they possess all the necessary information than when they lack some of the needed information, (2) when the problem that they face is well-structured rather than unstructured, (3) when their subordinates' acceptance of the decision is not critical for the effective implementation of the decision or when the prior probability of acceptance of an autocratic decision is high, and (4) when the personal goals of their subordinates are *not* congruent with the goals of the organization as manifested in the problem.

So far we have been talking about relatively common or widely shared ways of dealing with organizational problems. Our results strongly suggest that there are ways of "tailoring" one's approach to the situation that distinguish managers from one another. Theoretically, these can be thought of as differences among managers in decision rules that they employ about when to encourage participation. Statistically, they are represented as interactions between situational variables and personal characteristics.

Consider, for example, two managers who have identical distributions of the use of the five decision processes shown in Table I on a set of thirty cases. In a sense, they are equally participative (or autocratic). However, the situations in which they permit or encourage participation in decision making on the part of their subordinates may be very different. One may restrict the participation of his subordinates to decisions without a quality requirement, whereas the other may restrict their participation to problems with a quality requirement. The former would be more inclined to use participative decision processes (like GII) on such decisions as what color the walls should be painted or when the company picnic should be held. The latter would be more likely to encourage participation in decision making on decisions that have a clear and demonstrable impact on the organization's success in achieving its external goals.

Use of the standardized problem set permits the assessment of such differences in decision rules that govern choices among decision-making processes. Since the cases are selected in accordance with an experimental design, they can indicate differences in the behavior of managers attributable not only to the existence of a quality requirement in the problem but also in the effects of acceptance requirements, conflict, information requirements, and the like.

The research using both recalled and standardized problems has also enabled us to examine similarities and differences between the behavior of the normative model and the behavior of a typical manager. Such an analysis reveals, at the very least, what behavioral changes could be expected if managers began using the normative model as the basis for choosing their decision-making processes.

A typical manager says he would (or did) use exactly the same decision process as that shown in Figure 1 in 40 percent of the situations. In two thirds of the situations, his behavior is consistent with the feasible set of methods proposed in the model. In other words, in about one third of the situations his behavior violates at least one of the seven rules underlying the model.

The four rules designed to protect the acceptance or commitment of the decision have substantially higher probabilities of being violated than do the three rules designed to protect the quality or rationality of the decision. One of the acceptance rules, the Fairness Rule (Rule 6) is violated about three quarters of the time that it could have been violated. On the other hand, one of the quality rules, the Information Rule (Rule 1), is violated in only about 3 percent of occasions in which it is applicable. If we assume for the moment that these two sets of rules have equal validity, these findings strongly suggest that the decisions made by typical managers are more likely to prove ineffective due to deficiencies of acceptance by subordinates than due to deficiencies in decision quality.

Another striking difference between the behavior of the model and of the typical manager lies in the fact that the former shows far greater variance with the situation. If a typical manager voluntarily used the model as the basis for choosing his methods of making decisions, he would become both more autocratic and more participative. He would employ autocratic methods more frequently in situations in which his subordinates were unaffected by the decision and participative methods more frequently when his subordinates' cooperation and support were critical and/or their information and expertise were required.

It should be noted that the typical manager to whom we have been referring is merely a statistical average of the several thousand who have been studied over the last three or four years. There is a great deal of variance around that average. As evidenced by their behavior on standardized problems, some managers are already behaving in a way that is highly consistent with the model, while others' behavior is clearly at variance with it.

A New Technology for Leadership Development

The investigations that have been summarized here were conducted for research purposes to shed some light on the causes and consequences of participation in decision making. In the course of the research, we came to realize, partly because of the value attached to it by the managers themselves, that the data collection procedures, with appropriate additions and modifications, might also serve as a valuable guide to leadership development. From this realization evolved an important by-product of the research activities—a new approach to leadership development based on the concepts in the normative model and the empirical methods of the descriptive research.

This approach is based on the assumption stated previously that one of the critical skills required of all leaders is the ability to adapt their behavior to the demands of the situation and that one component of this skill involves the ability to select the appropriate decision-making process for each problem or decision he confronts.

Managers can derive value from the model by comparing their past or intended behavior in concrete decisions with that prescribed by the model and by seeing what rules, if any, they violate. Used in this way, the model can provide a mechanism for a manager to analyze both the circumstances that he faces and what decisions are feasible under these circumstances.

While use of the model without training is possible, we believe that the manager can derive the maximum value from a systematic examination of his leadership style, and its similarities to and dissimilarities from the model, as part of a formal leadership development program.

During the past two years we have developed such a program. It is not intended to "train" participants in the use of the model, but rather to encourage them to examine their own leadership style and to ask themselves whether the methods they are using are most effective for their own organization. A critical part of the program involves the use of a set of standardized cases, each depicting a leader faced with an administrative problem to solve. Each participant then specifies the decision-making process that he would use if faced with each situation. His responses are processed by computer, which generates a highly detailed analysis of his leadership style. The responses for all participants in the course are typically processed simultaneously, permitting the economical representation of differences between the person and other participants in the same program.

In its present form, a single computer printout for a person consists of three $15'' \times 11''$ pages, each filled with graphs and tables highlighting different features of his behavior. Understanding the results requires a detailed knowledge of the concepts underlying the model, something already developed in one of the previous phases of the training program. The printout is accompanied by a manual that aids in explaining results and provides suggested steps to be followed in extracting full meaning from the printout.

Following are a few of the questions that the printout answers:

1. How autocratic or participative am I in my dealings with subordinates in comparison with other participants in the program?

2. What decision processes do I use more or less frequently than the average?

3. How close does my behavior come to that of the model? How frequently does my behavior agree with the feasible set? What evidence is there that my leadership style reflects the pressure of time as opposed to a concern with the development of my subordinates? How do I compare in these respects with other participants in the class?

4. What rules do I violate most frequently and least frequently? How does this compare with other participants? On what cases did I violate these rules? Does my leadership style reflect more concern with getting decisions that are high in quality or with getting decisions that are accepted?

5. What circumstances cause me to behave in an autocratic fashion; what circumstances cause me to behave participatively? In what respects is the way in which I attempt to vary my behavior with the demands of the situation similar to that of the model?

When a typical manager receives his printout, he immediately goes to work trying to understand what it tells him about himself. After most of the major results have been understood, he goes back to the set of cases to re-read those on which he has violated rules. Typically, managers show an interest in discussing and comparing their results with others in the program. Gatherings of four to six people comparing their results and their interpretation of them, often for several hours at a stretch, were such a common feature that they have recently been institutionalized as part of the procedure.

We should emphasize that the method of providing feedback to managers on their leadership style is just one part of the total training experience, but it is an important part. The program is sufficiently new so that, to date, no long-term evaluative studies have been undertaken. The short-term results, however, appear quite promising.

Conclusion

The efforts reported in this article rest on the conviction that social scientists can be of greater value in solving problems of organizational behavior if their prescriptive statements deal with the complexities involved in the phenomena with which they study. The normative model described in this paper is one step in that direction. Some might argue that it is premature for social scientists to be prescriptive. Our knowledge is too limited and the issues too complex to warrant prescriptions for action, even those that are based on a diagnosis of situational demands. However, organizational problems persist, and managers cannot wait for the behavioral sciences to perfect their disciplines before attempting to cope with them. Is it likely that models that encourage them to deal analytically with the forces impinging upon them would produce less rational choices than those that they now make? We think the reverse is more probable—reflecting on the models will result in decisions that are more rational and more effective. The criterion for social utility is not perfection but improvement over present practice.

12 • THE "ELITE" DECISION MAKERS: WHAT MAKES THEM TICK?[1]

At one extreme, some executives can take what seemingly appears to be a simple situation, render it complex, zero in on the wrong problems, seek solutions that are peripheral to the core issues, and then take what seems forever to make a decision. At the other extreme, some executives have the ability to quickly reduce seemingly complex situations to their essentials, distill the problems or opportunities out of them, and then go straight to what seems at that point the obvious course of action.

The latter are the people who happen upon a foundering situation and immediately take charge because they know what to do next. Within organizations lucky enough to have one or more decision makers, they are the ones to whom others instinctively turn for confirmation of their own judgments. They emerge as *the* decision makers because of their track records, the apparent ease with which they make decisions, their propensity for making many of them, their high rate of visibility, and because their own judgments are expressed so positively and with such confidence that others, less sure of themselves, hesitate to quarrel with them.

These decision makers form a small, unique, and elite part of American business leadership. What makes them different? Are there *common* elements in their approaches to business problems and opportunities that give them the ability to rapidly assess a situation, get right to the heart of it, and then make a fast decision? There are. To find out what, we analyzed eight executives over a several year period on a basis of personal observation and confirmed the observations in discussions with their associates, subordinates, and others who were privy to their behavioral patterns. Four were independent businessmen, owners of their own businesses; two were corporate vice-presidents; and two were corporate presidents. Their ages varied from 32 to 58, their sales volumes from $2 million to $191 million. They were selected because of opportunity for observation, their cooperation and that of their subordinates, and because they appeared to fit the mold of the type of decision maker we wanted to examine.

While there are obviously many keys that make their unique decision-making processes work, we have selected the few that we found to have a high degree of commonality and which seemed to be essential to the process. Our analysis broke down into three categories:

Their approach to problems
Their approach to problem-decisions
Some pertinent personal traits

[1]From *Human Resource Management,* Vo. 16, No. 4 (Winter, 1977), pp. 14–20. Reprinted by permission of *Human Resource Management* and Charles H. Ford.
[2]Charles H. Ford, author, lecturer, and consultant on organizational problems and attitudes. He is also a co-owner of Duval Corporation, a Canton, Massachusetts, manufacturing company.

149

Where we have used quotes, they are as close to verbatim as possible. Case examples are expressed in their simplest terms in order to best illustrate what otherwise might be complex points. The cases themselves were selected because they were representatively typical. The words *tend* and *tendency* will appear frequently simply because, while the patterns of behavior we observed had very definite shapes, they lacked precise repetitive dimensions. Thus, we could determine, in the main, *what* the two groups (our elite decision makers and subordinate groups) did, *why* they did it, and *how*, but obviously could not say that in every case 100 percent of them in each group responded according to form.

APPROACH TO PROBLEMS

A Crux Sensitivity

"I feel it in my gut," said one executive when questioned about the basis of several of his decisions, inviting no further conversation on the subject. Another dismissed the question, "Why any damn fool can see it," with no explanation as to why any damn fool can see it. We discovered that unlike many of us who analyze a situation by painstakingly piling and dovetailing one fact upon another (subject to our interpretation of what is fact), separating the important from the unimportant (often unsuccessfully), fighting the tendency to get sidetracked by the tangential and irrelevant (again, often unsuccessfully)—*they* start with a crux-sensitivity in which their mental radars cut through the peripheral and lock in on the important, crucial, and relevant. They have the knack of developing generally accurate impressions, of quickly taking in a total situation and forming rapid interpretive judgments. If this ability to sense core issues is based on any dissection of the facts of a given situation and then reconstructing them in a usable form, it is done at such a speed as to defy recognition of the process.

Because this crux-sensitivity exposes the problem or opportunity in such great clarity, they are able to make decisions quickly—so quickly, in fact, that often we describe many of their judgments as being intuitive or instinctive. What we were looking for, however, were the keys to this process. How did it work? Why did it work? What were some of the underlying common approaches that produced these abilities to "impressionate" rapidly, to develop this crux sensitivity, to be able to expose a problem or opportunity so clearly?

As part of our analysis technique, we took several decisions in which our executives were individually involved and presented the same problems to several of the others (and, as a control mechanism, to groups of their subordinates). We then found the common denominators and compared these with the responses of their subordinate groups. It was these comparisons that verified the keys.

The First Key

The first key is the tendency of our decision makers, unlike other executives, to initially evaluate a situation *not* in terms of what appears to be the apparent problem but in terms of the *effect* of the problem—the problem impact.

This is a crucial distinction because these take-off points lead to entirely different sequences of thought. Problem impact is the broader view, and its initial identification permits a stripping away of the unimportant and peripheral in the evaluative process. Solutions appropriate to problem impact are generally far more responsive to the needs of the situation. As we will demonstrate, it is the keystone of the elite decision maker's approach.

A division of a miniconglomerate (a $191 million company) had a southern sewn garment plant located in a rural sparsely populated area. Unsuccessfully competing for labor with a machine tool plant whose hourly rates were much higher, its labor quality was poor and restless. In a highly competitive, labor intensive industry, it simply couldn't afford to raise its hourly rates.

In a meeting, the corporate personnel director, plant manager, and group VP wrestled with ways to improve labor quality and find a way to get more labor which was needed for growth. Their perception was that labor was the problem; and they approached its solution from the point of view of developing new incentive programs, inexpensive window-dressing fringe benefits, and so on as corrective steps.

The president had little patience with this approach. "A classic case of dead horse whipping," he hmmphed. His perception was that the labor problem created a situation which made the future of the plant untenable and this (the problem impact) is what had to be addressed. His decision: Relocate the plant to a labor surplus area. (Three out of five other decision makers arrived at the same conclusion. Four out of five subordinate groups, on the other hand, saw labor as the problem to be attacked through conventional personnel management techniques.)

A small packaging manufacturing company had a sharp, sudden upturn in sales. Coincidentally it faced a vacation shutdown in six weeks during which time essential equipment maintenance was scheduled. Its joint sales-production team decided to go on overtime and increase its inventory to carry it over the shutdown period. Three weeks later, the warehouse superintendent called a meeting: "My warehouse is bursting. I have no more room."

The group considered several alternatives, including asking customers to accept goods before scheduled shipping dates. The possibility of giving extra dating or temporary price reductions as added incentives was also considered. For what appeared to be valid reasons, the vice-president of sales ruled these out. Their overall conclusion: Shut down some equipment, reduce overtime, and, by being cleverly selective, keep to a minimum the hurt that would accrue to the company and its customers.

The mechanics of which equipment to shut down and which customers to affect were discussed. Two and a quarter hours into this complex, ramification-fraught rescheduling, the president walked in and was introduced to the problem. "We're going to have to cut back on production because we're loaded full up in the warehouse," he was told.

Dismayed, the president shook his head. "You can't penalize sales because the warehouse is full. The problem isn't too much production, it's too little space." Turning to the warehouse superintendent he directed, "Get on the phone, rent some trailers, park them in the yard and load them with your excess." His time input: a little less than two minutes.

This case was presented to five of our other decision makers as well as to their subordinate groups. The question was put simply in the form of, "Here's the problem this company faced. What would you do?" Figure 1 is a reconstruction of the approach each group used.

FIGURE 1
EXAMPLE OF PROBLEM RECONSTRUCTION

Breakdown Situation	3 out of 5 Decision Makers*	4 out of 5 Subordinate Groups*
What is the problem?	_____	Overcrowded warehouse
What is the problem impact?	Potential loss of sales	_____
What caused this problem?	_____	Too much production for warehouse capacity
What caused this problem impact?	Lack of space	_____
What to do about it?	Increase space	Cut back and reschedule production

* When the case company executives are included, the figures are actually 4 out of 6 for the decision makers, 5 out of 6 for the subordinate groups.

As these cases demonstrate, once the problem impact was zeroed in on, the decision maker's train of thought generally continued in a straight line to a determination of the causes of the problem impact and finally to an attack on or a reversal of those things causing the problem impact. Subordinate groups, starting with the problem and seldom getting to the problem impact, tended to flounder and narrowly evaluated the situation, with ultimate decisions unresponsive to the needs of the situation.

The Second Key

Most of us tend to evaluate problems in terms of their most familiar solutions, solutions over which we have in the past controlled similar situations, and to identify problems and analyze situations based on our acceptance of certain aspects of them which appear to be constants. We'll call this the principle of *precedent constraint.*

In the packaging company's case, the company's executives had had a great deal of experience in juggling machine schedules but virutally no experience in juggling warehouse space which was perceived as a constant. Their tendency, therefore, was to evaluate the situation crux and make decisions within the framework of this constant acceptance, not beyond it, and to make these judgments within the context of their past experience (juggling schedules).

The sewn garment plant's executives had had considerable experience in personnel management. The location of the plant was the constant. While they were bound by their most familiar experience (which had been used to control other but perhaps dissimilar labor situations) and the constant, the president's thinking was not so constrained and he had greater freedom in evaluating the situation and the problem-impact.

Why then are some executives bound by precedent constraint and others not?

One answer that surfaced was the matter of degree of profit awareness as opposed to a more limited job awareness. When subordinate group executives were asked to define their jobs, they tended to do so in terms of their direct managerial (functional) responsibilities: "My job is to manage this plant." "I'm responsible for marketing our product line."

The decision makers, on the other hand, related their answers to some aspect of their responsibility for making money for the company. "I'm in charge of the bottom line," said one president (in contrast to, "My job is to run the company"). "I've got plenty of competent people who can take in raw materials at one end and push out finished goods at the other," said one of our VPs. "My job is to see to it that they do it the best way at the least cost." Said our other vice-president (marketing): "I can sum it up in a few words. My job is to sell more than last year and make a good buck on everything I sell." Here again, the difference between the decision maker and other executives seems to turn on a simple basic attitudinal difference. The broader one sees his job in relation to the ultimate corporate goal of making money, the wider, more unconstrained, his range of thought and *the more apt he is to be sensitive to problem impact.*

The Third Key

Most of us, when presented a problem or opportunity situation, tend to reconstruct it in terms that are most meaningful to us and then progressively sort out the alternatives until we reach a conclusion (the Decision Tree, for example). The time span and range of words and thoughts leave ample room for tangential flights, mis-emphases and possibly loss of the core issues. The third key, therefore, is the element of time. It was common for our decision makers to make situation analyses in a matter of minutes and express most of these in a few brief sentences reflecting some variation of the train of thought previously noted (e.g., identification of problem impact, identification of causes creating problem impact and, finally, reversal or attack on those causes).

Their brevity of expression is obviously a reflection not only of economy of thought input (credit their ability to bypass the unimportant and irrelevant) but of their ability to reduce a situation to a few basic essential points. With subordinate groups, discussions tended to be prolonged and roamed widely. Inevitably, when reviewing situations given them for review, they asked for increasingly more information, much of it peripheral. Our impression was that this was due in part to a groping process. When our decision makers asked for more information, it was minimal and generally its purpose was to confirm their original evaluation of problem impact.

Time, in general, is an important element in the psyche of our decision makers. Patience is not one of their strong points. While their evaluative and decision processes are at work, tangential conversations, time spent on minor issues, and train-of-thought disruptions annoy them. Pending problems tend to make them irritable. "Let's think about it for a while," or "Let's sleep on it and talk about it tomorrow" tends to set their teeth on edge.

To save time, they are often willing to forego informational input. ("Never mind taking the time to develop those figures. I think we can make a pretty good stab at them—at least sufficient for our purposes at this time.")

While there is little question of the direct relationship of the two, to what extent brevity of time input is a factor in developing a crux sensitivity or the product of it is not clear. However, it's obvious that, when a situation is analyzed in a matter of a few cogent sentences, little time is available for the peripheral, unimportant, and irrelevant and that the *conditioning effect* is to think in core terms.

The Fourth Key

Thus far we have discussed problem situations in which the thrust is to correct something wrong. Opportunity situations are those in which the thrust is an *opportunity impact*—to gain an advantage from something new. Here, too, we find a common thread. Our decision makers are generally positive thinkers

FIGURE 2
POSITIVE AND NEGATIVE THINKING PATHS

Negative Thinkers	Anatomy of a Decision Relative to a New Idea	Positive Thinkers
Precipitate denigration	1.Statement of new idea (opportunity)*	
	2.Analysis or consensus of potential profitability of new idea (opportunity impact)	Evaluation of opportunity impact*
Magnification of implementary problems and risks	3.Analysis of implementary problems and risks*	
	4.Solutions to implementary problems and risk minimization	Analysis: Problems, risks, and solutions*
	5.Analysis of cost of step 4 above versus benefits new idea would produce	Profitability analysis*

* Possible abortion points

Note: For a comprehensive treatment of subject of positive versus negative thinking, the reader may wish to read "Good Ideas ÷ the Wrong Corporate Orientation = O," *Human Resource Management* (Fall, 1976), Graduate School of Business Administration, University of Michigan, and "How to Measure Your Organization's Negative Thinking," *Optimim*, Vol. 7, No. 4 (1976), Bureau of Management Consulting, Department of Supplies and Services, Canadian Government. Both articles were written by the author.

as contrasted to segments of the subordinate groups who tend to think more negatively.

To put this in perspective, Figure 2 may be useful. It is expressed in terms of the possible points at which a new idea may be aborted simply because this best demonstrates the different paths of thinking taken by positive and negative thinkers.

While negatively oriented subordinate groups tend to perceive new ideas primarily in terms of their implementary *problems* and *risks,* positively oriented executives perceive them primarily in terms of their profit-potential (opportunity impact). The distinction is crucial since it establishes two entirely different take-off points leading to completely different trains of thought. One is constructive to opportunity, the other destructive. For example, at the extreme, subordinate groups tended to concentrate on and abort new ideas at one of two stages. Either at the end of the first step (Figure 2) by precipitate denigration ("It'll never work." "It's not for us." "We've tried something like that before.") or at the end of Step 3 where implementary problems and risks tended to be magnified. The opportunity itself, whatever it may have represented, was not central to their response to the new idea.

Our decision makers, by contrast, focused their response on the opportunity impact. Problems and risks were considered; but the tendency was to consider them only *after* they had assessed the significance of the opportunity impact, and then they were considered in *context* with their solutions.

While they can abort the new idea at any stage (for example, they may not perceive the opportunity impact as significant in terms of profit potential), their reasons for abortion are obviously different from those of the negative thinker.

APPROACH TO DECISIONS

In their approach to decisions, perhaps the most profound characteristic that distinguished our decision makers from other executives is their propensity for making high risk decisions.

Obviously they are in a position to make decisions with more profound impact on the organization than on subordinates. But the difference, we found, goes beyond this. It involves a different philosophy. This philosophy can best be defined in terms of the difference between an incremental or palliative solution in which the problem is "nipped at" as opposed to *solution totality* (a term from one of our corporate presidents) in which the problem is totally attacked so that in most cases, after the solution is applied, it is no longer recognizable (even though the solution itself may create a whole new range of problems).

Incremental or palliative solutions, because of their nature, can be closely monitored. Taken in steps, they involve little risks and can often be reversed easily. Total solutions, however, generally call for wider sweeps of action whose ultimate results are often less predictable and which by their very scope call for more investment and/or bridge-burning.

We found that decision makers' propensity for higher risk-taking is a reflection of the last segment of their sequential train of thought (reverse those elements causing the problem impact). Whereas the problem impact (opportunity impact) is of a wider scope than the apparent problem, its solution is almost always more far-reaching and thus more risky. For example, a division of one of our reviewed companies depended upon its ability to bring out a constant stream of new frozen food products. The path went from R and D to test marketing to full-scale production and distribution. The time lapse, after release from R and D, was approximately ten to eleven months. "No good," said the president. "We've got to move faster. Of all the elements in the chain, market testing takes the longest." His subordinates, perceiving the problem as market testing, agreed that perhaps they could try reducing the testing time. "You missed the point," retorted the president who perceived an unacceptable repetitive time loss as the problem impact. "I don't want to reduce it. I want to eliminate it."

His subordinates agreed that perhaps someday they could eliminate testing and tentatively suggested trying it with one product. "Nope," said the president. "Not someday and no crutches. From here on, no more market testing—period. From now on our judgment is going to have to do what testing did for us." (An interesting footnote: The time lapse dropped to approximately five to six months. To date, of six products brought out without testing, four have been successful, the results of another are incomplete but indications point to success—and one bomb. This compared with approximately a 60 percent success rate previously.

Decision makers' thread of impatience is another trait which, as applied here, manifests itself in the desire to attack a problem quickly, get rid of it, and not have to face it again. "Some of our people can make a career out of one problem," said one of our vice-presidents. "They're comfortable with it. They temporize with it and it keeps coming back in one form or another. The last thing I ever want to see is the same problem twice." "If you peck away at a problem," said one of our independent businessmen, "it'll probably change at the same rate as your partial solutions so you end up spinning your wheels just to stay even. My feeling is that if you have a problem, zap it in one fell swoop. I don't have the temperament to deal with some variation of the same problem over and over again."

Further, they perceive risk as their responsibility. "Problems untouched get worse and opportunities are transient," said a corporate president. "Sometimes you've got to burn a bridge or risk a sizable investment to turn a problem or latch onto an opportunity. Most of my people don't appreciate this; so in the final analysis if I don't make the decision, who will?"

Some other reasons for high risk-taking we observed: Because of their confidence in the quality of their judgments, they don't actually see the same degree of risk in their decisions as others less sure of themselves see it. Therefore, what appears to be a high risk decision to some executives is often perceived as a lesser risk decision by our decision makers. Not being as highly protective of their jobs as subordinate group executives, they are more prone to take chances with less fear of the consequences of failure. And, endowed with a pretty healthy ego, they feel their desire to excel and to be recognized for achievement can best be demonstrated by decisions which can produce highly visible and profound results. These, of course, are generally the higher risk decisions.

SOME PERSONAL TRAITS

Four personal traits appeared to be significant in the elite decision makers.

1. A combination of self-confidence, self-assurance and impatience created a mixture resulting in a tendency to be abrupt, unsubtle, and often tactless with subordinates. In several cases the distinction between arrogance (as many subordinates saw them) and confidence-impatience (as they saw themselves) was not too clear. To their credit, four of our decision makers were conscious of this tendency and made efforts to subdue it. To two others, little conscious effort was required. With the remaining two, little attempt made to correct themselves, and not surprisingly their rate of subordinate turnover was high.

2. Despite this self-assurance and impatience, most of them (6) respected opposition or conflict, but generally only when it was on substantive issues and strongly asserted. "Tell me I'm wrong," said one. "If I am and you save me from making a mistake, you win points. But don't nitpick me to death. And be damn sure it's what you really think. Don't fight me just for the sake of arguing."

3. Overriding the whole process is their sense of security. Subordinates lacking this sense, who questioned their own judgments, who were highly protective of their jobs, revealed a tendency to make those decisions that could be defended with sound data-supported arguments. They sought confirming support from others and many times attempted to make decisions on a share-the-responsibility basis. They seemed more preoccupied with the possibility of having to defend a decision later than with the effect of the decision itself. The decision maker, on the other hand, tended to make more unilateral decisions with far less defense-oriented data and more prone, as previously noted, to defend a judgment with, "Why, any damn fool can see it." We noted that several subordinate executives exhibited many of our decision makers' traits and talents until it came down to the decision point. Then they tended to back off (although they knew they were right), fearful of the consequence of possible error. Their decisons then either erred on the side of caution (incremental solutions, for example) or were deferred while they looked for a more defensible solution. The decison makers were not so job protective. Of the three that did not either own their own businesses or possess a block of stock sufficient to make dislodgement difficult, they expressed the feeling that if they lost their jobs they would have no problem picking up the threads elsewhere with little break in continuity or scope of income.

4. *Tough-minded* has become a cliche in decision makers. As it came across to us, the decision makers' tough-mindedness simply resulted from their ability to narrow their field of vision between problem impact and solution—thus eliminating the peripheral. Unhappily, the fates of people who are adversely involved in many such decisions lie on the periphery. For example, they often fire subordinates easily. The fact that the subordinate is the problem is less important to them than the problem impact of his not getting the job done. If they close a plant resulting in an economic dislocation to the community, again it is because the plant closing is the straight line answer to problem impact.

Happily, not all our decision makers filled this mold in the conventional sense, and many times the human effect factor tempered final decisions. The distinction was that they backed off from their decisions to take the human factor into account rather than arriving at the decision which *first* took into account the human factor. We found this, not surprisingly, more pronounced among our independent businessmen than among our corporate executives.

If we have given the impression that subordinate groups are regarded by us as composed of floundering dolts and that our elite decision makers are some sort of omniscient supermen cloaked with mantles of infallability, we apologize. They are not.

Many members of the subordinate groups were highly competent and creative. Several individuals obviously represented the next generation of our elite decison makers who simply lacked at this point in their careers the rank to authoritatively express or implement their judgments.

So far as our elite decision maker is concerned, when he's right, he's very right. When he goofs, he goofs badly. Often we found that when he errs, he's quick to correct his mistake with the same total solution approach that brought about the original decision. But not always. Some—and this varies from case to case as well as from executive to executive—stick by their decisions reluctant to accept the fact that their judgment was wrong and perhaps their subordinates were right.

Identification of problem impact and assessment of the scope of opportunity impact is in the final analysis a judgmental evaluation. Decision makers can judge wrongly. They can be stubborn. Their self-confidence can cross the line to arrogance. But they do have unique problem and opportunity approach processes which we felt needed to be better understood. And whatever else, it can be said that by and large, they are the doers and the movers.

13 · ADAPTORS AND INNOVATORS—WHY NEW INITIATIVES GET BLOCKED[1]

M. J. Kirton[2]

BACKGROUND

The Adaption-Innovation theory defines and measures two styles of decision-making, [1-3] clarifying earlier literature on problem-solving and creativity which concentrates more on defining and assessing *level* rather than *style*. This shift of emphasis has advantages in the practical world of business, commerce and administration. The present measures of level are much criticized in terms of their reliability and validity, and in addition are contaminated by such factors as intelligence, know-how, and scope for individual action. A measure of style is not affected by these factors, however, and it may be possible to produce a measure that is more obviously valid.

According to the Adaption-Innovation Theory, everyone can be located on a continuum ranging from highly adaptive to highly innovative according to their score on the Kirton Adaption-Innovation Inventory. The range of responses is relatively fixed and stable,[3] and in the general population, approaches the normal curve distribution. For the purpose of clarity the following descriptions characterize those individuals at the extreme ends of the continuum.

Adaptors characteristically produce a sufficiency of ideas,[4] based closely on, but stretching, existing agreed definitions of the problem and likely solutions. They look at these in detail and proceed within the established mores (theories, policies, practices) of their organizations. Much of their effort in change is in improving and 'going better' (which tends to dominate management, e.g. Drucker). [4]

Innovators, by contrast, are more likely in the pursuit of change to reconstruct the problem, separating it from its enveloping accepted thought, paradigms and customary viewpoints, and emerge with much less expected,

[1] Reprinted with permission from *Long Range Planning,* Vol. 17, No. 2, M. J. Kirton, "Adaptors and Innovators—Why New Initiatives Get Blocked," Copyright 1984, Pergamon Press, Ltd.
[2] M. J. Kirton, Director, Occupational Research Centre, Hatfield Polytechnic, U.K.
[3] Test-retest coefficients of 0·82 for 6th formers *(N* = 412) on one New Zealand study[15] after 8 months; South African study (unpublished)[1A] after 5 months on *N* = 143, means: 91·18, S.D. 9·31; and 91·10, S.D. 8·52.
[4] Factor analyses show that total adaptor-innovator scores are composed of three traits: sufficiency versus proliferation of originality; degree of (personal) efficiency and degree of group-rule conformity. They are closely related respectively to Rogers'[6] creative loner; Weber's[7]; and Merton's[8] typical bureaucrat and bureaucratic behaviour.

and probably less acceptable solutions (see Fig. 1). They are less concerned with 'doing things better' than with 'doing things differently'.

The development of the A-I theory began with observations made and conclusions reached as a result of a study of management initiative. [5] The aim of this study was to investigate the ways in which ideas, which had led to radical changes in the companies studied, were developed and implemented. In each of the examples of initiative studied the resulting changes had required the co-operation of many managers and others in more than one department.

Numerous examples of successful 'corporate' initiative, such as the introduction of a new product or new accounting procedures were examined, and this analysis highlighted the stages through which such initiative passed on the way to becoming part of the accepted routine of the company, i.e. perception of the problem, analysis of the problem, analysis of the solution, agreement to change, acceptance of change, delegation and finally implementation. The study also looked at what went wrong at these various stages, and how the development of a particular initiative was thus affected. From this, a number of anomalies were thrown up that at the time remained unexplained.

(1) Delays in Introducing Change

Despite the assertion of managers that they were collectively both sensitive to the need for changes and willing to embark on them, the time lag between the first public airing of most of the ideas studied, and the date on which an idea was clearly accepted as a possible course of action, was a matter of years—usually two or three. Conversely, a few were accepted almost immediately, with the bare minimum of in-depth analysis. (The size of proposed changes did not much affect this time scale, although all the changes studied were large.)

(2) Objections to New Ideas

All too often, the new idea had been formally blocked by a series of well-argued and reasoned objections which were upheld until some critical event—a 'precipitating event'—occurred, so that none of these quondam cogent contrary arguments (lack of need, lack of resource, etc.) was ever heard again. Indeed, it appeared at times as if management had been hit by almost total collective amnesia concerning past objections.

(3) Rejection of Individuals

There was a marked tendency for the majority of ideas which encountered opposition and delays to have been put forward by managers who were themselves unacceptable to an 'establishment' group, not just before, but also after the ideas they advocated had not only become accepted, but even rated as highly successful. At the same time, other managers putting forward the more palatable ideas were themselves not only initially acceptable, but remained so, even if these ideas were later rejected or failed.

The A-I theory now offers a rational, measured explanation of these findings.

FIGURE 1

BEHAVIOUR DESCRIPTIONS OF ADAPTORS AND INNOVATORS

Adaptor	Innovator
Characterized by Precision, Reliability, Efficiency, Methodicalness, Prudence, Discipline, Conformity	Seen as Undisciplined, Thinking Tangentially, Approaching Tasks from Unsuspected Angles
Concerned with Resolving Problems Rather Than Finding Them	Could be Said to Discover Problems and Discover Avenues of Solution
Seeks Solutions to Problems in Tried and Understood Ways	Queries Problems' Concomitant Assumptions; Manipulates Problems
Reduces Problems by Improvement and Greater Efficiency, with Maximum of Continuity and Stability	Is Catalyst to Settled Groups, Irreverent of their Consensual Views; Seen as Abrasive, Creating Dissonance
Seen as Sound, Conforming, Safe, Dependable	Seen as Unsound, Impractical; Often Shocks his Opposite
Liable to Make Goals of Means	In Pursuit of Goals Treats Accepted Means with Little Regard
Seems Impervious to Boredom, Seems Able to Maintain High Accuracy in Long Spells of Detailed Work	Capable of Detailed Routine (System Maintenance) Work for Only Short Bursts. Quick to Delegate Routine Tasks
Is an Authority Within Given Structures	Tends to Take Control in Unstructured Situations
Challenges Rules Rarely, Cautiously, When Assured of Strong Support	Often Challenges Rules, Has Little Respect for Past Custom
Tends to High Self-doubt. Reacts to Criticism by Closer Outward Conformity. Vulnerable to Social Pressures and Authority; Compliant	Appears to Have Low Self-doubt When Generating Ideas, Not Needing Consensus to Maintain Certitude in Face of Opposition
Is Essential to the Functioning of the Institution All the Time, but Occasionally Needs to be 'Dug Out' of His Systems	In the Institution is Ideal in Unscheduled Crises, or Better Still to Help to Avoid them, if he Can be Controlled
When Collaborating with Innovators: Supplies Stability, Order and Continuity to the Partnership	*When collaborating with adaptors:* Supplies the Task Orientations, the Break with the Past and Accepted Theory
Sensitive to People, Maintains Group Cohesion and Cooperation	Appears Insensitive to People, Often Threatens Group Cohesion and Cooperation
Provides a Safe Base for the Innovator's Riskier Operations	Provides the Dynamics to Bring About Periodic Radical Change, Without which Institutions Tend to Ossify

Originally Published in the *Journal of Applied Psychology* (reference 11).

ADAPTORS AND INNOVATORS—TWO DIFFERENT STYLES OF THINKING

Adaptive solutions are those that depend directly and obviously on generally agreed paradigms, are more easily grasped intellectually, and therefore more readily accepted by most—by adaptors as well as the many innovators not so directly involved in the resolution of the problem under scrutiny. The familiar assumptions on which the solution depends are not under attack, and help 'butter' the solution advanced, making it more palatable. Such derived ideas, being more readily acceptable, favourably affect the status of their authors, often even when they fail—and the authors of such ideas are much more likely to be themselves adaptors, characterized as being personally more acceptable to the establishment with whom they share those underlying familiar assumptions. [1] Indeed, almost irrespective of their rank, they are likely to be part of that establishment, which in the past has led innovators to claim somewhat crudely that adaptors owe their success to agreeing with their bosses. However, Kirton [9] conducted a study in which KAI scores were compared with superior/subordinate identification in a sample of 93 middle managers. No connection was found between KAI scores and tendency to agree with one's boss. Instead a more subtle relationship is suggested, i.e. that those in the upper hierarchy are more likely to accept the same paradigms as their adaptor juniors, and that there is, therefore, a greater chance of agreement between them on broad issues and on approved courses of action. Where they disagree on detail within the accepted paradigm, innovators may be inclined to attach less significance to this and view the broad agreements reached as simple conformity.

It can thus be seen how failure of ideas is less damaging to the adaptor than to the innovator, since any erroneous assumptions upon which the ideas were based were also shared with colleagues and other influential people. The consequence is that such failure is more likely to be written off as 'bad luck' or due to 'unforeseeable events', thereby directing the blame away from the individuals concerned.

In stark contrast to this, innovative ideas, not being as closely related to the group's prevailing, relevant paradigms, and even opposing such consensus views, are more strongly resisted, and their originators are liable to be treated with suspicion and even derision. This rejection of individuals tends to persist even after their ideas are adopted and acknowledged as successful. [It should be noted that both these and the further descriptions to come are put in a rather extreme form (as a heuristic device) and usually therefore occur in a somewhat less dramatic form.]

DIFFERENCES IN BEHAVIOUR

Evidence is now accumulating from a number of studies [1,2,10] that *personality* is implicated in these characteristic differences between adaptors and innovators. Indeed it must be so, since the way in which one thinks affects the way in which one behaves, and is seen to behave, in much the same way as there are differences in personality characteristics between those who are left brain dominated and those who are right brain dominated—the former being described as giving rise to methodical, planned thinking and the latter to more intuitive thinking, [11] (there is a significant correlation between left-right brain preference scores and adaptation-innovation). The personality characteristics of adaptors and innovators that are part of their cognitive style are here described.

Innovators are generally seen by adaptors as being abrasive and insensitive, despite the former's denial of these traits. This misunderstanding usually occurs because the innovator attacks the adaptor's theories and assumptions, both explicitly when he feels that the adaptor needs a push to hurry him in the right direction or to get him out of his rut, and implicitly by showing a disregard for the rules, conventions, standards of behaviour, etc. What is even more upsetting for the adaptor is the fact that the innovator does not even seem to be aware of the havoc he is causing. Innovators may also appear abrasive to each other, since neither will show much respect for the other's theories, unless of course their two points of view happen temporarily to coincide. Adaptors can also be viewed pejoratively by innovators, suggesting that the more extreme types are far more likely to disagree than collaborate. Innovators tend to see adaptors as stuffy and unenterprising, wedded to systems, rules and norms which, however useful, are too restricting for their (the innovators') liking. Innovators seem to overlook how much of the smooth running of all around them depends on good adaptiveness [7,8] but are acutely aware of the less acceptable face of efficient bureaucracy. Disregard of convention when in pursuit of their own ideas has the effect of isolating innovators in a similar way to Rogers' creative loner. [6]

While innovators find it difficult to combine with others, adaptors find it easier. The latter will more rapidly establish common agreed ground, assumptions, guidelines and accepted practices on which to found their collaboration. Innovators also have to do these things in order to fit at all into a company but they are less good at doing so, less concerned with finding out the anomalies within a system, and less likely to stick to the patterns they help form. This is at once the innovators' weakness and source of potential advantage.

WHERE ARE THE INNOVATORS AND THE ADAPTORS?

Much of Kirton's earlier research was devoted to the description and classification of these two cognitive styles. More recently, attention has been focused on the issue of how they are distributed and whether any distinctive patterns emerge. It has been found from a large number of studies that KAI scores are by no means haphazardly distributed. Individuals' scores are derived from a 32-item inventory, giving a theoretical range of 32-160, and mean of 96. The observed range is slightly more restricted, 46-146, based on over 1000 subjects; the observed mean is near to 95 and the distribution conforms almost exactly to a normal curve. The studies have also shown that variations by identifiable subsets are predictable, their means shifting from the population mean in accordance with the theory. However, the groups' range of scores is rarely restricted—even smallish groups showing ranges of approximately 70-120—a finding with important implications for change, against the background of differences found at cultural level, at organizational level, between jobs, between departments and between individuals within departments. This is a somewhat arbitrary grouping since norms of cognitive style can be detected wherever a group of people define themselves as different or distinct from others, by whatever criteria they choose be it type of work, religion, philosophy, etc. However, while allowing for a certain amount of overlap, the majority of research studies can be classified according to these groupings.

INNOVATORS AND ADAPTORS IN DIFFERENT CULTURES

A considerable amount of research information has been accumulating regarding the extent to which mean scores of different samples shift from culture to culture. For example, published normative samples collected from Britain, [1,2,12,13] U.S.A., [14] Canada [12] and New Zealand [15] have all produced remarkably similar means. When the KAI was validated on a sample of Eastern Managers from Singapore and Malaysia [16] their mean scores of 95 (S.D. 12·6; $N = 145$) were compatible with those of their Western counterparts (e.g. U.K. managerial sample had a mean of 97; S.D. 16·9; $N = 88$) compared to general U.K. samples which together yielded a mean of 95·3, S.D. 17·5, $N = 532$).

However, samples of Indian and Iranian managers [17-19] ($\Sigma N = 622$) yielded lower means than similar samples from U.K., U.S.A., Canada and Singapore (91). More adaptive norms were also found in work still in progress in a sample of black South African business students. [1A] These differences may not simply be a split between Western and Chinese Western groups vs others, since tentative results from a sample of Flemish-speaking job applicants for professional posts in a leading Belgian pharmaceutical company [2A] have yielded an even more adaptive mean[5] (85·6, $N = 213$) than that of the South African sample. Clearly there may be cultural differences of adaptor innovator norms.

There is also a further speculation put forward by Kirton [20] that people who are most willing to cross boundaries of any sort are likely to be more innovative, and the more boundaries there are and the more rigidly they are held, the higher the innovative score should be of those who cross. In the Thomson study managers in Western-owned companies in Singapore scored higher in innovativeness than either those working for a private local com-

---

[5] Caution: based on a Dutch version of KAI which is still being tested.

pany or those in the Civil Service, and those in this last category had the most adaptive scores of the triad. Further evidence for cultural differences emerge in work inspired by Professor (Mrs.) P. Mathur on Indian and Iranian managers. [17,18,19] Here, it was found that, as expected, entrepreneurs scored higher on the KAI than non-entrepreneurs (97·9 and 90·5 as opposed to 77·2 for Government Officers), but Indian women entrepreneurial managers were found to be even more innovative than their male counterparts. They had had to cross two boundaries: they broke with tradition by becoming a manager in the first place, and they had succeeded in becoming a manager in a risky entrepreneurial business.

INNOVATORS AND ADAPTORS IN DIFFERENT ORGANIZATIONS

Organizations in general [7,21,22] and especially organizations which are large in size and budget [23,24] have a tendency to encourage bureaucracy and adaptation in order to minimize risk. It has been said by Weber, [7] Merton [8] and Parsons [25] that the aims of a bureaucratic structure are precision, reliability and efficiency, and that the bureaucratic structure exerts constant pressure on officials to be methodical, prudent and disciplined, and to attain an unusual degree of conformity. These are the qualities that the adaptor-innovator theory attributes to the 'adaptor' personality. For the marked adaptor, the longer an institutional practice has existed, the more he feels it can be taken for granted. So when confronted by a problem, he does not see it as a stimulus to question or change the structure in which the problem is embedded, but seeks a solution within that structure, in ways already tried and understood—ways which are safe, sure, predictable. He can be relied upon to carry out a thorough, disciplined search for ways to eliminate problems by 'doing things better' with a minimum of risk and a maximum of continuity and stability. This behaviour contrasts strongly with that of the marked innovator. The latter's solution, because it is less understood, and its assumption untested, appears more risky, less sound, involves more 'ripple-effect' changes in areas less obviously needing to be affected; in short, it brings about changes with outcomes that cannot be envisaged so precisely. This diminution of predictive certainty is unsettling and not to be undertaken lightly, if at all, by most people—but particularly by adaptors, who feel not only more loyal to consensus policy but less willing to jeopardize the integrity of the system (or even the institution). The innovator, in contrast to the adaptor, is liable to be less respectful of the views of others, more abrasive in the presentation of his solution, more at home in a turbulent environment, seen initially as less relevant in his thinking towards company needs (since his perceptions may differ as to what is needed), less concerned with people in the pursuit of his goals than adaptors readily tolerate. Tolerance of the innovator is thinnest when adaptors feel under pressure from the need for imminent radical change. Yet the innovators' very disadvantages to institutions make them as necessary as the adaptors' virtues in turn make them.

Every organization has its own particular 'climate', and at any given time most of its key individuals reflect the general outlook. They gradually communicate this to others in the organization, and in time due to recruitment, turn-over and such processes the cognitive styles will reflect the general organizational ethos. However, the range seems to remain unaffected, and this is critical when one wishes to consider who might be the potential agents for a change in the mode of the whole group.

Sufficient evidence has been collected to enable predictions to be made not only about the direction of, but the extent to which these shifts in KAI mean will occur from organization to organization. For example. Kirton [2,12] hypothesized that the mean scores of managers who work in a particularly stable environment will incline more towards adaption, while the mean scores of those whose environment could be described as turbulent will tend towards innovation. This hypothesis was supported by Thomson, [16] whose study, as we have already noted, showed that a Singapore sample of middle-ranking Civil Servants were markedly adaptor-inclined (mean = 89, S.D. 10·5) whereas the means of a sample of managers in multi-national companies were just as markedly innovator-inclined (mean = 107, S.D. 11·4).

A dissertation by Holland [26] suggests that bank employees are inclined to be adaptors; so are local government employees. [27] Employees of R & D oriented companies, however, show the opposite inclination. [28] Two of these studies support and refine the hypothesis that given time, the mean KAI score of a group will reflect its ethos. Both Holland and Hayward and Everett found that groups of new recruits had means away from those of the established group they were joining. However, within 3 (Holland) or at most 5 (Hayward and Everett) years, as a result of staff changes, the gaps between the means of the new groups and the established groups narrowed sharply.

If there are predictable variations between companies wherever selection has been allowed to operate for a sufficient length of time, then variations may be expected within a company as adaptors and innovators are placed in the parts of the organization which suit them best. It is unlikely (as well as undesirable), that any organization is so monolithic in its structure and in the 'demands' on its personnel that it produces a total conformity of supported by Kirton [12] when adaptors were found to be more at home in departments of a company that must concentrate on solving problems which mainly emanate from within their departmental system (e.g. production) and innovators tend to be more numerous in departments that act as interfaces (e.g. sales, progress chasing). Studies by Keller and Holland [14,28,29] in American R & D departments found that adaptors and innovators had different roles in internal company communications; adaptors being more valued for communications on the workings of the company and innovators being more valued for communications on advanced technological information. [28] Kirton [3,12] also found that managers who tend to select themselves to go on courses (i.e. selected) will have significantly different mean KAI scores from the managers on courses who were just sent as part of the general scheme (i.e. personally unselected), the former being innovator-inclined. Members of three groups of courses were tested: one British 'unselected', one British 'selected' and one Canadian 'selected'. The result [12] showed that the unselected managers scored significantly more adaptively than the selected groups. Among the Canadian sample of managers, there was sufficient information on their job titles to be able to divide them into two groups of occupations: those liable to be found in adaptor-oriented departments (e.g. line manager) and those liable to be found in innovator-oriented departments (e.g. personnel consultant). The latter group were found to be significantly more innovative than the former, having a mean of 116·4 for non-line managers as opposed to a mean of 100·14 for line managers.[6] These findings later led to a full-scale study [13] in which data on 2375 subjects collected in 15 independent studies were cross-tabulated with reference to different occupational types and varying degrees of self-selection to courses. Engineering instructors and apprentices were studied as examples of occupations involving a narrow range of paradigms, thorough rigid training and a closely structured environment, while research and development personnel were examined as examples of occupations involving a number of flexible paradigms and a relatively unstructured environment. The differences were large, significant and in the expected direction.

These variations which exist between companies and between occupational groups are also found within the relatively narrow boundaries of the job itself. For example, work in progress suggests that within a job there may be clear subsets whose tasks differ and whose cognitive styles differ, e.g. an examination of the job of quality control workers for a local government body revealed that the job contained two major aspects. One was the vital task of monitoring, and one was the task of solving anomalies which were shown up in the system from time to time. The first of these tasks was carried out by an adaptive inclined group, and the second by an innovative one.

Such knowledge about jobs and who is inclined to do them could eventually lead to a better integration of adaptors and innovators within a company.

WHO ARE THE CHANGE AGENTS?

It has already been noted that the mean adaptor-innovator score of a group may shift quite considerably depending on the population in question, whilst the range remains relatively stable. This suggests that many a person is part of a group whose mean adaptor-innovator score is markedly different from his[7] own. There are three possible reasons why these individuals should be

[6] Because of the nature of this course and selection system, both groups' means were displaced toward innovativeness.

[7] Throughout for he, him, his read she, her, hers.

caught up in this potentially stressful situation:

(a) they are in transit, for example, under training schemes;

(b) they are trapped, unhappy and may soon leave; [26,27]

(c) they have found a niche which suits them and have developed a particular role identity.

(These three categories should be regarded as fluid, since given a change in the individual's peer group, boss, department or even organizational outlook, he may well find himself shifting from one category to another.)

It is the identification of the third category which will most repay further investigation since it contains refinements of the A-I theory which have considerable practical implications, though these are as yet speculations and work is currently being undertaken to explore their ramifications more fully.

The individual who can successfully accept and be accepted into an environment alien to his own cognitive style must have particular survival characteristics, and it is those characteristics which make him a potential agent for change within that particular group. In order to effect a change an individual must first have job 'know-how' which is also an important quality keeping him functioning as a valuable group member when major changes are not needed. He must also be able to gain the respect of his colleagues and superiors, and with this comes commensurate status, which is essential if he wants his ideas to be recognized. Lastly, if a person is embarked on a course of action for change, he will of course require the general capacity, e.g. leadership, management qualities, to carry out such a task. His different cognitive style gives him a powerful advantage over his colleagues in being able to anticipate events which others may not see (since due to their cognitive styles, they may not think to look in that direction).

Therefore, the agent for change can be seen as a competent individual who has enough skill to be successful in a particular environment (which he may in fact have made easier by selecting or being selected for tasks within the unit less alien to his cognitive style). At this point he plays a supportive role to the main thrust of the group with its contrasting cognitive style. Given a 'precipitating event' however (particularly if he has anticipated and prepared for it), the individual becomes at once a potential leader in a new situation. In order to be able to take advantage of this position, he must have personal qualities to bring to bear, management must have the insight to recognize the position, and management development must have also played its part. However, this may need to be reinforced by individual and group counselling which makes use of an understanding of Adaption-Innovation theory. [3A,4A]

It should be emphasized here that the change agent can be either an adaptor or an innovator, and this is solely determined by the group composition, so that if it is an innovator group, the change agent will be an adaptor, and vice versa. This discovery challenges traditional assumptions that heralding and initiating change is the innovator's prerogative because a precipitating event could demand either an adaptive or innovative solution, depending on the original orientation of the group and the work. An example in which an adaptor is the change agent in a team of innovators might be where the precipitating event takes the form of a bank's refusal to give further financial support to a new business enterprise. At this stage the change agent (who may have been anticipating this event for months) is at hand with the facts, figures and a cost cutting contingency plan all neatly worked out. It is now that the personal qualities of know-how, respect, status and ability will be crucial for success. All this assumes that many groups will have means away from the centre. It seems likely that the more the mean is displaced in either direction, the harder it will be, the bigger the precipitating event, to pull the group back to the middle, which may be unfortunate both for the group and the change agent. However, an 'unbalanced' team is what may be required at any particular time. To hold such a position and yet to be capable of flexibility is a key task of management to which this theory may make a contribution.

In a wider context, it is hoped that the Adaption-Innovation theory will offer an insight into the interactions between the individual, the organization and change. By using the theory as an additional informational resource when forward planning, it may also be possible to anticipate, and retain control in the face of changes brought about by extraneous factors. This hopefully will enable such changes to take place amid less imbalance and confusion, thereby rendering them more effective.

Acknowledgment—Thanks are due to Miss Yvonne Deighan for her help in the preparation of this paper.

REFERENCES FOR ARTICLE

1. KIRTON, M. J. Adaptors and innovators: a description and measure, *Journal of Applied Psychology,* **61,** 622–629 (1976).
2. KIRTON, M. J. *Manual of the Kirton Adaption-Innovation Inventory,* National Foundation for Educational Research, London (1977).
3. KIRTON, M.J. Adaptors and innovators: the way people approach problems, *Planned Innovation,* **3,** 51–54 (1980).
4. DRUCKER, P. F. Managements' new role, *Harvard Business Review,* **47,** 49–54 (1969).
5. KIRTON, M. J. *Management Initiative,* Acton Society Trust, London (1961).
6. ROGERS, C. R. Towards a theory of creativity, in H. H. Anderson (Ed.), *Creativity And Its Cultivation,* Harper, New York (1959).
7. WEBER, M. in H. H. Gerth and C. W. MILLS (Eds. and trans.), *From Max Weber: Essays in Sociology,* Routledge & Kegan Paul, London (1970).
8. MERTON, R. K. (Ed.) Bureaucratic structure and personality, in *Social Theory and Social Structure,* Free Press of Glencoe, New York (1957).
9. KIRTON, M. J. Adaptors and innovators and superior-subordinate identification, *Psychological Reports,* **41,** 289–290 (1977).
10. CARNE, J. C. and M. J. KIRTON. Styles of creativity: test score correlations between the Kirton Adaption-Innovation Inventory and the Myers-Briggs Type Indicator, *Psychological Reports,* **50,** 31–36 (1982).

11. TORRANCE, E. P. Hemisphericity and creative functioning, *Journal of Research & Development in Education,* **15,** 29–37 (1982).
12. KIRTON, M. J. Adaptors and innovators in organizations, *Human Relations,* **3,** 213–224 (1980).
13. KIRTON, M. J. and S. R. PENDER. The adaption-innovation continuum: occupational type and course selection, *Psychological Reports,* **51,** 883–886 (1982).
14. KELLER, R. T. and W. E. HOLLAND. A cross-validation study of the Kirton Adaption–Innovation Inventory in three research development organizations, *Applied Psychological Measurement,* **2,** 563–570 (1978).
15. KIRTON, M. J. Have adaptors and innovators equal levels of creativity? *Psychological Reports,* **42,** 695–698 (1978).
16. THOMSON, D. Adaptors and innovators: a replication study on managers in Singapore and Malaysia, *Psychological Reports,* **47,** 383–387 (1980).
17. DEWAN, S. Personality characteristics of entrepreneurs, Ph.D. Thesis, Institute of Technology, Delhi (1982).
18. HOSSAINI, H. R. Leadership effectiveness and cognitive style among Iranian and Indian middle managers, Ph.D. Thesis, Institute of Technology, Delhi (1981).
19. KHANEJA, D. K. Relationship of the adaption-innovation continuum to achievement orientation in entrepreneurs and non-entrepreneurs, Ph.D. Thesis, Institute of Technology, Delhi (1982).
20. KIRTON, M. J. Adaptors and innovators in culture clash, *Current Anthropology,* **19,** 611–612 (1978).
21. BAKKE, E. W. Concept of the social organisation, in M. Haire (Ed.), *Modern Organization Theory,* Wiley, New York (1965).
22. MULKAY, M. S. *The Social Process of Innovation,* Macmillan, London (1972).
23. SWATEZ, G. M. The social organization of a university laboratory, Minerva, *A Review of Science Learning & Policy,* **VIII,** 36–58 (1970).
24. VEBLEN, T. *The Theory of the Leisure Class,* Vanguard Press, New York (1928).
25. PARSONS, T. *The Social System,* Free Press of Glenco, New York (1951).
26. HOLLAND, P. A. Creative thinking: an asset or liability in employment, M.Ed. Dissertation, University of Manchester (1982).
27. HAYWARD G. and C. EVERETT. Adaptors and innovators: data from the Kirton Adaption-Innovation Inventory in a local authority setting, *Journal of Occupational Psychology,* **56,** 339–342 (1983).
28. KELLER, R. T. and W. E. HOLLAND. Individual characteristics of innovativeness and communication in research and development organizations, *Journal of Applied Psychology,* **63,** 759–762 (1978).
29. KELLER, R. T. and W. E. HOLLAND. Towards a selection battery for research and development professional employees, *IEEE Transactions on Engineering Management,* **EM-26 (4)** November (1979).

Thanks are due for the use of their unpublished data to:
1A. POTTAS, C. D. University of Pretoria, South Africa.
2A. PEETERS, L. Janssen Pharmaceutical, Belgium.
3A. LINDSAY, P. (in Press), Cambridge Management Centre, U.K.
4A. DAVIES, G. B. (in preparation), Cambridge Management Centre, U.K.

14 • OPERATIONAL TECHNIQUES OF CREATIVE THINKING[1]

Charles S. Whiting[2]

The following discussion is based on a brainstorming session held at a New England manufacturing company last spring by our research group at the Harvard Business School. In order not to disclose the actual company, the product and circumstances have been disguised.

Chairman: "Gentlemen, today, we want to develop some new ideas to make the display of our paint line more effective at the dealer level. To solve this problem, we're going to use brainstorming, one of the operational techniques of creative thinking. Be sure to remember the two essential brainstorming rules. First, make no evaluation or criticism whatsoever. We only want ideas at this stage of the problem solving process. Second, try for unusual, even impractical ideas. By ranging far and wide, you'll be more apt to come up with a new approach. All set, let's start."

Advertising Manager: "What we need are some action display devices."

Sales Manager: "How about something that lights up—something that flashes on and off. Maybe it could go on and off when you approached it. You might even have a switch that works when someone steps on a certain floor board."

Advertising Agency Account Executive: "You could have a display in the window showing your entire line. Perhaps you could use light effectively to display the colors."

Marketing Director: "I've got an idea! Why don't you tie this in with the current do-it-yourself trend. Set up a film or slides in a machine in the window and show people the proper way to paint a house."

Advertising Manager: "Show them how to do all that kind of thing— lay bricks, paint, even how to hammer a nail properly. First show them a picture—then outline the steps—then give them an ad. You might even make them come into the store to get a brochure listing the various steps shown on the slides. That would be a good way to get them into the store— otherwise, they hardly ever come in unless they're ready to buy."

Agency Account Executive: "This do-it-yourself stuff is great! Why don't you get together with other firms in the home improvement field and sponsor do-it-yourself shows in local high school auditoriums. It's already been done in large cities, but I've never seen it done in a small town. You could show films and demonstrate techniques."

Product Designer: "On this do-it-yourself kick again. Why not put a loudspeaker outside the store with a taped instructional spiel on do-it-yourself."

[1] From *Advanced Management* (October, 1955), pp. 24-30. Reprinted by permission of *Advanced Management*.

[2] Clarles S. Whiting, associated with McCann-Erickson, Incorporated, New York City.

Agency Account Executive: "You know, I'll bet you could make a lot of money just supplying merchants with tape machines and taped advertising messages. Remind me to try that someday."

A little later:

Advertising Manager: "Let's have a miniature display—sort of a doll house affair showing painted walls—it could revolve."

Agency Account Executive: "That's not bad, but speaking of miniatures—why don't you have some miniature paint cans made up and send them out as a promotion—they could contain a sample of your paint."

Chairman: "Back to the doll house, I just had a crazy idea—it's no good to us, but what an idea! Have a doll house in which you do-it-yourself. I mean paper the walls, paint it, install miniature plumbing—perhaps even lay miniature bricks. Some toy manufacture should love that idea. It might even bring boys into the doll house market!"

Product Designer: "A minute ago you were speaking of displays. Why not a display in a supermarket with a pitchman or demonstrator. People have to eat so they get to the supermarket every week or so—they hardly ever get into our dealers' stores."

Agency Account Executive: "What an idea I've got—a new advertising medium. Why shouldn't local stores or even national advertisers buy advertising space on supermarket walls? Look at all the blank space behind the meat counter that people could look at while they're waiting to be served."

Sales Manager: "You might even use the ceiling, it's blank."

Marketing Director: "Here's the craziest one yet. Let's paint our different shades on the ceilings of our dealers' stores. You might even have a novelty room upside down on the ceiling."

Chairman: "They'd certainly flock in to see that—and think of the publicity value!"

Company Creative Programs

Brainstorming, as developed by Alex F. Osborn, is just one of the operational techniques of creative thinking which business organizations are beginning to use in order to enable their employees to produce more new ideas.

The whole field of creative thinking has been drawing a great deal of attention in the last few years although its application to business problems is not exactly new: General Electric has been running a creative engineering program since 1937, and Batten, Barton, Durstine and Osborn has been using brainstorming to solve certain client problems since 1939. More recently companies such as IBM, B. F. Goodrich and the AC Spark Plug Division of General Motors have started various programs designed to teach their employees to be more creative and Ethyl regularly sponsors a presentation of these techniques to its clients, by Charles Clark, one of the experts in the field. Universities too are beginning to experiment with new courses designing to teach students to utilize a more creative approach to problem solving. Professor John Arnold's creative enginnering course at

MIT is perhaps the best known of these, but Rutgers has a special course combining engineering and creative thinking and Columbia, Boston University, Buffalo University and a host of others offer courses in applied imagination or creative thinking.

Fundamentally, the theory of creative thinking is based on the following premises:

1. Everyone has some degree of creative ability.
2. Certain mental and social factors prevent people from fully utilizing their creative ability.
3. Through proper orientation, use of certain techniques, and through practice, these mental and social blocks can be eliminated and this innate creative capacity can be utilized to a greater extent, and perhaps the level of creative ability may even be raised somewhat by training.

Techniques and programs for stimulating creative thinking can be broken down into two types: educational and operational. Educational programs and techniques are primarily designed to make a person more aware of his creative ability, and through study of the creative process and use of certain imagination exercises, attempt to raise his level of creative ability or at least to teach him how to utilize it more effectively. A great deal has already been written on this aspect of creative thinking, therefore I am going to concentrate on the operational aspects of the subject. Operational creative thinking techniques are perceptual schemes or conference methods which an individual or group can use to produce more new ideas—faster.

Basic Operational Principles

Two of the basic principles upon which all the operational techniques of creative thinking rely are:

1. A positive attitude is established—criticism or evaluation is delayed until after the ideas have been produced. This elimination of judgment from the idea production stage is one of the strongest causes for the success these techniques have achieved. Since no evaluation is allowed, negative attitudes are eliminated and a climate is created in which the participants feel free to express ideas they might otherwise be reluctant to reveal.
2. Unusual ideas are sought by encouraging many unusual, even obviously impractical, ideas, and individuals or participants in group sessions become accustomed to breaking away from traditional approaches to their problems.

The Three Types of Operational Techniques

The operational techniques of creative thinking can be roughly broken down into three categories:

1. Analytical Techniques
2. Free Association Techniques
3. Forced Relationship Techniques

Analytical techniques provide a form in which to attack a problem. They usually also rely heavily on questioning the various elements of the object or problem under consideration. They force you to ask yourself whether this can be changed or eliminated, whether a different type of power might be used, and many similar questions. Three of the commonly used operational techniques that fit into this category are checklists, attribute listing, and the input-output technique.

Free Association techniques are designed to allow any idea that comes to mind to present itself. In these techniques the use of any evaluation whatsoever in the initial idea production stage is strongly discouraged. Included in this category are the brainstorming technique and variations such as Phillips 66 Buzz Sessions, and the Gordon Technique.

Forced Relationship techniques rely on an unnatural or unusual relationship which is forced either by mechanical means or is chosen in an arbitrary manner. Once this forced relationship is established, it is used as the starting point for a series of free associations that can produce a new idea. There are a number of different variations of this type of technique. The ones I will consider will be the listing technique, catalog technique, and the "focused object" technique.

One of the simplest and most commonly used analytical techniques is the checklist. Checklists have been developed for a myriad of special uses and are often very effective when searching for the solution to a specific problem. The principal reason for their effectiveness is that if properly constructed, they recall areas for investigation that might otherwise be neglected. One of the simplest and most effective general checklists is a basic nine category list developed by Alex F. Osborn, one of creative thinking's pioneers. Here it is in its simplest form:[3]

1. Put to other uses
2. Adapt
3. Modify
4. Magnify
5. Minify
6. Substitute
7. Re-arrange
8. Reverse
9. Combine

Checklists however have two rather obvious weaknesses. First, they rely on the historical accumulation of checkpoints; thus they may exclude categories that are important to the new problem being considered. Similarly, they may include many questions that are not necessary and thus may waste the user's time.

Attribute Listing

The attribute listing technique was developed by Professor Robert Platt Crawford of the University of Nebraska. Basically, it consists of listing all the attributes or qualities of an object or problem, then systematically considering each attribute or group of attributes in turn, trying

---

[3] An expanded version of this list appears on page 284 of Osborn's book *Applied Imagination*, Charles Scribner's Sons, New York, 1953.

to change them in as many ways as possible. An example of a number of variations that could be developed for a common wooden lead pencil through use of this technique is given in Figure 1.

FIGURE 1

EXAMPLE OF ATTRIBUTE LISTING

Attribute	*Possible Changes*
Lead produces writing	Light might be used to affect photographic paper. Heat might be used to affect a special paper. Could use a solution instead of solid lead or might use a chemical solution that reacted with the paper. (Some of these variations might lead to a pencil or writing instrument that never had to be sharpened or refilled.)
Wooden casing	Could be metal; plastic; entirely made of graphite.
Plain yellow color	Could be any color; carry advertising; or have a design. (Perhaps women would buy pens and pencils carrying the same designs as their dresses.)

The point of the example is only to demonstrate the technique. Clearly most of the ideas are neither new nor very practical, but several of them offer interesting possibilities. Remember, just one good idea can be the basis for an entire new product line or perhaps even a whole new industry.

The Input-Output Technique

The input-output technique has been used in the creative engineering program at General Electric. It is used principally in problems in which energy is involved. The following example quoted from *Imagination-Undeveloped Resource* [4] illustrates this technique very well.

"A dynamic system can be classified according to its (1) input, (2) output, and (3) limiting requirements or specifications. For example in designing a device to automatically shade a room during bright sunlight, the problem can be defined as follows:

Input—Solar energy.
Output—Making windows alternately opaque and transparent.
Specifications—Must be usable on various sized windows, must admit not more than 20 foot-candle illumination anywhere in the room, must not cost more than $100 per 40 square foot window.

"Once the definition is set up, means of bridging the gap between input and output are sought. At each step the question is asked—can this phenomenon (input) be used directly to shade the window (desired output)? Using the above example once again, we observe that solar energy is of two types, light and heat.

"Step 1: *What phenomena respond to application of Heat? Light?* —Are there vapors that cloud upon heating? Gases expand, metals expand, solids melt. Are there substances that cloud in bright light? Does light cause

[4] Pages 27-28, Imagination-Undeveloped Resource, Creative Training Associates, P.O. 913, Grand Central Station, New York, N.Y.

some materials to move or curl? Light causes photo-electric cells to produce current, chemicals to decompose, plants to grow.

"Step 2: *Can any of these phenomena be used directly to shade the window?*—Vapors that cloud on heating? Substances that cloud in bright light? Bi-metals warp. Slats of a blind could warp shut.

"Step 3: *What phenomena respond to step one outputs?*—Gases expand, could operate a bellows, etc. Photoelectric current, could operate a solenoid, etc. Solids melt, effect on electric conductivity, etc.

"Step 4: *Can any of these phenomena be used directly to shade the window?*—Bellows could operate a blind, etc.

"Step 5: *What phenomena respond to step three output?*—Bellows, solenoid, etc. could operate a solenoid switch or valve, which in turn could operate motors to draw the blind.

"In this manner a number of possible solutions can be developed for evaluation."

For most purposes either attribute listing or the input-output technique are probably more effective than checklists because they are based upon an individual analysis of the product or problem in question rather than on an historical accumulation of checkpoints. However the two techniques are not particularly suited to the same type of problem. Attribute listing is generally most effective when attempting to change or modify an existing object or procedure because it concentrates on the attributes of the object or procedure in question. The input-output technique on the other hand concentrates on the job to be done, thus it is probably best suited for seeking new or alternative ways to accomplish some objective.

Brainstorming

In our society, and throughout our educational process, hard sharp critical judgment has been held out as the mark of the capable man. The basic theory behind the brainstorming method is that many times this worship of critical judgment prevents people from expressing ideas that are a bit unorthodox. Thus, although this unorthodox idea might have been the best solution to the problem at hand, it is not revealed because its originator fears that his reputation for having good judgment may suffer. Furthermore, in many cases it is extremely easy to find fault with even the best idea. Thus in many cases when good ideas are expressed, they are quickly quashed by the exercise of judgment or criticism before they get a real chance.

In a brainstorming session, a climate that is most conducive to the production of ideas is set up. First, no judgment or evaluation is allowed at all. Secondly, the participants are encouraged to express ideas that are extremely impractical. Who knows, what at first may seem to be a poor idea may stimulate someone else to produce a better idea, or this poor idea itself might even be developed into something useful. In fact, General Electric demonstrates the effectiveness of the brainstorming method by deliberately taking the idea the group members consider the poorest, and developing it into something useful. In one session held at the Harvard Business School for members of the Advanced Management Program by people from General Electric, a toaster was the subject under consideration. Of all the suggested improvements for the toaster, the one the group considered the poorest concerned making toast or toasters mouseproof. Yet, perhaps this idea is not as silly as it sounds. Conceivably, toast or all food for that matter could be treated with some chemical which is offensive to rodents and insects, yet did not affect human beings or the taste of the product. If this process could be developed, the nature of the food preservation business might be drastically changed.

In addition to providing a climate encouraging ideas and freedom of expression, brainstorming works for several other good reasons:

1. Contagion of enthusiasm.
2. Competition, everyone tries to produce more and better ideas than the other participants.
3. It provides the opportunity to improve or change the ideas of others. What may seem absurd to one person, may stimulate someone else to suggest a useful variation.

Brainstorming can also be done on an individual basis. Simply follow the rule of no evaluation and turn off the judicial side of your mind during the idea production stage. After all the ideas have been produced, they can be evaluated, preferably at a later date. This is the time for sharp judgment, after you have the ideas.

A Phillips 66 Buzz Session is often applied to brainstorming with large groups. Basically, a large group is broken down into a number of smaller brainstorming groups. Each group appoints a chairman and proceeds to brainstorm. After they have produced a number of ideas, they select one or more of the better ideas. The chairman of each small group then presents the selected ideas to the entire group.

The Gordon Technique

The Gordon technique was developed by William J. J. Gordon of Arthur D. Little, Inc., a research and consulting firm in Cambridge, Mass. This technique is the basic method used by Arthur D. Little's Design Synthesis Group. This group invents new products to order for their clients. So far they have never failed to produce a requested invention. Among the products they have invented are a revolutionary new type of gasoline pump, a new type of can opener, and a new method of building construction.

The objective of a Gordon session is different from that of a brainstorming session. In a brainstorming session, a multiplicity of ideas is sought. In the Gordon method, only one radically new idea is wanted.

The principal characteristic of the Gordon discussion session is that only one man—the group leader—knows the exact nature of the problem to be solved. There are two main reasons why Gordon feels that the other panel members should not know what the problem is. First, he feels that brainstorming produces superficial ideas because solutions are arrived at too soon. He avoids early solutions by not revealing the problem. Secondly, he seeks to avoid "egocentric involvement." In other words, a participant in a brainstorming session may become infatuated with one of his own ideas—perhaps he may even go as far as to consider it the only logical solution. Naturally, such involvement can seriously hamper the participant's effectiveness.

Since the group members do not know the problem being considered, it is extremely important to choose a suitable subject for discussion, one that is related to the actual problem, yet which does not reveal its true nature. Here are a few examples of products and the discussion subject used: toys—play or enjoyment; fishing lures—persuasion; a new can opener—opening.

Here's an example of how a session using the Gordon technique might be conducted. Suppose the problem were to invent a new type of lawnmower. For this problem the subject for discussion could either be cutting or separation. In this case, separation would probably be the best choice because it encompasses a somewhat broader area. Cutting almost implies some sort of mechanical motion employing a blade or blades.

The session would probably open with a discussion of what separation means. The discussion would then probably move on to ways in which things are separated in nature, industry, or the home. A possible solution might be recognized by the group leader when someone talked about the rotary saw blade used in a sawmill to cut lumber. Perhaps a few years ago this idea might have led to the development of the rotary blade lawnmower now on the market. Next, someone might mention welding, and how a flame can be used to cut or separate a piece of metal into two pieces. Possibly this might lead to a solution in which a flame was used to singe the tops of the grass. Another and probably better variation might be a lawnmower that consisted merely of a single heated wire designed to accomplish the same thing. If such a lawnmower could be developed it might have several strong advantages: it would be light and easy to push and there would be no moving parts—thus it might be both safer and longer lasting. The sole purpose of this illustration is to show the kind of possibilities that occur to the group leader as the discussion moves along.

The sessions held at Arthur D. Little usually last three hours. This amount of time is necessary if a thorough discussion of the subject is to be held. After the initial idea is obtained, the group develops the idea into a finished, patented product by more conventional means.

Comparison of Systems

The principal weakness of the Gordon method is that so much of the success of the session depends upon the group leader. Unless he has the ability to see relationships quickly, the session can be a failure. Also, if the other members of the group had known the exact nature of the problem, they might have been able to see relationships the leader missed. Very possibly, these relationships might have led to even better solutions for the problem at hand.

Several procedures might be followed to overcome this weakness. In one case, the session would be conducted as at present and the proceedings would be tape recorded. Then, after the session was finished and the problem revealed, the other group members would listen to the recording to see whether there were other possibilities the group leader missed. In the other alternative method, half the group members would know the problem, the other half would not. In this case, three to five people can attempt to see the relationships leading to a solution.

Our research group at Harvard felt that for most purposes, the Osborn brainstorming system is most practical. Its rules are simple and easily understood. Furthermore, many business problems especially in the advertising, sales promotion, and merchandising area call for a wide variety of ideas. The brainstorming session is especially effective in producing a large number of different ideas.

The Gordon system on the other hand probes much deeper than the Osborn system. It goes back closer to natural phenomena and is therefore especially useful for deriving entirely new principles. However, it requires an extremely capable group leader and well-trained participants. Therefore this type of session cannot usually be successfully conducted by novices, whereas brainstorming sessions very often can. A summary of rules and suggestions for both types of group sessions is given in Figure 2 reproduced from *Imagination — Undeveloped Resource*.

Forced Relationship Techniques

The forced relationship techniques are not particularly suited to solving an existing problem except in the broadest sense. This is because they rely on a chance relationship which is almost impossible to relate to the particular problem at hand. However, they are extremely useful in the artistic or literary fields where the user is often seeking only a new and different idea rather than the solution to a specific problem.

One of the forced relationship techniques consists of making a list of objects or ideas which may or may not have some relationship to each other. The list is then numbered. The next step consists of considering the first item on the list in relationship with each of the other items in order. After item number one has been considered in relationship with each item on the list, item two is treated in a similar manner. This process continues until each item on the list has been considered in relationship with every other item on it. A variation of this technique consists of considering three or more items at the same time.

Catalog Technique

One of the favorite methods some cartoonists use to obtain a new idea is to take a Sears Roebuck catalog or a telephone book or any other source containing a large variety of different objects or categories, select two or more objects at random and force a relationship between them. This relation is then used as the basis for a cartoon idea. There are a number of other fields in which this technique or variations on the same theme can be useful.

FIGURE 2

SUMMARY OF RULES AND SUGGESTIONS FOR GROUP SESSIONS

Osborn Brainstorming
> Rules:
> 1. Judicial thinking or evaluation is ruled out.
> 2. Free wheeling is welcomed.
> 3. Quantity is wanted.
> 4. Combinations and improvements are sought.

> Suggestions for the Osborn technique:
> 1. Length: 40 minutes to one hour, sessions of ten to fifteen minutes can be effective if time is short.
> 2. Do not reveal the problem before the session. An information sheet or suggested reference material on a related subject should be used if prior knowledge of the general field is needed.
> 3. Problem should be clearly stated and not too broad.
> 4. Use a small conference table which allows people to communicate with each other easily.
> 5. If a product is being discussed, samples may be useful as a point of reference.

Gordon Technique
> Rules:
> 1. Only the group leader knows the problem.
> 2. Free association is used.
> 3. Subject for discussion must be carefully chosen.

> Suggestions for the Gordon technique:
> 1. Length of session: two to three hours are necessary.
> 2. Group leader must be exceptionally gifted and thoroughly trained in the use of the technique.

General Suggestions that Apply to Both Techniques

1. Selection of personnel: a group from diverse backgrounds helps. Try to get a balance of highly active and quiet members.
2. Mixed groups of men and women are often more effective, especially for consumer problems.
3. Although physical atmosphere is not too important, a relaxed pleasant atmosphere is desirable.
4. Group size: groups of from four to twelve can be effective. We recommend six to nine.
5. Newcomers may be introduced without disturbing the group, but they must be properly briefed in the theory of creative thinking and the use of the particular technique.
6. A secretary or recording machine should be used to record the ideas produced. Otherwise they may not be remembered later. Gordon always uses a blackboard so that ideas can be visualized.
7. Hold sessions in the morning if people are going to continue to work on the same problem after the session has ended, otherwise hold them late in the afternoon. (The excitement of a session continues for several hours after it is completed, and can effect an employee's routine tasks.)
8. Usually it is advisable not to have people from widely differing ranks within the organization in the same session.

The technique which I call the "focused object" technique contains elements of both the free association and the forced relationship techniques. It is especially useful for problems such as obtaining ideas for advertising layout or copy. The principal difference between this technique and the other forced relationship techniques is that one object or idea in the relationship is not selected at random, but deliberately chosen. The other object or idea is selected arbitrarily. The attribute or qualities of this second object or idea are then used as the starting point for a series of free associations. An attempt is made to adapt the resulting stream of free associations to the chosen object or problem. In the case of advertising copy and art ideas, the deliberately selected object is usually the product which is to be advertised.

The following example (Figure 3) shows how a common lampshade was used in a forced relationship associated with an automobile. The automobile was the pre-selected object. By focusing on the attributes of the lampshade, a chain of free associations was started, which led to other ideas. The third column shows the applications of the chain of free associations to the problem of obtaining copy and layout ideas for the automobile.

FIGURE 3

EXAMPLE OF FOCUSED OBJECT TECHNIQUE

Attribute of Lampshade	*Chain of Free Association*	*Application to Automobile*
Lampshade is shaped like a peak or volcano	Volcano	
	Volcanic power	
	Explosive power	"Engine has explosive power."
	Peak	"This automobile is the peak of
	Peak of perfection	perfection."
	Steep hill	"It has hill climbing ability."
The lampshade has form	Racing form	Use a layout showing individual
	Horses	horses to dramatize horsepower.
	Horsepower	
	Winner's circle	"This automobile is always in the
	Fine horses	winner's circle."
	Other fine things	"He likes fine horses, he likes fine
	Morocco leather	cars."
	Ivory chess sets	Associate car with fine things.
	Africa	Picture car in use in Africa and all over the world.

Place of These Techniques in Business

If treated in their proper perspective—as aids for better utilizing native creative capacity, and possibly increasing it somewhat—use of these operational techniques of creative thinking can greatly benefit most organizations. However, they should not be regarded as a panacea—they cannot replace good judgment and hard work.

In addition to providing a greater quantity of ideas, educational and operational programs for stimulating creative thinking provide several other benefits to companies using them. First, they clearly establish the idea in the employees' minds that the company wants new ideas. Secondly, through use of these techniques, employees usually become much more confident of their creative ability—this leads to increased self-confidence that can benefit the organization in many ways. By putting the spotlight on creativity, management itself becomes much more aware of the importance of new ideas and the many factors influencing creative output in an organization. Creativity is encouraged by a permissive atmosphere—that is, an organizational climate in which freedom of expression, mutual trust, and respect are present. Once management clearly becomes aware of this more organizations will take steps to see that such an atmosphere exists. Furthermore, by encouraging freer expression of ideas, management may do much to break down the rigid barriers that too often exist between the various echelons in an organization. Thus, flexibility and improved communications may be another side result of the teaching and use of the art of creative thinking.

However, the teaching of creative thinking still faces the problem of gaining industrial and educational acceptance. Part of the reason why some people consider the subject of creative thinking "illegitimate" is due to the way in which it is frequently presented. It is offered as a cure-all with all the fanfare of a medicine show. Naturally, thinking people tend to distrust such proffered panaceas. The net result is that many people are suspicious of and even antagonistic toward the subject. Therefore any company that contemplates using these techniques should be prepared to deal with resistance and perhaps even open antagonism. The proper way to handle this is to move into the area of creative thinking gradually. Be sure you know what you are attempting to do and what the limitations of creative training are. The proper type of program installation is essential. Judge the amount of resistance you expect to encounter and conduct a promotional campaign to overcome it.

Once the difficulties inherent in establishing a program have been overcome, your company can join the ranks of companies such as U.S. Rubber, Carborundum, H. J. Heinz, and Dow Chemical Company, that are already benefiting from their experiences with creative training, not only through a greater number of new ideas, but also in improved employee attitudes and better communication.

BIBLIOGRAPHY, CHAPTER 4

Berisahel, J. G. "Resolving Post-Decision Doubts." *International Management*, Vol. 29, No. 10, pp. 61-67.

Cummings, L., B. Hinton, and B. Goddel. "Creative Behavior as a Function of Task Environment." *Academy of Management Journal*, Vol. 18, No. 3 (September, 1973), pp. 489-499.

———— , and G. Mize. "Risk Taking and Organizational Creativity." *Personnel Administration*, Vol. 31, No. 1 (January-February, 1968), pp. 38-47.

Dery, David. "Decision-Making, Problem-Solving and Organizational Learning." *Omega: The International Journal of Management Science,* Vol. 11, No. 4 (1983), pp. 321-328.

Douglass, Merrill E. "How to Conquer Procrastination." *Advanced Management Journal* (Summer, 1978), pp. 40-50.

Ford, C. H. "Structuring the Organization for Fast Decision Making." *Human Resource Management,* Vol. 12, No. 2 (Summer, 1973), pp. 2-14.

Green, Thad B. "Problem Definition—Key to Effective Problem Solving." *Management Adviser,* Vol. 10, No. 6 (November-December, 1973), pp. 42-45.

Gruber, W. H. "How to Innovate in Management." *Organizational Dynamics,* Vol. 3, No. 2 (Fall, 1974), pp. 30-47.

Herbert, Theodore, and R. W. Estes. "Improving Executive Decisions by Formalizing Dissent: The Corporate Devil's Advocate." *Academy of Management Review,* Vol. 2, No. 4 (October, 1977), pp. 662-667.

Hespos, Richard F., and Paul A. Strassmann. "Stochastic Decision Trees for the Analysis of Investment Decisions." *Management Science,* Vol. 11, No. 10 (August, 1965), pp. 224-259.

Hodnett, Edward. *The Art of Problem Solving.* New York: Harper & Row, Publishers, Inc. 1955.

Isaack, Thomas S. "Intuition: An Ignored Dimension of Management." *Academy of Management Review,* Vol. 3, No. 4 (October, 1978), pp. 917-921.

Kaufmann, Felix. "Decision Making—Eastern and Western Style." *Business Horizons,* Vol. 13, No. 6 (December, 1970), pp. 81-86.

Kepner, Charles H., and Benjamin B. Tregoe. *The Rational Manager.* New York: McGraw-Hill Book Co., 1965.

Klatzky, S. "Automation, Size, and the Locus of Decision Making: The Cascade Effect." *The Journal of Business,* Vol. 43, No. 2 (April, 1970), pp. 141-151.

O'Reilly, Charles A. III. "Individuals and Information Overload in Organizations: Is More Necessarily Better?" *Academy of Management Journal,* Vol. 23, No. 4 (1980), pp. 684-696.

Pierson, David A. "A Technique for Managing Creative People." *Personnel* January-February, 1983), pp. 12-26.

Pollock, Alex J. "Computers Can't Walk or Talk." *Across the Board,* Vol. 20, No. 6 (June, 1983), pp. 1-3.

Robey, Daniel, and William Taggart. "Measuring Managers' Minds: The Assessment of Style in Human Information Processing." *Academy of Management Review,* Vol. 6., No. 3 (1981), pp. 375-383.

Rowan, Roy. "Those Business Hunches Are More Than Blind Faith." *Fortune,* Vol. 99, No. 8 (April 23, 1979), pp. 111-114.

Sinetar, Marsha. "Entrepreneur, Chaos, and Creativity—Can Creative People Really Survive Large Company Structure?" *Sloan Management Review,* Vol. 26, No. 2 (Winter, 1985), pp. 57-62.

Summers, Irvin, and D. E. White. "Creativity Techniques: Toward Improvement of the Decision Process." *Academy of Management Review,* Vol. 1, No. 2 (April, 1976), pp. 99-107.

Ulvila, Jacob W., and Rex V. Brown, "Decision Analysis Comes of Age." *Harvard Business Review,* Vol. 60, No. 5 (September-October, 1982), pp. 130-141.

White, Charles. "Problem Solving: The Neglected First Step." *Management Review* (January, 1983), pp. 52-58.

Chapter 5

Perspectives on
Decision Making

During the past 25 years, there has been a continuing interest in developing more sophisticated and "scientific" approaches to decision making. With the advent of expert systems of computer simulation of professional choices and the continuation of quantitative developments aiding decision, we have set forth powerful forces that are influencing how decisions are being made in organizations. The purpose of this chapter is to put these developments into perspective. Both Theodore Levitt and Roger Eck scrutinize management science models as to their real contribution to managing. Costigan presents the same view briefly and perhaps obliquely in the final article about how top executives think. It is obvious that executives who make more complex decisions do not think only in a sequential mode, as does a computer program. Nor do top management decision makers operate at the same level. Rather, they appear to relate variables and sequences of logic across several levels.

All of these negative thoughts about mathematic and automated decision making do not imply that such efforts are completely in vain. In fact, at some levels of the organization, these efforts toward automation and expert systems can be of substantial value. However, we have been saying this for a long time and have been waiting for these developments to occur at the top levels of the organization, but they have not. To some extent, these papers reflect that frustration of failure of scientific methods to progress beyond the routine levels of managerial decision making.

15 • A HERETICAL VIEW OF MANAGEMENT SCIENCE[1]

Theodore Levitt[2]

There is only one way to manage anything, and that is to keep it simple. Even if business is getting more complex, as many people claim, it doesn't follow that the organizational structures of today's companies have to be more involuted, planning more rigid and detailed, control systems more elaborate, or decision making more cumbersome and scientific.

Corporate affairs are indeed more complex than in times past, but companies are actually more manageable. That's because the things that need doing have been sensibly and systematically simplified. The larger the corporation, in fact, the better managed it generally is, even though those inside the corporation are not always so sure. Like soldiers in battle, they see a lot of confusion and mismanagement and therefore suffer a good deal of frustration and strain. From the heights of the command post, things look better.

A RETINUE OF EAGER SYCOPHANTS

Still, as a corporation gets better managed and more concerned with the quality and practice of management itself, its top people develop a powerful propensity to manage differently. They are encouraged in this by a rapidly expanding retinue of eager sycophants, equipped with new "scientific" tools and decision-making modes, who promise to free the manager from the inescapable uncertainties, risks, and traumas of running an enterprise. "Experts," trained to the teeth in the techniques (but not necessarily the practice) of management, are enlisted to do even better what people of native shrewdness, sound good sense, and abundant energy did quite beautifully before.

Management "scientists" in business schools, consulting organizations, and the large corporations themselves are pressing ever harder for the use of ever more elaborate forms of mathematicized analyses of an expanding variety of corporate activities. Exploiting the productive prowess of the computer, market researchers generate enormous masses of data that look with false precision and careless profligacy at every conceivable angle from which a subject can be viewed, regardless of relevance or realism. Model builders seek to simulate everything from cash flows and balance sheets twenty years hence to next year's labor negotiations. They build intricate decision trees whose pretension to utility is exceeded only by the awe in which high level line managers hold the technocrats who construct them.

Yet the modern corporation was built by people trained largely on the job. Command went to those whom natural selection shuffled to the top, and formal

[1]From *Fortune* (December 18, 1978), pp. 50–52. Reprinted by permission of *Fortune* magazine.
[2]Theodore Levitt, Professor of Business Administration, Harvard Business School.

managerial training was minimal. The Harvard Business School, one of the few training grounds in academe, contented itself with teaching students to think straight about practical matters and to take command. "Currently useful generalizations" were good enough and were constantly revised to suit the occasion. Case method pedagogy dominated management education.

All too quickly a lot of this has changed, especially at schools that are Harvard's more determined competitors and in the large corporations. Even at Harvard, social-climbing technocrats who pretend with increasing vigor to dispense grace and salvation have infiltrated the crevices of weakness and self-doubt. New tools of management, new concepts, special "advanced" ways of analyzing and simulating markets, customers, investments, balance sheets, distribution systems, and organizations—all these, with unctuous promises of mathematical and behavioral precision, tumble out from numerous graduate business schools in rising abundance. Increasingly scholasticism replaces common sense, formalism supersedes dexterity, organizational routines become more tortuous, and the staff dominates the line. "Methods" rivet the attention as much as results. Entropy threatens energy.

The modern corporation, wrongly thinking that larger size and rapid change require special managerial methods, now runs the risk of academicizing and ruining itself. That has already happened in the socialist countries where the "corporations" are entirely (except for ideology) in the tight grip of managerial technocrats—the learned graduates of the high academies. No wonder Soviet enterprise falls further and further behind, managing not even to manage what it borrows or buys or pilfers from abroad. And no wonder—to take an example from the industrialized countries in the West—that some Swedish corporations are in such a shambles, largely because of their long love affair with "behavioral science" experimentation in the work place and "scientific" methods in the marketplace.

THE DUMB DINOSAUR

Though doing business is less easy today, it has been made more complex by people who refuse to keep things simple. Mobil, Unilever, Xerox, Mitsui, Citicorp —none of these is inherently more complex than the small business firm, nor does its management require all that many new skills. The owner-manager of a small variety store with some 3,000 stockkeeping units, for instance, has a far more difficult and demanding task than the head of Kmart with his 1,492 stores. The owner-manager has to do everything, including the bookkeeping, purchasing, selling, repairs, even janitoring. The head of Kmart does none of these. Division heads and department heads under them do only one of those tasks. Their job may be big, but it's relatively simple compared with the owner-manager's. By subdividing work, Kmart has become simpler, more manageable, and thus bigger.

A company can grow in size and effectiveness only if it makes itself simple. Size did not kill the dinosaur any more than it killed W.T. Grant Co. and the Penn Central Railroad. What did kill the dinosaur was size wrongly managed. It remained slothfully where it was, rather than energetically going where it could survive. The dinosaur is a false metaphor for the dangers of size. The problem, as with thousands of other extinct species, was the absence not of physical agility but of mental ability—ability to make the right choices about the conditions of survival.

It can be said that the large corporation is more complex because of the number and diversity of tasks and units that need to be harmonized for a single corporate purpose. But what is being harmonized is the work of organizational units that support each other. The foundry supplies parts to the engine plant, and the engine plant to the assembly plant. Warehouses store the output and supply products for the sales department. The legal department helps with contracts, market research with data, finance with funds.

Smaller or less integrated corporations do not escape these tasks. If they do not perform them directly, they must buy them. In this respect the coordinating job is likely to be more difficult because it involves independent vendors or agents who march to their own tunes.

THOSE EMPTY FACTOIDS

Among the most empty factoids—as Norman Mailer calls "imagined facts" —habitually proclaimed these days is that the small company is naturally more flexible and more achieving than the large one. Proof is claimed by reference to a multiplicity of new companies in such fields as data processing, oil exploration, and retailing, where an I.B.M. or Exxon or Sears, Roebuck dominates. What is not mentioned are all the entrepreneurs in these fields who regularly fail, the numerous small companies congenitally incapable of escaping their juvenile weaknesses, and the thousands of exhausted small company managers mired deep in self-exploitation seven days a week.

If the large enterprise were, indeed, more complex and difficult to manage than the small one, we would hardly have so many thriving ones. Some are large because of technology, like steel mills. Some become large because of markets, like Coca-Cola. Most are large, however, because they've been managed well. Besides there is no presumption that ease and tranquility are God's prescription for corporate life anymore than for life any other place. As Winston Churchill said of representative democracy: "It is the worst of all forms of government, save for the alternatives."

Yet the corporation's zeal for managerial perfection threatens it with an excessive and paralyzing professionalization. The danger is less the stupefying bureaucratization of which Max Weber spoke nearly a century ago than the false pretensions of the complicators who buzz like swarming bees around the centers of power. They tend to disable the corporation by creating complexities.

In a fairly typical example, a large corporation spent $350,000 a year to build a financial planning model for asking *what if* questions, mostly about cash flows. Yet, a study published by the Marketing Science Institute—an organization financed by corporations, foundations, and trade associations—contends that such models have serious limitations because they are too simple. The authors of the study go on to say that ". . . [a corporate planning model should] proceed from a macromodel to an industry model to a firm model to a product model to a brand model and then on to such resource-oriented models as finance and production models."

BERT LANCE'S ADVICE

Professor Gordon C. Rausser, a prodigiously learned expert on mathematical modeling, has concluded that the analytical difficulties increase and the reliabilities decline disproportionately as the amounts of data and types of calculations rise. Rausser examined in excruciating depth every known method (*schemes* he called them) "to assist us in the assessment and evaluation of alternative policies . . ."—in this case as applied to national agricultural policy planning. Though his concluding words about the value of all this work was that "clearly the jury is still out," what seems clear is that when the jury comes in it will say that you will have to spend millions to bring any of these planning schemes even close to workability.

Indeed, a survey of 51 marketing model builders and model users published in the *Journal of Marketing Research* (November, 1977) revealed gross disagreement about the utility of the models being examined. When the presumptive Meistersingers of modern management technology disagree so extravagantly about the utility of their own doings, one is inclined to take Bert Lance's famous advice, "If it ain't broke, don't fix it."

Yet business schools competitively intent on proclaiming their superiority over each other teach this weighty vacuousness while the better professional business journals publish it with attitudinizing luxuriousness. Look also at the portentous agendas and the grave sermons from the expanding number of business research institutes, or at the cosmetic mathematizations from the business-consulting firms populated increasingly by articulate quantifiers and resolute social engineers. And look also at the pedigreed composition and overengineered output of the staff personnel of the more advanced large corporations. The situation is analagous to a point made by Professor Frank H. Knight, the late economist of the University of Chicago. He said as far back as 1940 that economists were ruining the economy, and asked: "When did doctors start making more people sick than well?"

There seems almost no recognition whatever in all this of the enormous contingency of the world in which business operates. What imaginably is added to the store of actionable knowledge by ever more intricate correlation analyses, multidimensional scaling, and conjoint analyses that, with data of uncertain accuracy, presume to explain market relationships of such fragility and instability that, like Heisenberg's principle, to observe them is to alter them? Of what earthly use is yet another regression analysis of past price and sales volume relationships when the data are less reliable than the precision of the tools to analyze them?

THE BIGGER, BETTER THEORY

It will be said that those who must make decisions will feel more comfortable with the help of such studies. In the present atmosphere an unpretentious study is not enough. A great many facts have to be marshaled and messaged, and the results elaborately presented. The more intricate the analyses and the more complicated the algorithms, then the more professionally contemporary one is presumed to be. The Harvard Law of Scientific Laws slips firmly into the secular world: "The bigger the theory, the better."

The best and the brightest who failed us so miserably for a decade in the affairs of state are now staking out turf in the affairs of business. Paradoxically they are accorded increasing respect in almost direct proportion to their increased incomprehensibility and declining relevance. Their power is expanding, though their testable utility declines. Claude Lévistrauss, the French anthropologist, said that, "Quesalid did not become a great shaman because he cured his patients; he cured his patients because he had become a great shaman."

It was not so long ago that people in business did not hesitate to say out loud in the presence of their peers that a certain article in, say, even the pragmatic *Harvard Business Review* was pure poppycock—pretentious intellectualizing pretending to spurious precision, full of wasteful elaboration leading nowhere. Now they hesitate for fear of seeming somehow to have missed the point or of lacking in modern management sensibilities.

Albert Einstein, whom nobody ever successfully accused of simplemindedness or oversimplifying, wrote in his *Autobiographical Notes* that there are two criteria according to which one can "criticize physical theories at all." First, "The theory must not contradict empirical facts." The facts don't have to confirm or prove the theory, so long as they don't disprove it. That kind of supreme faith in the power of inductive reasoning and aesthetic congruence over formal data-based analysis was reinforced by Einstein's second criterion which was concerned ". . . with what may briefly but vaguely be characterized as the 'naturalness' or 'logical simplicity' of the premises . . ."

Common sense is the managerial metaphor for *naturalness* and *logical simplicity*. It is rooted in years of experience and normal observation. Einstein told his assistant, Ernst Straus, "What I am really interested in is whether God could have made the world in a different way; that is, whether the necessity of logical simplicity leaves any freedom at all." Obviously he believed there was no truth other than that of logical simplicity.

Everywhere observation and experience proclaim for all with eyes to see the explanatory and operating power of simplicity and order—whether in technology, in systems, in controls, in organizations, or in human behavior. "The *focused factory,* to use Wickham Skinner's mellifluous term, is more productive and manageable than the diffused and diversified factory. It simplifies the work and the management of the work. The microprocessor is simpler in both conception and the method of its production than its predecessor combination of hundreds of handmade and hand-welded transistors, diodes, resistors, and rectifiers. The unit train, containerization, credit cards, supermarkets, travel agencies, theme and fast-food restaurants, computerized machine design, ambulatory medical clinics—all these and many more are simpler, more efficient, and more manageable than what they superseded or supplemented.

KEEP IT SIMPLE

When they attain a certain managerial altitude these days, managers need not trade what they know, and know how to do well, for the elaborate prescriptions of management science hucksters on the make. There are only a few things worth knowing well. Underpinning them all is the truth imposed by the necessity of nature itself: Keep it simple. Few things are more important than the clarity, focus, and greater functionality that derive from the implementation of this single rule. It applies to all fucntions, all product lines, all balance sheets, all organizations, and especially to all studies needed to direct, monitor, and run the organization.

There is the truth, too, that nothing is so important as energy and commitment—in the service, of course, of the proper purposes. There must be, in Arch Patton's felicitous phrasing, the "will to manage." This means, more than anything, a confident eagerness to act vigorously and cheerfully without fear in the face of uncertainty, unfettered by any need to examine in every possible detail from every possible angle with every possible method of analysis all the possible considerations and consequences at stake in any decision or action. This is not a license for foolishness or thoughtlessness. It is a call for sense and moderation.

16 • TREADING SOFTLY WITH MANAGEMENT SCIENCE[1]

Roger D. Eck[2]

Management science—known also as operations research, operations analysis and systems analysis—was a *cause célèbre* of the early 1960's. The prevailing opinion was that a blend of computers, science, and sophisticated mathematical techniques would bring dramatic changes to the executive suite. Now, after nearly two decades of gestation, we are discovering that management science is not living up to its advanced billing.

Organizations that employ computer specialists, management scientists, operations analysts, and other technical specialists have been, or soon will be, urged to reevaluate the role of such specialists. Three questions are pertinent: (1) In what respect has management science failed? (2) Why has management science failed? (3) What are appropriate organizational responses to management science? It is to these issues that this article is addressed.

As a foundation for discussion, it is useful to distinguish between the roles that have been historically assumed by the manager and by the management scientist.

MANAGER/MANAGEMENT SCIENCE

The *manager* has been traditionally concerned with planning, directing, coordinating, and controlling organizational activities. Of primary concern is the realization that managers state (subject to the approval of higher boards) organizational objectives and select the programs that will be employed to attain the objectives. The manager is held responsible for goal attainment, and managers quite reasonably consider a good decision to be a decision that attains the prescribed objectives. Because managers make decisions in an environment where a lack of information and risk predominate, the decision-making procedures that executives use incorporate historical experiences, intuition, thumb rules, and luck.

The management scientist normally serves as an advisor to the manager, and is most often found in a staff position or in a consulting capacity. The management scientist has been traditionally concerned with attempts to make the decision-making process more systematic. For example, the management scientist might attempt to specify the factors that should be (not "are") considered in selecting a new plant site. To the management scientist, a good decision is a decision that, irrespective of the final outcome, is made in a logical manner. Management scientists make extensive use of computers, statistical procedures, and other mathematical devices.

[1] From *Arizona Business*, Vol. XXII, No. 1 (January, 1975), pp. 3-7. Reprinted by permission of *Arizona Business*.
[2] Roger D. Eck, Assistant Professor of Quantitative Systems, Arizona State University.

The charges against management science concern the extent to which management scientists have been able to assist managers.

Criticisms

C. West Churchman charges that the preparation for dealing with "text-book uncertainty" that is afforded by such disciplines as management science has little to do with preparation for "executive uncertainty." [3] C. Jackson Grayson argues that "the impact of management science has been extremely small" and asserts that management science "appears to be unable to assist in a dynamic decision-making environment." [4] Herbert A. Simon suggests that science-oriented disciplines demand a commitment to knowledge creation that detracts from the advancement of an ability to use knowledge in the actual decision-making processes of organizations.[5]

UNDERLYING PROBLEMS

The implications of such charges are that management science does not directly confront the executive function, falls far short of providing the pragmatic insights that are needed for effective top-level management, and, in a dynamic environment, management science has a tendency to produce solutions for yesterday's problems.

The author, a management scientist, is of the opinion that the charges are well founded. Further, the author can find no substantial evidence to suggest that many of the shortcomings of management science will be rectified within the next few years. To understand why the charges against management science are valid, and, more importantly, to comprehend appropriate organizational responses, it is instructive to consider some of the problems that perplex management scientists.

Objectives

Most management science methods that are available at this time assume that organizational objectives can be clearly stated in a manner that is amenable to quantification. Further, the majority of successful applications of management science are found in contexts where there is a prepotent objective. When organizations are faced with multiple, potentially conflicting objectives, the management scientist can proceed only if it is possible to quantify the extent to which the organization would prefer greater attainment of one objective at the expense of lesser attainment of other objectives.

[3] C. West Churchman, "Management Education: Preparation for Uncertainty," *Organizational Dynamics* (Summer, 1972).

[4] C. Jackson Grayson, Jr., "Management Science and Business Practice," *Harvard Business Review*, Vol. LI, No. 4 (July-August, 1973), pp. 41-48.

[5] Herbert A. Simon, "The Business School: A Problem in Organizational Design," *The Journal of Management Studies*, Vol. IV, No. 1 (February, 1967), pp. 1-16.

The difficulties are further compounded when there is a conflict of interest among the participants who hold a claim on an organization (shareholders, creditors, management, labor, customers, suppliers, and so forth). Management scientists are typically unable to provide means of arriving at a "fair" compromise when there are conflicts of interest.

Problems related to the specification of organizational objectives are important for two reasons. First, it must be acknowledged that the specification of suitable organizational objectives is the most basic executive obligation. Until objectives have been formulated that motivate the continued support of various interested parties, there is no need to "manage." At this time organizational objectives seem to be established by an intuitive and little-understood process. The speciousness of statements of corporate goals that appear in annual reports need not necessarily be accidental. One thing that is clear is that today's management scientist is ill equipped to contribute to the formulation of organizational objectives. Management scientists tend to enter the picture after objectives have been formulated and attempt to specify the best means of meeting given objectives.

The second objective-related problem is that management scientists have had little success when the objectives are not fully quantifiable. In the face of "fuzzy" specifications for the desired tradeoffs among conflicting objectives, the management scientist is typically impotent.

Probability

When the eventual consequences of an organization's actions cannot be foretold with certainty management science techniques often assume that probabilistic assessments can be obtained. The type of assessments that are required by management scientists have a close connection to the requirements of mathematical probability theory. Two factors seem to introduce a gulf between the manager and the management scientist when uncertainty looms large. First, mathematical probability theory is abstract and often produces results that are contraintuitive. Therefore, the executive who attempts to cooperate with the management scientist can find himself faced with a request to implement a course of action that not only offends his common sense, but that was arrived at by an incomprehensible line of reasoning. Second, by asking the manager to make probability assessments and to act on the basis of such assessments, the management scientist is, in effect, asking the manager to document and assume responsibility for something that might eventually prove to be catastrophic. Even though the *logic* of such a request might be unassailable, there are strong behavioral motivations for ignoring logic. At this time the management scientist tends to respond by attempting to train the practicing manager in the fundamentals of probability theory. It is not at all clear that this response is sufficient for fruitful applications of management science in contexts where uncertainty is a major issue.

Models and Data

Management science methods assume that it is possible to mathematically state how attainment of an organization's objective(s) is (are) influenced by executive actions and other uncontrollable factors. If the "influence mechanism" is known and can be articulated, and if data are available to gauge the relative strengths of various influences, then model building and testing can be a relatively fast exercise. Unfortunately, many of the "influence mechanisms" are either not well known or organizations do not typically maintain the type of records that facilitate the model building and validation process. As a case in point, consider how little is known about the extent to which a two-column ad in the *New York Times* really influences profits.

Management science procedures are, at this time, based on models. Accordingly, management scientists are frequently unable to contribute to urgent concerns due to an inability to build an appropriate model. This is especially true when answers must be extracted from models in a compressed span of time.

Communications

Perhaps the most perplexing problem faced by contemporary management scientists is the problem of communication. By "communication" we mean an efficient and effective *two-way* rapport between the specialist and the manager. Unless both parties are more than minimally acquainted with the cognitive apparatus and *modus operandi* of the other party, errors of omission and oversimplification lead to breakdowns in communication. It is the opinion of many management scientists that management scientists can, and will, learn to think like managers. It is not at all clear that managers will learn to think like management scientists. The difficulty in developing this second direction in the communications process is that a good working grasp of management science seems to require extensive academic preparation. As an informal outline of the type of preparation that management scientists would like to find in the executive suite, it can be proposed that managers have one university-level course in each of the following areas: probability theory, classical statistics, Bayesian decision theory, operations research, and computer programming. It is not at all clear that it is possible for managers to obtain such an extensive background, and it is not at all clear that managers are eager to try.

A BALANCE SHEET FOR MANAGEMENT SCIENCE

From the preceding admittedly terse and by no means exhaustive list of unsolved problems in management science, there is ample cause for finding the charges of Churchman, Grayson, Simon, and others to be valid. On the other hand, it must be noted that the unsolved problems of the management scientist are also unsolved problems of the manager. Managers do not claim to know how to set good, feasible objectives, and managers do not claim to be infallible decision makers in the face of uncertainty. In large measure, the charges against management science are statements of disappointment. It had been hoped that management science would shed *more* light on the problems that confront and perplex executives.

It should also be recognized that management science *has* made contributions. The fact that statistical tests, simulation, linear programming, inventory formulas, PERT, and other management science tools are being used by a large number of organizations is presented as evidence of the contributions of management science. In view of the historical slowness of business to adopt new quantitative procedures—for example, Neil W. Chamberlain reports that it required about twenty years for a clear majority of our largest corporations to replace "payback" methods of investment analysis with more sophisticated "present worth" methods—the track record of management science cannot be considered to be totally inconsequential.[6]

SOME CORPORATE RESPONSES

This brings us to the point where it is time to consider appropriate organizational responses. With respect to the question, "Should we just ignore management science?" the consensus of responsible opinions appears to be an emphatic negative. The motivation for this response is that in the proper circumstances, management science has made important contributions and has paid for itself.

Current thinking is directed towards efforts to assure that management science will be applied in "proper circumstances" and with reasonable expectations. The following clearly contradictory suggestions can be gleaned from recent issues of such vehicles of emerging trends as the *Harvard Business Review:*

§ Confine management science inquiries to the well-structured problems.
§ Management scientists should stop refining approaches to already solved problems.
§ Management scientists should be held responsible for implementing solutions.
§ Management science should be regarded as being a provider of information inputs.
§ Management science should pay its own way.
§ It is unrealistic to evaluate the contributions of management science in terms of short-run accomplishments.
§ The management scientist should hold a high-level staff position where he is privy to the corridors of power.
§ The management scientist should be integrated into line units where he will experience operational problems.

[6] Neil W. Chamberlain, *The Firm: Micro-Economic Planning and Action* (New York: McGraw-Hill, Inc., 1962).

To make sense out of such seemingly contradictory suggestions, it would be prudent for an organization to first ask "Can we afford to support management science activities that might not, in the near future, lead to results that cover expenses?" Many smaller firms will probably have to answer "no" to this question. If this is the case, then management science activities should be directed to those areas where management science has had a historical record of success. This area is found at the lower "operating" levels of the organization where organizational entities have clear, unconflicting goals such as "increase product reliability," "increase product output," and "reduce downtime."

Lower Operating Levels. The fruitful areas for immediate results will be areas where the data that are needed for decision making can be gleaned from extant records, such as production records, the existing cost accounting system, specifications provided by the purchasing department, requirements provided by the marketing department, and so forth.

It should be noted that by directing attention to the lower operating levels of the organization, issues of uncertainty tend to be diminished. For example, a burning issue in the executive suite might be "What should our product line be?" but on the production line that uncertainty has been resolved.

Short-Run Payoff. There is a further motivation for confining attention to the lower levels of the organization when it is imperative that management science pay for itself in the short run. It is in the lower operating levels that we find the engineer, the accountant, the computer specialist, and the financial analyst who habitually work with, and make recommendations based on, computational procedures. Here one would anticipate that effective communications could most easily be established.

It is reasonable to anticipate that in lower-level operating positions, problems that are amenable to resolution by readily available management science techniques would not appear on a daily basis. If the management scientist is to pay his own way, he might have to do so by engaging in activities not strictly "management science." This realization suggests that the management scientist be integrated in a line position where he fully understands the operational aspects of a problem, is responsible for (limited) results, and need apply management science only when conditions are "perfect."

Long-Term Program

For the organization that can afford a long-term program of introspection and upgrading of executive capabilities, there seems to be a different set of appropriate responses. Because management science is poorly equipped to provide answers to the immediate problems that confront top executives, it could be autistic to suggest that management scientists be privy to the chambers of power for immediate purposes (other than the edification of the management scientist). Before the management scientist can become a consistent provider of executive-level answers, many current difficulties will have to be resolved.

By suggesting that management scientists who work at the higher corporate levels *not* be held responsible for implementing programs and demonstrating results, we differ sharply from the suggestions of others—most notably, Grayson. The main reason for differing with Grayson is the belief that, given current abilities, the only way that a management scientist can adequately function in the role of practicing top-level executive is by adopting the *modus operandi* of practicing executives—that is, by largely abandoning management science. Stated another way, it is suggested here that if an executive is needed, an executive should be hired.

This does not mean that it would be unreasonable to support a high-level management science activity. Quite the contrary! The management scientist is particularly well qualified to serve in the capacity of an in-house student of an organization.

Perhaps the most valuable—albeit, intangible—contribution of management science is to provide an alternative perspective of the management process. An investment in high-level management science could be viewed as analogous to purchasing an insurance policy to guard against executive complacency and organizational atrophy. Before dismissing this role for the management scientist, the executive is asked to count the number of critics of the organization who are both knowledgeable and on the side of the executive.

It is to be hoped that the management scientist will eventually be able to make positive contributions to the executive function. Because the actual implementation of management science findings in high-level, unstructured problem areas can be expected to be a long-run proposition, management scientists would be well advised to pay particular attention to executive concerns that are not likely to disappear in the near future. The budgeting process, cash management, dividend policy, standards of performance, the requirements for future management information systems, and the development of criteria for R & D management appear to be promising candidates for high-level, long-term investigation.

It is doubtful that any management scientist is fully knowledgeable in all of the many subfields of management science. If management scientists are to contribute by, first, learning more about the practice of management and, second, by developing and pioneering the application of science to top-level executive decision making, it is reasonable to anticipate that some form of group effort will be required. By turning to a high-level staff *group* of management scientists, the organization can take steps to foster an environment where: (1) management scientists can become more aware of the needs of executives, and (2) the contributions of the management scientist need not be restricted by the limitations of the isolated management scientist. The high-level management science staff group can be, in part, justified as a corporate resource for other management scientists who have been integrated into operating (line) positions.

CONCLUSION

As we tread softly with management science, we (managers and management scientists) have an opportunity to maximize hope. That, if the author understands Churchman, is progress.

17 • HOW TOP EXECUTIVES THINK[1]

Kelly Costigan

For years, it has been thought that the prerequisites for executive success were a high IQ and the right academic pedigree—including an MBA. But a wealth of new research is undoing that neat recipe. Professional success has now been linked to a special kind of intelligence, one not necessarily acquired in business school or measured by IQ tests.

Top-flight executives, studies show, have "practical intelligence" and think multidimensionally. This means that when they make a decision, they synthesize a jumble of information and integrate apparently unrelated considerations—including the consequences two or more steps down the road.

THE LONG-RANGE VIEW

The less multidimensional thinker may be guided in each decision by a single, immediate goal, such as making a profit in a takeover. But the more successful executive is always aware of how the ramifications of any decision may help or hurt his company. According to Siegfried Streufert, a behavioral scientist at Penn State's College of Medicine, he will consider factors beyond profit. What effect, for example, will an acquisition have on a competitor? When firing a subordinate, the executive may help him find another position in order to discourage him from divulging the company's secrets.

Moreover, the best managers are highly motivated individuals who advance themselves through their ability to make the most of every opportunity to display their skills. They "are always strategizing," says Streufert. "It's an overall approach. Most business schools don't teach this—they teach you *what* to think, not *how* to think."

Streufert, who summarizes his studies of top managers in a forthcoming book, *Complexity, Managers and Organizations,* says that multidimensional thinking manifests itself in three different kinds of abilities: planning in a long-term but flexible way; perceiving patterns in events as they are rapidly changing; and being selective about the information used to make a decision.

Superior mid- to top-level executives also have a remarkable ability to build networks and alliances among different groups in order to get a task accomplished, according to a study of 2,000 managers conducted by Richard Boyatzis, president of McBer, a Boston consulting firm. He cites as an example a marketing manager who, to persuade a company committee of manufacturing engineers to use more than one supplier for a product, called in design engineers to support his argument. Why? Because they spoke the same language that the committee members did.

A chief executive officer (CEO), moreover, must be able "to com-

[1] First appeared in *Science Digest* (January, 1985), p. 26, © 1985 by the Hearst Corporation. Reprinted by permission of Kelly Ellen Costigan.

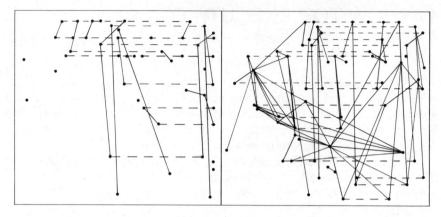

The diagrams above show strategic planning patterns and coordination of decisions by two executives. Horizontal lines connect decisions made repeatedly, such as "Hire/Fire/Reward Personnel" (top line). Diagonal lines connect strategically related decisions. The more multidimensional manager (right) always thinks ahead and links his decisions.[2]

municate in a few key words the mission of the company," explains another McBer official, George Klemp. He sees Chrysler CEO Lee Iacocca as exemplifying this trait.

Through advertising and television appearances, Iacocca articulated his commitment to revitalizing the ailing company by making quality cars competitive with foreign imports. "He made a personal statement," Klemp says, "In essence, he was saying, 'You're buying this car for me.' It's a real customer orientation, but one connected to a specific vision of quality." At the same time, Iacocca helped shore up morale among employees.

TOUGHNESS ISN'T CRUCIAL

The style in which executives work with others—how tough they are— is not a significant determinant of whether they will be successful or not, adds Klemp. The head of a brokerage house can be lean, mean and bottom-line oriented, and his staff will tolerate it, he says, if they see the reasoning behind it. More crucial to executive success, in addition to intellectual ability, are self-confidence, skill at influencing others and an overall drive for excellence, according to McBer's data.

These same attributes are enhanced by "practical intelligence" in those seeking to make it to the top, says psychologist Robert Sternberg of Yale University. In *The Journal of Personality and Social Psychology,* Sternberg and a colleague report that many of the superior managers whom they surveyed from the top 20 American companies demonstrated this kind of pragmatic approach. Answering test questions built around hypothetical situations (such as how to gain rapid promotion), these managers displayed

---

[2] Illustration by Susan Handman, based on research by Siegfried Streufert.

the following behavior: a habit of doing tasks that capitalized on their talents and would be noticed by superiors; a willingness to set their own work priorities, rather than doing only what is assigned; and a knowledge of what they should accomplish in their jobs and what responsibilities should be delegated to others.

Much of this kind of intelligence is "tacit," Sternberg notes. It's seldom taught in school or directly communicated by others. Can it be learned? For the most part, yes. McBer provides many Fortune 500 companies with training programs that grow out of research into the competencies involved in specific posts at individual companies. Yet Sternberg cautions against thinking that *everyone* can enhance his or her potential for ultimate success. "Lots of people want to be successful," he notes, "but for many reasons, they don't do anything about it—even with training."

BIBLIOGRAPHY, CHAPTER 5

Anderson, John C., and T. R. Hoffmann. "A Perspective on the Implementation of Management Science." *Academy of Management Review,* Vol. 3, No. 3 (July, 1978), pp. 563-571.

Bowman, Edward H. "Risk Seeking By Troubled Firms." *Sloan Management Review,* Vol. 23, No. 4 (1983), pp. 33-42.

Caldwell, David F., and Charles A. O'Reilly, III. "Responses to Failure: The Effects of Choice and Responsibility on Impressions Management." *Academy of Management Journal,* Vol. 25, No. 1 (1982), pp. 121-136.

Calhoun, S. Reed, and Paul Green. "Simulation: Versatile Aid to Decision Making." *Advanced Management* (April, 1958), pp. 11-16.

Creamens, John E. "The Trend in Simulation." *Computers and Automation,* Vol. 17, No. 1 (January, 1968), pp. 44-48.

DeWade, Martin. "Managerial Style and the Design of Decision Aids." *OMEGA,* Vol. 6, No. 1 (1978), pp. 5-13.

Dutton, J. M., and R. E. Walton. "Operational Research and the Behavioral Sciences. *Operations Research Quarterly,* Vol. 15, No. 3, pp. 207-217.

Grayson, C. J. "Management Science and Business Practice." *Harvard Business Review,* Vol. 51, No. 4 (July-August, 1973), pp. 41-48.

Hadar, Josef. "Learning with Deterministic Decision Rules." *Decision Sciences,* Vol. 7, No. 1 (January, 1976), 18-28.

Heenan, D. A., and R. B. Addleman. "Quantitative Techniques for Today's Decision Makers." *Harvard Business Review,* Vol. 54, No. 3 (May-June, 1976).

Herrmann, C. C. , and J. F. Magee. " 'Operations Research' for Management." *Harvard Business Review,* Vol. 41, No. 4 (1963), pp. 100-112.

Jewell, William S. "Risk Taking in Critical Path Analysis." *Management Science,* Vol. 11 (January, 1965), pp. 438-443.

Konter, Rosabeth Moss. "The Middle Manager as Innovator." *Harvard Business Review,* Vol. 60, No. 4 (July-August, 1982), pp. 95-105.

MacCrimmon, K. R., and J. K. Siv. "Making Trade-Offs." *Decision Sciences,* Vol. 5, No. 5 (December, 1974), pp. 77-121.

Pendse, S. G. "Category Perception, Language and Brain Hemispheres: An Information Transmission Approach." *Behavioral Science,* Vol. 23 (1978), pp. 421-427.

Stanley, John D. "Dissent in Organizations." *Academy of Management Review,* Vol. 6, No. 1 (1981), pp. 13-19.

Vroom, V. H., and A. G. Jago. "Decision Making as a Social Process: Normative and Descriptive Models of Leader Behavior." *Decision Sciences,* Vol. 5, No. 4 (October, 1974), pp. 743-769.

Weick, Karl E. "Misconceptions About Managerial Productivity." *Business Horizons,* Vol. 26, No. 4 (1983), pp. 47-52.

Weist, Jerome. "Heuristic Programs for Decision Making." *Harvard Business Review,* Vol. 44, No. 5 (September-October, 1966), pp. 129-143.

Wolfson, R. J., and T. M. Caroll. "Ignorance, Error, and Information in the Classic Theory of Decision." *Behavioral Sciences,* Vol. 21 (1976), pp. 107-115.

Wright, Peter. "The Harassed Decision Maker." *Journal of Applied Psychology,* Vol. 59, No. 5 (1974), pp. 555-561.

Section B

Planning

The decisions that management makes influence the future directions of the firm regardless of the type of decision under consideration. Yet is is the process of looking ahead to assess some future state of affairs and then to commit the firm to a plan of action based on that assessment that we refer to as planning.

For some types of plans such as corporate policy or objectives, the results are more or less permanent in the sense that they are not under frequent review or change. In contrast are the plans for monthly or quarterly budgets or schedules, which serve to guide behavior during a rather limited period. The latter plans change frequently in expectation of results. The differences in time perspectives—that is, short-term versus semipermanent plans—are reflected in the articles in the first of the two chapters devoted to planning.

It should be noted that there is a superior-subordinate twist to the different types of plans typically set forth by managers. Supposedly goals take precedence over long-range plans. Similarly short-range plans are subordinate to long-range decisions. Since corporate objectives, goals, and policies are long range in concept, they tend to take precedence and guide the formation of budgets and schedules as well as short-term plans.

Chapter 6

Goals and
Planning

In the first article Grossman and Lindhe review a short-term planning exercise—the budgeting process. They pay particular attention to relate budgets to other important considerations such as corporate goals and policies.

Quinn and Seashore both examine goals, primarily from the corporate point of view. If managers do not establish objectives for their organization, decisions will merely involve one side of the managerial equation—efficiency. The larger (or equally as important) question is effectiveness. Doing the right thing is as important as doing the thing right.

Operations research techniques often assume that the goal to be maximized has already been determined and that the only matter left for planning or decision-making purposes is to select the best means of achieving that particular goal. Yet the manager, at almost any level in an organization, has some choices with respect to the goals that subordinates and the organization are going to attempt to achieve. Of course, at the lower levels in the organization, the manager is constrained by the goals set by superiors. If the superior has emphasized cost reduction to the exclusion of all else, the subordinate may have little choice in setting any other goal. Usually, however, some freedom in goal determination exists at all levels. Of course, at the top management level of a company, the goal determination process is relatively free in comparison with that at lower levels; but there are constraints imposed on top management's selection of any goal it wants to achieve. For example, competition, size of potential market, the ethical climate, and legal restrictions all restrain top management from freely establishing its objectives.

Management has not always been explicit about the objectives that it desires the organization to achieve. Quinn explains why this is so as he details the uncertainties that prevent explicit goal statements, at least at the very top levels in an organization.

Quinn's approach contrasts somewhat with that of Seashore, who attempts to show the critical importance of preestablishing goals for a firm. He shows that it is not enough for a well-managed firm merely to assume that everyone is going to maximize profit as a natural course. In fact, top management may find it pertinent not to maximize profit, especially in the short run, if it is to achieve long-run goals.

One must consider the opinions of both of these respected authors. Where uncertainty reigns, the muddling-through approach to goals as set forth by Quinn may be appropriate. Seashore contends that with diligence and persistence, uncertainty can be reduced to the extent that meaningful goals can often be set. It appears useful first to attempt the Seashore approach. If reduction of uncertainty is incomplete or impossible, the uncertainty of the situation would require an incremental approach to the formulation of objectives.

18 • IMPORTANT CONSIDERATIONS IN THE BUDGETING PROCESS[1]

Steven D. Grossman[2]
Richard Lindhe[3]

The firm is a system; i.e., a series of interrelated elements working together to achieve a purpose. The well-managed firm has a sense of that interrelationship; management plans with that understanding and the budget reflects it.

Good management involves planning for both the long-term and the short-term. Planning of this sort builds upon the resources of the firm within the environment. If we can gain a reasonable feel for the possibilities of future conditions which could affect a firm, we can establish a long-term plan and a set of short-term plans within that plan for the firm. This process is called strategic planning, and it is the foundation of proper budgets.

The primary functions of the budget are to communicate expectations and to aid in the allocation of resources. There are certain steps that should be followed in the budgeting process. These steps involve goals and objectives, the environment, the availability of resources, and the establishment and implementation of strategy.

Budgets involve people. Therefore, motivation, participation, and communication are vital factors in the success of the budgeting process. A budget that is established without regard to these considerations is bound to fail.

THE LONG-TERM PLAN

The firm's management should decide what it wishes the organization to be like at some time in the future. The elements of the firm at that time are set in general terms: size, industry, products, etc. Of course, these elements must be feasible. The long-term strategy, then, is an action plan that is designed to achieve long-term objectives.

The long-term plan necessarily is general in nature and provides fairly broad guidelines rather than specific activities. Two aspects of this plan are of major concern to us. The first has to do with those actions which are specifically linked to long-term strategy. The second aspect of the long-term plan relates to the short-term activities which are necessary to carry out the long-term strategy as we face the near future.

As we picture the long-term strategy, we can see that it is composed of a series of short-term plans or strategies. Each of these short-term plans builds upon the one before it. Adjustments are made as needed to respond to changes in the environment, available resources, or even basic goals and objectives. Each of these short-term plans prepares the firm for the next short-term plan (see Figure 1).

[1] From *Managerial Planning* (September-October, 1982), pp. 24-29. Reprinted by permission of *Managerial Planning*.
[2] Steven D. Grossman, Associate Professor of Accounting, Texas A&M University.
[3] Richard Lindhe, Associate Professor of Accounting, Northeastern University.

FIGURE 1

LONG- AND SHORT-TERM STRATEGIES

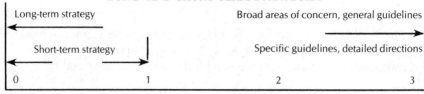

Years

   It is important to remember that these short-term strategies are subsets of the long-term strategy. When conditions cause changes to be necessary in the long-term, those changes should be reflected in the short-term as well. It is equally important to remember that these short-term strategies are individual steps which necessarily must be achieved in order to gain the larger goal. If each short-term plan is optimized separately, the long-term plan may not be achieved. The key to proper planning is to reach the end of one period in the best possible condition to implement the next short-term strategy. These short-term strategies are manifested in the operating budgets of the firm. The operating budget is often referred to as, simply, the budget.
   We shall think of the long-term strategy as a continuous process which is constantly being upgraded and fit to the nuances of the forecasted future. In this sense, the long-term plan or strategy has no end. The budget, too, is an unending process which shifts and changes with the strategy that it represents.

THE BUDGET

Both capital and operating budgets are meant to be reflections of their related strategies. Their primary functions, in this regard, are (1) to communicate expectations and, (2) to help allocate resources. These functions result in a series of highly complex actions, reactions, and interactions taking place.
   The steps inherent in strategic development are as follows:
   1. Establishment of goals and objectives.
   2. Scanning of the environment.
   3. Assessment of available resources.
   4. Establishment of the strategy.
   5. Implementation of the strategy.
These steps do not have to be carried out in this particular order. In fact, there may be considerable movement back and forth between steps as viability of purpose is tested. Moreover, this is not really a periodic event, although major emphasis may be given at specific points of time; rather it is a continuous process. Let us examine each of these briefly.

ESTABLISHMENT OF GOALS AND OBJECTIVES

An organization comes into being for a reason and stays in existence either for that reason or for some other. Accountants sometimes ascribe a particular objective to a firm—for example, maximization of profits or wealth—but, in fact, a firm may have a wide variety of objectives. The function of the accountant is not to set the goals and objectives for an organization, but to help in their achievement. Accountants also can help in the assessment of the viability and appropriateness of goals and objectives by supplying management with appropriate information.

Goals and objectives should be the focus for the firm, and the accountant must know and understand them. It is important that goals and objectives be enunciated, be communicated, and be reasonably well accepted. Otherwise, there can be no meaningful focus for the firm, and productive efforts may be dissipated.

THE ENVIRONMENT

The environment will be defined as the composite of all those factors which can affect the organization but over which the organization's management has little or no control. To add clarity to this description, we can divide the environment into four categories: (1) economic, (2) technical, (3) legal, and (4) social.

The economic environment is composed of such elements as general business activity, the activities of the industry or industries in which the organization functions, and the activities of governments. These are the factors that are embodied in the forecasts of firms.

Technical activity in the environment relates mainly to scientific development. New machines, new processes, and new products can have profound impacts upon the firm's future and, therefore, it is imperative that the firm be aware of all such developments.

Legal aspects of the environment relate to all legislation which can affect the organization. Legislation for our purposes refers to the three phases of laws: (1) the enactment of legislation, (2) the administration of legislation, and (3) the interpretation of legislation by the courts. The fact is that laws are administered differently in different places and at different times; in addition, a law may be expanded, diminished, or even abolished by the courts.

The social aspect of environment refers to the changing lifestyle of society. Changes in attitude, perspective, or moral sense may lead to changes in the other aspects of environment and have strong implications to the firm. In a sense, the social aspect may be considered to be the early warning part of the environment.

The environment may also be classified according to its predominant condition as: (1) stable, (2) dynamic, or (3) turbulent. A stable environment is relatively unchanging; firms concentrate upon the improvement of existing products and processes. A dynamic environment is a changing one in which forecasts are considered to be appropriate and can be made reasonably accurately. Most writers in business activities assume that a dynamic environment exists. A turbulent environment is so unstable that managers tend to have little faith in forecasts. Their natural tendency toward short-term planning and decision making is increased dramatically. The time of the oil embargo was such a time for many firms.

The environment contains both constraints and opportunities. The successful firm understands them and is able to operate within the constraints and take advantage of the opportunities.

AVAILABLE RESOURCES

A resource may be defined as anything which can help the firm achieve its objectives within the existing or future environment. Resources must be seen within a particular focus; their values are set by the environment and change as it does.

Notice the difference between resources as we have just defined them and assets as defined in accounting. An accounting asset may or may not be a resource: a resource may or may not be an accounting asset. A resource may be money, a building, or a machine. In addition, it may be executive ability, marketing experience, or a good reputation.

Accounting assets are measured in terms of their costs. Resources should be measured in terms of their ability to aid in goal achievement.

ESTABLISHMENT OF STRATEGY

Goals and objectives, the environment, and the available resources may be considered to be the building blocks of strategy, because the implementation of strategy must relate to them. Strategy is always tenuous—subject to change in the environment or, even, the purpose for which the firm exists. Thus, strategic development is always an ongoing process, and the budgets which reflect the strategy also must be in a continuous state.

In long-term strategy, the organization perceives a desired state of condition for that organization at some time (typically 5 to 10 years) in the future. Broad guidelines are established at this time for the functional areas such as marketing and finance.

Within this long-term plan, management sets desired conditions along the way—for example, at the end of each year. Obviously, these should not be rigid objectives, because the environment is likely to change in some way. The plan must be flexible so that it can be changed not simply in dimension but, if necessary, in its very basics.

It is clear that direction must be provided for all functions, for all divisions and for all departments. Although the ultimate focus of the firm must be long-term, this focus may be very difficult to maintain in the press of daily operations.

The short-term budget or operating budget is, then, a stage of the longer term. Operating budgets are, typically, for periods of one year with monthly updates. A number of firms follow the practice of setting a twelve month budget each month by adding a new month and dropping the past month.

IMPLEMENTING THE STRATEGY

The budget is the manifestation of the strategy and the most common way of implementing it. We shall see that the process of this implementation may be as important as the budget itself.

All of the essentials pertaining to measurement and behavior that are so crucial to the success of the plan are included in this process. If the costs that are measured are not the costs that are incurred, if the pattern of behavior that is assumed is not the actual pattern, if the way in which the measurements are used do not lead to appropriate behavior, then the plan must surely fail. Machines have behavior patterns; people have behavior patterns. The budget must reflect an understanding of these patterns and also the wide spectrum of human behavior which will do much to determine the success or failure of the budget.

The strategy and, hence, the budget which lead to the greatest profit for a particular period may not be the best choice for the firm. If that is so, then profit for the period may not be the best measure of success. Indeed, we need to measure success in terms of how well the firm moved along its strategic path. Each segment of the firm must perform its own unique function as intended, and its success must be measured in terms of that functional performance.

HUMAN BEHAVIOR AND THE BUDGET

When a machine has a cutting edge, it is normal for that cutting edge to become progressively more dull with use until it must be replaced. This variation in efficiency is normal to that machine. In this sense a human being, like the machine, has a normal variation in efficiency. We know that Monday mornings and Friday afternoons are usually less productive than other days. We also know that people are physically incapable of maintaining the same level of efficiency, and budgets need to reflect that normality.

There is, however, another side to human behavior. We have come to see that motivation is an important factor in performance, but we seldom explore the broader implications of human behavior in budgets. Just as there is a normal physical behavior pattern for a person, there is also a normal behavior which relates to that person's cultural and psychological side.

Our codes of behavior are set to a large extent by our cultures; that is, in fact, a distinguishing feature of a culture. Indeed, cultural impact is well recognized as a factor in behavior. We often overlook the fact that any large organization can be composed of a variety of disparate cultures.

Certainly, research scientists see a different role for themselves than finance people see either for themselves or for research scientists. Each group has its own culture; each sees a special set of rules for behavior; each has a set of normal behavior which is different than the other's.

We all "see" what we are conditioned to see. Accountants, marketing people, finance people, and others are each trained to look for certain things within an organization, and they will tend to "see" in terms of those things.

For example, assume that an engineer, an artist, and a psychologist all witness the same automobile accident. The odds are—and experience will verify—that each will see some things the others do not and, of course, miss something the others see.

The engineer is more likely to note the condition and performance of the automobiles, the psychologist is more likely to be aware of the behavior of the participants, and the artist is more likely to be attuned to the general scene. What they see will be partly determined by their perceptions—what they have been conditioned to see.

Suppose that the witnesses saw the event from different places—street level, fifth floor, front, back, etc. Now we can say that each witness had a different perspective and, therefore, was likely to see something different. This is why eyewitnesses sometimes report an incident in totally different ways.

Each group within the organization is likely to see the organization in terms of its own perceptions and from its own perspective. These perceptions and prospectives help to create normal behavior; they also create unique feelings about and reactions to the budget.

MOTIVATION

Budgets motivate people, although we have a lot to learn about how they do so. Since people relate to things as they perceive them, we must understand motivation within the unique worlds of varying cultures.

A simplistic way of describing motivation is to say that we can positively motivate people when we provide them with a climate in which they can meet their needs while they are meeting our needs. A firm can positively motivate people when they can work to meet their own needs by working to achieve the firm's goals and objectives.

Virtually every phase of the budget and its processes has the potential for impacting motivation by shaping the perceptions of the participants. If we can learn to "see" a bit from others' eyes, we might be able to understand better the psychology of budgets.

PARTICIPATION

While the traditional view of organizational behavior is that workers are motivated primarily by money, the more modern view is that workers are motivated by a wide variety of needs. An individual joins a firm and works for it as long as such action enables him to achieve his personal goals.

There seems to be relationship between the amount of participation and the quality of performance. Sometimes the relationship is positive due to the increased satisfaction by the members of the firm in utilizing their capabilities and achieving their objectives. However, the relationship may be negative if the members of the firm are reluctant to accept the risk of not achieving their own standards.

Although many people seem to accept the idea that participation in the budget process leads to better budget performance, it is not necessarily so. There are people who either cannot or do not wish to participate in the budget process. There are people who refuse to let a job be anything more than a means to other ends. They will do what they are told to do—and do it well—but they do not want any more involvement in the firm.

Some people may have difficulty understanding what is needed, others may not be able to communicate effectively, and still others may not have sufficient time available for meaningful participation. Meaningful participation can be very demanding.

In any case, if participation in the process is planned, it should be recognized that extensive preparation is necessary. New perceptions and new perspectives must be created for all parties if the process is to work.

Above all, there must be some minimum level of trust at all levels, and that trust must be deserved. Pseudo-participation can be very unproductive. Unless people believe that their actions have meaning, they will not provide meaningful input, and negative motivation is likely.

BUDGET COMMUNICATION

We said earlier that one of the purposes of the budget is to communicate expectations. The budget as a communication device plays a significant role in establishing the climate of the firm.

The effect that the message that is communicated by the budget has upon the members of the firm is established by their mental condition or mental set. This set will be established by:

1. Instruction—formal and informal.
2. Environment:
   a. The person's
   b. The firm's
3. The form of the message.
4. The budget system.
5. Knowledge about those in charge of the budget.

We shall look briefly at each of these elements in turn to see if we can gain some insights into the whole process.

Instructions

People will react to the budget, at least partly, in terms of the instructions that they have received about it. This instruction can be both formal and informal; it can be intentional and unintentional.

Although formal instruction is an imperative for a good budget, it is important that instructions be clear and complete. Too often, the instruction is, at best, cursory. Training tends to be informal. On-the-job training can be effective, however, if it is done properly.

Unintentional training is oftentimes both very effective and counter productive. Actions that are taken by budget managers or the inferences of such actions can have a strong impact in both the short-term and the long-term. Activities at this level can create misperceptions which can be very damaging. Time must be spent with operating managers so that they are not only clear in their understanding of budget operations but also are aware of the impact of their actions upon others.

Environment

People react to all sorts of stimuli—stimuli of the present or out of the past. The environment that has been created in the firm and individual perceptions are likely to be at least somewhat different for each person.

Although we cannot learn everything about each individual's background, we can gain a sense of the environment of the firm as perceived by the members of the firm in general and the key people in particular. Although the environment of the firm is difficult to articulate, it can be a significant part of the preparation of a successful budget.

Knowledge about the environment typically is determined by interviews and observations. Interviews must be carefully conducted and reinforced by observations. It is important to realize that the environment that we see may not be the environment that others see.

The attitude of managers at all levels will become incorporated into the budget. If managers tend to be uncommunicative, important questions about the budget may not only be unanswered, they may not even be asked. If managers generally are open and understanding, this attitude is likely to carry over into the budget.

The budget is part of the total environment of the firm, rather than separate and apart from it. The general feeling about the environment of the firm will transmit itself through the budget. Conversely, the spirit generated by the budget will be a tangible part of the environment of the firm.

The Form of the Message

Whether the budget process is communicating expectations or results, it is sending messages. Interestingly enough, we find that the way we send those messages can have a significant effect. The form of the message can be important. We know that people react differently to reports issued directly from a computer or apparently issued from a computer as compared to reports which are issued in other ways. Indeed, there is ample evidence that the form of the message affects behavior. The phenomena of primacy and recent effects in messages has been well documented and deserves attention.

The color and bordering of the report paper can affect the receiver. The size of the type, the order of presentation, the headings of the reports, the language and the symbols chosen all can create particular patterns of behavior.

Since the purpose of the budget is to create positive behavior, every aspect which can impact upon behavior in the budget process is important. Those who are in charge of the budget have a responsibility to see that the budget process is effective by doing whatever is necessary to ensure its success.

The use of accounting terminology, accounting titles, and accounting type reports should not be used when dealing with nonaccountants. Some remarkable improvements in the use of budgets and related materials can be achieved by fitting the form and format of the message to those who will use them. These improvements have been especially significant with regards to engineers, who like charts and graphs rather than accounting reports.

The Budget System

The more we study the budget as a system that is part of an information system, the more we learn about the complexities of a process that is used to measure, judge performance, and communicate results. We find that the final judgement on the efficacy of the budget system must be made on the basis of the total impact of the total process.

Time can be a significant factor in budget communication. Just as Friday afternoons and Monday mornings are bad production periods, they are poor periods for communications as well. People are not as likely to be as alert or responsive as they might be at other times.

If reports are regularly processed at particular times, deviations from the schedule can connote special significance. Obviously, if action is expected as a result of the budget report, it must be received in time for a meaningful response. If reports are received after action on a problem has already been taken, disfunctional behavior could result.

Studies have shown that delays in reporting can cause persons to be negative about the potential results and also to translate the report when it is received more negatively than would have been the case earlier. This suggests that every effort should be made to avoid delay in the reports and, if delay is unavoidable, the reason for the delay should be communicated early.

Positive reinforcement has been shown to improve both attitudes and efficiency, while negative reinforcements produces a deterioration of morale and productivity. In practice, the now traditional "management by exception" tends to concentrate on those things which are perceived as unfavorable. Since this is clearly negative reinforcement, we need to be concerned about the results. In fact, there are a lot of defensive actions under such conditions—actions which certainly do not add to either effectiveness or efficiency.

There is a tendency for budgets to cause a narrowing of perspective by highlighting only segmental concerns. The best way to counteract this might be to base budget analysis upon the interrelated factors of the budget. To be more specific, we need to provide measurements which relate to total impact and focus on that which relates to the total system.

Knowledge of the Source

Knowledge of the other party to communication can affect the impact of a message. Teachers with low expectations for the performance of their students actually tend to induce poor performance. If managers have low expectations for performance in a budget situation, these expectations are likely to be inadvertently communicated and thereby help to induce the expected behavior.

Historically, certain segments of an organization have held certain other segments in low regard. This attitude is prevalent among many engineers and research scientists about accountants, budgets, budget processes, and budget directors. Whether or not this attitude is justified, it can be detrimental to performance. In some cases, it may be necessary to use nonaccountants as sources for certain budget messages. In the long run, it is far better to work on the basic relationship to ensure a more productive condition.

SUMMARY

This article discussed three important aspects of the budgeting process. Each of these aspects should be considered carefully.

The long-term strategy is composed of a series of a short-term strategies. Conditions which cause changes in the long-term strategy should be reflected in the short-term strategies also. Each short-term plan is a step along the path of the long-term plan. The important consideration is whether the long-term strategy is achieved.

There are five steps that are inherent in the development of a firm's strategy. These steps include the establishment of goals and objectives, the scanning of the environment, the assessment of available resources, the establishment of the strategy, and the implementation of the strategy. These steps are interrelated and there is considerable movement back and forth between steps.

Human behavior is a vital consideration in the budget process. Almost every part of the budget process impacts motivation by shaping the perceptions of the personnel in the firm. Participation in the budgeting process may or may not be helpful. If participation is to be used, extensive preparation will be necessary.

The budget is an important communication device. A budget sends a message to the members of the firm. The effect of the message is established by the mental set of the members.

19 • STRATEGIC GOALS: PROCESS AND POLITICS[1]

James Brian Quinn[2]

Is a precise, measurable, cohesive package of strategic goals the hallmark of an effective top manager? To the contrary, this article suggests that the many executives who arrive at their goals through incremental "muddling" processes are using purposeful, politically astute, and effective management practices. The author documents why this is so and outlines how the techniques of broad goal setting and "logical incrementalism" can be used most effectively in your organization.

Executives are constantly under pressure to:

1. Define specific goals and objectives for their organizations
2. State these goals clearly, explicitly, and preferably quantitatively
3. Assign the goals to individuals or organizational units
4. Control the organization toward established measurable goals

These have become almost biblical mandates for most managers. Yet at the strategic level in large companies one often finds that successful executives announce only a few goals. These are frequently broad and general. Only rarely are they quantitative or measurably precise. Further, managements tend to arrive at their strategic goals through highly incremental "muddling" processes rather than through the kinds of structured analytical processes so often prescribed in the literature and "required" according to management dogma.

This article documents why top managers act as they do. It also asserts that their practices are purposeful, politically astute, and effective. They do not represent breakdowns in management technique, sloppiness, or lack of top management sophistication—as critics of these practices so often suggest. Managers at all levels can be more effective if they understand the logic and process considerations behind such broad goal setting and incremental techniques.

The conclusions in this article come from systematic observation of some ten organizations over a period of several years. Examples are selected from these observations, from secondary sources, and from a current project on "Strategy Formulation in Major Organizations," in which the author has interviewed some 100 top managers in large U.S. and European companies.

WHY NOT ANNOUNCE GOALS?

Why don't top executives simply arrive at goals and announce them in the precise, integrated packages advocated by theoretical strategists and expected by their

[1]Reprinted from *Sloan Management Review*, Vol. 19, No. 1 (October, 1977), pp. 21–37, by permission of the publisher. Copyright 1977 by the Sloan Management Review Association. All rights reserved.

[2]James Brian Quinn, Dartmouth College, Hanover, New Hampshire.

organizational constituents? In fact, they may establish a few broad goals by decree. But more often—and for good reason—they avoid such pronouncements. Why?

Undesired Centralization

Effective top managers understand that goal announcements centralize the organization. Such statements tell subordinates that certain issues are closed and that their thoughts about alternatives are irrelevant. Successful top executives know they cannot have as much detailed information about products, technologies, and customer needs as their line compatriots do. In formulating goals, they want both to benefit from this knowledge and to obtain the genuine participation and commitment of those who have it. For example:

> Mr. James McFarland said that shortly after he became Chief Executive Officer, "I asked myself what was expected of me as CEO. I decided that my role was really to build General Mills from a good into a great company. But I realized this was not just up to me. I wanted a collective viewpoint as to what makes a company great. Consequently, we took some thirty-five top people away for three days to decide what it took to move the company from 'goodness' to 'greatness.' Working in groups of six to eight, we defined the characteristics of a great company from various points of view, what our shortcomings were, and how we might overcome these." Over time these broad goals were translated into charters for specific divisions or groups. They became the initial guidelines that stimulated the company's very successful development over the next decade.

> The president of another large consumer products company was trying to develop a posture to deal with ever increasing government regulation in his field. He said, "I have started conversations with anyone inside or outside the company who can help me. I don't know yet what we should do. And I don't want to take a stand we can't all live with. Before we make any irrevocable decisions, I'll want a lot of advice from those people in the company who understand the specific problems better than I do. And I'll want everyone pulling together when we do set our course."

Far from stimulating desired participation, goal announcements can centralize the organization, rigidify positions too soon, eliminate creative options, and even cause active resistance to the goals themselves.

Focus for Opposition

Further, explicitly stated goals—especially on complex issues—can provide focal points against which an otherwise fragmented opposition will organize. Anyone with political sensibilities will understand this phenomenon. For example, President Carter's stated energy plan immediately drew the adverse comments of many parochial interests who only opposed a specific part of the plan. But soon these highly fragmented forces appeared unified in their opposition to the total plan, and each fragment gained added credibility from this apparent unity. In a like manner, a "land use plan" or a "zoning ordinance" quickly becomes a coalescing element for many disparate interests in a town. In industry, department or division heads, who compete fiercely on most issues, can become a formidable power bloc against some announced thrust which affects each only marginally. For example:

> In a textile fibers company strong marketing, production, and R&D managers—who fought each other constantly—formed a potent coalition to resist a "product management" scheme to coordinate the very things that caused their friction. And in decentralized companies powerful product division heads have forced new CEOs to give up, get out, or revert to acquisitions—rather than accept new interdivisional goals pushed from the top.

Because of such potential opposition, experienced executives are reluctant to put forward complete "goal packages" which could contain significant points of controversy. Instead they progress by building consensus around one—or a few —important new goal(s) at a time. This in part explains the "incrementalism" so often observed in organizations.

Rigidity

Once a top executive publicly announces a goal, it can become very difficult to change. Both the executive's ego and those of people in supporting programs become identified with the goal. Changing the goal broadcasts that the executive was in error and that all those pursuing the goal were on the wrong track. As a consequence, people doggedly prolong outmoded—but publicly committed— goals, rather than swallow losses and move on.

> The government constantly continues obsolete military, energy, and social programs for just such reasons. Corporate bankruptcy lists are rampant with conglomerates, banks, transportation companies, and real estate ventures under duress because their officers tried frantically to fulfill announced—but unrealistic—growth goals.

> By contrast, the vice-chairman of a multibillion dollar consumer products company said, "We don't announce growth goals in new areas precisely because we don't want to be trapped into doing something stupid. We might be tempted to acquire a company when we shouldn't. Or we might hang on to an operation we really should sell off. Public statements can sometimes generate powerful expectations—internally and externally—that can pressure you to do the wrong thing."

Top managers generally like to keep their options open as long as possible, consistent with the information they have. One way to accomplish this is to define only broad directions, then respond to specific, well-documented proposals. There is an additonal advantage to this approach. The proposers are more likely to identify with their proposition and see it through. Again, this is part of the logic behind incrementalism.

> As one vice-president in charge of diversification said, "Our management doesn't state a specific diversification goal requiring so many millions in profits and sales within five years. Instead we say 'we want to be a competitive factor in [a designated] industry in five years.' This keeps us free to approach each field flexibly as opportunities develop. And we don't get committed until we have concrete numbers and proposals to look at."

Security

There are still other good reasons why effective top managers do not announce goals explicitly or widely. In any healthy organization good people constantly bubble out to head other enterprises. Thus, top executives are justifiably reluctant to provide potential competitors with specific information about their future moves.

> When talking to the investment community or his vice-presidents, Tex Thornton was never very specific about the sequence and timing of his plan during Litton's rapid growth phase. Advance knowledge of Litton's interest could have inflated an acquisition's stock price, activated other potential acquirers, or caused third parties to intervene. With large numbers of Litton executives being sought by other companies, it would have been folly to disclose acquisition goals in detail. In addition, more general goals allowed Litton needed flexibilities to consider new opportunities as they became available.

Further, as one chief executive said, "the future can make fools of us all." There are many examples of former high executives ousted because unforeseen events made it impossible to fulfill ambitious announced goals.

> In the late 1960s the president of a large consumer products company announced to all his goal of 10 percent profit growth per year. But many in the company regarded this as his goal—not theirs. Despite some impressive successes, the president was hung for a failure to meet this goal in two successive years while he was trying to develop some entirely new ventures within the company. When these were slow in materializing, his vice-presidents gleefully saw that the original goal was well remembered at the board level. The embarrassed board, which had earlier approved the goal, terminated the president's career.

There are many other situations—like divestitures, consolidations, or plant closures—where managers may not announce goals at all until after they are accomplished facts. These are just some of the reasons why top managers do not follow the conventional wisdom about announcing goals. The few goals top managers do announce tend (1) to reflect or help build a developing consensus, (2) to be broad enough in concept to allow opportunism, and (3) to be sufficiently distant in time that a number of possible options could ensure their achievement.

WHEN SHOULD GOALS BE GENERAL?

Conventional wisdom also requires that effective goals be specific, measurable, and preferably quantitative. Many managers actually express embarrassment or frustration when they cannot reach this ideal. But more sophisticated executives find such highly precise goals useful only in selected circumstances. As an executive vice-president of a major automobile company said:

> The decisions where we can set specific numerical goals are the easy ones. Establishing the image of your car line, deciding what posture to take vis-à-vis developing legislation, determining what features the public will want in a car three years from now, setting goals for dealing with worker representation or host country demands abroad . . . those are the tough questions. And they don't have numerical answers.

One can attempt to be verbally precise in such areas. Yet very often a broad goal statement is more effective than its narrower, more measurable counterpart might be. Why?

Cohesion

A certain generality in goals actually promotes cohesion. Many can support continued growth, greater freedom, equal opportunity, full disclosure, or quality products, as organizational goals. But oddly enough, adding more specific dimensions to these broad concepts may quickly complicate communications, lose some individuals' support, and even create contention.

If a community tries to agree on its precise goals in building a new school, it may never reach a sufficient consensus for action. People can differ irreconcilably on whether a traditional, experimental, precollege, classical, or vocational approach should predominate. Yet they might easily agree on a goal to build a new school. Once the broad program is approved, they can resolve some very fundamental value differences by compromising on the much less emotionally charged architectural details.

Similarly, top managers can often avoid serious rifts by focusing agreement on very broad objectives where substantial agreement exists, then treating more specific goal issues as decisions about concrete proposals or program details. Again, incrementalism is logical. For example:

> The new principal stockholder in a mechanical equipment company wanted the company to grow relatively rapidly by selective acquisitions. One of the stockholder's board representatives prepared a detailed outline containing proposed areas for growth and diversification. Some other board members—based on limited experience —immediately took a rigid stance against one specific proposal, i.e. acquisitions in service areas supporting the company's line. Little progress could be made until the principal stockholder's representatives went back and sold the board on an idea they could all agree to, i.e. growth through acquisition. As the board becomes more comfortable with this broad concept, the principal stockholder's representatives still hope to bring in some service company candidates and allay their fellow directors' fears in terms of a specific example.

Identity and Élan

Broad goals can create identity and élan. Effective organizational goals satisfy a basic human need. They enable people to develop an identity larger than themselves, to participate in greater challenges, to have influence or seek rewards they could not achieve alone. Interestingly enough, many employees can better identify with broad goals like being the best or the first in an area than they can with more specific numerical goals. As the chief executive of a major consumer products company said:

> We have slowly discovered that our most effective goal is *to be best* at certain things. We now try to get our people to help us work out what these should be, how to define *best* objectively, and how to *become best* in our selected spheres. You would be surprised how motivating that can be.

Most companies devote great attention to measurable output goals—like size, productivity, profits, costs, or returns—that lack charisma and provide no special identity for their people. Yet they often fail to achieve these goals precisely because their people do not identify sufficiently with the company. To forge a common bond among individuals with widely diverse personal values, expectations, and capacities, such numerical goals must be teamed with goals that satisfy people's more basic psychological needs: to produce something worthwhile, to help others, to obtain recognition, to be free or innovative, to achieve security, to beat an opponent, or to earn community respect. While such organizational goals must be general enough to achieve widespread support, they must also clearly delineate what distinguishes *us* (the identity group) from *them* (all others).

To improve their competitive postures, executives often consciously define the uniqueness or niche of their company's products, processes, technologies, services, or markets. More thoughtful top managers also carefully analyze whether one strategic goal or another will better attract the skilled people and personal commitments they want. These people's talent and dedication then become the central strengths upon which the organization's success is built. An IBM salesman, a Bell Labs researcher, a *New York Times* stringer, or a Steuben glassblower all enjoy a special élan—as do millions of others whose organizations achieve a unique identity. This élan provides a special psychic compensation for the people involved, and symbiotically it becomes their organization's most priceless asset. More often than not such élan develops around broad conceptual goals rather than precise mathematical targets.

WHEN SHOULD GOALS BE SPECIFIC?

Contrary to conventional wisdom, relatively few strategic goals need to be mathematically precise. Properly derived, those few can provide essential focal points and stimuli for an organization. However, they should be generated with care and used with balance.

Precipitating Action

By making selected goals explicit at the proper moment, managers can create a challenge, precipitate desired discussions or analyses, or crystallize defined thrusts. For example:

> The president of a major packaging company wanted to move his organization in new directions. He first unleashed a series of management, staff, and consulting studies to help define the company's weaknesses and major opportunities for improvement. These were circulated as "white papers" for discussion by his top management team. After a while consensus began to emerge on critical issues and options. The president began to reinforce one: the need to work existing assets much harder. In further discussions his organization crystallized this concept into a specific target return on net assets—vastly higher than the current return—as a principal goal for 1981. This goal triggered the shutdown of excess facilities, a new focus on profitability rather than volume, and a profit-centered decentralization of the whole organization.

Under these circumstances, after building consensus around a broad goal, the top executive may merely approve its specific manifestation. Although the goal is a challenge, his own organization has recommended it. The executive knows that it is feasible, and key people understand and support the goal. The time horizon is sufficiently distant to allow for alternative approaches which will insure its achievement.

Major Transitions

Specific new goals also can help signal a major change from the past. Properly developed, they can challenge lower levels to propose specific solutions, yet not unduly constrain their approaches. To be effective they must build on some accepted values in the organization and leave time enough for proposed new programs to reach fruition. For example:

> After much discussion, an aerospace company's top management established the goal of moving 50 percent into nongovernmental business within a decade. This started a furor of creative proposals. Research put forward new technical concepts. Each division proposed how it could best realign its own business. Corporate staff units investigated industries and specific companies for acquisitions. The administrative vice-president recommended a new control system to handle diversification. Revised banking relations were proposed. And so on. From all these thrusts top management slowly chose its desired pattern of internal versus external growth, market sectors, organizational form, and financial structure. Throughout lower levels felt their ideas were appreciated, and they identified with changes made.

After a prolonged disaster or a major trauma, an organization often needs distinct and clear new goals. Typically these must combine a broad definition of long-term success and some specific, achievable, short-term goals to build confidence. Without visible intermediate goals, people can become frustrated and give up on the ultimate challenge.

Only A Few

At any given moment, an executive can push only a few specific new goals, giving them the attention and force they need to take hold. Fortunately a top executive rarely needs to press more than a few significant changes simultaneously. In fact, the essence of strategy is to identify this small number of truly essential thrusts or concepts and to consciously marshall the organization's resources and capabilities toward them. Then—to capture the organization's attention—the executive must consistently reinforce these strategic goals through his statements, his decision patterns, and his personnel assignments. He must be willing to put his credibility on the line and use the power and sanctions of his office to achieve them. Still, the typical organization's ongoing momentum and resource commitments will allow it to absorb only a few major changes at once.

Two examples illustrate the complex interactions that lead to success or failure when setting specific goals at the top level:

In 1969, RCA's chairman, Robert Sarnoff, initiated several major new thrusts simultaneously. While repositioning RCA in its traditional electronics-communications markets, he actively diversified the company through acquisitions. At the same time he also strove (1) to build RCA's computer activities into an effective direct competitor of IBM, (2) to move the company's technological efforts from research toward applications, and (3) to strengthen the company's lagging marketing capabilities. He implemented much of this through an enlarged central corporate staff. It was difficult for the organization to absorb so much top level initiated change at once. Various aspects of the program met intense resistance from existing divisions. The computer venture failed, and Mr. Sarnoff's credibility with the organization became strained to the breaking point.

By contrast, shortly after Philip Hofmann became chairman of Johnson and Johnson, he announced a specific new goal of $1 billion in sales (with a 15 percent after tax return on investment) before his retirement some seven years later. Annual sales were then approximately $350 million. Though the challenge was startling in scale, it built upon an established growth ethic in the company, and it did not constrain potential solutions. Instead it stimulated each division to define how it could best respond, thus maintaining the company's intended decentralization. It also allowed sufficient time for managers to propose, initiate, and carry out their new programs. Performance ultimately surpassed the goal by a comfortable margin.

At some point, of course, planning processes must refine goals into specific operational targets. As the examples of successful goal setting illustrate, this is best achieved through incremental, iterative processes which intimately involve those who have to implement the proposed strategic thrusts.

ARE EFFECTIVE GOALS SO IMPORTANT?

All the concepts above help insure that strategic goals are set (1) at the right time, (2) with maximum input from those who have the most specific knowledge, and (3) with the genuine commitment of those who must achieve results. Why should managers take such care in developing and expressing organizational goals? Effective strategic goals do more than provide a basis for direction setting and performance measurement. They are essential to establishing and maintaining freedom, morale, and timely problem sensing in an enterprise. The benefits of effective goal setting are greatest when people throughout the organization genuinely internalize the goals and make them their own.

Freedom with Control

If people share common purposes, they can self-direct their actions with minimum coordination from executive or staff groups. This is especially critical for creative groups like research, advertising, or strategic planning. Without such goal congruence, control of these activities is impossible. No amount of *ex post facto* performance measurement can insure that creative people imaginatively identify proper problems, generate imaginative alternatives, or invent new or responsive solutions. Such actions must be stimulated before the fact by ensuring that well-selected people understand and internalize goals.

Morale

Morale is a goal-oriented phenomenon. In a high morale organization people intensely share common performance goals. They ignore internal irritations and adapt rapidly to external stimuli which help or hinder goal accomplishment. Enterpreneurial organizations, project teams on urgent tasks, dedicated medical groups, or even whole societies (like Israel or Japan) exhibit these characteristics. A specific industrial example suggests how powerful the symbiotic effect of a stimulating goal and talented people can be:

> From 1970–1976 tiny KMS Industries supported the world's most advanced laser fusion program for commercial energy production. As one executive said, "I don't know any of us who didn't agree that this was the most important task in the world. We thought we could lick the fight. If successful, we would have a new basis for creating energy, hydrogen, and hydrocarbons. It would make the U.S. and other nations independent of world energy markets. People on the fusion program had extremely high morale. They would work all night. They were thoroughly committed." On May 1, 1974—despite much larger AEC and Russian expenditures in the field—a KMS team achieved the world's first "unambiguous" release of neutrons from laser fusion.

A contrasting example makes the opposite point:

> The dominantly shared goal of many a government (or staff) department is the preservation of its members' positions and budgets. Lacking shared—or often even understood—performance goals, such organizations become "hotbeds of inertia." They focus extraordinary energies on minor internal irritants. When disturbed by external stimuli they operate with awesome tenacity to reestablish accepted interpersonal and political equilibriums even to the point of negating their own output and jeopardizing their continuation.

Often managers spend enormous time trying to ease or resolve the interpersonal tensions in such organizations, but they accomplish little until they can get people to accept a new sense of common purpose.

Problem Sensing

Finally, goals help define problems. Organizations without a strong sense of broad purpose can precipitate their own demise by ignoring major problems or overlooking alternatives. Some companies define their services, concepts, and goals with such limited vision that they screen out major opportunities. Others have elaborately worked out goal statements covering broad issues, but their control and reward systems reinforce—and cause people to internalize—only a few. When people do not internalize an adequate range of goals, the consequences can be extremely costly.

> In the late 1960s many conglomerates proudly concentrated on "managing business as a financial enterprise." Their control and reward systems focused so much attention on continuously improving short-term financial performance that their managers often screened out other important issues as "nonproblems." This led them to under-

cut research and technology, product and personnel development, plant investments, international relations, and perhaps even ethics to an extent that sometimes jeopardized their companies' very viability.

Recently the chairman of a multibillion dollar diversified company publicly decried the $35 million his divisions would expend on depollution measures. It was clear that he perceived environmentalism only as a threat. Yet one division of his company (auto exhaust systems) was likely to sell an additional $600 + million of its product annually—with corresponding profits—because of the same environmental standards he resisted as a total loss to the company.

WILL CONVENTIONAL PROCESSES WORK?

If goals are to stimulate freedom with control, high morale, and creative problem solving, people throughout the organization must understand and actively identify with them. Usually this requires the genuine participation of many individuals in setting and modifying the goals. Yet the manager must not lose control over this vital process. He must carefully blend consultation, participation, delegation, and guidance to achieve his purposes. How can he manage this complex art?

Bottom Up

The philosophers' ideal is to arrive at goal consensus through democratic discussion or through bottom-up proposals. These views often prevail within small company, Japanese, or Theory *Y* managements, and they clearly have merit for some organizations.

However, such approaches are very time consuming and can prove to be frustrating, wasteful, or even divisive. Opaque committee discussions can go on endlessly and still leave individuals with different views of what goals were agreed on. People may expend extraordinary time and energy on proposals that management later rejects as irrelevant. They feel angry or manipulated when their carefully prepared proposals or goals are overruled for other organizational purposes only fully appreciated from on high.

Unwitting Bureaucracy

Managers of large enterprises rarely feel they can afford a purist approach to democratic goal setting. At the same time they sense the shortcomings of goals announced from above. Consequently, a pragmatic compromise emerges. Top managers often provide a framework of broad goals for their subordinate units. They then encourage lower level managers to make proposals which respond to these goals through planning, budgetary, and *ad hoc* processes. Before the proposals reach final approval stages, a series of staff interventions, personal discussions, and intermediate reviews tune them toward what various people think top management wants and will accept.

This process brings a kind of collective wisdom to bear. There is some personal involvement at all levels. But often a bland, committee-like consensus emerges. This process works moderately well for routine modifications of existing thrusts, but it discourages significant changes in organizational goals. Thus, unwittingly, most large enterprises become conservatively bureaucraticized. They continue existing momenta and overlook major external changes or new opportunities.

HOW DO MANAGEMENTS EVOLVE EFFECTIVE STRATEGIC GOALS?

Dramatic new strategic goal-sets rarely emerge full blown from individual bottom-up proposals or from comprehensive corporate strategic planning. Instead a series of individual, logical, perhaps somewhat disruptive decisions interact to create a new structure and cohesion for the company. Top managers create a new consensus through a continuous, evolving, incremental, and often highly political process that has no precise beginning or end. A well-documented example—one with which many readers will be familiar—illustrates important dimensions of this logical incremental approach to strategic goal setting.

> IBM's strategic goal of "introducing its 360 computers simultaneously as a single line with compatibility, standard interface, business and scientific capability, hybrid circuitry, and the capacity to open new markets" probably started in 1959 when T. Vincent Learson became head of the Data Systems and General Products divisions. The divisions' product lines had begun to overlap and proliferate, causing software, cost, and organizational problems. Top managers sensed this, but no clear solutions were at hand.
>
> In 1960–1961 various specific decisions began to eliminate alternatives and define key elements of the new goal. Proposals for two new computers, "Scamp" and the 8000 series, were killed to avoid further proliferation. In mid-1961 Learson and a subordinate, Bob O. Evans, arrived at a broad concept "to blanket the market with a single product line," and they initiated exploratory studies on a new product line called simply "NPL." During 1961 a special Logic Committee recommended that IBM use hybrid circuitry—rather than integrated circuits—in any major new line. In late 1961 NPL was foundering. Learson and chairman Watson started a series of dialogues on strategy with division heads, but no clear concept emerged. Consequently, they formed the SPREAD committee of key executives to hammer out basic concepts for a new line. In January, 1962, the committee reported and top management approved its recommended concepts for a new integrative product line, now worked out in some detail. Broad top management support and a genuine organization momentum were building behind the new concept.
>
> In 1962 development began in earnest, and IBM's board approved a $100 million manufacturing facility for hybrid circuits. Still, technical difficulties and differences in viewpoint persisted. In late 1962 a special programming meeting was held at Stowe to discuss software development, but major programming problems remained unresolved. In 1963 various groups openly resisted the new line. The opposition was broken up or removed. In December, 1963, Honeywell precipitated action by announcing a strong competitor for IBM's successful 1401 computer. Shortly thereafter, in January, 1964, Learson conducted a performance shoot-out between the 360/30 and the 1401. The 360/30 was judged good enough to go ahead. Final pricing, marketing, and production studies were now made. In March, 1964, top management approved the line in a final risk assessment session at Yorktown. And on April 7, 1964, Watson announced the 360 line. The decision now appeared irrevocable.
>
> But in 1965 and later, new time-sharing features, smaller and larger computers, and peripheral equipment units were announced or "decommitted." IBM raised $361

million of new equity in 1965 to support the line—ultimately investing some $4.5 billion in the 360. Further changes occurred in the line and its supporting hardware and software. Finally, well into the 1970s, the 360 series provided IBM's essential strategic strength, its massive installed computer base. The decision and its impact extended over some 15 years.

The pattern is common. At first there are simply too many unknowns to specify a cohesive set of new directions for the enterprise. More information is needed. Technical problems must be solved to determine feasibilities. Investments must be made in programs with long lead times. Trends in the market place must crystallize into sufficiently concrete demands or competitive responses to justify risk taking. Various resource bases must be acquired or developed. Different groups' psychological commitments must be diverted from ongoing thrusts toward a new consensus. Lead times for all these events are different. Yet logic dictates that final resource commitments be made as late as possible, consistent with the information available—hence incrementalism.

To reshape an organization's accepted culture significantly, an executive must often overcome some potent psychological/political forces. His success will depend on the very group whose perceptions he may want to change. If he moves too precipitously, he can undermine essential strengths of his organization. All too easily he can alienate his people, lose personal credibility, and destroy the power base his future depends on. Unless a crisis intervenes, he cannot change the organization's ethos abruptly. Instead he usually must build commitment— and his own political support—incrementally around specific issues or proposals. The real art is to thoughtfully blend these thrusts together, as opportunities permit, into patterns which slowly create a new logical cohesion.

Changing strategic goals typically involves managing a complex chain of interacting events and forces over a period of years. How do successful managers approach this challenge?

Managing the Incremental Process

For the reasons cited above, a kind of logical incrementalism usually dominates strategic goal setting. This process is purposeful, politically astute, and effective. It starts with needs that may only be vaguely sensed at first and incrementally builds the organization's awareness, support, and eventual commitment around new goals. The stages in this process—though not always the same—commonly recur. These are set forth below. The management techniques used at each stage —also outlined below—are not quite the textbook variety. But seeing these in the context of the total process helps explain their wide use and notable effectiveness. It also explains some of the seeming anomalies and real frustrations of management in large organizations. Managers at all levels should understand how this process operates and how they can best fit into and manage their roles in it.

Sensing Needs. Top executives very often sense needs for strategic change in quite vague or undefined terms, like IBM's *organizational overlap* or *too much proliferation.* Early signals may come from almost anywhere, and initially they may be quite indistinct. Long lead times are often needed to make significant changes. Consequently, effective executives—like Mr. Learson—consciously seek multiple contact points with managers, workers, customers, suppliers, technologists, outside professional and government groups, and so on. They purposely short-circuit all the careful screens an organization builds to tell the top only what it wants to hear and thus delay important strategic signals. They constantly move around, show up at unexpected spots, probe, and listen.

Building Awareness. The next step is very often to commission study groups, staff, or consultants to illuminate problems, options, contingencies, or opportunities posed by a sensed need. These studies sometimes lead to specific incremental decisions. More often they merely generate broadened or intensified perceptions of future potentials. At this stage managers may need to offset the frustration of study groups, who frequently feel they have failed because their studies do not precipitate direct action. But the organization is not yet ready for a decision. Key players are not yet comfortable enough with issues, variables, and options to take a risk. Building awareness, concern, and a comfort factor of knowledge about a situation is a vital early link in the practical politics of change.

Broadening Support. This stage usually involves much unstructured discussion and probing of positions. Earlier studies may provide data or the excuse for these discussions—as in the case of the strategic dialogues at IBM. At this stage top executives may actively avoid decisions, other than agreeing to explore options. Instead they may encourage other key players to see opportunities in a new light, define areas of indifference or concern, and identify potential opponents and points of contention. Whenever possible, the guiding executive lets others suggest new thrusts and maintains the originator's identity with the idea. He encourages concepts he favors, lets undesired or weakly supported options die, and establishes hurdles or tests for strongly supported ideas he may not agree with, but does not want to oppose openly. His main purpose is to begin constructive movement without threatening major power centers. Typically goals remain broad and unrefined.

Creating Pockets of Commitment. Exploratory projects—like NPL—may be needed to create necessary skills or technologies, test options, or build commitment deep within the organization. Initially projects may be small and *ad hoc*, rarely forming a comprehensive program. The guiding executive may shun identity with specific projects to avoid escalating attention to one too quickly or losing credibility if it fails. To keep a low profile he may encourage, discourage, or kill thrusts through subordinates, rather than directly. He must now keep his options open, control premature momentum, and select the right moment to meld several successful thrusts into a broader program or concept. His timing is often highly opportunistic. A crisis, a rash of reassignments, a reorganization, or a key appointment may allow him to focus attention on particular goals, add momentum to some, or perhaps quietly phase out others.

Crystallizing a Developing Focus. *Ad hoc* committees—like the SPREAD committee—are a favorite tool for this. By selecting the committee's membership, charter, and timing, the guiding executive can influence its direction. A committee can be balanced to educate, evaluate, or neutralize opponents. It can genuinely develop new options, or it can be focused narrowly to build momentum. Attention to the committee's dynamics is essential. It can broaden support and increase commitment significantly for new goals. Or it can generate organized opposition —and a real trauma—should top management later overrule its strong recommendations.

At crucial junctures the guiding executive may crystallize an emerging consensus by hammering out a few broad goals with his immediate colleagues and stating some as trial concepts for a wider group to discuss. He may even negotiate specific aspects with individual executives. Finally, when sufficient congruence exists or the timing is right, the goal begins to appear in his public statements, guidelines for divisions, and other appropriate places.

Obtaining Real Commitment. If possible, the executive tries to make some individual(s) explicitly accountable for the goal. But he often wants more than mere accountability—he wants real commitment. A major thrust, concept, product, or problem solution frequently needs the nurturing hand of someone who genuinely identifies with it and whose future depends on its success. In such cases, the executive may wait for a champion to appear before he commits resources, but he may assign less dramatic goals as specific missions for ongoing groups. Budgets, programs, proposals, controls, and reward systems must now reflect the new goal, whether or not it is quantitatively measurable. The guiding executive sees to it that recruiting and staffing plans align with the new goal and, when the situation permits, reassigns its supporters and persistent opponents into appropriate spots.

Continuing Dynamics. All the above may take years to effect—as it did in IBM's case. Over this time horizon, the process is rarely completely orderly, rational, or consistent. Instead the executive responds opportunistically to new threats, crises, and proposals. The decision process constantly molds and modifies his own concerns and concepts. Old crusades become the new conventional wisdom; and over time totally new issues emerge.

Once the organization arrives at its new consensus, the executive must move to ensure that this does not become inflexible. In trying to build commitment to a new concept, one often surrounds himself with people who see the world the same way. Such people can rapidly become systematic screens against other views. Hence, the effective executive now purposely continues the change process with new faces and stimuli at the top. He consciously begins to erode the very strategic goals he has just created—a very difficult psychological task.

CONCLUSION

Establishing strategic goals for complex organizations is a delicate art, requiring a subtle balance of vision, entrepreneurship, and politics. At the center of the art one finds consciously managed processes of broad goal setting and logical incrementalism. Management styles vary, but effective top executives in large enterprises typically state a few broad goals themselves, encourage their organizations to propose others, and allow still others to emerge from informal processes. They eschew the gimmickry of simplistic formal planning or MBO approaches for setting their major goals. Instead they tend to develop such goals through very complicated, largely political, consensus-building processes that are outside the structure of most formal management systems and frequently have no precise beginning or end.

Those who understand these processes can contribute more effectively, whatever their position in the organization. Those who wish to make major changes in organizations should certainly comprehend these processes, their rationale, and their implications. Those who ignore them may find the costs very high.

REFERENCES FOR ARTICLE

1. BOWER, J. L. "Planning within the Firm." *American Economic Review* (May, 1970).
2. BOWMAN, E. H. "Epistemology, Corporate Strategy, and Academe." *Sloan Management Review* (Winter, 1974), pp. 35–50.
3. COHEN, K. J., and R. M. Cyert. "Strategy, Formulation, Implementation, and Monitoring." *Journal of Business* (July, 1973).
4. FRANK, A. G. "Goal Ambiguity and Conflicting Standards." *Human Organization* (Winter, 1958).
5. GUTH, W. D. "Formulating Organizational Objectives and Strategy: A Systematic Approach." *Journal of Business Policy* (Autumn, 1971).
6. HALL, W. K. "Strategic Planning Models: Are Top Managers Really Finding Them Useful?" *Journal of Business Policy* (Winter, 1972/1973), pp. 33–42.
7. HUNGER, J., and C. STERN. "An Assessment of the Functionality of the Superordinate Goal in Reducing Conflict." *Academy of Management Journal* (December, 1976).
8. LATHAM, G. P., and G. A. YUKL. "Review of Research on the Application of Goal Setting in Organizations." *Academy of Management Journal* (December, 1975).
9. LINDBLOM, C. E. "The Science of 'Muddling Through.' " *Public Administration Review* (Spring, 1959).
10. MINTZBERG, H. "Strategy-Making in Three Modes." *California Management Review* (Winter, 1973).
11. PFIFFNER, J. M. "Administrative Rationality." *Public Administration Review* (1960), pp. 125–132.
12. SIMON, H. A. "On the Concept of Organization Goal." *Administrative Science Quarterly* (June, 1964).
13. SOELBERG, P. O. "Unprogrammed Decision Making." *Industrial Management Review* (Spring, 1967), pp. 19–29.
14. TOSI, H. L., J. R. RIZZO, and S. J. CARROLL. "Setting Goals in Management by Objectives." *California Management Review* (Summer, 1970), pp. 70–78.
15. VANCIL, R. F. "Strategy Formulation in Complex Organizations." *Sloan Management Review* (Winter, 1976), pp. 1–18.

20 • CRITERIA OF ORGANIZATIONAL EFFECTIVENESS[1]

Stanley E. Seashore[2]

Summary: Most organizations have many goals, not one. These goals are of unlike importance and their relative importance changes. Problems arise because these goals are sometimes competing (i.e., have trade-off value), and sometimes incompatible (negatively correlated). A strategy of optional realization of goals cannot be determined unless there exists some conception of the dimensions of performance, their relative importance, and their relationships with one another. These relationships may be one of causation, of simple correlation, of interaction; they may be linear and compensatory or nonlinear and noncompensatory. A framework is proposed for conceptualizing organizational performance, with distinctions among several different classes of performance dimensions and with consideration for several types of relationships among them.

MULTIPLE, CONFLICTING GOALS

The aim of the following discussion is to outline a way of viewing the relationships among the numerous criteria that might be considered in the evaluation of the performance of an organization. To understand such relationships we shall need to make some distinctions between different kinds of criterion measures. We shall need to create some encompassing conceptions that serve to aid the evaluation of performance when some desired measures are not available, or when the number of measures is inconveniently large.

The issues taken up here arise because most organizations have multiple goals rather than a single goal, and goal achievement may not be directly measurable. The formal objectives of the organization may themselves be multiple and, in any case, there are multiple shortrun goals and subgoals that need to be examined. The matter would be simple if the various goals were all of similar priority and combinable in some simple additive way; but this is not the situation. The manager making decisions that rest upon multivariate assessments of the performance of his organization has to calculate the weights and the correlation values that he will apply when estimating the net outcome of a course of action.

A typical example would be the case of a manager who wishes his firm to obtain a substantial profit, and at the same time to grow in size, to insure future profit by product improvements, to avoid financial risk, to pay a substantial annual dividend to his investors, to have satisified employees, and to have his firm respected in the community. He cannot maximize all of these simultaneously, as increasing one (e.g. dividends or risk avoidance)

---

[1] From *Michigan Business Review* (July, 1963), pp. 26-30. Reprinted by permission of *Michigan Business Review*.
[2] Stanley E. Seashore, Professor of Psychology and Assistant Director of the Institute for Social Research, the University of Michigan.

may imply reduced achievement on another (e.g. growth, product research). He must consider their "trade-off" value, their contingencies, and the presence of negative correlations among them. To estimate an optimum course of action he has to evaluate the dependability and relevance of the various measures and then estimate the way in which they combine to provide an overall evaluation of performance or a prediction of future change in performance. This task will be easier when we have for his use a theory to describe the performance of organizations. The following suggestions are a step in that direction.

CRITERIA AND THEIR USES

To begin with we need to make some distinctions among different kinds of criteria and their uses.

1. *Ends vs. means.* Some criteria are close to the formal objectives of the organization in the sense that they represent ends or goals that are valued in themselves; others have value mainly or only because they are thought to be necessary means or conditions for achieving the main goals of the organization. Substantial profit, for example, may be a goal sought by a business organization, while employee satisfaction may be valued because it is thought to be an aid in reaching the goal of substantial profit.

2. *Time reference.* Some criterion measures refer to a past time period (profit for the past year), others to current states (net worth), and still others to anticipated future periods (projected growth). Whatever their time reference, all may be used for drawing inferences about past or future conditions or changes.

3. *Long vs. short run.* Some criterion measures refer to a relatively short period of time, others to a longer period; they may refer to performances that are relatively stable (do not change much in the short run). The usefulness of a criterion measure is limited if the period covered is not appropriate to the usual or potential rate of change in the variable. [3]

4. *"Hard" vs. "soft."* Some criteria are measured by the characteristics of, or number or frequency of, physical objects and events, while others are measured by qualitative questions put to people. Dollar measures, for example, or tons of scrap, or number of grievances, are "hard" measures; while employee satisfaction, motivation to work, and cooperation, product quality, customer loyalty, and many others are usually "soft." The distinction is useful, but it contains a trap, for we commonly think of the hard variables as being in some way inherently more valid, more reliable, and relevant to the performance evaluation problem when

---

[3] Many firms, current operating and financial statistics, although appropriate for control and accounting purposes, prove to be of little value for performance evaluation for the reason that they are short-period measures of unstable performances. Monthly plant maintenance costs, for example, may be extremely variable (perhaps seasonal) and may be useful as a performance criterion measure only when applied to longer periods of time. In the short run, apart from other considerations, low maintenance costs may or may not be a favorable indicator.

this is not necessarily true. Profit rate, for example—a popular hard variable—is a rather vague concept to begin with (accountants dispute about definition and about conventions for measurement) and it is often in the short run unreliable as a performance and thus quite irrelevant to the evaluation problem, even for an organization whose long-run goals include making a profit. Similarly, a soft variable, such as one representing the intentions of key executves to stay with the organization, may be measured with high reliability in some circumstances and may be vital in the assessment of the organization's performance.

5. *Values.* Some variables appear to have a linear value scale (more is always better than less), while others have a curvilinear scale (some optimum is desired; more and less are both to be avoided). The shape of the curves determines in part the trade-off relationships among assessment variables under conditions where simultaneous optimization is not possible. Examples: profit rate is usually linear in value in the sense that more is better than less; maintenance costs, by contrast, are usually curvilinear in value in the sense that either excessively high or low costs may be judged to diminish overall firm performance.

THE HIERARCHY OF CRITERIA

A full accounting for the performance of an organization requires consideration for (1) achievement of the organization's main goals over a long span of time, (2) performance over shorter periods on each of those criteria that represent ends valued in themselves, and which, jointly, as a set, determine the net ultimate performance, and (3) performance on each of a number of subsidiary criteria that provide an immediate or current indication of the progress toward, or probability of achieving, success on end-result variables. The network of criteria of performance can be viewed as a pyramid-shaped hierarchy:

1. *At the top* is the "ultimate criterion"—some conception of the net performance of the organization over a long span of time in achieving its formal objectives, whatever they may be, with optimum use of the organization's environment resources and opportunities. The ultimate criterion is never measured (except possibly by historians); yet some concept of this kind is the basis for evaluation of lesser criteria of performance.
2. *In the middle* are the penultimate criteria. These are shorter run performance factors or dimensions comprised by the ultimate criterion. They are "output" or "results" criteria: things sought for their own value and having trade-off value[4] in relation to each other. Their sum, in some weighted mixture, determines the ultimate criterion. Typical variables of this class for business organizations are: sales volume, productive efficiency, growth rate, profit rate, and the like. There may be included some "soft" (usually behavioral) variables such as employee satisfaction or customer satisfaction. In case of some nonbusiness organizations these penultimate criteria might be predominantly of the behavioral kind, as in the case of a school whose output is judged in terms of learning rates,

---

[4] By trade-off value we mean only that an amount of one kind of performance may be substituted for an amount of another; for example, an increase in sales volume may be judged to offset a decline in profit rate per sales unit.

proportion of students reaching some standard of personal growth or development, etc.[5]

3. *At the bottom* of the hierarchy of assessment criteria are measures of the current organization functioning according to some theory of some empirical system concerning the conditions associated with high achievement on each of the penultimate criteria. These variables include those descriptive of the organization as a system and also those representing subgoals or means associated with penultimate criteria. The number of criteria in this class is very large (over 200 have been used in some studies without sensing that the limits were being approached), and they are interrelated in a complex network that includes casual, interactional, and modifier types of relationships. Included are some criteria that are not valued at all except for their power to reduce the amount of uncontrolled variance in the network. Among the "hard" criteria at this level, for a business organization, might be such as: scrappage, short-run profit, productivity against standards, meeting of production schedules, machine downtime, ratio of overtime to regular time, product return rate, rate of technological innovation, and the like. Among the "soft" criteria at this level may be such as these: employee morale, credit rating, communication effectiveness, absenteeism, turnover, group cohesiveness, customer loyalty, pride in firm, level of performance motivation, and others.

CHARACTERISTICS OF BEHAVIORAL CRITERIA

Such a model locates the behavioral criteria—those descriptive of the members (in this context, customers and clients are also "members") of the organization and of their values, attitudes, relationships, and activities—mainly in the lower regions of the network of assessment criteria, distant and perhaps only indirectly related to the ultimate goals by which the organization is eventually judged.

If behavioral criteria appear near the top of the network, it is because they are valued in themselves and have trade-off value in relation to other priority goals of the organization. In general, however, the hard—nonbehavioral—criteria are the preferred ones for most business organizations for the good reason that they are more relevant to the formal objectives of the organization.

The behavioral measures are presumed to have some stable relationships to the various nonbehavioral measures: these relationships may be causal, interactional, or merely one of covariance. It is further presumed that the criteria and their relationships are not entirely unique to each organization, nor transient, but are to some degree stable and to some extent common to all or many organizations. These presumptions appear to have some partial confirmation from analyses performed so far.[6]

[5] One large U. S. firm has published what appears to be a carefully consideration formulation of its own roster of assessment criteria at this penultimate level. It includes one behavioral category, "employee attitudes," which is further defined in operational terms in a manner compatible with the system outlined here.

[6] See "Applying Modern Management Principles to Sales Organizations," Foundation for Research on Human Behavior seminar report, 1963, for an illustration of the similarity across three sales organizations in the relevance of behavioral measures to hard penultimate criteria of organizational performance. Also, "Models of Organization Performance," an unpublished MS by Basil Georgopoulos, Stanley Seashore, and Bernard Indik; and "Relationships Among Criteria of Job Performance," by Stanley Seashore, Bernard Indik, and Basil Georgopoulos, *Journal of Applied Psychology, 44,* 1960, pp. 195-202.

We come now to the question of the role of behavioral criteria in the light of this broader conception of the evaluation of organizational performance. It appears that behavioral criteria are not likely, for most business organizations, to have a prominent place in the roster of penultimate criteria although they may and do appear there. Their chief role will arise from their power to improve the prediction of future changes in the preferred "hard" criteria, i.e., their power to give advance signals of impending problems or opportunities.

A second use that they may commonly have is to complement the available hard criteria in such a way as to give the manager a more balanced and more inclusive informational basis for his decisions in the case where the hard variable measures are incomplete or not reliable for short-run evaluation.[7]

In some rare instances, the behavioral criteria have to be used exclusively instead of the preferred hard criteria of organizational performance for the reason that measurements of hard criteria are not available at all or not a reasonable cost.

There are three basic strategies that may be applied in formulating a unique version of this general scheme that may be appropriate for a particular organization.

1. There exist several partially developed general theories concerning the survival requirements of organizations. These assumed requirements may be defined in performance terms and posited as the roster of penultimate criteria or organizational goals. From this starting point, a set of subsidiary goals and performance criteria may be considered on empirical grounds, on theoretical grounds, or on some combination of the two.

2. The existing personal values of the owners of a firm, or of the managers as representatives, may be pooled to form an agreed-upon roster of penultimate criteria together with their corresponding performance indicators, and from this starting point the set of subsidiary goals and performance criteria can be constructed.

3. Comparative empirical study can be made of the performance characteristics of a set of organizations assumed to share the same ultimate criterion but clearly differing in their overall success as judged by competent observers (for example, such a study might be made of a set of insurance sales agencies, some clearly prospering and others clearly headed for business failure). Using factorial analysis methods and actual performance data to identify the sets of lower-order performance criteria, and using trend and correlational analysis to detect the relationships among these sets of criteria over time, one can, in principle, draw conclusions about the penultimate components of performance

---

[7] An example, a decision to raise prices is likely to rest not only upon estimates of hard performances, past and future, but also upon estimates of political and economic climate, of customer loyalty, of the feasibility of alternatives such as employee collaboration in cost reduction, etc.

that bear upon organizational survival or failure in that particular line of business.

ALTERNATIVE THEORETICAL APPROACHES

These three approaches can and do produce strikingly different systems for describing the network of criteria to be used in evaluating organizational performance. One of the general theories, for example, proposes that there are nine basic requirements to be met, or problems to be continuously solved, for an organization to achieve its long-run goals; these include such requirements as adequate input of resources, adequate normative integration, adequate means of moderation of organization strain, adequate coordination among parts of the organization, etc. Theories of this kind are produced mainly by general organizational sociologists and stem from the view that an organization is a living system with intrinsic goals and requirements that may be unlike those of individual members. By contrast the second mentioned approach stems from the personal values of managers. The resulting networks of criteria are different.[8]

A start has been made at the Institute for Social Research in exploring such alternative strategies. With respect to the first approach, two theoretical models have been tested against empirical data from a set of organizations in a service industry, using executive judgments of unit overall effectiveness as the ultimate criterion. Both models proved to be about equally valid, but of limited utility in explaining variance on the ultimate criterion; each "accounted for" about half of the ultimate criterion variance, with the unexplained portion arising from measurement errors and/or faulty theory. An attempt to apply the wholly empirical approach to the same set of data proved to be a failure in the sense that it was no more powerful in explaining variance on the ultimate criterion than were the simpler, theory-based models, and furthermore the resulting roster of performance dimensions was not very satisfactory in common-sense terms.

A third effort is now in progress, using objective data about the performance of a set of insurance sales agencies over a span of twelve years; the early results look very promising on first examination. It appears that there will be identified a roster of about ten penultimate criteria of agency performance, each independent of the others and of varying weight in relation to ultimate performance, and each associated with a roster of subsidiary criteria of kinds that lend themselves to ready measurement and statistical combination. It remains to be seen whether these criteria are unique to this particular line of business, or have some applicability to other kinds of organizations.

[8] To illustrate, take the criterion of profit: in one case, profit is likely to be treated as one of a few penultimate criteria (ends valued in their own right), while in the other case profit is relegated to a subsidiary role as one of several alternative means for insuring adequate input of resources. If this seems implausible, note that some organizations—government, educational, and religious organizations, for example—have survived and prospered without profit from their own activities.

BIBLIOGRAPHY, CHAPTER 6

Anthony, Robert N. "The Trouble with Profit Maximization." *Harvard Business Review,* Vol. 38, No. 6 (November-December, 1960), pp. 126-134.

Argenti, John. "Defining Corporate Objectives." *Long Range Planning,* Vol. 1 (March, 1969), pp 24-27.

Beard, Donald W., and G. G. Dess. "Industry Profitability and Firm Performance: A Preliminary Analysis on the Business Portfolio Question." *Proceedings of Academy of Management Meetings,* (August, 1979), pp. 123-127.

Bourgeois, L. J. III. "Strategy and Environment: A Conceptual Integration." *Academy of Management Review,* Vol. 5, No. 1 (1980), pp. 25-39.

Branch, Ben. "Corporate Objectives and Market Peformance." *Financial Management,* Vol. 2, No. 2 (1973), pp. 24-29.

Brown, James K. "Corporate Soul-Searching: The Power of Mission Statements." *Across the Board,* Vol. 21, No. 3 (March, 1984), pp. 44-52.

Chidester, Thomas R., and W. Charles Grigsby. "A Meta-Analysis of the Goal-Setting Performance Literature." *Proceedings of Academy of Management Meetings,* (1984), pp. 202-206.

Eilon, S. "Goals and Constraints." *Journal of Management Studies,* Vol. 18 (1971), pp. 292-303.

Gross, Bertram. "What Are Your Organization's Objectives?" *Human Relations,* Vol. 18, No. 3 (1965), pp. 195-216.

Hayes, Douglas A. "Management Goals in a Crisis Society." *Michigan Business Review,* Vol. 22, No. 5 (November, 1970), pp. 7-11.

Kondrasuk, Jack N. "Studies in MBO Effectiveness." *Academy of Management Review,* Vol. 6, No. 3 (1981), pp. 419-430.

Lasagna, J. "Make Your MBO Pragmatic." *Harvard Business Review,* Vol. 49, No. 6 (November-December 1971), pp. 64-69.

Latham, Donald R., and David W. Stewart. "Organizational Objectives and Winning: An Examination of the NFL." *Academy of Management Review,* Vol. 24, No. 2 (June, 1981), pp. 403-408.

Latham, Gary ., and Timothy P. Steele. "The Motivational Effects of Participation Versus Goal Setting on Performance." *Academy of Management Journal,* Vol. 26, No. 3 (September, 1983), pp. 406-417.

McFarlane, Alexander N. "The Search for Purpose." *Conference Board Record,* Vol. 2, No. 2 (February, 1965), pp. 29-32.

Odiorne, George S. *Management by Objectives.* New York: Pitman Publishing Corp., 1965.

Richards, Max D. *Setting Strategic Goals and Objectives.* St. Paul, MN: West Publishing Co., 1986.

Rue, L. W. , and T. B. Clark. "Dangers Inherent in Growth Objectives." *Managerial Planning* (May-June, 1975), pp. 24-28.

Tolchinsky, Paul D. "Do Goals Mediate the Effects of Incentives on Performance?" *Academy of Management Review,* Vol. 5, No. 3 (1980), pp. 455-467.

Urwick, Lyndall F. "The Purpose of a Business." *Dun's Review and Modern Industry* (November, 1955), pp. 51, 52, 103-105.

Wieland, G. F. "The Determinants of Clarity in Organization Goals." *Human Relations,* Vol. 22, No. 2 (1969), pp. 161-172.

Chapter 7

Strategy and the Future

The previous chapter established where the organization is to aim, whereas the following articles examine the states in which the organization is likely to find itself in the future. Two types of forecasting are examined: the economic and demographic types of forecasting with which most firms of moderate to large size are familar. Moyer is definitive in pointing out the potential fallacies of such approaches and the dangers in relying upon plans based upon such forecasts. The question remains, however, of how the firm can reduce the uncertainty it faces. If not forecasts, then which techniques can the firm use to reduce uncertainty to an acceptable level? While there are techniques available for making decisions under uncertainty (or plain ignorance), the practical use of such techniques does not appear to have widespread acceptance. Estimates of future states appear necessary in modern planning. In addition to the usual economic and demographic forecasting, changes in social, psychologic, emotional, and political affairs will be as important as the economic states. Thus, the paper by Wilson outlining a method to assess future sociopolitical conditions is of relevance. The method is particularly applicable for companies engaging in the international arena, at times subject to massive changes or terrorist activities growing out of a mosaic of religious, nationalistic, or tribal foundations. Forecasting within a three- or four-dimensional matrix of factors influencing the organization demands all the help one can muster.

The other two articles are devoted to development of stategy given the environment and an assessment of the competency of the firm. While the process inferred in these articles is rather traditional, it is also rather complex. The leadership of the chief executive in planning efforts at the top level of the corporation is consequently seen as most important if the many phenomena are to be understood and used to the firm's ultimate benefit.

21 • THE FUTILITY OF FORECASTING[1]

Reed Moyer[2]

Samuel Goldwyn allegedly said: 'Never prophesy, particularly about the future'. A review of long-run forecasters' performance records shows that he may have a point. Evidence of forecast performance, analysis of factors contributing to forecast errors, and suggestions for coping with forecast uncertainty form the agenda for this article.

Assume that you, as a forecaster, had had to predict the following:

- In 1845, the 1855 California population.
- In mid-1929, the 1932 level of common stock prices on the New York Stock Exchange.
- In 1945, the demand in 1950 for pleasure aircraft.
- In 1955, the demand for hotel accommodation in 1970.
- In 1955, the installed capacity of nuclear power plants in 1965.
- In 1972, the price per barrel for U.S. crude oil imports in 1975.
- In December, 1978 the world price per ounce for gold in January, 1980. On the latter date, the gold price in mid-1982.
- In 1982, the demand in 1995 for retail banking facilities.

In some instances, wildly inaccurate forecasts of the foregoing phenomena exist; where none is available (e.g. 1855 California population) the possibility of large error is obvious. Some of these forecasts suffered from the intervention of unforeseen events such as the discovery of gold in California. Others fell victim to the effects of depression and inflation, both outside the forecaster's control (outside his ken?). A combination of social and political forces and myopia might have contributed to errors in the other forecasts. One common element exists in the first seven cases: it was easier to look back and see where events had led than to accurately forecast the future. (I include the eighth as an example of a current forecast likely to be off the mark.) No reasonable observer expects completely accurate long-range forecasts. But their importance in sound business planning requires far better results than many have shown.

FORECASTING PERFORMANCE

Obtaining a representative sample of long-range forecasts to test their accuracy is difficult. However, as an alternative, we have available William Ascher's compilation of results of over 165 forecasts in six subject areas. Table 1 summarizes his findings. Let's study them in detail, starting first

[1] Reprinted with permission from *Long Range Planning*, Vol. 17, No. 1, Reed Moyer, "The Futility of Forecasting," Copyright 1984, Pergamon Press, Ltd.
[2] Reed Moyer, Professor, Graduate School of Business Administration, University of California, Berkeley.

with population and economic forecasts that form the basis for many other detailed long-range forecasts.

Population Forecasts

Population forecasts assume special importance since a number of other projections are cast in *per capita* terms. The data in Table 1 on population forecasts reveal an apparently high level of accuracy that is misleading. Median forecast errors for the thirty one 5-, 10- and 20-year forecasts were 2.5, 6.2 and 8.7 per cent respectively.[3] Since over 80 per cent of the population forecasted 10 years hence are alive when a forecast is made, an 11.5 per cent forecast error (see Table 1, 10-year results) is substantial.

There were ten, 20-year forecasts. The 8.7% median referred to averages the two middle forecast even percentages of 5.8 and 11.5.

TABLE 1

LONG-RUN FORECASTING PERFORMANCE

Object of Forecast	No. of Forecasts	Date of Forecast	Period of Forecast	Margin of Error (Arithmetic Mean)
Nuclear power installed capacity	22	1954–1970	5 years	50%
Nuclear power installed capacity	13	Pre-1960	10 years	$4.0 \times$ [1.2]
Nuclear power installed capacity	11	Post-1960	10 years	$1.4 \times$ [1.2]
Electricity consumption	28	1953–1970	5 years	3.5%
Electricity consumption	23	1952–1965	10 years	6%
Electricity consumption	16	1952–1960	15 years	15%
General aviation aircraft sales	3	1944	5 years	224%
General aviation aircraft sales	3	1945	10 years	394%
General aviation aircraft sales	2	1947	8 years	369–381%
General aviation aircraft sales	1	1947	13 years	1310%
General aviation aircraft sales	10	1960–1970	5 years	1–18%
General aviation aircraft sales	3	1960–1970	10 years	19–23%
Commercial airline travel (revenue passenger miles)	n.a.	Post-1953	5 years	~15%
Commercial airline travel	n.a.	Post-1953	10 years	~40%
Commercial airline travel	4	1972	8 years	4.8%
Commercial airline travel	4	1973	7 years	4.0%
Commercial airline travel	2	1974	6 years	19.0%
Commercial airline travel	5	1975	5 years	25.6%
Computer capability	5	1966–1968	7–9 years	$1.6–20.1 \times$ [2]
Population	9	1928–1955	5 years	0.4–6.1%
Population	12	1928–1955	10 years	0.2–11.5%
Population	10	1928–1955	20 years	0.4–20.9%

[1] Median.
[2] Factor of error.
Source: William Ascher, *Forecasting: An Appraisal for Policy-Makers and Planners,* The Johns Hopkins Press, Baltimore (1978).

Accuracy of population forecasts has varied greatly depending on the year when the forecast was completed. A gloomy forecast at the depths of the Great Depression (1930) predicted a decline in U.S. population to 100m by the end of the 20th century.[4] A U.N. report in 1970 predicted a world population in the year 2000 of 7.5bn; 5 years later the estimate was reduced to 5.6bn![5] Forecasts including the period of the post-World War II baby boom were especially flawed. A 20-year forecast in 1938 erred by 17 per cent. One made 13 years earlier, however, that did not have to deal with that baby surge was only 3.4 per cent off target.

Economic Forecasts

Success rates for forecasts of GNP depend, as with population forecasts, partly on the date made and the effect of unforeseen intervening events. Ascher studied real GNP forecasts made by five private and governmental bodies between 1952 and 1968.[6] Predictions for 1965 erred by less than 5 per cent. The 1970 error rate ran from 5 to 10 per cent. GNP forecasts for 1975 made after 1965 had error rates of 15-20 per cent. Predictions of 1975 GNP made in the early part of the 1952-1968 period were no worse on average than those made in later years, and many were superior, despite the forecasts' longer time horizons.

One problem with economic forecasts is the transitory character of some of the forecasts' key elements. Constituents of a GNP forecast are the size of the work force, the unemployment level, the average number of hours worked per worker, and productivity growth. A GNP forecast for a particular year may badly miss the mark because of temporary economic slowdown accompanied by high unemployment and a reduced average work week. This fact should, therefore, condition evaluations of economic (and some other) forecasts. Analysts evaluating the reliability of long term economic forecasts might consider another factor. Ascher's review of 25 long-term forecasts made from 1952 to 1970 found 21 to be overly optimistic.[7] To deal with this condition may require that planners scale back *all* long-range economic forecasts before building their results into business plans.

A final note on economic and population forecasting: attention to the gross numbers for these and other forecasts (e.g. federal budget deficits) may obscure more important forecasting considerations. For example, a 10 per cent shortfall in an estimate of federal revenue receipts might trigger an enormous percentage error in the estimated budget deficit. Alan Reynolds, writing in 1983 during the debate over President Reagan's projected $200bn

---

[4] Julian L. Simon, *The Ultimate Resource,* p. 7, Princeton University Press, Princeton (1981).

[5] *Ibid.*

[6] William Ascher, *Forecasting: An Appraisal for Policy-Makers and Planners,* The Johns Hopkins Press, Baltimore (1978).

[7] *Ibid.,* p. 91.

deficit reinforces this point. He concludes that 'The federal budget deficits are wrong'.

That can be said with certainty, because estimated deficits are always wrong. The Office of Management and Budget was able to get within 25 per cent of estimating the following year's deficit in only three of 14 years. Deficits were underestimated before recessions, but overestimated in four other years by 44 to 141 per cent.[8]

These represent short- rather than long-range forecasts. Longer-term forecasts would presumably increase the size of the error.

Energy Forecasts

The large errors in forecasted installed capacity of nuclear power plants are similar to what we often associated with new technology. Nineteen of the twenty-two 5-year forecasts noted in Table 1 overestimated capacity. A 5 year Atomic Energy Commission capacity forecast as late as 1970 exceeded the actual figure by almost 50 per cent. Its 1980 forecast was 165 per cent too high.[9]

In retrospect, forecasters relied too heavily on estimates of technological development and nuclear power's presumed cost advantage over fossil fuel-fired power plants. These were essentially engineering-based forecasts that failed adequately to account for vital social and political factors. Nuclear power forecasters usually used a component approach whose components were total electrical capacity and nuclear's share of that total. Estimates of the latter were based on such factors as nuclear costs relative to alternative fuels and theoretical S-shaped growth curves. Regional fuel cost variations led to different projected nuclear 'capture' rates in different parts of the country. Site-safety tests and concern for safe waste disposal created delays and higher costs, throwing most of long-term forecasts into disarray. By late 1982, the nuclear power expansion program had ground to a halt.

Electricity consumption forecasts had lower error rates than did forecasts for nuclear power. Forecasts for 1970 made between 1952 and 1969 erred by 18-26 per cent for the early forecasts and less than 5 per cent for the later.[10] Most were *under*estimated. Forecasts for 1975 showed the same pattern until the late 1960s. Thereafter forecast error increased despite a shorter time horizon. Some forecasts issued as late as 1970-1973 overestimated 1975 consumption by 12-18 per cent. Forecasts as late as 1974 missed the mark by roughly 7-11 per cent. Every 1975 forecast made from 1961 to 1974 that Ascher studies (25 in all) overestimated consumption.

---

[8] Alan Reynolds, The OMB's questionable budget estimates, *The Wall Street Journal*, 18 January, p. 26 (1983).

[9] United States Atomic Energy Commission, *Forecast of Growth of Nuclear Power*, January (1971) in National Petroleum Council, *U.S. Energy Outlook: An Initial Appraisal, 1971-1985*, Vol. 1, July (1971).

[10] Ascher, *op. cit.*, p. 106.

The errors are partly due to two common forecasting deficiencies: an unwillingness or inability to recognize long-term trend line changes and a
failure to anticipate and even react to once-for-all trend-shattering events.
The 1970-1975 electricity growth rate fell 42 per cent from the 1965-1970
rate (from 7.9 per cent per year to 4.6 per cent). Part of the reduction
resulted from the aftershock of the 1973 oil crisis.

Forecasts for total energy consumption follow the error pattern of electricity consumption forecasts—generally improved results on 1975 forecasts
through the 1950s and 1960s followed by substantial overestimates thereafter.

Transportation Forecasts

Forecasts for commercial airline travel covered in Table 1 reveal an erratic
pattern. Five-year forecasts made since 1953 had a median error of around
15 per cent. From 1956 to 1959 nearly all of the 5-year forecasts were
overestimates; from 1960 to 1966 nearly all were *under*estimates. For the
next 4 years most forecasts were again optimistic. Longer-term forecasts,
e.g. 10 years, were almost uniformly underestimates. The shorter-term forecast errors point out the importance of such short-run factors as pricing
policies, economic and cost conditions and competitive considerations. The
forecasts covered by the median error of 25.6 per cent for the 5-year 1980
forecasts in Table 1 all represent underestimates. These errors reflected undue
pessimism over anticipated declines in air travel as a result of sharply higher
fuel costs. Longer-term forecast errors probably reflected an inability to
gauge accurately a feasible saturation rate for air travel. Forecasters apparently have been unable to determine the extent to which travellers have been
willing to substitute air travel for other travel modes.

Non-Ferrous Metals Forecasts

Many of the forecasts covered by Table 2 applied to new products and
services where one might expect high error rates. Table 2 presents data for
well-established products—18 non-ferrous metals and metal products.[11] It
compares levels of demand for the minerals in 1972 with those projected
by the Paley Commission 20 years earlier. Comparisons are made both for
the United States and for 'Other Market Economies' (Western Europe,
Canada, Australia and Japan).

Accuracy of the forecasts is less than commendable in both cases,
although the U.S. forecasts are superior to those for Other Market Economies
(OME). Seven of the eighteen U.S. minerals forecasts (39 per cent) are
within 20 per cent of the actual forecasts; none of the OME forecasts fall

---

[11] The material in this section is drawn from William Page and Howard Rush, The
accuracy of long-term forecasts for nonferrous metals, in Tom Wiston (ed.), *The Uses and
Abuses of Forecasting,* pp. 204-226, The Macmillan Press, London (1979).

within that range. By including other minerals forecasts made by the commission, however, the accuracy rate (± 20 per cent) is only 16 per cent. The error factor for the worst U.S. forecast—chromium—2.5; for the OME forecasts the worst performance applies to iron ore with an error factor of 5.6.

Earlier I noted the importance of economic and population variables in determining values for phenomena covered by other forecasts. One would expect an especially close correlation between growth of these basic variables and growth in the demand for minerals which are the building blocks of manufactured output. Table 3, in conjunction with Table 2, allows us to check whether such a correlation exists. This table compares forecasted and actual performance for a number of economic and demographic variables. Forecasted values for these variables buttressed the Paley Commission's minerals forecasts.

The first thing to note about Table 3 is the generally weak forecasting record for these variables. However, unlike the U.S. minerals forecasts which were predominantly optimistic, forecasts for the economic and demographic variables were mostly *under*estimates. Had the latter projections been more accurate (i.e. higher) the minerals forecasts presumably would have been even more inaccurate than they were. In the case of the OME, on the other hand, the commission underestimated economic growth. Improvement in predicting the economic variables doubtless would have improved minerals forecasts for the OME as well.

REASONS FOR ERRORS

Many forces contribute to long-range forecast errors in general. They include the following:

(1) Forecasters may analyse and measure only surface factors and ignore important underlying forces. For example, population projections consider such things as the number of fertile-age women and trend values for numbers of children per family. Equally important and often overlooked are the effects of birth rates on general economic conditions, the growing incidence of dual career families, and the changing social status of child-rearing. Coal demand forecasts have consistently overshot actual consumption. Such 'obvious' measures as long-run reserve availability and favorable cost comparisons *vis à vis* other fossil fuels generate optimistic coal demand forecasts. Analysts fail adequately to consider the negative drag on coal demand from the fuel's undesirable characteristics. Mining it creates safety and environmental hazards; burning it under certain conditions pollutes the atmosphere. In the long run its consumption could create a 'greenhouse' effect with enormously harmful consequences. These adverse characteristics breed political pressure to reduce its use. Failure of coal demand forecasts to factor in this political dimension leads to a continual upward bias.

(2) Long-range predictions pay too little attention to substitution effects. In addition to the factors mentioned above that might confound population

forecasts, couples might decide to substitute travel and other leisure-time activities for expenditures related to child-rearing. There is an infinite variety of expenditure-substitution possibilities. Sone involve the change of one product for another in a particular product class, e.g. coal for oil as a fuel, or electric-driven cars vs those powered by internal combustion engines. Substitution may also occur across product and activity classes—for example, leisure vs babies, or vacation homes vs educational expenditures. Some are hybrids: home video purchases (a capital expenditure for entertainment purposes) vs theater movies (services), or the purchase of personal computers plus assorted peripherals substituting for several products and services.

The more advanced a society economically, technologically and in educational attainment, the greater are substitution possibilities. These devel-

TABLE 2

PALEY COMMISSION: FORECASTED VS ACTUAL DEMANDS
FOR NON-FERROUS METALS, U.S. AND OTHER MARKET
ECONOMIES (THOUSAND TONS)

Mineral	U.S.			Other market economies		
	1970s' forecast	Actual 1972	Forecast/ actual %	1970s' forecast	Actual 1972	Forecast/ actual %
Iron ore	100,000	81,900	122	61,000	404,800	15
Crude steel products	150,000	124,500	138	124,000	280,900	44
Bismuth	1.75	1.46	120	—	—	—
Chromium	1960	558	351	1230	3500	35
Cobalt	20	19.5	103	13	39[1]	33
Manganese	1242	1366	91	—	—	—
Molybdenum	35	25.8	136	13.5	63	21
Nickel	200	246	81	64	309	21
Tungsten	7.5	7.1	106	27.5	35.3[2]	78
Aluminum	3600	4701	77	2400	5600	43
Antimony	28	19.9	141	50	29	170
Cadmium	12.5	6.3	198	6	12.4[1]	48
Copper	1800	1951	92	2050	4024	51
Lead	1200	954	126	1500	2201	68
Magnesium	500	1109	45	—	—	—
Mercury	2.4	2.0	118	—	—	—
Tin	94	49	192	122	199	61
Zinc	1500	1206	124	1700	3289	52

[1] 1974.
[2] Non-communist world production less U.S. consumption.
Source: William Page and Howard Rush, The accuracy of long-term forecasts for non-ferrous metals, in Tom Whiston (ed.), *The Uses and Abuses of Forecasting*, p. 207, The Macmillan Press, London (1979). Reprinted by permission of Macmillan, London and Basingstoke, and Holmes & Meier Publishers, Inc. (in the United States).

TABLE 3

PALEY COMMISSION: FORECASTED VS ACTUAL GROWTH
IN SELECTED ECONOMIC VARIABLES, 1950 TO 1970S[1]
(PERCENTAGE INCREASES)

Variable	Forecast for 1970s (%)	Actual 1972 (%)
Population	27	38
Labor force	27	39
Phones in use	50–85	156
Dwelling units in use	50	60
Gross national product	100	123
Residential construction	15	76
Private non-residential construction	50	380
Demand for new producer durable equipment	50	150
New passenger cars	15	39
New railroad equipment	100	33
Demand for new agricultural machinery	0	52
Demand for new consumer durables	40	285[2]
Shipbuilding	0	− 12

[1] The Paley Report forecasted values for the mid-1970s. 1972 was selected as the last year in the early 1970s that was free from boom or recession.
[2] Personal consumer expenditure on durable goods.
Source: William Page and Howard Rush, ibid., p. 210.

opments increase the number of branches in each person's lifetime decision tree. Since time is fixed for each individual, consumption patterns come close to being zero-sum games. Increased consumption of x may reduce the consumption of y. (This is not completely true since one can, for example, 'consume' both television and the electricity needed to power it as a leisure time substitute for book reading that, during the day at least, may entail no electricity consumption.) Also much increased consumption expenditure represents a move toward higher value added purchases rather than the consumption of more goods. One may acquire a Mercedes-Benz to replace a Chevrolet, or Gucci shoes for sandals. Nonetheless, increased affluence and an enlarged product and service menu fostered by technological developments continually enlarge consumption options. Thus they add to forecasting difficulty.

The substitution effect and the influence of technological developments on product substitution could have accounted for some of the Paley Commission's errors in forecasting minerals demand. For example, overestimates of demand in the United States for iron ore and steel products coupled with underestimates in demand for aluminum could be related if manufacturers substituted one metal product for the other. Moreover, the rapid technological progress that accompanied high economic growth rates in the period covered by Tables 2 and 3 may also have stimulated changes in production processes and the introduction of new products that, together, created unforeseen demand patterns for many minerals.[12]

(3) Assumption problems confound forecasting results. They may take several forms. C. W. Beck, Planning Director for Shell U.K. Ltd., points out one problem—the absence of independent forecasts among rival fore-casters of the same phenomenon. Concerned about the use of inaccurate forecasts in Shell's planning process, Beck found that there were few 'un-correlated estimates' in the work done by so-called independent forecasters whose output Shell tracked. The reason was that they tended to use the same assumptions, figures and theories.[13]

Another problem is what Ascher calls 'assumption drag', that is, the use of outmoded assumptions even when current data counter their validity.[14] This may occur for several reasons:

• Reluctance to question received doctrine.
• Doubt that the data, in fact, negate the assumptions—a feeling that the data represent merely a temporary 'blip'.
• Delay in getting the 'true' data.
• Delay also in constructing the forecast which may render assumptions obsolete.

(4) Other time factors may contribute to forecasting problems. Beck cites the failure of some forecasters to realize the time lags involved with certain developments.[15] Witness the delays associated with attempts in the United States to develop coal slurry pipelines and synthetic fuel plants. Even when technology has been perfected, political, social and economic forces may intervene to delay construction start-up. Also inauguration of other forecasted developments often depends upon phasing out existing facilities, and that may take more time than forecasters have predicted.

Another temporal variable is the forecast's time horizon. The longer the period between the time a forecast is made and its target date, the more opportunity there is for change in the major trend-determining factors. Iron-ically, in some cases longer time horizons lead to improved forecast results as two or more unforeseen developments cancel each other. This condition obtained with a 20 year population forecast made in 1928 that was more accurate than a 10 year forecast completed in the same year. This is an unusual occurrence. The length of forecasts and their degree of error are almost always directly related.

It also appears that some periods of time offer more hazards for fore-casters. A cataclysmic event such as World War II and its aftermath changed a lot of trend lines. Even if the war had been predicted, its social and economic consequences probably could not have been. The manifold in-

[12] See Page and Rush, pp. 209-211, for a review of attempts to account for errors in the Paley Commission's forecasts.

[13] C. W. Beck, Corporate planning for an uncertain future, *Long Range Planning*, 15(4), August (1982).

[14] Ascher, *op. cit.*, p. 53.

[15] Beck, *op. cit.*, p. 15.

crease in crude oil prices is another event with potential for disrupting many forecasts.

(5) Forecasts may err because of errors in forecasts of its components. Many forecasts are summations of predicted values for several constituents of the phenomenon being forecasted. For example steel demand forecasts may result from adding up separate forecasts for major end-use categories. Forecast components may take different forms in other cases. Example: population forecasts based on fertility, mortality and net migration rates. Forecast results may vary because forecasters choose different components. Thus components of an energy demand prediction may be end-user categories (industrial, commercial, residential), or a combination of such things as population and energy use *per capita*.

Forecast accuracy depends, therefore, not only on the choice of appropriate components but on the accurate prediction of the components' future values. The forecaster must contend with exogenous social, cultural and political events that may upset trend values for those components. Often, hard-to-predict technological developments may also alter forecasts. Consider the potential effect, for example, of development of a low cost, implantable artificial heart on population forecasts.

(6) Bias may cause forecast error. Critics of the Club of Rome's doomsday scenario attribute their gloomy resource forecasts to a predisposition to limit growth. Forecasts issued by political units are notoriously error-prone since political expediency often substitutes for objectivity.

HOW TO COPE WITH AN UNCERTAIN FUTURE

The inaccuracy of so many long-range forecasts leads one to question their value. It is unlikely that planners will dispense with them so it remains to consider how to improve them or at least adjust planning to their inaccuracy.

A corrective measure that one might take is to allow for the bias mentioned above. Bias may be self-generated—the planner or forecasters on his staff may naturally incline to optimism or pessimism. Recognizing the bias allows one to adjust to it. More likely is the existence of bias in forecasts issued by government agencies or industry groups either because they are too close to the trees to see the forest or because the forecast is used to further a policy aim. Example: exaggerated Defense Department forecasts of a Soviet military build-up to prod Congress into enlarging the defense budget. Here it pays to recognize the potential for self-interest in the forecast and to monitor the performance of those making the forecast. Evidence of bias should show up fairly quickly.

Bias may account for a familiar forecasting phenomenon—the 'hockey stick' forecast. Here the forecaster says, in effect, 'sales (or whatever else is being forecasted) are declining now, but we foresee them leveling off and then increasing in the future. A graph depicting this sales pattern resembles the configuration of a hockey stick. The Reagan Administration's economic forecasts throughout 1982 fell into the hockey stick category. Whether the optimistic bias was politically motivated, the result of inherent optimism, or the product of inept forecasting is hard to determine.

Government officials are not alone in the use of hockey stick forecasting. The phenomenon also prevails in business, perhaps for the same reasons that motivate its use by government agencies. A hockey stick forecast may reduce pressure on business managers from stockholders and other interested parties when a company's sales and profits decline. The 1981-1983 recession has spawned a surfeit of hockey stick forecasts in business. These forecasts are no better than the assumptions relating to general economic recovery that undergird them.

Checking the validity of forecasts' assumptions may reduce errors associated with them. Every forecast is premised on one or more assumptions covering external factors that affect either the phenomenon being forecast or directly related forces. The first requirement is to recognize and make explicit the assumptions that are built into the forecast. If y depends upon x, the manager should ask what outcome the absence of x implies. If x then does not occur, plans involving the occurrence of y need to be adjusted as quickly as possible. Consider how this approach might have worked when Congress in 1981 enacted tax legislation designed in part to foster increased savings that were expected to finance increased investment. Legislators might have asked: 'If this train of events does *not* occur, can we consider the legislation to have been a mistake, and therefore correct it?'

Having accounted for key assumptions underlying a forecast, continually monitoring them is the next requirement. Do values for the variables underlying the assumptions match one's expectations for them? Some variation is bound to exist. Significant deviation from expected values, however, should trigger an objective evaluation of the assumptions. The analyst should try to determine whether the 'surprises' represent temporary 'blips' or significant changes in trend lines. The latter calls for changes in the forecasts.

Ascher reaches a similar conclusion. Looking ahead, he foresees three developments designed to sensitize long-range forecasts to 'surprise' outcomes. First is the need, as I suggest, to account for deviations from previous patterns. He recommends establishing trend lines from the most current data. The second suggestion is to eliminate plausibility checks. This forecasting technique requires the forecaster to determine whether the forecast's outcome is implausible. If so, it is presumed to be incorrect. But it is in the nature of surprise events to create 'inplausible' outcomes. By eliminating these checks, the forecaster is freer to consider a forecast model's outcome that his intuition, based on conformity, might incorrectly reject. Third, Ascher recommends rejecting consensus forecasts since they tend to average high and low 'surprise' forecasts; hence they probably miss the actual surprise outcomes.

The above techniques may sensitize the forecaster to surprises, but they obviously cannot prevent their occurrence. Basing plans on scenarios rather than forecasts is one way to deal with the uncertainty of political, economic and social systems. P. W. Beck, who advocates using scenarios to overcome the uncertainty that hampers the use of forecasts, says that 'the greatest difference' [between forecasts and scenarios] is in the basic philosophies: forecasts are based on the belief that the future can be measured and controlled. Scenarios are based on the belief that it can not.[16] They have been defined as 'hypothetical sequences of events constructed for the purpose of focusing attention on causal processes and decision points'.[17]

Starting from the premise that business faces an uncertain future, Shell planners argue that their role is not to provide a 'single-line' numerical forecast but to 'promote conceptual understanding'.[18] The scenario says 'here are some of the key factors you have to take into account, and this is the way these factors could affect your line of business'.[19] Unlike the forecast which attempts to quantify the future, a scenario serves as a tool to aid the decision-making process. In practice planners construct multiple scenarios (since one would constitute a single-line forecast). Built into the scenario may be competititve, technical, social, political and economic factors that are woven into an internally consistent pattern.

There are obvious problems with reliance upon scenarios for business planning. One is the difficulty on encapsulating a number of unknowns into two or three tracks down which the firm may travel. Another is ensuring that the variables are internally consistent. Consistency based on past relationships may not apply to a future in which new developments break traditional patterns. How does one account for changes in expectations resulting from unique events that failed to influence previous relationships? For example, recent experience with high inflation rates and uncertainty about future rates of inflation may, for the time being at least, have altered the level of *real* interest rates. Thus a scenario based upon a low level of demand, a low inflation rate and correspondingly low level of interest rates would miss the mark. A firm whose success depended in large part on low interest rates might as a result base it plans on deceptively inaccurate scenarios.

Several management techniques can reduce the risks associated with potential forecasting error. The first is—to the extent possible—to implement plans on a step-by-step basis. This is true especially with capital expenditures and decisions involving product line expansion and market development. Expanding in small modules rather than through large-scale additions to capacity provides the flexibility necessary to respond to faulty forecasts. Avoiding vertical integration also contributes to flexibility. Managements inclined to its use might want to reconsider this policy. Recent research points to some of vertical integration's drawbacks.[20] Not the least of its

---

[16] Beck, *op. cit.*, p. 18.

[17] Herman Kahn and Anthony J. Wiener, *The Year 2000*, The Macmillan Co., New York (1967); Beck, p. 17.

[18] Beck, *op. cit.*, p. 17.

[19] Beck, *op. cit.*, p. 18.

[20] Robert D. Buzzell, Is vertical integration possible? *Harvard Business Review*, 83 (1), January-February (1983).

shortcomings is the increased financial commitment necessary to support plant expansions based on what might turn out to be erroneous forecasts.

This cautious approach obviously copes with overly optimistic forecasts—the usual event—but penalizes the firm when demand levels outpace projections. To allow for this possibility management can contract for a part of its output rather than produce it all itself. Being, say, 80 percent self-sufficient in production provides a comfortable 'fudge' factor in case demand lags forecasted levels, but may also create quick expansion opportunities when the reverse is true. The key here is to negotiate contracted-production arrangements that assure flexible output with acceptable quality control.

Long-range forecasters' ultimate asset may be an apparently ineluctable tendency of phenomena to move toward equilibrium. Force meets counterforce. A phenomenon moving in one direction sets in motion forces that will modify its course. Malthus' population theory recognizes this fact. Nature abounds with examples of the tendency toward homeostasis. Erosion in the demand for oil and in the crude oil price level in early 1983 is a dramatic business world example. There are countless other examples—business cycles, the ebb and flow of interest rates, pendulum swings of social mores and political orientations. Recognizing the existence of a tendency toward homeostasis may reduce forecast error. Still it will remain. Reducing error is a laudable goal but *coping* with it may be more important to the firm's welfare.

22 • PLAYING BY THE RULES OF THE CORPORATE STRATEGY GAME[1]

Walter Kiechel III

In the game of business, the best managers, like the best quarterbacks, have always had some notion of what their game plan should be. But nowadays managers, like quarterbacks, are increasingly looking for expert advice from the sidelines. To be sure, businessmen haven't really relinquished the strategic-planning function to management consultants. But corporations are finding that the tools devised by the consulting industry can help in some aspects of strategic planning—specifically when it comes to scouting out and understanding competitors' strengths and weaknesses and in figuring out how best to deploy their own corporate assets.

The rapid growth of a relatively new industry—strategy consulting—is testimony to the potent appeal of the various conceptual tools. This year companies will pay management consultants well over $100 million for work labeled *corporate strategy.* And talk of new strategic planning systems is cropping up in more and more annual reports.

The efflorescence of interest in strategy has been attributed in part to the increased uncertainty that businessmen feel these days when they contemplate the future—what will government intrusion, roaring inflation, or the sudden appearance of competition from abroad do to them next? If their businesses are going to be buffeted by uncontrollable forces, better to have a systematic plan for dealing with the aspects that *can* be predicted.

DEBUT OF THE S.B.U.

Two or three management-consulting firms, together with a few large corporations, seem to have developed most of the important strategic tools. General Electric, for example, with some help from McKinsey & Co., appears chiefly responsible for an organizational idea central to strategic thinking—the notion that a multiproduct company should be divided up according to the different product markets it serves. By late in the 1960's, GE had consolidated some product lines that were sold to the same customers, and broadened the scope of other operations to better serve particular markets—in one case, turning the "X-ray equipment business" into "medical systems," which in turn led to products exploiting new developments in cardiology and ultrasonics.

As a generic name for these newly defined component businesses, GE coined the term, *strategic business unit,* abbreviated as *s.b.u.* Then, as now, precisely delineating the boundaries of an s.b.u. is more art than science. If it's any help,

[1]From *Fortune* (September 24, 1979), pp. 110–115. Reprinted by permission of *Fortune* magazine.

an s.b.u. looks like a "natural business," could probably be a freestanding enterprise, and churns out, if not one product, a line of products sold to the same set of customers, generally against the same competitors.

The move to s.b.u.'s shifted the attention of GE's managers outward, toward the needs of the marketplace. With a relatively clear-cut idea of the market being served by an s.b.u., together with all the information he could muster on other players in the market, an s.b.u. manager could readily assess his competitive position.

Conceptual developments hatched in Boston around the same time helped to popularize this way of thinking. On July 1, 1963, Bruce Henderson, fresh from a falling out with Arthur D. Little, Inc., set up a one-man, one-desk management-consulting firm under the aegis of the Boston Safe Deposit & Trust Co. Henderson's operation, which eventually was named the Boston Consulting Group, started out to do general management consulting.

Rather quickly, however, B.C.G.'s practice began to tailor itself to fill the gaps that its chief perceived in the area of strategic planning. After attending another consulting outfit's conference on corporate planning, Henderson convened his own seminar on the subject in June, 1964, a response to his conclusion that "everybody was confusing long-range planning with five-year budgets." Pro forma extrapolations from past budgets, says Henderson, merely produced "a lot of lies."

B.C.G.'s first breakthrough idea—and one of the two or three concepts most important in popularizing strategy consulting—was the *experience curve*. It grew out of work done in 1966 for a General Instruments plant making television set components. In the process of studying the company's costs, Henderson discerned a pattern in the way unit costs declined as volume increased. Shortly afterward he read an article about the learning curve, which struck him as helpful in explaining what he had observed. Might not refinements on the old concept enable manufacturers to estimate their future costs at various levels of output? Later, working with data on General Instruments' costs in making semiconductors and with industry data on competitors, Henderson tested his hypothesis and found, in every case, that he could indeed predict cost behavior. He labeled his invention the experience curve.

What made the curve so interesting to businessmen was the linkage B.C.G. posited between it and the dynamics of market share. A company that produces and sells more units of a certain product than any of its competitors is, by definition, the market-share leader. Because it has the greatest volume of production, B.C.G. reasoned, this company should be farther down the experience curve than anyone else—that is, it should be able to turn out its product at the lowest cost per unit. If customers buy the product on the basis of price—a fundamental B.C.G. assumption—then the market leader should be able to steadily increase its share by keeping its prices lower than those of its competitors, whose unit costs, at least theoretically, should be higher.

By using the experience curve, a company can estimate what its costs will be upon achieving a given level of cumulative production. That could lead to a strategic decision to accept lower margins for the time being in order to expand market share, and perhaps the total market as well. Lower unit costs from higher volume later on will push margins up. The eventual outcome, of course, should be greater total profitability.

Assembling all the data that go into an experience curve can be educational in itself. To get information, consultants sometimes stake themselves out in public places, peering through the factory windows of a client's competitor, often with stopwatch in hand. Their mission: to get a fix on production line speed and, ultimately, comparative costs.

TELLING THEM WHAT TO DO

The visceral appeal of the experience curve to practicing managers appears obvious now—it seemed to tell them what to do, based on their product's position relative to the competition. Not airy banalities like "Set objectives" or "Develop a cost reduction program," but rather, "If your product is a strong No. 1 or No. 2, lower prices to gain share from weaker competitors." A product with a sixth or seventh rank market share should be critically examined, and perhaps eliminated.

With the experience curve underscoring the importance of market share, it took only about two years for B.C.G. to develop its second drop dead conceptual tool, the growth share matrix. While the curve might aid in positioning products, the new device promised to assist a corporation in its overall deployment of resources. The matrix seemed to explain how market share, market growth, and cash flows tied together.

In a recent interview, Henderson recounted the line of thought that produced the matrix: "If cost is a function of experience, and experience a function of volume, and volume a function of market share, then cost is a function of market share. But cash is a function of cost, so it too must be a function of market share. That led to the conclusion that, if you have high market share, you must be generating cash, but if you're also growing, you must have high cash use."

Like the experience curve, the growth share matrix offered the businessman a systematic approach to decision making. By arranging his product lines on a four-sector grid, he was able to isolate the businesses that would throw off cash and those that would devour it. The approach encouraged him to look beyond the current year's profit-and-loss statement and to think about where his resources should be deployed long-term.

The Boston Consulting Group was not alone in fostering the conceptual tools that underlie many of today's systematically developed corporate strategies. At approximately the same time that B.C.G. came up with its growth share matrix, McKinsey devised a roughly comparable nine-box matrix. And Texas Instruments built the experience curve into a means for disciplining follow-up to planning. The company requires its managers to "document the major cost-reduction steps that will keep product costs declining as planned."

But there, in most respects, the development of original concepts stopped. Since about 1970 neither B.C.G. nor apparently anyone else has been able to generate new ideas as exciting to businessmen as the s.b.u., experience curve, or the various matrices. A large measure of conceptual work done since then has consisted merely of building upon those devices, e.g., broadening the experience curve to embrace costs shared by different product lines, perhaps to show how one distribution system might be made to serve two products.

THE SEARCH FOR NATURAL LAWS

The failure to produce more breakthroughs is not for want of trying. Henderson, for example, tells visitors to his Boston headquarters that he has just about worked out a "synthetic theory of competition." The theory will "describe the innate behavioral characteristics of firms," and seems to be based in part on the work of nineteenth and twentieth century theorists of evolution. "It is almost a law of nature that if two competitors are identical one will eventually eliminate the other. You cannot find two species anywhere that get their food in exactly the same way." Talk of this sort tends to make some of the young B.C.G. consultants a bit uncomfortable.

Across the river, in Cambridge, the nonprofit Strategic Planning Institute pursues a similar effort, though one employing more rigorous statistical methodology. Under the direction of Sidney Shoeffler, a former economics professor at the University of Massachusetts, the Institute has been using a computer to study the histories of some 1,800 s.b.u.'s. The histories, coded and disguised to protect proprietary information, were submitted by 240 companies that pay $12,000 and up annually to be Institute members.

The Institute's main program, called PIMS—Profit Impact of Market Strategy—had its origins in a project begun at General Electric over a decade ago. Today, according to Shoeffler, the Institute is using this program "to transform the craft of strategic business management into a science," in part by laying bare the "laws of the marketplace."

For their money members get the benefit of the Institute's general conclusions, and the opportunity to try their own "what if" scenarios on its data base. While the Institute resists the idea of looking at particular industries, it will custom-tailor a computer run to discover what happened to businesses, say, with a 20 percent market share and a 5 percent return on assets when they cut back on research spending.

The notion that there are natural laws of business has been met with skepticism, even among consultants. But B.C.G., having gradually bought itself away from Boston Safe, has kept on growing. It now has consultants in seven offices around the world, generating around $35 million in revenues this year. Its clients don't even seem to worry if B.C.G. is working for their competitors. In the last few years, B.C.G. has got business from at least six forest-product companies: Hammermill Paper, International Paper, Mead, Crown Zellerbach, Boise Cascade, and Great Northern Nekoosa.

Thirteen offshoot firms have been established by former B.C.G. staffers. Most are so-called strategy boutiques. They don't do organizational design work, executive compensation studies, or any of the other specialties of the old-line management consultants. Two of them, Bain & Co. in Boston, with 150 consultants, and Strategic Planning Associates, of Washington, D.C., with 75 have already attracted clients with sales in billions of dollars.

Not surprisingly the emergence of these specialists has given rise to some agonizing strategic deliberations among the large general-practice consulting firms. B.C.G. and its progeny have clearly expanded the market for advice on corporate strategy and, in the process, have won business that theretofore would have gone to McKinsey, Arthur D. Little, or Booz, Allen & Hamilton. The traditional firms still suffer a bit from the common perception that they haven't come up with conceptual tools on the order of B.C.G.'s.

The upshot has been at once a scramble for expertise and a debate over the nature of strategy. Arthur D. Little, for example, hired a former employee of the Mead Corporation who had seen what B.C.G. had done in developing Mead's strategy. In August of this year, Booz, Allen persuaded John Roach, a senior consultant in B.C.G.'s Menlo Park office, to come over and help Booz, Allen develop its strategy practice.

On the intellectual front, the competition generally boils down to an argument over the importance of the various tools—curves, matrices—in strategy work. "One of the unfortunate things about the popularization of corporate strategy is that it has wedded people's attention to techniques," maintains Fred Gluck, who heads McKinsey's strategy practice. "The problem is not solely a need for new techniques, but for top management to use the ones we have." As might be expected, McKinsey stresses implementation, operating hand in hand with clients to get plans mutually arrived at to work. Such projects typically cost $100,000 and up.

THE COOKIE CUTTER CHARGE

To some extent, the debate over tools is a phony one, grounded in misunderstanding of what the competing firms actually do. B.C.G. consultants, for instance, while often accused of using a "cookie cutter," or formula, approach to each case, claim they typically spend 60 percent of their time on a detailed analysis of a client's and its competitors' costs for a particular product. Is the client properly spreading corporate expenses across product lines? Does he have a unique method of sale available to him to be used in undercutting the competition?

Such nuts-and-bolts analysis probably doesn't represent the future direction of the business, however. Most consultants are betting that strategy consulting in the eighties will focus on two different areas. The first, they say, will be to help managements cope systematically with problems that transcend concerns about their existing product lines. Can planning tools be devised to serve as a kind of radar that would enable top management to spot in advance public issues that will become entrenched as regulation? Or devices for better forecasting political risks abroad? Or systems useful in sharpening two of any company's most powerful competitive weapons—innovation and productivity? Consultants would have you think these things are doable.

But most managers are still experimenting with the strategic tools developed in the sixties, with mixed results. And almost all consultants think, along with McKinsey, that there will be plenty of business helping companies learn how to make them work. The consultants share a somewhat dirty little secret: Most believe that over 90 percent of American companies, their clients included, have so far proved incapable of developing and executing meaningful corporate strategies.

NO PATHWAY TO THE STARS

Horror stories abound. A Connecticut manufacturer cut prices to gain share, and four years later is still involved in a ruinous price war with competitors. A company with more than $3 billion in sales paid consultants millions to segment its business into 200 or so s.b.u.'s, but now can't do anything with them. And though companies have found the matrices useful in helping them think more clearly about their existing businesses, the grids don't suggest ways to find new stars.

The irony is that only after years of experience with the conceptual tools—pushing them to find out where they don't work and why—will management be able to assign them to their proper place in strategic planning. That done, businessmen will be freed to better use their imagination and inventiveness, qualities that no set of tools can replace.

In this, strategic concepts may be a bit like the rules of the Assassins. That curious medieval sect of Muslim fanatics, we are told, had several orders or ranks, each with its place in an ascending hierarchy. Upon being promoted into the next highest order, initiates would be given a new, and presumably loftier, set of rules to live by. After years during which these strictures became second nature to them, the devout might even find a place in the ninth, or highest order. These few would wait with hushed reverence as the sect's leader welcomed them individually into the elect, whispering into the ear of each the final, ultimate wisdom. The message: There are no rules.

23 • SOCIO-POLITICAL FORECASTING: A NEW DIMENSION TO STRATEGIC PLANNING[1]

Ian H. Wilson[2]

As with any current fancy, there is the danger that management's romance with socio-political forecasting will turn out to be a short-lived affair, weakened by lack of substantive contribution to business planning and crushed by the exaggerated claims of a few enthusiastic proponents.

This would be a pity, if it happened. The need for this new dimension to strategic planning is real and, to a large extent, recognized by managers. What is mainly lacking is an armory of analytical tools and techniques that are available to, say, economic and technological forecasting. And these take time, skill and discipline to develop. Now is the time, then, for a serious evaluation—by managers and forecasters alike—of the progress to date, the potential to be realized, and the programs of research and action to be implemented.

Social Change and the Need for Forecasting

The instincts of those pioneering companies which turned, in the late Sixties, toward some experimentation with social forecasting were right. Something basic *is* changing on the social scene, something that will have profound impact on business, something to which business needs time to adjust. And the hope was, and is, that this forecasting will provide the necessary lead time for companies to develop their "strategies of adjustment."

What are these changes? It is perhaps misleading, in an age and world of discontinuous change, to single out any one particular trend but, for purposes of this article, we can focus on the phenomenon of changing societal values and expectations and the resulting increased politicizing of our economy.

The years 1965-70 were a watershed in U.S. history. The analogy is apt for, since then, the streams of our social thinking have started to flow in quite different directions. We need only consider the changing values inherent in our new perceptions about the right relationship between man and woman, the majority and minorities, the individual and institutions, the economy and ecology, business and society. Among the consequences of these value shifts will be a re-writing of society's "charter of expectations" of corporate performance, and a shaking of what I have termed the "seven pillars of business," those basic values that we have up to now considered

[1] From *Michigan Business Review*, Vol. 26, No. 4 (July, 1974), pp. 15-25. Reprinted by permission from the July, 1974, issue of the *University of Michigan Business Review* published by the Graduate School of Business Administration, The University of Michigan.
[2] Ian H. Wilson, Consultant-Business Environment Studies, General Electric Company.

to be eternal verities undergirding our business system—growth; technology; profit; private property (as it applies to corporations); managerial authority; "hard work"; company loyalty.

Clearly, expectations are on the march and institutions must scurry to keep up with them. By 1970 it was obvious that business could no longer be satisfied with a complacent "other things being equal" formulation to cover the areas of its planning that lay outside traditional economic and technological forecasting. The impact of the various "movements" of the period broke suddenly and forcefully on the unprotected flanks of many companies, causing major disruptions in their plans of action. Lacking strategies to deal with these unexpected forces, companies were forced back on hastily improvised tactics that did little more than stave off one assault before another came.

Such a course of reluctant and belated *re*action is the antithesis of corporate enterprise and initiative on which companies pride themselves and which is an essential prerequisite for the future vitality and legitimacy of the corporation. If business is to reverse this situation and engage in *pro*active strategies to deal with changing social and political forces, it seems logical to conclude that it must, as one condition for success, expand its forecasting system to include these new factors.

A Critique of Objections

Up to this point there would most probably be general agreement with this line of reasoning: the need is apparent and managers are aware, if not of the rewards for success, at least of the penalties for failure. Where uncertainty, and perhaps disagreement, sets in is over the feasibility, scope and effectiveness of any formal venture into socio-political forecasting. The feeling is widespread that there is a basic incompatibility between the "soft" data of social and political analyses and the "hard" data of economic and technological forecasting: that the key strategic issues for business will be almost exclusively economic and financial; and that there is no satisfactory way of making socio-political forecasting contribute effective inputs into the strategic planning process.

Yet experience suggests that each one of these assumptions is subject to rebuttal. And the rebuttals are, of course, interlinked in their rationale.

First, the "hardness" of economic and technological forecasting data seems to be an assumption based on the fact that these data can be more easily quantified. Just how "hard" the data really may be is subject to question when one considers, for instance, the record in economic forecasting. This is said, *not* to damn economic forecasting, but simply to call in question the validity of this alleged dichotomy between "hard" and "soft" data. Forecasts may, in *any* classification, be "right" or "wrong"—which is surely an important and valid difference. But I think we should lay to rest any objection to socio-political forecasting that is based on a supposed incompatibility of data with the more traditional inputs to corporate planning.

A somewhat similar dichotomy appears to underlie the second objection which states, in effect, that the central issues for business will remain economic (market conditions, costs of labor and materials, etc.) and financial (cash flow, availability of capital, etc.), while social and political factors will be peripheral. Admittedly, the rebuttal involves a somewhat circular argument: namely, socio-political forecasting so far undertaken indicates the key importance to business of certain social and political issues which, in turn, argues the case for more such forecasting in the future. For instance, a priority analysis of social pressures on the corporation, undertaken in 1972 for the Public Issues Committee of General Electric's Board of Directors, highlighted the following as key corporate issues of the future:

1. Constraints on corporate growth—a spectrum of issues ranging from national growth policy through economic controls and environmental protection to questions of antitrust policy and industrial structure.

2. Corporate governance—including matters of accountability, personal liability of managers and directors, board representation, and disclosure of information.

3. Managing the "new work force"—dealing with the growing demands for job enlargement, more flexible scheduling, more equality of opportunity, greater participation and individualization.

4. External constraints on employee relations—the new pressures from government (EEO, health and safety, "federalization" of benefits), unions (coalition bargaining) and other groups (class-action suits, "whistle-blowing").

5. Problems and opportunities of business-government partnership—including a redefinition of the role of the private sector in public problem-solving.

6. "Politicizing" of economic decision-making—the growing government involvement in corporate decisions through consumerism, environmentalism, industrial reorganization, inflation control, etc.

It is quite beside the point to argue whether this (or some comparable) listing of issues is *more* or *less* important than economic, financial and technological issues. All that is needed is agreement that they are, and will be, *as* important and central to a corporation, and therefore deserve the same careful forecasting, monitoring and analysis that we now give to the state of the economy, the growth (or decline) of markets and the flow of funds.[3]

What, then, of the third objection? Are socio-political forecasts and analyses doomed forever to be interesting "coffee-table studies" and nothing more? Is it really true that there is no way of placing them in the mainstream of corporate planning? Here perhaps the best answer is provided by our early and, I think, promising experience at General Electric.

---

[3] One overclaim that must be guarded against is the reasoning that political decisions will be the major determinants of the economy, and that political forecasting is *the* crucial input to planning. As in any system, it is the interaction of *all* trends and factors that determines the outcomes, so I would argue that it is futile to argue for the primacy of any *one* type of forecasting.

Socio-Political Forecasting at General Electric

Socio-political forecasting emerged as a separate operation in General Electric in May, 1967, with the establishment of Business Environment Studies (BES) in the corporate-level Personnel and Industrial Relations component. (In retrospect, there is some organizational logic to the fact that this "people-oriented" forecasting grew up in the "people function" of the corporation.) At that time, with social and political change already starting to accelerate, it seemed to us that the Relations function of the business was in as much need of a forecasting operation and a futures dimension, in order to do an intelligent job of long-range planning, as were the marketing and technical functions of the company.

Personnel and industrial relations policies and practices are no exception to the general rule of institutional inertia. Indeed, the probability is that systemic change occurs more slowly here than in other areas of the business, if for no other reason than that it is inherently more sensitive and difficult a task to deal with people than with technologies. In this area above all, therefore, companies need lead time for strategies of adjustment. 1967 was, in other words, not too soon to be thinking about the relations policies that might be needed in 1974.

The area of our search lay in the broad sweep of social, political and economic trends in the United States over the next ten years or so (our original time-horizon was 1980). The tasks of the new BES operations were to identify and monitor these trends; to analyze them to determine their implications for relations planning and, hopefully, to catalyze those strategies of adjustment of which I have written. The last element of the task is, in a sense, the crucial one, for there is little point to gaining lead time if it is not put to good use.

The initial BES effort was a broad survey of the whole prospective business environment of the Seventies. In an effort to "make sense of change," to see a pattern in the kaleidoscope of prospective events, the BES group viewed social change as the interaction of eight developing forces for change:

1. Increasing affluence
2. Economic stabilization
3. Rising levels of education
4. Changing attitudes toward work and leisure
5. Increasing pluralism and individualism
6. Emergence of the post-industrial society
7. Growing interdependence of institutions
8. The urban/minority problem

This broad survey can be likened to a single 360° sweep of the early warning system radar, revealing a number of ill-defined "blips" on the screen. If left there, the survey might justifiably have been relegated to the "interesting, but ineffective" category of studies.

It was, however, only a beginning. It provided us with a frame of reference and a perspective on the future. More important, it established the priorities for more detailed studies and analyses. To continue the radar analogy, these subsequent studies examined the "blips" on the screen in greater detail in an effort to determine the exact nature, trajectory and impact points of the incoming "missiles." It was these studies (for example, on the future minority environment; women's rights in the Seventies, prospects for inflation) that, by focusing more sharply on specific policy implications, started to make the hoped-for contribution toward making personnel and industrial relations planning a more proactive affair. One indicator: whereas the minority study (1969), though focusing on the future, barely enabled us to keep pace with events, the women's rights study (1970) gave us enough of a jump on events that our own affirmative action guidelines on equal employment opportunity for women were published a year before the Federal guidelines.[4]

A "Four-Sided Framework" for Planning

Two years' experience with this new venture convinced us of its potential value to personnel relations planning. However, it became increasingly clear that many of the questions raised by our studies simply could not be answered within the framework of the personnel function. The implications of trend-analysis spilled over into matters of the social purpose of business, the structure and governance of the corporation, business-government relationships, production processes and market orientation. They could fit comfortably in only one frame of reference—corporate planning as a whole.

It would, however, have to be a different type of corporate planning from the past. Typically, corporate planning has based its strategies on inputs derived from economic forecasting (predictions about GNP, consumer and government spending, savings and investment, market analyses, etc.) and technological forecasting (assessments of "state of the art" developments, expected outputs from one's own and competitors' laboratories). The planning parameters of the past (and present) can, therefore, be conceptually represented by the model in Figure 1. Certainly these inputs have been, and will continue to be, vital to the planning process: change—and, therefore, forecasting—in these fields is becoming more complex and more needed. However, these inputs, our studies suggested, would no longer suffice, as the "exposed flanks" in this diagram might lead one to guess.

The typical business now finds itself the focal point for a bewildering array of external forces that impact on it from every angle. The larger the company, the more likely is this to be true. There is virtually no major trend in the social, political and economic arena, at home and abroad, that does not affect in some way the operations or future growth of the large corporation. To create an "early warning system" on only two fronts—economic

---

[4] Even this could not, of course, guarantee immunity from EEOC complaints and lawsuits as recent events have demonstrated.

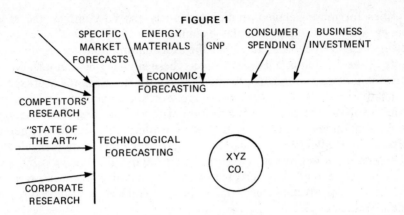

FIGURE 1

and technological—is, therefore, apt to leave a company highly vulnerable to attack from an unexpected quarter. Managers have been too ready to pretend that other factors were adequately covered by generalized assessments of the conventional and obvious political events—war, and election, or international trade agreements—or to rely on the caveat "other things being equal," which in the circumstances of today is a highly unsatisfactory (and unbusinesslike) treatment of vital factors.

If we have learned one lesson from the disruptions of accelerating change in the past decade, we should by now have recognized that "other things" have an uncomfortable habit of *not* being "equal." To look no further than at the outbursts in our cities and on our campuses, at the surge of a heightened ecological consciousness, at the proliferation of legislation on product safety, equal employment opportunity and occupational health, it should be obvious that social moods, personal attitudes, and political action have become dynamic and determinative forces for business.

The planning model for the future, therefore, will be more nearly represented by the four-sided framework illustrated in Figure 2.

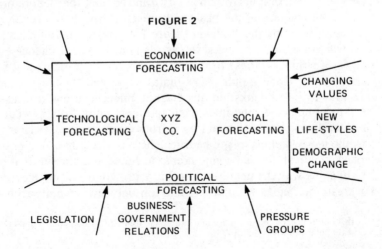

FIGURE 2

An approximation of this model was, in fact, incorporated as one element in the revamping of General Electric's strategic planning system in 1970. The starting point for the planning cycle is now the long-term environmental forecast. This establishes the basic premises from which can be deduced the strategies and policies that are likely to produce the best "fit" between the company and the future business environment. And it is in this larger context of environmental forecasting that socio-political forecasting finds its natural place.

Some Key Elements in the Process

Socio-political forecasting is nothing if not an art. By any standard, it is still far from being a science. However, even lacking the precision and instruments of science, it is evolving its own beginning processes, methodologies and discipline. Four key elements in the process bear examination:

1. *Continuous and comprehensive monitoring.* The paradox of forecasting in what Max Ways once called an "era of radical change" is that it becomes at once more necessary and more difficult. In a relatively stable society, in which tomorrow will predictably be pretty much like today, forecasting is relatively easy; but, by the same token, it is scarcely necessary since today's way of doing things will still be valid tomorrow. The more rapid, complex and pervasive change becomes, the more essential it is to try to "get a fix on the future." But, of course, the difficulties of forecasting increase geometrically with the number of sources of change.

The salient characteristics of a good monitoring system are continuity and comprehensiveness. A nonrepetitive scanning of the environment ("We did our 1980 study in 1970—and that's it!") will soon become an erroneous input to planning. Even a long-term forecast requires continuous updating, granted the rapidity of change and the present state of the art.

Whether the monitoring is actually done by company personnel or outside consultants remains a matter of choice. Probably the best self-operated system is, in fact, an industry-wide effort among life insurance companies, under the leadership of the Institute of Life Insurance (ILI). Their Trend Analysis Program (TAP) operates on the basis of a matrix, one axis of which is categories of publications (general press, business publications, academic journals, etc.), the other being segments of the environment (social change, technology, politics, etc.). "Monitors" are nominated to the Program by individual companies, and each is then assigned to a particular cell of the matrix to monitor a publication (or a set of them) for evidence of trends in that segment of the environment. Monitors' reports are collected, analyzed and synthesized into periodic reports by ILI, which distributes them to participating companies.

Most companies will find it imperative to supplement their own efforts, either by participating in a cooperative effort such as TAP or by purchasing monitoring services from outside organizations. Among the better known organizations are the Hudson Institute (Corporate Environment Program), the Futures Group ("Scout"), Institute for the Future ("Project Aware") and Daniel Yankelovich, Inc. ("Monitor," "Corporate Priorities")—however achieved, comprehensiveness must be a goal—and there is a large environment to monitor.

2. *Analyzing for critical business implications.* However the monitoring is done, the critical job of particularizing the findings to significance for a single company must, I think, be done internally. Only in this way can it become part of the thinking process of the management system of that company.

Here I would like to stress the importance of seeing *patterns* in trends and events. It is not sufficient merely to identify and monitor hundreds, maybe thousands, of separate items of change; to do only that would saturate the planning system with data. I appreciate that there is a very fine dividing line between objectively trying to find patterns in the trends, and subjectively imposing one's own pattern on them. Nevertheless, I think we must make this attempt and tread this fine line. I stress this need to see patterns in change because of its importance in enabling us to:

a. see the significance of isolated events;
b. analyze the cross-impacts of one trend on another (or others);
c. improve management's understanding of the probable future course of events.

Bringing the generalized forecast down to specific implications for a particular business may prove to be the most difficult part of all. We are all most apt to be blind in matters that closely affect us. But however difficult the exercise may be, we must make a thorough-going and conscientious effort to answer, in precise terms, the crucial questions: "What does this trend mean for me? For my work? For my company?" This exercise may be particularly difficult for managers because many of the implications will seem to challenge and even undermine some of their basic assumptions and values. These implications are, therefore, most apt to be set aside as mistaken interpretations, as "unthinkable," or as inconsistent with past experience and future forecasts along "traditional" lines. Yet it is precisely these seeming "wild cards" that our research must seek to uncover and evaluate.

3. *Developing tools and techniques.* As already noted, socio-political forecasting lacks the armory of analytical tools and techniques possessed by older forecasting disciplines. Trend projections, Delphi forecasting, scenarios, and "cross-impact analysis" are useful starts on forecasting methodologies, but the need for more tools remains great. With an acute awareness of their limitations and relative lack of sophistication, I offer for consideration two tools that we have found to be of some value.

(a) *Probability-Diffusion Matrix.* In predicting developments over a decade it is more meaningful to talk in terms of degrees of relative probability, than of certainty or "inevitability." In the final analysis, assigning probability to a trend or future event is a matter of judgment after weighing the known data and cross-checking with informed opinion. A further cross-check can be run by plotting the predictions along a probability axis so that their relative positions are made apparent.

It is also helpful to assess the probable "diffusion" of a trend or event— that is, the extent to which it is uniformly distributed over the population to which it applies (world, U.S.A., an industry, etc.) or relatively confined to a segment of that population. Again, plotting the predictions along a diffusion axis makes explicit, in a coordinated fashion, the relative weightings assigned in separate judgments.

Combining these two axes into a probability/diffusion matrix, as is done in Figure 3, serves as a check on the internal consistency of a relatively large number of predictions, from two viewpoints. By itself, such a matrix adds little to a scientific approach to environmental forecasting, but it does provide a way of looking at the future that may perhaps be helpful.

The plottings made in this matrix are largely for purposes of illustration, and not to be taken as final judgments. To the extent that they provoke debate, they will have at least demonstrated the value of making judgments clearly explicit so that planned action can more surely be taken.

FIGURE 3

PROBABILITY/DIFFUSION MATRIX FOR EVENTS AND TRENDS OCCURING IN U.S. AND WORLD BY 1980

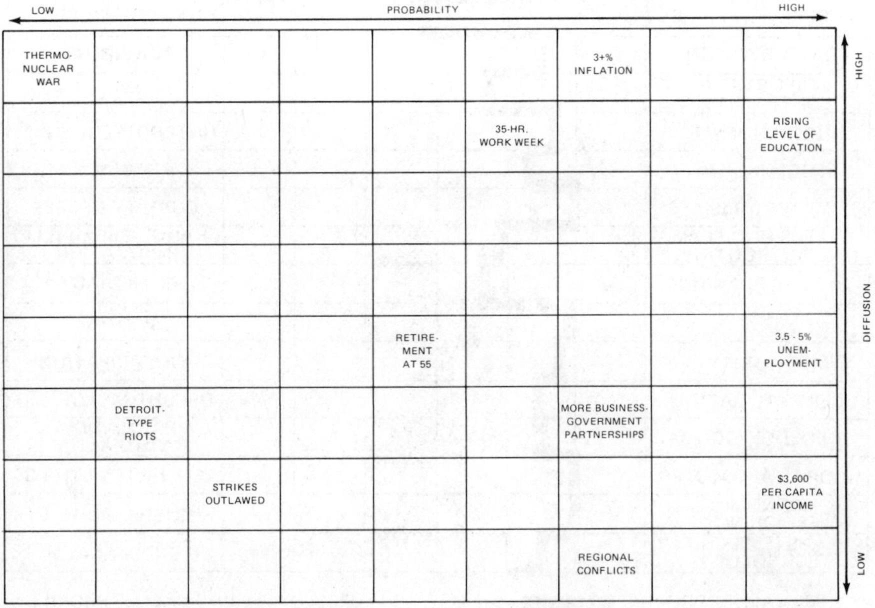

LOW ← PROBABILITY → HIGH (horizontal axis); HIGH → DIFFUSION → LOW (vertical axis, right side)

THERMO-NUCLEAR WAR							3+% INFLATION		
						35-HR. WORK WEEK			RISING LEVEL OF EDUCATION
					RETIREMENT AT 55				3.5 - 5% UNEMPLOYMENT
	DETROIT-TYPE RIOTS						MORE BUSINESS-GOVERNMENT PARTNERSHIPS		
		STRIKES OUTLAWED							$3,600 PER CAPITA INCOME
							REGIONAL CONFLICTS		

(b) *"Values Profile."* As we have already noted, changes in value systems may be the major determinants of social and political trends in the future, and business planning would be well advised to try to get a fix on these changes as one essential element in its forecasting system. One way of systematizing analysis of value trends is to develop a "values profile" (Figure 4). Like the probability/diffusion matrix, this chart should be viewed, not as a precise scientific measurement, but merely as a useful way of looking at the future. Like the matrix, too, it contains plottings that are meant to be indicative—pointing the way to a more comprehensive study—rather than definitive.

To point up the possible attitudinal changes as dramatically as possible, the chart has been made up of contrasting pairs of values (to a greater or lesser extent, that is, enhancement of one value implies a diminution of the other—e.g., war vs. peace; conformity vs. pluralism). Each society and generation has tended to seek its own new balance between these contrasting pairs, with the weight shifting from one side to the other as conditions and attitudes change.

FIGURE 4

PROFILE OF SIGNIFICANT VALUE-SYSTEM CHANGES: 1969-1980
AS SEEN BY GENERAL ELECTRIC'S BUSINESS ENVIRONMENT SECTION

1969   1980

WAR (MILITARY MIGHT)		PEACE (ECONOMIC DEVELOPMENT)
NATIONALISM		INTERNATIONALISM
FEDERAL GOVERNMENT		STATE/LOCAL GOVERNMENT
PUBLIC ENTERPRISE		PRIVATE ENTERPRISE
ORGANIZATION		INDIVIDUAL
UNIFORMITY/ CONFORMITY		PLURALISM
INDEPENDENCE		INTERDEPENDENCE
SOCIABILITY		PRIVACY
MATERIALISM		QUALITY OF LIFE
STATUS QUO/PERMA-NENCE/ROUTINE		CHANGE/FLEXIBILITY INNOVATION
FUTURE PLANNING		IMMEDIACY
WORK		LEISURE
AUTHORITY		PARTICIPATION
CENTRALIZATION		DECENTRALIZATION
IDEOLOGY/DOGMA		PRAGMATISM/ RATIONALITY
MORAL ABSOLUTES		SITUATION ETHICS
ECONOMIC EFFICIENCY		"SOCIAL JUSTICE"
MEANS (ESPECIALLY TECHNOLOGY)		ENDS (GOALS)

1969 VALUES PROFILE ■■■■■   ⋮⋮⋮⋮⋮ 1980 VALUES PROFILE

The chart also emphasizes the value changes likely to be most prevalent among the trend-setting segment of the population (young, well-educated, relatively affluent, "committed"). These are the people among whom companies recruit the managerial and professional talent they require.

The chart presents two value profiles—one representing the approximate balance struck by these trend-setters in 1969 (when our initial study was undertaken) between each pair of values; the other indicating the hypothetical balance that might be struck in 1980. It is important to stress that the chart attempts to predict value changes, *not* necessarily events. Even though trend-setters may value, say, arms control agreements, events may lag behind their influence (e.g., due to political thinking of the electorate as a whole) or lie outside their control (e.g., regional wars among developing nations).

4. *Integrating with other forecasts.* The essence of environmental forecasting, as has been mentioned, is the integration of the various conventional and nonconventional types of forecasting. The four-sided framework implies only four sets of inputs to the process; but this is merely a conceptual approach, and ideally the number should be higher. When the long-term environmental forecast was first undertaken in 1971 for our strategic planning, the number of initial inputs was set at nine (see Figure 5) —geopolitical/defense, international economic, social, political, legal, economic, technological, manpower and financial. In each of these, separate "tunnel visions" of specific aspects of the future we tried to (a) give a brief

FIGURE 5
**SCHEMATIC DESCRIPTION OF G.E.'S LONG-TERM
ENVIRONMENTAL FORECAST**

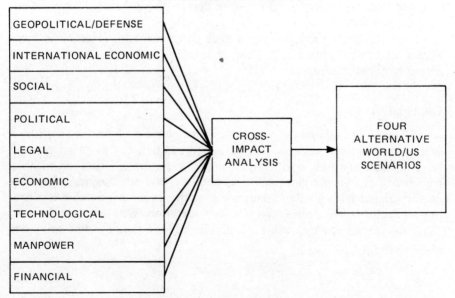

historical review (1960-70) as a jumping-off point for our analysis of the future; (b) analyze the major future forces for change—a benchmark forecast for 1970-80; (c) identify the potential discontinuities, i.e., those events which might have low probability, but high significance for General Electric; and (d) raise the first-order questions and policy implications suggested by these forecasts.

These were, by definition, *segmented* views of the future, and so inadequate as a final product. We proceeded to a "cross-impact analysis," selecting from the hundreds of trends/events in those nine environmental "slices" the 75 or so that had the highest combined rating of probability and importance. (Some events that were quite probable had little significance for General Electric; while others of low probability would have critical importance for the Company, should they occur.) On these 75 trends/events, we performed the sort of cross-impact analysis developed by Theodore J. Gordon, asking "If event A occurs, what will be the impact on the other 74? Will the probability of their occurrence increase? Decrease? Remain the same?" In effect, this process enabled us to build sets of "domino chains," with one event triggering another, and then to construct a small number of consistent configurations of the future.

The final step in the environmental forecasting process was the development of scenarios as an integrative mechanism for our work, pulling together the separate forecasts of the nine "slices," and blending quantitative and qualitative data. I must stress that we developed multiple scenarios; we did *not* take a single view of the future. In fact, we ended up with four possibilities:

—A benchmark forecast, which combined the "most probable" developments from the nine environmental "slices."

—Three variants which, in effect, were derived from varying combinations of discontinuities.

Significantly, I think, we rated even the benchmark forecast no more than a 50 percent probability. That, at least, is a measure of our own uncertainty about the future.

Conclusion

When all is said and done, of course, the element of chance or surprise will always remain. Indeed, one certain prediction is that managers will have to learn how to live with, and manage, uncertainty. However, within a framework of four (or nine) environmental parameters, business plans can be formulated with greater assurance that the major predictable environmental factors have been taken into consideration. With anything less, an otherwise sound strategy will remain vulnerable to the new discontinuities of our age.

24 • THE CORPORATE APPRAISAL: ASSESSING COMPANY STRENGTHS AND WEAKNESSES[1]

David E. Hussey[2]

In recent months much has been written about corporate long range planning, and many seminars have been held to bring this way of management to the attention of British industry. Because the subject is relatively new to the United Kingdom, most authors have provided an overview, rather than concentrating on individual aspects.

In my opinion this has led to an equation of corporate planning with the rather more romantic elements of long range strategy: acquisition and mergers, and major investment projects. But before strategy reaches this stage there is a good deal of hard work to be undertaken—at the end of which it may be decided that the company's path to greater profits may lie in improving present operations, rather than embarking on something new. This article is about some of that hard work.

ESTABLISHING THE CORPORATE IDENTITY

Good long range planning begins with the present, with an objective analysis of a company's strengths and weaknesses, and with decisions on the action that should be taken to correct those factors which inhibit the company's long term profitability. This stage might well be called establishing the corporate identity, for only by fully defining the factors that make up the company can the planner assist in setting it on the best path.

Perhaps this can be compared with the task of a career counsellor. It is relatively easy to make a list of the jobs available to a young man or woman, just as it is simple to produce a superficial list of investment opportunities open to a company. With the career counsellor the real skill comes in taking stock of each applicant, examining his qualifications, his personality and temperament, defining the areas in which some sort of further development may be required (for example, training), and matching these characteristics and the applicant's aspirations, against the various options open to him. There are well established techniques that can be used to find out most of what needs to be known about a person. Digging deep into the psyche of a company is a more complex operation, but no less important. Failure by the company in this area can be as stunting to future development in the corporate sense, as can the misplacement of a school-leaver in the personal sense.

[1] From *Long Range Planning*, Vol. 1, No. 2 (December, 1968), pp. 19-25. Reprinted by permission of Microforms International Marketing Corp., Elmsford, New York.
[2] David E. Hussey. Corporate Planning Officer, Elders & Fyffes, Ltd.

Basic Questions

But how can a company set about establishing its corporate identity? What should it seek to find out about itself? Every chief executive has some idea of what his company is best at, and what it is worst at. Unless he has devoted special efforts to this problem, it is likely that he will not know as much as he thinks he does. The larger the organization, the harder it becomes to know everything, and even in the smallest company, unless a formal analysis has been made of each area, the chances are that some things the company does will be the result of history rather than a decision that these things are right. The basic questions that should be asked are:

What are we doing now?
Why are we doing that?
Are there any alternative ways?
Should we be using these?

Strengths and Weaknesses

The study should lead to action. Immediate benefits can come from profit improvement schemes that will be suggested by the study—and it is well known that improvements frequently yield a higher return on investment than the best capital projects. Identification of weaknesses—which may be serious limiting factors to the company's long range plans—is the first step towards their removal. Obviously not all weaknesses are correctable, and there are some that every company has to live with—but knowledge of these means that the company can avoid decisions which put strain on areas that cannot withstand it. Some weaknesses can only be removed over a period of time—ways of doing this should be built into the long range plan.

A corollary is that the company will also identify its strong areas. The object of this is not to flatter management's ego, but to show some of the areas on which the company should concentrate its future efforts. Building on corporate strengths may be something of a hackneyed phrase but it is one which has a lot of truth in it. As a by-product of the study, opportunities may be identified for future expansion and development that would otherwise not have become apparent. The basic aim of long range planning must be to increase profits. The chief executive who begins his planning with this sort of study is likely to achieve greater success than his competitor who develops his plans in a vacuum.

THE INTERNAL EVALUATION

How should such an evaluation be carried out? For ease of discussion the evaluation can be considered under two major headings: internal and external (Figure 1). In reality the two areas combine to provide a single answer—for instance there may be little purpose in making production changes to a product unless it has market acceptance.

FIGURE 1

THE APPRAISAL OF THE COMPANY'S
STRENGTHS AND WEAKNESSES

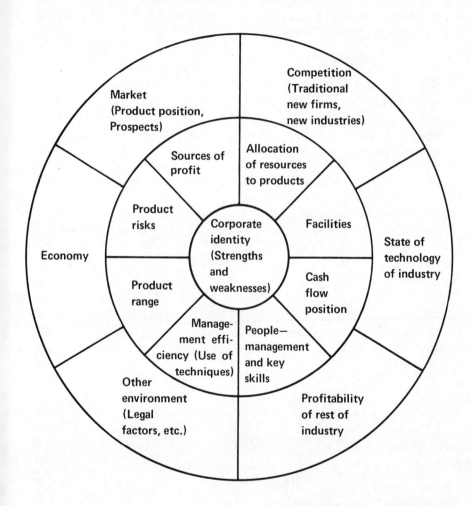

Outer circle—external factors
Middle circle—internal factors
Inner circle—the corporate identity

Profit Contribution

Perhaps the best place to start is the identification of the profit contribution of each area. What percentage of profits comes from where? The study should be made first by profit centers and then broken down by product. Of course, many companies will have this data as part of the normal management information system—although the remarks later in this article about the basis of cost allocation may be relevant. Having identified the profit strength of each product, it is wise to study past trends and internal opinions about the future prospects of each product. If, for example, the major contributors show signs of slipping, this should be known. By this stage the company should have an opinion of its present and future "breadwinners."

Allocation of Resources

The next step is very important. This is to examine the allocation of resources between products: not only resources of money and plant, but also the perhaps scarcer resources of management talent and technical skills. It so often happens that a declining product area is given to the best people to manage "to put it on its feet," when potentially more rewarding areas are not fully exploited because they are left to the second and third grades of management talent. This sort of analysis may show that R & D effort is misplaced. One so often sees in a company a prestige division which gets all the plums of personnel and finance because of its past glories, while other divisions with far greater potential have to take second place. The sort of decision that should come out of this analysis is where to change the emphasis.

Risks Involved

The wise investigator will also wish to examine the risks attached to each product. For instance:

How much dependence is there on one supplier for each type of raw material?

How much dependence is there on one or two customers for most of sales?

What happens to the product if one key person leaves (e.g. a designer in a fashion clothing business)?

Variety Reduction

Many companies take pride in their wide production range. The size of this is a fertile field for study since every additional product brings increases to inventories, clerical costs, and frequently to production costs. It is well worthwhile considering the savings that can take place from a reduction in the range. Expressing these potential savings in money terms gives an incentive to take action. In this analysis every pack should be considered as a product. The aim should be to remove all products with inadequate contribution (or potential) to profits, and to reduce the other products offered by making one do the work of several.

Realistic Allocation of Costs

In all the steps outlined so far, the cost added to the product by the business is of vital importance. In many cases the apportionment of costs between products is on some form of allocation basis. Now it is worthwhile studying the basis of allocation since although suitable for many purposes it may be inadequate for this study. Many allocations assume that costs fall in a normal distribution, for example that invoicing costs are a fixed percentage for all products. Inventories may be treated on the same basis. If costs are re-allocated on the basis of actual transactions two things may become apparent: a skewed distribution between products; a skewed distribtuion between different customers.

An example may make this clearer. A firm offering a lorry sales service is likely to express its sales/delivery costs as a percentage of the sales value—say 5 percent. The assumption is made that every £1 of sales bears the same percentage of cost—in other words that a normal distribution applies. In fact, everybody really knows that it costs less per unit to sell one customer 100 units than to sell 100 customers one unit each. In addition everybody knows that it takes more time and affort to reach a customer 10 miles away than one who is only one mile away. In other words costs do not fall in a normal distribution. Yet few companies organize their cost data so that they can make any decisions on this basis (Figure 2). The sort of decisions that have been made by companies applying this sort of analysis are: removal of service from many very small customers by a national distribution concern—resulting in a 20 percent cut in lorry fleet size, no loss of turnover because of the ability to concentrate efforts on a smaller area and a substantial increase in profits; the charging of a minimum price of £ 5 per order by an electronics company, forcing small customers to wholesalers; charging small orders a higher rate by a quarrying company.

Assessment of Company Resources

So far most of the discussion has been about the company's product. Some attention should be given to resources. Firstly an assessment should be made of the company's *production facilities*. Are they efficient? Is there surplus capacity? Is there room for expansion? Can two plants be rationalized under one roof? The list of questions can be increased.

One thing every company is likely to know is its *cash flow* position and its ability to raise money. At this stage a rough forecast of cash resources should be made, to give the company some guideline along which to develop future strategies. If money is going to be a problem the company's freedom of choice may be restricted. In such circumstances it may be important for the company to examine its credit policies, and vital for it to find ways of reducing capital tied up in inventories.

But money and plant are not the only ingredients of a successful business. Every company depends on people, and no company can afford to ignore this. The problem which is very much to the fore in many family businesses is top management succession. This is only one aspect, and the whole question of *recruitment and development of people* should be studied. If the company has difficulty attracting the right people there

FIGURE 2
THE REALISTIC ALLOCATION OF COSTS *

Example A: Delivery costs allocated as 2½% of sales

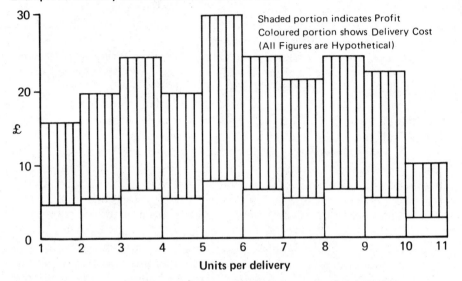

Shaded portion indicates Profit
Coloured portion shows Delivery Cost
(All Figures are Hypothetical)

Units per delivery

Example B: Delivery costs allocated at average call rate (£0.0914 per call)

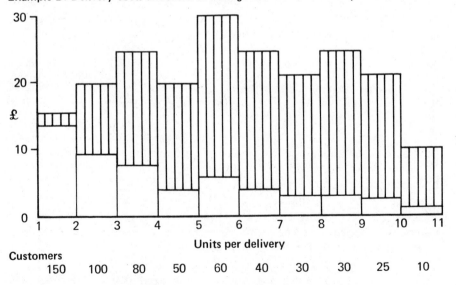

Units per delivery

Customers
150   100   80   50   60   40   30   30   25   10

* Both charts show contribution to delivery costs and profit.
    Note. Actual costs will not fit either pattern, although Example B is more accurate than Example A. A time study would show that the cost of delivering 10 units is more than the cost of delivering 1 unit—but perhaps only twice as much. More important, actual costs would fluctuate round the norm for each group, because of distances and other customer differences. Implications for policy are that many customers in the lower ranges will be served at a loss.

FIGURE 2—Continued

Example C: Number of customers and actual cost of serving

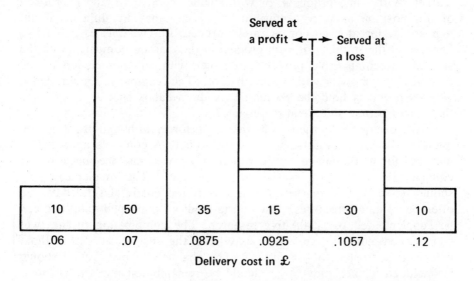

Note. Actual average cost of serving each of the 150 customers in the "over 1 but under 2 units" category is £0.0875 per call.

must be a reason—and there is little hope of improvement until this reason is identified. A careful stock should be taken of the ability of each key man-after all there is little point in launching new products if you know your marketing manager is not capable of making them profitable. As in all other points discussed, clear strategies should emerge to correct the position. Few companies can sack their total staff merely to replace them with better ones, and every chief executive has to manage with the human material he has in the company. But this does not mean that a bad situation has to be accepted, as positive action can be taken in the fields of training, recruitment, organization and re-deployment of people.

The planner should also be aware of the *management techniques* used within the company, the extent of their utilization, and the available techniques not at present being applied. By this I am not advocating the pinning of all hopes on the latest management fad, but on acceptance of the fact that present methods are not necessarily the best ones.

THE EXTERNAL EVALUATION

The consideration of internal evidence is only half of the picture, and will not yield the best results unless attention is given to the world outside the company. Because no company can make profits without customers, I should like to begin with the market place.

Market Standing

Firstly the company should find out what position each of its major products holds in the market, or more important in each segment of the market. With some products, or with smaller companies, the expression of this position as a percentage market share may be difficult, if not impossible. Great precision is rarely needed, but what is essential is a fair idea of the standing of each product in the market, compared with the standing of competitive products, together with an appreciation of the potential for growth within the market. The company should define why its products hold the position they do: what is special about them that makes people give them preference?

Much may be learned from the sales force, although there is frequently a bias in data obtained from this source. A complete appreciation may call for marketing research, which may investigate the image of the company, as well as the market for its products. The smaller company should not shrug off marketing research as too costly. Useful data can often be obtained from desk research (a study of published data) and can be supplemented by qualitative research. The combination of the two, which need not be expensive, may give the insight needed without incurring the cost of major surveys. The channels of distribution should be included in the study for it should be remembered that the channels used by the company will in many cases not be the only ones possible. The company should be sure that it understands its markets: that it knows what the consumer requires and whether this requirement is being satisfied.

Competition

Naturally competitive activity should also be studied, and an attempt should be made to define the strengths and weaknesses of each competitor. The danger here is lack of objectivity by those carrying out the study for it is too easy to underestimate the competition. Potential competition from new entrants to the industry should be considered. An industry which requires little capital or technical knowledge is always more vulnerable than one which is more difficult to enter. In this particular part of the investigation it is the degree of risk that has to be assessed.

Substitutes

One area of competition that is most important and most difficult to study is the coming from outside the traditional industry. The company must assess the vulnerability of its main products to substitutes, since unless it does this it may one day find itself in grave difficulties. It is significant that so many substitutes are developed by other industries—in the past we have seen plastic take over much from paper, cement roof tiles replace clay tiles, and synthetic fibres attacking the province of natural fibres. The process will continue since it is part of the developing technology, and if I were in the textile industry I would be worrying about I.C.I.'s announced new process to make the industry obsolete. Similarly the development of the electric car from sources outside the present motor industry is likely to affect manufacture, marketing channels and service stations. There is no easy solution. Each company must keep continuously aware of new developments and must always look out for this sort of opportunity from its own research wok. In my opinion the acceptance that things can change, and the freeing of the thoughts of those in the company to deliberately seek this change, is half the battle. At this stage in planning the company is more interested in establishing the status quo, for this is the first step to meeting change as an opportunity rather than as a threat.

Economics

Every company is affected by the economies of the countries in which it operates, but not all companies mirror the ups and downs of the trade cycle. The effect of economic changes on the company must be identified, since without this it becomes difficult to assess the vulnerability of future profits. Few companies have power to change the course of the economy, but all can alter their own balance of risks by diversification, or by extending their sales areas into different countries.

Interfirm Comparisons

The performance of other companies in the same industry should be studied. The lucky firms will be able to participate in a study by the Centre for Interfirm Comparisons: others will have to rely on the published accounts and public announcements of competitors. As with the other points discussed, the objective is to assess the reason for variances— not just to establish that they exist.

Stock-Market Valuation

Also of vital interest is an assessment of the company's vulnerability to takeover. To make this, the investigator should look at its own record, financial policies and balance sheet, against the background of activity in the market. Of course if the company *wants* to be acquired, it may develop a strategy that makes it more attractive to the roving eye of the hunter.

PREPARING THE REPORT

As listed above, the elements to be examined suggest a chain relationship, with item neatly following item. Of course reality is not like this at all, and the key elements—and there are others which have not been discussed—have a sort of spider's web relationship, with a central theme leading to a focal point; the uncovering of the corporate identity.

Factual Statements

With the data obtained, it will be possible to write down a series of factual statements about the company, together with the strategic implications (see Figure 3). How these statements are formulated depends on the complexity of the company—and the personal approach of the investigator. It is important that they be written, since in most companies there are likely to be areas of dispute (in fact it is almost possible to say dogmatically that if everyone agrees with the report, the job has not been done properly), and emotions will be involved. It is much easier to make an objective decision if all the evidence is fully documented.

Unpopular Conclusions

The reports may not always be pleasant. Few people enjoy trying to convince their chief executive that an area of the company which is dear to his heart should be closed down, or of similar unpopular measures. But this sort of study must be approached with integrity, for without a genuine attempt at honest appraisal the whole exercise may become a meaningless gesture.

Alternative Strategies

Also important is the consideration of alternative strategies to build on what is discovered. There is little point in deciding that the bottom is about to drop out of your market, and then sitting back and watching it happen. There are no rewards for prophets.

The Balance of Risks

The final report should show clearly the strong and weak points of the company. It should assess the vulnerability of the company to likely changes in the environment, and should establish what I like to call the company's "risk balance" (which put simply is the number of baskets the company has to keep its eggs in!) It is at this point that the company is ready to think seriously about its future profit targets, and the ways in which it will reach them.

The Team Approach

This sort of evaluation is complex, but not to be completed by any competent executive. If the company has a corporate planner, he should play a major part: indeed, in my opinion, the planner who does not attempt to define the company's strengths and weaknesses is not doing his job properly. I would recommend that a team approach be used, with people from line functions working with the planner. This goes to make for a greater involvement of operating management, and removes the feeling of imposition that may come from a purely staff investigation. In my view, this teamwork approach should be used for other planning prob-

FIGURE 3

EXAMPLE: ONE METHOD OF SUMMARIZING COMPANY STRENGTHS AND WEAKNESSES

Part 1: Weaknesses/Limiting Factors

Immediate Strategic Implications

1. Management
   a. Chief executive aged 65, no obvious successor.
   b. Weak middle management.

   c. Marketing manager incapable of handling any expansion.

a. Recruitment, merger, or sale of business.
b. Recruitment training (Position can be improved but some weakness will remain for 5 years).
c. A serious block. Solve by organization change or replacement.

2. Marketing
   a. 80 percent of profits emanate from product A market declining at 5 percent p.a. market share constant.

   b. 25 products contribute no profit and have no potential.

a. i. Reduce dependence.
    ii. Changed market strategy to improve performance.
    iii. Cost reduction to improve position—Introduce value analysis.
b. Cease production re-deploy resources.

Part 2: Strengths

1. People
   a. A high level of technical expertise in production departments.

2. Marketing
   a. Strong image among consumers, particularly for quality, performance and after-sales service.
   b. Five established brand names.

3. Finance
   a. £500,000 available for expansion from own resources. Up to 2 £m loan capital can be raised without difficulty.

Note. All statements would be supported in the Report.

lems, as it acts against what I regard as a dangerous tendency towards large planning departments. The fewer the staff people engaged in planning, the more work management will have to do—and this is where planning really belongs.

Self-deception

What I have been discussing is nothing more than a function of good management, and many may feel a defensive pride in their own way of running the company. Some companies may indeed already have much of the information available in different parts of the company. What is so often lacking is the drawing of all important data together to present the complete picture. The management casebooks are littered with the testimony of companies that found they did not have as perfect a knowledge of themselves as they once thought.

Of course this sort of analysis is not restricted to companies that practise long range planning. But the company that does it will suddenly realise that it is halfway to knowing what long range planning is all about—the way to better profits.

BIBLIOGRAPHY, CHAPTER 7

Ackoff, Russell L. *Concept of Corporate Planning*. New York: Wiley Interscience Division, John Wiley & Sons, Inc. 1970.

Anderson, Carl R., and F. T. Paine. "PIMS: A Reexamination." *Academy of Management Review*, Vol. 3, No. 3 (July, 1978), pp. 602-612.

Andrews, Kenneth R. "Strategic Planning of Mice and Men." *Across the Board*, Vol. 20, No. 10, pp. 6-9.

Ayal, Igal, and J. Zif. "Competitive Market Choice Strategies in Multinational Marketing." *Columbia Journal of World Business* (Fall, 1978), pp. 72-81.

Boulton, William R., *et al*. "Strategic Planning: Determining the Impact of Environmental Characteristics and Uncertainty." *Academy of Management Journal*, Vol. 25, No. 3 (September, 1982), pp. 500-509.

Buzzell, R. D., B. T. Gale, and R. G. M. Sulton. "Market Share—A Key to Profitability." *Harvard Business Review*, Vol. 53, No. 1 (1975), pp. 97-106.

Chandler, A. D., Jr. *Strategy and Structure*. Cambridge, MA: The M.I.T. Press, 1962.

Churchill, Neil C. "Budget Choice: Planning vs. Control." *Harvard Business Review*, Vol. 62, No. 4 (1984), pp. 150-162.

Crawford, C. Merle. "New Product Failure Rates—Facts and Fallacies." *Research Management*, Vol. 22, No. 5 (September, 1979), pp. 9-13.

Harrison, F. L. "How Corporate Planning Responds to Uncertainty." *Long-Range Planning*, Vol. 9, No. 2 (April, 1976), pp. 88-93.

Hedly, Barry. "Strategy and the 'Business Portfolio.' " *Long-Range Planning*, Vol. 10 (February, 1977), pp. 9-15.

Lorange, Peter, and R. F. Vancil. "How to Design a Strategic Planning System." *Harvard Business Review*, Vol. 54, No. 5 (September-October, 1976), pp. 75-81.

MacAvoy, Robert E. "Corporate Strategy and the Power of Competitive Analysis." *Management Review* (July, 1983), pp. 9-19.

Margulies, Newton, and Lora Calflesh. "A Socio-Technical Approach to Planning and Implementing New Technology." *Training and Development Journal* (December, 1982), pp. 16-29.

McCann, Joseph E., and John Selsky. "Hyperturbulence and the Emergence of Type 5 Environments." *Academy of Management Review*, Vol. 9, No. 3 (1984), pp. 460-470.

Mintzberg, Henry. "Planning on the Left Side and Managing on the Right." *Harvard Business Review*. Vol. 54, No. 4 (July-August, 1976), pp. 49-58.

Nair, Keshavan, and R. K. Sarin. "Generating Future Scenarios—Their Use in Strategic Planning." *Long-Range Planning*, Vol. 12 (June, 1979), pp. 57-61.

Naylor, T. H., and Daniel E. Gattis. "Corporate Planning Models." *California Management Review*, Vol. 28, No. 4 (Summer, 1976), pp. 69-77.

Quinn, James Brian. "Technological Forecasting." *Harvard Business Review*, Vol. 45, No. 2 (March-April, 1967), pp. 89-106.

Smallwood, J. "The Product Life Cycle: A Key to Strategic Marketing Planning." *MSU Business Topics*, Vol. 21, No. 1 (Winter, 1973), pp. 29-35.

Snyder, Neil H., and William F. Glueck. "Can Environmental Volatility Be Measured Objectively?" *Academy of Management Journal,* Vol. 25, No. 1, pp. 185-191.

Spivey, W. Allen. "Forecasting: A Perspective for Managers." *Journal of Contemporary Business,* Vol. 8, No. 3, pp. 61-78.

Thurston, P. "Make TF Serve Corporate Planning." *Harvard Business Review,* Vol. 49, No. 5 (September-October, 1971), pp. 98-102.

Venkatraman, N., and John C. Camillas. "Exploring the Concept of 'Fit' in Strategic Management." *Academy of Management Review,* Vol. 9, No. 3 (1984), pp. 513-525.

Wheelwright, Steven C., and D. G. Clarke. "Corporate Forecasting: Promise and Reality." *Harvard Business Review,* Vol. 54, No. 6 (November-December, 1976), pp. 40-42, 47-48, 52, 60, 64, 198.

Younger, Michael. "Assessing Opportunities for Diversification—An Analytical Approach." *Long-Range Planning,* Vol. 17, No. 4, pp. 10-15.

Section C

Controlling

Control may be considered a systemized way for an organization to achieve organizational learning. Control is predicated on the presumption that if individuals know how they have performed and if plans have been established as to how they should perform, the difference between the two provides a basis for correction of actual behavior compared with that described in the plans. The nature of the activity to be undertaken as well as the level of performance that is expected are established in the plan. A knowledge of the plan can provide a means for self-control by individuals who compare their behavior with the standard set forth in the plan.

The simplicity of the above statements concerning control are complicated in any large-scale organization, since operations in any part of a complex system are more or less dependent upon factors arising out of operations in another part of the system. Management's control is involved not only in comparing and correcting but also in identifying the causes of deviations that may result from activity outside the realm of the individual or group charged with the responsibility of achieving the plan.

Chapter 8 examines the basic nature of control and control systems. The organizational effects and the importance of control to managing a system as well as the impact of controls on individuals are examined as relevant to learning and behavior. Chapter 9 is an applied chapter in that it examines detailed control systems while relating them to overall planning and operation of the organization. Further, it reviews the theory of measurement and its application to control problems.

Chapter 8

The Meaning
of Control

Control is a corrective activity. In the control process, judgements about the adequacy of prior performance are made and corrective decisions undertaken. The essence of control is action that adjusts operations to predetermined standards, and its basis is information in the hands of managers. We cannot control behavior by organization structure. Job assignment is merely a plan or an expectation of what an individual is supposed to do in the organization—a condition that may or may not come to pass. Similarly, policies or goals guide behavior, but they do not control it since there is many a slip between expectations and reality. Thus, designers of control systems are dealing with the nonprogramable, the behavior deviating from expected results. It is that portion of the actions that cannot be dealt with a priori but rather is adjusted after results wander from the desired path.

Merchant reviews these concepts and adds meanings derived from modern research upon the subject. Hofstede criticizes much that has gone on under the aegis of modern control theory and suggests a change in the concept of managerial control to that akin to living systems that self-adjust to their environments as they experience success or failure. Self-correcting control systems would be much preferable to control by some managers who view behavior management as inimical or undesirable. Wouldn't it be a more attractive world if we as individuals were not expected to evaluate, let alone correct, the behavior of others? Yet managers are asked to do just that. The manager can consider himself or herself as part of the process or system that is operating and subject to control. If he or she can make such a conceptualization, then self-correction can take place, with the manager functioning as an actor rather than a controller in the system. Some may consider this technique, however, to be akin to sticking one's head in the sand to avoid the issue. Yet this view does consider the manager a part of instead of apart from the system.

25 • THE CONTROL FUNCTION
OF MANAGEMENT[1]

Kenneth A. Merchant[2]

After strategies are set and plans are made, management's primary task is to take steps to ensure that these plans are carried out, or, if conditions warrant, that the plans are modified. This is the critical control function of management. And since management involves directing the activities of others, a major part of the control function is making sure other people do what should be done.

The management literature is filled with advice on how to achieve better control. This advice usually includes a description of some type of measurement and feedback process:

> The basic control process, wherever it is found and whatever it controls, involves three steps: (1) establishing standards, (2) measuring performance against these standards, and (3) correcting deviations from standards and plans.[3]
>
> A good management control system *stimulates action* by spotting the *significant* variations from the original plan and highlighting them *for the people who can set things right.*[4]
>
> Controls need to focus on results.[5]

This focus on measurement and feedback, however, can be seriously misleading. In many circumstances, a control system built around measurement and feedback is not feasible. And even when feasibility is not a limitation, use of a feedback-oriented control system is often an inferior solution. Yet, good controls can be established and maintained using other techniques.

What is needed is a broader perspective on control as a management function: this article addresses such a perspective. The first part summarizes the general control problem by discussing the underlying reasons for implementing controls and by describing what can realistically be achieved. In the second part, the various types of controls available are identified. The last part discusses why the appropriate choice of controls is and should be different in different settings.

[1] Reprinted from "The Control Function of Management" by Kenneth A. Merchant, *Sloan Management Review*, Vol. 23, No. 4, pp. 43–55, by permission of the publisher. Copyright © 1982 by the Sloan Management Review Association. All rights reserved.

[2] Kenneth A. Merchant, Assistant Professor of Business Administration, Harvard University.

[3] See H. Koontz, C. O'Donnell, and H. Weihrich, *Management*, 7th ed. (New York: McGraw-Hill, 1980), p. 722.

[4] See W. D. Brinckloe and M. T. Coughlin, *Managing Organizations* (Encino, CA: Glencoe Press, 1977), p. 298.

[5] See P. F. Drucker, *Management: Tasks, Responsibilities, Practices* (New York: Harper & Row, 1974), p. 497.

WHY ARE CONTROLS NEEDED?

If all personnel always did what was best for the organization, control—and even management—would not be needed. But, obviously individuals are sometimes unable or unwilling to act in the organization's best interest, and a set of controls must be implemented to guard against undesirable behavior and to encourage desirable actions.

One important class of problems against which control systems guard may be called *personal limitations*. People do not always understand what is expected of them nor how they can best perform their jobs, as they may lack some requisite ability, training, or information. In addition, human beings have a number of innate perceptual and cognitive biases, such as an inability to process new information optimally or to make consistent decisions, and these biases can reduce organizational effectiveness.[6] Some of these personal limitations are correctable or avoidable, but for others, controls are required to guard against their deleterious effects.

Even if employees are properly equipped to perform a job well, some choose not to do so, because individual goals and organizational goals may not coincide perfectly. In other words, there is a *lack of goal congruence*. Steps must often be taken either to increase goal congruence or to prevent employees from acting in their own interest where goal incongruence exists.

If nothing is done to protect the organization against the possible occurrence of undesirable behavior or the omission of desirable behavior caused by these personal limitations and motivational problems, severe repercussions may result. At a minimum, inadequate control can result in lower performance or higher risk of poor performance. At the extreme, if performance is not controlled on one or more critical performance dimensions, the outcome could be organizational failure.

WHAT IS GOOD CONTROL?

Perfect control, meaning complete assurance that actual accomplishment will proceed according to plan, is never possible because of the likely occurrence of unforeseen events. However, *good* control should mean that an informed person could be reasonably confident that no major unpleasant surprises will occur. A high probability of forthcoming poor performance, despite a reasonable operating plan, sometimes is given the label "out of control."

Some important characteristics of this desirable state of good control should be highlighted. First, control is future-oriented: the goal is to have

---

[6] A recent summary of many of the findings in this area (illustrating such cognitive limitations as conservative revision of prior subjective probabilities when new information is provided, and the use of simplifying decision-making heuristics when faced with complex problems) is provided by W. F. Wright, "Cognitive Information Processing Biases: Implications for Producers and Users of Financial Information," *Decision Sciences* (April 1980): 284–298.

no unpleasant surprises in the future. The past is not relevant except as a guide to the future. Second, control is multidimensional, and good control cannot be established over an activity with multiple objectives unless performance on all significant dimensions has been considered. Thus, for example, control of a production department cannot be considered good unless all the major performance dimensions, including quality, efficiency, and asset management, are well controlled. Third, the assessment of whether good performance assurance has been achieved is difficult and subjective. An informed expert might judge that the control system in place is adequate because no major bad surprises are likely, but this judgment is subject to error because adequacy must be measured against a future that can be very difficult to assess. Fourth, better control is not always economically desirable. Like any other economic good, the control tools are costly and should be implemented only if the expected benefits exceed the costs.

HOW CAN GOOD CONTROL BE ACHIEVED?

Good control can be achieved by avoiding some behavioral problems and/ or by implementing one or more types of control to protect against the remaining problems. The following sections discuss the major control options.

Control-Problem Avoidance

In most situations, managers can avoid some control problems by allowing no opportunities for improper behavior. One possibility is *automation*. Computers and other means of automation reduce the organization's exposure to control problems because they can be set to perform appropriately (that is, as the organization desires), and they will perform more consistently than do human beings. Consequently, control is improved.

Another avoidance possibility is *centralization,* such as that which takes place with very critical decisions at most organization levels. If a manager makes all the decisions in certain areas, those areas cease to be control problems in a managerial sense because no other persons are involved.

A third avoidance possibility is *risk-sharing* with an outside body, such as an insurance company. Many companies bond employees in sensitive positions, and in so doing, they reduce the probability that the employees' behavior will cause significant harm to the firm.

Finally, some control problems can and should be avoided by *elimination* of a business or an operation entirely. Managers without the means to control certain activities, perhaps because they do not understand the processes well, can eliminate the associated control problems by turning over their potential profits and the associated risk to a third party, for example, by subcontracting or divesting.

If management cannot, or chooses not to, avoid the control problems caused by relying on other individuals, they must address the problems by implementing one or more control tactics. The large number of tactics that are available to help achieve good control can be classified usefully into three main categories, according to the *object* of control; that is, whether control is exercised over *specific actions, results,* or *personnel.* Table 1 shows many common controls classified according to their control object; these controls are described in the following sections.

TABLE 1

A CONTROL TOOL CLASSIFICATION FRAMEWORK

Object of Control		
Specific Actions	Results	Personnel

Behavioral Constraint:
—Physical (e.g., locks,
   security guards)
—Administrative (e.g.,
   separation of duties)
Action Accountability:
—Work Rules
—Policies and Proce-
   dures
—Codes of Conduct
Preaction Review:
—Direct Supervision
—Approval Limits
—Budget Reviews
	Results Accountability:
	—Standards
	—Budgets
	—Management by Ob-
	   jective (MBO)
		Upgrade Capabilities:
		—Selection
		—Training
		—Assignment
		Improve Communication:
		—Clarify Expectations
		—Provide Information for
		   coordination
		Encourage Peer Control:
		—Work Groups
		—Shared Goals

Control of Specific Actions

One type of control, specific-action control, attempts to ensure that individuals perform (or do not perform) certain actions that are known to be desirable (or undesirable). Management can limit the incidence of some types of obviously undesirable activity by using *behavioral constraints* that render occurrence impossible, or at least unlikely. These constraints include physical devices, such as locks and key-personnel identification systems, and administrative constraints, such as segregation of duties, which make it very difficult for one person to carry out an improper act.

A second type of specific-action control is *action accountability*—a type of feedback control system by which employees are held accountable for their actions. The implementation of action-accountability control systems requires: (1) defining the limits of acceptable behavior, as is done in procedures manuals; (2) tracking the behaviors that employees are actually engaged in; and (3) rewarding or punishing deviations from the defined limits. Although action-accountability systems involve the tracking and reporting of actual behaviors, their objective is to motivate employees to behave appropriately in the future. These systems are effective only if employees understand what is required of them, and they feel that their individual actions will be noticed and rewarded or punished in some significant way.

A third type of specific-action control is *preaction review*. This involves observing the work of others before the activity is complete, for example, through direct supervision, formal planning reviews, and approvals on proposals for expenditures. Reviews can provide effective control in several ways by: correcting potentially harmful behavior before the full damaging effects are felt; or influencing behavior just by the threat of an impending review, such as causing extra care in the preparation of an expenditure proposal. One advantage of reviews is that they can be used even when it is not possible to define exactly what is expected prior to the review.

Control of Results

Control can also be accomplished by focusing on results: this type of control comes in only one basic form, results accountability, which involves holding employees responsible for certain results. Use of results-accountability control systems requires: (1) defining the dimensions along which results are desired, such as efficiency, quality, and service; (2) measuring performance on these dimensions; and (3) providing rewards (punishments) to encourage (discourage) behavior that will lead (not lead) to those results. As with action-accountability systems, results-accountability systems are future-oriented; they attempt to motivate people to behave appropriately. But they are effective only if employees feel that their individual efforts will be noticed and rewarded in some significant way.

Control of Personnel

A third type of control can be called *personnel control* because it emphasizes a reliance on the personnel involved to do what is best for the organization, and it provides assistance for them as necessary. Personnel controls can be very effective by themselves in some situations, such as in a small family business or in a professional partnership, because the underlying causes of the needs for controls (personal limitations and lack of goal congruence) are minimal. However, even when control problems are present, they can be reduced to some extent by: (1) upgrading the capabilities of personnel in key positions, such as tightening hiring policies, implementing training programs, or improving job assignments; (2) improving communications to help individuals know and understand their roles better and how they can best coordinate their efforts with those of other groups in the organization; and (3) encouraging peer (or subordinate) control by establishing cohesive work groups with shared goals.

FEASIBILITY CONSTRAINTS ON THE CHOICE
OF CONTROLS

The design of a control system often depends partly on the feasibility of the various types of controls: not all of these tools can be used in every situation. Personnel controls are the most adaptable to a broad range of situations. To some extent, all organizations rely on their employees to guide and motivate themselves, and this self-control can be increased with some care in hiring, screening, and training. Even in a prison, where administrators are faced with a sharp lack of goal congruence and where few control options are available other than physical constraints, inmates are screened so that dangerous ones are not assigned to high-risk positions, such as in a machine shop.

Most situations, however, require reinforcing personnel controls by placing controls over specific actions, results, or a combination of the two. This is where feasibility becomes a limiting factor.

For control over specific actions, management must have some knowledge of which actions are desirable. While it may be easy to define precisely the required behavior on a production line, the definition of preferred behavior for a research engineer cannot be as precise. Being able to keep track of specific actions is also necessary to enforce actions accountability; however, this is usually not a limiting factor, except in rare situations such as a remote outpost, because actions can be observed directly or assessed indirectly through action reports, such as hours worked, sales calls made, or procedural violations.

For control over results, the most serious constraint is the ability to measure the desired results effectively. (Management usually knows what results are desirable.) Ideally, measurements should: (1) assess the *correct* performance areas—the ones for which results are truly desired; (2) be *precise*—not determined by only crude estimations; (3) be *timely* and (4) be *objective*—not subject to manipulation. While perfect measures are rarely available, reasonable surrogates can often be found or developed. For example, "complaints received" might be a good (negative) indicator of the performance of hotel staff personnel along the customer-service dimension. Significant difficulty in achieving any of these four measurement qualities, however, can lead to failure of a results-oriented control system.

Figure 1 shows how the two factors most limiting control feasibility—knowledge of desirable actions and the ability to measure results on the important performance dimensions—can influence the choice of controls used.[7] The most difficult control situation, shown in box 4 of Figure 1, is one in which the desirable actions are not known and the important result areas cannot be measured well. Only personnel controls (or problem avoidance) are available options. In a research laboratory, for example, success

[7] A similar scheme is presented in W. G. Ouchi, "A Conceptual Framework for the Design of Organizational Control Mechanisms," *Management Science* (September 1979): 833–848.

FIGURE 1

KEY CONTROL OBJECT FEASIBILITY DETERMINANTS

Ability to measure results
on important performance dimensions

		High	Low
Knowledge of which specific actions are desirable	Excellent	1. Specific-action and/or results control	2. Specific-action control (e.g., real-estate venture)
	Poor	3. Results control (e.g., movie director)	4. Personnel control (e.g., research laboratory)

might be difficult to assess for years, yet prescription of specific actions could be counter-productive. Fortunately, in this specific setting, control is not a serious problem because research scientists tend to be professional—well trained and responsible to the standards of their profession. They tend to control themselves, and consequently, control of research laboratories tend to be dominated by controls over personnel.

In box 3 of Figure 1, where knowledge of desirable specific actions is poor but good results measurements are available, control is best accomplished by controlling results. Movie production is a good example. It is probably impossible to dictate what a movie director should do or even to observe his or her behavior and predict whether the finished product will be good. It is, however, a relatively easy task to measure the economic performance of the movie and the artistic merit, if that is a concern. In this situation, the best control system would seem to be a results-accountability system that defines to the director the results expected, holds him or her responsible for achieving them, and provides some reinforcement in the form of compensation and/or recognition.

For similar reasons, results controls tend to be dominant at most upper-management levels. It is usually not possible to prescribe and keep track of the specific actions each manager should be performing, but it is relatively easy to define the results desired, in terms similar to those desired by shareholders.

Specific-action controls should dominate where there is knowledge about which actions are desirable but where results measurement is impossible or difficult, as indicated in box 2 of Figure 1. Consider, for example, control over a real-estate development business where large capital invest-

ment decisions are made frequently. Results of these decisions are difficult
to measure in a timely, accurate fashion because of their long-term nature;
they tend to be inseparable from the results of other actions and are con-
founded by changes in the environment. However, the techniques of investment analysis are well developed (e.g., net present value analysis with
tests of the sensitivity of assumptions), and control may be accomplished
by formally reviewing the techniques used and the assumptions made.

HOW TO CHOOSE AMONG THE FEASIBLE OPTIONS

Often managers cannot rely completely on the people involved in a given
area and cannot employ one or more of the avoidance strategies mentioned
earlier. When this is the case, the best situation is one in which either
specific-action or results controls, or both, can be chosen, as is shown in
box 1 of Figure 1. In general, the choice of one or more tools should involve
consideration of: (1) the total need for control; (2) the amount of control
that can be designed into each of the control devices; and (3) the costs of
each, both in terms of money spent and unintended behavioral effects, if
any. These decision parameters will be described more fully.

Need for Controls

The need for controls over any particular behavior or operation within an
organization depends very simply on the impact of that area on overall
organizational performance. Thus, more control should be exercised over a
strategically important behavior rather than over a minor one, regardless of
how easy it is to control each. For example, controlling the new-product-
development activity is far more important in many companies than making
sure that the production of existing products is accomplished as efficiently
as possible. Consequently, more resources should be devoted to controlling
the new-product activity, even though it is a far more difficult area to control.

Amount of Control Provided by Feasible Options

The amount of control provided by each of the control tools depends both
on their design and on how well they fit the situation in which they are
used. Personnel controls should usually provide some degree of control.
But although they may be totally effective in some situations, such as in a
small business, they provide little or no warning of failure. They can break
down very quickly if demands, opportunities, or needs change.

Specific-action and results controls can provide widely varying amounts
of control. In general, reasonably certain (or tight) control requires: (1)
detailed specification of what is expected of *each individual;* (2) prevention
of undesired actions, or effective and frequent monitoring of actions or
results; and (3) administration of penalties or rewards that are significant to
the individuals involved.

For example, with specific-action-accountability systems, the amount of control can be affected by changing one or more of the elements of the system. First, tighter control can be effected by making the definitions of acceptability more specific. This might take the form of work rules (e.g., no smoking) or specific policies (e.g., a purchasing policy to secure three competing bids before releasing the purchase order), as opposed to general guidelines or vague codes of conduct (e.g., act professionally). Second, control can be made tighter by improving the effectiveness of the action-tracking system. Personnel who are certain that their actions will be noticed relatively quickly will be affected more strongly by an action-accountability system than will those who feel that the chance of their being observed is small. Thus, constant direct supervision should provide tighter control than would an audit sampling of a small number of action reports some time later. Third, control can be made tighter by making the rewards or punishments more significant to the individuals involved. In general, this impact should vary directly with the size of the reward (or the severity of the punishment), although different individuals may react differently to identical rewards or punishments.

Results-accountability systems can be varied along similar lines. Expected performance can be defined broadly, for instance, with a goal for annual net income. Alternatively, expected performance can be defined in more detailed form by prescribing goals for specific result areas (for example, sales growth, efficiency, quality) and by using line items with short time horizons (e.g., month or quarter). Control is tighter when the performance dimensions for which results are desired are defined explicitly and, of course, correctly: this type of control is particularly effective if well-established results standards are available, perhaps in the form of output from an engineering study, industry survey, or historical analysis. Results-accountability control can also be tightened by improving the measurement of results. This can be accomplished by making the measures more precise, more timely, and/or less subject to manipulation.

In addition, reviews can be used to provide either tight or loose assurance. Tight assurance is more likely if the reviews are detailed, comprehensive, and frequent.

Of course, managers do not have to rely exclusively on a single type of control in a control system. Use of more than one type of control—in effect, overlapping controls—will often provide reinforcement. For example, most organizations rely on selecting good people, establishing some set procedures, implementing some accountability for results, and reviewing some key decisions before they are made.

Costs: Outlay and Behavioral

The cost of a control depends on two factors: the incremental dollar cost of the tool and the cost of any unintended behavioral effects. The actual dollar cost of a control might be considerably less than it first appears because some devices that provide control may already be in place for other reasons. For example, a budgeting process for a small firm does not have to justify its cost on the basis of control reasons alone. Creditors probably already require *pro forma* financial statements, so the incremental cost might involve only additional detail (e.g., down to the operations level) and involvement of a greater number of participants.

The costs of any unintended negative effects must also be considered, and these can be very significant. It is beyond the scope of this article to provide an exhaustive enumeration of the many negative side effects possible. Indeed, they come in many different forms, but it is nevertheless useful to mention a few examples.

A common problem with specific-action controls is that they cause operating delays. These can be relatively minor, such as delays caused by limiting access to a stockroom, but they can also be major. For example, after the executives of Harley-Davidson Motor Company bought the firm from AMF, Inc., they found that they were able to implement a rebate program in ten days, rather than the six to eight weeks it would have taken with all the reviews required in the multilayered AMF organization.[8] Obviously, where timely action is important, delays caused by control processes can be very harmful.

Another problem with specific-action controls is that they can cause rigid, bureaucratic behavior. Individuals who become accustomed to following a set routine are not as apt to sense a changing environment, nor are they likely to research for better ways of doing the tasks at hand in a stable environment.

Results controls can create severe, unintended negative effects when all the measurement criteria are not met satisfactorily. Perhaps the most serious common problem is a failure to define the results areas correctly. This causes "goal displacement," a situation where individuals are encouraged to generate the wrong results—in response to the goals defined in the control system—rather than those results truly needed by the organization. For example, a department store introduced an incentive compensation plan to pay employees on the basis of sales volume. The immediate impact was indeed an increase in sales volume, but the increase was accomplished in ways that were inconsistent with long-term organizational goals. The employees competed among themselves for customers and neglected important but unmeasured and unrewarded activities such as stocking and merchandising.[9] Another common example of goal displacement is caused by the practice of rewarding managers on the oft criticized return-on-investment criterion.[10]

[8] See H. Klein, "At Harley-Davidson, Life without AMF Is Upbeat but Full of Financial Problems," *Wall Street Journal*, 13 April 1982, p. 37.

[9] See N. Babchuk and W. J. Goode, "Work Incentives in a Self-Determined Group," *American Sociological Review* (1951):679–687.

[10] For a summary of criticisms of return-on-investment (ROI) measures of performance, see J. Dearden, "The Case against ROI Control," *Harvard Business Review*, May-June 1969, pp. 124–135.

Data distortion is another dangerous potential side effect of results controls. If the measurement methods are not objective, then the employees whose performances are being measured might falsify the data or change the measurement methods, and, in so doing, undermine the whole organization's information system.

Many of the ramifications of these unintended effects of control systems are not well understood, and their costs are very difficult to quantify. However, consideration of these effects is an important control-system design factor: they cannot be ignored.

WHERE DOES FEEDBACK FIT IN?

Because feedback does not appear prominently in the preceding discussion, it is useful for clarification purposes to consider where feedback fits in. Control is necessarily future-oriented, as past performance cannot be changed, but analysis of results and feedback variances can often provide a particularly strong addition to a control system. A prerequisite, of course, if the ability to measure results, so feedback can only be useful in the situations presented in boxes 1 and 3 of Figure 1.

There are three reasons why feedback of past results is an important part of many control systems. First, feedback is necessary as reinforcement for a results-accountability system. Even if the feedback is not used to make input adjustments, it signals that results are being monitored. This can heighten employee awareness of what is expected of them and should help stimulate better performance.

FIGURE 2

A SIMPLE FEEDBACK CONTROL MODEL

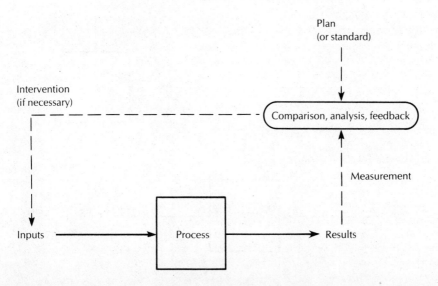

Second, in repetitive situations, measurement of results can provide indications of failure in time to make useful interventions. This is shown in the simple feedback control model presented in Figure 2. When the results achieved are not satisfactory, the inputs, which include the specific actions and types of persons involved, can be changed to provide different results. Obviously, these input adjustments are more likely to improve results when there is a good understanding of how inputs relate to results; otherwise, the interventions are essentially experiments.

Third, analysis of how the results vary with different combinations of inputs might improve understanding of how the inputs relate to results. This process is depicted in loop A of Figure 3, a slightly more complicated feedback control model. As this input/results understanding improves, it provides the opportunity to shift the control system from a results-oriented to a specific-action-oriented focus. If managers discover that certain specific actions produce consistently superior results, then it might be beneficial to inform employees of the specific actions that are expected of them, for example, by publishing these desired actions in a procedures manual. The greater the knowledge about how actions bring about results, the greater the possibilities of using a tight, specific-action-oriented control system.

Note that these latter two reasons for analyzing feedback—for making interventions and for learning—are only useful in situations that at least partially repeat themselves. If a situation is truly a one-time occurrence,

FIGURE 3

A FEEDBACK CONTROL MODEL WITH LEARNING

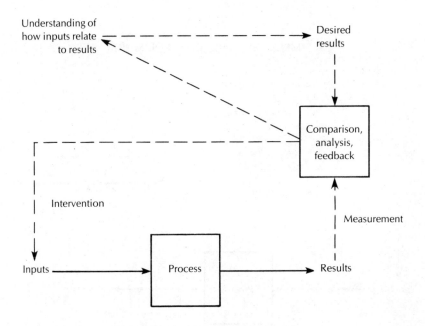

such as a major divestiture or a unique capital investment, management has little use for feedback information. In these cases, by the time the results are available, it is too late to intervene, and a greater understanding of how results are related to inputs is not immediately useful.

There are other circumstances where feedback need not, and perhaps should not, be a part of a good control system. In many cases, although feedback control systems are not really feasible, they are used anyway. This occurs because of the consistent tendency "to concentrate on matters that are concrete and quantifiable, rather than intangible concepts," which may be equally or more important.[11] Invariably, this will lead to dysfunctional effects, as will all other failures to satisfy the measurement criteria or to define results appropriately.

Cost considerations also commonly lead to decisions not to include feedback in a control system. The design, implementation, and maintenance of results-tracking information systems can often be very expensive. Thus, it is not feasible to have feedback as part of every control system, nor is it necessarily desirable even when feasibility constraints are not present.

THE DESIGN PROCESS

As discussed at the beginning of this article, management control is a problem of human behavior. The challenge is to have each individual acting properly as often as possible. Thus, it seems logical to start the control-system design process by considering the personnel component of the organization by itself. In some situations, well-trained, highly motivated personnel can be expected, with a high degree of certainty, to perform their jobs satisfactorily without any additional control steps being taken. A confident reliance on personnel controls is a very desirable situation because additional controls cost money and may have undesirable side effects.

If, however, management determines that personnel controls should be supplemented, the first step should be to examine the feasibility of the various control options. To do this, management must assess two factors: how much is known about which specific actions are desirable, and how well measurement can be accomplished in the important performance areas. This feasibility test might immediately determine whether the controls that can be added should be oriented toward specific actions or results. Control can be made tighter by strengthening the controls in place, along the lines discussed earlier, or by implementing overlapping controls, such as controls over results and specific actions.

In most cases, management has some, but less than complete, knowledge of which specific actions are desirable and some, but not perfect, ability to measure the important result areas. This situation usually calls for

---

[11] See D. Mitchell, *Control without Bureaucracy* (London: McGraw-Hill Book Company Limited, 1979), p. 6.

implementation of both specific-action and results controls, with feedback loops to improve understanding of the relevant processes.

AN EXAMPLE: CONTROL OF A SALES FORCE

The above observations about control can be illustrated by describing how control of a sales force might work. Generally, personnel controls are some part of every sales force control system. Consider, for example, this statement by a sales and marketing consultant:

> I think I can tell a good salesman just by being around him. If the guy is experienced, confident, well-prepared, speaks well, maintains control of situations, and seems to have his time planned, I assume I have a good salesman.

If a sales manager feels confident about all of the salespeople employed, he or she might wish to allow personnel controls to dominate the control system. This is likely, for example, in a small business with a sales force comprised solely of relatives and close friends. But most sales managers are not willing to rely exclusively on hiring and training good people.

What controls should be added? The answer, of course, depends on the type of sales involved. In a single-product, high-volume operation, the volume of sales generated is probably a good simple factor on which to base a results-oriented control system. It provides a reasonable, although not perfect, surrogate for long-range profitability, and the measurements are very inexpensive because the data are already gathered as a necessary input to the financial reporting system. The results-accountability system can then be completed by providing reinforcement in the form of sales commissions. This simple solution will also work where multiple products with varying profitabilities are involved, if the commission schedules are varied so that rewards are assigned in proportion to the profitability of the sales generated.

Consider, however, a situation where salespeople sell large-scale construction equipment and where sales come in very large but infrequent chunks. A commission-type, results-accountability system is still feasible. Measurement of results is not difficult and can be accurate to the penny. The amount of control provided, however, is not high because the measurements fail on the timeliness dimension. Because sales are infrequent, zero sales is not an unusual situation in any given month. Therefore, a salesperson could be drawing advances on hypothetical future commissions for many months without performing any of the desired promotional activities.

Two solutions are possible. One is to augment the commission system with some specific-action controls, such as activity reports. Some activities are probably known to be desirable, such as the number of hours worked and the quantity of calls made. If the product mix and market environment are fairly stable, then requiring and monitoring activity reports is not as costly as it might seem, because it could provide an important side benefit— an activity-oriented data base. The patterns in this data base can be analyzed and compared with results over time to add to knowledge about which activities yield the best results.

An alternate solution is to improve the results-accountability system. It might be possible to define some factors that are strong predictors of sales success, such as customer satisfaction with the salesperson or customer familiarity with the company's products. Measurement of these intangibles, of course, would have to be done by surveying customers. Even though these measures do not directly assess the desired result area (long-range profitability), and measurement is imprecise, they could provide a better focus for a results-oriented control system than a sales-generated measure because of the improvement in timeliness. Over time, it is likely that the choice of measures and measurement methodologies could be improved. The advantage of this results-oriented solution over an action-oriented system is that it is more flexible and less constraining to the salespeople; they can continue to use styles best suited to their personalities.

CONCLUSIONS

This article has taken a new look at the most basic organizational control problem—how to get employees to live up to the plans that have been established. In the course of discussion, the following major points were made:

1. Management control is a behavioral problem. The various control tools are only effective to the extent that they influence behavior in desirable directions.

2. Good control can often be achieved in several different ways. In some circumstances, the control problems can be avoided, for example, by centralizing or automating certain decisions. If problems cannot be avoided, one or more types of controls are usually desirable or necessary. The options can be classified according to the object of control, labeled in this article as specific actions, results, and personnel.

3. Not all types of controls are feasible in all situations. Figure 4 presents the questions to ask when assessing the feasibility of control types. If none of the controls is feasible, the probability of undesirable results occurring is high.

4. Control can be strengthened either by employing a tighter version of a single type of control or by implementing more than one type of control. However, tighter control is not always desirable because of additional system costs and the potential of undesirable side effects, such as destruction of morale, reduction of initiative, or displacement of employee focus toward measurable result areas only. Some of the qualities, benefits, and costs of each of the major control types are listed in Table 2.

5. The basic management control problems and alternatives are the same in all functional areas and at all levels in the organization, from the lowest supervisory levels to the very top levels of management. The best solutions, however, vary between situations.

FIGURE 4

QUESTIONS TO DETERMINE FEASIBILITY
OF CONTROL TYPES

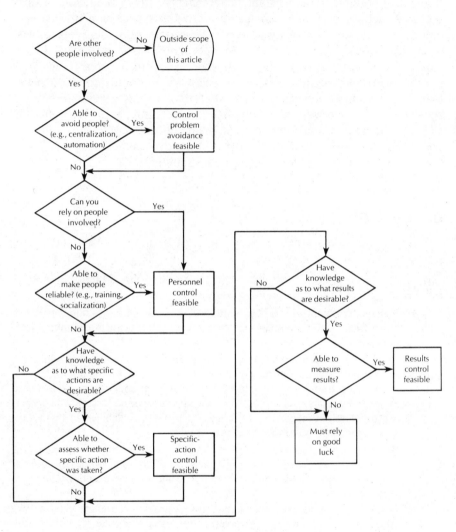

An understanding of control can be an important input into many management decisions. For example, control problems should be considered in
making some types of investments. An investemnt in an operation in which
control is very difficult—such as a highly specialized and technical area
where control must depend heavily on personnel controls—is, by definition,
risky. Thus, investments in such areas should promise high returns to compensate for this risk.

TABLE 2

QUALITIES OF CONTROL TOOLS

Object of Control:	Specific Actions		Results		Personnel
	Constraint	Accountability	Review	Accountability	
Amount of control provided (tight or loose)	Tight	Tight if specific; loose if vague	Tight if detailed and frequent	Tight if expectations are specific and detailed	Loose
Out-of-pocket-cost (relative)	Low	Low	High	High	Varies
Possible unintended effects (examples)	Slight operating delays	Rigid, bureaucratic behavior	Operating delays	Goal displacement data distortion	

Similarly, control considerations should affect the design of the other parts of the management system. Consider, for example, the organizational structure. If independent areas of *responsibility* cannot be carved out as part of the organizational structure, results-accountability control systems will not work well because employees will not feel that their individual actions have a noticeable effect on results. (It should be noted that many of the prescriptions calling for "responsibility accounting" only provide the illusion of results independence because of the many allocations of the costs and/or benefits of shared resources.) If independent areas of *authority* are not established, specific-action-accountability control systems cannot work. This principle underlies the internal control principle of "separation of duties." In addition, if tighter reviews of specific actions are necessary for adequate performance assurance, it is likely that the supervisory spans of control will have to be reduced. Similar observations can be made about other management functions, but they are beyond the scope of this article.

This article has attempted to provide a new look at this basic, but often overlooked, management problem. The control area is decidely complex, and there is much that is not known about how controls work and how employees respond to different types of controls. For example, it would be worthwhile to know more about how controls can be designed to maximize the amount of control provided while minimizing the cost in the form of employee feelings of lost autonomy. However, an increased awareness of the control problem, of what can be accomplished, and of the options available should provide a new perspective that will suggest ways to improve control systems and overall organizational performance.

The author wishes to acknowledge Robert N. Anthony, Peter Brownell, and Martha S. Hayes for their helpful comments.

26 • THE POVERTY OF MANAGEMENT CONTROL PHILOSOPHY[1]

Geert Hofstede[2]

The ineffectiveness of many management control systems is attributed to the cybernetic philosophy on which they are based. A distinction is made between routine industrial type processes, for which a homeostatic paradigm is more suitable, and nonroutine, nonindustrial type processes, for which a political paradigm is recommended. Attempts at enforcing a cybernetic paradigm on the latter processes, such as Program/Planning/Budgeting System and management by objectives, are bound to fail.

> Ja, mach' nur einen Plan!
> Sei nur ein grosses Licht!
> Und mach' dann noch 'nen Zweiten Plan,
> Geh'n tun sie beide nicht
> Bertolt Brecht, Die Dreigroschenoper.[3]

Anthony and Vancil [1, p. 5] define *management control* as "the process by which managers assure that resources are obtained and used effectively and efficiently in the accomplishment of the organization's objectives." Others narrow this definition down and distinguish *planning* (the setting of goals) from *control* (living up to the goals that were set). Whether we use the wider or the more limited definition, management control is the domain *par excellence* of formalized systems in organizations, and these systems tend to be designed according to a cybernetic philosophy.

By *cybernetic* is meant a process which uses the negative feedback loop represented by setting goals, measuring achievement, comparing achievement to goals, feeding back information about unwanted variances into the process to be controlled, and correcting the process. This is a much narrower use of the term *cybernetic* than that advocated by Wiener, who coined it to deal with the transfer of messages in the widest sense [17], but it corresponds more closely to its present use in practice. In spite of (or maybe owing to) its simplicity, the cybernetic-in-the-narrow-sense feedback loop has attained the status of a proper paradigm in a wide area of systems theory including, but not limited to, the management sciences [15]. A review of nearly 100 books and articles on management control theory issued between 1900 and 1972 [4] reflects entirely the cybernetic paradigm.

[1]From *Academy of Management Review,* Vol. 3, No. 3 (July, 1978), pp. 450–461. Reprinted by permission of *Academy of Management Review.*

[2]Geert Hofstede, Professor of Organizational Behavior at the European Institute for Advanced Studies in Management, Brussels, Belgium, and at INSEAD, Fontainebleau, France.

[3]Brecht's *Beggars Opera* may exist in an English translation but I have not been able to locate it. My own imperfect translation of these German lines is:
> "Just try to make a plan
> for which you pick your brain
> and after that, another plan:
> your toil will be in vain."

FIGURE 1

TECHNICAL CONTROL MODEL OF AN ORGANIZATIONAL CONTROL SYSTEM

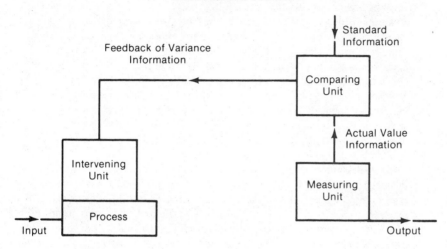

In the cybernetic view, a management control process in its most simplified form is similar to a technical control process, for example, control of the heat of a room by a thermostat (see Figure 1).

The model in Figure 1 uses only first order feedback. More sophisticated models for which technical analogues also can be found use higher order feedbacks to control the lower order controllers. Another possible control model used in technical devices is "feed forward," sometimes presented as an alternative for management control. Feed forward, however, assumes that interventions are programmable in advance as a known function of environmental disturbances—a condition unlikely to be fulfilled in most management control situations.

All cybernetic models of control have to assume that

1. There is a standard, corresponding to effective and efficient accomplishment of the organization's objectives.
2. Actual accomplishment can be measured. In Figure 1, the measuring unit is connected to the output of the process, but the measuring may include data about the input or about the ratio between output and input. For example, in an industrial production process, the quantity of various inputs (labor, materials, energy) for a given quantity of output may be measured.
3. When standard and measurement are compared and variance information is fed back, this information can be used to intervene in the process so as to eliminate unwanted differences between measurement and standard for the next round.

There is no doubt that the cybernetic model of control has been eminently successful in the design of machines, electronic circuits, or similar technical systems; but management control in an organization is a social process in a social, or maybe socio-technical system. The units (see Figure 1) in this case are people, or even groups of people. This subjects the use of the cybernetic model to severe limitations because

1. In many organizational situations, one or more of the three above-mentioned basic assumptions necessary for the validity of the cybernetic model are not justified: standards do not exist, accomplishment is not measurable, feedback information cannot be used. This is particularly the case for indirect (service) activities in industrial organizations and for all nonindustrial organizations, such as schools, hospitals, and public bodies. I became painfully aware of this when discussing classical industrial type management control [12] with a group of experienced management consultants working in nonindustrial settings. After finding out that the cybernetic paradigm did not apply to these consultants' daily practice, we even started to wonder to what extent it *really* applies in many industrial settings.

2. The three assumptions of the presence of a standard, the measurability of accomplishment, and the usability of feedback are most justified for routine, industrial type processes: industrial production and sales, and the supplying of routine services to clients. But even these relatively machinelike processes are in reality social: the cybernetic control process as pictured by the model is only one of many interpersonal processes going on among the same people at the same time. Other processes—some of them by-products of the control system—may interfere with the control process, and sometimes may even lead to an outcome which is the opposite of what was intended by the designers of the system [6].

One remarkable fact about control processes in organizations which have become associated with the cybernetic paradigm is that they are usually tied to a division of labor—different units in the model correspond to different people who are specialized in their tasks. Measuring and comparing are often done by staff personnel of a controller's department, standards are set by higher line management, intervening is the task of lower line management, while the actual process to be controlled is carried out by operating personnel (workers). In the last resort, it is usually these workers' response to the control process that determines whether the control has been effective.

Proper functioning of the control process presupposes *communication* [17]: the necessary messages should be sent and correctly received between the various specialized actors; it also presupposes that all will feel *motivated* to act according to the model [6]. Already the proper sending and receiving of the necessary messages poses many problems, since the various persons involved have different types of education, work experience, and hold different values. The latter also affects their motivation pattern.

A difference in values between people in controllers' departments and line management is evident to anyone familiar with organizational folklore; moreover, it is illustrated by research. For example [6, p. 236], controllers' department personnel in five Dutch companies felt more than line managers that working does not come naturally to most people and that people therefore need to be controlled and prodded (a Theory X point of view); they also showed themselves more concerned with the method of measuring performances than with the content of what was measured. In another study of an international group of middle management personnel [8], those in accounting and control departments, compared with others, showed low concern for the efficiency and effectiveness of their actions but high concern with orderliness, following a systematic approach, and doing things according to a schedule. Both studies quoted suggest that people in control departments tend to stress *form* whereas those in line roles tend to stress *content*.

In most cases, the controller's department is responsible not only for measuring and comparing, but also for design of the entire control system. An excessive stress on form rather than content explains why, at close scrutiny, many management control systems do *not* supply real control, but only pseudocontrol. *Pseudocontrol* is a state in which a system is under control on paper (the figures look right) but not in reality. There are several ways to achieve pseudocontrol; for example, by correcting the standards (rather than the process) whenever an important variance occurs, by choosing one's measures of performance so as to reflect the desired result (there are many ways to bend the figures without actually cheating), or by adjusting one element in the process at the expense of another which does not show in the figures (reducing cost at the expense of quality).

The value differences between the controller's department personnel and line management are just one type of social communication barriers in the system. We can also think of the way in which rank-and-file workers, with their particular education, work experience, and value systems, tend to react to control measures. We all know these are often met with considerable suspicion and resistance, going counter to the desired motivation, but control systems designers have been extremely slow to take account of these facts. As far back as 1953, Jonas [11, p. 188] signaled the tendency among cyberneticians to apply two kinds of doctrine—one to the people in their models, who are taken as robots, and another one to themselves: "He (the cybernetician) considers behavior, except his own; purposiveness, except his own; thinking, except his own." People usually dislike being taken as robots, and they will resist an organization built on such a double doctrine.

AN ALTERNATIVE PARADIGM: HOMEOSTASIS

While the cybernetic paradigm, by distinguishing various units in the control process, has undoubtedly contributed to the division of labor in control process tasks, there can be cybernetic control without division of labor. Division of labor in control of production tasks may have been a productive innovation in the days of F. W. Taylor who advocated" . . . taking the control of the machine shop out of the hands of the many workmen, and placing it completely in the hands of the management, thus superseding rule of thumb by scientific control" ("On the Art of Cutting Metals," 1906, p. 39; 4). It is recognized now that the separation of tasks and specialization which Taylor defended can go too far. What, among other factors, has changed since Taylor's days, at least in developed countries, is the worker. Today's worker is better educated; to escape from starvation is no longer his or her primary work motive, but he or she can afford to look for a task with some intrinsic reward to it. Entrusting, measuring, comparing, and intervening to specialized staff and line personnel implies an assumption that the operating personnel themselves cannot or do not want to adequately perform these tasks. This assumption, which is reinforced by the Theory X attitude found among certain people in controlling roles, may no longer be justified in many cases.

A fully documented example is available from a typewriter assembly workshop in Amsterdam [7]. Up to 1969, assembly took place in long lines of 60 to 70 operators each. The process was controlled by specialists in various ways. Engineers calculated time standards and divided the total assembly job into individual tasks of as equal as possible duration. For control purposes, the lines were further divided into five sections of 12 to 14 operators. Each section had its quality inspector to check the section's production; quality inspectors produced computerized defect lists for the line manager, and specialized repairmen repaired the defects. Five foremen, each assisted by a charge hand, supervised the five sections of two parallel assembly lines, so that each foreman was specialized in the supervision of one particular part of the assembly process. Foremen allocated workers to places, gave instructions, and watched over presence and absence; another computerized list showed the production and the various kinds of unproductive time for each worker. Specialized dispatchers provided the assembly operators with the parts they needed.

After extensive experiments the department was reorganized in 1971 into semiautonomous groups of 20 operators each. Operators divided the total assembly task among themselves according to each person's real capacities rather than based on a general standard. Quality defects were reported verbally within the group and corrected immediately; repairmen became superfluous and switched to production. Operators started ordering their own parts instead of waiting for the dispatcher. The foreman's task changed drastically; it now demanded less technical, more social leadership, representing the group to the rest of the organization. Operators arranged among themselves replacement for temporary absences, and the production recording was reduced to counting the number of finished machines at the end of the day. The various computer lists were discontinued. Productivity increased by 18 percent in two months and continued improving: in the two-and-a-half years following the reorganization the total gain was 46 percent, and quality improved.

The new situation also posed new problems. At the worker level training time for new operators increased. Since groups rather than individuals had become the basic elements in the production system, stability of group composition became much more of an issue than before. For these reasons rapid extension, change and reduction of production programs and levels posed more problems under the new system. The number of constraints for planning increased, the process became less flexible. An explosive production volume increase in 1974 led to severe productivity and quality problems in 1975. Another difficulty was that the new structure was limited to the worker level and was not reinforced by corresponding changes in structure and philosophy at higher levels in the hierarchy and in staff departments. People at the interface between the classical and the restructured part of the organization, such as supervisors, found their roles extremely difficult. As a result, the organization of the department moved back to more classical management control procedures in later years, although the small working groups with their aspect of job enlargement (work cycles of about ten minutes instead of three minutes in 1969) were retained.

The case shows that, under favorable circumstances, semiautonomous groups were created and took over most of the management control roles previously fulfilled by superiors and specialists. All tasks within the classical cybernetic control loop—measuring, comparing, feedback, intervening—were carried out within the group itself. Its links to the organization's needs were mainly established through the standards set by others in the organization for the group's tasks. Quality standards were given by the quality control department based on sales and customer service requirements, delivery programs by the production control department; productivity standards were present in the form of past production records. Rather than cybernetic, I would call such a control process *homeostatic.* Its analogy is not a technical device like a thermostat but a biological element represented by a *living cell,* which is equipped with internal processes capable of maintaining an equilibrium in a changing environment, provided that the environmental conditions do not become too unfavorable.

Like the word *cybernetic, homeostatic* can be used to mean different things; the term is used here because of its predominantly biological connotation. Homeostatic processes are composed of cybernetic elements, but without the division of labor between controlling and controlled units; control is exercised within the system itself. We could also call these processes self-regulating [14].

The switch from a technical to a biological paradigm also explains one other aspect of homeostatic control processes which was illustrated in the typewriter assembly case: whereas a technical control device can quickly be put together and can be repaired if it breaks down, a cell must grow (which takes time), and it can die. Homeostatic control processes, therefore, are more vulnerable than cybernetic processes.

The transfer from cybernetic to homeostatic management control systems will demand a drastically changed control philosophy, especially with regard to the traditional division of labor tied to the cybernetic model. Those in controllers' departments involved in the design and introduction of control systems will have to widen their outlook to include a broad view of the socio-psychological processes going on between people in an organization. The homeostatic approach needs a new type of controller. It may also need new types of information systems. Today considerable efforts are put into developing and improving management information systems, but here again the designers' basic assumptions about socio-psychological processes are often remarkably simplistic and shallow.

NONCYBERNETIC PROCESSES

So far we have dealt with control situations for which the three main conditions of the cybernetic model were fulfilled: a standard exists, accomplishment is measurable, feedback can be used for corrective intervention. If we consider the full range of human organizations in which control processes occur, those that satisfy the conditions for the cybernetic model tend to be the more structured, those which more or less fit a machine analog. In a criticism of the cybernetic paradigm in system theory in general, Sutherland [15] makes applicability of cybernetic control dependent on the determinedness of a system. If phenomena are completely determined, cybernetic control is obviously superfluous. It becomes useful for moderately stochastic phenomena. When phenomena are severely stochastic, cybernetic control becomes either technically or economically unfeasible. When phenomena are completely undetermined, cybernetic control has become meaningless. Translated in terms of everyday organization activities, Sutherland's moderately stochastic phenomena are the more structured: the routine industrial type processes referred to before. In many other organizational situations (indirect departments in industrial companies, public bodies, schools, hospitals, voluntary associations), we are in Sutherland's area of severely stochastic or even completely undetermined phenomena, and we meet with great problems in applying the cybernetic model. What we notice in practice when we try to follow a cybernetic approach is that (1) objectives may be missing, unclear, or shifting; (2) accomplishment may not be measurable; and/or (3) feedback information may not be usable. Each of these three conditions is illustrated here.

1. *Objectives are missing, unclear, or shifting.* If there is to be a standard, there should be objectives from which this standard is derived. Setting of standards presupposes clarity about the organization's objectives. Now social scientists have often stressed that to speak of an organization's objectives is unallowable; organizations cannot have objectives, only people can. We can speak of an organization's objectives only to the extent that there is either virtually complete consensus between all organization members about what should be done (for example, in a voluntary fire brigade); or a dominant coalition of persons within the organization with sufficient power to impose their objectives on all others, and with consensus among themselves (as in many business enterprises); or a single power holder whose objectives count as the organization's objectives (as in a small owner-controlled business firm).

    Many organizations do not satisfy any of these three conditions, and their objectives are therefore ambiguous. Examples are:
    a. Democratic institutions such as the city governments in most Western countries. In this case power is deliberately distributed among several persons or coalitions who hold different objectives for the entire organization; moreover, power is partly held by elected representatives, partly by permanent civil servants; the two groups differ considerably in their involvement with and expectations from the organization.
    b. Universities. Perhaps this is the extreme case of organizations in which power is widely distributed and different power groups hold very divergent views about objectives.

    c. Business organizations or parts of business organizations in which domi-
nant coalitions are not unanimous about objectives. Business employees
know that objectives may shift from one day to another, depending on who
has the upper hand. This becomes even more likely where societal changes,
such as attempts at establishing industrial democracy, bring new coalitions
of organization members into the objective-setting process.

In such cases, decisions, if they are consciously taken at all, are based on
processes of negotiation and struggle and cannot be derived from any prior organizational objective. Objectives may forever remain unclear. This may even be true if
someone in the organization publishes eloquent espoused objectives for public relations purposes—like those sometimes expressed in company charters. The objectives
in use in the real life situation of the organization's members are not necessarily the
same as the published ones.

2. *Accomplishment* may not be *measurable.* Even in cases where objectives are clear
    to all involved, it is often not possible to translate them into unambiguous,
    quantitative output standards against which performance can be measured. How
    should we measure the output of a police department? One of its final objectives
    is definitely to prevent crime; so we might consider the decrease of crime rates
    as an output measure. This assumes that other influences on crime rates can be
    neglected (which is not true) and that crime rates themselves can be measured
    objectively (whereas in fact they are partly derived from police reports). Low
    reported crime rates could also mean administrative incompetence of police per-
    sonnel to adequately register crimes. In such cases organizations often resort to
    surrogate measures of performance and to measures which are less directly tied
    to the organization's objectives but which are more easily measurable. In the case
    of the police department, the number of people arrested or the amount of fines
    levied could be such surrogate measures.

        For many organizations or activities within organizations, outputs can
    only be defined in qualitative and vague terms; the only thing really measur-
    able about such activities is their inputs—how much money and other re-
    sources will be allotted to them. These include most management and indirect
    activities in industrial organizations, such as advertising, personnel depart-
    ments, control activities in headquarters, research; most public bodies, such
    as municipal and government services; most activities in schools, universities,
    hospitals, and voluntary associations. In all these cases, the sole control of
    management exists at the time of resource allocation, but the criteria for
    resource allocation to this and not to that activity are judgmental. The essence
    of the process is negotiation, a political process in which many arguments
    other than the effective and efficient use of resources usually play a role—status
    of the negotiator, amount of support among influential persons which he or
    she might mobilize, personal relationship between negotiators, and sometimes
    nepotism.

        One frequently used control device is whether similar funds allocated last
    year were really spent; its main effect is the spending of unnecessary funds.
    Skillful negotiators have many ploys at their disposal, and skillful resource
    allocators have many counterploys [2, p. 249]. This is a part of the game of
    management control which has little to do with either effectiveness or effi-
    ciency of the organization—not because of anybody's evil intentions but sim-
    ply because nobody is able to predict which resource allocation corresponds
    to maximum effectiveness.

3. *Feedback information may not be usable.* The cybernetic model presupposes a recurring cycle of events: variance information is used to correct the present state of affairs to eliminate unwanted variances for the future. The model basically does not apply to one-time projects, like most investment projects, whether in private or in public organizations. Since the project in its present form never returns, even large differences between planned and actual cost and performance have no effect on future projects.

It is remarkable that many organizations do not even attempt to do any project cost accounting to check whether predictions at the time of proposal were really fulfilled; this can hardly be justified solely on the technical grounds that the benefits of one single project are difficult to disentangle. Once a proposal is accepted the resources allocated to it become sunk costs, and it is good management practice not to bother about such costs. However, this state of affairs stresses the negotiation element in the allocation of resources to investment projects even more. It is often hardly important whether the project's forecasted costs and performances are realistic—it is important that they look good to the person or persons who decide on the allocation. Once the decision is taken few people worry about real outcomes. This leads to deliberate underestimation of costs. A common practice in the game of investment budgeting is, for example, to budget for the price of a machine but not for its installation costs, auxiliary tools, or spare parts; once the machine is bought the organization is forced to buy these other items to get it going.

A few organizations do use regular evaluation studies of past investment projects; Hägg [5] studied these investment reviews and claims as one of their potential effects a "symbolic use." There is no change impact as far as planning of future projects is concerned. But managers use the review procedure by, for example, referring to it as a sign of progressive management. They can do this when asked questions about capital investment activities by researchers or superiors. The review procedure can also be looked upon as "institutionalized," as part of a tradition or a myth in the organization [5, pages 58–59]. Of course, it is also possible that reviews do have a change impact, or that they have no impact at all, not even a symbolic one. Hägg notes a general lack of interest by managers in the reviews; in cases where reviews could reveal outright failures in investment decisions, we could expect them to be unpopular among those who proposed and took these decisions.

ENFORCING A CYBERNETIC MODEL

With all its weaknesses, management control in situations which do meet the three basic conditions for applying the cybernetic model (presence of standards, measurable accomplishment, usable feedback) has still had a fair amount of success. In the developed countries of our world, an increasing part of the national income is spent on activities which do *not* meet these conditions—indirect departments in private organizations and all kinds of public activities, including education and health care.

Responsible managers have attempted to find ways to control the considerable resources spent on such activities. The success of the cybernetic model in other situations has led them to try to enforce a cybernetic approach for indirect and public activities as well. In practice this has been done by calling successful industrial consultants (McKinsey) to propose reorganizations for nonindustrial organizations—reorganizations which rarely have been carried out and even more rarely have been successful. The transfer of Robert McNamara from the Ford Corporation to the Secretary of Defense in the sixties began a movement in United States public agencies towards a planning/programming/budgeting system which became widely known as PPBS or PPB. PPBS has a number of objectives, but among these is control which it tries to execute by enforcing the cybernetic model, and in its most ambitious form it claims to apply to any organization. Reactions and experiences have been mixed. In 1967, C. L. Schultze, former Director, United States Bureau of the Budget, before a United States Senate Subcommittee, stated:

> I look forward to substantial improvements next year in terms of schedule, understanding of the role, and desired character of the Program Memoranda, and, perhaps more important, in terms of their analytic content. Analytic staffs have been assembled and have had a chance to shake down; a number of data collection efforts and long-term study efforts should reach fruition; and we are learning how to state program issues in a way that facilitates analysis and comparison. We have not yet by any means achieved my expectations for the system. That is partly because I have such high expectations for it. Ultimately I expect we will realize these expectations [1, page 702].

However, Wildavsky noted:

> PPBS has failed everywhere and at all times. Nowhere has PPBS been established and influenced governmental decisions according to its own principles. The program structures do not make sense to anyone. They are not, in fact, used to make decisions of any importance. Such products of PPBS as do exist are not noticeably superior in analytic quality or social desirability to whatever was done before [18, pp. 363–364].

The fundamental problem of an approach like PPBS—which has spread to other countries in spite of its ambiguous results in the United States—may be precisely that it extrapolates a cybernetic philosophy derived from industrial production and sales situations to organizations of a very different nature and that it never asked the basic question whether and when this extrapolation is justified. Within the public system there are activities that meet the criteria for a cybernetic control approach, such as quantifiable public services: garbage collection, public transport, the Post Office. Other activities miss one or more of the fundamental conditions for the cybernetic model; and no amount of trying harder, setting up analytic staffs (with all the value conflicts involved), and data collection will overcome this.

There is a certain parallel between PPBS in public administration and another popular technique of the sixties mainly used in private organizations: management by objectives (MBO). MBO is also based on a cybernetic philosophy [15]: objective setting (jointly between the employee, who is often himself a manager, and his superior), performance review, and corrective action. Not unlike PPBS, MBO is supported by believers but also is heavily attacked. Levinson calls it "one of the greatest management illusions" and "industrial engineering with a new name" [13]. Few cases of successful implementation of MBO have been reported —that is, cases in which others than the one responsible for the implementation claim it has been successful in improving performance. Ivancevich [9], besides reviewing the rare literature on research about MBO, reports on a three-year longitudinal study on the introduction of MBO in two out of three plants of one United States manufacturing company. The results were mixed, with one plant showing significant long-term improvement in performance and the other not. His study dealt with production workers and salesmen, organization members whose accomplishment is to some extent measurable. In these cases enforcement of a cybernetic control model by MBO may not be too difficult and, if the program is well managed, it may lead to performance improvement. However, MBO is also advocated and applied, for indirect jobs, in medical institutions, school systems, and government agencies. In these cases, accomplishment is much less measurable, and it is rare to find surrogates acceptable to both parties. If a commonly agreed measurement of accomplishment is lacking, the cybernetic model again does not apply, and MBO is simply bound to fail. A second reason why MBO may fail, even if the cybernetic model does apply, is that MBO is based on simplistic and mechanistic assumptions about the relationships among the people involved: it uses a reward-punishment psychology [13]. There is more going on between people than cybernetic objective setting and feedback alone.

POLITICAL CONTROL

Blanket application of a cybernetic philosophy to noncybernetic organization processes can only do more harm than good. This does not mean that the advantages of the cybernetic approach *to those cases where it applies* have to be dropped. Within most organizations, even indirect and public ones, there are activities that *can* be controlled in a cybernetic way: those which are mechanized so that individuals play no role in them; those where individuals play a role, but where there is consensus about what this role should be. However, it is necessary that performance be measurable so that standards can be set. In these cases, a cybernetic control philosophy—or preferably even a homeostatic philosophy—can make a real contribution. But often these cybernetic cases will be the exception. The more typically human and less mechanistic an activity, the less the chance that the conditions for a cybernetic approach will be met.

The essence of the noncybernetic situations is that they are *political;* decisions are based on negotiation and judgment (as an employee of a Dutch city government expressed it: on enlightenment by the Holy Spirit). Decisions often deal with *policies.* There is a well-known adage: There is no reason for it; it's just our policy. What this means is that policy is not merely composed of rational elements; its main ingredients are *values,* which may differ from person to person, and *norms,* which are shared within groups in society but vary over time and from group to group [16]. It makes little sense to speak of control processes here, at least in the formal sense in which such processes are described in cybernetic situations. It does make sense to speak of a control *structure,* taking into account the power positions of the various parties in the negotiations. Within this structure, we may study the control *games* played by the various actors [3]. Once resources are allocated, there is no automatic feedback on the effectiveness of their use; the only controls possible are whether the resources were really spent and if no funds were embezzled. Beyond that, it is a matter of trust in those in charge of carrying out the programs; the real control takes place through the appointment of a person to a task. Activities once decided upon will tend to perpetuate themselves; corrective actions in the case of ineffective or inefficient activities are not automatically produced by the control system but ask for a specific evaluation study; deciding upon such a study is in itself a political act which may upset an established balance of power.

As an example of a control aid that is still feasible in such a situation, Wildavsky [18, Ch. 19] describes the Public Expenditure Survey Committee (PESC) in the United Kingdom. The PESC is an interdepartmental group which establishes a yearly report showing the future cost of existing government policies, if these policies remain unchanged, over the next five years. The product of PESC is not planning or management control as such; it does not try to measure or evaluate outputs. It only presents an educated forecast of already committed inputs as a base line for governmental planning and policymaking. PESC does not assume any cybernetic model.

CONCLUSION: THE USE OF MODELS

In thinking about organizations, we cannot escape from using models. To see why this is so, I find it helpful to refer to the General Hierarchy of Systems which was first formulated in different ways by Von Bertalanffy and Boulding [10, pp. 7–9]. In the General Hierarchy of Systems, nine levels of complexity of systems are distinguished:

1. Static frameworks
2. Dynamic systems with predetermined motions
3. Closed loop control or cybernetic systems
4. Homeostatic systems like the biological cell
5. The living plant
6. The animal
7. Man
8. Human organizations
9. Transcendental systems

Every next level adds a dimension of complexity to the previous one.

So we find organizations at Level 8, where the complexity is overwhelming. Since the individual is at Level 7, it is fundamentally impossible for the human brain to grasp what goes on at Level 8. In order to think about organizations, we have to simplify: we use lower level systems which we can understand as models for what we cannot understand. Early thinkers about organizations focussed on the organization chart, a first level model. Scientific management was often concerned with procedures, second level models. The cybernetic control process is already a more complex third level model, and the homeostatic cell model is found at the fourth level.

One consequence of the use of lower level systems as models for organizations is that we automatically consider the people in the system (at least all except ourselves—see the quote from Jonas, page 266), as if they were things—as means to be used; the goals are supposed to be given. But, in fact, all organization goals derive from people: in the hierarchy of systems, the source of organization goals is at Level 7, with the individual. In an organization, the individual is *both goal and means;* but the use of lower level models implies dealing with people as means. We may do this only when there is consensus over goals, or goals can be imposed; so we see these are not just conditions for the applicability of the cybernetic model, but for any lower level model including biological ones.

In political situations there is no consensus about goals, and replacing the organizational reality by a model which treats people as means is no longer allowed. Using a cybernetic model such as PPBS, in such a case means a covering up of the real issues and will be perceived rightly by most people involved as an attempt by a technocratic coalition to impose their implicit goals on all others.

REFERENCES FOR ARTICLE

1. ANTHONY, R. N., J. DEARDEN, and R. F. VANCIL. *Management Control Systems: Text, Cases and Readings,* rev. ed. Homewood, Ill.: Richard D. Irwin, Inc., 1972.
2. ANTHONY, R. N., and R. HERZLINGER. *Management Control in Nonprofit Organizations.* Homewood, Ill.: Richard D. Irwin, Inc., 1975.
3. CROZIER, M. "Comparing Structures and Comparing Games." *European Contributions to Organization Theory,* edited by G. Hofstede and M. S. Kassem. Assens, Denmark: Van Gorcum, 1976, pp. 193–207.
4. GIGLIONI, G. B., and A. G. BEDEIAN. "A Conspectus of Management Control Theory: 1900–1972." *Academy of Management Journal,* Vol. 17 (1974), pp. 292–305.
5. HÄGG, I. "Reviews of Captial Investments." *Budgeting och Redovisning som Instrument for Styrning,* edited by S. Asztely. Stockholm: P. A. Norstedt, 1974, pp. 53–68.
6. HOFSTEDE, G. *The Game of Budget Control.* Assens, Denmark: Van Gorcum, and London: Tavistock Publications, 1967.
7. HOFSTEDE, G. *"Deux Cas de Changement."* Maitriser le Changement dans *l'Entreprise,* edited by H. C. de Bettignies. Paris: Les Editions d'Organisation, 1975, pp. 175–199.
8. HOFSTEDE, G. "Nationality and Espoused Values of Managers." *Journal of Applied Psychology,* Vol. 61, No. 2 (1976), pp. 148–155.
9. IVANCEVICH, J. M. "Changes in Performance in a Management by Objectives Program." *Administrative Science Quarterly,* Vol. 19 (1974), pp. 563–577.
10. JOHNSON, R. A., F. E. KAST, and J. E. ROSENZWEIG. *The Theory of Management of Systems.* New York City: McGraw-Hill, Inc., 1963.
11. JONAS, H. "A Critique of Cybernetics." *Social Research,* Vol. 20 (1953), pp. 172–192.
12. JURAN, J. M. *Managerial Breakthrough: A New Concept of the Manager's Job.* New York City: McGraw-Hill, Inc., 1964.

13. LEVINSON, H. "Management by Whose Objectives?" *Harvard Business Review,* Vol. 48, No. 4 (1970), pp. 125–134.
14. SANDKULL, B. "The Discontinuity of Modern Industry: A Quest for an Alternative Principle of Organizational Control." *Research Report, No. 31,* Linkoping, Sweden: Linkoping University, Department of Management and Economics, 1975.
15. SUTHERLAND, J. W. "System Theoretical Limits on the Cybernetic Paradigm." *Behavioral Science,* Vol. 20 (1975), pp. 191–200.
16. VICKERS, G. *Making Institutions Work.* London: Associated Business Programmes, 1973.
17. WIENER, N. *The Human Use of Human Beings: Cybernetics and Society.* 2nd rev. ed. Garden City, New York: Doubleday & Co., Inc., 1954.
18. WILDAVSKY, A. *Budgeting: A Comparative Analysis of the Budgetary Process.* Boston: Little, Brown & Company, 1975.

BIBLIOGRAPHY, CHAPTER 8

Anthony, Robert N. *Planning and Control Systems: A Framework for Analysis.* Cambridge, MA: Harvard University Press, 1965.
Arrow, Kenneth J. "Control in Large Organizations." *Management Science,* Vol. 10, No. 3 (April, 1964), pp. 397-408.
Beyer, Janice M., and Harrison M. Trice. "A Field Study of the Use and Perceived Effects of Discipline in Controlling Work Performance." *Academy of Management Journal,* Vol. 27, No. 4 (December, 1984), pp. 743-764.
Callahan, Robert E. "A Management Dilemma Revisited: Must Businesses Choose Between Stability and Adaptability?" *Sloan Management Review,* Vol. 21, No. 1 (Fall, 1979) pp. 25-33.
Cherrington, J. Owen, and D. J. Cherrington. "Budget Games for Fun and Frustration." *Management Accounting,* Vol. 57 (January, 1976), pp. 28-32.
Churchman, C. West, and P. Ratoosh. *Measurements: Definitions and Theories.* New York: John Wiley & Sons, Inc. 1959.
Daugherty, W., and D. Harvey. "Some Behavioral Implications of Budgeting Systems." *Arizona Business,* Vol. 20, No. 4 (April, 1973), pp. 3-7.
Dun and Bradstreet, Inc. *Cost Control in Business.* New York: Business Education Division, Dun and Bradstreet, Inc., 1967.
Follett, Mary Parker. "The Process of Control." From Gulick and Urwick (eds.). *Papers on the Science of Administration.* New York: Institute of Public Administration, 1937.
Haberstroh, Chadwick T. "Control as an Organization Process." *Management Science* (January, 1960), pp. 165-171.
Hall, W. N. "Methods of Evaluating Decentralized Operations." *Management Record,* Vol. 25, No. 1 (January, 1963), pp. 26-28.
Hamermesh, Richard G. "Responding to Divisional Profit Crises." *Harvard Business Review,* Vol. 55, No. 2 (March-April, 1977), pp. 124-130.
Herold, David M., and M. M. Greller. "Feedback: The Definition of a Construct." *Academy of Management Journal,* Vol. 20, No. 1 (March, 1977), pp. 142-147.

Higgins, J. C. "The Value of Accuracy in Information for Planning and Control." *Long-Range Planning,* Vol. 7, No. 4 (August, 1974), pp. 67-72.

How the duPont Organization Appraises its Performance. Financial Management Series 94, New York: American Management Association, Inc., 1950.

Jasinsky, Frank J. "Use and Misuse of Efficiency Controls." *Harvard Business Review,* Vol. 34, No. 4 (July-August, 1956), pp. 105-113.

Mauriel, John J., and Robert N. Anthony. "Misevaluation of Investment Center Performance." *Harvard Business Review,* Vol. 44, No. 2 (March-April, 1966).

McLean, John G. "Better Reports for Better Control." *Harvard Business Review,* Vol. 35, No. 3 (May-June 1957), pp. 95-104.

Parker, L. D. "Control in Organizational Life: The Contribution of Mary Parker Follett." *The Academy of Management Review,* Vol. 9, No. 4, pp. 736-745.

Prahalad, C. K. "An Approach to Strategic Control in MNC's." *Sloan Management Review,* Vol. 22, No. 4 (1980), pp. 5-13.

Reuter, Vincent G. "Utilization of Graphic Management Tools." *Arizona Business* (August-September, 1978), pp. 10-19.

Ridgeway, V. F. "Dysfunctional Consequences of Performance Measurement." *Administrative Science Quarterly* (September, 1956), pp. 240-247.

Sandretto, Michael J. "What Kind of Cost System Do You Need?" *Harvard Business Review,* Vol. 63, No. 1 (1985), pp. 110-118.

Schwartz, Bill N. "Implementing a Zero Base Budgeting System." *Arizona Business,* Vol. 27, No. 4 (April, 1980), pp. 9-18.

Searby, F. W. "Return to Return on Investment." *Harvard Business Review,* Vol. 53, No. 4 (March-April, 1975), pp. 113-119.

Terry, Herbert. "Comparative Evaluation of Performance using Multiple Criteria." *Management Science,* Vol. 9, No. 3 (April, 1963), pp. 432-441.

VanBreda, Michael F. "Integrating Capital and Operating Budgets." *Sloan Management Review,* Vol. 25, No. 2 (Winter, 1984), pp. 49-58.

Wiley, Mary Glenn, and Arlene Eskilson. "The Interaction of Sex and Power Base on Perceptions of Managerial Effectiveness." *Academy of Management Journal,* Vol. 25, No. 25 (September, 1982), pp. 671-676.

Chapter 9

Measurements
and Control

If we are to control, what is it that we are to control? In the first instance, the activity that is considered important to the goals of the organization appears most relevant. But it is not just a matter of identifying the most important behaviors that interests us. How do we measure those behaviors? To illustrate the problem that is presented in measuring performance of an organization, the financial theorists look for the long-term change in stockholder value, appropriately discounted, compared with alternate investments. Conversely, company managements might be seeking to maximize current returns on investment. Such a disagreement highlights the problem of deciding upon the proper measurement with which to evaluate behaviors. For it would be meaningless to correct performance to bring return on sales to an acceptable level if maximization of stockholder value were the most relevant measure of the phenomena of interest.

The problems of identifying proper behavior to control and the selection of the best measures of the behavior are the topics of most interest in this chapter. In the first paper Wilkinson provides a sweeping consideration of the measurement question, while Dewitt gets specific about ways to measure productivity of a firm relative to other firms in the industry.

In the last two articles the authors consider the process of control from an external perspective rather than from the point of view of the internal management of the enterprise. In their discussion of social audit, Davis and Blomstrom consider the issues of what constitutes proper social responsibility on the part of a corporation. While they write from the view of outsiders, it is possible that the firm can adopt these externally generated measures for its internal control efforts. Schell examines another externally generated set of measures for corporate performance from the viewpoint of the institutional investment community. The management of the firm may find these measures worth of its attention as well.

The papers in this chapter clearly show the necessity of selecting appropriate measures of the behavior we want to encourage or discourage. It is also clear that the authorship of the criteria may come from either internal or external sources.

27 • THE MEANINGS
OF MEASUREMENTS[1]

Managers are continuously preoccupied with problems relating to operational effectiveness and efficiency. They need up-to-date answers to such questions as: How well did the firm do last month in earning profits? Are we shipping orders to customers on time? Is the information system being used effectively? Are departmental managers controlling their resources properly? How productive are our employees? To gain the needed answers, managers perform a variety of measurements.

PREREQUISITES OF MEASUREMENTS

A prime prerequisite of performance measurements is that they provide quantitative indications of outputs related to objectives. An example of a measurement that well satisfies this prerequisite is the return on investment ratio, which yields a rate that is related to the profitability objective. Another prerequisite is that the measurement derives from a clear-cut and generally accepted process that involves precise and sensitive elements. Consider the measurement of inventory turnover which is computed as the ratio of cost of goods sold to average inventory. Because the process is unequivocal, and the two clearly defined elements are sensitive to the operations of a firm, the inventory turnover measurement is understandable and useful to a typical manager. On the other hand, the return on investment measurement does not meet this prerequisite very satisfactorily, since its elements are less clearly defined and sensitive. Assuming that the return on investment measurement pertains to an entire firm, the numerator may be variously specified as net income before income taxes, net income after income taxes, or net income before income taxes and bond interest. The investment in the denominator may be specified as gross assets, net assets, or owner's equity. During the process of computing the return on investment, the investment may or may not be averaged.

Other prerequisites of measurement are:

1. Timeliness. Each measurement should be available to the manager in time for him to take effective action, otherwise it has little value.

2. "Integrativeness." Each measurement should fit into the framework of measurements established by the firm and should exhibit characteristics that are appropriate to its position within the framework. Thus, measurements used for gauging the performance of high level managers or wide activity spans should be broad and

[1]From the Scottsdale Area Chapter of the National Association of Accountants, Vol. 57 (July, 1975), pp. 49–52.
[2]J. W. Wilkinson, Associate Professor of Accounting, Arizona State University, Tempe, Arizona.

related to strategic planning decisions; conversely, measurements used at low managerial levels or in narrow spans of activity should be pointed. Both the broad measurements and the narrow measurements should interlock.

3. Controllability. Each measurement used to gauge the performance of a manager must relate to factors that are controllable by the manager. For instance, a production manager should not be judged on the cost of raw materials used in production if he does not control the purchase of the materials.

Although few measurements in the real world meet all these prerequisites, most are useful if they meet only some of the prerequisites. In most instances a measurement could be employed if the value of the information that it provides exceeds the cost of generating the measurement. For example, the return on investment measurement is widely employed by firms because it yields a value that outweighs the shortcomings with respect to clarity and sensitivity. Furthermore, the cost required to produce the return on investment measurement is relatively small.

Figure 1 illustrates how performance measurements grow out of the objectives and policies established by top management as a result of long-term planning. Standard values are assigned to the respective measurements which are then compared with actual results. Significant deviations arising from the comparisons are fed back to signal the need for control decisions, corrective actions, or automatic adjustments. Multiple sets of measurements are usually desirable. For instance, as Figure 1 suggests, a set of measurements applicable to the information system of the firm may be developed parallel with the measurements that apply to the entire firm's operations. Both sets of measurements, however, blend into one overall control apparatus.

CLASSIFICATION OF MEASUREMENTS

A comprehensive set of performance measurements depends on adequate classifications. However, each individual measurement may be multidimensional and may be classified on the basis of more than one plan. Thus, gross profits per customer are measurable on the ratio scale, are related to the profitability objective and cost characteristic, fall within the marketing function, and are expressed in financial or monetary units. This feature of multidimensionality enables cross-checking among the respective classification plans, with the greater likelihood that all relevant measurements will be discovered. Listed below are five classification plans.

Measurability
1. Ratio scale: rate of return on investment, price earnings ratio, employee turnover
2. Interval scale: number of customer complaints, number of dollars in a particular account
3. Ordinal (ranking) scale: employee morale, product quality
4. Nominal scale: social responsibility, public representation

FIGURE 1

A MANAGEMENT CONTROL APPARATUS

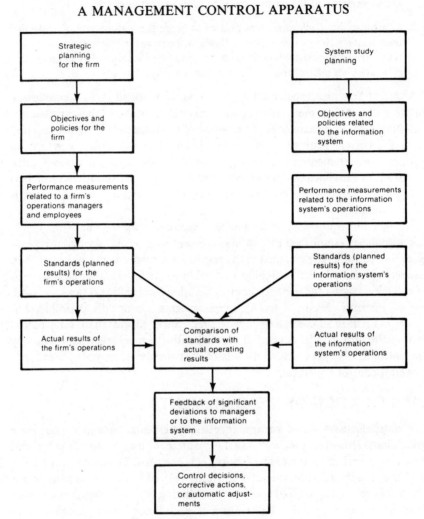

Objectives

1. Market standing: share of the market, price leadership
2. Profitability: rate of return on investment, rate of return on sales, contribution per product
3. Innovation: number of new products
4. Managerial and employee performance: budget variance for controllable costs, sales made per day, lines typed per hour
5. Managerial and employee development: number of hours devoted to training, number of promotions
6. Employee attitude: number of grievances, number of suggestions

7. Public responsibility: variety of public services performed
8. Customer relations: number of repeat sales
9. Productivity: number of units produced per man-hour or machine-hour, value added in relation to value distributed

Operating Function
1. Production: idle time (percentage of labor hours available), number of products rejected per day, percentage of production orders on schedule, percentage of scrap and rework, overhead variance
2. Marketing: gross profits per customer, increase or decrease in number of customers, number of new products, number of sales returns, number of customer complaints, share of the market sales quotas, number of calls made by salesmen
3. Personnel: employee turnover, absenteeism rate, grievances, number of new hires
4. Financial: current ratio, price earnings ratio, debt to equity ratio, receivables turnover

Operating Characteristics
1. Cost: overhead cost per unit produced, average cost per order processed
2. Time: length of time to check credit, length of time until manager answers customer inquiry, average throughput time in production for an order, percentage of orders shipped on schedule
3. Accuracy: number of errors made per invoice, average error in forecast sales
4. Reliability: number of machine breakdowns per month
5. Quality: length of product service life
6. Capacity: plant utilization (percentage of total capacity)
7. Efficiency: number of orders processed per man-hour

Unit of Measure
1. Financial: value added, profits, costs per cost center
2. Nonfinancial (operational): number of miles traveled per day, number of credit investigations, number of units produced per week

STANDARDS OF EVALUATION

A basis of comparison, or yardstick, is always needed to make effective use of each measurement. One commonly employed basis is time. Thus, a manager may compare the value of orders shipped last year against the value of orders shipped this year to see if business is growing. He may compare the value of orders shipped last month divided by last month's direct labor payroll (a measure on the ratio scale) against the value for the same ratio this month to determine whether scrap and rework losses are growing or declining.

Another basis that is often used is the standard measurement. Standards may be established in several different ways. One approach is to establish ideal, unattainable standards. Another approach is to employ normal standards based on the expected average performance for several future periods. A normal standard representing attainable performance is often used for such planning purposes as developing budgets. A normal, attainable, standard is generally believed to provide the greatest motivation to managers and employees.

A variety of techniques is often employed in setting specific values for different standards. Work measurement techniques, for instance, are most suitable for developing standard values related to the effectiveness of employees and machines that perform repetitive operations. Examples of such standards are the number of invoices typed per hour and the cost in dollars of direct labor per unit of product. The values of standards that gauge the effectiveness of managers (e.g., budgeted costs) are generally based on the experience and judgment of high level managers, plus the expectation of future events. The values of standards that take the form of financial ratios and key success factors are usually based on industry averages, statistical analysis of historical trends, and judgment.

Standard values are usually expressed in such units of measure as dollars, number of units per time period, or ratios. Thus, an example of a budget standard might be $100,000 of expenses for the machining department in 1972; while an example of a ratio standard might be 5 percent of back orders to total orders received. In some cases, standard values are expressed in a compound fashion. For instance, a service standard might state that at least 90 percent of the customers shall be waited on within two minutes. The values of standards may also change over extended periods of time as conditions change or as the firm adjusts to new situations. For example, during the years following the design of an improved information system, the percentage of back orders to total orders received might be assigned these standard values: 1971, 10 percent; 1972, 5 percent; 1973, 2.5 percent.

EXAMPLES OF PERFORMANCE MEASUREMENTS

Consider the development of performance measurements for a typical manufacturing firm. As a first step the president and the controller select measurements related to the overall firm. For each measurement they designate the responsible manager, based on established lists of responsibilities. Next they set standard values by reference to historical trends, averages, and expectations. Table 1 lists several of the resulting measurements and standard values. In order to provide comparisons, the controller computes current values. The president notes that in each case additional effort will be necessary to achieve the values established as standards.

As a second step, the controller meets with the director of information systems to select measurements related to the information system. After discussions between these two and other affected managers (i.e., the system operations manager and the system development manager), a list of systems related measures is prepared. Several of these measures appear in Table 2.

Throughout the following weeks the controller meets successively with the managers in charge of major activities. In all cases attainable standards are set. The standard values are established after reviews of historical records, studies of work measurement, and discussion with the responsible managers.

TABLE 1
OVERALL PERFORMANCE MEASURES

Measurement	Responsible Manager	Current Value	Standard Value
Rate of return on investment	President	2.3%	7.0%
Share of market	President	3.0%	6.0%
Current ratio	Financial vice-president	2:0	2:5
Plant utilization	Production vice-president	70.0%	85.0%
Contribution margin ratio for all products	Marketing vice-president	25.0%	30.0%
Public reputation	President	Good: 7 on scale of 10	Excellent: 9 on scale of 10

TABLE 2
SYSTEMS-RELATED PERFORMANCE MEASURES

Measure	Responsible Manager	Current Value	Standard Value
Data processing jobs completed on schedule	Systems operations manager	75.0%	99.0%
Downtime to productive computer time	Systems operations manager	8.0%	5.0%
Average cost per hour of computer productive time	Systems operations manager		
Average number of programming instructions prepared per day (by each programmer)	Systems development manager	85	100
Employee turnover per systems personnel only	Director of Systems	10.0%	5.0%

LIMITATIONS OF MEASUREMENTS

Although performance measurements are essential to the evaluation of activities, managers, and employees, relatively few measurements are ideal. For instance, in service activities where discretionary costs are significant and processes are relatively unstandardized (e.g., advertising, legal, research, public activities), the effectiveness of such activities is difficult to measure. Usually the best available type of measurement in such cases is a budgeted cost, even though a cost is a measurement of input rather than a measurement of effective output.

Frequently more than one measurement is needed to reflect the performance of a particular activity or manager, or to reveal the extent to which a specific objective is achieved. While a single composite measurement or index may be developed from the several individual measurements in such a case, seldom does an index provide suitable results. The weights that must be assigned to the individual measurements when compiling the indexes are necessarily based on arbitrary judgments.

Inappropriate and insufficient measurements can cause managers and employees to behave in undesirable ways. For instance, if salesmen are gauged and paid according to the sales volume that they generate rather than the profit that they produce, the salesmen will push the hottest items in the line rather than the more profitable items. Furthermore, unless additional measurements are employed, the salesmen will also tend to neglect customer service and to be casual concerning the maintenance of sales equipment. Generally the less quantifiable and longer range objectives tend to receive less attention than the clearly understandable, quantifiable, and shorter range objectives.

CONCLUSION

In spite of their limitations, measurements are vital to the evaluation of performance. A comprehensive plan of evaluation can be developed by:

1. Selecting suitable measurements
2. Selecting a sufficiently wide variety of measurements (with multiple classification plans)
3. Establishing attainable standard values for each of the quantifiable measurements
4. Comparing actual current values with standard values
5. Providing the resulting deviations to responsible managers

28 • A TECHNIQUE FOR MEASURING MANAGEMENT PRODUCTIVITY[1]

Frank Dewitt[2]

Assessing management effectiveness or productivity is becoming the concern of more people every day. Businesses are seeking management strengths through acquisitions, mergers, and intensive executive recruiting and training programs. Lending agencies are looking deeper into client firms' general management, along with specialized functions of financial management. Informed investors and financial analysts look upon management as the primary influence in corporate growth, enterprise survival, and increasing profits. Government regulatory agencies, as well as government buyers, inquire into management capabilities. And finally, corporate management continuously evaluates its own managerial force and processes, probing for strengths to be used and weaknesses to be overcome.

These groups all seek to identify responsible and productive management. But how can management productivity be measured with precision?

Need for Objective Standards

Qualitative analyses of the company's management principles and functional processes may reveal something about management effectiveness. However, analyses of this kind are limited, because the criteria cannot be expressed mathematically and the findings are not based on management results. Therefore, they should be supplemented by an evaluation of the company's performance.

Company performance, of course, can be measured and visualized in numerical terms that precisely reveal management accomplishments. In addition, application of principles and functional practices of management will be reflected in the results of company performance. Because management is wholly responsible for the operation of the enterprise and for the acquisition and employment of the enterprise's resources, it makes sense to measure its productivity in terms of the enterprise it manages.

The purpose of this article is to illustrate one quantitative technique for measuring management productivity. This method uses arrays (numbers of mathematical elements arranged in rows and columns) as an evaluation tool. It also requires that management be evaluated on the basis of the following results:

1. The performance of the managed enterprise.
2. The relationship of enterprise performance to the resources used to achieve it.
3. The position of the enterprise in its competitive environment.

[1] Reprinted by permission of the publisher from *Management Review*, June, 1970, © 1970 by the American Management Association, Inc., pp. 2-11.
[2] Frank DeWitt, Management Evaluation Specialist, United States Air Force Contract Division, Los Angeles, California.

Although this article will illustrate how arrays can be used to evaluate the management productivity of a business corporation, the method can also be applied to any kind of organization or enterprise, providing appropriate performance factors are used.

The specific performance factors that are relevant for a business corporation are revenues, operating income, and net earnings. Together these factors reflect the basic management purpose of maximizing returns and coverting them to profits. Management considerations of historical presentations and extrapolations of these factors provide a means of internal views of growth plans and operational decisions. However, they do not provide criteria by which management quality may be evaluated. Management must be evaluated on its ability to excel in competition and its ability to maximize enterprise performance with minimum resources. Performance factors, viewed alone, can only measure the size of enterprise accomplishments. They cannot relate to the influence of management.

Performance vs. Resources

Management's objective of using minimum resources to obtain maximum returns can be quantitatively expressed. Ratios of performance factors to resource factors provide a view of these relationships and may be formulated as follows:

$$\text{Management productivity} = \text{Performance} \div \text{Resources}.$$

For example:

Company *A* uses 61,500 employees (resource factor) to produce $950,000,000 in revenues (performance factor.)
Management productivity = $950,000,000 ÷ 61,500 = $15,447 revenues per employee.

This formula, however, does not indicate how well the personnel productivity of revenue is converted into personnel productivity of profits. To determine this, two more measures are needed—operating income per employee and net earnings per employee.

Two other aspects of management productivity that are easily measured are the efficiency with which physical facilities and capital resources are utilized. These are measured in the same way as personnel productivity. However, instead of dividing revenues, operating income, and net income by the number of employees, you divide by the number of dollars invested in plant and equipment and by the number of dollars of stockholders' equity.

It must be stressed again that the application of these formulas or ratios to a single enterprise can provide only limited information which is meaningless unless it is reviewed in light of historical and forecasted data. Standing alone, these criteria cannot provide management evaluation information. However, these productivity ratios do provide a means by which one enterprise may be compared with others. Arrays of these indicators make it possible to visualize various management accomplishments equitably in the competitive environment.

Competitive Environment

In the example of Company *A* cited earlier, the personnel productivity ratio was $15,447 revenues per employee. Compare this with the performance of Company *B*:

> Company *B* used 1,942 employees to produce $65,000,000 in revenues.
> Management productivity = $65,000,000 ÷ 1,942 = $33,471 revenues per employee.

These ratios, used by themselves, would indicate that Company *B* obtained a better productivity than Company *A*.

However, the competitive environment in which each company's management operated to attain these enterprise accomplishments is not revealed. Company *A* may have been delivering a mass-market product from a low-cost operation of high-volume production using a large number of employees. Its personnel productivity ratio of $15,447 may be higher than rival firms engaged in the same activity. Company *B* may have been working on a high-cost research and development assignment, and its ratio of $33,471 per employee may be lower than its competitors'. This clearly indicates that the productivity of management must be measured in terms of the environment in which the enterprise operates; in other words, the companies compared must be engaged in similar operations. When such a comparison is used, the ability of an enterprise to outperform competing organizations clearly indicates above-average management productivity.

Grouping of Similar Companies

How does a company go about making up a list of other firms that it can consider its competitors? Investment information services have drawn up various groupings of similar business corporations, and these often can be used for identifying a group of competitive companies for comparison. For the most part, however, these groups contain only those companies whose stocks are listed for public sale, and this may limit the selection.

The *Standard Industrial Classification Manual,* published by the government and available from the Superintendent of Documents, Government Printing Office, Washington, D.C., catalogues and describes various industries. These definitions may be used to categorize industrial companies for inclusion in a competitive group. For example, the groups of companies that will be used to judge management productivity are air transport corporations that fall within the following definition contained in the SIC Manual:

> **Industry Group 4511. Air Transportation, Certified Carriers**
> Companies holding certificates of public convenience and necessity under
> the Civil Aeronautics Act, operating over fixed routes on fixed schedules, or

in the case of certificated Alaskan carriers over fixed or irregular routes. These companies may be primarily engaged in the transportation of revenue passengers or in the transportation of cargo and freight.

The ratios proposed for measuring management productivity are comparable criteria. Arrays of these ratios provide the arrangements by which managment accomplishments can be compared. The *degree* or the extent of the numerical differences in these ratios is not important. The *position*, however, becomes of paramount interest.

For example, in an array of 11 competing airlines the highest value may be considered No. 1, the lowest No. 11, with the whole series chronologically listed from high to low or vice versa. Table 1 below illustrates the difference between degree and position arrays. The actual differences in the revenues of the 11 airlines constitute degree arrays. The order of rank is the position array.

TABLE 1

REVENUES OF SELECTED AIR TRANSPORT CORPORATIONS—1968

Corporation	Degree Arrays		Position Array
	* Revenues	Percent	
United Air Lines	$1,262	100.0%	1
Pan American World Airways	1,036	82.1	2
American Airlines	957	75.8	3
Trans World Airlines	948	75.1	4
Eastern Airlines	745	59.0	5
Delta Air Lines	432	34.2	6
Northwest Airlines	416	33.0	7
National Airlines	225	17.8	8
Western Air Lines	222	17.6	9
Continental Airlines	208	16.5	10
Seaboard World Airlines	65	5.2	11

* millions of dollars

All arrays used in this discussion will be position arrays. The evaluation question posed asks only whether management productivity is high or low. It is not concerned with how high or how low, but with whether performance is above or below the average. The average employed here is the position average, that is, the median. In the grouping of the 11 airlines, the company ranked No. 6 is in the median position.

The analysis concept used to measure the management productivity of the 11 airlines is the arrangement of the relationships of organizational accomplishments per units of resources to reveal the position of each enterprise in its competitive environment. All data used to develop the position arrays were derived from the 1968 annual stockholder reports issued by each of the corporations named.

Personnel Productivity

An array of the three personnel productivity indicators for the 11 airlines is shown in Table 2 below. "Revenues per Employee" is a measure of revenue productivity, while "Operating Income per Employee" and "Net Earnings per Employee" are both measures of profit productivity.

TABLE 2

PERSONNEL PRODUCTIVITY
AIR TRANSPORT CORPORATIONS—1968

Corporation	Revenues per Employee	Operating Income per Employee	Net Earnings per Employee
Northwest	1	1	1
Seaboard	2	4	4
National	3	2	2
Continental	4	6	9
American	5	8	6
Pan American	6 (median)	9	5
Delta	7	3	3
United	8	7	8
Western	9	5	7
Eastern	10	11	11
Trans World	11	10	10

This table permits the evaluation of personnel productivity or efficiency in terms of the enterprise management capability to obtain enterprise results through its employees. A cursory examination of Table 2 reveals that only three of the top five corporations in revenue productivity maintained top positions in both profit productivity indicators. It also shows that only one of the three was able to achieve a higher ranking in both profit indicators than it did in its revenue position. In addition, one corporation with low revenue productivity moved into a high position in both profit indicators.

Capital Productivity

Table 3 presents the same kind of array as Table 2, except that it depicts capital productivity. It relates stockholders' equity (resource factor) to the same three performance factors (revenues, operating income, and net earnings) and arranges them in the same way.

Management's effectiveness in making use of capital is shown in this table. None of the high revenue productivity firms was able to maintain relative positions in the profit productivity indicators, and only two remained above the median in operating income productivity and one in net earnings.

TABLE 3

CAPITAL PRODUCTIVITY
AIR TRANSPORT CORPORATIONS—1968

Corporation	Revenues per Stockholders Equity $	Operating Income per Stockholders Equity $	Net Earnings per Stockholders Equity $
Eastern	1	11	11
Seaboard	2	6	4
Continental	3	5	9
American	4	7	6
Western	5	4	7
United	6 (median)	8	8
Delta	7	2	2
Trans World	8	10	10
Pan American	9	9	5
National	10	1	1
Northwest	11	3	3

Facilities Productivity

Table 4 below reveals the capability of a company's management to make use of its facilities, or ihe plant and equipment employed in attaining enterprise performance. The value of plant and equipment as used in this indicator is the acquisition cost. The selection of these costs may be subject to question. However, acquisition costs, rather than depreciated or appraisal costs, were used to avoid complicated adjustments for comparability and to provide a uniform reference point in all accounting systems.

TABLE 4

FACILITIES PRODUCTIVITY
AIR TRANSPORT CORPORATIONS—1968

Corporation	Revenues per Plant & Equipment $	Operating Income per Plant & Equipment $	Net Earnings per Plant & Equipment $
Seaboard	1	4	1
Delta	2	1	4
American	3	5	2
National	4	3	3
Trans World	5	10	8
Eastern	6 (median)	11	11
Northwest	7	2	5
United	8	6	6
Pan American	9	8	7
Western	10	7	10
Continental	11	9	9

This decision is based on the practical management concept that there would be no excessive acquisition costs in the records if useless assets had been properly scrapped or sold. An asset's presence, therefore, implies that management has ruled it was needed for enterprise operations.

The facilities productivity table indicates that all of the first five airlines, except one, maintained their positions above the median, and that one improved its high revenue position in both profit indicators. It also shows that one low revenue productivity corporation moved to high profit positions.

Composite Picture. The three tables on personnel, capital, and facilities productivity illustrate a technique by which arrays may be used to visualize the productivity of management. If, at this point, the analysis phase were considered complete, it would be possible to use these tables to judge the relative merits of management quality at each of these corporations. This, of course, would be a three-pronged evaluation based on three separate questions, each contained within a single sphere of interest: Which companies obtain the best productivity from manpower? Which from capital? Which from facilities?

Management, however, is pervasive. It coordinates and makes use of all resource factors as an integrating force. This integrating skill of management is brought into focus by Table 5 on page 362, which is a composite of Tables 2, 3, and 4.

The translation of revenue productivity into profit productivity is basic to business management. Table 5 reveals that only National improved its revenue position in all profit productivity indicators. Although it is important that business management obtain high revenue productivity, it is even more important that revenue productivity be converted to profit productivity. This is why two profit indicators are used in the analysis. One— operating income—provides some insight as to whether the achievements were obtained through operational efficiencies. The other—net earnings —furnishes some visibility by which a management's belated realizations or discoveries of operating inefficiencies were covered by aggressive management action, such as asset sales, to increase net earnings.

Conclusion

The purpose of management is to achieve the objectives for which the enterprise it manages exists and to ensure the survival of the enterprise. To this end it selects, acquires, activates, and directs resources toward the attainment of enterprise goals of its own choosing. It creates, implements, and administers the systems, procedures, and methods by which the enterprise operates to attain its goals. Management changes, adjusts, and develops resource mixtures to maintain an enterprise thrust toward its objectives. Thus, the performance of an enterprise is directly attributable to management's influence. This fact suggests that management can be quantitatively measured in terms of enterprise performance.

TABLE 5

RECAPITULATION OF RESOURCES PRODUCTIVITY
AIR TRANSPORT CORPORATIONS—1968

Corporations	Revenues	Operating Income	Net Earnings	Revenues	Operating Income	Net Earnings	Revenues	Operating Income	Net Earnings
	Per Employee			Per Stockholders Equity $			Per Plant and Equipment $		
American	5	8	6	4	7	6	3	5	2
Continental	4	6	9	3	5	9	11	9	9
Delta	7	3	3	7	2	2	2	1	4
Eastern	10	11	11	1	11	11	6	11	11
National	3	2	2	10	1	1	4	3	3
Northwest	1	1	1	11	3	3	7	2	5
Pan American	6	9	5	9	9	5	9	8	7
Seaboard	2	4	4	2	6	4	1	4	1
Trans World	11	10	10	8	10	10	5	10	8
United	8	7	8	6	8	8	8	6	6
Western	9	5	7	5	4	7	10	7	10

The performance of a business enterprise is mathematically measured in terms of its revenue and profit factors. These factors alone cannot measure management. However, when they are related to the resources used to obtain the performance, these relationships provide a means by which the management influence may be made comparable. Thus, ratios of performance factors to resource factors become meaningful criteria by which one management may be compared with another. In this article, these ratios of performance to resource factors have been identified as management productivity indicators, that is, personnel productivity, capital productivity, and facilities productivity.

The positioning of each enterprise in a competitive group measures the ability of an enterprise to perform above or below the median of the group. Productivity indicators arrayed singly, in like manner, provide a means by which management effectiveness can be visualized in its separated uses of personnel, capital, and facilities.

Management, however, permeates the whole structure of the enterprise. It adjusts and coordinates resources, as considered necessary, in its drive for maximum results with minimum resources. This management influence is evidenced by the translation of revenues into profits. A single matrix including all productivity ratio arrays provides an analytical device by which the movement of revenue productivity positions to profit productivity positions can be visualized and evaluated.

29 • IMPLEMENTING THE SOCIAL AUDIT IN AN ORGANIZATION[1]

Keith Davis[2]
Robert L. Blomstrom[3]

The changing lifestyle of American society is requiring a concurrent change in the lifestyle of business because business exists to serve the needs of people. One significant change is in the direction of more social involvement and social responsibility on the part of business. Changing expectations of people are requiring business to be more concerned with the social consequences of all its activities.

Effective management practice requires that if a business moves into a new activity, it should periodically appraise how well it is doing with respect to that activity, so that the desired objective can be achieved. In the area of social involvement this means an entirely new development, the social audit. Perhaps a firm only peripherally involved in social issues will be content with top-of-the-head evaluations, but a firm that has employee time and resources committed to social involvement will certainly want to evaluate its performance with a social audit. The following discussion covers what a social audit is, what its benefits are, and how it can be implemented in an organization.

Defining the Social Audit

A social audit is a systematic study and evaluation of an organization's social performance, as distinguished from its economic performance. It is concerned with possible influences on the social quality of life instead of the economic quality of life. The social audit leads to a *social performance report* for management and perhaps outsiders also.

In this definition the term "social performance" refers to any organizational activities that affect the general welfare of society. The idea of social performance emphasizes total needs of the whole community and the whole society. It is a systemwide view. It tends to focus on general humanistic values while reducing traditional economic and technical values to subsystems within the larger social system. It is concerned with the social meaning of events.

The evaluation of social performance is not a wholly new idea. For many years organizations have been making judgments about how their activities affect society, but these judgments typically have been spur-of-the-moment and intuitive. The idea of a *systematic study and evaluation*

[1] From *Business & Society Review*, Vol. 16, No. 1 (Fall, 1975), pp. 13-18. Reprinted by permission from *Business & Society Review*, Fall 1975, © 1976 by Warren, Gorham, and Lamont, Inc., 210 South Street, Boston, Mass. All rights reserved.
[2] Keith Davis, Professor of Management, Arizona State University.
[3] Robert L. Blomstrom, Professor of Hospitality and Director of the School of Hotel, Restaurant and Institutional Management, Michigan State University.

or organizational social performance is relatively new, because only recently has society given major emphasis to social involvement by business. The social audit for business originally was proposed by Howard R. Bowen in 1953 in a brief discussion in his book, *Social Responsibilities of the Businessman* [2].

Features of a Social Audit

Areas for social audit include any activity which has significant social impact, such as actions affecting environmental quality and equal employment opportunity. Normally, a social audit can determine only what an organization is doing in social areas, not the amount of social good that results from these activities. It is a process audit rather than an audit of results. Social results are so nebulous that they are difficult to measure, and generally accepted social norms are almost nonexistent. There is a variety of opinions about what is "good" and what is "bad," and even when there is agreement about the desirability of a result, there are different measures of how much good is accomplished.

Social results are also difficult to audit because most of them occur outside an organization, so a firm has no way of securing data from these outside sources. Even when data are available, causes are so complex that a firm has no way of knowing how much of the results were caused by its actions. For example, violent crimes decreased four percent in an urban ghetto where a firm had a minority employment program. How much of the benefit, if any, was caused by this program? Even though results cannot be proved, an audit of what is being done still is considered desirable, because it shows the amount of effort that a business is making in areas deemed beneficial to society. Further, if effort can be measured, then informed judgments can be made about potential results.

Social audits can be made either by internal specialists, outside consultants, or a combination of the two. The internal auditor has the advantage of familiarity with the business, but his judgments might be influenced by company loyalties. An outside consultant has the advantage of an outsider's view, but he lacks familiarity with organizational activities, so he may overlook significant data. In any case, if audit information is to be released to the public, the outside auditor has more credibility.

A significant issue is whether the audit, or any portion of it, is to be made public by means of a social performance report. The philosophy of an open system suggests that the public interest is best served by public reporting; however, the present state of the art with social audits is so imprecise that public disclosure might do more harm than good. Imprecise data and informed judgments are helpful for internal decision-making, but they probably are not concrete enough to satisfy the public. Further, there are so many differences of opinion that almost anyone could find reasons for criticizing a firm's performance, and dissident groups could expand some detail far beyond its importance. The result could be that social conflict would increase and firms would withdraw from social programs in order to avoid reporting on them, thus defeating the original purposes of social reporting. Bowen's original proposal was that a social audit should be made by *outside* consultants for *inside* use only, and that it should be made only every five years.

Because of the problems involved, progress toward public disclosure of social audits will be slow. It seems wise to proceed with caution, but the eventual direction seems certain to be toward more social reporting. A few firms already have made extensive disclosures when they thought these disclosures would contribute to public understanding of an important issue. One corporation, for example, released detailed statistical and descriptive material about its employment practices in South Africa where racial discrimination in employment exists. It believed that its own practices were a sound alternative to activist proposals, and it wanted to replace rhetoric with facts in this public debate.

Use of Quantitative Data

Social audits use both quantitative and qualitative data. The pressures to use a quantitative approach are strong because of the respectability and apparent objectivity of this tactic. Quantitative data are precise and convincing, but in the area of social performance it is misleading to report only in quantitative terms. Numbers can communicate only a part of the total situation—only a part of the whole truth. Both qualitative and quantitative data are essential. Normally, a firm uses as much quantitative data as possible, provided it portrays the situation accurately, and then supplements this with qualitative data. Examples of useful quantitative data are proportions of minorities employed and costs of a pollution abatement program.

An example of the *misuse* of quantitative data is found in a potential public project in Britain which would have required demolition of a historic twelfth-century Norman church. A cost/benefit analysis of the proposed project calculated that the loss from demolition of the church would be only the face value of the fire insurance policy on the church. No consideration was given to the historic social value of the church.

In spite of the difficulties with quantification, the lure of objective figures remains, particularly dollar figures in the form of traditional accounting statements. For example, one firm made a genuine effort to conduct a social audit which it reported in dollar terms in its annual report [3]. The Social Income Statement attempted to portray social income that the firm provided for society, and in this context payments for benefits such as employee tuition reimbursement represented social income. Social costs were represented by such items as projected effects of layoffs and employee discharges. The difference between social income and social costs represented the net social income that the firm provided for society. There was also a related Social Balance Sheet which reported cumulative debits and credits.

While the foregoing approach is useful, its weakness is that it is limited to economic terms and may overlook the social meaning of activities. Purely dollar presentations show only part of the whole picture of a firm's social performance. This means that traditional accounting procedures cannot satisfy all the needs of social auditing.

The most progress in assigning dollar values to social data has been made with *human resource accounting* in employee relations [4]. Human resource accounting attempts to account for changes in the quality of a firm's human organization as represented by a firm's investments in people. Its purpose is to enable management to know whether its actions are increasing or decreasing the quality of human resources, and by approximately what amount. For example, investments in training are treated as a long-run improvement in the quality of the work force, so on the accounting statement they are considered capital investment.

Benefits of a Social Audit

Essentially an organization conducts a social audit because it exists in a social world and in order to live effectively in that world it needs social data to guide its actions. Within that broad context, what does an organization expect from a social audit? What benefits does an audit provide? Certainly one benefit is that is supplies data for comparison with policies and standards so that management can determine how well the organization is living up to its objectives. Many firms have established affirmative action programs, ecology programs, and similar activities, and they need to evaluate the progress made with these programs. Just as a spaceship in flight must know where it is in order to correct its flight pattern and reach its objective, a business must know where it is in relation to its objectives. An organization can also make comparisons over a period of time, to determine how fast it is moving toward its social objectives.

Related to the first benefit is the fact that a social audit encourages greater concern for social performance throughout the organization. It has been shown that subordinate managers and employees tend to give their attention to activities where reports are required and evaluations made by higher management. In the process of preparing reports and responding to evaluations, employees become more aware of social data and the social implications of their actions, and corporate social objectives are more strongly reinforced in all areas of the organization.

A third benefit of the social audit is that it provides data for comparing the effectiveness of different types of programs. In one branch plant, for example, a firm may emphasize counseling in the employment of hard-core unemployed persons, while in another branch it emphasizes an elaborate training program. An examination of the problems and progress made in each of these programs will give management useful inputs for establishing better programs.

A fourth benefit is the provision of cost data on social programs, so that management can relate this data to budgets, available resources, company objectives, and to projected program benefits. If a business is going to devote significant amounts of its resources to social programs, then it needs some evidence of what those programs cost. Direct costs, such as gifts, are easy to compute, but deriving indirect costs is more difficult. Should managers keep records of their time so that appropriate portions of their salaries can be charged to social programs? Shall a firm compute its opportunity costs for alternative uses of resources and charge those costs to social programs?

One example of an approach to computing opportunity costs is a bank which had a loan program for minority businesses. These loans were made at a lower interest rate than regular business loans, and the bank could have employed all of its funds in regular loans. In addition, the default rate for minority loans was higher than for regular loans, so a higher proportion of the average loan was lost by default. Available time studies on loans also showed that the processing time for minority loans was considerably longer because of such factors as additional business counseling. In order to determine extra costs of the minority loan program, the bank subtracted the minority loan yield from the regular loan yield to determine opportunity costs and then added the extra administrative costs of the minority loans.

A fifth benefit of a social audit is that it provides information for effective response to external groups which make demands on the organization. News reporters, minority groups, and a variety of others want to know what a business is doing in areas of their special interests, and a business needs to respond as effectively as possible. The social audit makes available to public groups concrete data about social performance, if it is required.

The foregoing benefits indicate that essentially an organization conducts a social audit to provide managers with information inputs about their firm's current state of social performance, so that better decisions may be made. Managers are key decision-makers in an organization, and the quality of their decisions is related to the quality and amount of information inputs they receive prior to making these decisions. For balanced decisions in a social world, they need dependable social inputs along with other inputs. This improvement in business decision-making eventually should lead to improved benefits for society. From society's point of view, rather than the firm's point of view, this is the ultimate benefit of a social audit. In the process, however, the firm also benefits because it increases its social viability.

Operation of Audit Programs

The social audit is such a new concept that there are very few guidelines for making it, and there is no standard procedure that will compare with the rather definite standards that exist for accounting audits. Most firms are at the beginning of the learning curve with respect to social audits. They are starting to experiment with them, but they have only limited success as of now. When firms do begin social audit procedures, they tend to find the process is more complex than originally contemplated. Everything is related to everything else. The following company experience illustrates the operation of an audit program [5].

> The board of directors determined that a social responsibility committee should be appointed by the board chairman to make a social audit for the firm. The committee consisted of two company officers and one public member. It found very few audit guidelines and had to develop its own program with the counsel of persons both inside and outside the company. Early in the program the committee recognized that the audit needed to be more comprehensive than anticipated and that social effects of company operations were more extensive than expected.
>
> Eventually six areas for audit were developed as follows: social importance of regular activities, consumerism, community service, environment, equal employment, and fixing responsibility within the firm for social performance. Audit programs were developed for each area, and both qualitative and quantitative data were sought. The entire process helped management translate vague ideas about social performance into hard realities.

Limited experience indicates that a social audit is a more massive undertaking than firms expect. Although some social data are available in existing records, much needed information is nonexistent and new procedures are required for measuring and reporting it.

When one considers the many difficulties involved in social auditing, such as credibility, identification of cause and effect, complexity, quantification, measurement, and absence of norms, it is evident that business faces a major task. Firms find that they need to move slowly. In the beginning most of them select only a few areas for audit, rather than try to conduct a complete audit of all operations. Progress toward social auditing and reporting is being made, but it will be slow evolution, not instant change. Even modest programs will give managers, and the public, useful information that they have not had earlier.

Conclusion

A social audit is a systematic study and evaluation of an organization's social performance, as distinguished from its economic performance. It is essential for a firm's internal decision-making and for external social reporting. It mostly reports what an organization is doing, rather than the difficult-to-measure social good that results from these activities. An audit is expressed in both quantitative and qualitative terms. Benefits of an audit include data for comparison with standards, increased concern for social performance, comparison of different types of programs, cost/benefit comparisons, and data for external social reporting.

This discussion has shown that a social audit needs to be made by any business that is substantially socially involved. It is essential for effective management of a firm's social response to changing life-styles and public expectations. Audits, however, tend to be more complex and difficult than most firms expect. Businesses need to proceed slowly as they move up the learning curve with the social audit. Since progress may be slow, this is one more reason to begin implementing social audits now.

REFERENCES FOR ARTICLE

1. Portions of this article are adapted from the authors' book, *Business and Society: Environment and Responsibility* (3d ed.; New York: McGraw-Hill Book Company, 1975).
2. HOWARD R. BOWEN, *Social Responsibilities of the Businessman* (New York: Harper & Brothers, Publishers, 1953), pp. 155-156. Bowen's proposal received reinforcement from Blum in a major article; see Fred H. Blum, "Social Audit of the Enterprise," *Harvard Business Review*, March-April, 1958, pp. 77-86.
3. RAYMOND A. BAUER, "The Corporate Social Audit: Where Does It Stand Today?" *Personnel* (July-August, 1973), pp. 8-18; and Raymond A. Bauer and Dan H. Fenn, Jr., "What Is a Corporate Social Audit?" *Harvard Business Review* (January-February, 1973), pp. 37-48. A related approach is the proposal for a Socioeconomic Operating Statement in David F. Linowes, *Strategies for Survival* (New York: AMACOM, 1973), pp. 169-178. See also John J. Corson and George A. Steiner, *Measuring Business' Social Performance: The Corporate Social Audit* (New York: Committee for Economic Development, 1975).
4. RENSIS LIKERT and DAVID G. BOWERS, "Improving the Accuracy of P/L Reports by Estimating the Change in Dollar Value of the Human Organization," *Michigan Business Review* (March, 1973), pp. 15-24.
5. BARRY RICHMAN, "New Paths to Corporate Social Responsibility," *California Management Review* (Spring, 1973), pp. 23-24.

30 • INDUSTRIAL ADMINISTRATION THROUGH THE EYES OF AN INVESTMENT COMPANY[1]

Erwin H. Schell[2]

The attempt by investment houses to measure the effectiveness of administrative or managerial ability in a manufacturing enterprise, apart from the technical approach of the security analyst is nothing new. As long ago as 25 years, the president of our oldest American investment trust stated that, in judging a security, he gave 50 percent weighting to the statistical report, and an equal amount of information gained from personal contacts with directors, executives, vendors, customers and community.

The justification for this paper, then, is less because of any innovational qualities, than because of the somewhat unusual objectives that it seeks to describe.

The investment company on whose board I serve as a representative of the public, offers to the buyers of securities a spectrum of ten Certificates of Participation, based upon an equal number of investment funds ranging in degree of conservatism from high-grade bonds to appreciation common stocks. The portfolios of each of these ten funds contain securities selected according to their consistent tendency to reflect the characteristics of their particular class.

The service rendered the investor is the assurance that he is buying what he thinks he is buying. Decisions as to *what* type of investment he should buy are his to make, with the aid of dealer counsel if he should so desire.

This investment company therefore is concerned chiefly with the selection and classification of securities into groups which may be depended upon to behave in a truly representative fashion in terms of their class. Moreover, it is important that this representation be a distinguished one; that the securities selected be leaders in their respective fields; and that this leadership be dependable. Clearly, this requirement of *consistent leadership* demands a choice of securities on a long-range basis— a quality which is provided only through long-term administration.

To a surprising degree the questions asked by this investment company are, therefore, the identical questions which an alert top executive will find valuable in assessing the quality and effectiveness of his long-term administration. For this reason I have asked permission of the president of my organization to present its procedure here.

Some years ago, the following question was put to us as directors:

> Assuming that you are personally considering investment in the securities of a given company, and that you have access to balance sheets,

---

[1] From *Appraising Managerial Assets—Policies, Practices and Organizations,* General Management Series No. 151. American Management Association, 1950, pp. 3-9. Reprinted by permission of the American Management Association.

[2] Erwin H. Schell, Member of the Board, Keystone Custodian Funds, Inc., 1950.

income statements and other statistical data, *what five questions would you ask*—over and above those which may be answered by analysis of statistical reports—in obtaining an objective measure of the quality of management of the company?

This question engendered a wide variety of responses which were classified and incorporated in part in the field questionnaire which forms a portion of the selective procedure employed.

It should go without saying that, whereas this form of managerial investigation is viewed as the most important of the several analyses undertaken, yet it is but one aspect of the economic, industrial and financial studies which also contribute their share to the final judgment.

CRITERIA FOR EVALUATING MANAGEMENT

Obviously, each manufacturing enterprise calls for a different type of leadership. Someone has said with considerable truth that a successful business requires the application of good standard practice of routine functions and the application of genius to the key activities. While we may not agree with this statement in full, we cannot evade the fact that businesses *are* different and call for varying talents in their administration.

Neverthless, there are certain criteria that appear to apply to so broad a field that they may be said to be generally indicative.

In the Management Evaluation Questionnaire, the more than 60 queries are arranged for convenience in the making of individual interviews. I have regrouped them under twelve headings in the order in which they would normally follow in preparing a final report.

Managerial Personnel

Here we refer to the executive staff—the principal officers and department heads. We are careful to obtain their respective ages, length of service with the company, nature of previous business experience, compensation and stock interest, if any. We are happy when we have a preponderance of upper-level executives in the middle-age group, with length of service sufficient to reflect stabilization, receiving compensation in accordance with an objectively designed salary plan, and with the future stimulus of a stock interest, where possible.

We have also discovered that the outside interests of these men throw considerable light on the probable depth and trend of their personal application to the business.

Casting this specific information against our previously prepared background of general business trends and special conditions in the industry of which this company is a part, enables us to assess whether, in general the company is staffed with "men of the hour" as well as "men who have what (specifically) it takes."

Additional calipers will be applied to this group under subsequent headings.

Administration

We are particularly interested in the composition and activities of the board of directors; who are the principal directors; their major interests and abilities, and to what extent they are members of executive or other board committees; on what other boards they serve.

We are hopeful of finding in this group men of sufficient competence, experience and judgment to make a direct and continuing contribution to the establishment of long-term company policy. We are hopeful that these men, in addition to their industrial or professional ability, will be "men of parts" having wide and varied contacts, including service on other boards. We are hopeful that the board will contain men representing management, stockholders and the public; that it will be a diversified group capable of making a directors' discussion broadly constructive.

We believe that boards of directors will be called upon in the future to play an even more active role in the conduct of a business than heretofore and we are gratified when we find a committee structure or other device in operation to implement and stimulate these activities. It is pleasing to discover a scattering of young men on these boards. They can be expected to bedevil the oldsters, but they do add precious leaven to the loaf.

Objectives

We are eager to learn what objectives are given highest priority by the company. This, we find, is a hard thing to get at. Searching as we are for establishments that provide distinguished leadership in their field, we anticipate that the basic problem of making a profit has been under control for some time, thus enabling other objectives to be given important and attentive consideration. The way we approach this matter is to inquire what are the most important problems that the company faces today for important objectives always meet important difficulties and it is in overcoming such difficulties that important problems are born.

To paraphrase an old saying: "Management is known by the problems it keeps."

It delights us when a company president can tell us precisely what he is shooting for (rifle, not shotgun); how he is organizing to accomplish his purpose; how far advanced he is on his program; and how he thinks he is getting along. Such information enables us more effectively to judge of his probable future success or failure and its effect upon the business which he directs.

Organization

While we have suggested to our field investigators several leading questions regarding organization—having to do with such matter as definite and clean-cut responsibilities and attending authority, and the presence of up-to-date manuals, charts and the like—yet we are chiefly interested to learn whether the top executive is convinced of the fact that in any establishment of reasonable size, current changes are so frequent as to make organization a continuing problem.

We look forward to the possibility that he not only believes this to be true, but has set up some sort of permanent committee, staff group, or outside counsel to assure the presence of this continuing scrutiny and adjustment to new needs.

As we make our constant round of investigations of the securities in our ten portfolios, it affords us no little satisfaction to find that progressive changes in organization are made apace with the changes in process, personnel or product.

The days when organizations receive only periodic refurbishings, like spring housecleaning, are gone. Constant evolutional change is the order of the day.

Plans

The long depression and the subsequent war were for many concerns periods of crisis-management rather than of long-term planning. We believe that tomorrow the far look ahead will become increasingly essential for any company which aspires to consistent and continuing leadership in its field.

Modern forecasting and planning techniques make use of Confucius' admonition: "We should make plans so that we may have plans to discard."

The fields of procurement of materials, distribution of product, financing, labor and executive requirements, plant growth and equipment purchase, long-term estimates reaching far forward at half-yearly intervals and subject to semi-annual revisions until the future becomes the present— all these enable industry to plan intelligently, explain the bases for alteration of plans as time passes and thus gain a firmer mind-hold upon what is to come.

Our questions relating to the presence of out-reaching devices for this dimensioning of the future are, in reality, designed to measure the degree to which top management is already dedicated to a program of planned rather than of fortuitous progress.

Control

An industrial analyst of earlier days once told me that the first thing he set about doing was finding the person in the company—whether executive, director or stockholder—who was in position to say "no," to mean it, and to enforce it.

Such people are rightfully still extant in industry, but we use the term somewhat more broadly. We feel that any management which aims at long-term distinction must of necessity have developed objectives, standards, supervision, evaluation and reward for the control of output, quality, materials, facilities, processes, costs, finances and indeed every active function of the business.

To put it bluntly, we welcome the presence of these control activities as proof that the operating executive is really running the business, rather than vice versa. We are pleased when we find such procedures long established and, in fact, taken for granted as inescapable elements of competent managerial operation.

Our questions here, therefore, are somewhat general in character and serve mainly to assure us that a long-accepted principle of good management has not been allowed to atrophy.

Nevertheless, these inquiries do, from time to time, reveal informal control structures that do not appear on the organization chart.

Upkeep

In our evaluation of management we are definitely and deeply concerned with management's policies and practices regarding upkeep. In today's industrial world, where obsolescence is increasingly outdistancing the effect of depreciation due to wear and tear, the problem of maintaining technical parity with the advancing state-of-the-art has become a major issue for well-nigh every manufacturer.

The problem is especially severe in areas of productive facilities. Most plants today have within their walls an assortment of equipment dating from the days of World War I to the present. Only a few have managed to keep the entire plant reasonably up-to-date. It is these latter organizations whose securities are apt to impress us favorably, for we have learned by experience that the greatest bulwark of competition is the continuing presence of modern facilities, irrespective of the age of the establishment.

Auxiliary areas of upkeep such as external plant appearance, housekeeping, and building maintenance reveal the presence or absence of standards of management which are vital to long-term leadership, as we see it.

Our questions are useful, then, in determining the *attitude* of management no less than the *action* of management with respect to upkeep as it exists in a rapidly advancing technology.

In this area, we also direct questions to those responsible for personnel and executive training. Upkeep of human resources is no less a managerial responsibility than the maintenance of physical equipment. We view continuing industrial training programs as the prime method by which obsolescence in workmen and managers may be combatted. Executive techniques no less than worker skills are experiencing marked changes as time passes. The state-of-the-art here is no less eruptive than in the more technical areas of equipment and process.

Improvement

It goes without saying that consistent long-term leadership today demands the presence of constant improvement in materials, processes, products, personnel and indeed all the active functions of management, if the position is to be maintained. Moreover, this improvement must be over and above that required to obtain parity with the general advancing state-of-the-art.

Our questions here are directed to determine the degree to which management has actually taken steps to insure and assure such progress. We ask, for example, about the presence of adequate provision for product research and development; how the research organization rates in the field of the industry; how research expense ratios compare with those of other progressive organizations; the extent to which current sales volume stems from past research and development. We ask about the status of market research; of the nature of current demand for company products. We ask whether management has ever summarized and evaluated its own management; whether management has made use of consultants in areas where improvements may be hastened through benefit of professional advice. We ask whether the company has been a leader in adopting the newest production methods; whether it has shown aggressive adaptability to meet changing conditions.

We view this section of our evaluations most importantly and want full assurance that the implements, engineering procedures and skilled personnel for the making of constant improvement are at hand.

Morale

So many people have confused morale with group enthusiasms or excitements that I hesitate to use the word out of its precise context. By morale we mean that temper of spirit which causes organizations to drive patiently, unromantically and increasingly through difficulty and disappointment; the quality of loyalty that causes older employees to try to get their sons and daughters jobs in the same organization; the kind of support that gives full obedience with a grin although honest differences of opinion still exist.

We want particularly to know whether there is a good working team upstairs. For example, it is an old banking rule in New England that no money is loaned to a business where a family row is in progress. We respect the soundness of this tradition. We want to know whether employees, in general, are sold on the company; whether they think it is a "good place to work."

We are interested in the history of the company's labor relations but we do not necessarily view past difficulties as diagnostic or current or future weakness. Often these early encounters when fairly adjudicated build for subsequent mutual respect and regard.

No area that we examine is more intangible than this. No area is more important.

Attitude

We are convinced that the personal attitudes of top executives toward their employees, their stockholders, their community, the public and the government, directly determine the success or the failure of these varied staff activities as conducted by subordinates farther down the line. We view it as vital to the managerial evaluation of any company that the attitudes of top management toward these five groups of interest be obtained.

To support and confirm responses to our questions, we also look at the record. We want to know whether the attitude as expressed has been put to use in a practical way. In each of these categories we ask whether there is any evidence that the record of the company in its chosen field has been outstanding; whether definite and clear-cut operating policies have been developed; organization problems solved; personnel appointed and programs designed, supervised and evaluated.

In this area of managerial attitude we rely heavily on the Biblical adage: "By his works shall ye know him."

Competitive Resource

The competitive position of the company in its industry is subject to statistical measurement and therefore not germane to these inquiries.

The nature and extent of competitive power, however, is a topic with which we are definitely concerned here. For example, we think it important to know why customers of the company under study buy in preference to competitiors. Is it price, quality, delivery, or what? We think it important to know whether this competitive strength resulted from planned developments within the company or from chance. We should like to know whether these competitive resources are the result of environmental advantages that will be permanent, or whether they are in current danger as a result of competitive research and development, patent termination or other causes.

Every going company produces a good to which its customers give preference over competitive goods. Too often, top management is not aware of exactly what its advantage consists, and does not recognize its loss until too late.

Reputation

Last in this company report, I put the topic of reputation. From the point of view of the field investigator, it again will be the last factor to be scrutinized. Too early knowledge of the opinion of others regarding a company may cause us unwittingly to develop prejudgments which may later color the facts as found.

Again, the nightmare of the investment analyst is the company which to all outward appearance is well managed, but which is undeservedly living on its reputation while dry-rot and senescence are at work within.

With these precautions in mind, our investigator turns to the company's competitiors, customers, bankers, to other investment underwriting houses, cooperating analysts, insurance companies and other sources, for comments and counsel. When these statements are at odds with his findings, the investigator returns to the company for recheck.

The final report, when combined with other studies of general business, of the industry in question, of the company's financial structure and condition, earnings and dividends, of internal market action, and certain other factors, permits of decision as to the precise position on the waiting list of our company's future purchases; or continuance in, or elimination from, current portfolios.

CONCLUSION

When we review the nature and purpose of our inquiries in these twelve fields—management, administration, objectives, organization, plans, control, upkeep, morale, improvement, attitude, competitive resource and reputation—we find that the times are requiring us to apply new yardsticks to managerial competence.

The depth and rapidity of economic and industrial change; the growth of application of democratic principles (I do not refer to politics here); the widening of active relationships with employees, stockholders, community, public and government—these three basic trends appear to be responsible for new and greater stress upon:

> vigor and versatility in operating management; breadth and variety of viewpoint in administration; vigilance in matters of organization; clarity and definiteness of long-term objectives; dependency upon far-reaching plans; maintenance of integrated controls; upkeep in harmony with an advancing art; improvement as a normal expectancy; effective (result-getting) managerial attitudes; creativeness through high morale; resources for increasing competition; reputation for consistently distinguished, long-term leadership in a specific industry.

In our field studies thus far, only a small proportion of the companies analyzed are rated as superior in terms of all these requirements.

Finally, investment analysis cannot be held to be scientific as we speak of science and technology. Intangible factors are difficult to get at, particularly difficult to measure and therefore susceptible to underemphasis.

We are continuing to discover revealing criteria in this nebulous area. You have been presented with our most recent thinking and procedures.

BIBLIOGRAPHY, CHAPTER 9

Bauer, Raymond A., L. T. Cauthorn, and R. P. Warner. "Auditing the Management Process for Social Performance." *Business and Society Review,* No. 15 (Fall, 1975), pp. 39-45.

Blodgett, Timothy. "Measuring the Impact of Inflation On Working Capital." *Harvard Business Review,* Vol. 61, No. 1 (1983), pp. 28-31.

Campfield, William L. "Auditing Management Performance." *Financial Executive,* Vol. 39, No. 1 (January, 1971), pp. 24-34.

Chow, Chee W., and William S. Waller. "Management Accounting and Organizational Control." *Management Accounting* (April, 1982), pp. 36-41.

Davis, K. "Five Propositions for Social Responsibility." *Business Horizons*, Vol. 18 (1975), pp. 19-23.

Doz, Yves L. "Headquarters Influence and Strategic Control in M.N.C." *Sloan Management Review*, Vol. 23, No. 1 (1981), pp. 15-29.

Edmunds, Stahrl W. "Unifying Concepts in Social Responsibility." *Academy of Management Review*, Vol. 2, No. 1 (January, 1977), pp. 38-45.

Foote, Susan Bartlett. "Changing Regulatory Strategies—What Managers Should Know about Federal Preemption." *Sloan Management Review*, Vol. 26, No. 1 (1985), pp. 69-78.

Hall, F. S. "Organization Goals: The Status of Theory and Research." From Livingstone, J. L. (ed.). *Managerial Accounting: The Behavioral Foundations*. Columbus, OH: Grid, Inc., 1975.

Hay, R. D. "Social Auditing: An Experimental Approach." *Academy of Management Journal*, Vol. 18, No. 4 (December, 1975), pp. 871-877.

"Improving the Company's Relations with Stockholders and the Financial Community." *Coordination and Communication Problems of the Financial Executive*, Financial Management Series No. 109. New York: American Management Association, Inc., 1954, pp. 22-40.

MacKay, A. E. "Management Control in a Changing Environment." *Financial Executive*, Vol. 47, No. 3, pp. 25-36.

Merrill, James. "Country Risk Analysis." *Columbia Journal of World Business*, Vol. 17, No. 1 (Spring, 1982), pp. 88-91.

Meyer, Dan D. "Adapting to Environmental Jolts." *Administrative Science Quarterly*, Vol. 27, No. 4 (December, 1982), pp. 515-537.

Scheel, Henry. "Measuring the Efficiency of Management from a Society's Viewpoint." *Advanced Management* (September, 1959), pp. 4-7, 11-13, 30.

Sethi, S. P. "Dimensions of Corporate Social Performance: An Analytical Framework." *California Management Review*, Vol. 17, No. 3, pp. 58-64.

_____ . "A Conceptual Framework for Environmental Analysis of Social Issues and Evaluation of Business Response Patterns." *Academy of Management Review*, Vol. 4, No. 1 (1979), pp. 63-74.

Simon, Jeffrey D. "Political Risk Assessment: Past Trends and Future Prospects." *Columbia Journal of World Business*, Vol. 17, No. 3 (Fall, 1982), pp. 62-71.

Steiner, G. A. "Should Business Adopt the Social Audit?" *The Conference Board Record*, Vol. 9, No. 5 (May, 1972), pp. 7-10.

Taylor, Bernard. "Turnaround, Recovery and Growth: The Way Through the Crisis." *Journal of General Management*, Vol. 8, No. 2, pp. 5-13.

Toan, Arthur B., Jr. "Measuring the Social Performance of Business." *Price Waterhouse & Co. Review*, Vol. 18, No. 2, pp. 4-9.

Zeithaml, Carl P., and Gerald P. Keim. "How to Implement a Corporate Political Action Program." *Sloan Management Review*, Vol. 26, No. 2 (Winter, 1985), pp. 23-32.

Section D

Directing

Many observers of the management scene would consider it ideal if employees, taking the plans that have been developed for the organization and receiving a position description of what they are to do, were to undertake their assignments without further instructions or interventions. Few organizations have achieved that ideal state of self-management on the part of employees. Rather, some translation of the plans and structure into more specific orders, directions, and suggestions is seen as important to the accomplishment of the purpose of the system.

Motivational theorists have extensively studied the subject of directing employees toward organizational goals. The scope of this examination is presented in a managerial framework in Chapter 10. The relevance of motivation questions allows managers to employ these motives in their workplace culture and relationships. If these factors are ignored, the manager loses considerable ability to influence employees toward the desired ends.

The quality of leadership as well as the factors that motivate employees are important in the equation of translating plans into purposeful action. The stereotype of the old bull-of-the-woods who ranted and raved in order to get things done in his shop has pretty much been supplanted by the concept of a more sophisticated and knowledgeable leader. Chapter 11 examines how the behavior of the modern leader differs from and is similar to that outmoded stereotype. Putting together the qualities of leadership needed in a particular situation with the factors that motivate employees provides a basis for modern sophisticated direction of employees toward the firm's goals. As we can provide the climates and conditions favorable to employee initiatives, the need for managerial interventions in directing employees will be reduced.

Chapter 10

Motivation and
Behavior

The black and white of motivation theory is outlined in the initial paper, a classic by Douglas McGregor in the form of theories X and Y. This conception is useful to us in discriminating among the several motivational ideas that can be used. It shows the contrasts and the differences in behavior that can be expected from operation under one or the other conceptualization. In the second article Yukl and Taber examine the use of power and the conditions under which it can be employed most effectively. In the rush to theory Y, we must remember that we undertake direction to accomplish results and that at times we need to apply power in order to achieve those results.

McClelland discusses achievement and outlines the basis for motivation in terms of achievement motivation, although a number of other needs exist (as he shows) in the theory from which this is derived. Finally, Cook takes the motivational ideas reviewed in these previous articles and evaluates how the manager can use them in managing their employees. This transition prepares us for the more detailed examination of leadership in Chapter 11. Of course, leadership cannot be undertaken in a vacuum of knowledge about motivation ideas. Cook's analysis aids in relating the two concepts with greater precision and with empirical research.

31 • THE HUMAN SIDE OF ENTERPRISE[1]

Douglas Murray McGregor[2]

It has become trite to say that industry has the fundamental know-how to utilize physical science and technology for the material benefit of mankind, and that we must now learn how to utilize the social sciences to make our human organizations truly effective.

To a degree, the social sciences today are in a position like that of the physical sciences with respect to atomic energy in the thirties. We know that past conceptions of the nature of man are inadequate and, in many ways, incorrect. We are becoming quite certain that, energy could become available within the organizational setting.

We cannot tell industrial management how to apply this new knowledge in simple, economic ways. We know it will require years of exploration, much costly development, research, and a substantial amount of creative imagination on the part of management to discover how to apply this growing knowledge to the organization of human effort in industry.

MANAGEMENT'S TASK: THE CONVENTIONAL VIEW

The conventional conception of management's task in harnessing human energy to organizational requirements can be stated broadly in terms of three propositions. In order to avoid the complications introduced by a label, let us call this set of propositions "Theory X":

1. Management is responsible for organizing the elements of productive enterprise—money, materials, equipment, people—in the interest of economic ends.
2. With respect to people, this is a process of directing their efforts, motivating them, controlling their actions, modifying their behavior to fit the needs of the organization.
3. Without this active intervention by management, people would be passive —even resistant—to organizational needs. They must therefore be persuaded, rewarded, punished, controlled—their activities must be directed. This is management's task. We often sum it up by saying that management consists of getting things done through other people.
4. The average man is by nature indolent—he works as little as possible.
5. He lacks ambition, dislikes responsibility, prefers to be led.
6. He is inherently self-centered, indifferent to organizational needs.
7. He is by nature resistant to change.
8. He is gullible, not very bright, the ready dupe of the charlatan and the demagogue.

[1] Reprinted, by permission of the publisher, from *Management Review,* November, 1957 © 1957 American Management Association, Inc. All rights reserved.
[2] Douglas Murray McGregor, School of Industrial Management, Massachusetts Institute of Technology.

The human side of economic enterprise today is fashioned from propositions and beliefs such as these. Conventional organization structures and managerial policies, practices, and programs reflect these assumptions.

In accomplishing its task—with these assumptions as guides—management has conceived of a range of possibilities.

At one extreme, management can be "hard" or "strong." The methods for directing behavior involve coercion and threat (usually disguised), close supervision, tight controls over behavior. At the other extreme, management can be "soft" or "weak." The methods for directing behavior involve being permissive, satisfying people's demands, achieving harmony. Then they will be tractable, accept direction.

This range has been fairly completely explored during the past half century, and management has learned some things from the exploration. There are difficulties in the "hard" approach. Force breeds counter-forces: restriction of output, antagonism, militant unionism, subtle but effective sabotage of management objectives. This "hard" approach is especially difficult during times of full employment.

There are also difficulties in the "soft" approach. It leads frequently to the abdication of management—to harmony, perhaps, but to indifferent performance. People take advantage of the soft approach. They continually expect more, but they give less and less.

Currently, the popular theme is "firm but fair." This is an attempt to gain the advantages of both the hard and the soft approaches. It is reminiscent of Teddy Roosevelt's "speak softly and carry a big stick."

IS THE CONVENTIONAL VIEW CORRECT?

The findings which are beginning to emerge from the social sciences challenge this whole set of beliefs about man and human nature and about the task of management. The evidence is far from conclusive, certainly, but it is suggestive. It comes from the laboratory, the clinic, the schoolroom, the home, and even to a limited extent from industry itself.

The social scientist does not deny that human behavior in industrial organization today is approximately what management perceives it to be. He has, in fact, observed it and studied it fairly extensively. But he is pretty sure that this behavior is *not* a consequence of man's inherent nature. It is a consequence rather of the nature of industrial organizations, of management philosophy, policy, and practice. The conventional approach of Theory X is based on mistaken notions of what is cause and what is effect.

Perhaps the best way to indicate why the conventional approach of management is inadequate is to consider the subject of motivation.

PHYSIOLOGICAL NEEDS

Man is a wanting animal—as soon as one of his needs is satisfied, another appears in its place. This process is unending. It continues from birth to death.

Man's needs are organized in a series of levels—a hierarchy of importance. At the lowest level, but pre-eminent in importance when they are thwarted, are his *physiological needs*. Man lives for bread alone, when there is no bread. Unless the circumstances are unusual, his needs for love, for status, for recognition are inoperative when his stomach has been empty for a while. But when he eats regularly and adequately, hunger ceases to be an important motivation. The same is true of the other physiological needs of man—for rest, exercise, shelter, protection from the elements.

A *satisfied need is not a motivator of behavior!* This is a fact of profound significance that is regularly ignored in the conventional approach to the management of people. Consider your own need for air: Except as you are deprived of it, it has no appreciable motivating effect upon your behavior.

SAFETY NEEDS

When the physiological needs are reasonably satisfied, needs at the next higher level begin to dominate man's behavior—to motivate him. These are called *safety needs*. They are needs for protection against danger, threat, deprivation. Some people mistakenly refer to these as needs for security. However, unless man is in a dependent relationship where he fears arbitrary deprivation, he does not demand security. The need is for the "fairest possible break." When he is confident of this, he is more than willing to take risks. But when he feels threatened or dependent, his greatest need is for guarantees, for protection, for security.

The fact needs little emphasis that, since every industrial employee is in a dependent relationship, safety needs may assume considerable importance. Arbitrarily management actions, behavior which arouses uncertainty with respect to continued employment or which reflects favoritism or discrimination, unpredictable administration of policy—these can be powerful motivators of the safety needs in the employment relationship *at every level,* from worker to the vice president.

SOCIAL NEEDS

When man's physiological needs are satisfied and he is no longer fearful about his physical welfare, his *social needs* become important motivators of his behavior—needs for belonging, for association, for acceptance by his fellows, for giving and receiving friendship and love.

Management knows today of the existence of these needs, but it often assumes quite wrongly that they represent a threat to the organization. Many studies have demonstrated that the tightly knit, cohesive work group may, under proper conditions, be far more effective than an equal number of separate individuals in achieving organizational goals.

Yet management, fearing group hostility to its own objectives, often goes to considerable lengths to control and direct human efforts in ways that are inimical to the natural "groupiness" of human beings. When man's social needs—and perhaps his safety needs, too—are thus thwarted, he behaves in ways which tend to defeat organizational objectives. He becomes resistant, antagonistic, uncooperative. But this behavior is a consequence, not a cause.

EGO NEEDS

Above the social needs—in the sense that they do not become motivators until lower needs are reasonably satisfied—are the needs of greatest significance to management and to man himself. They are the *egoistic needs,* and they are two kinds:

1. Those needs that relate to one's self-esteem—needs for self-confidence, for independence, for achievement, for competence, for knowledge.
2. Those needs that relate to one's reputation—needs for status, for recognition, for appreciation, for the deserved respect of one's fellows.

Unlike the lower needs, these are rarely satisfied; man seeks indefinitely for more satisfaction of these needs once they have become important to him. But they do not appear in any significant way until physiological, safety, and social needs are all reasonably satisfied.

The typical industrial organization offers few opportunities for the satisfaction of these egoistic needs to people at lower levels in the hierarchy. The conventional methods of organizing work, particularly in mass-production industries, give little heed to these aspects of human motivation. If the practices of scientific management were deliberately calculated to thwart these needs, they could hardly accomplish this purpose better than they do.

SELF-FULFILLMENT NEEDS

Finally—a capstone, as it were, on the hierarchy of man's needs—there are what we may call the *needs for self-fulfillment.* These are the needs for realizing one's own potentialities, for continued self-development, for being creative in the broadest sense of the term.

It is clear that the conditions of modern life give only limited opportunity for these relatively weak needs to obtain expression. The deprivation most people experience with respect to other lower level needs diverts their energies into the struggle to satisfy *those* needs, and the needs for self-fulfillment remain dormant.

MANAGEMENT AND MOTIVATION

We recognize readily enough that a man suffering from a severe dietary deficiency is sick. The deprivation of physiological needs has behavioral consequences. The same is true—although less well recognized—of deprivation of higher-level needs. The man whose needs for safety, association, independence, or status are thwarted is sick just as surely as the man who has rickets. And his sickness will have resultant consequences.

We will be mistaken if we attribute his resultant passivity, his hostility, his refusal to accept responsibility to his inherent "human nature." These forms of behavior are *symptoms* of illness—of deprivation of his social and egoistic needs.

The man whose lower-level needs are satisfied is not motivated to satisfy those needs any longer. For practical purposes they exist no longer. Management often asks, "Why aren't people more productive? We pay good wages, provide good working conditions, have excellent fringe benefits and steady employment. Yet people do not seem to be willing to put forth more than minimum effort."

The fact that management has provided for these physiological and safety needs has shifted the motivational emphasis to the social and perhaps to the egoistic needs. Unless there are opportunities *at work* to satisfy these higher-level needs, people will be deprived; and their behavior will reflect this deprivation. Under such conditions, if management continues to focus its attention on physiological needs, its efforts are bound to be ineffective.

People *will* make insistent demands for more money under these conditions. It becomes more important than ever to buy the material goods and services which can provide limited satisfaction of the thwarted needs. Although money has only limited value in satisfying many higher-level needs, it can become the focus of interest if it is the *only* means available.

THE CARROT-AND-STICK APPROACH

The carrot-and-stick theory of motivation (like Newtonian physical theory) works reasonably well under certain circumstances. The *means* for satisfying man's physiological and (within limits) his safety needs can be provided or withheld by management. Employment itself is such a means, and so are wages, working conditions, and benefits. By these means the individual can be controlled so long as he is struggling for subsistence.

But the carrot-and-stick theory does not work at all once man has reached an adequate subsistence level and is motivated primarily by higher needs. Management cannot provide a man with self-respect, or with the respect of his fellows, or with the satisfaction of needs for self-fulfillment. It can create such conditions that he is encouraged and enabled to seek such satisfactions for *himself*, or it can thwart him by failing to create those conditions.

But this creation of conditions is not "control." It is not a good device for directing behavior. And so management finds itself in an odd position. The high standard of living created by our modern technological know-how provides quite adequately for the satisfaction of physiological and safety needs. The only significant exception is where management practices have not created confidence in a "fair break"—and thus where safety needs are thwarted. But by making possible the satisfaction of low-level needs, management has deprived itself of the ability to use as motivators the devices on which conventional theory has taught it to rely—rewards, promises, incentives, or threats and other coercive devices.

The philosophy of management by direction and control—*regardless of whether it is hard or soft*—is inadequate to motivate because the human needs on which this approach relies are today unimportant motivators of behavior. Direction and control are essentially useless in motivating people whose important needs are social and egoistic. Both the hard and the soft approach fail today because they are simply irrelevant to the situation.

People, deprived of opportunities to satisfy at work the needs which are now important to them, behave exactly as we might predict—with indolence, passivity, resistance to change, lack of responsibility, willingness to follow the demagogue, unreasonable demands for economic benefits. It would seem that we are caught in a web of our own weaving.

A NEW THEORY OF MANAGEMENT

For these and many other reasons, we require a different theory of the task of managing people based on more adequate assumptions about human nature and human motivation. I am going to be so bold as to suggest the broad dimensions of such a theory. Call it "Theory Y," if you will.

1. Management is responsible for organizing the elements of productive enter-prise—money, materials, equipment, people—in the interest of economic ends.
2. People are *not* by nature passive or resistant to organizational needs. They have become so as a result of experience in organizations.
3. The motivation, the potential for development, the capacity for assuming responsibility, the readiness to direct behavior toward organizational goals are all present in people. Management does not put them there. It is a responsibility of management to make it possible for people to recognize and develop these human characteristics for themselves.
4. The essential task of management is to arrange organizational conditions and methods of operation so that people can achieve their own goals *best* by directing *their own* efforts toward organizational objectives.

This is a process primarily of creating opportunities, releasing potential, removing obstacles, encouraging growth, providing guidance. It is what Peter Drucker has called "management by objectives" in contrast to "management by control." It does *not* involve the abdication of management, the absence of leadership, the lowering of standards, or the other characteristics usually associated with the "soft" approach under Theory X.

SOME DIFFICULTIES

It is no more possible to create an organization today which will be a full, effective application of this theory than it was to build an atomic power plant in 1945. There are many formidable obstacles to overcome.

The conditions imposed by conventional organization theory and by the approach of scientific management for the past half century have tied men to limited jobs which do not utilize their capabilities, have discouraged the acceptance of responsibility, have encouraged passivity, have eliminated meaning from work. Man's habits, attitudes, expectations—his whole conception of membership in an industrial organization—have been conditioned by his experience under these circumstances.

People today are accustomed to being directed, manipulated, controlled in industrial organizations and to finding satisfaction for their social, egoistic, and self-fulfillment needs away from the job. This is true of much of management as well as of workers. Genuine "industrial citizenship"—to borrow again a term from Drucker—is a remote and unrealistic idea, the meaning of which has not even been considered by members of industrial organizations.

Another way of saying this is that Theory X places exclusive reliance upon external control of human behavior, while Theory Y relies heavily on self-control and self-direction. It is worth noting that this difference is the difference between treating people as children and treating them as mature adults. After generations of the former, we cannot expect to shift to the latter overnight.

STEPS IN THE RIGHT DIRECTION

Before we are overwhelmed by the obstacles, let us remember that the application of theory is always slow. Progress is usually achieved in small steps. Some innovative ideas which are entirely consistent with Theory Y are today applied with some success.

Decentralization and Delegation

These are ways of freeing people from the too-close control of conventional organization, giving them a degree of freedom to direct their own activities, to assume responsibility, and, importantly, to satisfy their egoistic needs. In this connection, the flat organization of Sears, Roebuck and Company provides an interesting example. It forces "management by objectives," since it enlarges the number of people reporting to a manager until he cannot direct and control them in the conventional manner.

Job Enlargement

This concept, pioneered by I.B.M. and Detroit Edison, is quite consistent with Theory Y. It encourages the acceptance of responsibility at the bottom of the organization; it provides opportunities for satisfying social and egoistic needs. In fact, the reorganization of work at the factory level offers one of the more challenging opportunities for innovation consistent with Theory Y.

Participation and Consultative Managment

Under proper conditions, participation and consultative management provide encouragement to people to direct their creative energies toward organizational objectives, give them some voice in decisions that affect them, provide significant opportunities for the satisfaction of social and egoistic needs. The Scanlon Plan is the outstanding embodiment of these ideas in practice.

Performance Appraisal

Even a cursory examination of conventional programs of performance appraisal within the ranks of management will reveal how completely consistent they are with Theory X. In fact, most such programs tend to treat the individual as though he were a product under inspection on the assembly line.

A few companies—among them General Mills, Ansul Chemical, and General Electric—have been experimenting with approaches which involve the individual in setting "targets" or objectives *for himself* and in a *self*-evaluation of performance semiannually or annually. Of course, the superior plays an important leadership role in this process—one, in fact, which demands substantially more competence than the conventional approach. The role is, however, considerably more congenial to many managers than the role of "judge" or "inspector" which is usually forced upon them. Above all, the individual is encouraged to take a greater responsibility for planning and appraising his own contribution to organizational objectives; and the accompanying effects on egoistic and self-fulfillment needs are substantial.

APPLYING THE IDEAS

The not infrequent failure of such ideas as these to work as well as expected is often attributable to the fact that management has "bought the idea" but applied it within the framework of Theory X and its assumptions.

Delegation is not an effective way of exercising management by control. Participation becomes a farce when it is applied as a sales gimmick or a device for kidding people into thinking they are important. Only the management that has confidence in human capacities and is itself directed toward organizational objectives rather than toward the preservation of personal power can grasp the implications of this emerging theory. Such management will find and apply successfully other innovative ideas as we move slowly toward the full implementation of a theory like Y.

THE HUMAN SIDE OF ENTERPRISE

It is quite possible for us to realize substantial improvements in the effectiveness of industrial organizations during the next decade or two. The social sciences can contribute much to such developments; we are only beginning to grasp the implications of the growing body of knowledge in these fields. But if this conviction is to become a reality instead of a pious hope, we will need to view the process much as we view the process of releasing the energy of the atom for constructive human ends— as a slow, costly, sometimes discouraging approach toward a goal which would seem to many to be quite unrealistic.

The ingenuity and the perseverance of industrial management in the pursuit of economic ends have changed many scientific and technological dreams into common place realities. It is now becoming clear that the application of these same talents to the human side of enterprise will not only enhance substantially these materialistic achievements, but will bring us one step closer to "the good society."

32 • THE EFFECTIVE USE OF MANAGERIAL POWER[1]

Gary Yukl[2]
Tom Taber[3]

Influence over the attitudes and behavior of subordinates is the essence of competent leadership. It is impossible to be an effective manager without influencing subordinates. Despite its obvious importance, however, the way in which managers exert their power has not been subjected to much research. There have been only a small number of studies on the relationship between leader power and effectiveness. In most of these studies, power was classified in terms of the taxonomy developed by J.R.P. French Jr. and B. Raven in 1959. This taxonomy identifies five distinct types of power:

- *Authority* (legitimate power): the legitimate right of the leader to make certain kinds of requests.
- *Reward power:* the leader's control over rewards valued by subordinates.
- *Coercive power:* the leader's control over punishments.
- *Expert power:* the leader's task-relevant knowledge and competence as perceived by subordinates.
- *Referent power:* subordinate loyalty to the leader and desire to please him or her.

The research revealed that effective leaders rely most on expert and referent power to influence subordinates. The use of expert and referent power was positively correlated with subordinate performance or satisfaction in most of the studies. Use of legitimate and coercive power tended to be negatively correlated with effectiveness, or to be uncorrelated with it. Results for reward power were mixed, with no clear trend across studies. The results from this research seem plausible, even though the correlations were not strong or consistent.

THE USE OF POWER AND SUBORDINATE REACTION

To understand how a leader's use of power can affect subordinate performance, it is necessary to consider such intervening processes as subordinate motivation and effort. The motivational outcome of an influence attempt by the leader can be classified according to whether it produces commitment, compliance, or resistance in the subordinate.

When subordinates are committed, they are enthusiastic about carrying out the leader's requests and make a maximum effort to do so. Committed

[1]Reprinted, by permission of the publisher, from *Personnel*, March-April 1983 © 1983 AMACOM Periodicals Division, American Management Associations, New York. All rights reserved.
[2]Gary Yukl, Professor, State University of New York at Albany.
[3]Tom Taber, Associate Professor, State University of New York at Albany.

employees accept the leader's goals and exert maximum effort to accomplish them. Simple compliance, on the other hand, is only a partially successful outcome of leader influence. Subordinates go along with the leader's requests without necessarily accepting the leader's goals. They are not enthusiastic and may make only the minimal acceptable effort in carrying out such requests. Resistance, as most managers know, is a clearly unsuccessful outcome. Subordinates reject the leader's goals and may pretend to comply, but, instead, intentionally delay or sabotage the task. Unfortunately, only a few studies have considered subordinate motivation as an intervening variable. From the limited evidence available, we can piece together a picture of the likely causal relationships between leader power bases and subordinate motivation.

As Figure 1 illustrates, expert and referent power tend to result in subordinate commitment, authority and reward power tend to result in compliance, and coercion tends to result in resistance. Because group performance is usually better when subordinates are highly motivated to do the task, the use of expert and referent power usually leads to a higher level of performance.

FIGURE 1

OUTCOMES THAT RESULT FROM DIFFERENT TYPES OF POWER

Power Source	Commitment	Compliance	Resistance
Authority	Possible	LIKELY	Possible
Reward Power	Possible	LIKELY	Possible
Coercive Power	Unlikely	Possible	LIKELY
Expert Power	LIKELY	Possible	Possible
Referent Power	LIKELY	Possible	Possible

The problem with most of the power research is that it overlooks the leader's skill in exercising power. The outcome of a particular attempt to influence subordinates will depend as much on the leader's skill as on the type of power used. It is quite possible that expert and referent power could result merely in compliance or even in resistance if not used skillfully. By the same token, authority and reward power could result in subordinate commitment when used in an appropriate situation by a very skilled leader. Coercion does not necessarily have to result in resistance; it may result in subordinate compliance if used skillfully.

Thus the power studies yield somewhat misleading findings. One gets the false impression that an effective leader uses only expert and referent power—with no need at all to use authority, rewards, or coercion. However, this impression is at odds with findings from motivation research that indicate that rewards can be very effective in increasing subordinate effort and performance in some situations. Motivation research also provides evidence that punishment is sometimes effective in getting subordinates to comply with rules and regulations. And various kinds of evidence indicate that exercising authority with a legitimate request is the most common approach used for influencing subordinates, and one that is quite important in the day-to-day operations of a work unit. Thus it is likely that effective leaders use all five types of power at one time or another. Leader effectiveness stems from knowing the appropriate type of power to use in each situation and how to exercise this power skillfully to maximize subordinate commitment.

THE LEADERSHIP MODEL

Figure 2 shows a model that depicts the relationship between power and leader effectiveness. The model differs in some important respects from traditional thinking about leader power. First, the model holds that mere possession of power by itself has no consistent effects on subordinate motivation; power merely acts as a moderator variable to condition the effects of a leader's influence attempts. Second, the model clearly distinguishes between having power and using it. The successful use of power requires the leader to have relevant skill and a desire to exercise power, as well as the power resources themselves. Finally, the feedback loops in the model, indicated by dashed lines, recognize that power relationships are reciprocal and historical. A leader's behavior over time can increase or diminish his or her power, and the leader's behavior is itself influenced by subordinate behavior and performance.

FIGURE 2

A MODEL OF LEADER POWER AND EFFECTIVENESS

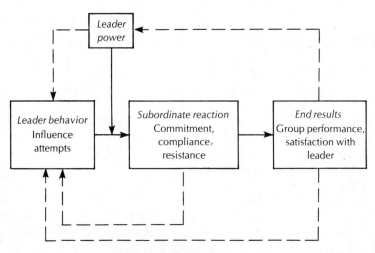

In the process of accumulating power and exercising it, leaders are confronted with an interesting paradox. Any increase in power gives a leader greater potential for influencing subordinates, but a power differential also increases the propensity for resistance. The existence of a power differential is generally disturbing to the person who has lower power and status. Subordinates are aware that a powerful leader has the potential to cause them great harm or inconvenience. For this reason, even a benevolent leader's subordinates tend to be very sensitive to the leader's behavior, including subtle indications of approval or disapproval. Involuntary dependence on the whims of a powerful authority figure can cause resentment as well as anxiety, particularly for subordinates with strong needs for esteem and independence. A leader who treats subordinates as somehow inferior—who acts arrogant, bossy, and manipulative—will quickly elicit resistance to requests and commands.

Thus successful use of power requires influence attempts that do not threaten the subordinates' self-esteem. A number of other factors contribute to the success of an influence attempt, such as clarity of communication, timing, and appropriateness of requests as well as the leader's ability to relate requests to subordinates' needs and concerns. Previous leadership research does not tell us much about the way to exercise power successfully. However, some useful insights are provided by studies of motivation, attitude change, counseling, and conflict resolution. From this research, we have learned enough to offer some tentative guidelines on how to use and maintain each of the five types of power.

GUIDELINES FOR USING AUTHORITY

Subordinates generally accept their boss's right to make requests and tell them what work to do. However, they do not like to be given orders in a way that implies they are not as good as the leader—people don't want to be treated like slaves. Thus effective leaders exercise authority by making polite requests, not by making arrogant demands.

Legitimate requests should be made in clear, simple language, and the leader should check to make sure subordinates understand what is required, especially if there is any indication that subordinates are confused. Whenever appropriate, the reason for the request should be explained so that subordinates understand why it is necessary. If anyone is likely to raise a question about the legitimacy of the leader's request, subordinates must be made to understand that it is indeed within the scope of the leader's formal authority to make such a request. Finally, the leader should follow up to verify that subordinates have complied with such requests. Subordinates who are reluctant to do something requested by the leader may wait to see if he or she is serious enough to insist on compliance. If the leader doesn't, subordinates may assume it is safe just to forget about it.

GUIDELINES FOR USING REWARDS

A common use of reward power is to offer specific incentives for doing what the leader wants. Incentive plans are usually very mechanical; subordinates automatically earn a bonus or commission for each item they make or sell. This type of mechanical incentive may be appropriate when there is a repetitious, tedious task with an objective output measure. But for more complex jobs, mechanical incentives are not the best way to exercise reward power. One danger in emphasizing explicit incentives is that subordinates quickly define their relationship to the leader in purely economic terms, and they come to expect special rewards every time the leader wants them to do something new or unusual. A much better relationship between leader and subordinate is one based on mutual loyalty and teamwork rather than an impersonal exchange of benefits.

There are other dangers in offering specific incentives. One is that they tend to make the leader appear manipulative—something subordinates may resent. Another limitation of incentives is that they are unlikely to result in commitment, even under the best of conditions. The typical response to specific incentives is to do only what is needed to earn the reward and no more. Subordinates may be tempted to neglect the less visible aspects of the task so they can complete it quickly.

Thus, in most situations, it is better to use rewards not as a bribe for doing what the leader wants, but rather to reinforce desirable behavior after it has already occurred. Tangible rewards can be used in conjunction with praise and recognition to communicate the message that the leader appreciates subordinates who are competent and committed. The size of the reward should be based on an evaluation of the subordinate's total performance, rather than on just some narrow aspect of it, as tends to be the case with incentives. The reward need not be limited to money. An effective leader will discover what other things subordinates value and use these as rewards also. It may be more time off, a better work schedule, or more desirable work assignments—but regardless of what type of reward is used, it is imperative to avoid the appearance of manipulation.

GUIDELINES FOR USING COERCION

Effective leaders generally avoid the use of coercive power except when absolutely necessary, because coercion is likely to create resentment and undermine their referent power. Coercion is most appropriately used to deter behavior that is very detrimental to the organization, such as violation of safety rules, reckless behavior endangering lives or valuable assets, and direct disobedience of legitimate requests. Skillfully used, coercion stands a reasonably good chance of getting subordinates to comply with rules, regulations, and orders.

Before criticizing or disciplining a subordinate, the leader should try to find out whether the subordinate is really at fault. A hasty reprimand that turns out to be unjustified can prove very embarrassing and seriously impair relations with subordinates. If a warning or punishment is needed, the leader should impose discipline promptly and consistently without showing any favoritism. Warnings should be stated in a way that avoids the appearance of personal hostility toward the subordinate. The leader should remain calm and convey a sincere desire to help the subordinate comply with rules and requirements to avoid the necessity for punishment. The subordinate should be invited to share in assuming responsibility for correcting disciplinary problems, including the setting of improvement goals and development of improvement plans. For all but the most serious of infractions, one or more warnings should be given before punishment is meted out. However, to protect the credibility of their coercive power, leaders should avoid issuing idle or exaggerated warnings that they are not prepared to carry out. Finally, when it is necessary to use punishment, the magnitude of the punishment should fit the seriousness of the infraction.

GUIDELINES FOR USING EXPERT POWER

Expert power depends on the subordinates' perception that the leader knows the best course of action in a given situation. A leader's expert power increases when he or she suggests a course of action that turns out to be highly successful. Expert power is decreased when the leader shows faulty judgment or makes decisions that lead to failure by the group. Thus, to accumulate expert power, a leader should foster an image of experience and competence. It is essential to preserve credibility by avoiding careless statements and rash decisions. The leader should keep informed about technical matters and outside developments that affect the group's work. In a crisis, it is essential to remain calm and act confident and decisive. A leader who appears confused, who vacillates or, even worse, is obviously panicked, will quickly lose expert power.

Like authority, expert power involves a risk of highlighting status differences between leader and subordinates. Leaders who act arrogant and talk down to subordinates encounter resistance to their directions. Comments that threaten subordinates' self-esteem are strictly taboo. Even leaders who are more knowledgeable than subordinates in a particular matter should show respect for subordinates' ideas and suggestions and try to incorporate these into plans whenever feasible. If subordinates have serious concerns about the leader's planned course of action, the leader should recognize these concerns and try to deal with them instead of simply dismissing them with such comments as, "Don't be ridiculous, you have nothing to worry about." The leader should carefully explain why the proposed plan of action is the best one possible and what steps will be taken to minimize any risk to subordinates.

GUIDELINES FOR USING REFERENT POWER

Referent power, like expert power, increases or decreases over the course of successive interactions between leader and subordinates. Referent power is increased by being considerate toward subordinates, showing concern for their needs and feelings, treating them fairly, and defending their interests when dealing with superiors and outsiders. Referent power is diminished when a leader expresses hostility, distrust, rejection, or indifference toward subordinates, or when the leader fails to defend subordinates' interests with superiors. Over time, actions speak louder than words, and a leader who tries to appear friendly but who takes advantage of subordinates or fails to stick up for them will eventually find that his or her referent power has eroded away.

One effective way to use referent power is to make a personal appeal that evokes subordinate feelings of loyalty. The leader should indicate that the request is personally very important and that he or she is counting on subordinates for their support and cooperation. The leader should be careful not to use personal appeals too often or to ask for more than is reasonable, given the nature of the relationship. There are limits to what can be asked in the name of loyalty and friendliness. If the request appears unreasonable to subordinates, the leader can end up with reduced referent power as well as resistance to the request.

A more indirect way to use referent power is through role modeling. Here the leader sets an example by behaving the way that subordinates should behave. Subordinates will tend to imitate a leader whom they admire, because they want to please him or her and because they want to be more like him or her. Thus a leader with considerable referent power can influence subordinates in a positive way without even making explicit requests.

A CALL FOR FURTHER RESEARCH

These guidelines for using each type of power are tentative, most require further confirmation and elaboration. Much basic research remains to be done on how leaders use or should use power effectively. Past research has not explored the subject deeply enough to reveal many of the subtle nuances and nonverbal behaviors involved in influencing subordinates. Nor has previous research examined the complex interaction among the various forms of influence. In addition to taking usual questionnaire approach, more observational studies are needed.

Researchers should also examine a broader range of influence behavior. It is now evident that the French and Raven taxonomy fails to include some forms of influence that can be very important to leaders or managers, such as inspirational appeals, informational control, situational engineering (including job design), and use of participation. Finally, as mentioned earlier, the dynamic nature of influence processes requires more longitudinal research to examine the evolution of influence relationships between leader and followers over time. Research on how to use power effectively offers tremendous benefits to practicing managers, and it is time now to start taking this kind of research more seriously.

33 • THAT URGE TO ACHIEVE[1]

David C. McClelland[2]

Most people in this world, psychologically, can be divided into two broad groups. There is that minority which is challenged by opportunity and willing to work hard to achieve something, and the majority which really does not care all that much.

For nearly twenty years now, psychologists have tried to penetrate the mystery of this curious dichotomy. Is the need to achieve (or the absence of it) an accident, is it hereditary, or is it the result of environment? Is it a single, isolatable human motive, or a combination of motives—the desire to accumulate wealth, power, fame? Most important of all, is there some technique that could give this will to achieve to people, even whole societies, who do not now have it?

While we do not yet have complete answers for any of these questions, years of work have given us partial answers to most of them and insights into all of them. There is a distinct human motive, distinguishable from others. It can be found, in fact tested for, in any group.

Let me give you one example. Several years ago, a careful study was made of 450 workers who had been thrown out of work by a plant shutdown in Erie, Pennsylvania. Most of the unemployed workers stayed home for a while and then checked back with the United States Employment Service to see if their old jobs or similar ones were available. But a small minority among them behaved differently; the day they were laid off, they started job-hunting.

They checked both the United States and the Pennsylvania Employment Office; they studied the "Help Wanted" sections of the papers; they checked through their union, their church, and various fraternal organizations; they looked into training courses to learn a new skill; they even left town to look for work, while the majority when questioned said they would not under any circumstances move away from Erie to obtain a job. Obviously the members of that active minority were differently motivated. All the men were more or less in the same situation objectively: they needed work, money, food, shelter, job security. Yet only a minority showed initiative and enterprise in finding what they needed. Why? Psychologists, after years of research, now believe they can answer that question. They have demonstrated that these men possessed in greater degree a specific type of human motivation. For the moment let us refer to this personality characteristic as "Motive A"

[1] From *Think* Magazine, Vol. 32, No. 6 (November-December, 1966), pp. 19-23. Reprinted by permission from *Think* Magazine, published by IBM, Copyright 1966 by International Business Machines Corporation.

[2] David C. McClelland, Chairman of the Department of Social Relations, Harvard University, Acting Chairman of the Center for Research and Personality.

and review some of the other characteristics of the men who have more of the motive than other men.

Suppose they are confronted by a work situation in which they can set their own goals as to how difficult a task they will undertake. In the psychological laboratory, such a situation is very simply created by asking them to throw rings over a peg from any distance they may choose. Most men throw more or less randomly, standing now close, now far away, but those with Motive A seem to calculate carefully where they are most likely to get a sense of mastery. They stand nearly always at moderate distances, not so close as to make the task ridiculously easy, nor so far away as to make it impossible. They set moderately difficult, but potentially achievable goals for themselves, where they objectively have only about a 1-in-3 chance of succeeding. In other words, they are always setting challenges for themselves, tasks to make them stretch themselves a little.

But they behave like this only if *they* can influence the outcome by performing the work themselves. They prefer not to gamble at all. Say they are given a choice between rolling dice with one in three chances of winning and working on a problem with a one-in-three chance of solving in the time allotted, they choose to work on the problem even though rolling the dice is obviously less work and the odds of winning are the same. They prefer to work at a problem rather than leave the outcome to chance or to others.

Obviously they are concerned with personal achievement rather than with the rewards of success *per se*, since they stand just as much chance of getting those rewards by throwing the dice. This leads to another characteristic the Motive A men show—namely, a strong preference for work situations in which they get concrete feedback on how well they are doing, as one does, say in playing golf, or in being a salesman, but as one does not in teaching, or in personnel counseling. A golfer always knows his score and can compare how well he is doing with par or with his own performance yesterday or last week. A teacher has no such concrete feedback on how well he is doing in "getting across" to his students.

The *n* Ach Men

But why do certain men behave like this? At one level the reply is simple: because they habitually spend their time thinking about doing things better. In fact, psychologists typically measure the strength of Motive A by taking samples of a man's spontaneous thoughts (such as making up a story about a picture they have been shown) and counting the frequency with which he mentions doing things better. The count is objective and can even be made these days with the help of a computer program for content analysis. It yields what is referred to technically as an individual's *n* Ach score (for "need for Achievement"). It is not difficult to understand why people who think constantly about "doing better" are more apt to do better at job-hunting, to set moderate, achievable goals for themselves, to dislike gambling (because they get no achievement satisfaction from success) and to prefer work situations where they can tell easily whether they are improving or not. But why some people and not others come to think this way is another question. The evidence suggests it is not because they are born that way, but because of special training they get in the home from parents who get moderately high achievement goals but who are warm, encouraging and nonauthoritarian in helping their children reach these goals.

Such detailed knowledge about one motive helps correct a lot of common sense ideas about human motivation. For example, much public policy (and much business policy) is based on the simpleminded notion that people will work harder "if they have to." As a first approximation, the idea isn't totally wrong, but it is only a half-truth. The majority of unemployed workers in Erie "had to" find work as much as those with higher *n* Ach, but they certainly didn't work as hard at it. Or again, it is frequently assumed that *any* strong motive will lead to doing things better. Wouldn't it be fair to say that most of the Erie workers were just "unmotivated"? But our detailed knowledge of various human motives shows that each one leads a person to behave in *different* ways. The contrast is not between being "motivated" or "unmotivated" but between being motivated toward A or B or C, etc.

A simple experiment makes the point nicely: subjects were told that they could choose as a working partner either a close friend or a stranger who was known to be an expert on the problem to be solved. Those with higher *n* Ach (more "need to achieve") chose the experts over their friends, whereas those with more *n* Aff (the "need to affiliate with others") chose friends over experts. The latter were not "unmotivated"; their desire to be with someone they liked was simply a stronger motive than their desire to excel at the task. Other such needs have been studied by psychologists. For instance, the need for Power is often confused with the need for Achievement because both may lead to "outstanding" activities. There is a distinct difference. People with a strong need for Power want to command attention, get recognition, and control others. They are more active in political life and tend to busy themselves primarily with controlling the channels of communication both up to the top and down to the people so that they are more "in charge." Those with high *n* Power are not as concerned with improving their work performance daily as those with high *n* Ach.

It follows, from what we have been able to learn, that not all "great achievers" score high *n* Ach. Many generals, outstanding politicians, great research scientists do not, for instance, because their work requires other personality characteristics, other motives. A general or a politician must be more concerned with power relationships, a research scientist must be able to go for long periods without the immediate feedback the person with high *n* Ach requires, etc. On the other hand, business executives, particularly if they are in positions of real responsibility or if they are salesmen, tend to score high in *n* Ach. This is true even in a Communist country like Poland: apparently there, as well as in a private enterprise economy, a manager succeeds if he is concerned about improving all the time, setting moderate goals, keeping track of his or the company's performance, etc.

Motivation and Half-Truths

Since careful study has shown that common sense notions about motivation are at best half-truths, it also follows that you cannot trust what people tell you about their motives. After all, they often get their own motives from common sense. Thus a general may say he is interested in achievement (because he has obviously achieved), or a businessman that he is interested only in making money (because he has made money), or one of the majority of unemployed in Erie that he desperately wants a job (because he knows he needs one); but a careful check of what each one thinks about and how he spends his time may show that each is concerned about quite different things. It requires special measurement techniques to identify the presence of *n* Ach and other such motives. Thus what people say and believe is not very closely related to these "hidden" motives which seem to affect a person's "style of life" more than his political, religious or social attitudes. Thus *n* Ach produces enterprising men among labor leaders or managers, Republicans or Democrats, Catholics or Protestants, capitalists or communists.

Wherever people begin to think often in *n* Ach terms things begin to move. Men with higher *n* Ach get more raises and are promoted more rapidly, because they keep actively seeking ways to do a better job. Companies with many such men grow faster. In one comparison of the two firms in Mexico, it was discovered that all but one of the top executives of a fast growing firm had higher *n* Ach scores than the highest scoring executive in an equally large but slow-growing firm. Countries with many such rapidly growing firms tend to show above-average rates of economic growth. This appears to be the reason why correlations have regularly been found between the *n* Ach content in popular literature (such as popular songs or stories in children's textbooks) and subsequent rates of national economic growth. A nation which is thinking about doing better all the time (as shown in its popular literature) actually does do better economically speaking. Careful quantitative studies have shown this to be true in Ancient Greece, in Spain in the Middle Ages, in England from 1400-1800, as well as among contemporary nations, whether capitalist or communist, developed or underdeveloped.

Contrast these two stories for example. Which one contains more *n* Ach? Which one reflects a state of mind which ought to lead to harder striving to improve the way things are?

Excerpt from story A (4th grade reader): "Don't Ever Owe a Man— The world is an illusion. Wife, children, horses, and cows are all just ties of fate. They are ephemeral. Each after fulfilling his part in life disappears. So we should not clamour after riches which are not permanent. As long as we live it is wise not to have any attachments and just think of God. We have to spend our lives without trouble, for is it not time that there is an end to grievances? So it is better to live knowing the real state of affairs. Don't get entangled in the meshes of family life."

Excerpt from story B (4th grade reader): "How I Do Like to Learn— I was sent to an accelerated technical high school. I was so happy I cried. Learning is not very easy. In the beginning I couldn't understand what the teacher taught us. I always got a red cross mark on my papers. The boy sitting next to me was very enthusiastic and also an outstanding student. When he found I couldn't do the problems he offered to show me how he had done them. I could not copy his work. I must learn through my own reasoning. I gave his paper back and explained I had to do it myself. Sometimes I worked on a problem until midnight. If I couldn't finish, I started early in the morning. The red cross marks on my work were getting less common. I conquered my difficulties. My marks rose. I graduated and went on the college."

Most readers would agree without any special knowledge of the *n* Ach coding system, that the second story shows more concern with improvement than the first, which comes from a contemporary reader used in Indian public schools. In fact the latter has a certain Horatio Alger quality that is reminiscent of our own McGuffey readers of several generations ago. It appears today in the textbooks of Communist China. It should not, therefore, come as a surprise if a nation like Communist China, obsessed as it is with improvement, tended in the long run to outproduce a nation like India, which appears to be more fatalistic.

The *n* Ach level is obviously important for statesmen to watch and in many instances to try to do something about, particularly if a nation's economy is lagging. Take Britain, for example. A generation ago (around 1925) it ranked fifth among 25 countries where children's readers were scored for *n* Ach—and its economy was doing well. By 1950 the *n* Ach level had dropped to 27th out of 39 countries—well below the world average—and today, its leaders are feeling the severe economic effects of this loss in the spirit of enterprise.

Economics and *n* Ach

If psychologists can detect *n* Ach levels in individuals or nations, particularly before their effects are widespread, can't the knowledge somehow be put to use to foster economic development? Obviously detection or diagnosis is not enough. What good is it to tell Britain (or India for that matter) that it needs more *n* Ach, a greater spirit of enterprise? In most such cases, informed observers of the local scene know very well that such a need exists, though they may be slower to discover it than the psychologist hovering over *n* Ach in individuals or nations.

Since about 1960, psychologists in my research group at Harvard have been experimenting with techniques designed to accomplish this goal, chiefly among business executives whose work requires the action characteristics of people with high *n* Ach. Initially, we had real doubts as to whether we could succeed, partly because like most American psychologists we had been strongly influenced by the psychoanalytic view that basic motives are laid down in childhood and cannot really be changed later, and partly because many studies of intensive psychotherapy and counseling have shown minor if any long-term personality effects. On the other hand we were encouraged by the nonprofessionals: those enthusiasts like Dale Carnegie, the communist ideologue or the church missionary, who felt they could change adults and in fact seemed to be doing so. At any rate we ran some brief (7 to 10 days) "total push" training courses for businessmen, designed to increase their *n* Ach.

Four Main Goals

In broad outline the courses had four main goals: (1) They were designed to teach the participants how to think, talk and act like a person with high *n* Ach, based on our knowledge of such people gained through 17 years of research. For instance, men learned how to make up stories that would code high in *n* Ach (i.e., how to think in *n* Ach terms), how to set moderate goals for themselves in the ring toss game (and in life). (2) The courses stimulated the participants to set higher but carefully planned and realistic work goals for themselves over the next two years. Then we checked back with them every six months to see how well they were doing in terms of their own objectives. (3) The courses also utilized techniques for giving the participants knowledge about themselves. For instance, in playing the ring toss game, they could observe that they behaved differently from others—perhaps in refusing to adjust a goal downward after failure. This would then become a matter for group discussion and the man would have to explain what he had in mind in setting such unrealistic goals. Discussion could then lead on to what a man's ultimate goals in life were, how much he cared about actually improving performance v. making a good impression or having many friends. In this way the participants would be freer to realize their achievement goals without being blocked by old habits and attitudes. (4) The courses also usually created a group *esprit de corps* from learning about each other's hopes and fears, successes and failures, and from going through an emotional experience together, away from everyday life, in a retreat setting. This membership in a new group helps a man achieve his goals, partly because he knows he has their sympathy and support and partly because he knows they will be watching to see how well he does. The same effect has been noted in other therapy groups like Alcoholics Anonymous. We are not sure which of these course "inputs" is really absolutely essential—that remains a research question—but we were taking no chances at the outset in view of the general pessimism about such efforts, and we wanted to include any and all techniques that were thought to change people.

The courses have been given: to executives in a large American firm, and in several Mexican firms; to underachieving high school boys; and to businessmen in India from Bombay and from a small city—Kakinada in the state of Andhra Pradesh. In every instance save one (the Mexican case), it was possible to demonstrate statistically, some two years later, that the men who took the course had done better (made more money, got promoted faster, expanded their businesses faster) than comparable men who did not take the course or who took some other management course.

Consider the Kakinada results, for example. In the two years preceding the course 9 men, 18 percent of the 52 participants, had shown "unusual" enterprise in their businesses. In the 18 months following the course 25 of the men, in other words nearly 50 percent, were unusually active. And this was not due to a general upturn of business in India. Data from a control city some forty-five miles away, show the same base rate of "unusually active" men as in Kakinada before the course—namely, about 20 percent. Something clearly happened in Kakinada: the owner of a small radio shop started a chemical plant; a banker was so successful in making commercial loans in an enterprising way that he was promoted to a much larger branch of his bank in Calcutta; the local political leader accomplished his goal (it was set in the course) to get the federal government to deepen the harbor and make it into an all-weather port; plans are far along for establishing a steel rolling mill, etc. All this took place without any substantial capital input from outside. In fact, the only costs were for four 10-day courses plus some brief follow-up visits every six months. The men are raising their own capital and using their own resources for getting business and industry moving in a city that had been considered stagnant and unenterprising.

The promise of such a method of developing achievement motivation seems very great. It has obvious applications in helping underdeveloped countries, or "pockets of poverty" in the United States, to move faster economically. It has great potential for businesses that need to "turn around" and take a more enterprising approach toward their growth and development. It may even be helpful in developing more *n* Ach among low-income groups. For instance, data show that lower-class Negro Americans have a very low level of *n* Ach. This is not surprising. Society has systematically discouraged and blocked their achievement striving. But as the barriers to upward mobility are broken down, it will be necessary to help stimulate the motivation that will lead them to take advantage of new opportunities opening up.

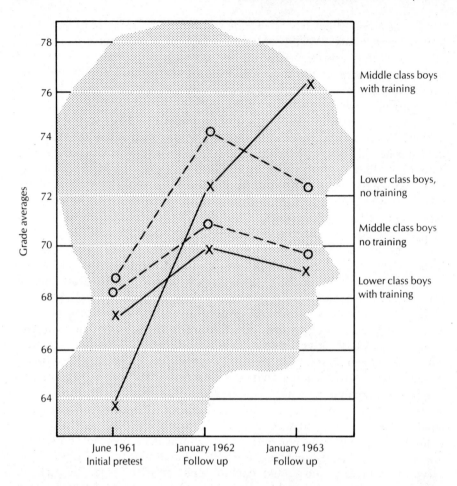

In a Harvard study, a group of underachieving 14 year-olds was given six-week course designed to help them do better in school. Some of the ooys were also given training in achievement motivation, or *n* Ach (solid lines). As graph reveals, the only boys who continued to improve after a two-year period were the middle-class boys with the special *n* Ach training. Psychologists suspect the lower-class boys dropped back, even with *n* Ach training, because they returned to an environment in which neither parents nor friends encouraged achievement.

Extreme Reactions

But a word of caution: Whenever I speak of this research and its great potential, audience reaction tends to go to opposite extremes. Either people remain skeptical and argue that motives can't really be changed, that all we are doing is dressing Dale Carnegie up in fancy "psychologese," or they become converts and want instant course descriptions by return mail to solve their local motivational problems. Either response is unjustified.

What I have described here in a few pages has taken 20 years of patient research effort, and hundreds of thousands of dollars in basic research costs. What remains to be done will involve even larger sums or more time for development to turn a promising idea into something of wide practical utility.

Encouragement Needed

To take only one example, we have not yet learned to develop *n* Ach really well among low-income groups. In our first effort—a summer course for bright underachieving 14-year-olds—we found that boys from the middle class improved steadily in grades in school over a two-year period, but boys from the lower class showed an improvement after the first year followed by a drop back in their beginning low grade average. (See chart on page 449.) Why? We speculate that it was because they moved back into an environment in which neither parents nor friends encouraged achievement or upward mobility. In other words, it isn't enough to change a man's motivation if the environment in which he lives doesn't support at least to some degree his new efforts. Negroes striving to rise out of the ghetto frequently confront this problem: they are often faced by skepticism at home and suspicion on the job, so that even if their *n* Ach is raised, it can be lowered again by the heavy odds against their success. We must learn not only to raise *n* Ach but also to find methods of instructing people in how to manage it, to create a favorable environment in which it can flourish.

Many of these training techniques are now only in the pilot testing stage. It will take time and money to perfect them, but society should be willing to invest heavily in them in view of their tremendous potential for contributing to human betterment.

34 · GUIDELINES FOR MANAGING MOTIVATION[1]

Curtis W. Cook[2]

Motivating employees is one of the most consistent challenges any manager faces. In dealing with this challenge, supervisors at all organizational levels have learned to rely on one or two sources of guidance. One is personal experience. From years of working with people a manager experiments and learns what seems to work more often than it fails. In addition to personal judgment, many managers seek ideas from training programs, seminars, and reading.

Undoubtedly the formal model of motivation most often encountered is the hierarchy-of-needs theory of the late Abraham Maslow, or one patterned after this pioneering work. Unfortunately people generally are not motivated by one theory alone, whether it be that of a psychologist or a supervisor. Behavioral science researchers have formulated and investigated motivational theories based on factors other than prepotent needs. However, these other streams of thought have been slow to have an impact on management action, apparently because the more a supervisor knows about motivation, the more confusing the issue appears to be—Catch 22.

There is no easy and fail-safe way to improve motivational management. But two approaches to the problem might help. One is to clear away some of the confusion about what researchers and theorists say about motivation by identifying the points of consistency among the major models. The second is to work from this synthesis of motivational knowledge to develop a series of practical guidelines for managing motivation. The objective is to explain systematically why and how motivation occurs, and then to suggest ways in which theory can be put into practice.

A MEANS TO AN END

Managers should be concerned with motivation because it affects performance. Performance is the target; motivation can be one means for getting there. From one managerial perspective, *performance* might mean maintaining or improving on a certain level of productivity. From another perspective, performance means the human factor—having employees who are reasonably satisfied. At yet a higher level the human performance factor involves personal (and team) growth or development. Employees acquire knowledge and skills which enable individuals and the organization to adapt to and undertake changes in job tasks and programs.

[1]From *Business Horizons,* Vol. 23, No. 2 (April, 1980), pp. 61–69. Copyright 1980 by the Foundation for the School of Business at Indiana University. Reprinted by permission of *Business Horizons.*

[2]Curtis W. Cook, Associate Professor of Management and Chairman of the Board of the Center for Management Studies at Southern Illinois University, Edwardsville, Illinois.

Obviously other factors besides motivation affect performance. The individual worker's job skills and knowledge, health, emotional state, and other personal factors bear on today's performance and tomorrow's growth potential. Also involved are the many factors of management and organization that are used to promote organizational predictability: equipment and facilities, job designs, organizational structure, policies and procedures, managerial style, and other such matters. It is important for the manager to realize that these factors which bear directly on performance also affect the individual worker's motivational state and may thus have a double impact on performance.

Motivation itself is intangible, little more than a concept that we use to explain a force within people. More precisely, it is a ubiquitous term used to make inferences about the direction and strength of human behavior. In work organizations, motivation is said to be reflected in what a person does and the manner in which it is done.

The directional aspect of motivation underlies in part the choice of behaviors. Where job design permits some flexibility among tasks, the reason why a worker engages in one activity more frequently than in others probably involves some personal state of motivational arousal. Something in the activity or the person activates and directs behavior toward that activity. For example, one worker will devote considerable time to cleaning up the work area, to make sure it is always tidy. Another frequently wanders around the plant "looking for something" and often is found talking to someone at the drinking fountain. Both these examples suggest a behavior-directing force, in one case presumably toward a selected facet of work, in the other case toward activities other than work (work avoidance behaviors).

Beyond channeling or directing behavior, motivation also involves the degree of energy or effort exerted toward a task, person, or object. Outwardly we pick up clues about motivation by making judgments about how hard someone tries. We use a variety of adjectives to label a person who seems motivated: diligent, persevering, industrious, enthusiastic, conscientious. The level of effort also can be explained by the degree to which a particular behavioral pattern is sustained over time. One employee, for example, may work at 100 percent of capacity one day and only 60 percent the next, while another sustains a consistent 90 percent effort.

WHAT DO EMPLOYEES EXPECT?

One of the newer formal theories of motivation incorporates a line of logical reasoning that has long been assumed by the practical-minded manager. But it took the research of scholars such as Victor Vroom, Ed Lawler, and Lyman Porter to develop a format framework called *expectancy theory*.[3] At the heart of

[3]V. H. Vroom, *Work and Motivation* (New York City: John Wiley & Sons, Inc., 1964); E. E. Lawler III, *Motivation in Work Organizations* (Monterey, Calif.: Brooks/Cole Publishing Company, 1973); L. W. Porter and E. E. Lawler III, *Managerial Attitudes and Performance* (Homewood, Ill.: Richard D. Irwin, Inc., 1968).

the expectancy model are three basic questions that most individuals inevitably raise about their work situations. Although the language may vary, and the sequence certainly is not formally patterned, these three questions are:

1. What's in it for me? How important to me are the available rewards or personal consequences of working at this job for this organization?
2. If I try harder, will it make a difference in my performance? Can I influence my level of performance through my level of effort?
3. Am I rewarded for what I produce? If I increase my level of performance, will I receive an increase in rewards or personal consequences and vice versa?

The usefulness of this framework of questions is the explicit focus on performance. Essentially the theory is based on the premise that workers are capable of and do attempt to define relationships among their motivational effort, their job performance, and available rewards or consequences. It suggests that individuals manage (or can regulate) personal motivations depending on what they expect in terms of the three-way relationship among effort, performance, and rewards. If the worker believes there is little relationship between effort and performance, or between performance and eventual rewards, or if the type and magnitude of rewards are not particularly valued, the worker may decide, What's the use?

Affirmative answers to all three (or perhaps two) questions should promote a higher level of effort. However, it may be that the worker perceives that only some activities within the job permit a positive fit among the three elements. Unfortunately the activities which are found to be rewarded may be ones that contribute little to (or even detract from) the primary task performance expected by management. Many socially or politically oriented behaviors are reactions to such environments, especially when work output results are ill defined or when formal performance evaluations focus more on personal traits than on accomplishments.

EMPLOYEE NEEDS

While expectancy theory is relatively new, Maslow's hierarchical need theory is the explanation of human motivation most widely known to managers. The model typically identifies five levels of needs (physical, safety, interpersonal, esteem, and self-actualization) and proclaims that higher needs are not activated until more basic needs (such as physical and safety) are satisfied. Such a presentation appears in practically all textbooks about management or supervision and finds its way into most seminars or training sessions that include a motivation component.

But when Maslow presented his pioneering theory in 1943, his model was based on observations about neurotic people in a clinical or therapy setting.[4] He

---

[4]A. H. Maslow, "A Theory of Human Motivation," *Psychological Review,* Vol. 50 (1943), pp. 370–396.

later expressed reservations about the way his model had been applied literally to industrial settings and had influenced the thinking of subsequent management scholars, such as Douglas McGregor and Fred Herzberg, and practioners.[5] Maslow later simplified his theory so that it corresponded with the theories which describe behavior as being directed or channeled either toward or away from something or someone.[6]

A simplified explanation of need theory relates directly to these opposing directions of behavior. There are some conditions (such as hunger, threats to security, nonacceptance by esteemed colleagues) that a person wants to avoid. If these conditions are experienced or are believed to be pending, they tap into deficiency-reduction needs (essentially lower orders on the original Maslow scale) and they trigger behaviors to get rid of or reduce the deficiency. Alternatively there are some things that a person actively seeks because they enable satisfaction of higher growth-aspiration goals. Growth-aspirational goals tend to be more personalized and unique among individuals than deficiency-reduction needs. Furthermore, personal growth or enrichment activity tends to be sustained—people seldom get too much of that which is personally meaningful.

Need theory is most useful when applied to the first question in the expectancy model: What's in it for me? To the extent that individual needs can be identified or personally meaningful goals articulated, then the supervisor has clues as to the types of rewards or consequences that are important to an employee. And to the extent that one (or more) growth-aspiration goals can be satisfied through work, there is a greater likelihood that a higher level of effort will be directed to sustain high task effort once relief is obtained from those annoyances or frustrations that are found in deficiency-reduction needs.

EFFORTS AND REWARDS

Another realm of theory concerns specific individual motives. While growth-aspiration goals are unlimited in variety and number, the realization that some people have strongly held specific motives can simplify the motivational management process. The motives which have been most widely explored in organizational settings by researchers such as David McClelland are the need to achieve, the need for power, and the need for affiliation.[7]

A person with a strong achievement motive is turned on by challenge, derives considerable satisfaction from success, and is fairly realistic about the limits of his or her personal competence. The individual motivated by power obtains satisfaction (not necessarily malicious) through influencing or controlling others.

---

[5]A. H. Maslow, *Eupsychian Management: A Journal* (Homewood, Ill.: Richard D. Irwin, Inc., 1965).

[6]A. H. Maslow, "Deficiency Motivation and Growth Motivation," *Nebraska Symposium on Motivation,* edited by M. R. Jones (Lincoln: University of Nebraska Press, 1955).

[7]D. C. McClelland, *The Achieving Society* (Princeton: D. Van Nostrand Company, 1961) and *Power: the Inner Experience* (New York City: Irvington Publishers, Inc., 1975).

The individual with a strong affiliation need finds satisfaction in being accepted and respected and in interacting on a personal basis with others.

Looking for clues to these personal motive areas provides a more specific way of mapping the meaningful goal structure of the individual. One employee asks for involvement in new tasks or projects and experiences a feeling of reward in being able to handle them successfully (achievement motive). Another likes to do battle in committees or enjoys being widely known by persons in high positions in the organization (power motive). A third is sought out by peers because he is sensitive and patient in helping others with problems (affiliation motive).

The important lesson about strongly held personal motives, once they are identified, is that the process of engaging in a motive-related activity often provides feelings of meaningful rewards. The activity itself serves to reinforce these behaviors with less need for externally administered rewards. The critical task is, first, to identify people within the work unit who seem to have any of these motives and, second, to seek some activity that might permit at least partial satisfaction of the motive.

EFFORTS AND PERFORMANCE

In most work situations, a manager would assume that employees would answer yes to the question, Does my effort affect performance? But employees often will not agree. They may believe that whatever results are achieved are due to chance or to the power of others, such as supervisors or others in the work group. They do not attribute the outcome to their own efforts. Or they do not perceive stability or predictability in their work situations. When events are random, or the supervisor acts capriciously, a strong blow is dealt to the possibility of motivating workers; a sustained high level of task effort is probable only when the employee sees himself or herself as influencing the task outcome.

Obviously these attributions may be incorrect (or partially in error). But when a worker believes task performance is not predictable from day to day (or project to project), and also perceives that the random results are caused by the whims of the supervisor (a powerful other), there is no way the employee's work behavior will be consistent.

However, a little known, yet potentially powerful, research finding is that internal attribution is related to the achievement motive. As Bernard Weiner explains, if a person can internalize success (I helped make it happen) and can also feel emotional satisfaction or pride in the accomplishment, then a foundation is provided on which an increased need to achieve might be developed.[8] Certainly the achievement motive is not the only personal motive that affects performance positively. But for most types of tasks where some element of individual initiative is desirable, it certainly increases the probability that the employee will be highly task motivated.

[8] B. Weiner, *Achievement Motivation and Attribution Theory* (Morristown, N. J.: General Learning Press, 1974).

PERFORMANCE AND REWARDS

Finally, we come to the issue of the relationship between rewards and performance. This becomes a sticky issue for many managers because formal compensation systems often are based on factors other than performance, such as job classification, seniority, or pay grade. For personal rewards to be related to performance, it is usually necessary to identify and use factors which are nonmonetary, such as feedback, job assignments, and praise. To understand the dynamics of the reward-performance process, two additional behavioral science concepts are helpful. One focuses on the issue of perceived equity, the other on reinforcement contingencies.

Feelings about inequity usually begin when an individual makes a personal input/output comparison, often in reference to others. Research by J. Stacey Adams suggests that if a person experiences inequitable or abusive treatment, he or she will attempt to reduce the inequity.[9] This can occur by direct behavior adjustment, especially when rewards are thought to be less than the effort exerted. The worker simply reduces effort and does not try as hard, that is, reduces motivation. Alternatively a perceptual adjustment may occur when the employee reconsiders output or effort in comparison with that of others in the work group or even outside the organization. An employee might resolve an initial inequity, for example, by thinking, I guess he really has been putting out more than I have.

The concept of reinforcement draws on B. F. Skinner's work on behavior modification. The central premise is that if fairly consistent consequences follow a particular behavior that behavior will be reinforced. Positive consequences (rewards) tend to strengthen a behavior, while negative consequences (punishment or adverse outcomes) tend to diminish a behavior.[10] The managerial objective of behavior modification techniques is to develop and provide a systematic reinforcer for desirable performance behavior.

HOW TO MANAGE MOTIVATION

The above ideas about motivation emphasize that motivation is not simply a force or condition that resides inside individuals. In addition to the personal side (personality and physical and emotional state), motivation is affected by the nature of the person's task or job requirements, the technology or physical support provided for the job, the actions of immediate supervisors and interactions with others in management, and the policies, rules, and structure of the organization.

Although complex, motivation can be positively influenced or managed. The following guidelines suggest a variety of techniques that managers might use to redirect an employee's task behavior or to strengthen the level of effort channeled

[9]J. S. Adams, "Inequity in Social Exchange," *Advances in Experimental Social Psychology,* Vol. 2, edited by L. Berkowitz (New York City: Academic Press, 1965), pp. 267–299.
[10]B. F. Skinner, *About Behaviorism* (New York City: Alfred A. Knopf, Inc., 1974).

into behaviors that lead to desired performance results. Generally these guidelines move from those that are relatively easy to implement (perhaps requiring only minor modification of the existing situation) to those that are more difficult. In all cases these guidelines are derived from and are consistent with the theoretical ideas presented earlier.[11]

1. *Clarify the task role.* While this may sound elementary, supervisors often take it for granted that employees fully understand their job or task role. The easiest way to test their understanding is to ask, "What is expected of you in this job?" What managers often find is that jobs are explained or described to employees in terms of duties and responsibilities. If an employee begins parroting back the "responsible for . . ." jargon, the manager should shift to an exploration of expected results. The practical issue is, "How do we both recognize adequate desired performance?" To a degree, some of the techniques involved in management by objectives (MBO) focus on this aspect of results-oriented role clarification. However, a manager does not need a formal MBO program to initiate greater role clarification. In fact, in many instances, the mechanics of formal MBO programs fail to accomplish this goal because they promote standardization and may be viewed as little more than a documentation process rather than as a technique for motivating employees.

2. *Provide positive feedback.* If expected results have been identified, and the manager is aware of employee behaviors that affect results, then appropriate behaviors or results ought to be recognized and feedback provided to the employee. One manager gave this advice: "Let the person know that you know and make sure he or she knows also. Don't assume that all employees realize when they are doing OK. Tell them how they have improved and why you believe it has happened." Verbal acknowledgment costs nothing and yet it provides reassurance to the employees that they are doing the right thing (or moving in the desired direction) and that their contribution is valued. A manager does not have to wait for magnificent improvements. Reinforce *any* improvement in behavior. In addition to performance feedback, keeping employees informed about job-related developments helps to build perceptions of equity and fair treatment.

3. *Personalize the causes of performance.* Many people never fully realize the impact of their behavior on performance. External attribution is an accepted outlook on life by employees—for some, because of childhood and youth experiences over which they felt they had no control; for others, because of experiences in organizations that seem capricious or run by political, technological, and bureaucratic factors. We are all aware that some supervisors or co-workers at times seize the glory of someone else's accomplishments. But to strengthen a desire to perform well, a supervisor should help the individual realize the ways in which personal efforts affect performance. It helps to be very specific, especially when output problems arise. Rather than berating an employee by saying, "You're always goofing up this job," turn the situation around and demonstrate exactly what personal actions can lead to acceptable performance.

[11]The guidelines are also consistent with compensation and rewards, according to research findings supported by Southern Illinois University Research and Projects Grant 90702.

4. *Make apparent the personal gains.* If system-administered benefits (choice of job assignments, promotions, special privileges) are to serve as motivational inducements, they need to be specified in advance. This goes beyond the day-to-day feedback by attempting to focus employee attention on long-term performance benefits: "Here's what you stand to gain by continuing to perform at this level." But do not assume that all such rewards are equally attractive to all people. Using this approach successfully requires knowing something about the special motives, interests, goals, concerns, and needs of each individual. Observing what they enjoy talking about and doing is one source of clues about relevant rewards. Discussing aims and preferences with individual workers is another way of seeking out what might be meaningful. Then attaching performance contingencies to the relevant reward and periodically reviewing progress toward that target may keep the incentive value of the future reward alive.

5. *Personalize pride in accomplishment.* Feedback and clarification of how personal actions affect performance are a necessary starting point for developing internal attribution of success. But to stimulate a higher level of task motivation it is also useful to make sure the employee is enjoying the feeling of success. It may be necessary to explore with the person how he or she feels when a task is performed successfully. Feelings of pride in accomplishment are not as common as managers might think, especially given the tendency to see powerful other persons or chances as keys to the results. It is necessary to get people who seldom display pride to talk about their emotional responses to task improvement. The manager may have to provide clues that help the employee identify and articulate the emotions of feeling proud or satisfied. This process of working with them to internalize feelings of accomplishment may advance the need for achievement from a latent to an active place in the person's motive structure.

6. *Encourage personal goal clarification.* Many people have vague expectations about how organizational involvement contributes to personal goals or growth. Unless a person is strongly committed to a particular career path, he or she may simply drift, accepting the path of least resistance. Personal lives often are divorced from organizational involvement. Obviously some types of jobs contribute little to the employee except income and job security. But frequently there is more to be gained in terms of personal development than the individual realizes. While at first glance this may appear to be the same as the fourth guideline, in practice it involves a higher degree of thinking and soul-searching. The manager must work with the individual to help define personal goals that are to some degree organizationally aligned by focusing on identifying and elaborating on what the person wants from work now and at specified times in the future. Then career strategies can be cooperatively developed for achieving some growth-aspiration goals that currently are not realized in the organization.

7. *Match the job with personal motives.* Ultimately this may suggest that some people be transferred to other jobs. In the short run it means that, to the extent that there is some variety of work tasks within the unit, selective assignments may be made on the basis of recognized motives. The person with a discernible need for achievement is involved in special projects or troubleshooting. The one with a high need for affiliation might take on major responsibilities

for interfacing with the public, if that is part of the unit task requirement. A highly power-motivated individual might serve well as a representative to negotiating sessions. Enabling employees to engage in tasks where the required behavior is compatible with their underlying need will provide internalized satisfaction directly and require fewer external (supervisor-administered) reinforcers.

8. *Remove supervisory roadblocks.* Now comes the tough part. It is a rare supervisor who does not (at least on occasion) abuse subordinates, creating for them unnecessary hassles and obstacles. For example, in trying to treat employees equally, inconsistencies may be created; if two workers have demonstrated a marked degree of self-reliance, then the close supervision that may be required for others would be inconsistent with the higher level of job maturity demonstrated by the dependable two. Or supervisors can fail to back up an employee who has, perhaps, suggested means for cutting costs. Perhaps the greatest danger here is in falling victim to routine, of taking employees for granted, and of failing to be observant of changes in their expectations or behavior.

9. *Remove organizational roadblocks.* Superior performance cannot be expected if resources are not provided or if obstacles surround the employee. Every organization can stand some housecleaning of policies and administrative procedures that are meant to bring a high degree of uniformity (conformity) to organizational activity. But when excessive energy is diverted away from productive ends for the sake of conformity, individuals affected by such practices lose the enthusiasm and commitment to performance they might have had at an earlier time. In effect, the organization causes them to become dismotivated.

Performance is generally more positively affected by intelligent motivational efforts than by forcing or coercing a certain kind of behavior from employees or by imposing rigid constraints on them. The suggested guidelines can be used selectively to strengthen the level of task effort we call motivation. When tempered with personal experience and used in conjunction with a knowledge of the employees supervised, these techniques can pay off in better motivational management.

BIBLIOGRAPHY, CHAPTER 10

Ackerman, Leonard. "Let's Put Motivation Where It Belongs—Within the Individual." *Personnel Journal,* Vol. 49, No. 7 (July, 1970), pp. 559-562.

Babb, Harold W., and D. G. Kopp. "Applications of Behavior Modification in Organizations: A Review and Critique." *Academy of Management Review,* Vol. 3, No. 2 (April, 1978), pp. 281-292.

Broedling, Laurie A. "The Uses of the Intrinsic-Extrinsic Distinction in Explaining Motivation and Organizational Behavior." *Academy of Management Review,* Vol. 2, No. 2 (April, 1977), pp. 267-276.

Campbell, *et al.* Managerial Behavior Performance and Effectiveness. New York: McGraw-Hill Book Co., 1970.

DeVries, M. F. R. K. "Organizational Stress: A Call for Management Action." *Sloan Management Review,* Vol. 21, No. 1 (Fall, 1979), pp. 3-14.

Dewhirst, H. Dudley, and R. D. Arvey. "Range of Interests vs. Job Performance and Satisfaction." *Research Management,* Vol. 14, No. 4 (July, 1976), pp. 18-23.

Geare, A. J. "Productivity from Scanlon Type Plans." *Academy of Management Review,* Vol. 1, No. 3 (July, 1976), pp. 99-108.

Giblin, E. J. "Motivating Employees: A Closer Look." *Personnel,* Vol. 55, No. 2 (February, 1976).

Herzberg, Frederick. *The Motivation to Work,* New York: John Wiley & Sons, Inc., 1959.

Hunt, J. G., and J. W. Hill. "The New Look in Motivation Theory for Organizational Research." *Human Organization,* Vol. 2 (Summer, 1969).

Kempner, Thomas. "Motivation and Behavior—A Personal View." *Journal of General Management,* Vol. 9, No. 1, pp. 51-57.

Kerr, S. "On the Folly of Rewarding *A,* While Hoping for *B."* Academy of Management Journal, Vol. 18, No. 4 (December, 1975), pp. 769-783.

Kreitner, Robert. "Managing the Two Faces of Stress." *Arizona Business,* Vol. 24, No. 8 (October, 1977), pp. 9-14.

Locke, Edwin A. "The Ubiquity of the Technique of Goal Setting in Theories of and Approaches to Employee Motivation." *Academy of Management Review,* Vol. 3, No. 3 (July, 1978), pp. 594-601.

Mankoff, A. W. "Values—Not Attitudes—Are the Real Key to Motivation," *Management Review,* Vol. 63, No. 12, pp. 23-29.

Maslow, A. H. *Motivation and Personality.* New York: Harper & Row, Publishers, Inc., 1954.

McClelland, David C. *The Achieving Society.* New York: Van Nostrand Reinhold Co., 1961.

Mitchell, Terence. "Motivation: New Directions for Theory, Research, and Practice." *Academy of Management Review,* Vol. 7, No. 1 (1982), pp. 80-88.

Murthy, K. R. S. and M. S. Salter. "Should CEO Pay Be Linked to Results?" *Harvard Business Review,* Vol. 52, No. 3 (May-June, 1975), pp. 66-73.

Pate, Larry E. "Cognitive versus Reinforcement View of Intrinsic Motivation." *Academy of Management Review,* Vol. 3, No. 3 (July, 1978), pp. 505-514.

Proodian, Ralph. "There Are No Dull Subjects." *Wall Street Journal,* January 14, 1985.

Rabinowitz, William, *et al.* "Worker Motivation: Unsolved Problem or Untapped Resource?" *California Management Review,* Vol. 25, No. 2 (January, 1983), pp. 45-56.

Richardson, Peter R. "Courting Greater Employee Involvement through Participative Management." *Sloan Management Review,* Vol. 26, No. 2 (Winter, 1985), pp. 33-44.

Schein, Edgar H. "Coming to a New Awareness of Organizational Culture." *Sloan Management Review,* Vol. 25, No. 2 (1984), pp. 3-15.

Schwartz, Howard S. "Maslow and the Hierarchical Enactment of Organizational Reality." *Human Relations,* Vol. 36, No. 10, pp. 933-956.

Seashore, S. E., and T. D. Taber. "Job Satisfaction Indicators and their Correlates." *American Behavioral Scientist,* Vol. 18, No. 3 (January-February, 1975), pp. 333-368.

Steers, Richard M., and R. T. Mowday. "The Motivational Properties of Tasks." *Academy of Management Review* (October, 1977), pp. 645-658.

_____ , and D. G. Spencer. "Achievement Needs and MBO Goal Setting." *Personnel Journal,* Vol. 57, No. 1 (January, 1978), pp. 26-28.

Stone, Eugene, and Hal G. Gueutal. "On the Premature Death of Need-Satisfaction Models: An Investigation of Salancik and Pfeffer's Views on Priming and Consistency Artifacts." *Journal of Management,* Vol. 10, No. 2 (Summer, 1984), pp. 237-249.

Stonich, Paul J. "The Performance Measurement and Reward System: Critical to Strategic Management." *Organization Dynamics* (Winter, 1984), pp. 45-57.

Ungson, Gerardo Rivera, and Richard M. Steers. "Motivation and Politics in Executive Compensation." *Academy of Management Review,* Vol. 9, No. 2 (1984), pp. 313-323.

Vroom, Victor H. *Work and Motivation.* New York: John Wiley & Sons, Inc., 1964.

Walton, Eugene, and Frank Friedlander. "Positive and Negative Motivations Toward Work." *Administrative Science Quarterly,* Vol. 9 (June, 1964-March, 1965), pp. 194-207.

Weaver, Charles N. "What Workers Want from their Jobs." *Personnel,* Vol. 53, No. 3 (May-June, 1976), pp. 48-54.

Whyte, William F., *et al. Money and Motivation,* New York: Harper & Row, Publishers, Inc., 1955.

Wiener, Yoash. "Commitment in Organizations: A Normative View." Academy of Management Review, Vol. 7, No. 3 (1982), pp. 418-428.

Wofford, J. C. "A Goal-Energy-Effort Requirement Model of Work Motivation." *Academy of Management Review,* Vol. 4, No. 2 (1979), pp. 193-201.

Zaleznik, A., C. R. Christensen, and F. J. Roethlisberger. *The Motivation, Productivity and Satisfaction of Workers.* Boston: Division of Research, Graduate School of Business, Harvard University, 1958.

Chapter 11

<hr>

Leadership

The basic thesis of Tannenbaum and Schmidt's discourse is that leadership is exercised in different places in different ways with different subordinates and leaders. As a consequence, there is no single best way to lead people. Rather, there are several appropriate leadership styles or methods depending upon the situation, the leader, and the follower. Tannenbaum and Schmidt have developed a conditional theory of leadership. The condition determines the approach to leadership that is most appropriate.

Yet the challenge to managerial leadership is even greater than that implied in the above-mentioned article. Howard and Wilson show that over a period of years, the values held by individuals in society and the workplace have substantially changed. The implication of these work ethic changes can be substantial. The managers of tomorrow will be faced with motivating individuals to perform under conditions in which work is seen as less valued than it was in previous times. How can we motivate people when they are less interested in the outcomes? The cultures that fostered the protestant work ethic appear to be much weaker today in the United States than they were 50 years ago. If this is true, must firms go to Korea, for example, to get the work done at a cost that makes the firm competitive? The answers are fewer than the questions raised here.

In the final article Watson puts leadership in a total managerial perspective along with strategy, organizational structure, information systems, and so on. In other words, we need to go beyond the conditional concepts of Tannenbaum and Schmidt to the total managerial situation to resolve the issue of how leadership should be exercised. Yet even Watson's analysis does not completely resolve the longitudinal issues set forth by Howard and Wilson. How to get people to work in a culture that devalues work has been resolved by slavery and war in prior civilizations, but these "solutions" certainly appear inimical to current cultural values.

35 • HOW TO CHOOSE A LEADERSHIP PATTERN[1]

Robert Tannenbaum[2]
Warren H. Schmidt[3]

● "I put most problems into my group's hands and leave it to them to carry the ball from there. I serve merely as a catalyst, mirroring back the people's thoughts and feelings so that they can better understand them."

● "It's foolish to make decisions oneself on matters that affect people. I always talk things over with my subordinates, but I make it clear to them that I'm the one who has to have the final say."

● "Once I have decided on a course of action, I do my best to sell my ideas to my employees."

● "I'm being paid to lead. If I let a lot of other people make the decisions I should be making, then I'm not worth my salt."

● "I believe in getting things done. I can't waste time calling meetings. Someone has to call the shots around here, and I think it should be me."

Each of these statements represents a point of view about "good leadership." Considerable experience, factual data, and theoretical principles could be cited to support each statement, even though they seem to be inconsistent when placed together. Such contradictions point up the dilemma in which the modern manager frequently finds himself.

NEW PROBLEM

The problem of how the modern manager can be "democratic" in his relations with subordinates and at the same time maintain the necessary authority and control in the organization for which he is responsible has come into focus increasingly in recent years.

Earlier in the century this problem was not so acutely felt. The successful executive was generally pictured as possessing intelligence, imagination, initiative, the capacity to make rapid (and generally wise) decisions, and the ability to inspire subordinates. People tended to think of the world as being divided into "leaders" and "followers."

New Focus

Gradually, however, from the social sciences emerged the concept of "group dynamics" with its focus on *members* of the group rather than solely

[1] From *Harvard Business Review* (March-April, 1958), pp. 95-101. Reprinted by permission of Robert Tannenbaum, Warren H. Schmidt, and *Harvard Business Review*.
[2] Robert Tannenbaum, Professor of Personnel Management, Institute of Industrial Relations, University of California at Los Angeles.
[3] Warren H. Schmidt, Professor of Personnel Management, Human Relations Research Group, University of California at Los Angeles.

on the leader. Research efforts of social scientists underscored the importance of employee involvement and participation in decision making. Evidence began to challenge the efficiency of highly directive leadership, and increasing attention was paid to problems of motivation and human relations.

Through training laboratories in group development that sprang up across the country, many of the newer notions of leadership began to exert an impact. These training laboratories were carefully designed to give people first-hand experience in full participation and decision making. The designated "leaders" deliberately attempted to reduce their own power and to make group members as responsible as possible for setting their own goals and methods within the laboratory experience.

It was perhaps inevitable that some of the people who attended the training laboratories regarded this kind of leadership as being truely "democratic" and went home with the determination to build fully participative decision making into their own organizations. Whenever their bosses made a decision without convening a staff meeting, they tended to perceive this as authoritarian behavior. The true symbol of democratic leadership to some was the meeting—and the less directed from the top, the more democratic it was.

Some of the more enthusiastic alumni of these training laboratories began to get the habit of categorizing leader behavior as "democratic" or "authoritarian." The boss who made many decisions himself was thought of as an authoritarian, and his directive behavior was often attributed solely to his personality.

New Need

The net result of the research findings and of the human relations training based upon them has been to call into question the sterotype of an effective leader. Consequently, the modern manager often finds himself in an uncomfortable state of mind.

Often he is not quite sure how to behave; there are times when he is torn between exerting "strong" leadership and "permissive" leadership. Sometimes new knowledge pushes him in one direction (I should really get the group to help make this decision"), but at the same time his experience pushes him in another direction ("I really understand the problem better than the group and therefore I should make the decision"). He is not sure when a group decision is really appropriate or when holding a staff meeting serves merely as a device for avoiding his own decision-making responsibility.

The purpose of our article is to suggest a framework which managers may find useful in grappling with this dilemma. First we shall look at the different patterns of leadership behavior that the manager can choose from in relating himself to his subordinates. Then we shall turn to some of the questions suggested by this range of patterns. For instance, how important is it for a manager's subordinates to know what type of leadership he is using in a situation? What factors should he consider in deciding on a leadership pattern? What difference do his long-run objectives make as compared to his immediate objectives?

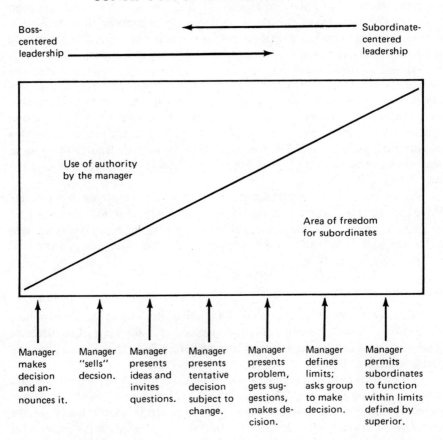

EXHIBIT 1

CONTINUUM OF LEADERSHIP BEHAVIOR

Boss-centered leadership ← → Subordinate-centered leadership

Use of authority by the manager

Area of freedom for subordinates

| Manager makes decision and announces it. | Manager "sells" decsion. | Manager presents ideas and invites questions. | Manager presents tentative decision subject to change. | Manager presents problem, gets suggestions, makes decision. | Manager defines limits; asks group to make decision. | Manager permits subordinates to function within limits defined by superior. |

RANGE OF BEHAVIOR

Exhibit I presents the continuum or range of possible leadership behavior available to a manager. Each type of action is related to freedom available to his subordinates in reaching decisions. The actions seen on the extreme left characterize the manager who maintains a high degree of control while those seen on the extreme right characterize the manager who releases a high degree of control. Neither extreme is absolute; authority and freedom are never without their limitations.

Now let us look more closely at each of the behavior points occurring along this continuum.

The Manager Makes the Decision and Announces It. In this case the boss identifies a problem, considers alternative solutions, chooses one of them, and then reports this decision to his subordinates for implementation. He may or may not give consideration to what he believes his subordinates will think or feel about his decision; in any case, he provides no opportunity for them to participate directly in the decision-making process. Coercion may or may not be used or implied.

The Manager "Sells" His Decision. Here the manager, as before, takes responsibility for identifying the problem and arriving at a decision. However, rather than simply announcing it, he takes the additional step of persuading his subordinates to accept it. In doing so, he recognizes the possibility of some resistance among those who will be faced with the decision, and seeks to reduce this resistance by indicating, for example, what the employees have to gain from his decision.

The Manager Presents His Ideas, Invites Questions. Here the boss who has arrived at a decision and who seeks acceptance of his ideas provides an opportunity for his subordinates to get a fuller explanation of his thinking and of his intentions. After presenting the ideas, he invites questions so that his associates can better understand what he is trying to accomplish. This "give and take" also enables the manager and the subordinates to explore more fully the implications of the decision.

The Manager Presents a Tentative Decision Subject to Change. This kind of behavior permits the subordinates to exert some influence on the decision. The initiative for identifying and diagnosing the problem remains with the boss. Before meeting with his staff, he has thought the problem through and arrived at a decision—but only a tentative one. Before finalizing it, he presents his proposed solution for the reaction of those who will be affected by it. He says in effect, "I'd like to hear what you have to say about this plan that I have developed. I'll appreciate your frank reactions, but will reserve for myself the final decision."

The Manager Presents the Problem, Gets Suggestions, and Then Makes His Decision. Up to this point the boss has come before the group with a solution of his own. Not so in this case. The subordinates now get the first chance to suggest solutions. The manager's initial role involves identifying the problem. He might, for example, say something of this sort: "We are faced with a number of complaints from newspapers and the general public on our service policy. What is wrong here? What ideas do you have for coming to grips with this problem?"

The function of the group becomes one of increasing the manager's repertory of possible solutions to the problem. The purpose is to capitalize on the knowledge and experience of those who are on the "firing line." From the expanded list of alternatives developed by the manager and his subordinates, the manager then selects the solution that he regards as most promising.[4]

The Manager Defines the Limits and Requests the Group to Make a Decision. At this point the manager passes to the group (possibly including himself as a member) the right to make decisions. Before doing so, however, he defines the problem to be solved and the boundaries within which the decision must be made.

An example might be the handling of a parking problem at a plant. The boss decides that this is something that should be worked on by the people involved, so he calls them together and points up the existence of the problem. Then he tells them:

> There is the open field just north of the main plant which has been designated for additional employee parking. We can build underground or surface multilevel facilities as long as the cost does not exceed $100,000. Within these limits we are free to work out whatever solution makes sense to us. After we decide on a specific plan, the company will spend the available money in whatever way we indicate.

The Manager Permits the Group to Make Decisions Within Prescribed Limits. This represents an extreme degree of group freedom only occasionally encountered in formal organizations, as, for instance, in many research groups. Here the team of managers or engineers undertakes the identification and diagnosis of the problem, develops alternative procedures for solving it, and decides on one or more of these alternative solutions. The only limits directly imposed on the group by the organization are those specified by the superior of the team's boss. If the boss participates in the decision-making process, he attempts to do so with no more authority than any other member of the group. He commits himself in advance to assist in implementing whatever decision the group makes.

KEY QUESTIONS

As the continuum in Exhibit I demonstrates, there are a number of alternative ways in which a manager can relate himself to the group or individuals he is supervising. At the extreme left of the range, the emphasis is on the manager—on what *he* is interested in, how *he* sees things, how *he* feels about them. As we move toward the subordinate-centered end of the continuum, however, the focus is increasingly on the subordinates—on what *they* are interested in, how *they* look at things, how *they* feel about them.

When business leadership is regarded in this way, a number of questions arise. Let us take four of especial importance.

Can a Boss Ever Relinquish His Responsibility by Delegating It to Someone Else? Our view is that the manager must expect to be held

---

[4] For a fuller explanation of this approach, see Leo Moore, "Too Much Management, Too Little Change," *Harvard Business Review* (January-February, 1956), p. 41.

responsible by his superior for the quality of the decisions made, even though operationally these decisions may have been made on a group basis. He should, therefore, be ready to accept whatever risk is involved whenever he delegates decision-making power to his subordinates. Delegation is not a way of "passing the buck." Also, it should be emphasized that the amount of freedom the boss gives to his subordinates cannot be greater than the freedom which he himself has been given by his own superior.

Should the Manager Participate with His Subordinates Once He Has Delegated Responsibility to Them? The manager should carefully think over this question and decide on his role prior to involving the subordinate group. He should ask if his presence will inhibit or facilitate the problem-solving process. There may be some instances when he should leave the group to let it solve the problem for itself. Typically, however, the boss has useful ideas to contribute, and should function as an additional member of the group. In the latter instance, it is important that he indicate clearly to the group that he sees himself in a *member* role rather than in an authority role.

How Important Is It for the Group to Recognize What Kind of Leadership Behavior the Boss Is Using? It makes a great deal of difference. Many relationship problems between boss and subordinate occur because the boss fails to make clear how he plans to use his authority. If, for example, he actually intends to make a certain decision himself, but the subordinate group gets the impression that he has delegated this authority, considerable confusion and resentment are likely to follow. Problems may also occur when the boss uses a "democratic" facade to conceal the fact that he has already made a decision which he hopes the group will accept as its own. The attempt to "make them think it was their idea in the first place" is a risky one. We believe that it is highly important for the manager to be honest and clear in describing what authority he is keeping and what role he is asking his subordinates to assume in solving a particular problem.

Can You Tell How "Democratic" a Manager Is by the Number of Decisions His Subordinates Make? The sheer *number* of decisons is not an accurate index of the amount of freedom that a subordinate group enjoys. More important is the *significance* of the decisions which the boss entrusts to his subordinates. Obviously a decision on how to arrange desks is of an entirely different order from a decision involving the introduction of new electronic data-processing equipment. Even though the widest possible limits are given in dealing with the first issue, the group will sense no particular degree of responsibility. For a boss to permit the group to decide equipment policy, even within rather narrow limits, would reflect a greater degree of confidence in them on his part.

DECIDING HOW TO LEAD

Now let us turn from the types of leadership that are possible in a company situation to the question of what types are *practical* and *desirable*. What factors or forces should a manager consider in deciding how to manage? Three are of particular importance:

1. Forces in the manager.
2. Forces in the subordinates.
3. Forces in the situation.

We should like briefly to describe these elements and indicate how they might influence a manager's action in a decision-making situation.[5] The strength of each of them will, of course, vary from instance to instance, but the manager who is sensitive to them can better assess the problems which face him and determine which mode of leadership behavior is most appropriate for him.

Forces in the Manager

The manager's behavior in any given instance will be influenced greatly by the many forces operating within his own personality. He will, of course, perceive his leadership problems in a unique way on the basis of his background, knowledge, and experience. Among the important internal forces affecting him will be the following:

1. *His Value System.* How strongly does he feel that individuals should have a share in making the decisions which affect them? Or, how convinced is he that the official who is paid to assume responsibility should personally carry the burden of decision making? The strength of his convictions on questions like these will tend to move the manager to one end or the other of the continuum shown in Exhibit I. His behavior will also be influenced by the relative importance that he attaches to organizational efficiency, personal growth of subordinates, and company profits.[6]
2. *His Confidence in His Subordinates.* Managers differ greatly in the amount of trust they have in other people generally, and this carries over to the particular employees they supervise at a given time. In viewing his particular group of subordinates, the manager is likely to consider their knowledge and competence with respect to the problem. A central question he might ask himself is: "Who is best qualified to deal with this problem?" Often he may, justifiably or not, have more confidence in his own capabilities than in those of his subordinates.
3. *His Own Leadership Inclinations.* There are more managers who seem to function more comfortably and naturally as highly directive leaders. Resolving problems and issuing orders come easily to them. Other managers seem to operate more comfortably in a team role, where they are continually sharing many of their functions with their subordinates.

[5] See also Robert Tannenbaum and Fred Massarik, "Participation by Subordinates in the Managerial Decision-Making Process," *Canadian Journal of Economics and Political Science* (August, 1950), pp. 413-418.
[6] See Chris Argyris, "Top Management Dilemma: Company Needs vs. Individual Development," *Personnel* (September, 1955), pp. 123-134.

4. *His Feelings of Security in an Uncertain Situation.* The manager who releases control over the decision-making process thereby reduces the predictability of the outcome. Some managers have a greater need than others for predictability and stability in their environment. This "tolerance for ambiguity" is being viewed increasingly by psychologists as a key variable in a person's manner of dealing with problems.

The manager brings these and other highly personal variables to each situation he faces. If he can see them as forces which, consciously or unconsciously, influence his behavior, he can better understand what makes him prefer to act in a given way. And understanding this, he can often make himself more effective.

Forces in the Subordinate

Before deciding how to lead a certain group, the manager will also want to consider a number of forces affecting his subordinates' behavior. He will want to remember that each employee, like himself, is influenced by many personality variables. In addition, each subordinate has a set of expectations about how the boss should act in relation to him (the phrase "expected behavior" is one we hear more and more often these days at discussions of leadership and teaching). The better the manager understands these factors, the more accurately he can determine what kind of behavior on his part will enable his subordinates to act most effectively.

Generally speaking, the manager can permit his subordinates greater freedom if the following essential conditions exist:

1. If the subordinates have relatively high needs for independence. (As we all know, people differ greatly in the amount of direction that they desire.)
2. If the subordinates have a readiness to assume responsibility for decision making. (Some see additional responsibility as a tribute to their ability; others see it as "passing the buck.")
3. If they have a relatively high tolerance for ambiguity. (Some employees prefer to have clear-cut directives given to them; others prefer a wider area of freedom.
4. If they are interested in the problem and feel that it is important.
5. If they understand and identify with the goals of the organization.
6. If they have the necessary knowledge and experience to deal with the problem.
7. If they have learned to expect to share in decision making. (Persons who have come to expect strong leadership and are then suddenly confronted with the request to share more fully in decision making are often upset by this new experience. On the other hand, persons who have enjoyed a considerable amount of freedom resent the boss who begins to make all the decisions himself.)

The manager will probably tend to make fuller use of his own authority if the above conditions do *not* exist; at times there may be no realistic alternative to running a "one-man show."

The restrictive effect of many of the forces will, of course, be greatly modified by the general feeling of confidence which subordinates have in the boss. Where they have learned to respect and trust him, he is free to vary his behavior. He will feel certain that he will not be perceived as an authoritarian boss on those occasions when he makes decisions by himself. Similarly, he will not be seen as using staff meetings to avoid his decision-making responsibility. In a climate of mutual confidence and respect, people tend to feel less threatened by deviations from normal practice, which in turn makes possible a higher degree of flexibility in the whole relationship.

Forces in the Situation

In addition to the forces which exist in the manager himself and in his subordinates, certain characteristics of the general situation will also affect the manager's behavior. Among the more critical environmental pressures that surround him are those which stem from the organization, the work group, the nature of the problem, and the pressures of time. Let us look briefly at each of these.

Type of Organization. Like individuals, organizations have values and traditions which inevitably influence the behavior of the people who work in them. The manager who is a newcomer to a company quickly discovers that certain kinds of behavior are approved while others are not. He also discovers that to deviate radically from what is generally accepted is likely to create problems for him.

These values and traditions are communicated in many ways—through job descriptions, policy pronouncements, and public statements by top executives. Some organizations, for example, hold to the notion that the desirable executive is one who is dynamic, imaginative, decisive, and persuasive. Other organizations put more emphasis upon the importance of the executive's ability to work effectively with people—his human relations skills. The fact that his superiors have a defined concept of what the good executive should be will very likely push the manager toward one or the other of the behavioral range.

In addition to the above, the amount of employee participation is influenced by such variables as the size of the working units, their geographical distribution, and the degree of inter-and intra-organizational security required to attain company goals. For example, the wide geographical dispersion of an organization may preclude a practical system of participative decision making, even though this would otherwise be desirable. Similarly, the size of the working units or the need for keeping plans confidential may make it necessary for the boss to exercise more control than would otherwise be the case. Factors like these may limit considerably the manager's ability to function flexibily on the continuum.

Group Effectiveness. Before turning decision-making responsibility over to a subordinate group, the boss should consider how effectively its members work together as a unit.

One of the relevant factors here is the experience the group has had in working together. It can generally be expected that a group which has functioned for some time will have developed habits of cooperation and thus be able to tackle a problem more effectively than a new group. It can also be expected that a group of people with similar backgrounds and interests will work more quickly and easily than people with dissimilar backgrounds, because the communication problems are likely to be less complex.

The degree of confidence that the members have in their ability to solve problems as a group is also a key consideration. Finally, such group variables as cohesiveness, permissiveness, mutual acceptance, and commonality of purpose will exert subtle but powerful influence on the group's functioning.

The Problem Itself. The nature of the problem may determine what degree of authority should be delegated by the manager to his subordinates. Obviously he will ask himself whether they have the kind of knowledge which is needed. It is possible to do them a real disservice by assigning a problem that their experience does not equip them to handle.

Since the problems faced in large or growing industries increasingly require knowledge of specialists from many different fields, it might be inferred that the more complex a problem, the more anxious a manager will be to get some assistance in solving it. However, this is not always the case. There will be times when the very complexity of the problem calls for one person to work it out. For example, if the manager has most of the background and factual data relevant to a given issue, it may be easier for him to think it through himself than to take the time to fill in his staff on all the pertinent background information.

The key question to ask, of course, is: "Have I heard the ideas of everyone who has the necessary knowledge to make a significant contribution to the solution of this problem?"

The Pressure of Time. This is perhaps the most clearly felt pressure on the manager (in spite of the fact that it may sometimes be imagined). The more that he feels the need for an immediate decision, the more difficult it is to involve other people. In organizations which are in a constant state of "crisis" and "crash programming" one is likely to find managers personally using a high degree of authority with relatively little delegation to subordinates. When the time pressure is less intense, however, it becomes much more possible to bring subordinates in on the decision-making process.

These, then, are the principal forces that impinge on the manager in any given instance and that tend to determine his tactical behavior in relation to his subordinates. In each case his behavior ideally will be that which makes possible the most effective attainment of his immediate goal within the limits facing him.

LONG-RUN STRATEGY

As the manager works with his organization on the problems that come up day by day, his choice of a leadership pattern is usually limited. He must take account of the forces just described and, within the restrictions they impose on him, do the best that he can. But as he looks ahead months or even years, he can shift his thinking from tactics to large-scale strategy. No longer need he be fettered by all of the forces mentioned, for he can view many of them as variables over which he has some control. He can, for example, gain new insights or skills for himself, supply training for individual subordinates, and provide participative experiences for his employee group.

In trying to bring about a change in these variables, however, he is faced with a challenging question: At which point along the continuum *should* he act?

Attaining Objectives

The answer depends largely on what he wants to accomplish. Let us suppose that he is interested in the same objectives that most modern managers seek to attain when they can shift their attention from the pressure of immediate assignments:

1. To raise the level of employee motivation.
2. To increase the readiness of subordinates to accept change.
3. To improve the quality of all managerial decisions.
4. To develop teamwork and morale.
5. To further the individual development of employees.

In recent years the manager has been deluged with the flow of advice on how best to achieve these long-run objectives. It is little wonder that he is often both bewildered and annoyed. However, there are some guidelines which he can usefully follow in making a decision.

Most research and much of the experience of recent years give a strong factual basis to the theory that a fairly high degree of subordinate-centered behavior is associated with the accomplishment of the five purposes mentioned.[7] This does not mean that a manager should always leave all decisions to his assistants. To provide the individual or the group with greater freedom than they are ready for at any given time may very well tend to generate anxieties and therfore inhibit rather than facilitate the attainment of desired objectives. But this should not keep the manager from making a continuing effort to confront his subordinates with the challenge of freedom.

CONCLUSION

In summary, there are two implications in the basic thesis that we have been developing. The first is that the successful leader is one who is keenly aware of those forces which are most relevant to his behavior

---

[7] For example, see Warren H. Schmidt and Paul C. Buchanan, *Techniques that Produce Teamwork* (New London: Arthur C. Croft Publications, 1954); and Morris S. Viteles, *Motivation and Morale in Industry* (New York: W. W. Norton & Company, Inc., 1953).

at any given time. He accurately understands himself, the individuals and group he is dealing with, and the company and broader social environment in which he operates. And certainly he is able to assess the present readiness for growth of his subordinates.

But this sensitivity or understanding is not enough, which brings us to the second implication. The successful leader is one who is able to behave appropriately in the light of these perceptions. If direction is in order, he is able to direct; if considerable participative freedom is called for, he is able to provide such freedom.

Thus, the successful manager of men can be primarily characterized neither as a strong leader nor as a permissive one. Rather, he is one who maintains a high batting average in accurately assessing the forces that determine what his most appropriate behavior at any given time should be and in actually being able to behave accordingly. Being both insightful and flexible, he is less likely to see the problems of leadership as a dilemma.

36 • LEADERSHIP IN A DECLINING WORK ETHIC[1]

Ann Howard[2]
James A. Wilson[3]

In the last decade, as the baby boom generation entered adulthood, one fact has emerged. This post-war generation, born in the joy of victory and a surge of unprecedented affluence, represents a sharp change in the social fabric of American life. In stark contrast to the overly ambitious hopes of their parents, the baby boomers are less motivated toward success, less optimistic, and certainly less committed to the large institutions that make up this society than any previous generation of Americans.

Nowhere does this sharp break with traditional values cause more consternation than in the U.S. corporate world, which built its strength on competition and on the Horatio Alger myth of personal success through the scramble for leadership. As the baby boom generation meets the corporation, one wonders, Is this the proverbial clash of irresistible force and immovable object? Will the corporation change to accommodate these young people weaned on immediate gratification and wedded to notions of rampant individualism, or are these youngsters-in-anomie simply aliens passing through without leaving a mark on the corporation? Will a renewed emphasis on participative management engage the hearts and minds of these disaffected young people, or will the team approach simply hasten the demise of the work ethic? Can organizations negotiate a safe journey through the turbulent times ahead if leadership falls to those who would rather not lead?

HARD DATA FROM AT&T

In the late 1970s the American Telephone and Telegraph Company began its second major longitudinal study of managers, eager to see if new college graduates entering the management work force of the Bell System's twenty-three operating companies were comparable to a similar group of twenty years before. Ability measures used in the study brought good news: the new generation did indeed match the former managerial group. But when it came to measures of motivation, the research data delivered a formidable shock. By and large the new recruits were inclined neither to push their way up the organizational hierarchy nor to lead others. In short, the new managers weren't motivated to act like managers.

[1] © 1982 by the Regents of the University of California. Reprinted from *California Management Review*, Vol. XXIV, No. 4, pp. 33 to 46 by permission of the Regents.
[2] Ann Howard, Manager of Basic Human Resources Research, American Telephone and Telegraph Company.
[3] James A. Wilson, Associate Professor/Assistant to the Dean, Graduate School of Business, University of Pittsburgh.

The data producing these startling conclusions were extensive and comprehensive. The original longitudinal study of managers, the Management Progress Study (MPS), was initiated at AT&T in 1956 by Dr. Douglas W. Bray, who continues to direct it as the participants crest middle age and prepare for retirement. The second project, the Management Continuity Study (MCS), which Bray and the senior author of this article began in 1977, was designed to parallel the college graduate subsample of MPS as closely as possible. Participants in both studies constituted those newly hired into first-level general management jobs.

The MPS sample was selected from six Bell operating companies; the average age was twenty-four. The later MCS group came from a broader range of thirteen telephone companies, and the average age was twenty-five. The new sample was better educated; 45 percent had attempted postgraduate training compared with only 11 percent of the previous cohort. The 274 participants in the earlier study were all white males, but by the time of the new study, the management population was more diverse, including other race groups and females. Consequently, of the 204 participants in the MCS sample, one-half were women and one-third minorities, a reflection of the hiring mix in the Bell companies.

For both longitudinal studies, data collection began with three days at an assessment center. Participants were evaluated by a team of assessors after completing a variety of exercises, including ability tests, personality, motivation, and attitude questionnaires, simulations and group discussions, and interviews and projective techniques. For both samples, the assessors were psychologists from both inside and outside the Bell System. Three of the eight assessors employed each year were the same as for the MPS group (assessed 1956-1960) and the MCS group (assessed 1977-1979), and efforts were made to keep standards identical across both samples.

Narrative reports and quantitative results of the assessment process were read aloud at staff integration sessions, and the assessors rated each participant on twenty-six dimensions that were considered critical to managerial ability and motivation. In addition, predictions were made as to whether each assessee had the potential for middle management and whether he or she could be expected to remain with the Bell System for a normal career life. Follow-ups have included a number of interviews with participants and their bosses and two three-day reassessments eight and twenty years later for the original MPS men.

The two samples were not dissimilar in all aspects of motivation. In what might be called motivation for accomplishment, they were remarkably alike. For example, on the Edwards Personal Preference Schedule (a forced-choice questionnaire based on Henry Murray's "needs") scale measuring "need for achievement," both groups were similar in their preferences for goals such as accomplishing something of great significance or doing a difficult job well. The focus in the scale is on mastery of challenging tasks, with no assumptions about extrinsic or accompanying rewards like money or promotions. A comparison of the two samples showed no significant differences in average score on this scale; the MPS (1950s) participants scored at the sixty-second percentile and the MCS (1970s) at the sixtieth of 1958 Bell System college recruit norms.

After the assessment staff heard all data regarding motivation for accomplishment, they rated assessees on the dimension "inner work standards," the extent to which the individual would want to do a good job even if a less good one were acceptable to the boss and others. Here, too, there was no difference in average rating between the two cohorts. To the extent that performance on a management job provides challenge and a sense of accomplishment, the new group of recruits should be as motivated to perform well as the former. Yet it is important not to be misled by the willingness of the young people to "work hard," for, as we shall see, their reasons for doing so differ from those that operated in the past.

Moreover, high standards for task accomplishment, while essential for the technical specialist, may not be as critical for the general manager. What differentiates the manager is that he or she is expected to rise to higher and higher levels within the company, directing others and taking the broad view of the organization, rather than focusing on individual task goals. On exercises designed to measure the desire to advance oneself, however, the 1970s recruits showed a disappointing lack of interest.

One of these exercises was a short questionnaire measuring desires for upward mobility or motivation toward powerful, high-status and well-paying positions. As the left side of Figure 1 illustrates, the average score for the 1950s MPS participants on the questionnaire was at the fifty-second percentile; twenty years later the MCS average was at the twenty-ninth percentile of the same MPS norms, a statistically significant difference. The 1970s participants scored significantly lower than those of the 1950s on all the advancement items in the questionnaire as well as on half the general and money-related items. Although the new recruits seemed to be motivated internally toward task accomplishment, if the challenge they seek in their work is not readily available, it is unlikely that money or advancement opportunities will inspire their work efforts.

This seeming apathy toward climbing the corporate ladder was matched by a decline in the new recruits' expectation level. In an expectations inventory, the recruits were asked to speculate five years ahead and indicate what they foresaw for a variety of situations. The items concerned not only advancement and salary but more generalized aspects of managerial life, such as intellectual stimulation from peers, access to company information and resources, and geographic desirability of work location. The average MCS (1970s) score, shown on the right-hand side of Figure 1, was only at the seventeenth percentile of the 1950s MPS norms.

In fairness, this score should not be interpreted as unbridled negativism toward the corporation, but rather a dampened optimism toward many aspects of work life. The questionnaire explored internal beliefs or attitudes

Article 36 • LEADERSHIP IN A DECLINING WORK ETHIC

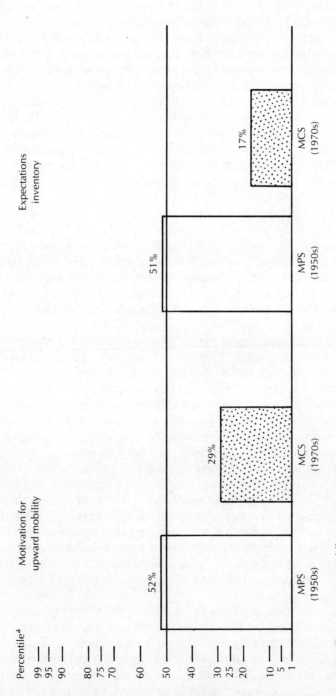

FIGURE 1

CAREER ORIENTATION

Average score

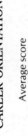

^aMPS college norms; group difference, p < .001.

and the participants in one or both samples could be misreading the system. Alternatively, they could have been moved to provide "socially acceptable" responses, acceptable for their own times.

But for whatever reasons, the new recruits indicated beliefs that the future has less to offer. For example, while 60 percent of the 1950s sample strongly affirmed that in five years they would hold a challenging job with the opportunity to learn and accomplish new things, only 45 percent of the 1970s group were this positive. Of the expectation that the company would make a strong effort to furnish all the resources needed to do a good job, 58 percent of the 1950s group were strongly positive compared to only 27 percent of the latter group. Even with respect to building deep friendships with at least two or three work associates, 75 percent of the last generation had the highest expectations compared to only 46 percent of the current one.

When asked to list which of the expectations inventory items they most wanted to be true, about the same proportion of MCS and MPS participants claimed they wanted a challenging job and one that would pay at least a middle manager's salary. But 54 percent of the 1950s sample also chose advancing to middle management as something they most wanted, while only 34 percent of the latter sample chose that item. Clearly, the new generation doesn't want as much from a managerial career and doesn't expect as much.

Other assessment center exercises confirmed the generational differences in motivation. Projective techniques, including two incomplete sentence tests and stories written to six Thematic Apperception Test (TAT) cards, revealed that while the newer recruits were as directed as the former toward individual task accomplishment, they were less concerned about personal advancement. Personal interviews also revealed negativism toward advancement. Illustrative was the comment, "The higher you go up in management, the more time your have to put in your work. I plan to do my job the best I can, but my loyalty is to my family."

Interview comments revealed less commitment to a business career as such, which is, perhaps, consistent with the less favorable responses to the expectations inventory. Many of the new recruits expressed their intention to return to graduate school, thus implying that neither their formal education nor their career plans were as yet final. One, explaining his reluctance to form a close allegiance with a large organization, said, "I want to lead a life style that isn't all work." He claimed he would secretly "like to be an actor or an artist."

Any comparison of the MPS and MCS participants should, of course, take into account the impact of race and sex differences within the MCS sample. With respect to task accomplishment, career advancement, and expectations, sex differences were negligible and not statistically significant. The only meaningful difference here was that more women were expected to leave the company voluntarily since they anticipated career/family conflicts in the years to come. The minorities scored significantly higher than whites in advancement motivation and expectations. But interview information, as well as an examination of the relevant items in the questionnaire measure of upward mobility, revealed that the primary motivation of the minority group was not for the power or challenge associated with advancement, but to gain financial rewards. Flagging ambitions were somewhat more a white phenomenon than a minority trait, and a comparison of whites alone across the two generations signalled even greater disparities.

Advancement in a managerial career nearly always results in assuming leadership responsibilities and directing others in the organization. A hierarchical organizational structure requires that fewer and fewer managers at higher levels be accountable for greater and greater numbers of managers and workers at lower levels. It is imperative that an upwardly mobile manager appreciate, respond to, and indeed thrive on leadership responsibilities.

One measure of the motivation toward leadership comes from the "dominance" scale of the Edwards Personal Preference Schedule. Respondents indicate 'on this scale their preferences for such activites as leading and directing others, assuming leadership of groups to which they belong, and persuading and influencing others to follow their wishes. As shown in Figure 2, the MCS (1970s) managers were much less favorably inclined toward

FIGURE 2

LEADERSHIP

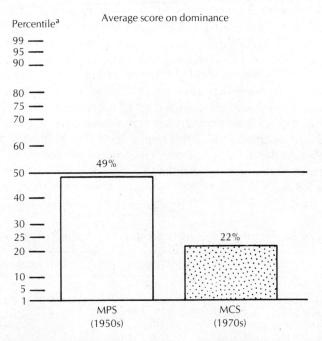

Percentile[a]   Average score on dominance

aEdwards personal preference schedule, 1958 Bell System college recruit norms, N = 585; group differences, p < .001.

these items than were the MPS (1950s) managers, producing an average score at only the twenty-second percentile compared to the forty-ninth percentile for their predecessors. The females were partially responsible for this downward shift, as they scored significantly lower than the males, but that was only a small part of the difference. The average "dominance" score for the MCS males was only at the twenty-eighth percentile, still markedly lower than the scores of their MPS counterparts. Race differences on this scale were not significant.

The desire to lead and direct others expressed on the dominance scale should not be construed as a predilection for an authoritarian, rule-oriented, inflexible use of power. In fact, on a revised version of the California F-scale measuring authoritarianism, the MCS recruits were not any less rigid or dogmatic than their peers of the previous generation. The new managers appear to reject leadership roles regardless of leadership style.

Their rejection of leadership does not necessarily imply a preference for followership. On the Edwards scale of "deference," indicating a tendency to follow instructions, follow others, and defer to if not revere those in higher positions, the MCS (1970s) managers also scored lower than their MPS (1950s) counterparts, although this difference was not quite statistically significant, primarily because the minority males were more deferent than others in the group. More convincing evidence of the lack of deference came from the interviews and projective tests, so that the rating of the assessors on the dimension "need for superior approval," shown in Table 1, showed a marked discrepancy between the two generations. While 68 percent of the MPS participants had been rated high on this dimension, only 37 percent of the MCS participants were judged this way, with no significant race or sex differences. Said one participant, describing his reluctant acceptance of the subordinate role, "People with authority often earn it with time rather than ability. My ambition is to never have a company, government, or person capture my soul and spirit because of financial shackles."

The organizational hierarchy seems to have been attacked from both flanks. The new managers neither aspire to higher-level jobs nor defer to those who have them. To paraphrase Shakespeare's Polonius, the philosophy of this generation might be "Neither a follower nor a leader be."

This evidence does not clearly indicate what these young managers do

TABLE 1

FOLLOWERSHIP: ASSESSMENT DIMENSION, NEED FOR SUPERIOR APPROVAL

	MPS (1950s)	MCS (1970s)
High	68%	37%
Moderate	21	39
Low	11	24
	100%	100%
N	274	204

Group differences, p < .004.

want. Since the Edwards test is a forced-choice questionnaire, less desire for some scales is necessarily counterbalanced by stronger desires for others. The two scales that are notably higher for the new managers both related to emotional support. Providing such support is the content domain of the "nurturance" scale, shown on the left side of Figure 3. Items refer to assisting others less fortunate, treating others with kindness and sympathy, or being generous with others. The MCS (1970s) recruits scored significantly higher than MPS (1950s) on this scale; their average was at the seventy-fourth percentile compared to the forty-ninth for the previous generation. Race and sex difference were inconsistent, since among whites the males scored slightly higher and among minorities the females scored higher.

The new managers apparently want to receive as well as to give emotional support. This is reflected in the Edwards "succorance" scale, shown on the right side of Figure 3. Scale items reflect wanting others to offer help when in trouble, seeking encouragement from others and gaining their sympathy and understanding for personal problems. Again, the 1970s managers scored high compared to those in the past, their average score topping the eightieth percentile compared to an average score at the sixty-sixth percentile for the 1950s group. There were no race differences but a small significant sex difference; still, the MCS males logged in an average score at the seventy-sixth percentile, a significant increase over the previous group of males.

Those who view business executives as cold-hearted, status-oriented, impersonal machines will no doubt rejoice at this apparent shift toward humanism. These new managers may reject the exercise of authority and offer their subordinates instead an atmosphere of collegial sharing of emotions and feelings that will lead to the release of spontaneous creativity. But a practical organization with goals of efficient production and service might well wonder if these young managers will occupy themselves with the personal problems of their subordinates to the neglect of legitimate business concerns. Moreover, the aura of pessimism that pervades the responses of the recruits suggests that their embrace of emotional supportiveness may be more a cry of anguish than a business goal that they seek on the basis of moral principles.

One reading of these data could be that a dispirited new generation of managers, unsure of future direction, wants primarily an interesting job and emotional sustenance from peers, with no heavy commitment to the organization. With little desire to advance, pessimism about organizational rewards, little inclination to assume leadership and equal disdain for following others, these new college graduates may not be well suited to managing a large, traditional, hierarchical organization like the current Bell System.

THE CULTURE BEYOND

In looking at these two widely disparate groups of Bell System employees, one must question whether the differences between the two groups were not

FIGURE 3

GIVING AND RECEIVING EMOTIONAL SUPPORT

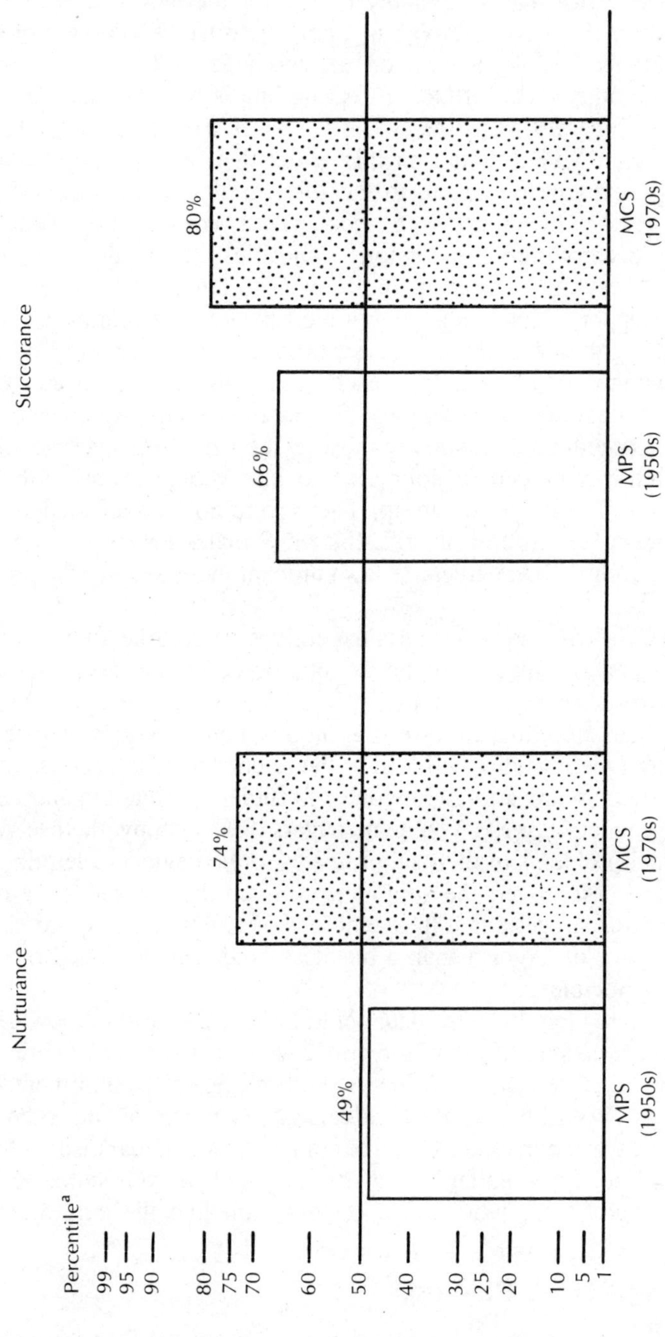

aEdwards personal preference schedule, 1958 Bell System college recruit norms, N = 585; group differences, p < .001.

a function of the Bell System itself—its recruiting practices over the years or the type of college graduate it attracted during the 1950s and the 1970s. Though it may be true that those most interested in power and quick business success would probably choose individual ventures rather than a large corporation, there is no reason to believe this would be more true in the 1970s than in the 1950s. Moreover, the Bell System of the 1950s had something of a homelike, small town character in its individual companies not present today, when the corporation's monopoly status has been challenged and it is learning to compete in world markets. Thus, noncompetitive, security-oriented college graduates should have found it more appealing in the past than in the present.

To find out whether similar problems are being experienced elsewhere, AT&T researchers have invited other organizations to participate in an interbusiness testing study. Although the data are just beginning to come in, the initial results show a similar pattern of differences between younger and older managers. In the meantime, other evidence also suggests that the MCS findings reflect a trend broader than the experience of just one corporate entity.

In 1974, Dr. John Miner predicted a shortage of individuals with the personality traits needed to manage large, hierarchical, bureaucratic organizations.[4] He based his predictions on responses from college students, usually those in undergraduate business courses, using the Miner Sentence Completion Scale. This projective instrument is predicated on the notion that certain motivational patterns should match up with the role prescriptions of hierarchical organizations. These motivations include a favorable attitude toward people in authority positions and the desire to compete, to exercise power over others, to assert oneself, to stand out from a group, and to perform routine administrative duties responsibly.

Data using the Miner scale have now been extended to more than twenty-five different samples, geographically dispersed and traversing a period of twenty years from 1960 to 1980.[5] A decline in scores first appeared in 1962 or 1963 with younger students and continued for a period of ten years. Scores remained at this plateau until 1980, with the average student responding negatively to managerial cues more often than positively. Female students, though originally significantly below the males, dropped relatively less over time, so that in 1980 the two sexes were indistinguishable in terms of their managerial motivation—they were equally low.

The thrust of the results with the Miner scale not only confirms the Bell findings in a much broader context, but suggests the problem may have manifested itself in new management recruits before 1977 had such characteristics been explored. The combination of the two sets of results suggests

---

[4] John B. Miner, *The Human Constraint: The Coming Shortage of Managerial Talent* (Washington: D.C.: The Bureau of National Affairs, 1974).

[5] John B. Miner, "The Human Constraint over Twenty Years," presentation at American Psychological Association Convention, Montreal (1980).

potential problems for business with respect to leadership in the coming years.

The declining desire to manage is no doubt related to the emergence of a new breed of workers described recently by the survey firm of Yankelovich, Skelly and White.[6] Their research points to a declining work ethic in which loyalty to the organization has been replaced by loyalty to the self, where concern for work has been superseded by concern for leisure, and identification with a work role has devolved to preoccupation with individual needs and pleasures. Respect for authority and a belief in the importance of rules, once taken for granted in the corporate setting, are increasingly drowned in a pool of skepticism and cynicism.

The firm's survey results also indicate a challenge to the time-honored reward systems of work. Belief in meritocracy has been upstaged by a psychology of entitlements, so that rewards are no longer reserved for the deserving. In the current value system, such things as a good job, health care, and a secure retirement are considered inalienable rights. As government guarantees of financial subsistence plus two-paycheck families mitigate the threat of job loss, traditional penalties for poor performance become impotent. Money is less a symbol of success than a facilitator of one's leisure activities and personal life style. Present sacrifice and hard work as a means to later rewards is now thought to be foolish; immediate gratification and living for today set the style. Goals in life are described subjectively in terms of fulfilling one's own potential with little respect for the outward manifestations of success, such as money or social and organizational status.

Other accounts in the popular literature bolster these findings and impressions. A survey of *Esquire* readers in 1979 found that men under thirty wanted more time for what they called ''personal growth,'' though they did not want to work hard.[7] They aspired to a life perfectly balanced between love, leisure, and personal expression; they rejected ambition and effective leadership skills as important values in life. The most negative prospect to these men was to follow their father's footsteps in a pattern of early marriage, family responsibilities, and long years on a narrow corporate track in hope of some later rewards.

About the same time, *Technology Review* reported that MBAs at even the most prestigious schools placed a premium on individual values,[8] and *U.S. News and World Report* noted that money and power were losing favor as motivators at work.[9] In 1980 *Fortune,* in a report of new high potential

---

[6] Daniel Yankelovich, ''The New Psychological Contracts at Work,'' *Psychology Today* (May 1978).

[7] Gail Sheehy, ''Introducing the Postponing Generation,'' *Esquire* (October 1979), pp. 25-33.

[8] ''Technology and the Workplace—Changing Values of the MBA.'' *Technology Review* (June/July 1979), p. 78.

[9] ''Why 'Success' Isn't What It Used To Be,'' *U.S. News and World Report* (30 July 1979), p. 48.

twenty-five-year-olds in business, found them arrogantly confident that they would rise to high places.[10] To these young achievers, business was a quick means to gratify frankly materialistic requirements. The group considered corporate loyalty a misfortune suffered by their parents and many sought to begin their own businesses in their early thirties. This, they believe, would best help them realize their goals of self-actualization, autonomy, and freedom from monetary worries.

It appears that many young people today are encapsulated in the notion of privatism, avoiding involvement in anything beyond their immediate interests. Since they believe their "real life" begins after work hours, there is sometimes painful fragmentation between work and leisure. If work is not life, then commitment to the institution providing work seems ill considered.

The corporation is not the only institution spurned by the value system of the emerging young adult population. Church, family, the political arena, government, and military all come in for well-aimed scorn as they face challenges to their authority and increasing skepticism about the institution's ability to solve society's problems and offer hope for the future. They, too, detect a flowering of narcissism among the "Me Generation," a crisis of authority, and an age of cynics.

The signs of value change and discontent extend beyond U.S. borders. Recently, youth in Switzerland pressed their demands for a youth center by raining destruction on the *Bahnhofstrasse*. As reported in *New York Times Magazine,* this "movement of the discontented" rebelled against conformity, materialism, militarism, and male chauvinism.[11] Though fiercely critical of older values and "bourgeois ambition," their own values and motivations were unclear and nebulous except for the certainty that they did not want to waste themselves in hard work. A problem for the authorities in dealing with them was that their motto was "No leaders"—there were no spokespersons or structures with whom to negotiate.

These various accounts of new values share common themes: pervasive cynicism, self-righteous individualism, and condemnation of the values of the previous generation. One must conclude that sometime between the days of the MPS recruitment (1956-1960) and that of MCS (1977-1979), the cultural environment, especially values, shifted sharply. We assume that the characteristics of the Bell System's new managers, described previously, are not substantively different from those of new managers elsewhere in large U.S. organizations; all seem to be cut from the same cloth.

[10] Gwen Kinkead, "On a Fast Track to the Good Life," *Fortune* (7 April 1980), pp. 74-84.
[11] Paul Hofmann, "The Swiss Malaise," *The New York Times Magazine* (8 February 1981), pp 35 ff.

HISTORICAL DEVELOPMENTS

The causes of cultural change dwell somewhere in the realm of theory. Explanations are merely speculations, but the effort can allay the discomforts of ignorance. Writers indulge in the art of clarifying what seems illogical by reordering history to their own ends. We, too, will indulge.

Most historians, economists, writers, social critics, and others attempting to explain the source of the new values begin with the post-World War II period. Up until that time, dating at least from the Reformation, the dominant value scheme in Western civilization was what Max Weber called the "Protestant work ethic." Religious in basis, the Protestant work ethic equated hard work and self-denial with walking in the paths of righteousness. The Calvinists, in fact, practiced austere asceticism as a measure of spiritual discipline. Man was urged to advance by habits of industry, sobriety, moderation, self-discipline, and avoidance of debt. Self-indulgence was considered not only socially undesirable but morally reprehensible.

Masculinity, in this scheme, was intertwined with being a good provider, and loss of one's job was akin to loss of social respectability. Under these traditional values, women stayed home if they could afford to and dedicated themselves to housewifery and motherhood. Men, in turn, directed their efforts to providing for their families. They expected security from their jobs and hoped for money and status as well. They repaid the corporation with their loyalty, tolerating its various drawbacks, inconveniences, and work requirements. They postponed their gratifications and rewards, working preparation for some distant future by patient and painstaking accumulation of skills, credibility, and cash.

Following World War II, in a country elated by victory and sudden prosperity, Americans approached life with a new confidence in the future. The idea that women's role was solely to bear and rear children so dominated this time of affluence that it resulted in the largest baby boom in the nation's history. From 1946 (peaking in 1957) until its decline in the early 1960s, an ethic of procreation permeated every race, class, and education group. Elaborating on the theory of economist Richard Easterlin, Landon Jones, in his book *Great Expectations,* described how the sheer size of this new generation has affected everything from cultural values to divorce rates and crime statistics.[12]

To the baby boom parents of the late 1940s and 1950s (themselves emerging from the Great Depression), familial life was equated with material possession; their children were to have everything. Never would they know the deprivation and hardship experienced by their parents. Hand in hand with this child-centeredness went progressive education. Whether a reaction to war, a revolt against the strict scheduling of Watson's behaviorism, or something else not yet suspected, permissiveness characterized modern

[12] Landon Y. Jones, *Great Expectations: American and the Baby Boom Generation* (New York: Coward, McCann, and Geoghegan, 1980).

child-rearing practices. Schools emphasized social values of getting along (perhaps as a way to manage the great influx of children), and academic standards declined. This permissiveness and emphasis on social interaction, in turn, began to undermine the Protestant work ethic. Although, at the emotional level, parents may have wanted their children to accept their values, practices recommended by Dr. Spock and progressive educators may have undermined their efforts to instill them.

Thanks to the achievements of the still hardworking older generation, consumer goods abounded and an upwardly spiraling standard of living sharply challenged the ethic of deferred gratification. The new American, courted by advertising, became even more sought after as consumer than as producer. Labor was no longer a moral obligation for a life of righteousness; its value lay in providing the means to purchase the accoutrements of the good life.

According to Jones, as this enormous and pampered cohort of boom babies advanced through adolescence into college in unprecedented numbers, they became competitors for the scarce resources of an academic community unprepared for the influx. Their response was reaction, as they became "the most fiercely anticompetitive generation in our history."[13] The turbulence and conflicts of the sixties, fueled by events like the Kennedy assassination and the Vietnam War, may have been by-products of the massive size of this youthful generation struggling in prolonged adolescence. Ultimately, they began to create a culture of their own.

The Flower Children were the extreme expression of this anticompetitive culture. Repulsed by their parents' overstriving and disillusioned by the war in Vietnam, they rejected hard work as an unfulfilling and meaningless activity. In fact, true to the absolutist thinking of youth, their rejection of parental values was total. Condemning the older generation's world as militaristic, repressive, corrupt, materialistic, and joyless, they defined their own values in direct opposition, loudly proclaiming adherence to personal freedom, openness, joy, and love. The achievement ethic was replaced by the pleasure principle. Their hedonistic indulgences in sex, drugs, and "rap sessions" stressed a togetherness which required neither labor nor commitment.

The extremes of the hippie counterculture did not last, but a quieter challenge has replaced them. The dramatic clash between the Protestant work ethic of their parents' generation and the hippie counterculture intensified the struggle of the young to fashion an identity of their own. Lacking the religious and moral fervor of their parents, they nevertheless found little that was viable in the counterculture. Sexual freedom brought sophistication but little intimacy and an inability to commit to others or to specific ideals. The ties of marriage and children were often postponed or broken. Similarly, they reasoned that jobs which became boring could simply be changed.

[13] Ibid., p. 84.

The boom generation, in an existential crisis with no clear alternatives, is still plagued by uncertainty about what it should be or become. Wandering in anomie, finding no suitable role models, this generation has been forced to look inside itself. This focus on self developed in the 1970s into the narcissistic excesses of the Me Decade. If the Calvinists were compulsively industrious in their flights from sin, the narcissists were equally obsessive in attempting to infuse their aimless lives with meaning.[14] Their flirtations with cults, drugs, therapies, sports, and diversions can be viewed as desperate attempts at self-definition. With their avoidance of genuine commitment or strong family ties, their emotional outreachings seem less a goal than a sustenance.

Just as the original altruism has turned to narcissism, early optimism has turned to pessimism. The anticompetitiveness bred in crowded colleges was reinforced when the boom generation faced their peers again in the employment market. Many could not find jobs or learned that a college education brought fewer rewards than their parents had promised. Promotions seemed less probable when so many of this generation vied for them. According to Jones, the realization that the unrealistically high parental dreams for this affluent, educated generation were unachievable resulted in lowered expectations and an unwillingness to truly compete. They appear less ambitious, have lesser expectations, and are apathetic about advancing in organizational life.

They must face not only the realization that their numbers put them at a disadvantage in the competition of the work environment, but that the earth's resources are limited too. These children of affluence will have to adjust to a world of scarcity. While the energy crisis continues and inflation erodes investments and savings, the call to buy now and pay later seems ever more sensible. Said historian Christopher Lasch, "As the future becomes menacing and uncertain, only fools put off until tomorrow the fun they can have today."[15]

The result is that the new narcissists have learned to live for the moment. History, rather than providing a reservoir of experience from which to guide their lives, has become irrelevant, and the future looks too dismal and unpredictable to warrant attention. Immediate gratification is the new order of the day as society shifts from the ascendance of superego values and self-restraint to the self-indulgence of the id.

Today, the affluence this generation experienced early in life has been translated into a psychology of entitlements, with little appreciation for the role of sacrifice and commitment. Perhaps fueled by the government follies of Vietnam and Watergate, today's young generation has little respect for authority or experience as stabilizing elements in life. Yet it is the older adults, acting out of their own historic forces, who failed to convince the

[14] Christopher Lasch, *The Culture of Narcissm: American Life in an Age of Diminishing Expectations* (New York: W.W. Norton and Company, 1978).
[15] Ibid., p. 53.

younger generation of their capacity to lead the country toward moral and incorruptible goals. And now it is the older adults who will have to fill the leadership vacuum in organizations, for those in the younger generation are preoccupied with themselves.

FUTURE DIRECTIONS

Though private industry may bemoan its destiny, there are those who will welcome and laud the turning away from materialism, power-seeking, upward-striving, and competition and the movement toward individual freedom, leisure, and cooperation. Environmentalists and others have questioned the imperatives of economic progress, high technology, and material abundance. Simultaneously, social movements have emphasized relaxation, inner peace, and harmony rather than the conquest of nature. The orientation of these social movements was illustrated when the MCS (1970s) recruits ranked eighteen terminal values on the Rokeach Values Inventory. When compared with seventy-one older (by fifteen years, on the average) fourth- and fifth-level high-potential Bell managers, the MCS managers gave significantly higher ranks to "inner harmony," "wisdom," and "true friendship." The older managers scored higher on "conquer the environment," type values—"a sense of accomplishment," "freedom," and "an exciting life."

With forces pulling in both directions, our culture may be at a turning point. Sociologist Amitai Etzioni has suggested three possible future directions for Americans.[16] In his first scenario, the erosion of modernity, the pace of the economy would slow, with people becoming less driven to achieve. This could yield greater pleasure and relaxation but also result in lowered productivity, less efficiency, and, perhaps, more corruption. The Fall-of-Rome alternative is unlikely to be popular with the older generation.

The second scenario, reindustrialization or restoration, is a return to the past, where old virtues and taboos take on a new urgency. This would satisfy the longing many feel to return to a respect for authority, rules, and responsibilities. Accompanying this would be development of energy sources and a rededication to efficiency, productivity, and economic progress. This approach is exemplified by the Reagan administration's "New Beginning" and the conservative temper. Business should be pleased by the economic possibilities, but a return to sexual and social repressions could create a serious backlash, particularly among the freedom-loving and socially tolerant young. Perhaps more significantly, elimination of such social programs as job training, income supports, and mass transit funding could lead to a new backlash from the underprivileged.

---

[16] Amitai Etzioni, "Work in the American Future: Reindustralization or Quality of Life," in Clark Kerr and Jerome M. Rosow (eds.), *Work in America: The Decade Ahead* (New York: Van Nostrand Reinhold, 1979).

The third scenario, a quality-of-life society, would focus more on culture and recreation and less on materialism, more on living in harmony with the environment and less on a conquest of the environment or exploitation of nature. Social progress would get more attention than economic progress. In a similar fusion, Yankelovich argues for an ethic of commitment, away from both self-denial (old values) and self-fulfillment (new values) and toward a connectedness with others.[17] He visualizes integrating the instrumental and expressive sides of life, just as others have rejected old, "macho" values in favor of an androgynous blend of the traditionally masculine with the traditionally feminine.

Aspects of Etzioni's third scenario have been pursued in various forms by quality-of-life enthusiasts in industry with the thought that more fulfilling work or shorter working hours might lead to a revitalized interest in work and more productivity. Changing work values are cited increasingly by these supporters to justify their pleas for greater worker participation in decision making and democracy in the work place. Recent questionnaires show growing favor for the notion that workers should take part in decisions affecting their jobs—not surprising considering the declining voice of authority and rising psychology of entitlements.

An organizational approach to coming to terms with the new values may consist of restructuring the organization, reducing the hierarchical impact, and dispersing power and authority to a wider segment of the work force. Some organizations have introduced matrix management, worker councils, sociotechnical systems, autonomous work groups, quality circles, and other versions of "industrial democracy" which increase worker participation and reduce the need for extended chains of command.

These measures have not won unqualified acceptance. Some, including union leaders, have criticized efforts at humanizing the work place for creating a false image of democracy while actually leaving workers in a more helpless position than before. Lasch claims that the decline of authority at work, just as in the family, leads not to the collapse of restraints but to depriving them of a rational basis. The so-called democratic techniques soften the adversary relationship between supervisor and subordinate (as between management and labor) and make it more difficult for the workers to resist the demands of the corporation.[18] Thus, the "workers' control" movement, ostensibly aimed at a redistribution of power, has been castigated as but a more sophisticated method used by the truly powerful to pressure workers toward greater production.

Without considering the merit or demonstrated effectiveness of the industrial democracy alternatives, it could be argued that they do not adequately address the current generation's lack of interest in leadership or advancement. These methods have been tried primarily with nonmanage-

[17] Daniel Yankelovich, *New Rules: Searching for Self-Fulfillment in a World Turned Upside Down* (New York: Random House, 1981).
[18] Lasch, op. cit.

ment employees, who may or may not share the new values of their college-educated peers. While production workers may replace some lower-level managers, the motivation to manage is less critical for this group. The real problem in this new approach is that quality circles or similar self-regulating groups and committees create an even greater demand for social and leadership skills and managerial motivation among those who remain in the higher echelons.

Other organization changes in the quality of work life domain may raise the work satisfaction of new-values employees and perhaps even foster loyalty. Suppose an organization were avant garde with respect to sex roles and decided neither women nor men employees should have to sacrifice family for career. By offering a package of alternatives such as flextime, shared jobs, geographical moves geared to couples, child care, and paternity leaves, the organization might find itself in a buyer's market for managerial and professional talent. Similarly, "cafeteria" benefit plans and various time options, like sabbaticals, flexiyear contracts, and trade-offs of time and income, could replace rewards like money and advancement in vying for workers' commitment. Of course, there is no guarantee that any new consonance between individual values and an organization's benefits would result in higher productivity or performance. Like many well-meant social engineering schemes, this could, in fact, boomerang into a tangle of expensive and difficult to administer human resource programs that attract the laziest and least promising employees and encourage the achievers to follow suit.

Though some organizations may be willing to adjust their implied psychological contracts with employees, resistance to major structure change is apt to be intense, especially if change were to threaten traditional power and authority relationships. Coming from an age in which humans were to serve the organization, it is heresy to suggest that organizations serve the people within them. Realistically, some organizations, like the Marine Corps, may be incapable of functioning participatively, or at least so we believe. Moreover, in those organizations already threatened by outside forces, radical change may be particularly ill advised. The Bell System, currently in the throes of a major government-ordered restructuring into separate subsidiaries, comes to mind. One might argue, in fact, that never before has Bell had so great a need for strong traditional forms of leadership.

If the organization cannot or will not undergo a major transformation to accommodate the new values, what alternatives remain for meeting the potential leadership crisis? One classic approach is to cull the applicant population, using advanced personnel selection techniques, for managers whose values are more old than new. One Bell System division traditionally has looked for only the most advancement-oriented recruits, luring them with promises of better positions and higher starting salaries at the second rather than the first level of management. The commitment is to a fast track of promotions for those who prove their merit and dismissal for those who don't.

Twenty-two such recruits were assessed with the MCS participants in the late 1970s; the results showed that the selection process had indeed been working. They outshone their peers on nineteen of the twenty-six managerial dimensions, including very high needs for advancement and strong leadership skills and motivation. Not all young people are alike, and sophisticated organizations can still skim the cream off the top if they can muster the recruiters and incentives to capture what may be, or become, a rare breed. Yet even among this elite, upwardly mobile group, some of the new values crept through; they were more noticeably selfish than their peers, equally low on deference to superiors, and some blatantly planned to exploit the company for a brief experience before moving on to something else, such as starting their own business.

There are reasons to hope that in a few years there may be more of the traditionally motivated young people in the applicant pool. Several questionnaire studies on college campuses show a slight upturn in responses to questions about interest in business, administrative positions, or making money. A recent readministration of the Miner test to business students also hinted that the downward trend in managerial motivation may at last be reversing itself.[19] The trials of the first baby boomers may have exhausted the pendulum swing toward nonwork anomie as their younger siblings realize they have to eat. Social change is often dialectic, and perhaps it is time for a return swing to a more moderate position.

In the meantime, what to do with the dispirited cohort already lolling in the lower ranges of management? Perhaps their motivation for challenge and accomplishment, thankfully still alive, could be tied to the carrot of advancement. Or perhaps the special attention of an early career development program might be warranted. Young people may have to be taught the meanings, virtures, and strengths of power and leadership—their value in instilling good ideas, making positive things happen, and directing organizations and society toward new goals as well as old. Sympathetic mentors, role models, and counselors may help by giving feedback and advice as well as interpreting and teaching the values and mores of the firm. Opportunities to learn about their own and other organizations and cultures, by formal development programs or temporary assignments in other organizations or overseas, may help put self- and organization-oriented goals in perspective while fostering creative approaches to management. If the new managers are unconvinced that higher management jobs will, on balance, offer them more of the good life than "merely" higher status, perhaps we should be grateful for what remains of the work ethic, and hope that a new crop of recruits can be found to pass them by on the hierarchical success ladder.

---

[19] K.M. Bartol, C.R. Anderson, and C.E. Schneier, "Motivation to Manage Among Business Students: A Reassessment," *Journal of Vocational Behavior*, Vol. 17 (1980), pp. 22-32.

To adapt to the new values of young managers, one can change the organization, change the reward system, recruit differently, or provide early career development experience. But this holds all variables constant, in a sense. Both human institutions and human motivations flow from the spiritual ethos or *Zeitgeist* created by conditions of the times. As the culture evolves, so do people, values, and organizations, so that new people and new modes of work can exist in a reformulated consonance.

At first blush it might appear that the quality-of-life reformers and new-values employees were made for each other. Yet the root ideas for humanizing the work place are not really new. During the 1940s, when Abraham Maslow and Carl Rogers began to speak of man's actualizing tendency, participative management was introduced into a pajama factory. Efforts in this vein did not entirely die out, and in the early 1970s, the quality-of-life movement was revitalized as a systems approach.

Still, it is no more plausible to say that quality-of-life reforms were a response to new workers' demands than to hypothesize that the young people of the 1970s, in their existential angst were easy prey for the quality-of-life reformers. More likely both emanated from a common evolving *Zeitgeist*, reflecting two sides of the same coin. Whether this coin can buy much-needed productivity is the critical but unanswered question.

That organizations and current personal value systems are out of phase suggests an effort should be made to restore the balance lest we sacrifice the viability of contemporary organizations. Yet because of cultural drives toward homeostasis, it may not be mere wishful thinking to expect a naturally evolving balance.

Calvinsim once united virtue, salvation, work, and motivation in a productive package, but that package has come undone. Perhaps people now look only to themselves for the motivation that used to be supplied externally and emerge prisoners of their own insularity. The fire to lead others may soon be rekindled under a reformulated ethos, but the legacy of these shifting values in our culture may be a firm warning from humans that corporations and organizations in general can no longer with impunity take their loyalty and involvement for granted.

37 • LEADERSHIP, MANAGEMENT, AND THE SEVEN KEYS[1]

Craig M. Watson[2]

In recent years a good deal of excitement has grown around the implications and significance of the 7-S organizational framework,[3] stemming both from the insights the system yields into organizational effectiveness and from the explanation it provides for consistently outstanding performance by excellent companies.[4]

In brief, the theory holds that traditional view of organizations pivots on three axes: *strategy,* which leads almost implicitly to organization *structure,* and *systems* which orchestrate complex functions resulting in performance. The 7-S construct, by contrast, suggests that four additional S's are critical to achieving and understanding the effectivness of excellent management: *style,* the patterns of action, symbolic and actual, which top management communicates to the organization at large, and which the organization itself ultimately adopts as a cultural orientation; *staff,* meaning the people side of the organization equation, especially the socialization and development process which molds managers into effective, acculturated performers; *skills,* the company's unique competences and dominating attributes; and *superordinate (or shared) goals,* the set of values or aspirations which underpin what a company stands for and believes in.[5]

The significance of the new framework (as others have stated) is in the attention it draws to the "soft," informal facets of organization which formerly were considered insufficiently systematic or "hard" to be of interest. The traditional approach focuses on the relatively easy-to-change strategy, structure, and systems, while the new approach alerts us to the crucial role played by the more elusive features.

The key factors distinguishing the 7-S framework from the traditional approach to organizational effectiveness, in fact, focus on the change levers which leaders, as distinct from managers, have always manipulated to effect organizational change and to achieve superior performance. By extension, much of what the 7-S approach embodies is the direct result of observing organizations run by leaders as opposed to managers.

---

[1] From *Business Horizons,* Vol. 26, No. 2 (March-April, 1983), pp. 8-13. Reprinted by permission of *Business Horizons.*

[2] Craig M. Watson, Financial Director of Business Projects and Planning, Merck & Co., Inc.

[3] Robert H. Waterman, Jr., Thomas J. Peters, and Julien R. Phillips, "Structure Is Not Organization," *Business Horizons,* June 1980: 14–26.

[4] See, for example, Thomas J. Peters, "Putting Excellence Into Management," *The McKinsey Quarterly,* Autumn 1980: 31–41, and Anthony G. Athos and Richard Pascale, *The Art of Japanese Management* (New York: Simon & Schuster, 1981).

[5] Each of the seven S's is defined more fully in "Structure Is Not Organization" (see note 1). Also, see Robert H. Waterman, Jr., "The Seven Elements of Strategic Fit," *The Journal of Business Strategy,* Winter 1982:69–73.

The implications of this perspective are manifold. For example:

- If one believes that there is a difference between leadership and management, then there is some question as to whether managers can achieve 7-S performance at all.
- Society produces far few leaders than it does managers. The socialization process which cultivates managers also reinforces tradition, whereas leaders succeed in making change.
- Some cultures more naturally incline toward utilization of both the hard and the soft levers to effect change and achieve performance. This, in fact, has been called the "art of Japanese management." Does this imply that certain cultures are more naturally adept at creating leaders than others?
- Achieving 7-S management is a long-term undertaking. There is some question as to whether the predominantly short-term orientation of American management can be modified sufficiently to make the transition successfully.
- Finally, our management education system reinforces the traditional view of organization performance. The relative novelty of the 7-S framework makes it unlikely that the approach will be adopted quickly by the educational system.

These issues, while indeed speculative, are worth raising because it is easy to embrace new techniques and approachs as panaceas before fully appreciating their implications. Thus they are put forth as cautions. This having been said, let us return to the distinctions between leadership and management.

The seminal work on the difference between leadership and management is Abraham Zaleznik's 1977 McKinsey award-winning contribution.[6] Zaleznik explores the distinctions in attitudes toward goals, conceptions of work, relations with others, senses of self, and manner of development. Using these basic headings, I will underscore the correspondence between the leader's broad focus on multiple elements of the seven keys, and contrast this with the manager's traditional attention to the more limited set of organization factors.

ATTITUDES TOWARD GOALS

Goal-setting is a central element in the guidance of organizatonal achievement. Through setting an overall target on performance and focusing group effort, the executive—leader or manager—implicitly concentrates organizational energies in a given direction.

Zaleznik argues that "Managers tend to adopt impersonal, if not passive, attitudes toward goals. Managerial goals arise out of necessities rather than desires, and, therefore, are deeply embedded in the history and culture

---

[6] Abraham Zaleznik, "Managers and Leaders: Are They Different?" *Harvard Business Review*, May-June 1977:67–78.

of the organization."[7] In contrast, leaders "are active instead of reactive, shaping ideas instead of responding to them. Leaders adopt a personal and active attitude toward goals. The influence a leader exerts in altering moods, in evoking images and expectations, and in establishing specific desires and objectives determines the direction of business takes. The net result is to change the way people think about what is desirable, possible and necessary."[8]

This fundamental distinction in goal-setting attitudes is expressed in the way goals are set in organizations and in the goals which result. The *manager* is more likely to identify threats and opportunities and mobilize to respond to them in a systematic fashion through focus on *strategy*. The *leader,* on the other hand, tends to define a *superordinate goal,* such as product leadership, quality, service, or being number one; in working to achieve that goal, the leader commands outstanding performance. To leaders, strategy is the overall pattern of executing goal achievement. Managers are more likely to see strategy, or a component of it, such as product differentiation or lowest cost, as the overriding issue, rather than the corporate goal itself. Semantics play a part, but not a big one: lowest cost is a strategy; "number one" is a value.

In McKinsey's studies of excellent companies Thomas Peters states, "The operating principle at well-managed companies is to do one thing well. At IBM, the all-pervasive value is customer service. At Dana it is productivity improvment. At 3M and H-P it is new product development. At P&G it is product quality. At McDonald's it is customer service, quality, cleanliness and value . . . At all these companies, the values are pursued with an almost religious zeal . . . "[9]

CONCEPTIONS OF WORK

Irrespective of how goals are set, organizations must deal, operationally, with the mundane details of getting things done. They must organize and execute the thousands of tasks which, collectively, result in performance, for better or for worse. In the course of this activity, there are decisions made, resources allocated, and positions taken which, in substance, form the work of the organization. In this context, Zaleznik underscores distinctions between managers and leaders in the areas of choice and risk-taking.

"In order to get people to accept solutions to problems, managers need to coordinate and balance continually . . . The manager aims at shifting balances of power toward solutions acceptable as a compromise among conflicting values."[10] The leader, alternatively "needs to project his ideas

[7] Zaleznik: 70.
[8] Zaleznik: 74.
[9] Peters: 88.
[10] Zaleznik: 72.

into images that excite people, and only then develop choices that give the projected images substance. Consequently, leaders create excitement in work . . . [U]nless expectations are aroused and mobilized, with all the expectations inherent in heightened desire, new thinking and new choice can never come to light.''[11]

These conceptions of work manifest themselves both in managed and in led organizations: Leaders are inclined to make work exciting by encouraging an organizational *style* that is intuitive, highly personal, and tied in closely to the ''carrots'' that motivate key players to perform. Moreover, the leader's company is more likely to promote entrepreneurial autonomy at appropriately low levels in the organization, as a way of motivating people to make choices for themselves which, collectively, improve the performance of the whole. Peters reports: ''Well-managed companies authorize their managers to act like entrepreneurs . . . As a result, these managers develop unusual programs with results that far exceed those of a division or corporate staff.''[12] In so doing, leaders use *structure* to advantage as a motivational extension of their leadership style.

Inherent in the decentralized structure is a higher level of risk, since the choices made are more removed from the leader's direct control. A higher degree of remoteness from operating decisions is accepted by leaders, because they tend to ''work from high-risk positions, indeed often are temporarily disposed to seek out risk and danger, especially where opportunity and reward appear high.''[13] Thus, in the leader's *style* we see an inherent capacity to invest faith in people's desire to respond to excitement, risk and opportunity. This faith can only exist, however, when the leader has assembled appropriate staff and skills necessary to ensure high levels of performance. In consequence, the leader is more comfortable placing his faith in his own or in his key executive's judgment than in analysis, quantitative methods, and other potential assurances. He knows the difference between ''computer printout'' decisions and ''cigar and brandy'' decisions and is comfortable with either when he has faith in the people involved or in his own judgment. Because he is willing to take risks on people, the leader depends less on *structure* to dampen the impact of risk, and even less on *systems* to gather information and to make things happen.

Managers, alternatively, in their need to coordinate and balance, place a great deal of faith in *systems* and *structures*. Thus, we see managers' companies *dominated* by planning, forecasting, capital budgeting, and other systems which, at the extreme, can actually supplant judgment.

From the standpoint of risk, Zaleznik points out that for ''those who become managers, the instinct for survival dominates their need for risk, and their ability to tolerate mundane, practical work assists their survival.''[14]

---

[11] Zaleznik.
[12] Peters.
[13] Zaleznik.
[14] Zaleznik: 73.

Again we see systems coming to the rescue, with major challenges or unique opportunities continually staffed out for study and analysis, and returned with balanced (read: low-risk) recommendations. Similarly, an overly managerial environment tends to be one in which new ideas wither and die, largely because top management is perceived as so risk-averse that venturesome ideas are viewed as having little chance of approval.

RELATIONS WITH OTHERS

Human relationships, in one form or another, are the essential ingredients of organization performance. The manner in which these relationships unfold and operate in the organization determines the quality of organizational performance. As expected, managers and leaders see their relations with others differently.

Zaleznik tells us managers seek out activities with people, but at the same time, "maintain a low level of emotional involvment in these relationships . . . The manager's orientation to people, as actors in a sequence of events, deflects his or her attention away from the substance of people's concerns and toward their roles in a process."[15] Leaders, on the other hand, empathize. "Empathy is not simply a matter of paying attention to other people. It is also the capacity to take in emotional signals and to make them mean something in a relationship with an individual . . . The distinction is simply between a manger's attention to *how* things get done and a leader's to *what* the events and decisions mean."[16]

Again, the manager's emphasis is on *systems,* possibly even viewing people as part of a framework of processes, while the leader's focus is on meaning as the foundation of motivation. The ability to empathize, to receive and send signals, and to impute meaning to work are all elements of the leader's *style* and *skill,* constituting his mastery of the soft S's of effectiveness.

Another facet of relationships with others concerns the manager's striving to convert win-lose decisions into win-win situations through compromise. On its face, this seems desirable, but in practice, Zaleznik observes, the result is defective both in the manner of achievement and in the choices which ultimately emerge. Specifically, Zaleznik identifies three tactics by which managers seek to convert win-lose to win-win decisions:

- Focus on procedure, not substance.
- Use of indirect signals rather than direct messages.
- Manipulation of time and delay to reduce the sting of losing.

The ultimate result is an organization steeped in bureaucracy (emphasis on structure) and political intrigue.

---

[15] Zaleznik.
[16] Zaleznik: 74.

The focus of leadership in the face of win-lose decisions stands in sharp relief. Leaders are more apt to cast situations in their worst case form. They are more likely to face reality, make hard decisions, and absorb their consequences. Perhaps because of this, Zaleznik asserts leaders "attract strong feelings of identity and difference, or of love and hate . . . leader-dominated structures often appear turbulent, intense, and at times even disorganized. Such an atmosphere intensifies individual motivation. . . . "[17] Here, again, the leader's style plays a crucial role.

SENSES OF SELF

Much of the distinction between managers and leaders stems from differences in their perceptions of themselves. "Managers see themselves as conservators and regulators of an existing order of affairs with which they personally identify and from which they gain rewards. Perpetuating and strengthening existing institutions enhances a manager's sense of self-worth: he or she is performing in a role that harmonizes with the ideals of duty and responsibility."[18]

The implication of this is that profound change—perhaps even when it is most emphatically needed for the survival of a company—is not normally within the province of managers. This may be one reason why so often a dramatic shift in corporate focus is accompanied by a wholesale management change, as well. Conversely, when organizations achieve desired levels of performance—for example, after a turnaround or following a period of rapid growth—they appoint managers to install systems, procedures and structures designed to consolidate their positions. Managers, in the traditional sense, are not sought out to make change.

In contrast, Zaleznik sees leaders as working in, but never belonging to, organizations. "Their sense of who they are does not depend upon memberships, work roles, or other social indicators of identity . . . [They] search out opportunities for change. The methods to bring about change may be technological, political, or ideological, but the object is the same: to profoundly alter human economic and political relationships."[19]

In summary, these differences imply that leaders have an inherent inclination to utilize the soft S's of style, skills, staff and shared goals. Managers, alternatively, tend toward reliance on the traditional triad of strategy, structure, and systems. Organizationally, the extreme result is likely to be leader-run companies high in performance, energy, focus and motivation, in contrast to manager-run companies with mediocre performance, bureaucratic structures, and ponderous decision-making systems.

[17] Zaleznik.
[18] Zaleznik: 75.
[19] Zaleznik.

426 LEADERSHIP • *Chapter 11*

CONFLICT, CONVERGENCE AND CULTURE

Ironically, the 7-S framework offers two contrasting perspectives on the future potential of management.

- First, if the points made in this article are valid, 7-S management is the province of leaders, and managers per se will not ordinarily be capable of achieving sufficient mastery of all seven keys to attain consistently superb performance.
- Alternatively, the framework suggests that the effects of leadership (or, at least, its visible instruments) can possibly be *developed consciously and applied systematically by managers* to beneficial effect, by paying attention to the soft as well as the hard S's.

Proponents of the new framework say it is indeed possible to make managers more effective by focusing attention on the soft seven keys. Conversely, the point can equally be made that leaders can become more effective managers by focusing more effort on the traditional strategy, structure, and systems. In this sense, the 7-S framework underscores the importance of balance, of attention to style, shared values, systems, structure, and so forth equally, in the enlightened interplay of the hard and the soft. The whole can become larger than the sum of the parts; management and leadership can be made to converge.

In practice, the best performing companies have, or have had, leaders at the top reinforcing values, lending style, molding staff, and developing unique skills. At the same time, in rare cases, these leaders also possess superior traditional managerial skills. Where both facets are not present in the same individual, hierarchy assumes great significance. For example, where the leader occupies high position, managers below him are likely to be well-motivated and the organization's performance correspondingly impressive. By contrast, when leader personalities work under traditional managers, there is likely to be friction and frustration, ultimately resulting in high turnover. The key complaints of those leaving are an inability to get ideas heard, perception of threats or opportunities unheeded by the firm at large, and a prevailing managerial attitude prone to delusions about competitive realities or internal capabilities.

It is in countering the negative impact of these potential conflicts that particularly creative organizations are apparently successful. Excellent companies encourage ideas from all quarters. They keep structures lean and simple and encourage operational autonomy.[20]

On the issue of culture and its impact (whether Japan, for example, is more likely to produce leaders than the West), the 7-S framework offers important insights. First good management does not depend on the presence of leadership, although in many cases, it is enhanced by leadership qualities. What is crucial is the presence of the soft and the hard instruments in balance.

[20] Peters: 32.

Second, the Japanese are, apparently, more inclined to use the soft tests of management—as an extension of their cultural norms—than are Western managers whose culture stresses different values.[21] Third, managerial performance is multivariate. Culture certainly plays a part, but what is more significant is that excellent performance in organizations in Japan or in the West depends on achieving harmony among all seven keys to organization.

• • •

The awareness created by the 7-S approach to organizational effectiveness should benefit organizations run by either leaders or traditional managers, as we have used the terms. Outstanding companies are distinguished not by the leaders who head them or by the managers who run them, but rather by the manner in which leadership and management are harmonized to create a climate which work is both uncommonly meaningful and unusually effective.

BIBLIOGRAPHY, CHAPTER 11

Balakrishnan, K. "Corporate Power: Benign or Malignant?" *Vikalpa,* Vol. 5, No. 1 (January, 1980), pp. 1-12.

Barrow, Jeffrey C. "The Variables of Leadership: A Review and Conceptual Framework." *Academy of Management Review,* Vol. 2, No. 2 (April, 1977), pp. 231-251.

Bass, Bernard M., and V. J. Shackleton. "Industrial Democracy and Participative Management: A Case for a Synthesis." *Academy of Management Review,* Vol. 4, No. 3 (1979), pp. 393-404.

Bennis, Warren G. "Leadership Theory and Administrative Behavior: The Problem of Authority." *Administrative Science Quarterly,* Vol. 4 (December, 1969), pp. 259-301.

———. "The Artform of Leadership." *Training and Development Journal* (April, 1982), pp. 44-46.

Davidson, H. Justin. "The Top of the World Is Flat." *Harvard Business Review,* Vol. 55, No. 2 (March-April, 1977), pp 89-99.

Davis, Tim R. V., and F. Luthans. "Leadership Reexamined: A Behavioral Approach." *Academy of Management Review,* Vol. 4, No. 2 (1979), pp. 237-248.

Falbe, Cecilia M. "Leadership Behavior and Organization Performance: A Model of Social Influence at the Macro Level." *Proceedings of Academy of Management Meetings* (1984), pp. 173-177.

Fleenor, C. Patrick, David L. Kurtz, and Louis E. Boone. "The Changing Profile of Business Leadership." *Business Horizons,* Vol. 26, No. 4 (July-August, 1983), pp. 43-46.

Gabarro, John J., and J. P. Kotter. "Managing Your Boss." *Harvard Business Review,* Vol. 58, No. 1 (January-February, 1980), pp. 92-100.

---

[21] Athos and Pascale.

Graeff, Claude L. "The Situational Leadership Theory: A Critical View." *Academy of Management Review*, Vol. 8, No. 2 (1983), pp. 285-291.

Helmrich, D. L. "The Executive Interface and President's Leadership Behavior." *Journal of Business Research*, Vol. 3, No. 1 (January, 1975), pp. 43-52.

Howell, Jon P., and Peter W. Dorfman. "Substitutes for Leadership." *Academy of Management Journal*, Vol. 24, No. 4 (1981), pp. 714-728.

Kemelgor, Bruce H. "Power and the Power Process: Linkage Concepts." *Academy of Management Review*, Vol. 1, No. 4 (October, 1976), pp. 143-149.

Krein, Theodore J. "How to Improve Delegation Habits." *Management Review* (May, 1982), pp. 58-61.

Liden, Robert C., and George Graen. "Generalizability of the Vertical Dyad Linkage Model of Leadership." *Academy of Management Journal*, Vol. 23, No. 3 (September, 1980), pp. 405-421.

Madison, Dan L., *et al.* "Organizational Politics: An Exploration of Managers' Perceptions. *Human Relations*, Vol. 33, No. 2 (1980), pp. 79-100.

Mayes, Bronston T., and R. W. Allen. "Toward a Definition of Organizational Politics." *Academy of Management Review*, Vol. 2, No. 4 (October, 1977), pp. 672-678.

McMurry, R. N. "Power and the Ambitious Executive." *Harvard Business Review*, Vol. 51, No. 6 (November-December, 1973), pp. 140-145.

Nord, Walter R. "Dreams of Humanization and the Realities of Power." *Academy of Management Review*, Vol. 3, No. 3 (July, 1978), pp. 674-679.

Walsh, Kieron, *et al.* "Power and Advantage in Organizations." *Organizational Studies*, Vol. 2, No. 2 (1981), pp. 131-152.

Weihrich, Heinz. "How to Change a Leadership Pattern." *Management Review*, Vol. 68, No. 4 (1979), pp. 26-40.

White, Bernard J. "Union Response to the Humanization of Work: An Explanatory Proposition." *Human Resource Management*, Vol. 14, No. 3 (Fall, 1975), pp. 2-9.

Zaleznik, A. "The Dynamics of Subordinancy." *Harvard Business Review*, Vol. 43, No. 3 (May-June, 1965) pp. 119-131.

Section E

Organizing

The design or redesign of organizational structure must consider two masters. On the one hand, we are concerned with providing a vehicle for smoothly accomplishing the goals of the organization. On the other hand, we need a design that allows satisfaction of employees' needs. Without provision for the human equation, of course, it will be difficult to achieve economic goals. Structure is said to follow strategy in the sequence of decisions in the firm. Thus, the rationale of structure is said to follow the goals of the organization. This forthright approach is subject to considerable qualification, as the series of articles on structure show.

In Chapter 12 Galbraith examines the factors that bear upon the type of structure to be developed. There is considerable distance between the vision of the organization design and operation of the enterprises according to that vision. The bare bones of designing task roles for a series of positions, combining these positions into linking groups, developing hierarchy, and so on are merely the first tentative step in developing a high-achievement organization. The designer is frustrated by an inability to anticipate behavior patterns. It is not until the system starts operating that its complexity and the cultural development of the enterprise ensue. These informal interrelationships flesh out the formal preselected structure that originated in the mind of the designer.

Chapter 13 looks at structural characteristics that either influence design or to which the system should strive. As a basis for design or redesign, the variables to which one need attend bear analysis. Of course, the initial design of an organization is a rare event. It is the redesign of existing systems that is the frequent case. As any of the factors that entered into the initial design change, the relevance of the existing structure must be questioned. Acquisitions, closing of plants, mergers, and introduction of new products are everyday strategic events that require structural alterations. Many minor changes also dictate structural change, as the information in Chapter 13 emphasizes.

Chapter 12

Establishing
Structure

The purpose of this chapter is to provide a basic understanding of the design process and factors relevant to structural issues. The articles address this purpose in a somewhat indirect manner. By examining structure as it relates to innovating organizations, excelling teams, or diversifying groups, we also receive a picture of the total design process.

Galbraith has long been associated with organizational structure choices. He recently has been dealing with research and development as well as entrepreneurial systems. The distillation of these experiences in the form of the design of innovating organizations is the basis of this work. Following in the same vein is the report by Sweeney and Allen about teams that excel. If we observe the characteristics of these high-performance groups, we may be able to instill these factors in groups with which we deal. The danger that is raised, however, is the apparent temporary nature or the short life span of these teams. Further, pressure from peer organizations appears to jeopardize the continuance of these excelling teams.

Next Lorsch reviews structural mapping upon the strategy of the organization. As firms diversify, greater structural differentiation is needed.

The matrix form of organization structure is one that has received a great deal of attention as a way of accommodating the offsetting requirements of tasks relating to a product with the tasks indigenous to the business functions (e.g., marketing, research and development, and manufacturing). Yet the tradeoffs are difficult to make and are not resolved by mere structural arrangements. Leadership of high integrity and vision is also required in order to make it work. For this reason we do not find a great number of matrix organizations.

Finally, the issues of accommodating the uniqueness of individuals in the way we assign tasks and build structures from positions and small groups constitute the topic of Edward Lawler's article. Shall we put individuals into structures and jobs that are designed to meet the effectiveness needs of the organization? Or shall we design jobs to meet the skills, aptitudes, and interests of the individuals and let the organization use that output as best it can? The individualized organization is mostly dream rather than reality, but its message is useful for determining what kind of organization we want to have.

38 • DESIGNING THE INNOVATING ORGANIZATION[1]

Jay R. Galbraith[2]

Innovation is in. New workable, marketable ideas are being sought and promoted these days as never before in the effort to restore U.S. leadership in technology, in productivity growth, and in the ability to compete in the world marketplace. Innovative methods for conserving energy and adapting to new energy sources are also in demand.

The popular press uses words like *revitalization* to capture the essence of the issue. The primary culprit of our undoing, up until now, has been management's short-run earnings focus. However, even some patient managers with long-term views are finding that they cannot buy innovation. They cannot exhort their operating organizations to be more innovative and creative. Patience, money, and a supportive leadership are not enough. It takes more than these things to achieve innovation.

It is my contention that innovation requires an organization specifically designed for that purpose—that is, such an organization's structure, processes, rewards, and people must be combined in a special way to create an innovating organization, one that is designed to do something for the first time. The point to be emphasized here is that the innovating organization's components are completely different from and often contrary to those of existing organizations, which are generally operating organizations. The latter are designed to efficiently process the millionth loan, produce the millionth automobile, or serve the millionth client. An organization that is designed to do something well for the millionth time is not good at doing something for the first time. Therefore, organizations that want to innovate or revitalize themselves need two organizations, an operating organization and an innovating organization. In addition, if the ideas produced by the innovating organization are to be implemented by the operating organization, they need a transition process to transfer ideas from the innovating organization to the operating organization.

This article will describe the components of an organization geared to producing innovative ideas. Specifically, in the next section of this article, I describe a case history that illustrates the components required for successful innovation. Then I will explore the lessons to be learned from this case history by describing the role structure, the key processes, the reward systems, and the people practices that characterize an innovating organization.

---

[1] From *Organizational Dynamics* (Winter, 1982), pp. 5–24. Reprinted by permission of Jay R. Galbraith.
[2] Jay R. Galbraith, Director of a management consulting firm, Denver, Colorado.

THE INNOVATING PROCESS

Before I describe the typical process by which innovations occur in organizations, we must understand what we are discussing. What is innovation? How do we distinguish between invention and innovation? Invention is the creation of a new idea. Innovation is the process of applying a new idea to create a new process or product. Invention occurs more frequently than innovation. In addition, the kind of innovation in which we are interested here is the kind that becomes necessary to implement a new idea that is not consistent with the current concept of the organization's business. Many new ideas that are consistent with an organization's current business concept are routinely generated in some companies. Those are not our current concern; here we are concerned with implementing inventions that are good ideas but do not quite fit into the organization's current mold. Industry has a poor track record with this type of innovation. Most major technological changes come from outside an industry. The mechanical typewriter manufacturers did not introduce the electric typewriter; the electric typewriter people did not invent the electronic typewriter; vacuum tube companies did not introduce the transistor, and so on. Our objective is to describe an organization that will increase the odds that such nonroutine innovations can be made. The following case history of a nonroutine innovation presents a number of lessons that illustrate how we can design an innovating organization.

THE CASE HISTORY

The organization in question is a venture that was started in the early seventies. While working for one of our fairly innovative electronics firms, a group of engineers developed a new electronics product. However, they were in a division that did not have the charter for their product. The ensuing political battle caused the engineers to leave and form their own company. They successfully found venture capital and introduced their new product. Initial acceptance was good, and within several years their company was growing rapidly and had become the industry leader.

However, in the early 1970s Intel invented the microprocessor, and by the mid-to-late seventies, this innovation had spread through the electronic industries. Manufacturers of previously "dumb" products now had the capability of incorporating intelligence into their product lines. A competitor who understood computers and software introduced just such a product into our new venture firm's market, and it met with high acceptance. The firm's president responded by hiring someone who knew something about microcomputers and some software people and instructing the engineering department to respond to the need for a competing product.

The president spent most of his time raising capital to finance the venture's growth. But when he suddenly realized that the engineers had not made much progress, he instructed them to get a product out quickly. They did, but it was a half-hearted effort. The new product incorporated a microprocessor but was less than the second-generation product that was called for.

Even though the president developed markets in Europe and Singapore, he noticed that the competitor continued to grow faster than his company and had started to steal a share of his company's market. When the competitor became the industry leader, the president decided to take charge of the product-development effort. However, he found that the hardware proponents and software proponents in the engineering department were locked in a political battle. Each group felt that its "magic" was the more powerful. Unfortunately, the lead engineer (who was a co-founder of the firm) was a hardware proponent, and the hardware establishment prevailed. However, they then clashed head-on with the marketing department, which agreed with the software proponents. The conflict resulted in studies and presentations, but no new product. So here was a young, small (1,200 people) entrepreneurial firm that could not innovate even though the president wanted innovation and provided resources to produce it. The lesson is that more was needed.

As the president became more deeply involved in the problem, he received a call from his New England sales manager, who wanted him to meet a field engineer who had modified the company's product and programmed it in a way that met customer demands. The sales manager suggested, "We may have something here."

Indeed, the president was impressed with what he saw. When the engineer had wanted to use the company's product to track his own inventory, he wrote to company headquarters for programming instructions. The response had been: It's against company policy to send instructional materials to field engineers. Undaunted, the engineer bought a home computer and taught himself to program. He then modified the product in the field and programmed it to solve his problem. When the sales manager happened to see what was done, he recognized its significance and immediately called the president.

The field engineer accompanied the president back to headquarters and presented his work to the engineers who had been working on the second-generation product for so long. They brushed off his efforts as idiosyncratic, and the field engineer was thanked and returned to the field.

A couple of weeks later the sales manager called the president again. He said that the company would lose this talented guy if something wasn't done. Besides, he thought that the field engineer, not engineering, was right. While he was considering what to do with this ingenious engineer, who, on his own had produced more than the entire engineering department, the president received a request from the European sales manager to have the engineer assigned to him.

The European sales manager had heard about the field engineer when he visited headquarters, and had sought him out and listened to his story.

The sales manager knew that a French bank wanted the type of application that the field engineer had created for himself; a successful application would be worth an order for several hundred machines. The president gave the go-ahead and sent the field engineer to Europe. The engineering department persisted in their view that the program wouldn't work. Three months later, the field engineer successfully developed the application, and the bank signed the order.

When the field engineer returned, the president assigned him to a trusted marketing manager who was told to protect him and get a product out. The engineers were told to support the manager and reluctantly did so. Soon they created some applications software and a printed circuit board that could easily be installed in all existing machines in the field. The addition of this board and the software temporarily saved the company and made its current product slightly superior to that of the competitor.

Elated, the president congratulated the young field engineer and gave him a good staff position working on special assignments to develop software. Then problems arose. When the president tried to get the personnel department to give the engineer a special cash award, they were reluctant. "After all," they said, "other people worked on the effort, too. It will set a precedent." And so it went. The finance department wanted to withhold $500 from the engineer's pay because he had received a $1,000 advance for his European trip, but had turned in vouchers for only $500.

The engineer didn't help himself very much either; he was hard to get along with and refused to accept supervision from anyone except the European sales manager. When the president arranged to have him permanently transferred to Europe on three occasions, the engineer changed his mind about going at the last minute. The president is still wondering what to do with him.

There are a number of lessons about the needs of an innovative organization in this not uncommon story. The next section elaborates on these lessons.

THE INNOVATING ORGANIZATION

Before we can draw upon the case history's lessons, it is important to note that the basic components of the innovating organization are no different from those of an operating organization. That is, both include a task, a structure, processes, reward systems, and people, as shown in Figure 1. Figure 2 compares the design parameters of the operating organization's components with those of the innovating organization's components.

This figure shows that each component must fit with each of the other components and with the task. A basic premise of this article is that the task of the innovating organization is fundamentally different from that of the operating organization. The innovating task is more uncertain and risky, takes place over longer time periods, assumes that failure in the early stages

FIGURE 1

ORGANIZATION DESIGN COMPONENTS

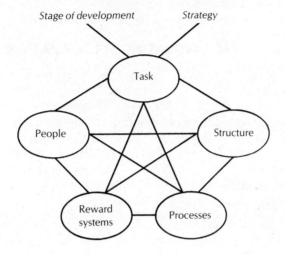

FIGURE 2

COMPARISON OF COMPONENTS OF OPERATING AND
INNOVATING ORGANIZATIONS

	Operating Organization	Innovating Organization
Structure	Division of labor	Roles:
	Departmentalization	Orchestrator
	Span of control	Sponsor
	Distribution of power	Idea generator (champion)
		Differentiation
		Reservations
Processes	Providing information and	Planning/funding
	communication	Getting ideas
	Planning and budgeting	Blending ideas
	Measuring performance	Transitioning
	Linking departments	Managing programs
Reward systems	Compensation	Opportunity/autonomy
	Promotion	Promotion/recognition
	Leader style	Special compensation
	Job design	
People	Selection/recruitment	Selection/self-selection
	Promotion/transfer	Training/development
	Training/development	

may be desirable, and so on. Therefore, the organization that performs the innovative task should also be different. Obviously, a firm that wishes to innovate needs both an operating organization and an innovating organization. Let's look at the latter.

STRUCTURE OF THE INNOVATING ORGANIZATION

The structure of the innovating organization encompasses these elements: (1) people to fill three vital roles—idea generators, sponsors, and orchestrators; (2) differentiation, a process that differentiates or separates the innovating organization's activities from those of the operating organization; and (3) "reservations," the means by which the separation occurs—and this may be accomplished physically, financially, or organizationally.

The part that each of these elements plays in the commercialization of a new idea can be illustrated by referring to the case history.

Roles

Like any organized phenomenon, innovation is brought about through the efforts of people who interact in a combination of roles. Innovation is not an individual phenomenon. People who must interact to produce a commercial product—that is, to innovate in the sense we are discussing—play their roles as follows:

• Every innovation starts with an *idea generator* or idea champion. In the above example, the field engineer was the person who generated the new idea—that is, the inventor, the entrepreneur, or risk taker on whom much of our attention has been focused. The case history showed that an idea champion is needed at each stage on an idea's or an invention's development into an innovation. That is, at each stage there must be a dedicated, full-time individual whose success or failure depends on developing the idea. The idea generator is usually a low-level person who experiences a problem and develops a new response to it. The lesson here is that many ideas originate down where "the rubber meets the road." The low status and authority level of the idea generator creates a need for someone to play the next role.

• Every idea needs at least one *sponsor* to promote it. To carry an idea through to implementation, someone has to discover it and fund the increasingly disruptive and expensive development and testing efforts that shape it. Thus idea generators need to find sponsors for their ideas so they can perfect them. In our example, the New England sales manager, the European sales manager, and finally the marketing manager all sponsored the field engineer's idea. Thus one of the sponsor's functions is to lend his or her authority and resources to an idea to carry the idea closer to commercialization.

The sponsor must also recognize the business significance of an idea. In any organization, there are hundreds of ideas being promoted at any one time. The sponsor must select from among these ideas those that might become marketable. Thus it is best that sponsors be generalists. (However, that is not always the case, as our case history illustrates.)

Sponsors are usually middle managers who may be anywhere in the organization and who usually work for both the operating and the innovating organization. Some sponsors run divisions or departments. They must be able to balance the operating and innovating needs of their business or function. On the other hand, when the firm can afford the creation of venture groups, new product development departments, and the like, sponsors may work full time for the innovating organization. In the case history, the two sales managers spontaneously became sponsors and the marketing manager was formally designated as a sponsor by the president. The point here is that by formally designating the role or recognizing it, funding it with monies earmarked for innovation, creating innovating incentives, and developing and selecting sponsorship skills, the organization can improve its odds of coming up with successful innovations. Not much attention has been given to sponsors, but they need equal attention because innovation will not occur unless there are people in the company who will fill all three roles.

• The third role illustrated in the case history is that of the *orchestrator*. The president played this role. An orchestrator is necessary because new ideas are never neutral. Innovative ideas are destructive; they destroy investments in capital equipment and people's careers. The management of ideas is a political process. The problem is that the political struggle is biased toward those in the establishment who have authority and control of resources. The orchestrator must balance the power to give the new idea a chance to be tested in the face of a negative establishment. The orchestrator must protect idea people, promote the opportunity to try out new ideas, and back those whose ideas prove effective. This person must legitimize the whole process. That is what the president did with the field engineer; before he became involved, the hardware establishment had prevailed. Without an orchestrator, there can be no innovation.

To play their roles successfully, orchestrators use the processes and rewards to be described in the following sections. That is, a person orchestrates by funding innovating activities and creating incentives for middle managers to sponsor innovating ideas. Orchestrators are the organization's top managers, and they must design the innovating organization.

The typical operating role structure of a divisionalized firm is shown in Figure 3. The hierarchy is one of the operating functions reporting to division general managers who are, in turn, grouped under group executives. The group executives report to the chief executive officer (CEO). Some of these people play roles in both the operating and the innovating organization.

The innovating organization's role structure is shown in Figure 4. The chief executive and a group executive function as orchestrators. Division

FIGURE 3

TYPICAL OPERATING STRUCTURE OF DIVISIONALIZED FIRM

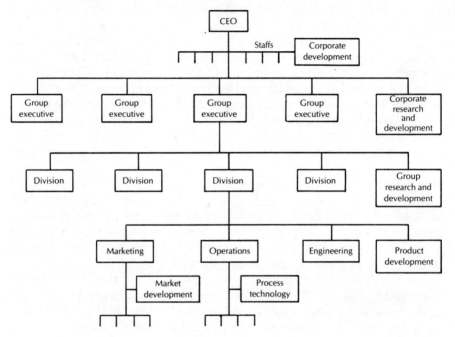

managers are the sponsors who work in both the operating and the innovating organizations. In addition, several reservations are created in which managers of research and development (R&D), corporate development, product development, market development, and new process technology function as full-time sponsors. These reservations allow the separation of innovating activity from the operating activity. This separation is an organizing choice called differentiation. It is described next.

Differentiation

In the case history we saw that the innovative idea perfected at a remote site was relatively advanced before it was discovered by management. The lesson to be learned from this is that if one wants to stimulate new ideas, the odds are better if early efforts to perfect and test new "crazy" ideas are differentiated—that is, separated—from the functions of the operating organization. Such differentiation occurs when an effort is separated physically, financially, and/or organizationally from the day-to-day activities that are likely to disrupt it. If the field engineer had worked within the engineering department or at company headquarters, his idea probably would have been snuffed out prematurely.

FIGURE 4

AN INNOVATING ROLE STRUCTURE (DIFFERENTIATION)

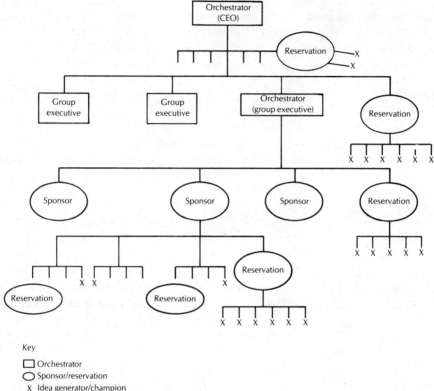

Key

☐ Orchestrator
◯ Sponsor/reservation
X Idea generator/champion

Another kind of differentiation can be accomplished by freeing initial idea tests from staff controls designed for the operating organization. The effect of too much control is illustrated by one company in which a decision on whether to buy an oscilloscope took about 15 to 30 minutes (with a shout across the room) before the company was acquired by a larger organization. After the acquisition, that same type of decision took 12 to 18 months because the purchase required a capital appropriation request. Controls based on operating logic reduce the innovating organization's ability to rapidly, cheaply, and frequently test and modify new ideas. Thus, the more differentiated an initial effort is, the greater the likelihood of innovation.

The problem with differentiation, however, is that it decreases the likelihood that a new proven idea will be transferred back to the operating organization. Herein lies the differentiation/transfer dilemma: The more differentiated the effort, the greater the likelihood of producing a new business idea, but the less likelihood of transferring the new idea into the operating organization for implementation. The dilemma occurs only when the organization needs both invention and transfer. That is, some organizations may not need to transfer new ideas to the operating organization. For example, when Exxon started its information systems business, there was no intention to have the petroleum company run this area of business. Exxon innovators had to grow their own operating organizations; therefore, they could maximize differentiation in the early phases. Alternatively, when Intel started work on the 64K RAM (the next generation of semiconductor memories, this random access memory holds roughly 64,000 bits of information), the effort was consistent with their current business and the transfer into fabrication and sales was critical. Therefore, the development effort was only minimally separated from the operating division that was producing the 16K RAM. The problem becomes particularly difficult when a new product or process differs from current ones, but must be implemented through the current manufacturing sales organizations. The greater the need for invention and the greater the difference between the new idea and the existing business concept, the greater the degree of differentiation required to perfect the idea. The only way to accomplish both invention and transfer is to proceed stagewise. That is, differentiate in the early phases and then start the transition process before development is completed so that only a little differentiation is left when the product is ready for implementation. The transition process is described in the section on key processes.

In summary, invention occurs best when initial efforts are separated from the operating organization and its controls—because innovating and operating are fundamentally opposing logics. This kind of separation allows both to be performed simultaneously and prevents the establishment from prematurely snuffing out a new idea. The less the dominant culture of the organization supports innovation, the greater is the need for separation. Often this separation occurs naturally as in the case history, or clandestinely, as in "bootlegging." If a firm wants to foster innovation, it can create reservations where innovating activity can occur as a matter of course. Let us now turn to this last structural parameter.

Reservations

Reservations are organizational units, such as R&D groups, that are totally devoted to creating new ideas for future business. The intention is to reproduce a garage-like atmosphere where people can rapidly and frequently test their ideas. Reservations are havens for "safe learning." When innovating, one wants to maximize early failure to promote learning. On reservations that are separated from operations, this cheap, rapid screening can take place.

Reservations permit differentiation to occur by housing people who work solely for the innovating organization and by having a reservation manager who works full time as a sponsor. They may be located within divisions and/or at corporate headquarters to permit various degrees of differentiation.

Reservations can be internal or external. Internal reservations may include some staff and research groups, product and process development labs, and groups that are devoted to market development, new ventures, and/or corporate development. They are organizational homes where idea generators can contribute without becoming managers. Originally, this was the purpose of staff groups, but staff groups now frequently assume control responsibilities or are narrow specialists who contribute to the current business idea. Because such internal groups can be expensive, outside reservations like universities, consulting firms, and advertising agencies are often used to tap nonmanagerial idea generators.

Reservations can be permanent or temporary. The internal reservations described above, such as R&D units, are reasonably permanent entities. Others can be temporary. Members of the operating organization may be relieved of operating duties to develop a new program, a new process, or a new product. When developed, they take the idea into the operating organization and resume their operating responsibilities. But for a period of time they are differentiated from operating functions to varying degrees in order to innovate, fail, learn, and ultimately perfect a new idea.

Collectively the roles of orchestrators, sponsors, and idea generators working with and on reservations constitute the structure of the innovating organization. Some of the people, such as sponsors and orchestrators, play roles in both organizations; reservation managers and idea generators work only for the innovating organization. Virtually everyone in the organization can be an idea generator, and all middle managers are potential sponsors. However not all choose to play these roles. People vary considerably in their innovating skills. By recognizing the need for these roles, developing people to fill them, giving them opportunity to use their skills in key processes, and rewarding innovating accomplishments, the organization can do considerably better than just allowing a spontaneous process to work. Several key processes are part and parcel of this innovating organizational structure. These are described in the next section.

KEY PROCESSES

In our case history, the idea generator and the first two sponsors found each other through happenstance. The odds of such propitious match-ups can be significantly improved through the explicit design of processes that help sponsors and idea generators find each other. The chances of successful match-ups can be improved by such funding, getting ideas, and blending ideas. In addition, the processes of transitioning and program management move ideas from reservations into operations. Each of these is described below.

Funding

A key process that increases our ability to innovate is a funding process that is explicitly earmarked for the innovating organization. A leader in this field is Texas Instruments (TI), a company that budgets and allocates funds for both operating and innovating. In essence the orchestrators make the short-run/long-run tradeoff at this point. They then orchestrate by choosing where to place the innovating funds—with division sponsors or corporate reservations. The funding process is a key tool for orchestration.

Another lesson to be learned from the case history is that it frequently takes more than one sponsor to launch a new idea. The field engineer's idea would never have been brought to management's attention without the New England sales manager. It would never have been tested in the market without the European sales manager. Multiple sponsors keep fragile ideas alive. If engineering had been the only available sponsor for technical ideas, there would have been no innovation.

Some organizations purposely create a multiple sponsoring system and make it legitimate for an idea generator to go to any sponsor who has funding for new ideas. Multiple sponsors duplicate the market system of multiple bankers for entrepreneurs. At Minnesota Mining and Manufacturing (3M), for example, an idea generator can go to his or her division sponsor for funding. If refused, the idea generator can then go to any other division sponsor or even to corporate R&D. If the idea is outside current business lines, the idea generator can go to the new ventures group for support. If the idea is rejected by all possible sponsors, it probably isn't a very good idea. However, the idea is kept alive and given several opportunities to be tested. Multiple sponsors keep fragile young ideas alive.

Getting Ideas

The process of getting ideas occurs by happenstance as it did in the case history. The premise of this section is that the odds of match-ups between idea generators and sponsors can be improved by organization design. First, the natural process can be improved by network-building actions such as multidivision or multireservation careers or company-wide seminars and conferences. All of these practices plus a common physical location facilitate matching at 3M.

The matching process is formalized at TI, where there is an elaborate planning process called the *o*bjectives, *s*trategies and *t*actics or OST system, which is an annual harvest of new ideas. Innovating funds are distributed to managers of objectives (sponsors) who fund projects based on ideas formulated by idea generators, and these then become tactical action programs. Ideas that are not funded go into a creative backlog to be tapped throughout the year. Whether formal, as at TI, or informal, as at 3M, it is noteworthy that these are known systems for matching ideas with sponsors.

Ideas can also be acquired by aggressive sponsors. Sponsors sit at the crossroads of many ideas and often arrive at a better idea by putting two or more together. They can then pursue an idea generator to champion it. Good sponsors know where the proven idea people are located and how to attract such people to come to perfect an idea on their reservation. Sponsors can go inside or outside the organization to pursue these idea people.

And finally, formal events for matching purposes can be scheduled. At 3M, for example, there's an annual fair at which idea generators can set up booths to be viewed by shopping sponsors. Exxon Enterprises held a "shake the tree event" at which idea people could throw out ideas to be pursued by attending sponsors. The variations of such events are endless. The point is that by devoting time to ideas and making innovation legitimate, the odds that sponsors will find new ideas are increased.

Blending Ideas

An important lesson to be derived from our scenario is that it is no accident that a field engineer produced the new product idea. Why? Because the field engineer spent all day working on customer problems and also knew the technology. Therefore, one person knew the need and the means by which to satisfy that need. (An added plus: The field engineer had a personal need to design the appropriate technology.) The premise here is that innovation is more likely to occur when knowledge of technologies and user requirements are combined in the minds of as few people as possible—preferably in that of one person.

The question of whether innovations are need-stimulated or means-stimulated is debatable. Do you start with the disease and look for a cure, or start with a cure and find a disease for it? Research indicates that two-thirds of innovations are need-stimulated. But this argument misses the point. As shown in Figure 5(a), the debate is over whether use or means drives the downstream efforts. This thinking is linear and sequential. Instead, the model suggested here is shown in Figure 5(b). That is, for innovation to occur, knowledge of all key components is simultaneously coupled. And the best way to maximize communication among the components is to have the communication occur intrapersonally—that is, within one person's mind. If this is impossible, then as few people as possible should have to communicate or interact. The point is that innovative ideas occur when knowledge of the essential specialties is coupled in as few heads as possible. To encourage such coupling, the organization can grow or select individuals with the essential skills or it can encourage interaction between those with meshing skills. These practices will be discussed in a people section.

A variety of processes are employed by organizations to match knowledge of need and of means. At IBM they place marketing people directly in the R&D labs where they can readily interpret the market requirement documents for researchers. People are rotated through this unit, and a net-

FIGURE 5

LINEAR SEQUENTIAL COUPLING COMPARED WITH
SIMULTANEOUS COUPLING OF KNOWLEDGE

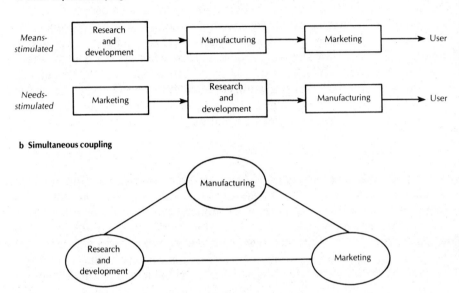

a **Linear sequential coupling**

b **Simultaneous coupling**

work is created. Wang holds an annual users' conference at which customers
and product designers interact and discuss the use of Wang products. Lanier
insists that all top managers, including R&D management, spend one day
a month selling in the field. It is reported that British scientists made remarkable progress on developing radar after actually flying missions with
the Royal Air Force. In all these cases there is an explicit matching of the
use and the user with knowledge of a technology to meet the use. Again
these processes are explicitly designed to get a user orientation among the
idea generators and sponsors. They increase the likelihood that inventions
will be innovations. The more complete a new idea or invention is at its
inception, the greater the likelihood of its being transferred into the operating
organization.

Transitioning

Perhaps the most crucial process in getting an innovative product to market
is the transitioning of an idea from a reservation to an operating organization
for implementation. This process occurs in stages, as illustrated in the case
history. First, the idea was formulated in the field before management knew

about it. Then it was tested with a customer, the French bank. And finally, at the third stage, development and full-scale implementation took place. In other cases, several additional stages of testing and scale-up may be necessary. In any case, transitioning should be planned in such stages. At each stage the orchestrator has several choices that balance the need for further invention with the need for transfer. The choices and typical stages of idea development are shown in Figure 6.

FIGURE 6

TRANSITIONING IDEAS BY STAGES

	Stages			
Choices	I	II	Nth	Implementation
Sponsor	Corporate	Corporate	. . .	Division
Champion	Corporate	Corporate	. . .	Division
Staffing	Corporate	Corporate-division	. . .	Division
Location	Corporate	Corporate	. . .	Division
Funding	Corporate	Corporate	. . .	Division
Autonomy	Complete	Complete	. . .	Minimal

At each stage these choices face the orchestrator: Who will be the sponsor? Who will be the champion? Where can staff be secured for the effort? At what physical location will work be performed? Who will fund the effort? How much autonomy should the effort have, or how differentiated should it be? For example, at the initial new idea formulation stage the sponsor could be the corporate ventures group with the champion working on the corporate reservation. The effort could be staffed with other corporate reservation types and funded at the corporate level. The activity would be fully separate and autonomous. If the results were positive, the process could proceed to the next stage. If the idea needed further development, some division people could be brought in to round out the needed specialties. If the data were still positive after the second stage, then the effort could be transferred physically to the division, but the champion, sponsor, and funding might remain at the corporate level. In this manner, by orchestrating through choices of sponsor, champion, staff, location, funding, and autonomy, the orchestrator balances the need for innovation and protection with the need for testing against reality and transfer.

The above is an all-too-brief outline of the transition process; entire books have been written on the subject of technology transfer. The goal here is to highlight the stagewise nature of the process and the decisions to be made by the orchestrator at each stage. The process is crucial because it is the link between the two organizations. Thus to consistently innovate, the firm needs an innovating organization, an operating organization, and a process for transitioning ideas from the former to the latter.

Managing Programs

Program management is necessary to implement new products and processes within divisions. At this stage of the process, the idea generator usually hands the idea off to a product/project/program manager. The product or process is then implemented across the functional organization within the division. The systems and organizational processes for managing projects have been discussed elsewhere and will not be discussed here. The point is that a program management process and skill is needed.

In summary, several key processes—that is, funding, getting ideas, blending ideas, transitioning, and managing programs—are basic components of the innovating structure. Even though many of these occur naturally in all organizations, our implicit hypothesis is that the odds for successful innovation can be increased by explicitly designing these processes and by earmarking corporate resources for them. Hundreds of people in organizations choose to innovate voluntarily, as did the field engineer in the case history. However, if there were a reward system for people like these, more would choose to innovate, and more would choose to stay in the organization to do their innovating. The reward system is the next component to be described.

REWARD SYSTEM

The innovating organization, like the operating organization, needs an incentive system to motivate innovating behavior. Because the task of innovating is different from that of operating, the innovating organization needs a different reward system. The innovating task is riskier, more difficult, and takes place over longer time frames. These factors call for some adjustment of the operating organization's reward system, the amount of adjustment depending on how innovative the operating organization is and how attractive outside alternatives are.

The functions of the reward system are threefold: First, the rewards must attract idea people to the company and the reservations and retain them. Because various firms have different attraction and retention problems, their reward systems must vary. Second, the rewards provide motivation for the extra effort needed to innovate. After 19 failures, for example, something has to motivate the idea generator to make the 20th attempt. And, finally, successful performance deserves a reward. These rewards are primarily for idea generators. However, a reward-measurement system for sponsors is equally important. Various reward systems will be discussed in the next sections.

Rewards for Idea Generators

Reward systems mix several types of internal motivators, such as the opportunity to pursue one's ideas, promotions, recognition, systems, and special compensation. First, people can be attracted and motivated intrinsically by simply giving them the opportunity and autonomy to pursue their own ideas. A reservation can provide such opportunity and autonomy. Idea people—who are internally driven—such as the field engineer in our story can come to a reservation, pursue their own ideas, and be guided and evaluated by a reservation manager. This is a reward in itself, albeit a minimal reward. If that minimal level attracts and motivates idea people, the innovating organization need go no further in creating a separate reward system.

However, if necessary, motivational leverage can be obtained by promotion and recognition for innovating performance. The dual ladder—that is, a system whereby an individual contributor can be promoted and given increased salary without taking on managerial responsibilities—is the best example of such a system. At 3M a contributor can rise in both status and salary to the equivalent of a group executive without becoming a manager. The dual ladder has always existed in R&D, but it is now being extended to some other functions as well.

Some firms grant special recognition for high career performance. IBM has its IBM fellows program in which the person selected as a fellow can work on projects of his or her own choosing for five years. At 3M, there is the Carlton Award, which is described as an internal Nobel Prize. Such promotion and recognition systems reward innovation and help create an innovating culture.

When greater motivation is needed, and/or the organization wants to signal the importance of innovation, special compensation is added to the aforementioned systems. Different special compensation systems will be discussed in the order of increasing motivational impact and of increasing dysfunctional ripple effects. The implication is that the firm should use special compensation only to the degree that the need for attraction and for motivation dictate.

Some companies reward successful idea generators with one-time cash awards. For example, International Harvester's share of the combine market jumped from 12 percent to 17 percent because of the introduction of the axial flow combine. The scientist whose six patents contributed to the product development was given $10,000. If the product continues to succeed, he may be given another award. IBM uses the "Chairman's Outstanding Contribution Award." The current program manager on the 4300 series was given a $5,000 award for her breakthrough in coding. These awards are made after the idea is successful and primarily serve to reward achievement rather than to attract innovators and provide incentive for future efforts.

Programs that give a "percentage of the take" to the idea generator and early team members provide even stronger motivation. Toy and game companies give a royalty to inventors—both internal and external—of toys and games they produce. Apple Computer claims to give royalties to employees who write software programs that will run on Apple equipment. A chemical company created a pool by putting aside 4 percent of the first five years' earnings from a new business venture, which was to be distributed to the initial venture team. Other companies create pools from percentages that range from 2 to 20 percent of cost savings created by process innovations. In any case, a predetermined contract is created to motivate the idea generator and those who join a risky effort at an early stage.

The most controversial efforts to date are attempts to duplicate free-market rewards within the firm. For example, a couple of years ago, ITT bought a small company named Qume that made high-speed printers. The founder became a millionaire from the sale; he had to quit his previous employer to found the venture capital effort to start Qume. If ITT can make an outsider a millionarie, why not give the same chance to entrepreneurial insiders? Many people advocate such a system but have not found an appropriate formula to implement the idea. For example, one firm created five-year milestones for a venture, the accomplishment of which would result in a cash award of $6 million to the idea generator. However, the business climate changed after two years, and the idea generator, not surprisingly, tried to make the plan work rather than adapt to the new, unforeseen reality.

Another scheme is to give the idea generator and the initial team some phantom stock, which gets evaluated at sale time in the same way that any acquisition would be evaluated. This process duplicates the free-market process and gives internal people the same venture capital opportunities and risks as they would have on the outside.

The special compensation programs produce motivation and dysfunctions. People who contribute at later stages frequently feel like second-class citizens. Also, any program that discriminates will create perceptions of unfair treatment and possible fallout in the operating organization. If the benefits are judged to be worth the effort, however, care should be taken to manage the fallout.

Rewards for Sponsors

The case history also demonstrates that sponsors need incentives, too. In the example, because they were being beaten in the market, the sales people had an incentive to adopt a new product. The point is that sponsors will sponsor ideas, but these may not be innovating ideas unless there's something in it for them. The orchestrator's task is to create and communicate those incentives.

Sponsor incentives take many forms. At 3M, division managers have a bonus goal that is reached if 25 percent of their revenue comes from products introduced within the previous five years. When the percentage falls below the goal, and the bonus is threatened, these sponsors become amazingly receptive to new product ideas. The transfer process becomes much easier as a result. Sales growth, revenue increase, numbers of new products, and so on, may be the bases for incentives that motivate sponsors.

Another controversy can arise if the idea generators receive phantom stock. Should the sponsors who supervise these idea people receive phantom stock, too? Some banks have created separate subsidiaries so that sponsors can receive stock in the new venture. To the degree that sponsors contribute to idea development, they will need to be given such stock options, too.

Thus, the innovating organization needs reward systems for both idea generators and sponsors. It should start with a simple reward system and move to more motivating, more complex, and possibly more upsetting types of rewards only if and when attraction and motivation problems call for them.

PEOPLE

The final policy area to be considered involves people practices. The assumption is that some people who are better at innovating are not necessarily good at operating. Therefore, the ability of the innovating organization to generate new business ideas can be increased by systematically developing and selecting those people who are better at innovating than others. But first the desirable attributes must be identified. These characteristics that identify likely idea generators and sponsors are spelled out in the following sections.

Attributes of Idea Generators

The field engineer in our case history is the stereotype of the inventor. He is not mainstream. He's hard to get along with, and he wasn't afraid to break company policy to perfect his idea. Such people have strong egos that allow them to persist and swim upstream. They generally are not the type of people who get along well in an organization. However, if an organization has reservations, innovating funds, and dual ladders, these people can be attracted and retained.

The psychological attributes of successful entrepreneurs include great need to achieve and to take risks. But, to translate that need into innovation, several other attributes are needed. First, prospective innovators have an irreverence for the status quo. They often come from outcast groups or are newcomers to the company; they are less satisfied with the way things are and have less to lose if there's a change. Successful innovators also need "previous programming in the industry"—that is, an in-depth knowledge of the industry gained through either experience or formal education. Hence, the innovator needs industry knowledge, but not the religion.

Previous startup experience is also associated with successful business ventures. As are people who come from incubator firms (for example high-technology companies) and areas (such as Boston and the Silicon Valley) that are noted for creativity.

The amount of organizational effort needed to select these people varies with the ability to attract them to the organization in the first place. If idea people are attracted through reputation, then by funding reservations and employing idea-getting processes, idea people will, in effect, select themselves—they will want to work with the organization—and over time their presence will reinforce the organization's reputation for idea generation. If the firm has no reputation for innovation, then idea people must be sought out or external reservations established to encourage initial idea generation. One firm made extensive use of outside recruiting to accomplish such a goal. A sponsor would develop an idea and then attend annual conferences of key specialists to determine who was most skilled in the area of interest; he or she would then interview appropriate candidates and offer the opportunity to develop the venture to those with entrepreneurial interests.

Another key attribute of successful business innovators is varied experience, which creates the coupling of a knowledge of means and of use in a single individual's mind. It is the generalist, not the specialist, who creates an idea that differs from the firm's current business line. Specialists are inventors; generalists are innovators. These people can be selected or developed. One ceramics engineering firm selects the best and the brightest graduates from the ceramics engineering schools and places them in central engineering to learn the firm's overall system. They are then assigned to field engineering where they spend three to five years with customers and their problems and then they return to central engineering product design. Only then do they design products for those customers. This type of internal coupling can be created by role rotation. Some aerospace firms rotate engineers through manufacturing liaison.

People who have the characteristics that make them successful innovators can be retained, however, only if there are reservations for them and sponsors to guide them.

Attributes of Sponsors and Reservation Managers

The innovating organization must also attract, develop, train, and retain people to manage the idea development process. Because certain types of people and management skills are better suited to managing ideas than others, likely prospects for such positions should have a management style that enables them to handle idea people, as well as early experience in innovating, the capability to generate ideas of their own, the skills to put deals together, and generalist business skills.

One of the key skills necessary for operating an innovating organization is the skill to manage and supervise the kind of person who is likely to be an idea generator and champion—that is, people who, among other characteristics, do not take very well to being supervised. Idea generators and champions have a great deal of ownership in their ideas. They gain their satisfaction by having "done it their way." The intrinsic satisfaction comes from the ownership and autonomy. However, idea people also need help, advice, and sounding boards. The successful sponsor learns how to manage these people in the same way that a producer or publisher learns to handle the egos of their stars and writers. This style was best described by a successful sponsor:

It's a lot like teaching your kids to ride a bike. You're there. You walk along behind. If the kid takes off, he or she never knows that they could have been helped. If they stagger a little, you lend a helping hand, undetected preferably. If they fall, you catch them. If they do something stupid, you take the bike away until they're ready.

This style is quite different from the hands-on, directive style of managers in an operating organization. Of course, the best way to learn this style is to have been managed by it and seen it practiced in an innovating organization. Therefore, experience in an innovating organization is essential.

More than the idea generators, the sponsors need to understand the logic of innovation and to have experienced the management of innovation. Its managers need to have an intuitive feel for the task and its nuances. Managers whose only experience is in operations will not have developed the managerial style, understanding, and intuitive feel that is necessary to manage innovations because the logic of operations is counterintuitive in comparison with the logic of innovations. This means that some idea generators and champions who have experienced innovation should become managers as well as individual contributors. For example, the president in our case history was the inventor of the first-generation product and therefore understood the long, agonizing process of developing a business idea. It is also rare to find an R&D manager who hasn't come through the R&D ranks.

The best idea sponsors and idea reservation managers, therefore, are people who have experienced innovation early in their careers and are comfortable with it. They will have been exposed to risk, uncertainty, parallel experiments, repeated failures that led to learning, coupling rather than assembly-line thinking, long time frames, and personal control systems based on people and ideas, not numbers and budget variances. Sponsors and reservation managers can be developed or recruited from the outside.

Sponsors and reservation managers need to be idea generators themselves. Ideas tend to come from two sources. The first is at low levels of the organization where the problem gap is experienced. The idea generator who offers a solution is the one who experienced the problem and goes to a sponsor for testing and development. One problem with these ideas is that they may offer only partial solutions because they come from specialists whose views can be parochial and local. But sponsors are at the crossroads of many ideas. They may get a broader vision of the emerging situation as a result. These idea sponsors can themselves generate an idea that is suitable for the organization's business, or they can blend several partial ideas into a business-adaptable idea. Sponsors and reservation managers who are at the crossroads of idea flow are an important secondary source of new ideas. Therefore, they should be selected and trained for their ability to generate new ideas.

Another skill that sponsors and especially reservation managers need is the ability to make deals and broker ideas. Once an idea has emerged, a reservation manager may have to argue for the release of key people, space, resources, charters, for production time, or a customer contact. These deals all require someone who is adept at persuasion. In that sense, handling them is no different than project or product management roles. People do vary in their ability to make deals and to bargain and those who are particularly adept should be selected for these roles. However, those who have other idea management skills may well be able to be trained in negotiating and bargaining.

And, finally, sponsors and reservation managers should be generalists with general business skills. Again, the ability to recognize a business idea and to shape partial ideas into business ideas are needed. Sponsors and reservation managers must coach idea generators in specialties in which the idea generator is not schooled. Most successful research managers are those with business skills who can see the business significance in the good ideas that come from scientists.

In summary, the sponsors and reservation managers who manage the idea-development process must be recruited, selected, and developed. The skills that these people need relate to their style, experience, idea-generating ability, deal-making ability, and generalist business acumen. People with these skills can either be selected or developed.

Thus some of the attributes of successful idea generators and idea sponsors can be identified. In creating the innovating organization, people with these attributes can be recruited, selected, and/or developed. In so doing, the organization improves its odds at generating and developing new business ideas.

SUMMARY

The innovating organization described is one that recognizes and formalizes the roles, processes, rewards, and people practices that naturally lead to innovations. The point we have emphasized throughout this article is that the organization that purposely designs these roles and processes is more likely to generate innovations than is an organization that doesn't plan for this function. Such a purposely designed organization is needed to overcome the obstacles to innovation. Because innovation is destructive to many established groups, it will be resisted. Innovation is contrary to operations and will be ignored. These and other obstacles are more likely to be overcome if the organization is designed specifically to innovate.

Managers have tried to overcome these obstacles by creating venture groups, by hiring some entrepreneurs, by creating "breakthrough funds," or by offering special incentives. These are good policies but by themselves will not accomplish the goal. Figure 1 conveyed the message that a consistent set of policies concerning structure, process, rewards, and people are needed. The innovating organization is illustrated in Figure 7. It is the combination of idea people, reservations in which they can operate, sponsors to supervise them, funding for their ideas, and rewards for their success that increase the odds in favor of innovation. Simply implementing one or two of these practices will result in failure and will only give people the impression that such practices do not work. A consistent combination of such practices will create an innovating organization that will work.

FIGURE 7

AN INNOVATING ORGANIZATION'S DESIGN COMPONENTS

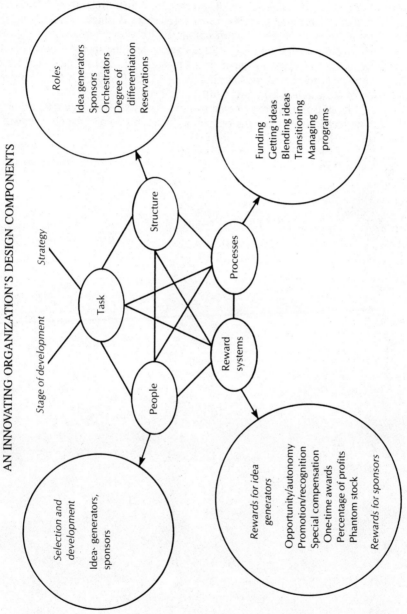

SELECTED BIBLIOGRAPHY

The basic ideas of organization design and of blending structure, processes, rewards, and people practices are described in my earlier book, *Organization Design* (Addison-Wesley, 1978). The idea of differentiation comes from Paul Lawrence and Jay Lorsch's *Organization and Environment* (Harvard Business School, 1967). One can also find there the basic ideas of contingency theory.

The structure of the innovative organization and the three roles involved are similar to those identified in the investment idea and capital budgeting process. These have been identified by Joseph Bower in *The Resource Allocation Process* (Division of Research at Harvard University, 1968).

Innovation itself has been treated in various ways by many people. Some good ideas about technological innovation can be found in Lowell Steele's *Innovation in Big Business* (Elsevier, 1975).

39 • TEAMS WHICH EXCEL[1]

Patrick J. Sweeney[2]
Douglas M. Allen[3]

In 1969, the U.S. Air Force Weapons Laboratory (AFWL) had a critical requirement to solve several major problems in laser technology, which did not appear to have any straightforward, simple solutions. The Air Force Aero Propulsion Laboratory was asked to provide technical assistance in solving these problems and did so by forming a ten-man group to work specifically on the laser problems. In the first year of operation, this group solved more than 12 major problems, won a major technical award, and developed a highly regarded reputation for excellence. This laser group is an example of what Peter Vaill, a behavioral scientist at George Washington University, has described as a "High Performing System" (HPS).

Although an HPS is rare, nearly everyone has been exposed to this type of organization at one time or another. According to Vaill an HPS exists when "a set of men utilizing some collection of technologies is performing, in relation to some predefined goals or standards, in a way which may be described as "excellent" or "outstanding" or "high performing." A method for analyzing the HPS is to observe several such systems and determine the similarity of operations within the systems. Vaill did this by basing his observations on HPSs such as athletic teams, performing arts groups, and the crew of a racing sailboat.[4] He listed 39 such observations which were subsequently summarized into 21 organizational traits in four basic groups by H. Shepard, of Shepard Associates.[5] This list is very important in the understanding of an HPS and is included below with explanations.

HPS ORGANIZATIONAL TRAITS

Behavior

1. *Language*—A private language develops for communication within the system and about its performance and problems. The language is highly functional for communicating system subtleties and complexities and much of it may be nonverbal. Outsiders may experience the language as unintelligible jargon.

2. *Task-Maintenance*—Completing tasks and feeling good are accomplished in unison. The activities involved in doing the work and maintaining team spirit appear to be identical or so intertwined as to be inseparable.

[1] From *Research Management*, Vol. 27, No. 1 (January-February, 1984), pp. 19–22. Reprinted by permission of *Research Management*.
[2] Patrick J. Sweeney, Associate Professor, University of Dayton, Dayton, Ohio.
[3] Douglas M. Allen, Vice-President of IDEA.
[4] Notes from P. Vaill, unpublished.
[5] Notes from H. Shepard, unpublished.

3. *Leadership*—Leaders tend to be viewed by members as experts in the system's basic activity. Generally the leaders are pacesetters and system role models. They tend to work well with others. When a person has been the leader of an HPS for an extended period, he or she becomes a quasi-mythical figure embodying in his person much of the meaning which the system has for its members. Vince Lombardi and Knute Rockne demonstrated this typical leadership characteristic.

4. *Experimentation*—Invariably there exists much tinkering, fiddling, experimenting with different roles, testing, rearranging, and trying new ways of operating the system.

5. *Execution*—Every HPS has its own equivalent of what in sports is termed execution, a set of actions that must be accomplished with great precision in relation to each other action. There must be a cleanness and exactness of performance and an accuracy of timing. Members take great pride in their ability to execute, and failures in execution are dismaying and very upsetting. To observers, members may seem to be taking themselves too seriously.

6. *Process Awareness*—Members of HPSs seem to have a heightened awareness of how things are going. They examine not only what they're doing but how they're doing it. Sometimes there are members in specialized roles who feed back constantly to the members exactly how the process is working.

7. *Fragility*—HPSs are in a way fragile and require some buffering from the external environment. Members also pay a lot of attention to arranging the environment in which they're going to work. Things have to be just right.

System/Environment Relations

8. *System-specific Performance Criteria*—Members often develop a unique set of performance standards for their own system, which may be quite different from the way outsiders evaluate their performance. When the system is not operating well by these special standards, members experience failure and mental anguish.

9. *On/Off*—To observers, HPS systems do not have clear on/off characteristics. The intertwining of task and maintenance (see 2 above) may be a factor of this perception by outsiders.

10. *Communication with Environment*—It is difficult for HPS members to explain to the outside world what they're doing or how they do it. They would rather just say, "Watch me." In fact, members are not highly motivated to tell the outside world, since the meaning of the activity to the member is in the doing, not the explaining.

11. *Environment's Reception of Output*—The HPS's output does not automatically please the environment, for the performance criteria that are important to members tend to be the unique internal criteria mentioned in **8,** above.

12. *Boundary Management*—The system needs to be buffered against disturbing interferences. In some fields, agents or managers are employed to negotiate with the outside world.

13. *Interface Management*—When the outputs of several HPSs need to be coordinated, a special system of rules is often developed, which is implemented and policed by individuals or groups that do not have membership in any of the HPSs. In other instances, there is sufficient commitment to superordinate goals to support flexibility and adaptability among HPSs, so that the supersystem becomes an HPS itself.

14. *Rule-Book Modification*—There may be a set of rules or a policy manual, but actual HPS behavior rarely conforms very closely to these because of the tendency to experiment continuously to bring the system closer to some desired state. Performance breakthroughs occur in unplanned ways because members are constantly experimenting and making discoveries about the technology and their personal potentials. Thus, with frequent and rapid changes, the rule book is always out of date.

15. *Equipment Modification*—What is true of the set of rules is also true of equipment. Members elaborate and modify it continuously to improve system operation.

16. *Organic Relationship with Equipment*—HPS members experience the system's technology as an extension of themselves.

17. *Biology of Equipment*—Equipment in an HPS develops a perceived psychology and biology. Equipment becomes an animate part of the system and often is given a human or animal name.

Feelings

18. *Intense Commitment*—There is an extremely high level of commitment to the objectives of the activity and to each member's success in the activity. Members don't opt out of an HPS. They freely choose to stay with the people, the activity, and the HPS even when there are supposedly more attractive opportunities elsewhere.

19. *Consciousness of History*—There is a deep consciousness of the lore and history of the activity. New members are recruited with this pride in tradition in mind, looked over very carefully to see if they fit, and indoctrinated in the system's lore.

20. *Varieties of Motivation*—Simplistic theories of motivation just don't account for the behavior of HPS members. Esthetic motivation, the seeking of beauty in the operation of the system, or possibly thrill-seeking, the thrill of victory, may explain the extremely high motivation of HPS members.

21. *Rhythm*—HPSs exhibit a rhythm of operation which members experience and observers can often see. Until the rhythm is achieved members are dissatisfied and continue to strive. After rhythm is achieved an improved performance results with much less apparent effort.

NECESSARY CONDITIONS

With the HPS now defined, the next question is "why?" The theory which is presented here provides a dual answer to the question; that is, there are two conditions which must be present in parallel for an HPS to occur. In general, the first of these deals with the people who make up the organization and the second is concerned with the interfaces between the organization and its environment.

The first condition is composed of two parts—the people in the organization must be both mentally and physically competent to fulfill the basic duties required of them and the people must also be creative. For example, athletes must not only be intelligent enough to thoroughly understand the rules and strategies of the sport, but must also be in peak physical condition to produce an outstanding performance. In a research laboratory, the scientists must understand the basics of the technologies, the state-of-the-art, and be able to operate the delicate and precise equipment necessary to perform experiments. These are obvious situations for an HPS. However, in a great majority of cases where these conditions exist, the organization still does not even approach the levels of performance which would qualify it as an HPS.

The second part of this first HPS condition concerns the creativity of the decision makers in the organization. Creativity must exist at the critical level in the organization, where decisions directly affect organization performance. This is at the lowest decision making level. This part of the condition is based upon a comparison of the HPS observations with research upon creative people and the similarities between the two. In fact, the HPS observations mentioned earlier which do not exhibit these similarities (for example, Leadership and Boundary Management) deal with the group only as opposed to the people in the group. The aspect of this theory which deals with creativity benefits as a function of the hierarchy of decision makers in an organization was originally primarily intuitive, but has been substantiated by observation. Returning to the examples of the sports team and the research laboratory, it is evident that creativity has the most benefits at the coaching (or management) level in sports, in which the team strategies are developed, but it has more benefits to the scientists (or "working level") in the research lab. In each case, this is the lowest level of decision making.

Support of this concept was noted in a table developed by John Morse and Jay Lorsch in 1970 which compares the characteristics of a manufacturing and a scientific organization.[6] Both were "high-performing organizations." Their table shows that the freedom to be creative was found only in the management levels in the high performing manufacturing plant, in which those below the management level have little decision making authority. It was noted, however, that the scientific organization appears to allow creativity at all levels.

[6] Morse, J. and Lorsch, J., "Beyond Theory Y," *Harvard Business Review,* May–June 1970: pp. 61–68.

It is again evident that the above conditions are not complete. There are examples of cases in which these conditions were met and yet an HPS did not occur. Moreover, there are also examples of HPSs which, after a while, ceased to be an HPS although no personnel changes occurred.

The second necessary condition is an environment which *allows* the HPS to happen. The word allow is important because this kind of high performance in an organization cannot be accomplished through any directives, awards, or restrictions; it can only happen if the decision makers are motivated and given the freedom to do what they believe needs to be done.

In order to illustrate this principle of motivation and freedom, let's consider the laser group example which introduced the concept of an HPS at the beginning of this article.[7] The ten people who formed the group were chosen because of their various technical expertise and past R&D performance (or creativity). Most of them had never worked together and they came from several different technical disciplines. In addition to the ten people in the group, the lab designated a manager to function as the link between the group and its environment, and to shelter the group from the external environment. The group agreed to the concept only under the following circumstances, which were granted:

- Time freedom: Flextime (flexible working schedules).
- Travel freedom: Group members would be permitted to travel wherever and whenever they believed it was necessary.
- Top priorities: Supplies and equipment were to be procured as top priority items.
- Administrative activities: Group members were not to have any administrative responsibilities.
- Customer Relations: Group members were permitted to deal directly with the customer, AFWL.

The group office was a single large room which tended to improve interaction. The members of the group usually worked in teams ranging in size from two people to all ten. The group tended not only to work together, but also socialized together during off-duty hours about once a week, usually on Saturdays.

The group constantly exhibited a tremendous amount of creativity and innovation. For example, when it was determined that a laser beam was to be transmitted from a source inside an aircraft to a target outside the aircraft, it was necessary that a hole be created in the aircraft and a turrett be inserted. However, it was not known what effect this would have on the aircraft. There was nothing in the literature but a quick answer was needed. The group drilled a hole in the roof of one member's car and inserted a turrett. They then used a cassette recorder to record the acoustical effects of the hole and turrett as they drove the car on an aircraft runway at 120 MPH.

---

[7] Private Conversation with R. Barthelemy, Air Force Wright Aeronautical Laboratories.

This speed was then translated to a Mach number and results were interpreted to determine the effects.

The group often took other innovative approaches to solving problems. They solved at least 12 of the major problems presented to the group by the AFWL in the first year. They never formalized their results into reports or papers, but instead dealt directly with the Weapons Laboratory, thus "instantly" incorporating their results in the lab's laser systems efforts.

The group quickly gained an outstanding reputation. Internally, the group was characterized as having high group spirit and creativity. Although there were often disagreements, they were always based on technical correctness and not on petty personal differences. The group's manager acted in many ways as the manager of a rock group—he handled all of the group's outside needs while not interfering with its performance.

After its first year the group developed opponents within the Propulsion Lab. These people did not believe the freedom which the group exhibited was proper or fair to the other members of the laboratory.

About this time a newly appointed laboratory commander decided to formalize the group. The group was incorporated into the existing laboratory as one of three branches in one of the laboratory's five divisions. The group then reported to a division director instead of the laboratory director. They were required to document their results, handle administrative duties, and compete for travel and supplies (it should be noted that the group originally operated at a very low cost and its travel was in line with other groups of similar size during the first year).

These changes created large conflicts between the group members and the new structure. During the next three months, the group remained internally compatible, but it was spending time and energy fighting the new environment. The group's productivity dropped substantially. Soon the conflict with the outside world snowballed into the group. Conflict began between group members and also between the group and its customer, AFWL. Eventually, people started leaving the group. When two members had left, the laboratory decided that the group's manager was needed for another position in the lab. His replacement was viewed by the group as an outsider. Eventually, more of the group members moved on. At about two years after the initial formation of the group, it was dissolved due to very low productivity and the conflict which it was causing within the laboratory.

Although impossible to prove that the changes in the environment caused the group to evolve from an HPS to a group with poor productivity, it is possible to hypothesize such a conclusion from the group history. Thus, the freedom which an organization is permitted is an imperative condition for the development and operation of an HPS.

In conclusion, the conditions that must exist for the organization and operation of a high performing system are: 1. Members must be mentally and/or physically competent, 2. Decision makers must be creative, 3. An HPS must be *permitted* (not forced) to happen, 4. Members must be highly motivated and group results must be desired. This theory is not validated outside of what is presented in this article. It is interesting that Vaill made his observations in 1975 and to date, those doing research on this topic can be counted on the fingers of one hand. We would postulate that research and experimentation on HPSs could have a substantial impact on the operations and productivity of many types of organizations.

40 • ORGANIZING FOR DIVERSIFICATION[1]

Jay W. Lorsch[2]

INTRODUCTION

"No creation of the U.S. economy reflects the vigor, imagination, and sheer brass of the 1960's more than the conglomerate corporations. Wheeling and dealing with panache and merging with seeming haste all over the lot, they have shattered the cautious business cliches that have prevailed since the Depression. In so doing, they have mushroomed suddenly into the nation's largest industrial empire. Now they are in trouble." [3] Thus began another article in the seemingly endless reporting by national news media on this new business phenomenon. Whether or not there is complete truth to all of the specifics described in this colorful journalese, one thing is clear: it is another piece of evidence that the public, management, and investor interest in the so-called "conglomerate" company is exceedingly high. While we may question whether the blanket statement "Now they are in trouble" is valid, it does seem reasonable to conclude that these large and highly diversified enterprises face unusual and difficult internal management problems which must be solved if they are to survive as a viable business institution. It is to these internal management issues that I wish to devote my attention in this paper.

In commenting on these issues, I will draw on the research in which my colleague Stephen Allen and I are currently engaged.[4] Although this research program is still in progress, the underlying conceptual scheme and preliminary findings seem sufficiently interesting to report them. While these ideas have particular relevance for understanding the organizational and management issues facing conglomerate companies, we feel they also are more generally applicable to the internal organizational issues faced by all multi-divisional companies.

Our research is being conducted in four conglomerate companies with current sales in the range of 300 to 500 million dollars. In selecting the companies for study, we have sought companies whose managements are devoting considerable attention to the control and development of the internal operation of their diversified enterprises. To state our selection criteria the other way around—we have excluded from our sample companies whose management we considered to be principally engaged in the financial manipulation of price earnings ratios and not in the long term internal development of the enterprise and its organization. So far, the analysis of data on two of these companies—one highly effective and one

[1] From Proceedings of the Annual Meeting of the Academy of Management (December, 1968), Chicago, pp. 87-100. Reprinted by permission of the Academy of Management and Jay W. Lorsch.
[2] Jay W. Lorsch, Harvard University, Cambridge, Massachusetts.
[3] *Business Week* (November 30, 1968), p. 74.
[4] This project is being supported by the Division of Research, Harvard University Graduate School of Business Administration.

less so—has been completed.[5] These are the findings to which I will refer, but our data from the other firms appear to be supporting these general conclusions.

THE BASIC CONCEPTS—DIFFERENTIATION AND INTEGRATION

The concepts which underlie our attempts to understand the internal functioning of these highly diversified companies are the same concepts that Paul Lawrence and I utilized in our recent study.[6] In that study, attention was focused on the functioning of organizations in a single business or marketing a single family of products. Our concern was to understand how functional units within such an organization became differentiated from each other as the members of each unit dealt with their specified part of the organization's environment and how integration was achieved among these units to accomplish the organization's superordinate objectives. Without reviewing those findings in detail, let me summarize three general conclusions which are helpful to understanding the present discussion:

1. We found that single-business organizations operating effectively in different environments had different patterns of differentiation, and had developed different organizational mechanisms to achieve this differentiation and the integration required in their environment. In essence, different organizational patterns were required to be effective in different businesses.
2. In all the organizations studied, we found that the states of differentiation and integration were essentially antagonistic. The more different the orientations and behavior patterns of units were in relation to the demands of their particular tasks, the more difficult it was to achieve integration between them.
3. The economically effective firm, as I suggested in (1) above, achieved the required states of differentiation and integration in the face of this underlying antagonism by having appropriate integrating mechanisms, but also by having developed a pattern of behavior among its members which effectively managed and resolved conflict to reach integrated decisions.

DIFFERENTIATION IN DIVERSIFIED CORPORATIONS

This general view of the functioning of single business organizations can be used to understand one important aspect of the organization of a highly diversified firm, if we recognize that these firms segment their activities into a number of product divisions. In fact, several of the organizations studied in our earlier research were product divisions of diversified chemicals, food, or container corporations. What these findings suggested to us about the organizational issues facing a highly diversified firm was that in each effective product division, managers would have developed organizational practices, orientations, and a management style which was consis-

---

[5] A full report of the findings in these first two companies is contained in Stephen Allen, "Managing Organization Diversity: A Comparative Study of Corporate-Divisional Relations" (unpublished doctoral thesis, Harvard Business School).

[6] Paul R. Lawrence and Jay W. Lorsch, *Organization and Environment: Managing Differentiation and Integration,* Division of Research, HBS, 1967.

tent with their particular business environment. While there was a need for differentiation and integration among the functions within each division's organization, there would also be differentiation in orientation and organization among the product divisions as each worked to meet the demands of its particular environment. This basic notion has been confirmed by our preliminary data in the present study. We have found that the managers in various product divisions develop goal orientations and time perspectives and related behavior which are in tune with the nature of their division's operating environment.

But these product divisions are not the only differentiated units in the organization of a conglomerate company. The corporate headquarters unit is another. Just as there is differentiation among the operating divisions related to differences in their operating environment, we predicted, and our preliminay data confirm, that there are differences in outlook between corporate managers on the one hand and divisional managers on the other. These differences also seem to be related to differences in the part of the corporation's environment on which the corporate executive focuses and that part of the environment which is of concern to the managers in the various divisions. As we have indicated, each division management focuses on its own operating environment, but corporate management focuses primarily on what we can label the financial environment (See Figure 1). Thus, where division executives are concerned with their respective divisional profits and operating goals, corporate executives are more financially oriented. They are concerned with the effect of activities on stock prices, the corporation's capacity to borrow, banker and stockholder relationships, etc. In addition they tend to have a longer term time orientation than their divisional subordinates. Finally, whereas in general the organizational practices of the divisions tend to be more formalized, those in the corporate headquarters are less so. This is appropriate for the problem solving, long-term task in which corporate management is involved. All of these differences mean that managers in the various divisions and managers at the corporate levels will seek different solutions to common problems. Each will have a natural tendency to want his point of view to carry the day.

We can summarize our discussion to this point by raising two of the internal organizational issues highly diversified companies face. Based on the evidence in *Organization and Environment* and our current study, it is clear that for each division to be effective, it must develop organizational states and processes consistent with the demands of its environment. In companies with divisions in distinctly different business, this means these divisions will be highly differentiated in terms of style of management and managerial orientations. Thus, one issue for an effective diversified firm will be how to create sufficient autonomy and minimize constraints so that each division can, in the current phrase, "do its own thing." But our preliminary data also point to the differences in orientations and behavior between corporate executives and those at the division level. In the more

FIGURE 1
DIFFERENTIATION AND ENVIRONMENT

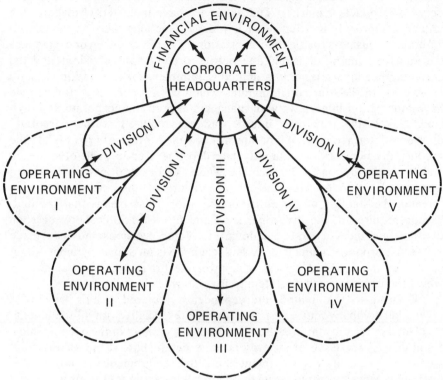

Arrows represent required information flows: (a) across the organization's boundary and (b) among organizational units

effective company, in fact, these differences are greater than in the less effective one. This is consistent with our original prediction and our findings reported in *Organization and Environment,* given the differences in their respective parts of the environment. In the effective companies, both divisional managers and corporate executives are focusing on their own issues and problems. This may produce more conflict, but, tentatively, we can also conclude that it produces better results. Corporate managers stay out of the hair of divisional level managers and let them operate in terms of the demands of their business. The second implication for managing diversified companies, then, is how to maintain the necessary differences between corporate level and division management. But maintaining these differences among divisions and behavior corporate and divisional management is only part of the total problem. Managers must also find ways of achieving integration in the face of these differences.

INTEGRATION IN DIVERSIFIED COMPANIES

In understanding the issue of achieving integration while still maintaining the necessary differentiation in a diversified company, it is necessary to identify where and what type of integration is required among the various divisional and corporate units. To start with, it is clear that when product divisions are formed, they are structured around the critical interdependence of product or market. That is, as we have indicated elsewhere, the critical reciprocal interdependence among functions must be managed within each business (division) organization.[7] Therefore, when one examines the interface among divisions and between the various divisions and the corporate headquarters, only a limited requirement for integration is found (Figure 1). In the four conglomerates which we are currently studying we have found from interviews with managers at both the corporate and divisional levels that the only interdependence required at the corporate-divisional interface is what Thompson has called a pooled type. While the product divisions are not directly interdependent upon each other, each makes a contribution to the financial whole, and each draws financial and managerial resources from the whole. Failure of any one division may threaten the stability of the entire organization. This means that the integration required of the divisional level and upward is only between each division and the corporate headquarters. Joint decisions must be made between corporate management and each division's management about economic and financial issues, to control the broad areas of business in which the company will operate and to control profitability.

Pointing to the limited interdependence required at this level of a diversified company may come as a surprise, especially with all the emphasis placed in the current literature on obtaining synergy in these companies. I will discuss the issue of synergy in more detail shortly, but at this point I do want to qualify my statement about the requirement for only pooled interdependence by emphasizing that I am talking about four firms which had not adopted a strategy of either forward or backward integration, but in which the strategy was clearly diversification. While this is also true of most of the so-called conglomerates, there are obviously many other multi-divisional companies which have operating divisions which are interdependent as suppliers and/or customers. Where this is the case, a requirement for integration among these divisions obviously exists.

Given the requirement for this limited interdependence among the corporate headquarters and the operating divisions, we still were predicting that the effective firms would achieve better quality integration than the less effective ones. Our preliminary data support this prediction. Thus, we find that a third issue facing the management of diversified companies is how to achieve effective integration between the corporate headquarters and its divisions. This is a particular thorny issue if we reintroduce two facts raised earlier. First, in the more effective company, the differences in orientations and points of view are greater than in the less effective one.

---

[7] Jay W. Lorsch and Paul R. Lawrence, "Environmental Factors and Organizational Integration." Paper prepared for 63rd Annual Meeting of the American Sociological Association, August, 1968, Boston, Mass. A similar point is also made by James D. Thompson in *Organizations in Action* (New York: McGraw-Hill Book Company, 1967).

But we have also mentioned, based on the *Organization and Environment* study, that greater differentiation between units creates more problems of achieving integration. The more difficult the viewpoints of the two parties, the more difficult it is for them to communicate. Thus, a more comprehensive statement of the management issue is how to achieve a high quality of integration between the corporate headquarters and the various divisions, while still permitting the differences in outlook necessary for all parties to work on their particular tasks. The key to performing this balancing act seems to rest in developing organizational mechanisms to facilitate the flow of information necessary to achieve integration, and also developing conflict resolution practices in the organization which allow managers at the two levels to reach joint decisions. We will briefly look at the organizational vehicles established in diversified organizations to achieve integration and will then take a longer look at conflict resolution practices in these firms.

ORGANIZATIONAL DEVICES FOR ACHIEVING INTEGRATION

With the only interdependence required at this level of the organization being of the pooled type, one might expect, following Thompson and March and Simon, that the necessary integration could be achieved through the management hierarchy and through management control systems, such as budgets, business plans, etc.[8] While this is basically what we have found in the four companies studied, there are two aspects of these devices which are worthy of brief comment.

First, apropos of the use of the hierarchy to achieve integration at this level, one clear trend in the four companies studied, as well as in other diversified firms, is the establishment of a new level of management called the "group level." These group vice president positions in the firms we have studied have been set up as part of corporate management to be a bridge between top corporate management and divisional management. Most of the time of the executives in these positions is devoted to achieving integration between the divisions in their group and the corporate management above them. Since these positions exist in all the companies in our study, it is not possible to say whether they help achieve integration while maintaining differentiation. But their existence in all four firms suggests that such positions are a minimal condition for achieving both differentiation and integration at this level, as firms become more diversified.

A second issue about the integrating mechanism utilized is the extent to which each company uses formalized paper information systems to facilitate communication between corporate and divisional levels and the extent to which they rely upon direct face to face contact. While the theories of Thompson and March and Simon would suggest that pooled interdependence can be managed without heavy reliance on face to face contact, it was our view that high quality face to face interaction would also have to

[8] J. G. March and H. S. Simon, *Organizations* (New York: John Wiley & Sons, Inc., 1958).

be used to manage these interdependencies. It is too early for us to reach a firm conclusion on this point, but our preliminary data suggest that in our four firm sample, the more effective firms are characterized by a higher quality of face to face interaction between corporate level and divisional executives. To understand why this is so, it is necessary to turn to the topic of conflict management in these firms.

CONFLICT MANAGEMENT IN DIVERSIFIED COMPANIES

As we have pointed out, the differentiated outlook of corporate and divisional management is inevitably going to lead to conflict which somehow must be managed and resolved. The fact that these differences are wider in effective firms makes it difficult to rely on only paper systems to achieve integration. In working out plans and budgets managers in each division are going to be working from the point of view of their division while corporate managers will usually have a point of view different from that of any one division. This means that direct face to face negotiations and discussion must take place to resolve these conflicting view points. This process is further complicated at this level of the organization by the nature of the conflict involved.

In *Organization and Environment* we pointed out that the conflicts which existed among functional units within a business are usually of the type where the potential benefits for the parties involved are not fixed. Though interests may conflict, there is always the possibility of finding an ingenious solution that satisfies all parties and optimizes total business results.[9] There is, however, another type of conflict situation—what game theorists call the zero-sum game. In such a case, each party has a stake in the conflict so that a gain for one is a loss for the other. While we do not view these two categories of conflict as pure types or as mutually exclusive, our study of diversified companies so far has lead us to the conclusion that the pooled interdependence among divisions causes managers to see the conflict as more of the zero-sum type at the corporate-divisional interface. While the possibility always exists of changing the rules of the game so that conflict at this level is seen less as zero-sum, as long as division managers are rewarded and highly controlled for divisional profits under a profit center concept, there is a tendency for them to see conflicts with the corporate headquarters and indirectly through the headquarters with other divisions as zero-sum. This fact suggests that it is even more necessary for effective, direct face-to-face contact to take place between divisional and corporate level executives. With the divisional profit center concept pushing the situation toward zero-sum, one practical way to redefine the situation is to have corporate executives give signals to divisional executives that total corporate objectives are also important. For these reasons, then, we expected that in effective firms we would find a higher quality of face-to-face contact to achieve integration and less strict reliance on the paper budgeting and planning systems.

[9] Lawrence and Lorsch, *op. cit.*, p. 204.

Given this broad view of the nature of conflict at this level, let us turn to more specific predictions and preliminary findings about the factors affecting conflict management in diversified firms. We will then elaborate our findings about communication flows and put them in the context of the conflict management process.

First we predicted that in effective firms the managers centrally involved in achieving integration between the corporate and divisional level would have a balanced viewpoint between the position of these two groups. This followed from our findings about the balanced orientations of integrators in *Organization and Environment.* [10] Obviously one set of managers involved in this integration activity are the Group Vice Presidents. Unfortunately, the sample of Group Vice Presidents from the two firms in which the study has been completed is so small that we can reach no conclusion about whether those in the more effective firm have a more balanced viewpoint. However, another set of positions involved in achieving integration between corporate headquarters and the divisions is the division general managers. Here we do have sufficient data to draw at least a tentative conclusion, and we have found that the Division General Managers in the more effective organization do have a more balanced orientation between those of their divisional subordinates and corporate executives than do general managers in the less effective firm. This then generally substantiates our prediction.

A second factor connected to conflict management with which we were concerned was the influence or power over policy decisions held by corporate and divisional managers. We predicted, and our preliminary data in two firms have substantiated, that in the effective firm the distribution of power over policy decisions would be more balanced between corporate and divisional executives than in the less effective firms. In the effective firm we have found that corporate and divisional managers have almost equal influence over policy decisions. In the less effective firm, the corporate management group is perceived to have considerably more power than the divisional managers. Our explanation of why this relative balance of power is important stems from two sources. First, we believe that having considerable influence over policy decisions is an important source of motivation for divisional managers. In essence, it provides them with a real sense of being part of the action. Second, and closely connected to this, when the divisional managers have relatively high power, they will be able to maintain the differentiated position necessary to operate their respective divisions effectively. Conflicts will be resolved, but not at the expense of divisional differentiation and autonomy. Although we have no data on the opposite situation, it seems equally obvious that if division managers had power which was excessively higher than that of corporate management, conflicts would be resolved in favor of the various divisions to the potential detriment of the whole. In sum, an approximate balance of power between

[10] *Ibid.,* Ch. II.

corporate and divisional managers seems necessary so that conflicts are resolved in a manner which balances the concerns of divisional managers and those of corporate managers. In this way, both differentiation and integration can be achieved.

Based on our findings in *Organization and Environment*, we are also predicting that a third conflict management factor which will be important is the mode of behavior utilized to resolve conflicts.[11] In the type of conflict situations involved in the single business organizations studied in our earlier research, we found that confrontation of conflict was a more pre-dominate behavioral pattern for resolving conflict in effective organizations. Managers in the effective organizations used more confronting and less forcing and smoothing behavior to resolve conflict than did managers in less effective ones. However, given the tendency for zero-sum conflict to emerge at this level of diversified companies and following Walton and McKersie, we conjectured that perhaps bargaining or compromise behavior would lead to more effective integration in these situations.[12] Our findings in the two companies studied to date, however, clearly indicate that con-frontation is a more practiced mode of resolving conflict in the effective firm than in the less effective one. We feel that the contradiction with Walton and McKersie's findings is more apparent than real. In essence, by con-fronting conflict, the managers in the effective firms seem to be able to keep the rules of the conflict game from becoming zero-sum. As a result, they work out the resolution which makes sense from the point of view of the total enterprise.

Let us return to the subject of communication flow, a factor which also helps to keep the conflict from being a zero-sum game. We predicted that in effective firms the quality of communication in both directions would be higher than in less effective ones. What we have found so far in the two firms for which we have complete data is that in the effective firm the down-ward flow of communication is superior, while in the less effective firm the upward flow of communication is superior. In the effective firm, there is a higher quality of information flowing from the corporations to the divisions. While some of this downward information moves through paper systems, most of it is transmitted in face-to-face interaction. In fact, there is clear evidence in the effective firm that the corporate executives are much more approachable on an informal basis than in the less effective firm. On the other hand, the higher quality and quantity of information moving upward in the less effective firm are a result of a very sophisticated and elaborate formalized management information system.

What does this mean for the process of conflict resolution? Our tenta-tive conclusion is that the downward flow of information in the effective firm is more crucial than the upward flow in the less effective one. This is so, as we have already pointed out, because the direct face-to-face contact

---

[11] *Ibid.*, Chs. III, IV.
[12] R. E. Walton and R. B. McKersie, *A Behavioral Theory of Labor Negotiations: A Social Interaction System* (New York: McGraw-Hill Book Company, 1965).

which accompanies the downward flow of information in the effective firm facilitates the process of conflict resolution. It helps to convert the potentially zero-sum conflict situation into an integrative one. As managers at the divisional level learn about corporate objectives and progress, they are more apt to see the relevance of corporate goals and are less likely to rigidly stand on parochial divisional interests. On the other hand, the upward flow of more formal information in the less effective firm does little to facilitate conflict resolution. Corporate management may learn how well the various divisions are doing, but the division managers learn nothing about corporate goals. In fact, the elaborate upward reporting of divisional results tends to emphasize to divisional managers the importance of their own divisional results. If they are reported upward in such detail and so frequently, they must be important factors in judging their performance. As a result, they are more apt to view any conflict situation as a zero-sum game between themselves and other divisions and an integrative solution is less likely.

A vivid example of the dynamics of the whole conflict management process can be seen by examining how the two firms on which we have complete data handled the problem of a division which was in serious profit difficulties. While in both firms communications between low performing divisions and headquarters were less good than communications between both performing divisions and headquarters, this situation was markedly accentuated in the low performing firm. In this company, the two-way interchange of information outside the formal reporting system almost stopped except for corporate demands that things improve. The balance of power between corporate and division management was heavily in favor of corporate management. As a result there was even less confronting behavior than between the high performing division managements and corporate managers in the same company. In the low peforming company, corporate management in effect demanded improved results but cut off all problem solving contact. As a result it was harder for division management to explain the need for more resources and to work jointly with corporate management to develop programs for remedial action.

In the effective firm the flow of communication, while reduced, remained open on a face-to-face basis. Pressure for improved performance was evident from corporate management, but it was done in a climate of a mutual exchange of views. Conflict was still confronted. The balance of power over decision was still present and division managers were able to work with corporate managers to resolve their problems. Rather than being demotivated and cut off from corporate help and resources, contact was maintained and they were able to present and understand their views in the context of total corporate goals. Instead of seeing themselves as losers in a zero-sum game with other divisions, they were able to recognize the need for decisions which went against them in terms of the corporate whole. As a result, in the effective firm, corporate and divisional managers jointly reached decisions about capital programs and business plans to solve the profit difficulties of the low performing divisions. In the less effective firm, there was less evidence of progress in this direction.

We have dwelt on these conflict management issues at some length because we believe, and our tentative data substantiate our belief, that the effective management of conflict is the key lever to achieving the differentiation and integration necessary for a diversified organization to function effectively. Without effective management of conflict, it seems difficult, if not impossible, for the management of a diversified firm to solve the twin issues of allowing each division management to "do its own thing" while still getting the maximum profit contribution for the corporate whole.

From our viewpoint, managing conflict to achieve the necessary differentiation and integration to run a diversified organization seems to be a delicate balancing act. It requires a balance between divisional autonomy and corporate control, so that there is a balance of power between levels. It requires managers at the head of the division and presumably at the group level of the corporation who have a balanced concern for the corporate viewpoint and the divisional viewpoint. Finally, it requires managers on both sides of the corporate divisional interface who have the skill to confront conflict and work at problems until a desirable resolution is achieved. At least these are the major factors which our tentative data suggest are important, if a firm is to effectively organize for diversity. But it is important to emphasize that these conclusions are drawn from a study of firms where the interdependence among divisions was of a pooled nature. If these firms had attempted to encourage more active collaboration among operating divisions, so that sequential or reciprocal interdependence among divisions was required, the organizational problems would be even more complex. Although the four conglomerates we are studying have not made a major attempt to achieve such interdivisional integration, we want to briefly discuss some of the issues connected with it, because such interdivisional collaboration is at the heart of current discussions about synergy in these diversified firms.

SYNERGY IN DIVERSIFIED ORGANIZATIONS

Many writers about conglomerate companies have suggested that the major economic justification for such enterprises is that they achieve synergy. That is, the output of the whole firm somehow becomes greater than the sum of the individual parts operating separately. On first glance our findings would suggest, if the four firms we are studying are typical, that little synergy actually exists in such conglomerate firms. Actually, whether or not this is true depends upon how you define the term synergy. We have found it useful to distinguish between three groups of synergy—financial, managerial, and operating. By financial synergy we mean the opportunities for the combined parts of the firm more effectively to obtain, manage, and utilize capital resources. This, based on our interviews with the managers in these companies, appears to be a form of synergy, which all four firms are achieving to some degree.

By managerial synergy we mean the opportunity for the combined divisions to more effectively utilize management techniques and managerial manpower than they could as independent enterprises. This involves sharing of knowledge about common managerial problems and working together to fill each other's managerial manpower needs. Although there is greater disparity among our four firms in this area than in the financial area, all are also striving to achieve this managerial synergy.

It is in the area of what we call operating synergy that these firms are making the least attempts to take advantage of their combined opportunities. By operating synergy we mean somehow getting divisions to join forces in manufacturing, marketing, and innovating products so as to take advantage of each division's particular competitive strength or to achieve more economically efficient operations. Examples of operating synergy might be one division manufacturing a product for a second division or one division marketing products for another, or perhaps two divisions combining their marketing and manufacturing know-how to produce a product system which neither could produce alone.

The reason that these firms rarely try to achieve this type of synergy and, even when they do, find it difficult to accomplish, is not hard to understand. Whereas financial and managerial synergy require only pooled interdependence at the corporate-divisional interface, operating synergy requires sequential and even reciprocal interdependence among divisions. In essence, it means that the divisions not only have to coordinate their efforts through the corporate headquarters, but also that they must actively integrate their efforts with another division's directly.

Given our discussion above about the tendency for conflict at this level of the organization to be seen as a zero-sum game, it is not hard to envisage why such interdivisional collaboration is difficult to achieve. Even in a firm which has achieved the delicate balances we have referred to, it is going to require even more working through of conflict, more direct face-to-face decisions between corporate and divisional executives and among executives from the divisions concerned. Finally, we suspect that it may even require some alteration of the divisional profit center concept, so that division managers on joint projects can resolve conflicts around the relevant criteria of joint contribution to corporate profits.

Given the amount of time and effort which would be required to effectively manage conflict and achieve the interdivisional integration required to gain operating synergy, it is not surprising, then, that these firms have not yet made major strides in this direction.[13] The problems of managing conflict to achieve differentiation and integration around the pooled interdependence required for financial and managerial synergy are sufficiently time consuming and complex that it would seem even the managers of effective conglomerates have all they can handle. But it is our prediction that in the future there will be more and more of a tendency in the direction of operating synergy. As the social and technical problems which provide

[13] John Kitching, "Why Do Mergers Miscarry?," *Harvard Business Review,* (November-December, 1967).

market opportunities become increasingly complex, they will require the joint efforts of several product divisions for solution. As this happens, the organizational issues of achieving differentiation and integration through conflict management will become increasingly complex. I hope that studies such as this can throw light on these issues and help management to deal with them.

CONCLUSION

In conclusion I would like to briefly mention a few of the broader implications of understanding the sorts of organizational issues I have been discussing. While this discussion has focused on the newer and more glamorous forms of diversified companies, as I pointed out earlier, it obviously also has relevance for the older more established diversified firms in such industries as metals, papers, and chemicals, if we recognize the different types of interdependencies which may be involved. Beyond this, it also has relevance for all multinational firms. While the diversity in these cases may be territorial as well, and the interdependencies more complex, the issues confronting mangement are similar. Finally, it occurs to me that many of the organizational problems facing the federal, state, and local governments as they strive to solve the urban crisis are similar to those we have been discussing. How different from the problem I have discussed are the problems of achieving inter-agency collaboration among federal departments or between state and local agencies? My hunch is that they are very similar and as we learn about organizing for diversity in business organizations, we should hopefully be able to shed some light on these same issues in these other institutions.

But to gain the understanding of such organizational issues means we must continue to free ourselves of the shibboleths about the one best way to organize. Instead, we must develop an understanding of how organizations function in relation to the demands of their task or environment and given the needs of their members. This is the broadest objective of the research program I have described. While our problem interest is diversified organizations, our continuing theoretical objective is to enhance our understanding of the contingent relations among the organization, its environment, and the men who manage and work in it.

41 • MATRIX ORGANIZATION DESIGNS[1]

Jay R. Galbraith[2]

Each era of management evolves new forms of organization as new problems are encountered. Earlier generations of managers invented the centralized functional form, the line-staff form, and the decentralized product division structure as a response to increasing size and complexity of tasks. The current generation of management has developed two new forms as a response to high technology. The first is the free-form conglomerate; the other is the matrix organization, which was developed primarily in the aerospace industry.

The matrix organization grows out of the organizational choice between project and functional forms, although it is not limited to those bases of the authority structure.[3] Research in the behavioral sciences now permits a detailing of the choices among the alternate intermediate forms between the project and functional extremes. Detailing such a choice is necessary since many businessmen see their organizations facing situations in the 1970's that are similar to those faced by the aerospace firms in the 1960's. As a result, a great many unanswered questions arise concerning the use of the matrix organization. For example, what are the various kinds of matrix designs, what is the difference between the designs, how do they work, and how do I choose a design that is appropriate for my organization?

The problem of designing organizations arises from the choices available among alternative bases of the authority structure. The most common alternatives are to group together activities which bear on a common product, common customer, common geographic area, common business function (marketing, engineering, manufacturing, and so on), or common process (forging, stamping, machining, and so on). Each of these bases has various costs and economies associated with it. For example, the functional structure facilitates the acquisition of specialized inputs. It permits the hiring of an electromechanical and an electronics engineer rather than two electrical engineers. It minimizes the number necessary by pooling specialized resources and time sharing them across products or projects. It provides career paths for specialists. Therefore, the organization can hire, utilize, and retain specialists.

These capabilities are necessary if the organization is going to develop high technology products. However, the tasks that the organization must perform require varying amounts of the specialized resources applied in varying sequences. The problem of simultaneously completing all tasks on time, with appropriate quality and while fully utilizing all specialist

---

[1] From *Business Horizons,* Vol. XIV, No. 1 (February, 1971), pp. 29-40. Reprinted by permission of *Business Horizons*.
[2] Jay R. Galbraith, faculty member of the Alfred P. Sloan School of Management, Massachusetts Institute of Technology, Cambridge, Massachusetts.
[3] See John F. Mee, "Matrix Organization," *Business Horizons* (Summer, 1964), p. 70.

resources, is all but impossible in the functional structure. It requires either fantastic amounts of information or long lead times for task completion.

The product or project form of organization has exactly the opposite set of benefits and costs. It facilitates coordination among specialties to achieve on-time completion and to meet budget targets. It allows a quick reaction capability to tackle problems that develop in one specialty, thereby reducing the impact on other specialties. However, if the organization has two projects, each requiring one half-time electronics engineer and one half-time electromechanical engineer, the pure project organization must either hire two electrical engineers—and reduce specialization—or hire four engineers (two electronics and two electromechanical)—and incur duplication costs. In addition, no one is responsible for long-run technical development of the specialties. Thus, each form of organization has its own set of advantages and disadvantages. A similar analysis could be applied to geographically or client-based structures.

The problem is that when one basis of organization is chosen, the benefits of the others are surrendered. If the functional structure is adopted, the technologies are developed but the projects fall behind schedule. If the project organization is chosen, there is better cost and schedule performance but the technologies are not developed as well. In the past, managers made a judgment as to whether technical development or schedule completion was more important and chose the appropriate form.

However, in the 1960's with a space race and missile gap, the aerospace firms were faced with a situation where both technical performance and coordination were important. The result was the matrix design, which attempts to achieve the benefits of both forms. However, the matrix carries some costs of its own. A study of the development of a matrix design is contained in the history of The Standard Products Co., a hypothetical company that has changed its form of organization from a functional structure to a matrix.

A COMPANY CHANGES FORMS

The Standard Products Co. has competed effectively for a number of years by offering a varied line of products that were sold to other organizations. Standard produced and sold its products through a functional organization like the one represented in Figure 1. A moderate number of changes in the product line and production processes were made each year. Therefore, a major management problem was to coordinate the flow of work from engineering through marketing. The coordination was achieved through several integrating mechanisms:

> *Rules and procedures.* One of the ways to constrain behavior in order to achieve an integrated pattern is to specify rules and procedures. If all personnel follow the rules, the resultant behavior is integrated without having to maintain on-going communication. Rules are used for the most predictable and repetitive activities.

FIGURE 1
STANDARD'S FUNCTIONAL ORGANIZATION

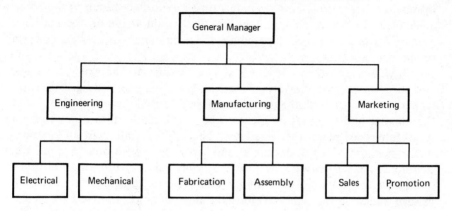

Planning processes. For less repetitive activities, Standard does not specify the procedure to be used but specifies a goal or target to be achieved, and lets the individual choose the procedure appropriate to the goal. Therefore, processes are undertaken to elaborate schedules and budgets. The usefulness of plans and rules is that they reduce the need for on-going communication between specialized subunits.

Hierarchical referral. When situations are encountered for which there are no rules or when problems cause the goals to be exceeded, these situations are referred upward in the hierarchy for resolution. This is the standard management-by-exception principle. This resolves the nonroutine and unpredictable events that all organizations encounter.

Direct contact. In order to prevent top executives from becoming overloaded with problems, as many problems as possible are resolved by the affected managers at low levels by informal contacts. These remove small problems from the upward referral process.

Liaison departments. In some cases, where there is a large volume of contracts between two departments, a liaison department evolves to handle the transactions. This typically occurs between engineering and manufacturing in order to handle engineering changes and design problems.[4]

The Standard Products Co. utilized these mechanisms to integrate the functionally organized specialties. They were effective in the sense that Standard could respond to changes in the market with new products on a timely basis, the new products were completed on schedule and within budget, and the executives had sufficient time to devote to long-range planning.

Matrix Begins Evolution

A few years ago, a significant change occurred in the market for one of Standard's major product lines. A competitor came out with a new design utilizing an entirely new raw material. The initial success caused Standard

---

[4] For a more detailed explanation, see Jay R. Galbraith, *Organization Design* (Reading, Mass.: Addison-Wesley Publishing Co., Inc., 1971).

to react by developing one of their own incorporating the new material. They hired some specialists in the area and began their normal new product introduction activities. However, this time the product began to fall behind schedule, and it appeared that the product would arrive on the market at a time later than planned. In response, the general manager called a meeting to analyze the situation.

Task Force. After a briefing, it was obvious to the general manager and the directors of the three functions what was happening. Standard's lack of experience with the new material had caused them to underestimate the number and kinds of problems. The uncertainty led to a deterioration in usefulness of plans and schedules. The problems affected all functions, which meant that informal contacts and liaison processes were cumbersome; therefore, the majority of the problems were referred upward. This led to overloads on the directors of the functions and the general manager, which in turn added to the delays. Thus, the new situation required more decision making and more information processing than the current organization could provide.

The directors of engineering and manufacturing suggested that the cause of the problem was an overly ambitious schedule. More time should have been allowed for the new product; if realistic schedules were set, the current coordination processes would be adequate. They proposed that the schedules be adjusted by adding three to six months to the current due dates, which would allow more time to make the necessary decisions.

The director of marketing objected, reporting that the company would lose a good percentage of the market if the introduction was delayed. A number of big customers were waiting for Standard's version of the new product, and a delay would cost the company some of these customers. The general manager agreed with the marketing director. He proposed that they should not change the schedule to fit their current coordination processes, but that they should introduce some new coordination mechanisms to meet the scheduled due dates.

The group agreed with the general manager's position and began to search for alternative solutions. One of the solution requirements suggested was to reduce the distance between the sources of information and the points of decision. At this point the manufacturing director cautioned them about decentralizing decisions: He reminded them of previous experiences when decisions were made at low levels of the engineering organization. The data the decision makers had were current but they were also local in scope; severe problems in the manufacturing process resulted. When these decisions were centralized, the global perspective prevented these problems from developing. Therefore, they had to increase decision-making power at lower levels without losing the inputs of all affected units. The alternative that met both requirements was a group with representation from all the major departments to enter into joint decisions.

The group was appointed and named the "new product task force." It was to last as long as cross-functional problems occurred on the new product introduction. The group was to meet and solve joint problems within the budget limits set by the general manager and the directors; prob-problems requiring more budget went to the top management group. The purpose was to make as many decisions as possible at low levels with the people most knowledgeable. This should reduce the delays and yet ensure that all the information inputs were considered.

The task force consisted of nine people; three, one from each function, were full-time and the others were part-time. They met at least every other day to discuss and resolve joint problems. Several difficulties caused them to shift membership. First, the engineering representatives were too high in the organization and, therefore, not knowledgeable about the technical alternatives and consequences. They were replaced with lower level people. The opposite occurred with respect to the manufacturing repre-sentatives. Quite often they did not have either information or the authority to commit the production organization to joint decisions made by the task force. They were replaced by higher level people. Eventually, the group had both the information and the authority to make good group decisions. The result was effective coordination: coordination $= f$ (authority $\times$ information).

Creation of the task force was the correct solution. Decision delays were reduced, and collective action was achieved by the joint decisions. The product arrived on time, and the task force members returned to their regular duties.

Teams. No sooner had the product been introduced than salesmen began to bring back stories about new competitiors. One was introducing a second-generation design based on improvements in the raw material. Since the customers were excited by its potential and the technical people thought it was feasible, Standard started a second-generation redesign across all its product lines. This time, they set up the task force structure in advance and committed themselves to an ambitious schedule.

Again the general manager became concerned. This time the product was not falling behind schedule, but in order to meet target dates the top management was drawn into day-to-day decisions on a continual basis. This was leaving very little time to think about the third-generation product line. Already Standard had to respond twice to changes initiated by others. It was time for a thorough strategy formulation. Indeed, the more rapid the change in technology and markets, the greater the amount of strategic deci-sion making that is necessary. However, these are the same changes that pull top management into day-to-day decisions. The general manager again called a meeting to discuss and resolve the problem.

The solution requirements to the problem were the same as before. They had to find a way to push a greater number of decisions down to lower levels. At the same time, they had to guarantee that all interdepen-dent subunits would be considered in the decision so that coordination would be maintained. The result was a more extensive use of joint decision making and shared responsibility.

The joint decision making was to take place through a team structure. The teams consisted of representatives of all functions and were formed around major product lines. There were two levels of teams, one at lower levels and another at the middle-management level. Each level had defined discretionary limits; problems that the lower level could not solve were referred to the middle-level team. If the middle level could not solve the problem, it went to top management. A greater number of day-to-day operating problems were thereby solved at lower levels of the hierarchy, freeing top management for long-range decisions.

The teams, unlike the task force, were permanent. New products were regarded as a fact of life, and the teams met on a continual basis to solve recurring interfunctional problems. Task forces were still used to solve temporary problems. In fact, all the coordination mechanisms of rules, plans, upward referral, direct contact, liaison men, and task forces were used, in addition to the teams.

Product Managers. The team structure achieved interfunctional coordination and permitted top management to step out of day-to-day decision making. However, the teams were not uniformly effective. Standard's strategy required the addition of highly skilled, highly educated technical people to continue to innovate and compete in the high technology industry. Sometimes these specialists would dominate a team because of their superior technical knowledge. That is, the team could not distinguish between providing technical information and supplying managerial judgment after all the facts were identified. In addition, the specialists' personalities were different from the personalities of the other team members, which made the problem of conflict resolution much more difficult.[5]

Reports of these problems began to reach the general manager, who realized that a great number of decisions of consequence were being made at lower and middle levels of management. He also knew that they should be made with a general manager's perspective. This depends on having the necessary information and a reasonable balance of power among the joint decision makers. Now the technical people were upsetting the power balance because others could not challenge them on technical matters. As a result, the general manager chose three technically qualified men and made them product managers in charge of the three major product lines.[6] They were to act as chairmen of the product team meetings and generally facilitate the interfunctional decision making.

Since these men had no formal authority, they had to resort to their technical competence and their interpersonal skills in order to be effective. The fact that they reported to the general manager gave them some additional power. These men were successful in bringing the global, general

---

    [5] See Paul R. Lawrence and Jay Lorsch, "Differentiation and Integration in Complex Organizations," *Administrative Science Quarterly* (June, 1967).
    [6] Paul R. Lawrence and Jay Lorsch, "New Management Job: the Integrator," *Harvard Business Review* (November-December, 1967).

manager perspective lower in the organization to improve the joint decision-making process.

The need for this role was necessitated by the increasing differences in attitudes and goals among the technical, production, and marketing team participants. These differences are necessary for successful subtask performance but interfere with team collaboration. The product manager allows collaboration without reducing these necessary differences. The cost is the additional overhead for the product management salaries.

Product Management Departments. Standard Products was now successfully following a strategy of new product innovation and introduction. It was leading the industry in changes in technology and products. As the number of new products increased, so did the amount of decision making around product considerations. The frequent needs for tradeoffs across engineering, production, and marketing lines increased the influence of the product managers. It was not that the functional managers lost influence; rather, it was the increase in decisions relating to products.

The increase in the influence of the product managers was revealed in several ways: First, their salaries became substantial. Second, they began to have a greater voice in the budgeting process, starting with approval of functional budgets relating to their products. The next change was an accumulation of staff around the products, which became product departments with considerable influence.

At Standard this came about with the increase in new product introductions. A lack of information developed concerning product costs and revenues for addition, deletion, modification, and pricing decisions. The general manager instituted a new information system that reported costs and revenues by product as well as by function. This gave product managers the need for a staff and a basis for more effective interfunctional collaboration.

In establishing the product departments, the general manager resisted requests from the product managers to reorganize around product divisions. While he agreed with their analysis that better coordination was needed across functions and for more effective product decision making, he was unwilling to take the chance that this move might reduce specialization in the technical areas or perhaps lose the economies of scale in production. He felt that a modification of the information system to report on a product and a functional basis along with a product staff group would provide the means for more coordination. He still needed the effective technical group to drive the innovative process. The general manager also maintained a climate where collaboration across product lines and functions was encouraged and rewarded.

The Matrix Completed

By now Standard Products was a high technology company; its products were undergoing constant change. The uncertainty brought about by the new technology and the new products required an enormous amount of decision making to plan-replan all the schedules, budgets, designs, and so on. As a result, the number of decisions and the number of consequential decisions made at low levels increased considerably. This brought on two concerns for the general manager and top management.

The first was the old concern for the quality of decisions made at low levels of the organization. The product managers helped solve this at middle and top levels, but their influence did not reach low into the organization where a considerable number of decisions were made jointly. They were not always made in the best interest of the firm as a whole. The product managers again recommended a move to product divisions to give these low-level decisions the proper product orientation.

The director of engineering objected, using the second problem to back up his objection. He said the move to product divisions would reduce the influence of the technical people at a time when they were having morale and turnover problems with these employees. The increase in joint decisions at low levels meant that these technical people were spending a lot of time in meetings. Their technical input was not always needed, and they preferred to work on technical problems, not product problems. Their dissatisfaction would only be aggravated by a change to product divisions.

The top management group recognized both of these problems. They needed more product orientation at low levels, and they needed to improve the morale of the technical people whose inputs were needed for product innovations. Their solution involved the creation of a new role—that of subproduct manager.[7] The subproduct manager would be chosen from the functional organization and would represent the product line within the function. He would report to both the functional manager and the product manager, thereby creating a dual authority structure. The addition of a reporting relation on the product side increases the amount of product influence at lower levels.

The addition of the subproduct manager was intended to solve the morale problem also. Because he would participate in the product team meetings, the technical people did not need to be present. The subproduct manager would participate on the teams but would call on the technical experts within his department as they were needed. This permitted the functional department to be represented by the subproduct manager, and the technical people to concentrate on strictly technical matters.

Standard Products has now moved to a pure matrix organization as indicated in Figure 2. The pure matrix organization is distinguished from the previous crossfunctional forms by two features. *First,* the pure matrix has a dual authority relationship somewhere in the organization. *Second,* there is a power balance between the product management and functional sides. While equal power is an unachievable razor's edge, a reasonable

[7] Jay Lorsch, "Matrix Organization and Technical Innovations," Jay Galbraith, ed., *Matrix Organizations: Organization Design for High Technology* (Cambridge, Mass.: The M.I.T. Press, 1971).

FIGURE 2

STANDARD'S PURE MATRIX ORGANIZATION

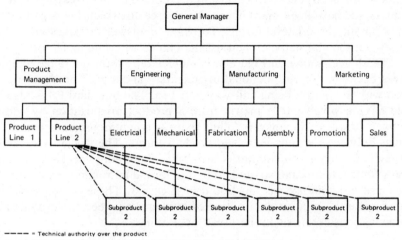

----- = Technical authority over the product

——— = Formal authority over the product (in product organization, these relationships may be reversed)

balance can be obtained through enforced collaboration on budgets, salaries, dual information and reporting systems, and dual authority relations. Such a balance is required because the problems that the organization faces are uncertain and must be solved on their own merits—not on any predetermined power structure.

Thus over a period of time, the Standard Products Co. has changed from a functional organization to a pure matrix organization using dual authority relationships, product management departments, product teams at several levels, and temporary task forces. These additional decision-making mechanisms were added to cope with the change in products and technologies. The changes caused a good deal of uncertainty concerning resource allocations, budgets, and schedules. In the process of task execution, more was learned about the problem causing a need for rescheduling and rebudgeting. This required the processing of information and the making of decisions.

In order to increase its capacity to make product relevant decisions, Standard lowered the level at which decisions were made. Coordination was achieved by making joint decisions across functions. Product managers and subproduct managers were added to bring a general manager's perspective to bear on the joint decision-making processes. In addition, the information and reporting system was changed in order to provide reports by function and by product. Combined, these measures allowed Standard to achieve the high levels of technical sophistication necessary to innovate products and simultaneously to get these products to the market quickly to maintain competitive position.

HOW DO I CHOOSE A DESIGN?

Not all organizations need a pure matrix organization with a dual authority relationship. Many, however, can benefit from some cross-functional forms to relieve top decision makers from day-to-day operations. If this is so, how does one choose the degree to which his organization should pursue these lateral forms? To begin to answer this question, let us first lay out the alternatives, then list the choice determining factors.

The choice, shown in Figure 3, is indicated by the wide range of alternatives between a pure functional organization and a pure product organization with the matrix being half-way between. The Standard Products Co. could have evolved into a matrix from a product organization by adding functional teams and managers. Thus there is a continuum of organization designs between the functional and product forms. The design is specified by the choice among the authority structure; integrating mechanisms such · as task forces, teams and so on; and by the formal information system. The way these are combined is illustrated in Figure 3. These design variables help regulate the relative distribution of influence between the product and functional considerations in the firm's operations.

FIGURE 3

THE RANGE OF ALTERNATIVES

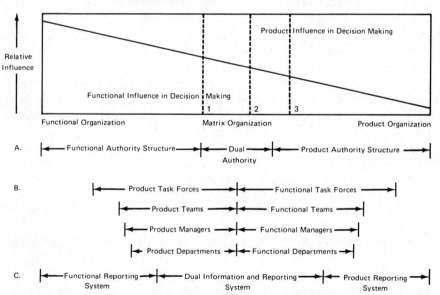

The remaining factors determining influence are such things as roles in budget approvals, design changes, location and size of offices, salary, and so on. Thus there is a choice of integrating devices, authority structure, information system, and influence distribution. The factors that determine choice are diversity of the product line, the rate of change of the product line, interdependencies among subunits, level of technology, presence of economies of scale, and organization size.

Product Lines

The greater the diversity among product lines and the greater the rate of change of products in the line the greater the pressure to move toward product structures.[8] When product lines become diverse, it becomes difficult for general managers and functional managers to maintain knowledge in all areas; the amount of information they must handle exceeds their capacity to absorb it. Similarly, the faster the rate of new product introduction, the more unfamiliar are the tasks being performed.

Managers are, therefore, less able to make precise estimates concerning resource allocations, schedules, and priorities. During the process of new product introduction, these same decisions are made repeatedly. The decisions concern tradeoffs among engineering, manufacturing, and marketing. This means there must be greater product influence in the decision process. The effect of diversity and change is to create a force to locate the organization farther to the right in Figure 3.

Interdependence

The functional division of labor in organizations creates interdependencies among the specialized subunits. That is, a problem of action in one unit has a direct impact on the goal accomplishment of the other units. Organizations usually devise mechanisms that uncouple the subunits, such as in-process-inventory and order backlogs. The degree to which inventories and backlogs develop is a function of how tight the schedule is. If there is a little slack in the schedule, then the functional departments can resolve their own problems. However, if rapid response to market changes is a basis of competition, then schedules are squeezed and activities run in parallel rather than series.[9] This means that problems in one unit directly affect another. The effect is a greater number of joint decisions involving engineering, manufacturing, and production. A greater need for product influence in these decisions arises due to the tight schedule. Thus the tighter the schedule, the greater the force to move to the right in Figure 3.

Although the tightness of the schedule is the most obvious source of interdependence, tight couplings can arise from reliability requirements and other design specifications. If the specifications require a more precise fit and operation of parts, then the groups designing and manufacturing the parts must also "fit and operate" more closely. This requires more coordination in the form of communication and decision making.

---

[8] For product line diversity, see Alfred Chandler, *Strategy and Structure* (Cambridge, Mass.: The M.I.T. Press, 1962); for product change rate, see Tom Burns and G. M. Stalker, *Management and Innovation* (London: Tavistock Publications, 1958).

[9] For a case study of this effect, see Jay Galbraith, "Environmental and Technological Determinants of Organization Design" in Jay Lorsch and Paul R. Lawrence, eds., *Studies in Organization Design* (Homewood, Ill.: Richard D. Irwin, Inc., 1970).

Level of Technology

If tight schedules and new products were the only forces operating, every organization would be organized around product lines. The level of technology or degree to which new technology is being used is a counter-acting force. The use of new technologies requires expertise in the technical specialties in engineering, in production engineering, in manufacturing, and market research in marketing. Some of the expertise may be purchased outside the organization.

However, if the expertise is critical to competitive effectiveness, the organization must acquire it internally. If the organization is to make effective use of the expertise, the functional form of organization is superior, as described earlier in the article. Therefore the greater the need for expertise, the greater the force to move to the left in Figure 3.

Economies of Scale and Size

The other factor favoring a functional form is the degree to which expensive equipment in manufacturing, test facilities in engineering, and warehousing facilities in marketing are used in producing and selling the product. (Warehousing introduces another dimension of organization structure, for example, geographical divisions. For our purposes, we will be concerned only with product and function dimensions.) It is usually more expensive to buy small facilities for product divisions than a few large ones for functional departments. The greater the economies of scale, the greater the force to move to the left in Figure 3. Mixed structures are always possible. That is, the capital intensive fabrication operation can organize along functional process lines, and the labor intensive assembly operation can organize along product lines.

The size of the organization is important in that it modifies the effect of expertise and economies of scale. That is, the greater the size of the organization the smaller the costs of lost specialization and lost economies of scale when the product form is adopted. Thus while size by itself has little effect on organization structure, it does moderate the effects of the previously mentioned factors.

The Choice

While research on organizations has not achieved a sophistication that would allow us to compute the results of the above factors and locate a point in Figure 3, we can still make our subjective weightings. In addition, we can locate our present position and make changes in the appropriate directions as product lines, schedules, technologies, and size change during the normal course of business. The framework provides some basis for planning the organization along with planning the strategy and resource allocations.

If the organization's present structure is on the left side of the figure, many of the symptoms occurring in the Standard Products example signal a need for change. To what degree are communication overloads occurring? Are top executives being drawn into day-to-day decisions to the detriment of strategy development? How long does it take to get top level decisions made in order to continue work on new products? If the answers to these questions indicate an overload, then some movement toward a matrix is appropriate. Probably a sequence of moves until the bottlenecks disappear is the best strategy; this will allow for the proper attitudinal and behavioral changes to keep pace.

If the organization is product organized, then movements to the left toward a matrix are more subtle. They must be triggered by monitoring the respective technological environments.

An example from the aerospace industry may help. In the late fifties and early sixties the environment was characterized by the space race and missile gap. In this environment, technical performance and technology development were primary, and most firms adopted organizations characterized by the dotted line at "1" in Figure 3. The functional departments had the greatest influence on the decision-making process. During the McNamara era, they moved to point "2." The environment shifted to incentive contracts, PERT-cost systems, and increased importance of cost and schedule considerations.

Currently, the shift has continued toward point "3." Now the environment is characterized by tight budgets, a cost overrun on the C-5 project, and Proxmire hearings in the Senate. The result is greater influence by the project managers. All these have taken place in response to the changing character of the market. A few firms recently moved back toward point "2" in response to the decreasing size of some firms. The reduction in defense spending has resulted in cutbacks in projects and employment. In order to maintain technical capabilities with reduced size, these firms have formed functional departments under functional managers with line responsibility. These changes show how changes in need for expertise, goals, and size affect the organization design choice.

Many organizations are experiencing pressures that force them to consider various forms of matrix designs. The most common pressure is increased volume of new products. Organizations facing this situation must either adopt some form of matrix organization, change to product forms of organization, or increase the time between start and introduction of the new product process.

For most organizations, the matrix design is the most effective alternative. Managers must be aware of the different kinds of matrix designs and develop some basis for choosing among them.

42 • THE INDIVIDUALIZED ORGANIZATION: PROBLEMS AND PROMISE[1]

Edward E. Lawler, III[2]

Two easily identified and distinctly different approaches to the study of behavior in organizations have dominated the organizational behavior literature for the past half century. One emphasizes the differences among people, the other the similarities.

The first and least dominant approach has its foundation in differential psychology and is concerned with the study of individual differences. The basic assumptions underlying this approach are that people differ in their needs, skills, and abilities, that these differences can be measured, that valid data about people's competence and motivation can be obtained by organizations and that these data can be used to make organizations more effective.

When behavioral scientists who take this approach look at organizations, they tend to see selection and placement. Their concern is with selecting those people who are right for a given job by measuring the characteristics of both the people and jobs and then trying to achieve the best fit. Their paradigm of the ideal organization would seem to be one where everyone has the ability and motivation to do the job to which he is assigned. Rarely do behavioral scientists with this orientation try to change the design of jobs or of organizations. Jobs are taken as a given and the focus is on finding the right people for them. Where efforts at job redesign have been made, they typically are instituted in the tradition of human engineering. That is, jobs have been made simpler so that more people can do them.

What is needed if this approach is to work?

1. People must differ in meaningful ways.
2. Valid data about the characteristics of people must exist.
3. People who are suited for the jobs must apply.
4. A favorable selection ratio must exist (a large number of qualified applicants must apply for the job).

The second approach has generally assumed that all employees in an organization are similar in many ways and that certain general rules or principles can and should be developed for the design of organizations. It is universalistic, propounding that there is a right way to deal with all people in organizations. This type of thinking is present in the work of such traditional organization theorists as Urwick and Taylor. It is also present in the writings of the human relations theorists such as Mayo and in the work of the human resource theorists such as McGregor and Likert. As John Morse notes, all these approaches contain either implicitly or explicitly the assumption that there is a right way to manage people [1].

[1] From *California Management Review*, Vol. XVII, No. 2 (Winter, 1974), pp. 31-39. Copyright 1974 by the Regents of the University of California. Reprinted from *California Management Review*, Vol. XVII, No. 2, by permission of the Regents.
[2] Edward E. Lawler, III, Professor of Psychology and Program Director, Institute for Social Research, University of Michigan.

Douglas McGregor's discussion of Theory X and Theory Y points out that, although scientific management and the more modern theories make different assumptions about the nature of man, both emphasize the similarities among people rather than the differences [2]. Based upon the Theory Y view of the nature of people, McGregor develops a normative organization theory that, like Theory X, stresses universal principles of management. For any of the universality theories to be generally valid, a certain type of person must populate society: one that fits its assumptions about the nature of people. In the case of the human resource theorists, this universal person will respond favorably to such things as enriched jobs, participative leadership, and interpersonal relationships characterized by openness, trust, and leveling. For the scientific management theorists, the universal type responds well to the use of financial rewards and the simplification of work. Thus, the validity of all these theories rests upon the correctness of the assumptions about the nature of people.

The work of those behavioral scientists who are concerned with individual differences suggests that the assumptions of all the universal theorists are dangerous over-simplifications for one very important reason: they fail to acknowledge the significant differences (in needs, personalities, and abilities) that cause individuals to react differently to organization practices concerned with job design, pay systems, leadership, training, and selection. Although many studies of individual behavior in organizations have not looked for individual differences, there are some that have found significant diversities. They are worth reviewing briefly since they clearly illustrate what is wrong with all organization theories which make universal assumptions about the nature of people.

Job Design

Job enrichment is one of the key ideas in most of the recent human resource theories of organization. According to the argument presented by Frederick Herzberg and others, job enrichment can lead to appreciable increases in employee motivation, performance and satisfaction [3]. In fact, there is a fairly large body of evidence to support this view [4].

There is, however, also a considerable amount of evidence that all individuals do not respond to job enrichment with higher satisfaction, productivity, and quality. In many studies the researchers have not been concerned with explaining these individual differences and have treated them as error variance. In others, however, attempts have been made to find out what distinguishes those people who respond positively to job enrichment. It has been pointed out that the type of background a person comes from may be related to how he or she responds to an enriched job [5]. According to some analyses, employees from rural backgrounds are more likely to respond positively to enrichment than are workers from urban environments.

More recent findings have shown that individual differences in need strength determine how people respond to jobs; the reason previous researchers have found urban-rural differences to be important lies in the kind of needs that people from these backgrounds have [6]. Rural background people have stronger higher-order needs (self-actualization, competence, self-esteem), and people with these needs respond positively to job enrichment, while those who don't fail to respond. It is argued that job enrichment creates conditions under which people can experience growth and self-esteem, motivating them to perform well. Clearly, for those employees who do not want to experience competence and growth, the opportunity to experience them will not be motivating, and not everyone should be expected to respond well to enriched jobs [7].

Pay Systems

The scientific management philosophy strongly emphasizes the potential usefulness of pay as a motivator as in many piece rate, bonus, profit sharing, and other pay incentive plans. There is abundant evidence to support the point that, when pay is tied to performance, motivation and performance are increased [8]. However, there is also evidence to indicate that not everyone responds to pay incentive plans by performing better. In one study, certain types of employees responded to a piece rate incentive system while others did not [9]. Who responded? Workers from rural backgrounds who owned their homes, were Protestants, and social isolates—workers who, in short, saw money as a way of getting what they wanted and for whom social relations were not highly important.

There are many different kinds of pay incentive systems; and the kind of pay system that will motivate one person often does not motivate others. For example, group plans apparently work best with people who have strong social needs [10]. This suggests that not only do the members of an organization have to be treated differently according to whether they will or will not respond to a pay incentive, but that those who will respond to pay systems may have to be subdivided according to the type of system to which they will respond.

There is abundant evidence that individuals differ in their responses to the fringe benefits they receive. Large differences, determined by such things as age, marital status, education, and so on, exist among individuals in the kinds of benefits they want and need [11]. Most organizations ignore this and give everyone the same benefits, thereby often giving high cost benefits to people who do not want them. Maximizing individual satisfaction with fringe benefits would require a unique plan for each employee.

Leadership

Research on leadership style during the past two decades has stressed the advantages that can be gained from the use of the various forms of power equalization. Participation, flat organizations, decentralization, and group decision-making are all power equalization approaches to motivating and satisfying employees. There is a considerable body of evidence to suggest that power equalization can lead to higher subordinate satisfaction, greater subordinate motivation, and better decision-making [12]. Unfortunately, much of this literature has only given brief mention to the fact that not all subordinates respond in the same way to power equalization and the fact that not all superiors can practise power equalization.

Victor Vroom was one of the first to point out that at least one type of subordinate does not respond positively to participative management [13]. His data show that subordinates who are high on the F-scale (a measure of authoritarianism) do not respond well when they are subordinates to a boss who is oriented toward participative management. Later studies have shown that at times the majority of the membership of a work group may not respond positively to power equalization efforts on the part of superiors [14].

Many superiors cannot manage in a democratic manner [15]. This, combined with the poor responses of many employees to democratic management styles, raises the question of whether it is advisable even to think of encouraging most managers to lead in a democratic manner. Many superiors probably *cannot* adopt a democratic leadership style, and because of the likely responses of some of their subordinates they *shouldn't*— regardless of task and situational considerations.

Training

To most modern organization theorists, training is an important element of organization design. It is particularly helpful in resolving individual differences. T-groups, managerial grid seminars, and leaderships courses are some examples of the kinds of human relations training that organizations use. These training approaches help assure that most people in the organization have certain basic skills and abilities and that some valid assumptions about the capacity of the people in the organization can be made.

Once again, the problem is that the very individual employee differences greatly affect the ability to learn from things such as T-groups and managerial grid seminars; this type of training is simply wasted on many people [16]. In fact, the training may end up increasing the range of individual differences in an organization rather than reducing it. It is also likely that while one type of human relations training may not affect a person, another type could have a significant impact. The same point can be made with respect to training people in the area of occupational skills. One person may learn best from a teaching machine while another learns the same material best from a lecture format.

Selection

In the work on selection the assumption has typically been made that people are sufficiently similar so that the same selection instruments can be used for everyone. Thus, all applicants for a job are often given the same battery of selection criteria—overlooking the fact that different instruments might work better as predictors for some groups than for others. This would not be a serious problem if individual difference factors were not related to the ability of the selection instruments to predict performance; but recent evidence suggests that they are. Certain kinds of tests work better for some segments of the population than for others [17]. However, this uniformity in selection testing is not the only reason for poor job performance prediction.

Differential psychologists have developed numerous valid tests of people's ability to perform jobs, but they have failed to develop tests that measure how employees will fit into particular organizational climates and how motivated they will be in particular organizations. All too often they have tried to predict individual behavior in organizations without measuring the characteristics of the organization. Trying to predict behavior by looking only at personal characteristics must inevitably lead to predictions whose validity is questionable..

All this is beginning to change, but it is doubtful if highly accurate predictions will ever be obtained. The measurement problems are too great and both organizations and people change too much. The research evidence also shows that people sometimes don't give valid data in selection situations and that some important determinants of individual behavior in organizations are difficult to measure [18].

Individual Differences

One clear implication of the research on individual differences is that for any of the universalistic theories to operate effectively in a given organization or situation, one of two things must occur: either the organization must deal with the individuals it hires so that they will change to meet the assumptions of the theory, or it must hire only those individuals who fit the kind of system that the organization employs. Unfortunately, there is no solid evidence that individuals can be trained or dealt with in ways that will increase the degree to which they respond to such things as enriched jobs and democratic supervision. Proponents of job enrichment often stress that people will come to like it once they have tried it, but this point remains to be proved.

The validity of most selection instruments is so low that organizations should not count on finding instruments that will allow them to select only those who fit whatever system they use. There is always the prospect that the differential psychologist can develop appropriate measures and that this will lead to organizations being able to select more homogenous work forces. This, in turn, would allow approaches such as the human resources approach to be effectively utilized in some situations. However, it seems unlikely that they could ever be used in large complex organizations. Even if measures are developed, it may not be possible for large homogenous populations of workers to be selected by organizations. Effective selection depends on favorable selection ratios, which are rare, and on the legal ability of organizations to run selection programs. It is also obvious that there has been and will continue to be a large influx into the labor market and into organizations of people from different socio-economic backgrounds. This has and will continue to create more diversity rather than homogeneity in the work forces of most organizations, decreasing the likelihood that large organizations can ever be completely staffed by people who fit the assumptions of scientific management, Theory X, Theory Y, or any other organization theory that is based upon the view that people are similar in important ways.

Further, it soon may not be legally possible for organizations to conduct the kind of selection programs that will by themselves produce good individual-organization fits. The federal government restrictions on testing for selection purposes soon could create conditions under which testing will no longer be practical. Organizations may find themselves in a situation where they must randomly select from among the "qualified applicants" for a job. Thus, even if valid tests were developed, work forces probably could not be selected that would contain only people that fit either the human resources or the scientific management assumptions about people.

There is evidence in the literature that some organization theorists are moving away from the view that one style of management or one organization design is right for most organizations [19]. However, the focus so far has been on environmental variables such as degree of uncertainty and stability, and production variables such as whether the task is predictable and whether the product can be mass, process, or unit produced. The researchers point out that different structures and different management styles are appropriate under different conditions. Some of the evidence they present is persuasive: products and environmental factors need to be considered when organizations are being designed. However, they often fail to point out that the nature of the work force also needs to be considered and they fail to suggest organization structures that allow for the fact that the people in any organization will vary in their response to such things as tight controls, job enrichment, and so on.

What seems to be needed is an organization theory based upon assumptions like the following, which recognize the existence of differences among individuals:

1. Most individuals are goal-oriented in their behavior but there are large differences in the goals people pursue.
2. Individuals differ both in what they enjoy doing and in what they can do.
3. Some individuals need to be closely supervised while others can exercise high levels of self-control.

In order to design an organization based on these assumptions, it is necessary to utilize various normative theories as guides to how different members of the same organization should be treated. In addition measures of individual needs and abilities, like those developed by differential psychologists, are needed. As will become apparent, it probably also is necessary to depend on the ability of individuals to help make decisions about where and how they will work. In short, it requires a synthesis of the individual differences approach and the work of the organization theorists into a new paradigm of how organizations should be designed—a new paradigm that emphasizes structuring organizations so that they can better adapt themselves to the needs, desires, and abilities of their members.

Structuring the Individualized Organization

The research on job design, training, reward systems, and leadership provides a number of suggestions about what an organization designed on the basis of individual differences assumptions would look like. A brief review will help to illustrate how an individualized organization might operate and identify some of the practical problems of the approach.

The research on job design shows that jobs can be fit to people if organizations can tolerate having a wide range of jobs and tasks. One plant in Florida has done this by having an assembly line operating next to a bench assembly of the same product. Employees are given a choice of which kind of job they want. The fact that some want to work on each kind is impressive evidence of the existence of individual differences. Robert Kahn has suggested that the fit process can be facilitated by allowing individuals to choose among different groups of tasks or modules that would be several hours long [20]. In his system, workers would bid for those tasks which they would like to do. For this system to work, all individuals would, of course, have to know a considerable amount about the nature of the different modules, and the approach would probably have to take place in conjunction with some job enrichment activities. Otherwise, the employee might be faced with choosing among modules made up of simple, repetitive tasks, thus giving them no real choice. As Kahn notes, the work module concept is also intriguing because it should make it easier for individuals to choose not to work a standard forty-hour work week. This is important because of the differences in people's preferences with respect to hours of work. The whole module approach rests on the ability of individuals to make valid choices about when and where they should work.

The leadership research shows that people respond to different types of leadership. This could be handled by fitting the superior's style to the personality of subordinates—the superior who can only behave in an authoritarian manner will be given subordinates who perform well under that type of supervision; the superior who can only behave participatively could be given only people who respond to that style; and the superior who is capable of varying his style could be given either people who respond to different styles in different conditions or a mix of people with which he or she would be encouraged to behave differently.

The research shows that training needs to be individualized so that it will fit the needs and abilities of the employee. Implementation requires careful assessment of the individual's abilities and motivation, and good career counseling. Once it has been accepted that not everyone in the organization can profit from a given kind of training, then training becomes a matter of trying to develop people as much as possible with the kind of training to which they will respond. It requires accepting the fact that people may develop quite different leadership styles or ways of behaving in general and trying to capitalize on these by fitting the job the person holds and the groups he supervises to his style.

The research shows that pay systems need to be fit to the person. Fringe benefit packages are a good example of this; several companies have already developed cafeteria-style fringe benefit packages that allow employees to select the benefits they want. The research also suggests that those individuals whose desire for money is strong should be placed on jobs that lend themselves to pay incentive plans.

In summary, an organization based on individual differences assumptions would have a job environment for each person which fits his or her unique skills and abilities. It would accomplish this by a combination of good selection and self-placement choices in the areas of fringe benefits, job design, hours of work, style of supervision, and training programs. But creating truly individualized job situations presents many practical problems in organization design—it is difficult to create gratifying jobs for both the person who responds to an enriched job and the person who responds to a routinized job. One way of accomplishing this could be by creating relatively autonomous subunits that vary widely in climate, job design, leadership style, and so on. For example, within the same organization the same product might be produced by mass production in one unit and by unit production using enriched jobs in another. One subunit might have a warm, supportive climate while another might have a cold, demanding one. The size of the subunit would also vary depending upon the type of climate that is desired and the type of production it uses. This variation is desirable as long as the placement process is able to help people find the modules that fit them.

An organization would have to have an immense number of subunits if it were to try to have one to represent each of the possible combinations of climate, leadership style, incentive systems, and job design. Since such a large number is not practical, a selection should be made based on a study of the labor market, attention to the principles of motivation and satisfaction, and the nature of the product and market. A study of the labor market to see what type of people the organization is likely to attract should help determine what combinations will be needed to fit the characteristics of most of the workers. In most homogenous labor markets, this may be only a few of the many possible combinations. Traditional selection instruments can help the organization decide who will fit into the subunits; and, if individuals are given information about the nature of the subunits, they can often make valid decisions themselves.

Motivation theory argues that when important rewards are tied to performance, it is possible to have both high satisfaction and high performance [21]. This suggests that all new work modules must meet one crucial condi-

tion: some rewards that are valued by members of that part of the organization must be tied to performance. This rules out many situations. For
example, a situation in which no extrinsic rewards such as pay and promotion
are tied to performance and which has authoritarian management and repetitive jobs should not exist. Finally, the research on job design and organization structure shows that the type of product and type of market limit the
kind of subunit which can be successful. For example, authoritarian management, routine jobs, and tall organization structures are not effective when the
product is technically sophisticated and must be marketed in a rapidly
changing environment.

Creating subunits with distinctly different climates and practices is one
way, but not the only way, to create an individualized organization. In small
organizations this probably is not possible; thus, it is important to encourage
differences within the same unit. This may mean training supervisors to deal
differently with subordinates who have distinctly different personal characteristics. It may also mean designing jobs that can be done in various ways.
For example, in one group a product might be built by a team and passed
from one member to another while in another group everyone might build
the entire product without help. Obviously, this approach generally will not
allow for as much variation as does the approach of building distinctive
subunits, but it permits some degree of individualization.

It is not yet entirely clear how such divergent organization practices as
work modules, cafeteria style pay plans, and job enrichment that is guided
by individual difference measures can be integrated in practice. Research on
how organizations can be individualized and on how individual differences
affect behavior in organizations is sorely needed.

Research on Individual Differences

The work on measuring individual differences that has been done so far
has focused largely on measuring the "can do" aspects of behavior for the
purpose of selection. The effective individualization of organizations depends
on the development of measures which tap the "will do" aspects of behavior,
such as measures of motivation and reactions to different organizational
climates, and measures that can be used for placing people in positions that
best fit their needs.

This is not to say that selection should be ignored; the kinds of individual differences that exist in an organization should be kept at a manageable number and those who clearly cannot do the job should be excluded.
But it is important that, in selection, measures of such things as motivation,
reactions to different leadership styles, and preferred organization climate
be collected and evaluated in relationship to the climate of the organization,
the psychological characteristics of the jobs in the organizations, and the
leadership style of various managers. The same measures are obviously
relevant when consideration is given to placing new employees in different
parts of the organization or in different jobs. The difficulty in doing this kind

of selection and placement is that there are few measures of the relevant individual differences, of the organization climate, and of the psychological characteristics of jobs. In many cases, it is not even known what the relevant individual difference variables are when consideration is being given to predicting how people will react to different administrative practices, policies, and to different organization climates. This is where the differential psychologist can make a major contribution.

Also needed is research on selection that is responsive to the new demands that society is placing on organizations and which recognizes that individuals can contribute to better selection decisions. Since organizations are rapidly losing the ability to select who their members will be, research is needed on how the selection situation can be turned into more of a counseling situation so that enlightened self-selection will operate. There is evidence that when job applicants are given valid information about the job, they will make better choices. Joseph Weitz showed this long ago with insurance agents, and more recently it has been illustrated with West Point cadets and telephone operators [22]. In the future the most effective selection programs will have to emphasize providing individuals with valid data about themselves and about the nature of the organization. After this information is presented to the applicants, they will make the decision of whether to join the organization. Before this kind of "selection" system can be put into effect, however, much research is needed to determine how this process can be handled. We need to know, for example, what kind of information should be presented to individuals and how it should be presented. However, the problems involved in the approach are solvable and, given the current trends in society, this approach represents the most viable selection approach in many situations.

Conclusions

The research on reward systems, job design, leadership, selection, and training shows that significant individual differences exist in how individuals respond to organizational policies and practices. Because of this, an effective normative organization theory has to suggest an organization design that will treat individuals differently. Existing normative theories usually fail to emphasize this point. There are, however, a number of things that organizations can do now to deal with individual differences. These include cafeteria style pay plans and selective job enrichment. Unfortunately, a fully developed practical organization theory based upon an individual difference approach can not be yet stated. Still, it is important to note that approaches to shaping organizations to individuals are developing. It seems logical, therefore, to identify these and other similar efforts as attempts to individualize organizations. It is hoped that the identification of these efforts and the establishment of the concept of individualization will lead to two very important developments: the generation of more practices that will individualize organizations and work on how these different practices can simultaneously be made operational in organizations. Only if these developments take place will individualized organizations ever be created.

REFERENCES FOR ARTICLE

1. JOHN J. MORSE, "A Contingency Look at Job Design," *California Management Review* (Fall 1973), pp. 67-75.
2. DOUGLAS MCGREGOR, *The Human Side of Enterprise* (New York: McGraw-Hill, 1960).
3. FREDERICK HERZBERG, *Work and the Nature of Man* (Cleveland: World, 1966).
4. ROBERT BLAUNER, *Alienation and Freedom* (Chicago: University of Chicago, 1964); and Edward E. Lawler, "Job Design and Employee Motivation," *Personnel Psychology,* Vol. 22 (1969), pp. 426-435.
5. ARTHUR TURNER and PAUL R. LAWRENCE, *Industrial Jobs and the Worker* (Boston: Harvard University School of Business Administration, 1965); and Charles L. Hulin and Milton R. Blood, "Job Enlargement, Individual Differences, and Worker Responses," *Psychological Bulletin,* Vol. 69 (1968), pp. 41-55.
6. J. RICHARD HACKMAN and EDWARD E. LAWLER, "Employee Reactions to Job Characteristics," *Journal of Applied Psychology,* Vol. 55 (1971), pp. 259-286.
7. JOHN J. MORSE, "A Contingency Look at Job Design," *op. cit.*
8. EDWARD E. LAWLER, *Pay and Organizational Effectiveness: A Psychological View* (New York: McGraw-Hill, 1971).
9. WILLIAM F. WHYTE, *Money and Motivation* (New York: Harper, 1955).
10. EDWARD E. LAWLER, *Pay and Organizational Effectiveness: A Psychological View, op. cit.*
11. STANLEY NEALY, "Pay and Benefit Preferences," *Industrial Relations,* Vol. 3 1963), pp. 17-28.
12. CHRIS ARGYRIS, "Personality and Organization Revisited," *Administrative Science Quarterly,* Vol. 18 (1973), pp. 141-167.
13. VICTOR H. VROOM, *Some Personality Determinants of the Effects of Participation* (Englewood Cliffs, New Jersey: Prentice Hall, 1960).
14. JOHN R. P. FRENCH, J. ISRAEL, and DAGFIN AS, "An Experiment on Participation in a Norwegian Factory," *Human Relations,* Vol. 13 (1960), pp. 3-19; and George Strauss, "Some Notes on Power-Equalization," in H. J. Leavitt (ed.), *The Social Science of Organizations* (Englewood Cliffs, New Jersey: Prentice-Hall, 1963).
15. FREDERICK E. FIEDLER, "Predicting the Effects of Leadership Training and Experience from the Contingency Model," *Journal of Applied Psychology,* Vol. 56 (1972), pp. 114-119.
16. JOHN P. CAMPBELL and MARVIN D. DUNNETTE, "Effectiveness of T-Group Experiences in Managerial Training and Development," *Psychological Bulletin,* Vol. 70 (1968), pp. 73-104.
17. EDWIN E. GHISELLI, "Moderating Effects and Differential Reliability and Validity," *Journal of Applied Psychology,* Vol. 47 (1963), pp. 81-86.
18. ROBERT M. GUION, *Personnel Testing* (New York: McGraw-Hill, 1965).
19. JOAN WOODWARD, *Industrial Organization: Theory and Practice* (London: Oxford University Press, 1965); Paul R. Lawrence and Jay W. Lorsch, *Organization and Environment* (Boston: Division of Research, Graduate School of Business Administration, Harvard University, 1967); Chris Argyris, *Integrating the Individual and the Organization* (New York: John Wiley, 1964); and Tom Burns and G. M. Stalker, *The Management of Innovation* (London: Tavistock Publications Limited, 1961).

20. ROBERT KAHN, "The Work Module—A Tonic for Lunchpail Lassitude," *Psychology Today,* Vol. 6 (1973), pp. 94-95.
21. VICTOR VROOM, *Work and Motivation* (New York: Wiley, 1964).
22. JOSEPH WEITZ, "Job Expectancy and Survival," *Journal of Applied Psychology,* Vol. 40 (1956), pp. 245-247: and John P. Wanous, "Effect of a Realistic Job Preview on Job Acceptance, Job Survival and Job Attitudes," *Journal of Applied Psychology,* in press.

BIBLIOGRAPHY, CHAPTER 12

Allen, Stephen A. "Organizational Choices and General Management Influence Networks in Divisionalized Companies." *Academy of Management Journal,* Vol. 21, No. 3 (September, 1978), pp. 341-365.

Babbitt, H. Randolph, Jr., and J. D. Ford. "Decision Maker Choice as a Determinant of Organizational Structure." *Academy of Management Review,* Vol. 5, No. 1 (1980), pp. 13-23.

Blackburn, Richard S. "Dimensions of Structure: A Review and Reappraisal." *Academy of Management Review,* Vol. 7, No. 1 (1982), pp. 59-66.

Dalton, Dan R., *et al.* "Organization Structure and Performance: A Critical Review." *Academy of Management Review,* Vol. 5, No. 1 (1980), pp. 49-64.

Davis, Stanley M., and P. R. Lawrence. "Problems of Matrix Organizations." *Academy of Management Review,* Vol. 56, No. 3 (May-June, 1978), pp. 131-142.

Filley, Alan C., and R. J. Aldag. "Characteristics and Measurement of an Organizational Typology" *Academy of Management Journal,* Vol. 21, No. 4 (December, 1978), pp. 578-591.

Harvey, E. "Technology and the Structure of Organizations." *American Sociological Review,* Vol. 33 (1968), pp. 247-259.

Hickson, D. J., D. S. Pugh, and D. C. Pheysey. "Operations Technology and Organization Structure." *Administrative Science Quarterly,* Vol. 14 (1969), pp. 378-397.

Hoffman, John, and Orry Shackney. "Assessing the Productivity of Corporate Staff Services." *Business Horizons,* Vol. 26, No. 4 (July-August, 1983), pp. 53-57.

Huber, George P., J. Ullman, and R. Leifer. "Optimum Organization Design: An Analytic Adoptive Approach." *Academy of Management Review,* Vol. 4 (1979), pp. 567-578.

Hunt, Raymond G., "Technology and Organization," *Academy of Management Journal,* No. 31 (September, 1970), pp. 235-252.

Mansfield, R., D. Todd, and J. Wheeler. "Company Structure and Market Strategy," *Omega,* Vol. 6, No. 2 (1978), pp. 133-138.

Matthews, Glenn H. "Run Your Business or Build An Organization?" *Harvard Business Review,* Vol. 62, No. 2 (1984), pp. 34-44.

Nicholas, Ian J. "Organizational Climate and Strategic Decision-Making," *Journal of General Management,* Vol. 7, No. 3, pp. 57-71.

Nystrom, Paul C., and William H. Starbuck. "Organizational Facade." *Academy of Management Review,* Vol. 9 (1984), pp. 182-185.

Robbins, Stephen. "The Theory of Organization from a Power-Control Perspective." *California Management Review,* Vol. 25, No. 2 (January, 1983), pp. 67-75.

Schreyögg, Georg. "Contingency and Choice in Organizational Theory." *Organizational Studies,* Vol. 1, No. 4 (1980) pp. 305-326.

Slocum, John W., Jr., and H. P. Sims, Jr. "A Typology for Integrating Technology, Organization, and Job Design." *Human Relations,* Vol. 33, No. 3 (1980), pp. 193-212.

Smith, H. R. "A Socio-Biological Look at Matrix." *Academy of Management Review,* Vol. 3, No. 4 (October, 1978), pp. 922-926.

Ulrich, David, and Jay B. Barney. "Perspectives in Organizations: Resource Dependence, Efficiency and Population." *Academy of Management Review,* Vol. 9, No. 3 (1984), pp. 471-481.

Van de Ven, A. H. "A Framework for Organizational Assessment." *Academy of Management Review,* Vol. 1, No. 1 (1976), pp. 64-78.

VanFleet, David D. "Span of Management Research and Issues." *Academy of Management Journal,* Vol. 26, No. 3 (September, 1983), pp. 546-552.

Woodman, Richard W., and D. C. King. "Organizational Climate: Science or Folklore?" *Academy of Management Review,* Vol. 3, No. 4 (October, 1978), pp. 816-826.

Woodward, Joan. *Industrial Organization: Theory and Practice.* London: Oxford University Press, 1965.

Chapter 13

Organization Analysis and Change

The need for organization change is developed further by Lifson, who maintains that organizational health is dependent upon a respect for, analysis of, and willingness to engage in organization change. It is a truism throughout the world, including the United States, that inertia to strategic and structural changes has sapped the strength of whole industries. Twenty years of easy management such as the United States steel industry experienced between 1955 and 1975 allowed competitors from abroad to build strength and develop superior capabilities.

Greiner examines the process of change itself. An understanding of some sequence of actions is needed to engender change. Often this process of change cannot be carried out successfully within the organization. Rather, an outside "change agent" may be necessary to create the sense of danger in the realization of the need to change.

Hendrick provides us with a method of organization analysis that is useful for identifying the problem. He advocates a self-directed approach to redesign, although this is not a necessary outgrowth of the analytic source of information that his method develops. This report is useful in another way in that it gets right down to undebatable figures that provide a common basis for determining how the organization is to proceed. In the final article Burgelman reviews a function not usually appearing on the organizational charts of a great number of companies—venturing. If it were to appear, it would probably occur in research and development or engineering. But venturing is more than that. Renewal of the firm is a never-ending activity. Provision for renewal in the organization is important. Change in the organization depends upon changes in the firm and its procedures. Thus, recognition of the venturing activity is undertaken at this point.

43 • ADAPTATION: A KEY TO ORGANIZATIONAL HEALTH[1]   Thomas B. Lifson[2]

Adaptation—the systematic change of practice as informed by on-going developments in the environment—is one of the keys to organizational health in any society, culture, or industry. We live in a dynamic environment and there's no question that those who fail to change become former leaders and suffer the fate of followers.

It is my thesis that one of the keys to Japan's economic success has been the cumulative enhancement of the ability of Japanese organizations to adapt—both at an individual firm level and at an industry and indeed societal level. In many respects, this adaptive skill was not chosen as a goal by the Japanese but was, rather, thrust upon them by historical circumstances.

Change is one of the most difficult things for an organization to live with. It involves threats to existing situations, to existing distributions of power, to existing ideas that people are very loathe to relinquish. It is really only the specter of a larger threat that can motivate people to give up the security of their existing practice.

Twice in the last century or so, Japan has faced the need to make drastic changes in the organization of her government, society, and economy. In both cases, the impetus came from America. In the last half of the Nineteenth Century, Commodore Perry set off the events which catapulted Japan from an isolated feudal society to a modern industrial and military power in half a century. And the American victory and occupation forced a rethinking and restructuring that was nearly as sweeping. In both cases, the need to adapt was obvious and inescapable.

Broadly speaking, there are two forms of change. One is adaptation, or piece-by-piece change, where a small change is made, it is observed that other pieces are affected by this change, they then have to change, and so on. It's a slow iterative process.

The second variety of change is often called catastrophic change. I prefer to call it frame change because it involves the simultaneous changing of several variables that create an entirely new framework of operations.

Both forms of change have occurred in Japan. The frame change was literally catastrophic, coming as it did in the wake of military defeats, but the adaptive change has been the more pervasive because it has endured. I would posit that catastrophic changes are faster but much more unpleasant. Our real choice is adaptive change if we wish to improve ourselves and our competitive position.

[1] From *Research Management,* Vol. 27, No. 4 (July-August, 1984), pp. 37–40. Reprinted by permission of *Research Management.*

[2] Thomas B. Lifson, Associate Professor, Harvard University.

I shall now consider the overall management and organizational system in Japan which I believe has been responsible for a very good record of adaptive change. I would debunk the notion that Japanese culture is somehow extraordinarily different from our own or that it accounts for a great part of Japan's success in business and industry. Most of the success of Japanese business can be attributed to good management and good strategy, which is not culture-specific. On the other hand, the context of that managerial and business success includes both culture and institutions. These are anchored in the social environment, which is slow to change but which may indeed be flexible.

One must also recognize that there is no such thing as Japanese management any more than there is such a thing as American management. Companies in Japan differ quite dramatically in their corporate cultures, both between industries and within single industries. Sony is quite different from Matsushita and both are really quite dissimilar from Mitsubishi Electric. These companies have their own histories and their own indigenous corporate cultures.

MEMBERSHIP IS A SOURCE OF REWARD

There *are* some important generalizations about Japanese culture as it affects management, however. One is the difference in terms of individual orientation; that is, orientation toward the individual as the center of society versus the group as the center of society. This is not an absolute distinction but rather a matter of degree. In Japan, people identify themselves when they meet someone primarily by the group or the company in which they are a member. If you are introduced to someone in Japan, the Japanese phrase goes, "I am Mitsubishi's Lifson, not I am Lifson of Mitsubishi or I am Lifson the industrial engineer." The membership comes first and then the individual comes and only after that comes the functional specialization.

Membership is a source of reward in Japan. For example, the ranking of organizations is a very pervasive element of Japanese popular culture. There is a great consciousness of who ranks first along almost any dimension and polls are constantly being taken of this nature—who has the most prestige, who is the most desirable employer, which is the most effective organization, and so on. These rankings are not only pervasive, they're widely shared. There is kind of a snowball or a halo effect that takes place so that a very definite social reward adheres to even a chauffeur or a warehouse worker who works for a large, prestigious company. In other words, membership becomes the reward in and of itself, as well as a part of identity. This reward aspect of membership is enhanced by corporate practices which tend in many ways to deemphasize a hierarchy within the organization and emphasize the common nature of all those who are members of the family, as it were, of the organization.

NO PLACE FOR LEGALISM

Another, and I think perhaps much more important difference that deserves attention, is the place of legalism in the society. Japan, as it exists today, has been influenced to a degree that we often fail to appreciate by Confucian ideas. For the 250 years preceding Japanese intercourse with the rest of the world, when it lived in isolation, the official ideology was a form of Confucianism. One important element of Confucianism is a great suspicion of the process of setting down absolute rules and using them as an inflexible guide to behavior. Rules, regulations and so forth are seen as, at best, a single source of information which must be interpreted with great care by leaders who are, most of all, informed by a kind of a humanism, an understanding of the nature of the human being and a willingness to adapt the rules and regulations to the situation at hand. Consequently, it often strikes Japanese observers and others coming from a Confucian tradition as quite ridiculous the way in which Americans insist on putting everything into a contract and specifying down to the last comma, what should take place and even more ridiculously, when some new situation develops, litigating it quite torturously and interpreting these rather artificial and formal regulations or documents as if they could comprehend the complexity and dynamism of a real business or social situation. Legalism, in other words, is a simplistic and often inhuman form of regulating the decision making process, according to this philosophy. I think that this tradition has had a very wide-ranging impact on corporate practices today.

One of these practices is the use of formal financial planning devices such as internal rates of return or return on equity for research budgeting and resource allocation. In my consulting practice with Japanese firms, I have found a great many of them are quite sophisticated about applying these tools, but I've also found a rather sophisticated suspicion of their being the sole device for allocating funds. They are treated by and large as a single source of information that has to be combined with all the other sources of information. The best source is a skilled decision maker's judgment of the people and of the situation. The formal decision making tools which we have developed into a high art at the Harvard Business School, for instance, are treated as rather simplistic, although occasionally useful devices.

HUMAN RESOURCES: FOUNDATION OF THE ENTERPRISE

Everyone is familiar with the vaunted life-time employment which is, in fact, a myth in Japan. What is not a myth, however, is that large corporations make about a 35-year commitment to employ a group of people from their college graduation until their mid-to-late fifties; and to promote them very slowly at first, with very little hierarchical differentiation among the people who entered at the same time. They keep people promoted in lockstep for about the first half of their career and then only gradually promote some faster than others until by the time they reach their late forties and early fifties, a few have ascended to the height of perhaps heading a division or to membership on the board of directors, while the slow runners merely stay in the ranks of middle management.

I consider this a very important set of practices and it is one, incidentally, that is coming under increased criticism in Japan. The key is that this system enables long term relationships to be forged among managers of the same age cohort within and between Japanese corporations. That is, those who enter the firm know that for about the next 15 years they're going to be rising in lockstep and they're going to be dealing with a fairly steady group of people who are their age cohorts in the firm and in the major client firms or subcontracting firms.

This forms what I call a pattern of parallel hierarchies; that is, if you're in the research and development side of the firm, which typically has its own career track, you know that your colleagues in marketing or manufacturing are going to be promoted in lockstep with you, and as you rise in responsibility they are going to rise in responsibility as well. This has the effect of deterring people quite strongly from playing short-term games, from putting all the blame on the other person and looking good in the short run and then moving on.

Related to this is the difficulty of leaving a Japanese corporation. There are those who are pushing a line that once you enter a Japanese firm it's all harmony and everything is wonderful. I see it much more as a competitive world but one in which the competition is constrained by the fact that you really can't jump ship and go on to join an equally prestigious and rewarding organization. Consequently people form long-lasting ties and they know that in the long run they're going to share the same fate. If the company fails in the marketplace it means that their future career prospects are quite poor. If they do a poor job, or if they are poor at human relations, those people they work with will be around to point a finger of blame later on.

I consider this extremely important to understanding corporate behavior in Japanese organizations, and I think it's one reason why you see very high levels of skill in mutual accommodation in all aspects of Japanese corporations, particularly in the relationship between R&D on the one hand and the marketing and manufacturing functions on the other. There is a very strong incentive for these people to work well together and to mutually accommodate one another—to pay attention when one person says, "Hey, that change will have an implication for me, it will force me to do things differently and if I do things differently, it's going to cost me something and in fact it's going to have some implications for either you or for somebody else in the organization." This long term career perspective in the context of parallel hierarchies forces people to really think about how others are affected by their own actions.

SOCIAL CONTRACTING

This leads to a form of decision making that I call social contracting; that is, a commitment to mutually work out the details of a project as they arise.

Rather than setting down details in an elaborate set of planning documents, a broad goal is adopted. It is understood that goals and ideas will change, that unforeseen things will happen, and that credit and blame will eventually be distributed. This kind of targeted but flexible change process can take place through social contracting. The notion is that you and I must work together, that we must agree to make changes and that some of those changes will be costly to different people in the organization, but those costs must be understood and somehow repaid, and it may not be possible to repay them in the short run. However, the Japanese firms have very long memories, partly because there's very little turnover, partly because people are crammed together in Japanese offices and everybody overhears what everybody else is saying and doing, and partly because Japanese people in general have a very strong orientation toward finding out what everybody else is up to and in comparing notes about who did what. The uncharitable word for this is gossip.

In fact, this relates to a form of cultural or social wisdom that we are not lacking in our society, but which we, for some reason, choose largely to ignore: the distinction between what the Japanese call the *honne*, the real intention or the real plan, and the *tatemae* which is the story for public consumption. This is something that we are aware occurs, but we consider a bad thing, believing that somehow we ought to all be just very sincere and talk about what we really mean. In Japan, it's understood that any social reality has these two natures to it and that it's up to the observer, by talking and observing very carefully, to deduce what the real intentions are, what the *honne* is. The search for this is a managerial obsession in most organizations, and it accounts for a good deal of the gossip and socializing that takes place.

PRODUCT CHAMPIONS CAN EMERGE

This form of social contracting, of informally allocating credit and informally evaluating who has done what, makes it quite possible for informal product champions or innovation champions to emerge in organizations. In other words, it's possible for people who see the necessity for even a very small change—it might be as small as retiming a cycle on a particular piece of machinery—or for something that's very big, to champion and to go out and speak to all those who might be affected by it and to gain their concurrence in making the change; and finally to see the change through to implementation. Such championing takes place at all levels of an organization. It can only take place in an environment in which it's not thought that change must come from the top and that change must be a formal process initiated by documentation. Rather, change must be seen as a process which occurs at all levels and in which credit can be incrementally allocated to the different people, and in which cost can be repaid over a long period of time.

This actually rests on a philosophic presumption which is not any more imbedded in Japanese culture than in our own: that change can come from those who are actually doing things, and ought to in many cases. It's often pointed out that the quality circle techniques were invented in the United States and adapted in Japan. I think that comes from the notion I introduced earlier that changes come out of threat and necessity, and the creation of threat is, I believe, a key to this. That the Japanese had perhaps the historical fortune to be devastated, led to a flexibility of mind and a willingness to look for the tools that work. This is something that has been perfected in Japan, and it's nothing that's alien to our own theories or practice.

Finally, there is an institution that is, again, not invented in Japan but which has been raised to something of an art form there; linking separate firms together, not through a formal process of drawing up contracts as we do in the United States, but through the process of simply agreeing to work together very closely and building ties of various sorts between the corporations. These ties perhaps begin with, and are most influenced by, the personal ties that develop between members of the organizations at all levels, what I earlier called the parallel hierarchies. But they are also reinforced by other forms of ties such as cross ownership of stock, offering debt financing between companies, and by agreeing to share confidential data from the very earliest stages.

This has grown up into an institution that's known in Japanese as the *Keiretsu,* which includes a variety of institutional arrangements but which we most frequently think of as the subcontracting relationship. The very close relationship that exists between large and small firms in Japan enables the Japanese automobile industry, with fewer employees than GM, to out-produce the total American auto industry. This is not purely a matter of superior labor productivity; it's also a matter of judicious subcontracting, of sharing information, plans, and production technology.

One bit of research that I did in Japan was to look at a process industry that had a good many downstream users. I interviewed both technology and marketing managers who were responsible for the relationships with the downstream ''subcontractors'' who were producing the final products and who were buying all of their raw materials from the upstream process industry. I was amazed at the degree of contact that existed between the R&D and the marketing people and their downstream users. They were involved at all levels of these firms. They knew their financial story, and they knew their production technology intimately. When a downstream user came up with a small innovation in terms of the machinery they were using which had an implication for the upstream processor's large scale technology in terms of adapting the product so it could be fabricated more economically, these changes were adapted very, very quickly. There was a tremendous amount of sharing of information that would ordinarily be kept secret between a customer and a supplier in this country, and in fact which might be legally constrained in terms of sharing in this country. In this situation, where the company has the understanding that they work together indefinitely and they will both share in the long term productivity gains that would result, they were unable to implement changes rather rapidly. ·

WHAT THE U.S. CAN LEARN

As we think about what we have to learn from Japan and indeed from elsewhere in the world, I think in a way it's quite our misfortune to have been the undisputed leader of the entire world in technology, productivity, financial resources and natural resources at the end of World War II. It has shaped our thinking and our institutions in profound ways and in ways that are perhaps no longer well adapted to our true situation. We still have a consciousness of the domestic market as being the most important market, we still have a consciousness of "Made in the U.S.A." as meaning the best, although this is beginning to fade rather rapidly. Most especially, we have not developed any kind of institutions, as well as a mentality, toward learning from overseas models.

Rather, the way we have typically incorporated learning from overseas is through immigration. We have benefited tremendously from appropriating to ourselves the best human capital from other parts of the world. I expect this to continue to be one major channel of adaptation. But we still have not developed the institutions to systematically go out and examine the way in which other productive systems work and to look for small, as well as large, lessons that can be learned at home.

But we're beginning to change. I think Japan has done us a tremendous favor by being so successful and by challenging some of our previous assumptions about ourselves, but I think we're also beginning to face up to the reality that we are no longer Number One in every area of endeavor. At the moment we are searching for a magic bullet that will solve all our problems, and this is not the way adaptation works. It's a matter of continually looking, sifting, refining, trying, finding failures and successes, readapting, tracing out the implications, and only at the final stage, incorporating change.

We are critically deficient in many areas, particularly in foreign languages. We have very few skilled managers or researchers who are fluent in foreign languages, not to mention Japanese. There are probably fewer than 1,000 Americans in any field of industrial endeavor who speak any kind of fluent Japanese, and if you look at the upper managerial ranks of major American corporations, there are precious few people who speak Japanese or for that matter many of the European languages well.

It requires a very close examination of the situation as it is, not the situation as it is interpreted, both literally and figuratively, to begin to find the true lessons from abroad. I think most of all we need the efforts of many people, and that includes not just the foreign language speakers but those who are affected by the changes that are brought to their attention in closely and critically monitoring practices and developments overseas. We need a very broad base of examination and a very broad base of personal contact at all levels, and in all functions of an organization, to really begin the process of adaptive change in learning from Japan.

It also may require some fairly heavy thinking about the nature of the institutions to which we have been attached in this country. When we get to the really systematic or frame adaptation level, I think we need to reexamine our labor markets which encourage job hopping and which encourage people to go for short term gains, our antitrust laws, our attachment to legalism and to very formalistic bureaucratic practices; and to our notion of leadership which is that the leader is the one who is the virtuoso, who is the doer, rather than the leader who is the facilitator and who helps others in their activity, the one who gets credit not for what he or she did, but for what he or she facilitated in those that work under him or her.

Moreover, Japan is not a static target, it's a moving target, and the Japanese reality is changing quite rapidly, not only because of its technological and management prowess but because the nature of Japanese society is changing rapidly. The baby boom in Japan was far greater than it was in the United States following World War II, and the lump is moving through the snake of the population age structure so that there is a great surplus now of lower and middle level managers and quite a shortage of entry level people in Japan. This is having profound influences on human resource practices in Japan and they will be changing. Various Japanese industries are maturing, their practices are changing and perhaps most importantly, the follower status of Japan, getting all the easy adaptation gains from examining the practice of the leader, is rapidly diminishing in many industries and forcing Japan to be more innovative on the basis of its internal innovations.

On the other hand, I'm quite optimistic because as we are moving into a follower status in various fields we are beginning to develop the skills of adaptation. We have a great many of the gains to be made on the steep end of this learning curve and we have barely begun to scratch the potential of learning from overseas, of learning through the adaptive method. I believe that therein lies great hope for us both as members of companies and as a society.

44 • PATTERNS OF ORGANIZATION CHANGE[1]

Larry E. Greiner[2]

Today many top managers are attempting to introduce sweeping and basic changes in the behavior and practices of the supervisors and the subordinates throughout their organizations. Whereas only a few years ago the target of organization change was limited to a small work group or a single department, especially at lower levels, the focus is now converging on the organization as a whole, reaching out to include many divisions and levels at once, and even the top managers themselves. There is a critical need at this time to understand better this complex process, especially in terms of which approaches lead to successful changes and which actions fail to achieve the desired results.

REVOLUTIONARY PROCESS

The shifting emphasis from small- to large-scale organization change represents a significant departure from past managerial thinking. For many years, change was regarded more as an evolutionary than a revolutionary process. The evolutionary assumption reflected the view that a change is a product of one minor adjustment after another, fueled by time and subtle environmental forces largely outside the direct control of management. This relatively passive philosophy of managing change is typically expressed in words like these:

> Our company is continuing to benefit from a dynamically expanding market. While our share of the market has remained the same, our sales have increased 15 percent over the past year. In order to handle this increased business, we have added a new marketing vice president and may have to double our sales force in the next two years.

Such an optimistic statement frequently belies an unbounding faith in a beneficient environment. Perhaps this philosophy was adequate in less competitive times, when small patchwork changes, such as replacing a manager here and there, were sufficient to maintain profitability. But now the environments around organizations are changing rapidly and are challenging managements to become far more alert and inventive than they ever were before.

[1] From *Organizational Change and Development* (Homewood, Ill.: Richard D. Irwin and the Dorsey Press, 1970), by Gene W. Dolton, Paul Lawrence, and Larry E. Greiner, pp. 213-228. Reprinted by permission of Richard D. Irwin, Inc.

[2] Larry E. Greiner, Harvard University.

[3] AUTHOR'S NOTE: This article is part of a larger study on organizational development, involving my colleagues Louis B. Barnes and D. Paul Leitch, which is supported by the Division of Research, Harvard Business School.

Management Awakening

In recent years more and more top managements have begun to realize that fragmented changes are seldom effective in stemming the underlying tides of stagnation and complacency that can subtly creep into a profitable and growing organization. While rigid and uncreative attitudes are slow to develop, they are also slow to disappear, even in the face of frequent personnel changes. Most often these signs of decay can be recognized in managerial behavior that (a) is oriented more to the past than to the future, (b) recognizes the obligations of ritual more than the challenges of current problems, and (c) owes allegiance more to department goals than to overall company objectives.

Management's recent awakening to these danger signs has been stimulated largely by the rapidly changing tempo and quality of its environment. Consider:

> Computer technology has narrowed the decision time span.
> Mass communication has heightened public awareness of consumer products.
> New management knowledge and techniques have come into being.
> Technological discoveries have multiplied.
> New world markets have opened up.
> Social drives for equality have intensified.
> Governmental demands and regulations have increased.

As a result, many organizations are currently being challenged to shift, or even reverse, gears in order to survive, let alone prosper.

A number of top managements have come around to adopting a revolutionary attitude toward change, in order to bridge the gap between a dynamic environment and a stagnant organization. They feel that they can no longer sit back and condone organizational self-indulgence, waiting for time to heal all wounds. So, through a number of means, revolutionary attempts are now being made to transform their organizations rapidly by altering the behavior and attitudes of their line and staff personnel at all levels of management. While each organization obviously varies in its approach, the overarching goal seems to be the same: to get everyone psychologically redirected toward solving the problems and challenges of today's business environment. Here, for example, is how one company president describes his current goal for change:

> I've got to get this organization moving, and soon. Many of our managers act as if we were still selling the products that used to be our bread and butter. We're in a different business now, and I'm not sure that they realize it. Somehow we've got to start recognizing our problems, and then become more competent in solving them. This applies to everyone here, including me and the janitor. I'm starting with a massive reorganization which I hope will get us pulling together instead of in 50 separate directions.

Striking Similarities

Although there still are not many studies of organization change, the number is growing; and a survey of them shows that it is already possible to detect some striking similarities running throughout their findings. I shall report some of these similarities, under two headings.

1. *Common approaches* being used to initiate organization change.

2. *Reported results*—what happened in a number of cases of actual organization change.

I shall begin with the approaches, and then attempt to place them within the perspective of what has happened when these approaches were applied. As we shall see, only a few of the approaches used tend to facilitate successful change, but even here we find that each is aided by unplanned forces preceding and following its use. Finally, I shall conclude with some tentative interpretations as to what I think is actually taking place when an organization change occurs.

COMMON APPROACHES

In looking at the various major approaches being used to *introduce* organization change, one is immediately struck by their position along a "power distribution" continuum. At one extreme are those which rely on *unilateral* authority. More toward the middle of the continuum are the *shared* approaches. Finally, at the opposite extreme are the *delegated* approaches.

As we shall see later, the *shared* approaches tend to be emphasized in the more successful organization changes. Just why this is so is an important question we will consider in the concluding section. For now, though, let us gain a clearer picture of the various approaches as they appear most frequently in the literature of organization change.

Unilateral Action

At this extreme on the power distribution continuum, the organization change is implemented through an emphasis on the authority of a man's hierarchical position in the company. Here, the definition and solution to the problem at hand tend to be specified by the upper echelons and directed downward through formal and impersonal control mechanisms. The use of unilateral authority to introduce organization change appears in three forms.

By Decree. This is probably the most commonly used approach, having its roots in centuries of practice within military and government bureaucracies and taking its authority from the formal position of the person introducing the change. It is essentially a "one-way" announcement that is directed downward to the lower levels in the organization. The spirit of the communication reads something like "today we are this way—tomorrow we must be that way."

In its concrete form it may appear as a memorandum, lecture, policy statement, or verbal command. The general nature of the decree approach is impersonal, formal, and task-oriented. It assumes that people are highly rational and best motivated by authoritative directions. Its expectation is that people will comply in their outward behavior and that this compliance will lead to more effective results.

By Replacement. Often resorted to when the decree approach fails, this involves the placement of key persons. It is based on the assumption that organization problems tend to reside in a few strategically located individuals, and that replacing these people will bring about sweeping and basic changes. As in the decree form, this change is usually initiated at the top and directed downward by a high authority figure. At the same time, however, it tends to be somewhat more personal, since particular individuals are singled out for replacement. Nevertheless, it retains much of the formality and explicit concern for task accomplishment that is common to the decree approach. Similarly, it holds no false optimism about the ability of individuals to change their own behavior without clear outside direction.

By Structure. This old familiar change approach is currently receiving much reevaluation by behavioral scientists. In its earlier form, it involved a highly rational approach to the design of formal organization and to the layout of technology. The basic assumption here was that people behaved in close agreement with the structure and technology governing them. However, it tended to have serious drawbacks, since what seemed logical on paper was not necessarily logical for human goals.

Recently attempts have been made to alter the organizational structure in line with what is becoming known about both the logics and nonlogics of human behavior, such as engineering the job to fit the man, on the one hand, or adjusting formal authority to match informal authority, on the other hand. These attempts, however, still rely heavily on mechanisms for change that tend to be relatively formal, impersonal, and located outside the individual. At the same time, however, because of greater concern for the effects of structure on people, they can probably be characterized as more personal, subtle, and less directive than either the decree or replacement approaches.

Sharing of Power

More toward the middle of the power distribution continuum, as noted earlier, are the shared approaches, where authority is still present and used, yet there is also interaction and sharing of power. This approach to change is utilized in two forms.

By Group Decision Making. Here the problems still tend to be defined unilaterally from above, but lower level groups are usually left free to develop alternative solutions and to choose among them. The main assumption tends to be that individuals develop more commitment to action when they have a voice in the decisions that affect them. The net result is that power is shared between bosses and subordinates, though there is a division of labor between those who define the problems and those who develop the solutions.

By Group Problem Solving. This form emphasizes both the definition and the solution of problems within the context of group discussion. Here power is shared throughout the decision process, but, unlike group decision making, there is an added opportunity for lower level subordinates to define the problem. The assumption underlying this approach is not only that people gain greater commitment from being exposed to a wider decision-making role, but also that they have significant knowledge to contribute to the definition of the problem.

Delegated Authority

At the other extreme from unilateral authority are found the delegated approaches, where almost complete responsibility for defining and acting on problems is turned over to the subordinates. These also appear in two forms.

By Case Discussion. This method focuses more on the acquisition of knowledge and skills than on the solution of specific problems at hand. An authority figure, usually a teacher or boss, uses his power only to guide a general discussion of information describing a problem situation, such as a case or a report of research results. The "teacher" refrains from imposing his own analysis or solutions on the group. Instead, he encourages individual members to arrive at their own insights, and they are left to use them as they see fit. The implicit assumption here is that individuals, through the medium of discussion about concrete situations, will develop general problem-solving skills to aid them in carrying out subsequent individual and organization changes.

By T Group Sessions. These sessions, once conducted mainly in outside courses for representatives of many different organizations, are increasingly being used inside individual companies for effecting change. Usually, they are confined to top management, with the hope that beneficial "spill-over" will result for the rest of the organization. The primary emphasis of the T group tends to be on increasing an individual's self-awareness and sensitivity to group social processes. Compared to the previously discussed approaches, the T group places much less emphasis on the discussion and solution of task-related problems. Instead, the data for discussion are typically the interpersonal actions of individuals in the group; no specific task is assigned to the group.

The basic assumption underlying this approach is that exposure to a structureless situation will release unconscious emotional energies within individuals, which, in turn, will lead to self-analysis, insight, and behavioral change. The authority figure in the group, usually a professional trainer, avoids asserting his own authority in structuring the group. Instead, he often attempts to become an accepted and influential member of the group. Thus, in comparison to the other approaches, much more authority is turned over to the group, from which position it is expected to chart its own course of change in an atmosphere of great informality and highly personal exchanges.

REPORTED RESULTS

As we have seen, each of the major approaches, as well as the various forms within them, rests on certain assumptions about what *should* happen when it is applied to initiate change. Now let us step back and consider what actually *does* happen—before, during, and after a particular approach is introduced.

To discover whether there are certain dimensions of organization change that might stand out against the background of characteristics unique to one company, we conducted a survey of 18 studies of organization change. Specifically, we were looking for the existence of dominant patterns of similarity and/or difference running across all of these studies. As we went along, relevant information was written down and compared with the other studies in regard to (a) the conditions leading up to an attempted change, (b) the manner in which the change was introduced, (c) the critical blocks and/or facilitators encountered during implementation, and (d) the more lasting results which appeared over a period of time.

The survey findings show some intriguing similarities and differences between those studies reporting "successful" change patterns and those disclosing "less successful" changes—i.e., failure to achieve the desired results. The successful changes generally appear as those which:

Spread throughout the organization to include and affect many people.
Produce positive changes in line and staff attitudes.
Prompt people to behave more effectively in solving problems and in relating to others.
Result in improved organization performance.

Significantly, the less successful changes fall short on all of these dimensions.

"Success" Patterns

Using the category breakdown just cited as the baseline for "success," the survey reveals some very distinct patterns in the evolution of change. In all, eight major patterns are identifiable in five studies reporting successful change, and six other success studies show quite similar characteristics, although the information contained in each is somewhat less complete. . . .

Consider:

1. The organization, and especially top management, is under considerable external and internal pressure for improvement long before an explicit

organization change is contemplated. Performance and/or morale are low. Top management seems to be groping for a solution to its problems.

2. A new man, known for his ability to introduce improvements, enters the organization, either as the official head of the organization, or as a consultant who deals directly with the head of the organization.

3. An initial act of the new man is to encourage a reexamination of past practices and current problems within the organization.

4. The head of the organization and his immediate subordinates assume a direct and highly involved role in conducting this reexamination.

5. The new man, with top management support, engages several levels of the organization in collaborative, fact-finding, problem-solving discussions to identify and diagnose current organization problems.

6. The new man provides others with new ideas and methods for developing solutions to problems, again at many levels of the organization.

7. The solutions and decisions are developed, tested, and found creditable for solving problems on a small scale before an attempt is made to widen the scope of change to larger problems and the entire organization.

8. The change effort spreads with each success experience, and as management support grows, it is gradually absorbed permanently into the organization's way of life.

The likely significance of these similarities becomes more apparent when we consider the patterns found in the less successful organization changes. Let us briefly make this contrast before speculating further about why the successful changes seem to unfold as they do.

"Failure" Forms

Apart from their common "failure" to achieve the desired results, the most striking overall characteristic of seven less successful change studies is a singular lack of consistency—not just between studies, but within studies. Where each of the successful changes follow a similar and highly consistent route of one step building on another, the less successful changes are much less orderly. . . .

There are three interesting patterns of inconsistency:

1. The less successful changes begin from a variety of starting points. This is in contrast to the successful changes, which began from a common point—i.e., strong pressure both externally and internally. Only one less successful change, for example, began with outside pressure on the organization; another originated with the hiring of a consultant; and a third started with the presence of internal pressure, but without outside pressure.

2. Another pattern of inconsistency is found in the sequence of change steps. In the successful change patterns, we observe some degree of logical consistency between steps, as each seems to make possible the next. But in the less successful changes, there are wide and seemingly illogical gaps in sequence. One study, for instance, described a big jump from the reaction to outside pressure to the installation of an unskilled newcomer who immediately attempted large-scale changes. In another case, the company lacked the presence of a newcomer to provide new methods and ideas to the organization. A third failed to achieve the cooperation and involvement of top management. And a fourth missed the step of obtaining early successes while experimenting with new change methods.

3. A final pattern of inconsistency is evident in the major approaches used to introduce change. In the successful cases, it seems fairly clear that *shared* approaches are used—i.e., authority figures seek the participation of subordinates in joint decision making. In the less successful attempts, however, the approaches used lie closer to the extreme ends of the power distribution continuum. Thus, in five less successful change studies, a *unilateral* approach (decree, replacement, structural) was used, while in two other studies a *delegated* approach (data discussion, T group) was applied. None of the less successful change studies reported the use of a *shared* approach.

How can we use this lack of consistency in the sequence of change steps and this absence of shared power to explain the less successful change attempts? In the next section, I shall examine in greater depth the successful changes, which, unlike the less successful ones, are marked by a high degree of consistency and the use of shared power. My intent here will be not only to develop a tentative explanation of the more successful changes, but in so doing to explain the less successful attempts within the same framework.

POWER REDISTRIBUTION

Keeping in mind that the survey evidence on which both the successful and the less successful patterns are based is quite limited, I would like to propose a tentative explanatory scheme for viewing the change process as a whole, and also for considering specific managerial action steps within this overall process. The framework for this scheme hinges on two key notions:

1. Successful change depends basically on a *redistribution of power* within the structure of an organization. (By *power,* I mean the locus of formal authority and influence which typically is top management. By *redistribution,* I mean a significant alteration in the traditional practices that the power structure uses in making decisions. I propose that this redistribution move toward the greater use of *shared* power.)
2. Power redistribution occurs through a *developmental process of change*. (This implies that organization change is not a black to white affair occurring overnight through a single causal mechanism. Rather, as we shall see, it involves a number of phases, each containing specific elements and multiple causes that provoke a needed *reaction* from the power structure, which, in turn, sets the stage for the next phase in the process.)

Using the survey evidence from the successful patterns, I have decided the change process into six phases, each of them broken down into the particular stimulus and reaction which appear critical for moving the power structure from one phase to another. Exhibit I represents an abstract view of these two key notions in operations.

Let us now consider how each of these phases and their specific elements make themselves evident in the patterns of successful change, as well as how their absence contributes to the less successful changes.

1. Pressure and Arousal

This initial stage indicates a need to shake the power structure at its very foundation. Until the ground under the top managers begins to shift, it seems unlikely that they will be sufficiently aroused to see the need for change, both in themselves and in the rest of the organization.

The success patterns suggest that strong pressures in areas of top management responsibility are likely to provoke the greatest concern for organization change. These pressures seem to come from two broad sources: (a) serious environmental factors, such as lower sales, stockholder discontent, or competitor breakthroughs; and (b) internal events, such as a union strike, low productivity, high costs, or interdepartmental conflict. These pressures fall into responsibility areas that top managers can readily see as reflecting on their own capability. An excerpt from one successful change study shows how this pressure and arousal process began:

> "Pressure" was the common expression used at all levels. Urgent telephone calls, telegrams, letters and memoranda were being received by the plant from above and cognizant of Plant Y's low performance position, the manager knew that he was, as he put it, "on the spot." [4]

EXHIBIT 1

DYNAMICS OF SUCCESSFUL ORGANIZATION CHANGE

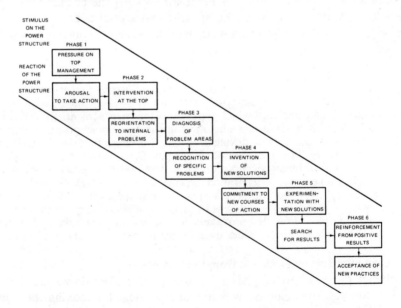

As this example points out, it is probably significant when both environmental and internal pressures exist simultaneously. When only one is

---

[4] Robert H. Guest, *Organizational Change: The Effect of Successful Leadership* (Homewood, Ill.: Dorsey Press, Inc., 1962), p. 18.

present, or when the two are offsetting (e.g., high profits despite low morale), it is easier for top management to excuse the pressure as only temporary or inconsequential. However, when both are present at once, it is easier to see that the organization is not performing effectively.

The presence of severe pressure is not so clearly evident in the less successful changes. In one case, there was internal pressure for more effective working relations between top management and lower levels; yet the company was doing reasonably well from a profit standpoint. In another case, there was environmental pressure for a centralized purchasing system, but little pressure from within for such a change.

2. Intervention and Reorientation

While strong pressure may arouse the power structure, this does not provide automatic assurance that top management will see its problems or take the correct action to solve them. Quite likely, top management, when under severe pressure, may be inclined to rationalize its problems by blaming them on a group other than itself, as "that lousy union" or "that meddling government."

As a result, we find a second stage in the successful change patterns— namely, intervention by an outsider. Important here seems to be the combination of the fact that the newcomer enters at the top of the organization and the fact that he is respected for his skills at improving organization practices. Being a newcomer probably allows him to make a relatively objective appraisal of the organization; entering at the top gives him ready access to those people who make decisions affecting the entire organization; and his being respected is likely to give added weight to his initial comments about the organization.

Thus we find the newcomer in an ideal position to reorient the power structure to its own internal problems. This occurs in the successful changes as the newcomer encourages the top managers to reexamine their past practices and current problems. The effect appears to be one of causing the power structure to suspend, at least temporarily, its traditional habit of presuming beforehand where the "real" problems reside. Otherwise, we would not find top management undertaking the third stage—identifying and diagnosing organizational problems. We can see how an outsider was accomplishing this reorientation in the following comment by the plant manager in one successful change study:

> I didn't like what the consultant told me about our problems being inside the organization instead of outside. But he was an outsider, supposedly an expert at this sort of thing. So maybe he could see our problems better than we could. I asked him what we ought to do, and he said that we should begin to identify our specific problems.[5]

[5] From my unpublished doctoral dissertation, "Organization and Development" (Harvard Business School, June 1965).

Three of the less successful changes missed this step. Two of the three attempted large-scale changes without the assistance of an outsider, while the third relied on an outsider who lacked the necessary expertise for reorienting top management.

3. Diagnosis and Recognition

Here, we find the power structure, from top to bottom, as well as the newcomer, joining in to assemble information and collaborate in seeking the location and causes of problems. This process begins at the top, then moves gradually down through the organizational hierarchy. Most often, this occurs in meetings attended by people from various organization levels.

A *shared* approach to power and change makes itself evident during this stage. Through consulting with subordinates on the nature of problems, the top managers are seen as indicating a willingness to involve others in the decision-making process. Discussion topics, which formerly may have been regarded as taboo, are now treated as legitimate areas for further inquiry. We see the diagnosis and recognition process taking place in this example from one successful change study:

> The manager's role in the first few months, as he saw it, was to ask questions and to find out what ideas for improvement would emerge from the group as a whole. The process of information gathering took several forms, the principal one being face-to-face conversations between the manager and his subordinates, supervisors on the lower levels, hourly workers, and union representatives. Ideas were then listed for the agenda of weekly planning sessions.[6]

The significance of this step seems to go beyond the possible intellectual benefits derived from a thorough diagnosis of organization problems. This is due to the fact that in front of every subordinate there is evidence that (a) top management is willing to change, (b) important problems are being acknowledged and faced up to, and (c) ideas from lower levels are being valued by upper levels.

The less successful changes all seem to avoid this step. For example, on the one hand, those top managements that took a *unilateral* approach seemed to presume ahead of time that they knew what the real problems were and how to fix them. On the other hand, those that took a *delegated* approach tended to abdicate responsibility by turning over authority to lower levels in such a nondirective way that subordinates seemed to question the sincerity and real interest of top management.

4. Invention and Commitment

Once problems are recognized, it is another matter to develop effective solutions and to obtain full commitment for implementing them. Traditional practices and solutions within an organization often maintain a hold that is difficult to shed. The temptation is always there, especially for the power

[6] Guest, *op. cit.*, p. 50.

structure, to apply old solutions to new problems. Thus, a fourth phase—the invention of new and unique solutions which have high commitment from the power structure—seems to be necessary.

The successful changes disclose widespread and intensive searches for creative solutions, with the newcomer again playing an active role. In each instance the newcomer involves the entire management in learning and practicing new forms of behavior which seek to tap and release the creative resources of many people. Again, as in the previous phase, the method for obtaining solutions is based on a *shared* power concept. Here the emphasis is placed on the use of collaboration and participation in developing group solutions to the problems identified in phase 3.

The potency of this model for obtaining both quality decisions and high commitment to action has been demonstrated repeatedly in research. In three successful changes, the model was introduced as a part of the phase 3 diagnosis sessions, with the newcomer either presenting it through his informal comments or subtly conveying it through his own guiding actions as the attention of the group turned to the search for a solution. In two other studies, formal training programs were used to introduce and to help implement the model. For all successful changes, the outcome is essentially the same—a large number of people collaborate to invent solutions that are of their own making and which have their own endorsement.

It is significant that none of the less successful changes reach the fourth stage. Instead, the seeds of failure, sown in the previous phases, grow into instances of serious resistance to change. As a result, top management in such cases falls back, gives up, or regroups for another effort. Because these studies conclude their reports at this stage, we are not able to determine the final outcome of the less successful change attempts.

5. Experimentation and Search

Each of the successful change studies reports a fifth stage—that of "reality testing" before large-scale changes are introduced. In this phase not only the validity of specific decisions made in phase 4, but also the underlying model for making these decisions (*shared* power), falls under careful organization scrutiny. Instead of making only big decisions at the top, a number of small decisions are implemented at all levels of the organization. Further, these decisions tend to be regarded more as experiments than as final, irreversible decisions. People at all organization levels seem to be searching for supporting evidence in their environment—e.g., dollar savings or higher motivation—before judging the relative merits of their actions. This concern is reflected in the comment of a consultant involved in one successful change:

> As might be expected, there was something less than a smooth, unresisted, uncomplicated transition to a new pattern of leadership and organizational activity. Events as they unfolded presented a mixture of successes and failures, frustrations and satisfactions. . . . With considerable apprehension,

the supervisors agreed to go along with any feasible solution the employees might propose.[7]

This atmosphere of tentativeness is understandable when we think of a power structure undergoing change. On the one hand, lower level managers are undoubtedly concerned with whether top management will support their decisions. If lower level managers make decisions that fail, or are subsequently reversed by top levels, then their own future careers may be in jeopardy. Or, on the other hand, if higher level managers, who are held responsible for the survival of the firm, do not see tangible improvements, then they may revert to the status quo or seek other approaches to change.

Thus, with these experimental attempts at change and the accompanying search for signs of payoff, there begins a final stage where people receive the results and react to them.

6. Reinforcement and Acceptance

Each of the studies of successful change reports improvements in organization performance. Furthermore, there are relatively clear indications of strong support for change from all organization levels. Obviously, positive results have a strong reinforcing effect—that is, people are rewarded and encouraged to continue and even expand the changes they are making. We see this expansion effect occurring as more and more problems are identified and a greater number of people participate in the solution of them. Consider this comment by a foreman in one study:

> I've noticed a real difference in the hourly workers. They seem a lot more willing to work, and I can't explain just why it is, but something has happened all right. I suppose it's being treated better. My boss treats me better because he gets treated better. People above me listen to me, and I hope, at least, that I listen to my people below me.[8]

The most significant effect of this phase is probably a greater and more permanent acceptance at all levels of the underlying methods used to bring about the change. In each of the successful changes, the use of *shared* power is more of an institutionalized and continuing practice than just a "one shot" method used to introduce change. With such a reorientation in the decision-making practices of the power structure, it hardly appears likely that these organizations will "slip back" to their previous behavior.

LOOKING AHEAD

What is needed in future changes in organization is less intuition and more consideration of the evidence that is now emerging from studies in this area. While it would be unwise to take too literally each of the major patterns identified in this article (future research will undoubtedly dispel,

[7] S. E. Seashore and D. G. Bowers, *Changing the Structure and Functioning of an Organization* (Ann Arbor: Survey Research Center, University of Michigan, Monograph No. 33, 1963), p. 29.
[8] Guest, *op. cit.*, p. 64.

modify, or elaborate on them), their overall import suggests that it is time to put to bed some of the common myths about organization change. As I see it, there are four positive actions called for.

1. *We must revise our egocentric notions that organization change is heavily dependent on a master blueprint designed and executed in one fell swoop by an omniscient consultant or top manager.*

The patterns identified here clearly indicate that change is the outgrowth of several actions, some planned and some unplanned, each related to the other and occurring over time. The successful changes begin with pressure, which is unplanned from the organization's point of view. Then the more planned stages come into focus as top management initiates a series of events designed to involve lower level people in the problem-solving process. But, even here, there are usually unplanned events as subordinates begin to "talk back" and raise issues that top management probably does not anticipate. Moreover, there are the concluding stages of experiencing success, partly affected by conscious design but just as often due to forces outside the control of the planners.

2. *We too often assume that organization change is for "those people downstairs," who are somehow perceived as less intelligent and less productive than "those upstairs."*

Contrary to this assumption, the success patterns point to the importance of top management seeing itself as part of the organization's problems and becoming actively involved in finding solutions to them. Without the involvement and commitment of top management, it is doubtful that lower levels can see the need for change or, if they do, be willing to take the risks that such change entails.

3. *We need to reduce our fond attachment for both unilateral and delegated approaches to change.*

The *unilateral* approach, although tempting because its procedures are readily accessible to top management, generally serves only to perpetuate the myths and disadvantages of omniscience and downward thinking. On the other hand, the *delegated* approach, while appealing because of its "democratic" connotations, may remove the power structure from direct involvement in a process that calls for its strong guidance and active support.

The findings discussed in this article highlight the use of the more difficult, but perhaps more fruitful, *shared* power approach. As top managers join in to open up their power structures and their organizations to an exchange of influence between upper and lower levels, they may be unleashing new surges of energy and creativity not previously imagined.

4. *There is a need for managers, consultants, skeptics, and researchers to become less parochial in their viewpoints.*

For too long, each of us has acted as if cross-fertilization is unproductive. Much more constructive dialogue and joint effort are needed if we are to understand better and act wisely in terms of the complexities and stakes inherent in the difficult problems of introducing organization change.

45 • ORGANIZATIONAL STRUCTURE: THE SOURCE OF LOW PRODUCTIVITY[1]

Gregory Hendrick[2]

American managers have become enamored of the frequent television documentaries showing Japanese factory workers running to and fro on the plant floor, singing the national anthem as they determinedly boost output per worker each and every hour. The message is clear: Thanks to Japan Inc.'s methods for improving motivation, quality, and productivity, it's taking over the world while American industry stands by in awe.

In reality, it is questionable whether the Japanese model is that good and whether it would make our factories more efficient. It is also questionable whether the Japanese methods should be applied to our white collar work-force, though we hear more and more about using these methods to increase American white collar productivity and to reduce our overhead costs. But that would be no solution for us either; in fact, it would only compound the productivity problems that American business already has.

The solution lies within ourselves. American management must look at itself and at the overstaffed bureaucracies it has created at the administrative and management levels if it is to regain a position of leadership as a productive nation. The key to the problem is the often overlooked basic of *organizational structure*. It is overlooked, if not ignored, because management traditionally doesn't regard its organization as relevant to productivity, whether in the office or in the plant.

But consider: A midwestern manufacturing company in one of the process industries was having difficulties with its engineering staff. Turnover was high even though salaries were the best in the area, and it was increasingly difficult to get the engineers to do important projects competently and on time. Efforts at job enrichment through job design (emphasizing motivation through the work itself) failed, as did other new but ultimately conventional approaches.

Finally, the company began looking at lines of authority and the reporting system and found that its 18 engineers reported to nine different supervisors, several of whom were not engineers themselves. In addition, there were seven layers of management reaching up to the top. For the company president to get an order or directive to his engineering staff, he had to contact eight different people who in turn had to meet with their subordinates, who then had to repeat the process once more to get the message down to the engineers.

[1] From *S.A.M. Advanced Management Journal*, Vol. 47, No. 1 (Winter, 1982), pp. 20–30. Reprinted by permission of the Society for Advancement of Management.
[2] Gregory Hendrick, President, SMC Hendrick Co.

Upon further examination, it was found that the engineers were spending only 20 percent to 25 percent of their time on engineering. The remainder was devoted to work that was secondary to their skills and training or not essential to their mission (for example, attending meetings, filling out reports, and doing menial tasks).

With the problem identified, the corporate structure was reorganized along the lines of the corporation's mission so that the number of middle managers could be reduced to eliminate duplication of management efforts and the engineers freed of secondary work. The result was an almost immediate improvement in productivity and efficiency, a substantial reduction in costs, and a stabilizing of the engineering staff.

IMPORTANCE OF STRUCTURE

As with this company, businesses of every size usually wait until a crisis develops to search deeply for the underlying causes. And when the problem is finally recognized, the usual response is to attempt a reorganization based on conventional methods—redrawing organization charts, realigning the top levels of the organization, and dismissing workers at the lower levels. This approach ignores the mission of the functional areas and the outputs of each entity within the organization.

A NEW APPROACH

Now, however, a new concept about organizational analysis is providing solutions that work. It is different in that, first, it is data-based and quantifiable. Second, it assumes that structure should be designed so that workers can accomplish the tasks and activities of the organization. And, third, it makes possible a comprehensive evaluation of the functions, activities, and utilization of a company's entire management and professional staff, from chief executive officer through first-line supervisors.

A FRESH LOOK AT STRUCTURE

This approach has been applied successfully to more than two hundred companies in a variety of industries.

The first step in implementing it is for management to recognize that the conventional organization chart is obsolete. Most companies' organization charts are hopelessly out of date, confusing, and ineffective as management tools. They are used merely to communicate the structure and do not portray structural strengths and weaknesses. In short, they describe bureaucracy but give management little information on which to act.

The approach advocated here replaces conventional organization charts with statistically based charts that can be used by management as ongoing tools. Called house plots, they provide a clear diagnostic blueprint that a company can use to increase productivity, improve efficiency, and reduce

FIGURE 1

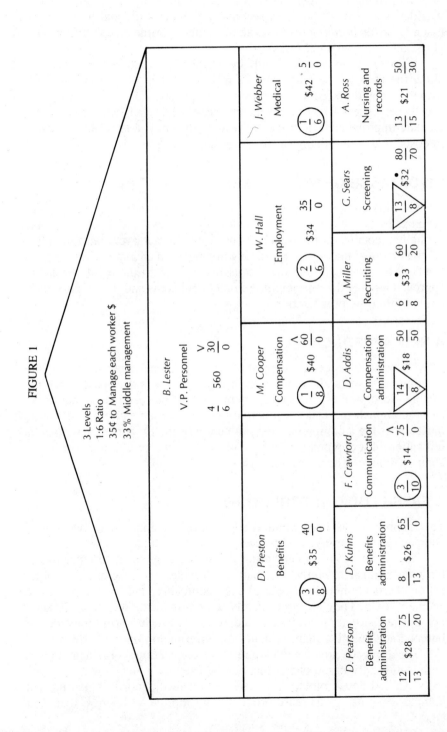

3 Levels
1:6 Ratio
35¢ to Manage each worker $
33% Middle management

overhead costs. Figure 1 shows the reporting relationships and structural data that house plots provide. They show:

- Number of levels.
- Ratios of managers to workers.
- Percent salary compression (the salary differential between a lower and the next higher position is less than a specific percentage—in this case, 25 percent, shown as the dots in the "A. Miller" and "G. Sears" boxes).
- Cost to manage each dollar of worker payroll (manager dollars divided by worker dollars).
- Number of one over ones (managers who supervise only one manager—see "M. Cooper" and "J. Webber").
- Percent middle management (the number of managers between top- and bottom-level management divided by the total number of managers at the company).
- Number of overstretched managers (shown as inverted triangles) and understretched managers (shown as circled fractions). (In both instances, the numerator shows how many are being supervised and the denominator how many could be supervised by this manager.)

Additional information is given for each position within a house plot (see Figure 2).

ANALYSES AND IMPLEMENTATION

Basic to this new approach to organizational structure are three important concepts: (1) Managers should manage (the concept of a full-time manager); (2) a reward system should recognize the contribution of technical input (Many companies make the mistake of promoting their best technicians to managers in order to put them in a higher salary grade. The result? Loss of a good technician and gain of a poor manager); and (3) people are not opposed to change—they are opposed to not participating in the change process.

FIGURE 2

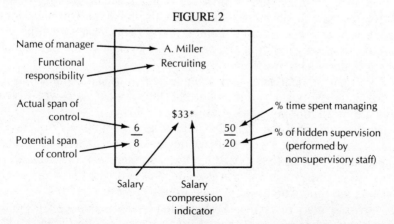

Each of these concepts is taken into account throughout the formal analysis.

The first step is to form a task force of company managers to study the data and develop recommendations—that is, let those to be responsible for managing the company be responsible for organizing it. Each house should have a representative on the task force to serve as its subject-matter expert; others can serve as consultants to aid the expert in developing recommendations for that house.

The data derived from this analysis provide the basis for the organizational analysis, which examines:

- Within each house, groups of adjacent units performing similar or related activities that conceivably could be combined under one functional manager.
- Nonmanagement activities performed by unit managers that can be eliminated, absorbed by workers within the unit, or transferred to other areas of the company.
- The number of managers with limited spans of control (understretched) who can absorb additional workers (actual span is less than 60 percent of span norm).
- Overstretched managers where actual span is greater than can be handled effectively by a full-time manager (actual span is greater than 150 percent of span norm).
- The time spent managing to indicate whether managers are spending more or less time managing than they should relative to the number of workers managed.

Working within houses, when restructuring is indicated, those units identified as most needed are then subject to an in-depth analysis.

In addition to the organizational data provided, this process relies heavily upon the experience, judgement, and knowledge of the people in the organization. For this reason, the approach must be built around key executives who are assigned as a task force of coconsultants to gather and analyze data and make presentations to the managers.

It is also important to note that the evaluation is directed toward the need for managerial positions, not for the incumbents. The management structure is redesigned from the bottom up by considering what the prime or mission work is within the first and second levels and determining management requirements from this.

The organizational analysis is complemented by a work analysis. The data used in the work analysis provide vital statistics that show where payroll dollars are or are not being spent effectively.

Thus a work analysis identifies units with high amounts of secondary and fragmented work that coconsultants review to determine where probable savings exist—that is, they ask which tasks are necessary, is there a better way of organizing work, and can it be done at less cost?

There are three key displays used in this process:

1. *Master activity listing*—Displays the time and dollars expended for every activity by employee, organizational unit, and total organization. In

most companies, about 20 percent of the activities absorb 80 percent of the payroll costs. An 80/20 analysis of the activity costs in each organization, arrayed from high cost to low cost, provides a method of examining those activities representing 80 percent of total expenditures. Thus it is possible to determine if excessive amounts are being expended on a given activity within a house or for the entire company. (See Table 1.)

2. *Cost panel*—Provides a profile of each activity expense grouped by

TABLE 1

ACTIVITY COSTS—HIGH TO LOW

Code		Total Dollars	Percent	Cum Percent	Equiv. People
001	Supervising Direct	919.2	10.3	10.3	63.8
227	Clerical Work	508.7	5.7	16.0	66.9
221	Training Participation	408.5	4.5	20.5	28.1
232	Secretarial/Steno/Typing	391.5	4.3	24.8	43.4
081	Proofing-Encoding	379.8	4.2	29.0	43.8
054	Real Estate Loan Processing	300.0	3.3	32.3	43.3
191	Internal Auditing	265.5	2.9	35.2	16.8
022	Corporate Business-Existing	233.7	2.6	37.8	31.1
095	Inquiries-Internal	217.4	2.4	40.2	28.9
089	Statement Filing	214.0	2.4	42.6	15.3
037	Credit Collection	207.7	2.3	44.9	26.7
035	Credit-Analysis	183.0	2.0	46.9	17.5
003	Supervising-Assist	179.7	2.0	48.9	13.1
302	Commercial Teller	144.6	1.6	50.5	11.9
096	Inquiries-External	139.8	1.5	52.0	11.3
194	Special Projects	138.7	1.5	53.5	16.1
031	Credit Documentation-Nonregulatory	132.2	1.4	54.9	17.7
231	Mail	131.6	1.4	56.3	10.0
012	Planning	131.0	1.4	57.7	14.2
240	Messenger Work	130.2	1.4	59.1	9.9
053	Appraisals	128.2	1.4	60.5	18.2
142	Data Input-on Line	125.0	1.4	61.9	9.1
030	Credit Approvals	117.1	1.3	63.2	14.7
033	Loan Approval	108.1	1.2	64.4	16.9
189	Examination-Credit	106.1	1.1	65.5	11.9
002	Supervising-Indirect	100.0	1.1	66.6	7.0
141	Data Input-Keypunch	97.4	1.0	67.6	14.0
083	Reconciling	93.1	1.0	68.6	13.6
196	Community Relations	85.2	0.9	69.5	11.3
084	Adjustments	78.9	0.8	70.3	8.2
153	Liaison-Internal	78.2	0.8	71.1	8.9
085	Difference Location	74.1	0.8	71.9	7.0
016	Corporate Business-New	74.0	0.8	72.7	11.8
190	General Ledger Control	71.0	0.7	73.4	11.4
124	Security	70.8	0.7	74.1	7.8
090	Recapping	70.2	0.7	74.8	4.5
192	Reporting-Financial	67.6	0.7	75.5	7.1

TABLE 2

COST PANEL

	Description	People Equiv.	People Actual	Total Dollars (Thousands)	F%	S%
073	Marketing Strategies	2	17	89.2	12	21
074	Market Information	1	8	20.5	12	60
075	Market Analysis	4	11	60.8	36	22
076	Selling	4	16	110.8	25	14
077	Products and Services	1	10	33.5	10	58
078	Advertising	1	9	30.6	11	60
079	Marketing Retention	2	11	47.1	18	32
	Marketing	15	82	392.5		
084	Policy/Procedure	2	35	110.1	6	17
085	Functional Product Administra-tion	1	7	25.8	14	
086	Quality Control	12	101	330.3	12	29
087	Collection	0	7	12.0	6	35
088	Leasing	1	6	23.5	17	34
089	Commercial Loan Sales	1	5	30.2	20	100
090	Product Accounting and Admin-istration	1	8	16.3	12	100
091	Branch Inquiries	16	122	330.4	13	19
092	Customer Inquiries	6	49	89.1	12	82
093	Home Relocation	2	8	39.1	25	
094	Commercial Loan Administration	1	12	30.4	8	100
095	Commercial Loan Underwriting	1	12	20.6	8	100
	Product Services	44	372	1,057.8		
	Marketing and Product Services	59	454	1,450.3		

F% = fragmentation percentage (equivalent number of people divided by actual number of people).
S% = percent secondary work.

subfunction companywide, the full-time equivalent number of employees, and the total number of employees who perform the activity. (See Table 2.)

3. *Misplaced work display*—Exhibits in a matrix format the dollars expended for each activity within each major organizational area. These are also totaled by subfunction to show the functional costs by organizational groupings. With this information, we can determine if work is being performed by the most appropriate responsibility area. (See Table 3.)

In actual studies, it is not unusual to find that the ratio of managers to workers has worsened to the point where there is one for every three or four workers. But probably the greatest impact on productivity and a major factor that has contributed to inflation in the United States is the amount of secondary or nonessential work being performed by corporations. Some of this work is due to government regulations, but most of it has come from the bureaucracies that have been built up in organizations over time.

TABLE 3

MISPLACED WORK

Activity Chart	Chairman	Information Service	Administrative Service	Personnel	Premises	Finance and Commerce Audit	Controller	Investment Service	Trust Service	Operations
						Planning				
011 Tax Planning							8.4			
012 Tax Accounting							11.9	1.4	1.8	
013 Cost Studies	25.0	23.4	3.2		4.1	3.8		3.7	19.4	2.0
014 Insurance							7.1			
015 Planning-Operational	17.4		3.2	3.7	3.2	1.8			7.7	9.8
016 Profit Planning	9.4	2.7	2.1	4.6	1.2			3.2	10.6	10.1
017 Profit Plan-Corporate	15.9		.9	12.6	1.2					
018 Financial Modelling	3.0						20.8			
Subfunction Totals	70.6	26.1	10.0	20.9	9.9	5.6	48.3	8.4	39.7	21.9
						Control				
029 Accounts Payable	1.4	6.2	12.4	4.4	29.1		15.9	1.7	4.9	12.9
030 Expense Processing	.7		7.9				4.0	.7	.7	2.9
031 Cash Position							5.3	10.1	5.8	
032 Fund Valuation							14.9	3.1		
033 General Ledger Control			1.2	1.0	7.5		57.2	29.1	11.9	7.7
034 Financial Reporting	2.8		1.9		13.7		112.3	83.1	2.5	1.6
035 Regulatory Reporting	3.0			4.0					1.9	
036 MCS Reporting		8.4	.6	3.4			4.2	3.2	14.5	7.9
037 Audit/Scope						7.2				
038 Auditing/Quality Control		1.9	1.4			314.2			10.8	
039 Security		.8	.6		32.9		24.0		1.1	
Subfunction Totals	8.0	17.5	26.2	12.9	83.3	321.4	268.1	130.3	53.7	32.5

Another factor contributing to a decline in productivity is the change in the mix of white collar and blue collar workers. The increase in white collar workers has raised the total compensation per hour of labor in this country.

An examination of this condition offers a major opportunity for productivity improvement. If a task performed by an employee earning $30,000 a year is transferred to an employee earning $15,000, the cost is reduced by 50 percent even though the same number of hours and employees are required. In the case of the process engineers cited earlier, it was determined that 60 percent of their activities could be handled effectively by employees with a high school education, thus offering a major opportunity to reduce the cost-per-hour portion of the output of the engineering unit.

CONCLUSION

The problems of declining productivity have numerous causes, but many of them are rooted in a company's structure and the misapplication of outdated principles. If productivity is to be improved, there must be a stated corporate productivity objective that senior management establishes and supports. Secondly, there must be an understanding that senior management, and it alone, is responsible for productivity. Middle managers address utilization of workers. First-line supervisors are responsible for efficiency of workers. But senior managers, by defining organizational structure, are the ones charged with seeing that their companies produce quality products and services at the lowest cost.

The solutions to productivity problems begin when senior management starts to look at itself through the organization structure.

46 • MANAGING THE INTERNAL CORPORATE VENTURING PROCESS[1]

Robert A. Burgelman[2]

Many large established firms currently seem to be trying hard to improve their capacity for managing internal entrepreneurship and new ventures. Companies like Du Pont and General Electric have appointed CEOs with a deep understanding of the innovation process.[3] IBM has generated much interest with its concept of "independent business units."[4] To head its new ventures division, Allied Corporation has attracted the person who ran 3M's new ventures group for many years.[5] These are only some of the better publicized cases.

Most managers in large established firms will probably agree that internal corporate venturing (ICV) is an important avenue for corporate growth and diversification. However, they will also probably observe that it is a hazardous one, and will be ready to give examples of new ventures (and managerial careers) gone for naught.

Systematic research suggests that such apprehension is not unfounded. In a large sample study of firms attempting to diversify through internal development, Ralph Biggadike found that it takes on the average about eight years for a venture to reach profitability, and about ten to twelve years before its ROI equals that of mainstream business activities.[6] He concludes his study with the caveat that new business development is "not an activity for the impatient or for the fainthearted." Norman Fast did a study of firms that had created a separate new venture division to facilitate internally developed ventures.[7] He found that the position of such new venture divisions was precarious. Many of these were short-lived, and most others suffered rather dramatic changes as a result of often erratic changes in the corporate strategy

[2] Robert A. Burgelman, Assistant Professor of Management, Graduate School of Business, Stanford University.

[3] See "DuPont: Seeking a Future in Biosciences," *Business Week*, 24 November 1980, pp. 86–98; "General Electric: The Financial Wizards Switch Back to Technology," *Business Week*, 16 March 1981, pp. 110–114.

[4] See "Meet the New Lean, Mean IBM," *Fortune*, 13 June 1983, pp. 68–82.

[5] "Allied after Bendix: R&D Is the Key," *Business Week*, 12 December 1983, pp. 76–86.

[6] See R. Biggadike, "The Risky Business of Diversification," *Harvard Business Review*, May-June 1979, p. 111.

[7] See N.D. Fast, "The Future of Industrial New Venture Departments," *Industrial Marketing Management* (1979): 264–273.

and/or in their political position. An overview of earlier studies on new ventures is provided by Eric von Hippel, who observed a great diversity of new venture practices.[8] He also identified some key factors associated with the success and failure of new ventures, but did not document how the ICV *process* takes shape.

The purpose of this article is to shed additional light on some of the more deep-rooted problems inherent in the ICV *process* and to suggest recommendations for making a firm's ICV strategy more effective. This article presents a new model capable of capturing the intricacies of managerial activities involved in the ICV process. This model provides a fairly complete picture of the organizational dynamics of the ICV process. By using this new tool, we can identify and discuss key problems and their interrelationships and then suggest some ideas for alleviating, if not eliminating, these deep-rooted problems.

A NEW MODEL OF THE ICV PROCESS

The hazards facing internal corporate ventures are similar in many ways to those confronting new businesses developed by external entrepreneurs. Not surprisingly, the ICV process has typically been conceptualized in terms of a "stages model" which describes the evolution and organization development of a venture as a *separate* new business. Such a model emphasizes the *sequential* aspects of the development process, and focuses on problems within the various stages and on issues pertaining to the transitions between stages. For example, Jay Galbraith has recently proposed a model of new venture development that encompasses five generic stages: (1) proof of principle, prototype; (2) model shop; (3) start-up volume production; (4) natural growth; (5) strategic maneuvering.[9] He discusses the different requirements of these five stages in terms of tasks, people, rewards, processes, structures, and leadership.

Such a stages model is useful for helping managers to organize their experiences and to anticipate problems of fledgling businesses. However, it does not really address the problems of growing a new business *in a corporate context*. Many difficult problems generated and encountered by ICV result from the fact that related strategic activities take place at multiple levels of corporate management. These must be considered *simultaneously* as well as sequentially in order to understand the special problems associated with ICV.

---

[8] See E. von Hippel, "Successful and Failing Internal Corporate Ventures: An Empirical Analysis," *Industrial Marketing Management* (1977): 163–174. Some of the diversity found by von Hippel, however, may be due to a somewhat unclear distinction between new product development and new business development.

[9] See J. R. Galbraith, "The Stages of Growth," *Journal of Business Strategy* 4 (1983) pp. 70–79.

A Process Model of ICV

The work of Joseph Bower and his associates has laid the foundation for a "process model" approach which depicts the simultaneous as well as sequential managerial activities involved in strategic decision making in large complex firms.[10] Recently, I have proposed an extension of this approach that has generated a new model of the ICV process.[11] This new model is based on the findings of an in-depth study of the complete development process of six ICV projects in the context of the new venture division of one large diversified firm. These ICV projects purported to develop new businesses based on new technologies, and constituted radical innovation efforts from the corporation's viewpoint. The Appendix provides a brief description of the methodology used in the study. Figure 1 shows the new model of ICV.

Figure 1 shows the *core* processes of an ICV project and the *overlaying* processes (the corporate context) in which the core processes take shape. The core processes of ICV comprise the activities through which a new

FIGURE 1

KEY AND PERIPHERAL ACTIVITIES IN A PROCESS MODEL OF ICV

	Core Processes		Overlaying Processes	
Levels	Definition	Impetus	Strategic Context	Structural Context
Corporate management	Monitoring	Authorizing	Rationalizing	Structuring
			Selecting	
NVD management	Coaching Stewardship	Strategic building	Organizational championing / Delineating	Negotiating
		Product championing		
Group leader Venture leader	Technical & need linking	Strategic forcing	Gatekeeping Idea generating Bootlegging	Questioning

☐ = Key Activities.

Source: Reprinted from "A Process Model of Internal Corporate Venturing in the Diversified Major Firm" by R.A. Burgelman, published in *Administrative Science Quarterly,* Vol. 28, No. 2, June 1983 by permission of *The Administrative Science Quarterly.* Copyright 1983 Cornell University.

[10] See J. L. Bower, *Managing the Resource Allocation Process* (Boston: Graduate School of Business Administration, Harvard University, 1970).

[11] See R. A. Burgelman, "Managing Innovating Systems: A Study of the Process of Internal Corporate Venturing" (unpublished doctoral dissertation, Columbia University, 1980); R. A. Burgelman, "A Process Model of Internal Corporate Venturing in the Diversified Major Firm," *Administrative Science Quarterly,* June 1983, pp. 223–244.

business becomes defined (definition process) and its development gains momentum in the corporation (impetus process). The overlaying processes comprise the activities through which the current corporate strategy is extended to accommodate the new business thrusts resulting from ICV (strategic context determination), and the activities involved in establishing the administrative mechanisms to implement corporate strategy (structural context determination).

The model shows how each of the processes is constituted by activities of managers at different levels in the organization. Some of these activities were found to be more important for the ICV process than others. These key activities represent new concepts which are useful to provide a more complete description of the complexities of the ICV process. Because they allow us to refer to these complexities in a concise way, they also serve to keep the discussion manageable. The process model shown in Figure 1 is *descriptive*. It does *not* suggest that the pattern of activities is optimal from a managerial viewpoint. In fact, many of the problems discussed below result from this particular pattern that the ICV process seems to take on naturally.

MAJOR PROBLEMS IN THE ICV PROCESS

The process model provides a framework for elucidating four important problem areas observed in my study:

- Vicious circles in the definition process,
- Managerial dilemmas in the impetus process,
- Indeterminateness of the strategic context of ICV development, and
- Perverse selective pressures exerted by the structural context on ICV development.

Table 1 serves as a road map for discussing each of these problem areas.

Vicious Circles in the Definition Process

The ICV projects in my study typically started with opportunistic search activities at the group leader level (first-level supervisor) in the firm's research function. Technical linking activities led to the assembling of external and/or internal pieces of technological knowledge to create solutions for new or known, but unsolved, technical problems. Need linking activities involved the matching of new technical solutions to new or poorly served market needs. Both types of linking activities took place in an iterative fashion. Initiators of ICV projects perceived their initiatives to fall outside of the current strategy of the firm, but felt that there was a good chance they would be included in future strategic development if they proved to be successful.

At the outset, however, project initiators typically encountered resistance and found it difficult to obtain resources from their managers to

TABLE 1

MAJOR PROBLEMS IN THE ICV PROCESS

Levels	Core Processes		Overlaying Processes	
	Definition	Impetus	Strategic Context	Structural Context
Corporate management	Top management lacks capacity to assess merits of specific new venture proposals for corporate development.	Top management relies on purely quantitative growth results to continue support for new venture.	Top management considers ICV as insurance against mainstream business going badly. ICV objectives are ambiguous & shift erratically.	Top management relies on reactive structural changes to deal with problems related to ICV.
NVD management	Middle-level managers in corporate R&D are not capable of coaching ICV project initiators.	Middle-level managers in new business development find it difficult to balance strategic building efforts with efforts to coach venture managers.	Middle level managers struggle to delineate boundaries of new business field. They spend significant amounts of time on political activities to maintain corporate support.	Middle-level managers struggle with unanticipated structural impediments to new venture activities. There is little incentive for star performers to engage in ICV activities.
Group leader Venture leader	Project initiators cannot convincingly demonstrate in advance that resources will be used effectively. They need to engage in scavenging to get resources.	Venture managers find it difficult to balance strategic forcing efforts with efforts to develop administrative framework of emerging ventures.	Project initiators do not have clear idea of which kind of ICV projects will be viable in corporate context. Bootlegging is necessary to get new idea tested.	Venture managers do not have clear idea of what type of performance will be rewarded, except fast growth.

demonstrate the feasibility of their project. Hence, the emergence of *vicious circles;* resources could be obtained if technical feasibility was demonstrated, but such a demonstration required resources. Similar problems arose with efforts to demonstrate commercial feasibility. Even when a technically demonstrated product, process, or system existed, corporate management was often reluctant to start commercialization efforts, because they were unsure about the firm's capabilities to do this effectively.

Product championing activities, which have been well documented in the literature, served to break through these vicious circles.[12] Using bootlegging and scavenging tactics, the successful product champion was able to provide positive information which reassured middle-level management and provided them with a basis for claiming support for ICV projects in their formal plans. As the product initiator of a medical equipment venture explained:

> When we proposed to sell the ANA product by our own selling force, there was a lot of resistance, out of ignorance. Management did numerous studies, had outside consultants on which they spent tens of thousands of dollars; they looked at ZYZ company for a possible partnership. Management was just very unsure about its marketing capability. I proposed to have a test marketing phase with twenty to twenty-five installations in the field. We built our own service group; we pulled ourselves up by the "bootstrap." I guess we had more guts than sense.

Why Does the Problem of Vicious Circles Exist? The process model provides some insight about this by showing the connection between the activities of the different levels of management involved in the definition process (see Table 1). Operational-level managers typically struggled to conceptualize their somewhat nebulous (at least to outsiders) business ideas, which made communication with management difficult. Their proposals often went against conventional corporate wisdom. They could not clearly specify the development path of their projects, and they could not demonstrate in advance that the resources needed would be used effectively in uncharted domains.

Middle-level managers in corporate R&D (where new ventures usually originated) were most concerned about maintaining the integrity of the R&D work environment, which is quite different from a business-oriented work environment. They were comfortable with managing relatively slow-moving exploratory research projects and well-defined development projects. However, they were reluctant to commit significant amounts of resources (especially people) to suddenly fast-moving areas of new development activity that fell outside of the scope of their current plans and that did not yet have demonstrated technical and commercial feasibility. In fact, the middle-level manager often seemed to encourage, not just tolerate, the sub-rosa activities of a project's champion. As one such manager said, "I encourage them to

[12] See D. A. Schon, "Champions for Radical New Inventions," *Harvard Business Review,* March-April 1963, pp. 77–86; E. B. Roberts, "Generating Effective Corporate Innovation," *Technology Review,* October-November 1977, pp. 27–33.

do 'bootleg' research; tell them to come back (for support) when they have results.''

At the corporate level, managers seemed to have a highly reliable frame of reference to evaluate business strategies and resource allocation proposals pertaining to the main lines of the corporation's business. However, their capacity to deal with substantive issues of new business opportunities was limited, and their expectations concerning what could be accomplished in a short time frame were often somewhat unrealistic. Also, ICV proposals competed for scarce top management time. Their relatively small size combined with the relative difficulty in assessing their merit made it at the outset seem uneconomical for top management to allocate much time to them.

The process model shows the lack of articulation between the activities of different levels of management; this may, to a large extent, account for the vicious circles encountered in the definition process.

Managerial Dilemmas in the Impetus Process

Successful efforts at product championing demonstrated that the technical and commercial potential of a new product, process, or system was sufficient to result in a sizeable new business. This, in turn, allowed an ICV project to receive ''venture'' status: to become a quasi-independent, embryonic new business organization with its own budget and general manager. From then on, continued impetus for its development seemed entirely dependent on achieving fast growth in order to convince top management that it could grow to a $50 to $100 million business within a five- to ten-year period.

My findings suggest that this created a *dilemmatic* situation for the venture manager: maximizing growth with the one product, process, or system available versus building the functional capabilities of the embryonic business organization. Similarly, the middle-level manager was confronted with a *dilemmatic* situation: focusing on expanding the scope of the new business versus spending time coaching the (often recalcitrant) venture manager.

Ironically, my study indicates that new product development was likely to be a major problem of new ventures.[13] Lacking the carefully evolved relationships between R&D, engineering, marketing, and manufacturing typical for the mainstream operations of the firm, the venture's new product development schedules tended to be delayed and completed products often showed serious flaws. This was exacerbated by the tendency of the venture's emerging R&D group to isolate itself from the corporate R&D department, partly in order to establish its own ''identity.'' A related, and somewhat disturbing, finding was that new venture managers seemed to become the victims of their own success at maintaining impetus for the venture's development. Here are some examples from my study:

[13] One of the key problems encountered by Exxon Enterprises was precisely the existence of these new product development problems in the entrepreneurial ventures (Qyx, Quip, and Vydec) it had acquired and was trying to integrate. See ''What's Wrong at Exxon Enterprises,'' *Business Week,* 24 August 1981, p. 87.

- In an environmental systems venture, the perceived need to grow very fast led to premature emphasis on commercialization. Instead of working on the technical improvement of the new system, the venture's resources were wasted on (very costly) remedial work on systems already sold. After a quick rise, stagnation set in and the venture collapsed.
- In a medical equipment venture, growth with one new system was very fast and could be sustained. However, after about five years, the new products needed for sustaining the growth rate turned out to be flawed. As one manager in the venture commented: "Every ounce of effort with Dr. S. [the venture manager] was spent on the short run. There was no strategizing. New product development was delayed, was put to corporate R&D. Every year we had doubled in size, but things never got any simpler."

In both cases the venture manager was eventually removed.

How Do These Dilemmas Arise? The process model shows how the strategic situation at each level of management in the impetus process is different, with fast growth being the only shared interest (see Table 1).

At the venture manager level, continued impetus depended on strategic forcing efforts: attaining a significant sales volume and market share position centered on the original product, process, or system within a limited time horizon.[14] To implement a strategy of fast growth, the venture manager attracted generalists who could cover a number of different functional areas reasonably well. Efficiency considerations became increasingly important with the growth of the venture organization and with competitive pressures due to product maturation. New functional managers were brought in to replace the generalists. They emphasized the development of routines, standard operating procedures, and the establishment of an administrative framework for the venture. This, however, was time-consuming and detracted from the all-out efforts to grow fast. Growth concerns tended to win out, and organization building was more or less purposefully neglected.

While the venture manager created a "beachhead" for the new business, the middle-level manager engaged in strategic building efforts to sustain the impetus process. Such efforts involved the conceptualization of a master strategy for the broader new field within which the venture could fit. They also involved the integration of projects existed elsewhere in the corporation, and/or of small firms that could be acquired with the burgeoning venture. These efforts became increasingly important as the strategic forcing activities of the venture manager reached their limit, and major discontinuities in new product development put more stress on the middle-level manager to find supplementary products elsewhere to help maintain the growth rate. At the same time, the administrative problems created by the strategic forcing efforts increasingly required the attention of the venture manager's manager.

---

[14] The need for strategic forcing is consistent with findings suggesting that attaining large market share fast at the cost of early profitability is critical for venture survival. See Biggadike (May-June 1979).

Given the overwhelming importance of growth, however, the coaching activities and organization building were more or less purposefully neglected.

The decision by the corporate-level management to authorize further resource allocations to a new venture was, to a large extent, dependent on the credibility of the managers involved. Credibility, in turn, depended primarily on the quantitative results produced. Corporate management seemed to have somewhat unrealistic expectations about new ventures. They sent strong signals concerning the importance of making an impact on the overall corporate position soon. This, not surprisingly, reinforced the emphasis to achieve growth on the part of the middle and operational levels of management. One manager in a very successful venture said, "Even in the face of the extraordinary growth rate of the ME venture, the questions corporate management raised when they came here concerned our impact on the overall position of GAMMA, rather than the performance of the venture per se."

Indeterminateness of the Strategic Context of ICV

The problems encountered in the core process of ICV are more readily understood when examining the nature of the overlaying processes (the corporate context) within which ICV projects took shape. My findings indicated a high level of indeterminateness in the strategic context of ICV. Strategic guidance on the part of top management was limited to declaring corporate interest in broadly defined fields like "health" or "energy." Also, there seemed to be a tendency for severe oscillations in top management's interest in ICV—a "now we do it, now we don't" approach. It looked very much as if new ventures were viewed by top management as insurance against mainstream business going badly, rather than as corporate objective per se.[15] As one experienced middle-level manager said:

> They are going into new areas because they are not sure that we will be able to stay in the current mainstream businesses. That is also the reason why the time of maturity of a new venture is never right. If current business goes OK, then it is always too early, but when current business is not going too well, then we will just jump into anything!

In other words, corporate management's interest in new ventures seemed to be activated primarily by the expectation of a relatively poor performance record with mainstream business activities—a legacy most top managers want to avoid. Treating ICV as "insurance" against such an undesirable situation, however, implies the unrealistic assumption that new ventures can be developed at will within a relatively short time frame, and plays down the importance of crafting a corporate development strategy in substantive

---

[15] See Entrepreneurial activity used as insurance against environmental turbulence was first documented by R. A. Peterson and D. G. Berger, "Entrepreneurship in Organizations: Evidence from the Popular Music Industry," *Administrative Science Quarterly* 16 (1971): 97–106; R. A. Burgelman, "Corporate Entrepreneurship and Strategic Management: Insights from a Process Study," *Management Science* 29 (1983): 1649–1664.

terms. Lacking an understanding of substantive issues and problems in particular new venture developments, top management is likely to become disenchanted when progress is slower than desired. Perhaps not surprisingly, venture managers in my study seemed to prefer less rather than more top management attention until the strategic context of their activities was more clearly defined.

Why This Indeterminateness? In determining the strategic context (even more than the impetus process), the strategies of the various levels of management showed a lack of articulation with each other. The process model in Table 1 allows us to depict this.

Corporate management's objectives concerning ICV seemed to be ambiguous. Top management did not really know which specific new businesses they wanted until those businesses had taken some concrete form and size, and decisions had to be made about whether to integrate them into the corporate portfolio through a process of retroactive rationalizing. Top management's actual (as opposed to declared) time horizon was typically limited to three to five years, even though new ventures take between eight and twelve years on the average to become mature and profitable.

Middle managers were aware that they had to take advantage of the short-term windows for corporate acceptance. They struggled with delineating the boundaries of a new business field. They were aware that it was only through their strategic building efforts and the concomitant articulation of a master strategy for the ongoing venture initiatives that the new business fields could be concretely delineated and possible new strategic directions determined. This indeterminateness of the strategic context of ICV required middle-level managers to engage in organizational championing activities.[16] Such activities were of a political nature and time-consuming. As one venture manager explained, these activities required an "upward" orientation which is very different form the venture manager's substantive and downward (hands-on) orientation. One person who had been general manager of the new venture division said: "It is always difficult to get endorsement from the management committee for ventures which require significant amounts of resources but where they cannot clearly see what is going to be done with these resources. It is a matter of proportion on the one hand, but it is also a matter of educating the management committee which is very difficult to do."

The middle-level manager also had to spend time working out frictions with the operating system that were created when the strategies of the venture and mainstream businesses interfered with each other. The need for these

---

[16] The importance of the middle-level manager in ICV was already recognized by E. von Hippel (1977). The role of a "manager champion" or "executive champion" has also been discussed by: I. Kusiatin, "The Process and Capacity for Diversification through Internal Development" (unpublished doctoral dissertation, Harvard University, 1976); M. A. Maidique, "Entrepreneurs, Champions, and Technological Innovation,' *Sloan Management Review,* Winter 1980, pp. 59–76.

activities further reduced the amount of time and effort the middle-level manager spent coaching the venture manager.

At the operational level, managers engaged in opportunistic search activities which led to the definition of ICV projects in new areas. These activities were basically independent of the current strategy of the firm. The rate at which mutant ideas were pursued seemed to depend on the amount of slack resources available at the operational level. Many of these autonomous efforts were started as "bootlegged" projects.

Perverse Selective Pressures of the Structural Context

Previous research indicates that reaching high market share fast has survival value for new ventures.[17] Hence, the efforts to grow fast which I found pervading the core processes correspond to the managers' correct assessment of the external strategic situation.

My study, however, suggests that the firm's structural context exerted *perverse selective pressures* to grow fast which exacerbated the external ones. This seemed in part due to the incompleteness of the structural context in relation to the special nature of the ICV process. Establishing a separate new venture division was useful for nurturing and developing new businesses that fell outside of the current corporate strategy. (It was also convenient to have a separate "address" for projects that were "misfits" or "orphans" in the operating divisions.) However, because the managerial work involved in these was very different from that of the mainstream business, the corporate measurement and reward systems were not adequate, and yet they remained in effect, mostly, in the new venture division (NVD).

Another part of the structural context problems resulted from the widely shared perception that the position of the NVD was precarious.[18] This, in turn, created an "it's now or never" attitude on the part of the participants in the NVD, adding to the pressures to grow fast.

How Do These Selective Pressures Arise? Table 1 shows the situation at each of the management levels. Corporate management did not seem to have a clear purpose or strong commitment to new ventures. It seemed that when ICV activities expanded beyond a level that corporate management found opportune to support in light of their assessment of the prospects of mainstream business activities, changes were effected in the structural context to "consolidate" ICV activities. These changes seemed reactive and indicative of the lack of a clear strategy for diversification in the firm. One high-level manager charged with making a number of changes in which the NVD would operate in the future said:

---

[17] See Biggadike (May-June 1979).
[18] See Fast (1979).

To be frank, I don't feel corporate management has a clear idea. Recently, we had a meeting with the management committee, and there are now new directives. Basically, it de-emphasizes diversification for the moment. The emphasis is on consolidation, with the recognition that diversification will be important in the future . . . . The point is that we will not continue in four or five different areas anymore.

At the middle level, the incompleteness of the structural context also manifested itself in the lack of integration between the ICV activities and the mainstream businesses. Middle-level managers of the new venture division experienced resistance from managers in the operating divisions when their activities had the potential to overlap. Ad hoc negotiations and reliance on political savvy substituted for long-term, joint optimization arrangements.[19] This also created the perception that there was not much to gain for middle-level star performers by participating directly in the ICV activities. In addition, the lack of adequate reward systems also made middle-level managers reluctant to remove venture managers in trouble. One middle-level manager talked about the case of a venture manager in trouble who had grown a project from zero to about $30 million in a few years:

When the business reached, say, $10 mmillion, they should have talked to him; have given him a free trip around the world, $50 thousand, and six months off; and then have persuaded him to take on a new assignment. But that's not the way it happened. For almost two years, we knew that there were problems, but no one would touch the problem until it was too late and he had put himself in a real bind. We lost some good people during this period, and we lost an entrepreneur.

At the operational level, managers felt that the only reward available was to become general manager of a sizeable new business in the corporate structure. This "lure of the big office" affected the way in which they searched for new opportunities. One high-level manager observed, "People are looking around to find a program to latch onto, and that could be developed into a demonstration plan. Business research always stops after one week, so to speak."

MAKING THE ICV STRATEGY WORK BETTER

Having identified major problem areas with the help of the process model, we can now propose recommendations for improving the strategic management of ICV. They serve to alleviate, if not eliminate, the problems by making the corporate context more hospitable to ICV. This could allow management to focus more effectively on the problems inherent in the core processes.

There are four "themes" for the recommendations which correspond to the four major problem areas already discussed:

- Facilitating the definition process,

[19] These frictions are discussed in more detail in R. A. Burgelman, "Managing the New Venture Division: Research Findings and Implications for Strategic Management," *Strategic Management Journal*, in press.

- Moderating the impetus process,
- Elaborating the strategic context of ICV, and
- Refining the structural context of ICV.

Each of these themes encompasses more specific action items for management. Table 2 summarizes the various recommendations and their expected effects on the ICV process.

Facilitating the Definition Process

Timely assessment of the true potential of an ICV project remains a difficult problem. This follows from the very nature of such projects: the many uncertainties around the technical and marketing aspects of the new business, and the fact that each case is significantly different from all others. These factors make it difficult to develop standardized evaluation procedures and development programs, without screening to death truly innovative projects.

Managing the definition process effectively poses serious challenges for middle-level managers in the corporate R&D department. They must facilitate the integration of technical and business perspectives, and they must maintain a life line to the technology developed in corporate R&D as the project takes off. As stated earlier, the need for product championing efforts, if excessive, may cut that life line early on and lead to severe discontinuities in new product development after the project has reached the venture stage. The middle-level manager's efforts must facilitate both the product championing efforts and the continued development of the technology base by putting the former in perspective and by making sure that the interface between R&D and businesspeople works smoothly.

Facilitating the Integration of R&D-Business Perspectives. To facilitate the integration of technical and business perspectives, the middle manager must understand the operating logic of both groups, and must avoid getting bogged down in technical details yet have sufficient technical depth to be respected by the R&D people. Such managers must be able to motivate the R&D people to collaborate with the businesspeople toward the formulation of business objectives against which progress can be measured. Formulating adequate business objectives is especially important if corporate management becomes more actively involved in ICV and develops a greater capacity to evaluate the fit of new projects with the corporate development strategy.

Middle-level managers in R&D must be capable of facilitating give-and-take between the two groups in a process of mutual adjustment toward the common goal of advancing the progress of the new business project. It is crucial to create mutual respect between technical and businesspeople. If the R&D manager shows respect for the contribution of the businesspeople, this is likely to affect the attitudes of the other R&D people. Efforts will probably be better integrated if regular meetings are held with both groups to evaluate, as peers, the contribution of different team members.

TABLE 2

RECOMMENDATIONS FOR MAKING ICV STRATEGY WORK BETTER

Levels	Core Processes		Overlaying Processes	
	Definition	Impetus	Strategic Context	Structural Context
Corporate management	ICV proposals are evaluated in light of corporate development strategy. Conscious efforts are made to avoid subjecting them to conventional corporate wisdom.	New venture progress is evaluated in substantive terms by top managers who have experience in organizational championing.	A process is in place for developing long-term corporate development strategy. This strategy takes shape as result of ongoing interactive learning process involving top & middle levels of management.	Managers with successful ICV experience are appointed to top management. Top management is rewarded financially & symbolically for long-term corporate development success.
NVD management	Middle-level managers in corporate R&D are selected who have both technical depth & business knowledge necessary to determine minimum amount of resources for project, & who can coach star players.	Middle-level managers are responsible for use & development of venture managers as scarce resources of corporation, & they facilitate intrafirm project transfers if new business strategy warrants it.	Substantive interaction between corporate & middle-level management leads to clarifying merits of new business field in light of corporate development strategy.	Star performers at middle level are attracted to ICV activities. Collaboration of mainstream middle level with ICV activities is rewarded. Integrating mechanisms can easily be mobilized.
Group leader Venture leader	Project initiators are encouraged to integrate technical & business perspectives. They are provided access to resources. Project initiators can be rewarded by means other than promotion to venture manager.	Venture managers are responsible for developing functional capabilities of emerging venture organizations, & for codification of what has been learned in terms of required functional capabilities while pursuing new business opportunity.	Slack resources determine level of emergence of mutant ideas. Existence of substantive corporate development strategy provides preliminary self-selection of mutant ideas.	A wide array of venture structures & supporting measurement & reward systems clarifies expected performance for ICV personnel.

The Middle Manager as Coach. Such meetings also provide a vehicle to better coach the product champion, who is really the motor of the ICV project in this stage of development. There are some similarities between this role and that of the star player on a sports team. Product champions are often viewed in either/or terms: either they can do their thing and chances are the project will succeed (although there may be discontinuities and not fully exploited ancillary opportunities), or we harness them but they will not play.

A more balanced approach is for the middle-level manager to use a process that recognizes the product champion as the star player, but that, at times, challenges him or her to maintain breadth by having to respond to queries:

- How is the team benefiting more from this particular action than from others that the team may think to be important?
- How will the continuity of the team's efforts be preserved?
- What will the next step be?

To support this approach, the middle manager should be able to reward team members differently. This, of course, refers back to the determination of the structural context, and reemphasizes the importance of recognizing, at the corporate level, that different reward systems are necessary for different business activities.

Moderating the Impetus Process

The recommendations for improving the corporate context (the overlaying processes) of ICV, have implications for the way in which the impetus process is allowed to take shape. Corporate management should expect the middle-level managers to think and act as corporate strategists and the operational-level managers to view themselves as organization builders.

The Middle-Level Managers as Corporate Strategists. Strategy making in new ventures depends, to a very great extent, on the middle-level managers. Because new ventures often intersect with multiple parts of mainstream businesses, middle managers learn what the corporate capabilities and skills—and shortcomings—are, and they learn to articulate new strategies and build new businesses based on new combinations of these capabilities and skills. This, in turn, also creates possibilities to enhance the realization of new operational synergies existing in the firm. Middle-level managers can thus serve as crucial integrating and technology transfer mechanisms in the corporation, and corporate management should expect them to perform this role as they develop a strategy for a new venture.

The Venture Managers as Organization Builders. Pursuing fast growth and the administrative development of the venture simultaneously is a major challenge during the impetus process. This challenge, which exists for any start-up business, is especially treacherous for one in the context of an established firm. This is because managers in ICV typically have less control over the selection of key venture personnel, yet, at the same time, have access to a variety of corporate resources. There seems to be less pressure on the venture manager and the middle-level manager to show progress in building the organization than there is to show growth.

The recommendations concerning measurement and reward systems should encourage the venture manager to balance the two concerns better. The venture manager should have leeway in hiring and firing decisions, but should also be held responsible for the development of new functional capabilities and the administrative framework of the venture. This would reduce the probability of major discontinuities in new product development mentioned earlier. In addition, it would provide the corporation with codified know-how and information which can be transferred to other parts of the firm or to other new ventures, even if the one from which it is derived ultimately fails as a business. Know-how and information, as well as sales and profit, become important outputs of the ICV process.

Often the product champion or venture manager will not have the required capabilities to achieve these additional objectives. The availability of the compensatory rewards and of avenues for recycling the product champion or venture manager would make it possible for middle management to better tackle deteriorating managerial conditions in the new business organization. Furthermore, the availability of a competent replacement (after systematic corporate search) may induce the product champion or venture manager to relinquish his or her position, rather than see the venture go under.

Elaborating the Strategic Context of ICV

Determining the strategic context of ICV is a subtle and somewhat elusive process involving corporate and middle-level managers. More effort should be spent on developing a long-term corporate development strategy explicitly encompassing ICV. At the same time measures should be taken to increase corporate management's capacity to assess venture strategies in substantive terms as well as in terms of projected quantitative results.

The Need for a Corporate Development Strategy. Top management should recognize that ICV is an important source of strategic renewal for the firm and that it is unlikely to work well if treated as insurance against poor mainstream business prospects. ICV should, therefore, be considered an integral and continuous part of the strategy-making process. To dampen the oscillations in corporate support for ICV, top management should create a process for developing an explicit long-term (ten to twelve years) strategy for corporate development, supported by a resource generation and allocation strategy. Both should be based on ongoing efforts to determine the remaining growth opportunities in the current mainstream businesses and the resource levels necessary to exploit them. Given the corporate objectives of growth and profitability, a resource pool should be reserved for activities outside the mainstream business. This pool should not be affected by short-term fluctuations in current mainstream activities. The existence of this pool of "slack" (or perhaps better, "uncommitted") resources would allow top management to affect the rate at which new venture initiatives will emerge (if not their particular content). This approach reflects a broader concept of strategy making than maintaining corporate R&D at a certain percentage of sales.

Substantive Assessment of Venture Strategies. To more effectively determine the strategic context of ICV and to reduce the political emphasis in organizational championing activities, top management should increase their capacity to make substantive assessments of the merits of new ventures for corporate development. Top management should learn to assess better the strategic importance of ICV projects to corporate development and their degree of relatedness to core corporate capabilities. One way to achieve this capacity is to include in top management people with significant experience in new business development. In addition, top management should require middle-level organizational champions to explain how a new field of business would further the corporate development objectives in substantive rather than purely numerical terms and how they expect to create value from the corporate viewpoint with a new business field. Operational-level managers would then be able to assess better which of the possible directions their envisaged projects could take and would be more likely to receive corporate support.

Refining the Structural Context of ICV

Refining the structural context requires corporate management to use the new venture division design in a more deliberate fashion, and to complement the organization design effort with supporting measurement and reward systems.

More Deliberate Use of the New Venture Division Design. Corporate management should develop greater flexibility in structuring the relationships between new venture projects and the corporation. In some instances, greater efforts would seem to be in order to integrate new venture projects directly into the mainstream businesses, rather than transferring them to the NVD because of lack of support in the operating division where they originated. In other cases, projects should be developed using external venture arrangements. Where and how a new venture project is developed should depend on top management's assessment of its strategic importance for the firm, and of the degree to which the required capabilities are related to the firm's core capabilities. Such assessments should be easier to implement by having a wide range of available structures for venture-corporation relationships.[20]

Also, the NVD is a mechanism for decoupling the activities of new ventures and those of mainstream businesses. However, because this decoupling usually cannot be perfect, integrative mechanisms should be established to deal constructively with conflicts that will unavoidably and unpredictably arise. One such mechanism is a "steering committee" involving managers from operating divisions and the NVD.

Finally, top management should facilitate greater acceptance of differences between the management processes of the NVD and the mainstream businesses. This may lead to more careful personnel assignment policies and to greater flexibility in hiring and firing policies in the NVD to reflect the special needs of emerging businesses.

Measurement and Reward Systems in Support of ICV. Perhaps the most difficult aspect concerns how to provide incentives for top management to seriously and continously support ICV as part of corporate strategy making. Corporate history writing might be an effective mechanism to achieve this. This would involve the careful tracing and periodical publication (e.g., a special section in annual reports) of decisions whose positive or negative results may become clear only after ten or more years. Corporate leaders (like political ones) would, presumably, make efforts to preserve their position in corporate history.[21] Another mechanism is to attract "top performers" from the mainstream businesses of the corporation to ICV activities. To do this, at least a few spots on the top management team should always be filled with managers who have had significant experience in new business development. This will also eliminate the perception that NVD participants are not part of the real world and, therefore, have little chance to advance in the corporation as a result of ICV experience.

The measurement and reward systems should be used to alleviate some of the more destructive consequences of the necessary emphasis on fast growth in venture development. This would mean, for instance, rewarding accomplishments in the areas of problem finding, problem solving, and knowhow development. Success in developing the administrative aspects of the emerging venture organization should also be included, as well as effectiveness in managing the interfaces with the operating division.

---

[20] An overview of different forms of corporate venturing is provided in E. B. Roberts, "New Ventures for Corporate Growth," *Harvard Business Review,* July-August 1980, pp. 132–142.

A design framework is suggested in R. A. Burgelman, "Designs for Corporate Entrepreneurship in Established Firms," *California Management Review,* in press.

[21] Some firms seem to have developed the position of corporate historian. See "Historians Discover the Pitfalls of Doing the Story of a Firm," *Wall Street Journal,* 27 December 1983.

Without underestimating the difficulties such a position is likely to hold, one can imagine the possibility of structuring it in such a way that the relevant data would be recorded. Another instance, possibly a board-appointed committee, could periodically interpret these data along the lines suggested.

At the operational level where some managerial failures are virtually unavoidable, top management should create a reasonably foolproof safety net. Product champions at this level should not have to feel that running the business is the only possible reward for getting it started. Systematic search for and screening of potential venture managers should make it easier to provide a successor for the product champion *in time*. Avenues for recycling product champions and venture managers should be developed and/or their reentry into the mainstream businesses facilitated.

Finally, more flexible systems for measuring and rewarding performance should accompany the greater flexibility in structuring the venture-corporate relations mentioned earlier. This would mean greater reliance on negotiation processes between the firm and its entrepreneurial actors. In general, the higher the degree of relatedness (the more dependent the new venture is on the firm's resources) and the lower the expected strategic importance for corporate development, the lower the rewards the internal entrepreneurs would be able to negotiate. As the venture evolves, milestone points could be agreed upon to revise the negotiations. To make such processes symmetrical (and more acceptable to the nonentrepreneurial participants in the organization), the internal entrepreneurs should be required to substitute negotiated for regular membership awards and benefits.[22]

CONCLUSION: NO PANACEAS

This article proposes that managers can make ICV strategy work better if they increase their capacity to conceptualize the managerial activities involved in ICV in process model terms. This is because the process model approach allows the managers involved to think through how their strategic situation relates to the strategic situation relates to the strategic situation of managers at different levels who are simultaneously involved in the process. Understanding the interplay of these different strategic situations allows managers to see the relationships between problems which otherwise remain unanticipated and seemingly disparate. This may help them perform better as *individual* strategists while also enhancing the *corporate* strategy-making process.

Of course, by focusing on the embedded, nested problems and internal organizational dynamics of ICV strategy making, this article has not addressed other important problems. I believe, however, that the vicious circles, managerial dilemmas, indeterminateness of the strategic context, and perverse selective pressures of the structural context are problem areas that have received the least systematic attention.

The recommendations (based on this viewpoint) should result in a somewhat better use of the individual entrepreneurial resources of the corporation,

---

[22] Some companies have developed innovative types of arrangements to structure their relationships with internal entrepreneurs. Other companies have established procedures to help would-be entrepreneurs with their decision to stay with the company or to spin off. Control Data Corporation, for example, has established an "Employee Entrepreneurial Advisory Office."

and, therefore, in an improvement of the corporate entrepreneurial capability. Yet, the implication is not that this process can or should become a planned one, or that the discontinuities associated with the entrepreneurial activity can be avoided. ICV is likely to remain an uncomfortable process for the large complex organization. This is because ICV upsets carefully evolved routines and planning mechanisms, threatens the internal equilibrium of interests, and requires revising a firm's self-image. The success of radical innovations, however, is ultimately dependent on whether they can become institutionalized. This may pose the most important challenge for managers of large established firms in the eighties.

APPENDIX: A FIELD STUDY OF ICV

A qualitative method was chosen as the best way to arrive at an encompassing view of the ICV process.

Research Setting

The research was carried out in one large, diversified, U.S.-based, high technology firm, which I shall refer to as GAMMA. GAMMA had traditionally produced and sold various commodities in large volume, but it had also tried to diversify through the internal development of new products, processes, and systems in order to get closer to the final user or consumer and to catch a greater portion of the total value added in the chain from raw material to end products. During the sixties, diversification efforts were carried out within existing operating divisions, but in the early seventies, the company established a separate new venture division (NVD).

Data Collection

Data were obtained on the functioning of the NVD. The charters of its various departments, the job descriptions of the major positions in the division, the reporting relationships and mechanisms of coordination, and the reward system were studied. Data were also obtained on the relationships between the NVD and the rest of the corporation. In particular, the collaboration between the corporate R&D department and divisional R&D groups were studied. Finally, data were also obtained on the role of the NVD in the implementation of the corporate strategy of unrelated diversification. These data describe the historical evolution of the structural context of ICV development at GAMMA before and during the research period.

The bulk of the data was collected by studying the six major ICV projects in progress at GAMMA at the time of the research. These ranged from a case where the business objectives were still being defined to one where the venture had reached a sales volume of $35 million.

In addition to the participants in the six ICV projects, I interviewed NVD administrators, people from several operating divisions, and one person from corporate management. A total of sixty-one people were interviewed. The interviews were unstructured and took from 1½ to 4½ hours. Tape recordings were not made, but the interviewer took notes in shorthand. The interviewer usually began with an open-ended invitation to discuss work-related activities and then directed the interview toward three major aspects of the ICV development process: the evolution over time of a project, the involvement of different functional groups in the development process, and the involvement of different hierarchical levels in the development process. Respondents were asked to link particular statements they made to statements of other respondents on the same issues or problems and to give examples where appropriate. After completing an interview, the interviewer made a typewritten copy of the conversation. About 435 legal-size pages of typewritten field notes resulted from these interviews.

The research also involved the study of documents. As it might be expected, the ICV project participants relied little on written procedures in their day-to-day working relationships with other participants. One key set of documents, however, was the written corporate long-range plans concerning the NVD and each of the ICV projects. These official descriptions of the evolution of each project between 1973 and 1977 were compared with the interview data.

Finally, occasional behavioral observations were made, for example when other people would call or stop by during an interview or in informal discussions during lunch at the research site. These observations, though not systematic, led to the formulation of new questions for further interviews.

Conceptualization

The field notes were used to write a case history for each of the venture projects which put together the data obtained from all participants on each of the three major aspects of venture development. The comparative analysis of the six ICV cases allowed the construction of a stages model that described the sequence of stages and their key activities. The process model results from combining the analysis at the project level with the data obtained at the corporate level.

BIBLIOGRAPHY, CHAPTER 13

Bohlander, George W. "Implementing Quality-of-Work Programs: Recognizing the Barriers." *MSU Business Topics,* Vol. 27, No. 2 (Spring, 1979), pp. 33-40.

Brooker, W. M. A. "The Content and Process of Adaptive Change." *Advanced Management Journal,* Vol. 30, No. 2 (April, 1965), pp. 21-24.

Byrd, Richard E. "Developmental Stages in Organizations: As the Twig is Bent, So Grows the Tree." *Personnel* (March-April, 1982), pp. 12-25.

Conner, Daryl R., and Robert W. Patterson. "Building Commitment to Organizational Change." *Training and Development Journal* (April 1982), pp. 18-30.

Crockett, W. J. "For Those Who Want to Take Organizational Development Seriously." *Management Review,* Vol. 62, No. 6 (1973), pp. 13-19.

Dettleback, W., and P. Kraft, "Organization Change through Job Enrichment." *Training and Development Journal,* Vol. 25, No. 8 (August, 1971), pp. 2-6.

Gaertner, Gregory H., Karen N. Gaertner, and David M. Akinnusi. "Environment, Strategy, and the Implementation of Administrative Change: The Case of Civil Service Reform." *Academy of Management Journal,* Vol. 27, No. 3 (1984), pp. 525-543.

Guest, Robert H. "Quality of Work Life—Learning from Tarrytown." *Harvard Business Review,* Vol. 57, No. 4 (July-August, 1979), pp. 76-87.

Kirton, Michael. "Adaptors and Innovators in Organizations." *Human Relations,* Vol. 33, No. 4 (1980), pp. 213-224.

Lindgren, N. "Organizational Change Has to Come through Individual Change." *Innovation,* Vol. 23 (1971), pp. 36-43.

Louis, Meryl R., Barry Z. Posner, and Gary N. Powell. "The Availability and Helpfulness of Socialization Practices." *Personnel Psychology,* Vol. 36 (1983), pp. 857-866.

Miller, Danny, and Peter H. Friesen. "Structural Change and Performance: Quantum versus Piecemeal—Incremental Approaches." *Academy of Management Journal,* Vol. 25, No. 4 (1984), pp. 867-892.

Ouchi, William G., and A. M. Jaeger. "Type Z Organization: Stability in the Midst of Mobility." *Academy of Management Review,* Vol. 3, No. 2 (April, 1978), pp. 305-314.

Parke, E. Lauck, and C. Tausky. "The Mythology of Job Enrichment: Self Actualization Revisited." *Personnel,* Vol. 53, No. 5 (September-October, 1975), pp. 12-21.

Pierce, Jon L., and A. L. Delbecq. "Organization Structure, Individual Attitudes and Innovation." *Academy of Management Review,* Vol. 2, No. 1 (January, 1977), pp. 27-37.

Porras, Jerry I., and P. O. Berg. "The Impact of Organization Development." *Academy of Management Review,* Vol. 3, No. 2 (April, 1978), pp. 249-266.

Ramaprasad, Arkalgud. "Revolutionary Change and Strategic Management." *Behavioral Science,* Vol. 27, No. 4 (1982), pp. 387-392.

Rohan, Thomas M. "Making the Leap to New Technology." *Industry Week,* Vol. 217, No. 6, pp. 56-59.

Sayles, Leonard. "The Change Process in Organizations." *Human Organization* (Summer, 1962), pp. 62-67.

Slatter, Stuart St. P. "The Impact of Crisis on Managerial Behavior." *Business Horizons,* Vol. 27, No. 3 (1984), pp. 65-68.

Slocum, John W., Jr., and D. Hellriegel. "Using Organizational Designs to Cope with Change." *Business Horizons,* Vol. 22, No. 6 (December, 1979), pp. 65-76.

Stanislas, Joseph, and Bettie C. Stanislas. "Dealing with Resistance to Change." *Business Horizons,* Vol. 26, No. 4 (July-August, 1983), pp. 74-78.

Watson, Tony J. "Group Ideologies and Organizational Change." *Journal of Management Studies,* Vol. 19, No. 3 (1982), pp. 259-275.

Zmud, Robert W., and A. A. Armenakis. "Understanding the Measurement of Change." *Academy of Management Review,* Vol. 3, No. 3 (July, 1978), pp. 661-669.

Section F

Staffing

The final group of articles concern the organization's need to acquire human resources to carry out the tasks required for achievement of its objectives. We are particularly interested in the managerial resources needed. One cannot just walk down the street and randomly select individuals to fulfill the roles required to manage the enterprise. Managing is not a natural activity that all of us have in abundance. It is even difficult to find persons with a natural and untrained managerial ability that will stand that organization in good stead over many years under varying conditions. Rather, managing is a learned activity, one dependent upon experience, education, or both. Organizations are aggregates of people, fiscal resources, and physical assets. Juggling these disparate resources and their behavior becomes a complex task. The number of managers who can do this well is strictly limited.

To make the best use of the managerial resource, it is important to identify what it is that managers do. In this way we can best estimate what types of persons are likely to be good at it and design the systems that will identify people in the organization who would excel at the specific managerial job. What does it take? And who is likely to be good at it? Since expertise in managing comes from experience and education, we need to maximize the managerial knowledge and skills of persons whom we identify as likely to be superior in this respect. Management development has become big business for a number of universities specializing in management education, because most firms cannot leave the important task of improving managerial skills to chance.

Chapters 14 and 15 are devoted to the staffing function. The roles of identifying and selecting managers and potential managers are covered in Chapter 14, and the additional developmental training of managers or potential managers is discussed in Chapter 15.

Having studied these reports, we have taken a first step in immersing ourselves in the tasks of the manager. In many ways, an understanding of the principles discussed in this book merely introduces us to the complexities of managing. Many persons will seek to extend this knowledge. The bibliographies to the chapters and articles are a good place to start.

Chapter 14

Managing Managers

The purpose of this chapter is to set forth the criteria for identifying and selecting managers together with an explanation of the processes by which these tasks can be accomplished. A number of articles previously considered in this book are relevant to the task of identifying what it is we are looking for when we seek a manager. In Chapter 11, for example, we review the skills and competencies useful for becoming a good leader. Similarly, Chapter 1 deals with the nature of management. These articles not only suggest the nature of management but also imply, at least, the kinds of behaviors sought by persons who aspire to higher level managerial positions.

In the first article Aggarwal criticizes deviations of managerial choices from maximizing the value of the enterprise. He sees the task of management as being vigilant in preventing suboptimal and oblique choices from dominating managerial behavior in the firm. Of course, the future is uncertain and optimality elusive. Yet without incessant attention to optimizing choice on the part of managers, an organization runs higher risks of failure.

The article by Katz is a classic widely employed in managerial education. Katz's description of human, technical, and administrative skills as a basis for managing is quite useful for evaluating our own preparation for managing as well as for helping subordinates or others to prepare themselves.

At some point top management will want to look at its cadre of managerial personnel in order to assess its present capabilities and its potential for the future. In their discussion of the career plateau, Terence, Stoner, and Warren provide a truly useful framework for assessing the state and status of managers' competencies and suggest what should be done with each status category.

In the final article Meyer reviews performance appraisal as a basis for identifying individual and group strengths and weaknesses. This appraisal is most useful in terms of applying the results to the manager's present job assignment rather than to some hypothetical position the person may have in the future. Other than reassignment, the appraisal points to what development could be undertaken to improve results.

47 • MANAGER, MANAGE THYSELF![1]

Sumer C. Aggarwal[2]

Politicians, journalists, academicians, and corporate managers all give their particular prescriptions for reversing economic decline, but few of their ideas address managerial causes for losses in productivity. In my various contacts with government and corporate managers, I have found repeatedly that these managers know pretty well what causes such losses in their respective organizations. But they are not willing to tell publicly what they know because it concerns them and their colleagues.

I shall explain that (1) the selfish attitudes and greed of the managers are the main roadblocks to economic recovery, and (2) the large number of overhead managers and their support staffs represent the largest single cause of economic decline.

UNREALISTIC EXPECTATIONS AND GREED

During the early fifties, a middle manager in a U.S. corporation was getting a salary of $6,000-$7,000; a mechanic made about $2.00 per hour; an office worker $1.00 per hour; and a construction worker nearly $2.50 per hour. In comparison to that, during 1981 a middle manager made $50,000 to $60,000, whereas the mechanic made about $10 per hour, an office worker $5 per hour, and a construction worker $18 per hour.[3] This means that during the last thirty years, the managerial salaries have gone up by about eight times, whereas the workers' wages have increased by about five times. In addition the benefits and perquisites now available to managers have increased by a much higher proportion than the benefits available to lower-level employees. The rate of these increases has been much higher for top corporate managers. During these thirty years, as professional managers gained more and more control of corporations, they rewarded themselves with a larger and larger share of the profits. As the percentage share of profits going to managers increased, the share going to investors and employees decreased. This is nothing but the sheer greed of the managerial class.

As managers were expanding their share, the unions, office employees, service workers, and retailers also expected larger rewards. Expectations rose constantly during these three decades of prosperity. The increases in salaries and wages were reasonable as long as productivity gains could

[1] From *Business Horizons*, Vol. 26, No. 1 (January-February, 1983), pp. 25–30. Reprinted by permission of *Business Horizons*.

[2] Sumer C. Aggarwal, Professor of Management Science and Operations Management, The Pennsylvania State University.

[3] *Pennsylvania Business Survey*, (University Park, Pa.: The College of Business Administration, The Pennsylvania State University, 1950, 1981).

support these extra costs. However, with rising expectations, work content and output of most groups in the work force was decreasing because technological advances were constantly transferring work from humans to machinery. This resulted in a decreasing workload and a decreasing commitment to work output.

These opposing trends began causing noticeable problems in 1979 when steel companies, auto manufacturers, electronic appliance producers, and others started losing money, layoffs became common, and some plants had to be shut down. Companies blamed excessive government regulations, excessive demands by labor unions, and unfair foreign competition. But little was said about the inertia of managers, their excessive support staffs, or their self-indulgence in personal and political cliques with their suppliers, customers, and colleagues. Corporate staffs have been growing like amoebas in a warm pool. A hundred are doing what was once done by ten, and it seems as if one thousand will soon take the place of the hundred. Exploding staff populations required modern buildings, fancy limousines, jet aircraft, yachts, antiques, and paintings. A sea of paper, corporate meetings, extensive travels, and unnecessary surveys generated by managers filled the need to keep everyone busy. Hardly anybody cared about costs; everybody was having too much fun. The spectacle bolstered managerial reputations and individual egos.

Let me illustrate this type of climate by describing the confusing but comfortable situation in a large plant in central Pennsylvania where I was invited to help with a productivity problem. The plant employs nearly 3,000 persons. Nearly 1,000 are direct-production employees; another 500 look after materials, maintenance, tooling, and so on. The remaining 1,500 are analysts, supervisors, and managers. The plant makes an excellent profit of nearly 23 percent before taxes. The majority of the middle-level and senior managers make from $50,000 to $100,000. Most employees are receiving an average wage or salary which is about $100 per week more than the salaries of employees of any other company within a 50-mile radius of the plant. The managers told me that the employees and management staff expect even higher salaries because they are aware of the higher profit level of the plant. I questioned the managers about the value of several large support staffs (forecasting, scheduling, planning, data processing, and so on). They were not at all sure about what these support services added, but they all thought it was nice to have such extensive staffs.

Regarding productivity, we discussed the plant's recent installation of a huge complex of machinery for producing a specific group of items, at a cost of $15 million. The new complex has replaced an old group of machines. This new complex required only seven persons for operation, compared to thirty-six persons for the old equipment. However, the new complex required eleven additional white-collar workers: planners, data processing personnel, and so on. The net savings in payroll was about $20,000 per month, but the monthly cost of invested capital and capital consumption was estimated to be $324,500. The managers sincerely believed they had increased productivity; in reality, they were spending about $304,500 per month more on the same level of production with no increase in profits. However, the managers were quite comfortable because they thought they could write off the entire $15 million cost during the next three years under President Reagan's Investment Tax Credit Incentive programs. However, discussions revealed that the new complex may not be used at full capacity during the coming years because the demand for its product group is decreasing.

Further, the plant manager recognized that during the last twenty years of his career at this plant, each time some high technology group of machines was added for improving productivity, the demand of the related products/components fell considerably between the time the machines were ordered and the time they became operational. Each time, only the costs went up; both the production efficiency and the profit contribution went down. Each time, management had only the satisfaction of having decreased the output/direct man hours ratio. At this stage, I told the management that they did not have any desire or motivation for increased productivity; during day-long discussions, they had rejected all my suggestions about reductions in overhead and other indirect costs. Just before my departure from the plant, the plant manager and I agreed that only when the Japanese or German competition moved in would managers think seriously about improving productivity. Now the situation is too comfortable for anyone in the plant to accept any changes, let alone cuts in the operating budgets or overheads.

INTOLERABLE OVERHEADS

Gradually, 90 percent of the U.S. working population has moved into non-productive status. Only the remaining 10 percent make goods, grow food, or dig out minerals. Most people agree that the fast-growing numbers of attorneys, accountants, analysts, supervisors, managers, and a host of other ''non-productive'' professionals add little to national productivity. Most organizations allocate anywhere between 30 percent to 70 percent of their total expenditures to overhead functions. The most common types of over-heads may be grouped under the three categories in the accompanying Table.

Most of these overhead costs are not kept in check because these are the favorites of managers. During normal as well as prosperous times, overhead costs keep growing with the help of managers' exotic justifications. It is not uncommon to find that several sections within the same organization are engaged in the same type of nearly equivalent overhead activity. A large portion of the overhead costs results from the irrelevance of the overhead services and their inefficient use.

Underutilization of overhead services or the waste of overhead services is promoted by the kingdom-building practices of various departments or sections of the organizations.

Any time an organization conducts value analysis of its overhead services, it is sure to find that the majority of these services add little to the products/services being generated by it. A few services may have marginal

THE MOST COMMON OVERHEADS

Necessary and Required Overhead Services	Services Whose Tangible Value is Questionable	Popular Overhead Services
Accounting and auditing	Public relations office	Photocopying
Personnel	Corporate lawyers	Telephones
R&D (focused)	Advertisements	Entertainment
Planning and forecasting	In-house newspaper	Travel
Plant engineering	Counseling	Luxury offices and personal
Sales and brand man-agement	Productivity office/ef-ficiency improve-	conference rooms
Corporate offices and general managers	ment office	Personal secretaries
Depreciation of capital facilities	Training	Corporate jets
	Elaborate audio-visual services	Expensive paintings
	Superfluous data pro-cessing services	Antiques

value and often may not be available when needed. For example, the controller's department of a Pennsylvania company was providing certain cost control reports to manufacturing about two months after the completion of each order. The purpose was to educate manufacturing sections about high-cost items. Because these reports were received two months after the fact, the supervisors and foremen did not bother to look at them. By this time, many factors had changed, and they were busy with problems at hand.

Normally, each large corporation wants to employ the best specialist in the scientific fields related to their products and services. In reality, the company's needs may best be served by specialists of average ability because the best specialists are usually more concerned with their professional excellence rather than with adding value to the products and services of their employer. For example, the market researchers of a company in Maryland were planning during August 1980 to promote a declining product, at the same time that the top executive committee was debating about whether to continue with this product at all.

The focus of some of the overhead services is often to please their superiors rather than to serve the goals of the organization. In such an organizational climate, section heads often ignore cost-savings considerations. For example, the manager of the general services section of a company in upstate New York wanted a promotion and a higher salary. He concentrated on pleasing each of the company vice-presidents. He succeeded in expanding his section's budget so that he could provide modern furniture, fancy rugs, paintings, expensive decorations, and a variety of telephone and audio-visual gadgets to each of these vice-presidents. He did get his targeted promotion and a big raise, but about a year later, expenditures on the luxury items were strongly criticized by the comptroller's office in an overall performance review meeting. At this time, most of the vice-presidents agreed that they were misguided by the general services manager. The manager was fired but a large sum of money had already been wasted.

Contrary to all the logic and principles of scientific management, managerial promotions in private companies and government departments alike are dependent upon (1) the number of persons the candidate supervises and (2) the size of the operating budget he or she controls. In normal times, both these factors motivate the managers to add more personnel to their departments and to push for a larger operating budget each year. If some manager attempts to realize substantial savings from his or her budget, the supervisor may suspect either that the manager has been inefficient in the past or has been neglecting certain important functions such as preventive maintenance, training, and R&D.

A large portion of the overhead expenditures may be attributed to the personal preferences of managers and is of a discretionary nature; hence managers are responsible for most of the non-value-adding overheads. A cost-conscious manager should be able to eliminate all such brightwork.

VALUE ANALYSIS FOR SLASHING OVERHEADS

In a great many cases, a sincere and focused value analysis of overhead[4] can result in decreasing overhead costs by 30 to 50 percent. However, thousands of small and unrelated activities constitute overheads, and arbitrary cuts in overhead expenditures can be damaging to the integrated goals of the company. Therefore, much care should be taken in distinguishing between wasteful and valuable overheads. The value analysis of overheads must be jointly conducted by the user-managers and supplier-managers of overhead services. The final cost control decisions must be made by the top management. The estimates of several corporations indicate that the overhead value analysis of an organization employing about 2,000 persons can be completed in about four months.

The value analysis of overheads requires going through four stages in a definite sequence. These are:

Stage 1: Chief executive officer appoints a high-level task force consisting of the most efficient and creative departmental managers. This task force appoints value analysis challenge teams for each of the major overhead functions. Each team includes the section head of the overhead service, the heads of its major user sections, and one or two experts, such as an industrial engineer, a value specialist, a cost accountant, and others. The task force sets the goals in terms of cost reduction percentages for each of the challenge teams. However, no special targets are singled out and no specific overhead services are pin-pointed as possible culprits.

[4] John L. Neuman, "Make Overhead Cuts That Last," *Harvard Business Review,* May-June 1975: 116–126.

Stage 2: Each challenge team identifies the demands for overhead services and asks the users to put a dollar value on the services they receive. The team then challenges the concerned head to justify the value of services supplied by his or her section.

Stage 3: Each challenge team attempts to develop options for cutting or reducing the overhead services under consideration. The team holds several meetings and investigates thoroughly each of the major overhead services under its purview. The team can make use of a typical Options Form (see the accompanying Figure) to facilitate their analysis. The Options Form forces the team members (section heads) to consider all possible means

OPTIONS FORM

Overhead Section						
Overhead Service	Eliminate	Defer	Reduce Quality	Reduce Amount	Reduce Frequency	Substitute
Reports						
1					•	
2			•			
3	•					
4				•		
Analyses						
1						•
2		•				
3	•					
Decisions						
1	•					
2						•
Plans						
1	•				•	
2						•
3				•		
4		•				
5			•			
Recommendations						
1						
2				•		
3	•					
4						
5						
Additional Suggestions						
1						
2						
3						
4						
5						

for reducing or reorganizing overhead services by requiring them to list all the possible options on the form no matter how radical or crazy they may seem. The receivers, who may become quite value conscious if they are made to pay for the services they receive, may put forth the most imaginative and creative options.

Stage 4: The possible cost reductions from individual options proposed by challenge teams may look small, but when hundreds of them are added together, they become significant. The challenge teams can assign rankings or priorities for each of the proposed options. This can be of considerable help to the task force and the top management. Next, all options are reviewed by the task force, which chooses some options from those proposed by all the challenge teams. Then the task force assigns its ranking to the chosen options. Finally, the shortened and combined list of options reaches the top management executive committee, and they decide on cuts, reductions, eliminations, or substitutions. Thus, the final decisions become the shared responsibility of suppliers, receivers, and managers of overhead services. The overhead cuts may involve elimination of some jobs, but any tough and objective management can handle it. The difficulties and risks involved in implementing reductions and cuts are not as great as they often look.

To illustrate how value analysis of overhead works, I give a brief account of three successful cases:

• Value analysis of the purchase function of a manufacturing company indicated that personnel were spending too much time on expediting the 10 percent of the requisitions which allowed less than adequate lead time. Top management decided that the purchasing department would bill the requisitioning department for expediting such rush acquisitions; the requisitioners were to pay out of their operating budgets. Soon afterward, the purchasing department was able to release three of its staff members to other sections.

• Value analysis of the check processing section of a bank showed that the interest money available from the float of the checking accounts was not sufficient to pay for free checking services to the customers. The bank management quickly changed its policy of no minimum balance to a minimum balance of $300 during each calendar month. Otherwise, each customer would have to pay a $2 monthly service charge. The new policy generated enough float that the interest earnings could more than pay for the free checking services.

• In one wholesale distribution center, the workers who filled orders had almost nothing to do on Mondays but worked overtime every Friday because the standing policy was to fill every order by noon Friday. This situation created unnecessary idle time costs and overtime costs. After a value analysis study, the management of the distribution center introduced a system of workload forecasts and flexible scheduling of order fillers. Further, they changed their Friday noon deadline policy to one that allowed an order to be filled within 24 hours after it was received. This way, all the orders received on Fridays could be filled on Mondays, and the problem of drastic fluctuations in workload disappeared.

• • •

Suffice it to say that managers' attitudes, intentions, and motivations are the prime movers that drive the economic health and vigor of a company. Managers need to be objective and conscientious about their personal gains and comforts. They must be able to isolate and eliminate wasteful and non-value-adding overhead functions that provide prestige, power, and ego satisfaction only to them. Given such managers, a company will be more able to avoid its economic decline, low productivity, dwindling profits, and low morale among its employees.

48 • SKILLS OF AN EFFECTIVE ADMINISTRATOR[1]

Robert L. Katz[2]

Although the selection and training of good administrators is widely recognized as one of American industry's most pressing problems, there is surprisingly little agreement among executives or educators on what makes a good administrator. The executive development programs of some of the nation's leading corporations and colleges reflect a tremendous variation in objectives.

At the root of this difference is industry's search for the traits or attributes which will objectively identify the "ideal executive" who is equipped to cope effectively with any problem in any organization. As one observer of American industry recently noted:

> "The assumption that there is an executive type is widely accepted, either openly or implicitly. Yet any executive presumably knows that a company needs all kinds of managers for different levels of jobs. The qualities most needed by a shop superintendent are likely to be quite opposed to those needed by a coordinating vice president of manufacturing. The literature of executive development is loaded with efforts to define the qualities needed by executives, and by themselves these sound quite rational. Few, for instance would dispute the fact that a top manager needs good judgment, the ability to make decisions, the ability to win respect of others, and all the other well-worn phrases any management man could mention. But one has only to look at the successful managers in any company to see how enormously their particular qualities vary from any ideal list of executive virtues."[3]

Yet this quest for the executive stereotype has become so intense that many companies, in concentrating on certain specific traits or qualities, stand in danger of losing sight of their real concern: *what a man can accomplish.*

It is the purpose of this article to suggest what may be a more useful approach to the selection and development of administrators. This approach is based not on what good executives *are* (their innate traits and characteristics), but rather on what they *do* (the kinds of skills which they exhibit in carrying out their jobs effectively). As used here, a *skill* implies an ability which can be developed, not necessarily inborn, and which is manifested in performance, not merely in potential. So the principal criterion of skillfulness must be effective action under varying conditions.

This approach suggests that effective administration rests on *three basic developable skills* which obviate the need for identifying specific

[1] From the *Harvard Business Review* (January-February, 1955), pp. 33-42. Reprinted by permission of the *Harvard Business Review*.

[2] Robert L. Katz, The Amos Tuck School of Business Administration, Dartmouth College, 1955.

[3] Perrin Stryker, "The Growing Pains of Executive Development," *Advanced Management* (August, 1954), p. 15.

traits and which may provide a useful way of looking at and understanding the administrative process. This approach is the outgrowth of firsthand observation of executives at work coupled with study of current field research in administration.

In the sections which follow, an attempt will be made to define and demonstrate what these three skills are; to suggest that the relative importance of the three skills varies with the level of administrative responsibility; to present some of the implications of this variation for selection, training, and promotion of executives; and to propose ways of developing these skills.

THREE-SKILL APPROACH

It is assumed here that an administrator is one who (a) directs the activities of other persons and (b) undertakes the responsibility for achieving certain objectives through these efforts. Within this definition, successful administration appears to rest on three basic skills, which we will call *technical, human, and conceptual.* It would be unrealistic to assert that these skills are not interrelated, yet there may be real merit in examining each one separately, and in developing them independently.

Technical Skill

As used here, technical skill implies an understanding of, and proficiency in, a specific kind of activity, particularly one involving methods, processes, procedures, or techniques. It is relatively easy for us to visualize the technical skill of the surgeon, the musician, the accountant, or the engineer when each is performing his own special function. Technical skill involves specialized knowledge, analytical ability within that specialty, and facility in the use of the tools and techniques of the specific discipline.

Of the three skills described in this article, technical skill is perhaps the most familiar because it is the most concrete, and because, in our age of specialization, it is the skill required of the greatest number of people. Most of our vocational and on-the-job training programs are largely concerned with developing this specialized technical skill.

Human Skill

As used here, human skill is the executive's ability to work effectively as a group member and to build cooperative effort within the team he leads. As *technical* skill is primarily concerned with working with "things" (processes or physical objects), so *human* skill is primarily concerned with working with people. This skill is demonstrated in the way the individual perceives (and recognizes the perceptions of) his superiors, equals, and subordinates, and in the way he behaves subsequently.

The person with highly developed human skill is aware of his own attitudes, assumptions, and beliefs about other individuals and groups; he is able to see the usefulness and limitations of these feelings. By accepting the existence of viewpoints, perceptions, and beliefs which are different from his own, he is skillful in understanding what others really mean by their words and behavior. He is equally skillful in communicating to others, in their own contexts, what he means by *his* behavior.

Such a person works to create an atmosphere of approval and security in which subordinates feel free to express themselves without fear of censure or ridicule, by encouraging them to participate in the planning and carrying out of those things which directly affect them. He is sufficiently sensitive to the needs and motivations of others in his organization so that he can judge the possible reactions to, and outcomes of, various courses of action he may undertake. Having this sensitivity, he is able and willing to *act* in a way which takes these perceptions by others into account.

Real skill in working with others must become a natural, continuous activity, since it involves sensitivity not only at times of decision making but also in the day-by-day behavior of the individual. Human skill cannot be randomly applied, nor can personality traits be put on or removed like an overcoat. Because everything which an executive says and does (or leaves unsaid or undone) has an effect on his associates, his true self will, in time, show through. Thus, to be effective, this skill must be naturally developed and unconsciously, as well as consistently, demonstrated in the individual's every action. It must become an integral part of his whole being.

Because human skill is so vital a part of everything the administrator does, examples of inadequate human skill are easier to describe than are highly skillful performances. Perhaps consideration of an actual situation would serve to clarify what is involved:

> When a new conveyor unit was installed in a shoe factory where workers had previously been free to determine their own work rate, the production manager asked the industrial engineer who had designed the conveyor to serve as foreman, even though a qualified foreman was available. The engineer, who reported directly to the production manager, objected, but under pressure he agreed to take the job "until a suitable foreman could be found," even though this was a job of lower status than his present one. Then the following conversation took place:
>
> *Production Manager:* "I've had a lot of experience with conveyors. I want you to keep this conveyor going at all times except for rest periods, and I want it going at top speed. Get these people thinking in terms of 2 pairs of shoes a minute, 70 dozen a day, 350 dozen pairs a week. They are all experienced operators on their individual jobs, and it's just a matter of getting them to do their jobs in a little different way. I want you to make that base rate of 250 dozen pair a week work!" [Base rate was established at slightly under 75% of the maximum capacity. This base rate was 50% higher than under the old system.]
>
> *Engineer:* "If I'm going to be foreman of the conveyor unit, I want to do things my way. I've worked on conveyors, and I don't agree with you on first getting people used to a conveyor going at top speed. These people have never seen a conveyor. You'll scare them. I'd like to run the conveyor at one-third speed for a couple of weeks and then gradually increase the speed."

"I think we should discuss setting the base rate [production quota before incentive bonus] on a daily basis instead of a weekly basis. [Workers had previously been paid on a daily straight piece work basis.]

"I'd also suggest setting a daily base rate at 45 or 40 dozen pair. You have to set a base rate low enough for them to make. Once they know they can make the rate, they will go after the bonus."

Production Manager: "You do it your way on the speed; but remember it's the results that count. On the base rate, I'm not discussing it with you; I'm telling you to make the 250 dozen pair a week work. I don't want a daily base rate."[4]

Here is a situation in which the production manager was so preoccupied with getting the physical output that he did not pay attention to the people through whom that output had to be achieved. Notice, first, he made the engineer who designed the unit serve as foreman, apparently hoping to force the engineer to justify his design by producing the maximum output. However, the production manager was oblivious to (a) the way the engineer perceived this appointment, as a demotion, and (b) the need for the engineer to be able to control the variables if he was to be held responsible for output. Instead the production manager imposed a production standard and refused any changes in the work situation.

Moreover, although this was a radically new situation for the operators, the production manager expected them to produce immediately at well above their previous output—even though the operators had an unfamiliar production system to cope with, the operators had never worked together as a team before, the operators and their new foreman had never worked together before, and the foreman was not in agreement with the production goals or standards. By ignoring all these human factors, the production manager not only placed the engineer in an extremely difficult operating situation but also, by refusing to allow the engineer to "run his own show," discouraged the very assumption of responsibility he had hoped for in making the appointment.

Under these circumstances, it is easy to understand how the relationship between these two men rapidly deteriorated, and how production, after two months' operation, was at only 125 dozen pairs per week (just 75% of what it had been under the old system.)

Conceptual Skill

As used here, conceptual skill involves the ability to see the enterprise as a whole; it includes recognizing how the various functions of the organization depend on one another, and how changes in any one part affect all the others; and it extends to visualizing the relationship of the individual business to the industry, the community, and the political, social, and economic forces of the nation as a whole. Recognizing these relationships and perceiving the significant elements in any situation, the admin-

[4] From a mimeographed case in the files of the Harvard Business School; copyrighted by the President and Fellows of Harvard College.

istrator should then be able to act in a way which advances the over-all welfare of the total organization.

Hence, the success of any decision depends on the conceptual skill of the people who make the decision and those who put it into action. When, for example, an important change in marketing policy is made, it is critical that the effects on production, control, finance, research, and the people involved be considered. And it remains critical right down to the last executive who must implement the new policy. If each executive recognizes the over-all relationships and significance of the change, he is almost certain to be more effective in administering it. Consequently the chances for succeeding are greatly increased.

Not only does the effective coordination of the various parts of the business depend on the conceptual skill of the administrators involved, but so also does the whole future direction and tone of the organization. The attitudes of a top executive color the whole character of the organization's response and determine the "corporate personality" which distinguishes one company's ways of doing business from another's. These attitudes are a reflection of the administrator's conceptual skill (referred to by some of his "creative ability")—the way he perceives and responds to the direction in which the business should grow, company objectives and policies, and stockholders' and employees' interests.

Conceptual skill, as defined above, is what Chester I. Bernard, former president of the New Jersey Bell Telephone Company, implies when he says: ". . . the essential aspect of the [executive] process is the organization as a whole and the total situation relevant to it."[5] Examples of inadequate conceptual skill are all around us. Here is one instance:

> In a large manufacturing company which had a long tradition of job-shop type operations, primary responsibility for production control has been left to the foremen and other lower-level supervisors. "Village" type operations with small working groups and informal organizations were the rule. A heavy influx of orders following World War II tripled the normal production requirements and severely taxed the whole manufacturing organization. At this point, a new production manager was brought in from the company, and he established a wide range of controls and formalized the entire operating structure.
>
> As long as the boom demand lasted, the employees made every effort to conform with the new procedures and environment. But when demand subsided to prewar levels, serious labor relations problems developed, friction was high among department heads, and the company found itself saddled with a heavy indirect labor cost. Management sought to reinstate its old procedures; it fired the production manager and attempted to give greater authority to the foreman once again. However, during the four years of formalized control, the foremen had grown away from their old practices, many had left the company, and adequate replacements had not been developed. Without strong foreman leadership, the traditional job-shop operations proved costly and inefficient.

In this instance, when the new production controls and formalized organizations were introduced, management did not foresee the con-

[5] *Functions of the Executive* (Cambridge: Harvard University Press, 1948), p. 235.

sequences of this action in the event of a future contraction of business. Later, when conditions changed and it was necessary to pare down operations, management was again unable to recognize the implications of its action and reverted to the old procedures, which, under existing circumstances, were no longer appropriate. This compounded *conceptual* inadequacy left the company at a serious competitive disadvantage.

Because a company's over-all success is dependent on its executives' conceptual skill in establishing and carrying out policy decisions, this skill is the unifying, coordinating ingredient of the administrative process, and of undeniable over-all importance.

RELATIVE IMPORTANCE

We may notice that, in a very real sense, conceptual skill embodies consideration of both the technical and human aspects of the organization. Yet the concept of *skill*, as an ability to translate knowledge into action, should enable one to distinguish between the three skills of performing the technical activities (technical skill), understanding and motivating the individuals and groups (human skill), and coordinating and integrating all the activities and interests of the organization toward a common objective (conceptual skill).

This separation of effective administration into three basic skills is useful primarily for purposes of analysis. In practice, these skills are so closely interrelated that it is difficult to determine where one ends and another begins. However, just because the skills are interrelated does not imply that we cannot get some value from looking at them separately, or by varying their emphasis. In playing golf the action of the hands, waists, hips, shoulders, arms, and head are all interrelated; yet in improving one's swing it is often valuable to work on one of these elements separately. Also, under different playing conditions the relative importance of these elements varies. Similarly, although all three are of importance at every level of administration, the technical, human, and conceptual skills of the administrator vary in relative importance at different levels of responsibility.

At Lower Levels

Technical skill is responsible for many of the great advances of modern industry. It is indispensable to efficient operation. Yet it has greatest importance at the lower levels of administration. As the administrator moves further and further from the actual physical operation, this need for technical skill becomes less important, provided he has skilled subordinates and can help them solve their own problems. At the top, technical skill may be almost nonexistent, and the executive may still be able to perform effectively if his human and conceptual skills are highly developed.

We are all familiar with those "professional managers" who are becoming the prototypes of our modern executive world. These men shift with great ease, and with no apparent loss in effectiveness, from one industry to another. Their human and conceptual skills seem to make up for their unfamiliarity with the new job's technical aspects.

At Every Level

Human skill, the ability to work with others, is essential to effective administration at every level. One recent research study has shown that human skill is of paramount importance at the foreman level, pointing out that the chief function of the foreman as an administrator is to attain collaboration of people in the work group.[6] Another study reinforces this finding and extends it to the middle management group, adding that the administrator should be primarily concerned with facilitating communication in the organization.[7] And still another study, concerned primarily with top management, underscores the need for self-awareness and sensitivity to human relationships by executives at the level.[8] These findings would tend to indicate that human skill is of great importance at every administrative level, but notice the difference in emphasis.

Human skill seems to be most important at lower levels, where the number of direct contacts between administrators and subordinates is greatest. As we go higher and higher in the administrative echelons, the number and frequency of these personal contacts decrease, and the need for human skill becomes proportionately, although probably not absolutely, less. At the same time, conceptual skill becomes increasingly more important with the need for policy decisions and broad-scale action. The human skill of dealing with individuals then becomes subordinate to the conceptual skill of integrating group interests and activities into a coordinated whole.

In fact, a recent research study by Professor Chris Argyris of Yale University has given us the example of an extremely effective plant manager who, although possessing little human skill as defined here, was nonetheless very successful:

> This manager, the head of a largely autonomous division, made his supervisors, through the effects of his strong personality and the "pressure" he applied, highly dependent on him for most of their "rewards, penalties, authority, perpetuation, communication, and identification."
>
> As a result, the supervisors spent much of their time competing with one another for the manager's favor. They told him only the things they thought he wanted to hear, and spent much time trying to find out his desires. They depended on him to set their objectives and to show them how to reach them. Because the manager was inconsistent and unpredictable in his behavior, the supervisors were insecure and continually engaged in interdepartmental squabbles which they tried to keep hidden from the manager.

[6] A. Zaleznik, *Foreman Training in a Growing Enterprise* (Boston: Division of Research, Harvard Business School, 1951).

[7] Harriet O. Ronken and Paul R. Lawrence, *Administering Changes* (Boston: Division of Research, Harvard Business School, 1952).

[8] Edmund P. Learned, David H. Ulrich, and Donald E. Booz, *Executive Action* (Boston: Division of Research, Harvard Business School, 1950).

Clearly, human skill as defined here, was lacking. Yet, by the evaluation of his superiors and by his results in increasing efficiency and raising profits and morale, this manager was exceedingly effective. Professor Argyris suggests that employees in modern industrial organizations tend to have a "built-in" sense of dependence on superiors which capable and alert men can turn to advantage.[9]

In the context of the three-skill approach, it seems that this manager was able to capitalize on this dependence because he recognized the inter-relationships of all the activities under his control, identified himself with the organization, and sublimated the individual interests of his subordinates to *his* (the organization's) interest, set his goals realistically, and showed his subordinates how to reach these goals. This would seem to be an excellent example of a situation in which strong conceptual skill more than compensated for a lack of human skill.

At the Top Level

Conceptual skill, as indicated in the preceding sections, becomes increasingly critical in more responsible executive positions where its effects are maximized and most easily observed. In fact, recent research findings lead to the conclusion that at the top level of administration this conceptual skill becomes the most important ability of all. As Herman W. Steinkraus, president of Bridgeport Brass Company, said:

> "One of the most important lessons which I learned on this job [the presidency] is the importance of coordinating the various departments into an effective team, and, secondly, to recognize the shifting emphasis from time to time of the relative importance of various departments to the business."[10]

It would appear, then, that at lower levels of administrative responsibility, the principal need is for technical and human skills. At higher levels, technical skill becomes relatively less important while the need for conceptual skill increases rapidly. At the top level of an organization, conceptual skill becomes the most important skill of all for successful administration. A chief executive may lack technical or human skills and still be effective if he has subordinates who have strong abilities in these directions. But if his conceptual skill is weak, the success of the whole organization may be jeopardized.

IMPLICATIONS FOR ACTION

This three-skill approach implies that significant benefits may result from redefining the objectives of executive development programs, from reconsidering the placement of executives in organizations, and from revising procedures for testing and selecting prospective executives.

---

[9] *Executive Leadership* (New York: Harper & Brothers, 1953); see also "Leadership Pattern in the Plant," HBR (January-February, 1953), p. 63.

[10] "What Should a President Do?" *Dun's Review* (August, 1951), p. 21.

Executive Development

Many executive development programs may be failing to achieve satisfactory results because of their inability to foster the growth of these administrative skills. Programs which concentrate on the mere imparting of information or the cultivation of a specific trait would seem to be largely unproductive in enhancing the administrative skills of candidates.

A strictly informative program was described to me recently by an officer and director of a large corporation who had been responsible for the executive development activities of his company, as follows:

> "What we try to do is to get our promising young men together with some of our senior executives in regular meetings each month. Then we give the young fellows a chance to ask questions to let them find out about the company's history and how and why we've done things in the past."

It was not surprising that neither the senior executives nor the young men felt this program was improving their administrative abilities.

The futility of pursuing specific traits becomes apparent when we consider the responses of an administrator in a number of different situations. In coping with these varied conditions, he may appear to demonstrate one trait in one instance—e.g., dominance when dealing with subordinates—and the directly opposite trait under another set of circumstances —e.g., submissiveness when dealing with superiors. Yet in each instance he may be acting appropriately to achieve the best results. Which, then, can we identify as a desirable characteristic? Here is a further example of this dilemma:

> A Pacific Coast sales manager had a reputation for decisiveness and positive action. Yet when he was required to name an assistant to understudy his job from among several well-qualified subordinates, he deliberately avoided making a decision. His associates were quick to observe what appeared to be obvious indecisiveness.
>
> But after several months had passed, it became clear that the sales manager had very unobtrusively been giving the various salesmen opportunities to demonstrate their attitudes and feelings. As a result, he was able to identify strong sentiments for one man whose subsequent promotion was enthusiastically accepted by the entire group.

In this instance, the sales manager's skillful performance was improperly interpreted as "indecisiveness." Their concern with irrelevant traits led his associates to overlook the adequacy of his performance. Would it not have been more appropriate to conclude that his human skill in working with others enabled him to adapt effectively to the requirements of a new situation?

Cases such as these would indicate that it is more useful to judge an administrator on the results of his performance than on his apparent traits. Skills are easier to identify than are traits and are less likely to be misinterpreted. Furthermore, skills offer a more directly applicable frame of reference for executive development, since any improvement in an administrator's skills must necessarily result in more effective performance.

Still another danger in many existing executive development programs lies in the unqualified enthusiasm with which some companies and colleges have embraced courses in "human relations." There would seem to be two inherent pitfalls here: (1) Human relations courses might only be imparting information or specific techniques, rather than developing the individual's human skill. (2) Even if individual development does take place, some companies, by placing all of their emphasis on human skill, may be completely overlooking the training requirements of top positions. They may run the risk of producing men with highly developed human skill who lack the conceptual ability to be effective top-level administrators.

It would appear important, then, that the training of a candidate for an administrative position be directed at the development of these skills which are most needed at the level of responsibility for which he is being considered.

Executive Placement

This three-skill concept suggests immediate possibilities for the creating of management teams of individuals with complementary skills. For example, one medium size midwestern distributing organization has as president a man of unusually conceptual ability but extremely limited human skill. However, he has two vice presidents with exceptional human skill. These three men make up an executive committee which has been outstandingly successful, the skills of each member making up for deficiencies of the others. Perhaps the plan of two-man complementary conference leadership proposed by Robert F. Bales, in which the one leader maintains "task leadership" while the other provides "social leadership," might be an example in point.[11]

Executive Selection

In trying to predetermine a prospective candidate's abilities on a job, much use is being made these days of various kinds of testing devices. Executives are being tested for everything from "decisiveness" to "conformity." These tests, as a recent article in *Fortune* points out, have achieved some highly questionable results when applied to performance on the job.[12] Would it not be much more productive to be concerned with skills of doing rather than with a number of traits which do not guarantee performance?

This three-skill approach makes trait testing unnecessary and substitutes for it procedures which examine a man's ability to cope with the actual problems and situations he will find on his job. These procedures, which indicate what a man can *do* in specific situations, are the same for selection and for measuring development. They will be described in the section on developing executive skills which follows.

[11] "In Conference," HBR (March-April, 1954), p. 44.
[12] William H. Whyte, Jr., "The Fallacies of 'Personality' Testing," *Fortune* (September, 1954), p. 117.

This approach suggests that executives should *not* be chosen on the basis of their apparent possession of a number of behavior characteristics or traits, but on the basis of their possession of the requisite skills for the specific level of responsibility involved.

DEVELOPING THE SKILLS

For years many people have contended that leadership ability is inherent in certain chosen individuals. We talk of "born leaders," "born executives," "born salesmen." It is undoubtedly true that certain people, naturally or innately, possess greater apptitude or ability in certain skills. But research in psychology and physiology would also indicate, first, that those having strong aptitudes and abilities can improve their skill through practice and training, and, secondly, that even those lacking the natural ability can improve their performance and effectiveness.

The *skill* conception of administration suggests that we may hope to improve our administrative effectiveness and to develop better administrators for the future. This skill conception implies *learning by doing*. Different people learn in different ways, but skills are developed through practice and through relating learning to one's own personal experience and background. If well done, training in these basic administrative skills should develop executive abilities more surely and more rapidly than through unorganized experience. What, then, are some of the ways in which this training can be conducted?

Technical Skill

Development of technical skill has received great attention for many years by industry and educational institutions alike, and much progress has been made. Sound grounding in the principles, structures, and processes of the individual specialty, coupled with actual practice and experience during which the individual is watched and helped by a superior, appear to be most effective. In view of the vast amount of work which has been done in training people in the technical skills, it would seem unnecessary in this article to suggest more.

Human Skill

Human skill, however, has been much less understood, and only recently has systematic progress been made in developing it. Many different approaches to the development of human skill are being pursued by various universities and professional men today. These are rooted in such disciplines as psychology, sociology, and anthropology.

Some of these approaches find their application in "applied psychology," "human engineering," and a host of other manifestations requiring technical specialists to help the businessman with his human problems. As a practical matter, however, the executive must develop his own human skill, rather than lean on the advice of others. To be effective, he must develop his own personal point of view toward human activity, so that he will (a) recognize the feelings and sentiments which he brings to a situation; (b) have an attitude about his own experiences which will enable him to re-evaluate and learn from them; (c) develop ability in understanding what others by their actions and words (explicit or implicit) are trying to communicate to him; and (d) develop ability in successfully communicating his ideas and attitudes to others.[13]

This human skill can be developed by some individuals without formalized training. Others can be individually aided by their immediate superiors and an integral part of the "coaching" process to be described later. This aid depends for effectiveness, obviously, on the extent to which the superior possesses the human skill.

For larger groups, the use of case problems coupled with impromptu role playing can be very effective. This training can be established on a formal or informal basis, but it requires a skilled instructor and organized sequence of activities.[14] It affords as good an approximation to reality as can be provided on a continuing classroom basis and offers an opportunity for critical reflection not often found in actual practice. An important part of the procedure is the self-examination of the trainee's own concepts and values, which may enable him to develop more useful attitudes about himself and about others. With the change in attitude, hopefully, there may also come some active skill in dealing with human problems.

Human skill has also been tested in the classroom, within reasonable limits, by a series of analyses of detailed accounts of actual situations involving administrative action, together with a number of role-playing opportunities in which the individual is required to carry out the details of the action he has proposed. In this way an individual's understanding of the total situation and his own personal ability to do something about it can be evaluated.

On the job, there should be frequent opportunities for a superior to observe an individual's ability to work effectively with others. These may appear to be highly subjective evaluations and to depend for validity on the human skill of the rater. But does not every promotion, in the last analysis, depend on someone's subjective judgement? And should this subjectivity be berated, or should we make a greater effort to develop people within our organizations with the human skill to make such judgments effectively?

Conceptual Skill

Conceptual skill, like human skill, has not been very widely understood. A number of methods have been tried to aid in developing this ability, with varying success. Some of the best results have always been

---

[13] For a further discussion of this point, see F. J. Roethlisberger, "Training Supervisors in Human Relations," HBR (September, 1951, p. 47.
[14] See, for example, A. Winn, "Training in Administration and Human Relations," *Personnel* (September, 1953), p. 139; see also, Kenneth R. Andrews, "Executive Training by the Case Method," HBR (September, 1951), p. 58.

achieved through the "coaching" of subordinates by superiors.[15] This is no new idea. It implies that one of the key responsibilities of the executive is to help his subordinates to develop their administrative potentials. One way a superior can help "coach" his subordinate is by assigning a particular responsibility, and then responding with searching questions or opinions, rather than giving answers, whenever the subordinate seeks help. When Benjamin F. Fairless, now chairman of the board of the United States Steel Corporation, was president of the corporation, he described his coaching activities as follows:

> "When one of my vice presidents or the head of one of our operating companies comes to me for instructions, I generally counter by asking him questions. First thing I know, he has told me how to solve the problem himself." [16]

Obviously, this is an ideal and wholly natural procedure for administrative training, and applies to the development of technical and human skills, as well as to that of conceptual skill. However, its success must necessarily rest on the abilities and willingness of the superior to help the subordinate.

Another excellent way to develop conceptual skill is through trading jobs, that is, by moving promising young men through different functions of the business but at the same level of responsibility. This gives the man the chance literally to "be in the other fellow's shoes."

Other possibilities include: special assignments, particularly the kind which involve inter-departmental problems; and management boards, such as the McCormick Multiple Management plan, in which junior executives serve as advisers to top management on policy matters.

For larger groups, the kind of case-problems course described above, only using cases involving broad management policy and interdepartmental coordination, may be useful. Courses of this kind, often called "General Management" or "Business Policy," are becoming increasingly prevalent.

In the classroom, conceptual skill has also been evaluated with reasonable effectiveness by presenting a series of detailed descriptions of specific complex situations. In these the individual being tested is asked to set forth a course of action which responds to the underlying forces operating in each situation and which considers the implications of this action on the various functions and parts of the organization and its total environment.

On the job, the alert supervisor should find frequent opportunities to observe the extent to which the individual is able to relate himself and his job to the other functions and operations of the company.

Like human skill, conceptual skill, too, must become a natural part of the executive's makeup. Different methods may be indicated for develop-

---

[15] For a more complete development of the concept of "coaching," see Myles L. Mace, *The Growth and Development of Executives* (Boston: Division of Research, Harvard Business School, 1950).

[16] "What Should a President Do?" *Dun's Review* (July, 1951), p. 14.

ing different people, by virtue of their backgrounds, attitudes, and experience. But in every case that method should be chosen which will enable the executive to develop his own personal skill in visualizing the enterprise as a whole and in coordinating and integrating its various parts.

CONCLUSION

The purpose of this article has been to show that effective administration depends on three basic personal skills, which have been called *technical, human,* and *conceptual.* The administrator needs: (a) sufficient technical skill to accomplish the mechanics of the particular job for which he is responsible; (b) sufficient human skill is working with others to be an effective group member and to be able to build cooperative effort within the team he leads; (c) sufficient conceptual skill to recognize the interrelationships of the various factors involved in his situation, which will lead him to take the action which achieves the maximum good for the total organization.

The relative importance of these three skills seems to vary with the level of administrative responsibility. At lower levels, the major need is for technical and human skills. At higher levels, the administrator's effectiveness depends largely on human and conceptual skills. At the top, conceptual skill becomes the most important of all for successful administration.

This three-skill approach emphasizes that good administrators are not necessarily born; they may be developed. It transcends the need to identify specific traits in an effort to provide a more useful way of looking at the administrative process. By helping to identify the skills most needed at various levels of responsibility, it may prove useful in the selection, training, and promotion of executives.

49 • MANAGING THE CAREER PLATEAU[1]

Thomas P. Ference[2]
James A. F. Stoner[3]
E. Kirby Warren[4]

A *plateau* is defined as the point in a career where the likelihood of additional hierarchical promotion is very low. Career plateaus are a natural consequence of the way organizations are shaped. Since there are fewer positions than aspirants at each higher rung of the organizational ladder, virtually all managers reach positions from which further upward mobility is unlikely.

Unfortunately the term *career plateau* has a negative tone, suggesting failure and defeat, which hinders understanding and management of this aspect of careers. Discussions of plateaued managers have focused largely on problem situations: shelf sitters, dead enders, deadwood, and so on [7, 18, 21]. But there is nothing inherently negative about the notion of a career plateau. To say that a person has plateaued tells us nothing about that person's performance on the job, morale, ambition, or any other personal or behavioral characteristic. It simply describes that individual's current career status within a particular organization.

During the past few years, the authors have discussed the career plateau phenomenon with experienced managers in a variety of organizations. The observations and conceptual model presented here are based on exploratory interviews conducted with 55 senior executives in nine major organizations. The interview sample was composed of senior personnel, management development executives, and division level line and staff management. The organizations were drawn from the following industries: banking, insurance, entertainment, paper manufacturing, petroleum, pharmaceutical, technical products, steel, and electrical equipment. (For a full report of the total study, see Stoner *et al.* [27].)

The interviews were intended to elicit the reactions of these executives to the conceptual model we were formulating and to obtain their insights into major issues associated with managerial career plateaus. This article describes a method of viewing the career plateau in the context of the entire organizational career and presents a series of issues associated with plateauing, as well as suggestions as to how organizations might manage this phenomenon more effectively.

A MODEL OF MANAGERIAL CAREERS

The first parameter in a model for classifying managerial career states is the likelihood of future promotion—the organization's estimate of the individual's

[1]From *Academy of Management Review*, Vol. 2, No. 4 (October, 1977), pp. 602–612. Reprinted by permission of *Academy of Management Review*.
[2]Thomas P. Ference, Director of the Master's Degree Program for Executives and Adjunct Associate Professor at the Graduate School of Business, Columbia University, New York City.
[3]James A. Stoner, Associate Professor at the Joseph P. Martino Graduate School of Business Administration, Fordham University, New York City.
[4]E. Kirby Warren, Professor of Management at the Graduate School of Business, Columbia University, New York City.

chances for receiving a hierarchical promotion. The second characteristic is performance in present position—how well the individual is seen by the organization as doing his or her present job. By classifying individuals as high or low on these two parameters, we can produce a straightforward classification of managerial career states, as shown in Figure 1. Naturally a more detailed model would allow for finer gradations of each characteristic or would introduce other dimensions. Some elaborations on the basic model are discussed below and in a subsequent paper [10].

The four principal career states in the model are:

1. *Learners* or *comers.* These individuals have high potential for advancement but presently perform below standard. Obvious examples are trainees who are still learning their new jobs and are not yet integrated into the organization's culture. Also included are longer service managers who have recently been promoted to new positions which they have not yet mastered.
2. *Stars.* These persons presently do outstanding work and are viewed as having high potential for continued advancement. They are on the high potential, fast track career paths. They are a readily identifiable group in most organizations, and probably receive the most attention in development programs and managerial discussions.
3. *Solid citizens.* Their present performance is rated satisfactory to outstanding, but they are seen as having little chance for future advancement. These individuals are probably the largest group in most organizations and perform the bulk of organizational work. Management effort and research seldom has focused on them.
4. *Deadwood.* These individuals have little potential for advancement, and their performance has fallen to an unsatisfactory level. These people have become problems, whether for reasons of motivation, ability, or personal difficulty. Probably a small group in most organizations, they are often the recipients of considerable attention, either for rehabilitation or dismissal.

The individuals on the left-hand side of the model—the solid citizens and the deadwood—are the plateaued managers. The solid citizens are effective pla-

FIGURE 1
A MODEL OF MANAGERIAL CAREERS

Current Performance	Likelihood of Future Promotion	
	Low	High
High	Solid Citizens (effective plateauees) Organizationally Plateaued Personally Plateaued	Stars
Low	Deadwood (ineffective plateauees)	Learners (comers)

teauees; the deadwood are ineffective. For most organizations, only individuals in the deadwood category are seen as current problems.

Formulation of the model in this manner suggests three major implications. First, an important challenge for management is to prevent solid citizens from slipping into the deadwood category. Second, different managerial approaches and styles are likely to be needed for effective management of individuals in each career state. Third, while there is considerable technology in place for dealing with managers in these three categories, few measures are available for dealing with the solid citizen. There are highly developed assessment and training programs for learners [4, 5], development programs for stars [24], and rehabilitation or outplacement programs for deadwood [7, 17]. Ironically the largest group, the effective solid citizens, frequently must fend for themselves.

SOME ELABORATION OF THE CAREER MODEL

The basic model can be elaborated to analyze sources of plateauing and to consider different types of effective plateauees. It is also amenable to an analysis of the development of careers over time.

Types of Effective Plateauees

Respondents indicated more than one identifiable subgroup within the solid citizen (effective plateauee) category. Individuals may become plateaued for reasons that can be grouped into two broad categories:

1. Some are *organizationally plateaued,* although having the ability to perform well in higher level jobs, because of lack of openings.

2. Some are *personally plateaued,* because they are seen by the organization either as lacking in *ability* for higher level jobs or as *not desiring* a higher level job.

The most important source of organizational plateauing is the narrowing pyramid (or cone) as diagrammed by Schein [25]. At each sequentially higher level, there are fewer positions above (the pool of opportunities shrinks) and more positions below (the pool of potential candidates increases). For a specific manager, jumping a major hurdle, such as obtaining a general management position by age 35, may indicate many opportunities ahead with few true competitors, an apparent broadening of the funnel. But for all managers as a group, the probability that each promotion will be the last increases with every step.

Other sources of organizational plateauing include:

1. *Competition.* For a given position, the individual may be seen as less qualified than other candidates, including some presently outside the organization.

2. *Age.* The individual may be seen as a less desirable candidate because of the need to utilize the position for training young, high potential managers who might have longer useful lives with the organization.

3. *Organizational needs.* The individual may be seen as too valuable in his or her present position to be spared for other, albeit higher level, work.

These considerations may or may not be seen as equitable from the perspective of a given individual, but they are part of an individual organizational decision-making process.

For individuals who are *personally* plateaued, promotion to a higher level position is unlikely even if openings occur. The organization's judgment might be based on a number of personal factors and qualities, including:

1. *Lack of technical and managerial skills.* This includes absence of job context (interpersonal competence) or job content (technical proficiency) skills needed for effective work at the next level. Skill deficiencies could arise from lack of aptitude, lack of exposure to responsibility or development opportunities, or lack of ability to respond to changing job requirements.

2. *Lack of career skills.* Some individuals are organizationally naive and lack an adequate understanding of the complexity of organizational realities [12]. Others tend to stay within a limited definition of their present job, failing to take active steps to move along a viable career path; they may be sidetracked too long in a job that has been mastered.

3. *Lack of sufficient desire.* Some individuals explicitly make known their desires not to be promoted further; others send ambiguous signals or place constraints on proposed promotions and transfers. An individual classified as a star by the organization may not desire additional promotion; such a person may become increasingly frustrated by the organization's efforts at advancement and development [2].

Cognizance of an individual's career state and how he or she got there is an essential input to management decisions about that individual. Different management styles and strategies should be adopted for different managers. Individuals who are organizationally plateaued because of lack of openings may thrive on managerial job enrichment efforts which distribute some of the boss's responsibility downwards. The same approach might overwhelm managers who are personally plateaued because their abilities are being fully utilized in their present job.

The Elusive Learners

In discussing the learner or comer category, several managers indicated difficulty identifying specific individuals currently in that category. Yet they recognized the category as logically consistent. They offered three major reasons for their difficulty in citing examples of learners. First, many managers above entry level positions learn new jobs and achieve high performance quickly, and thus are learners only a short time. Second, some managers are prepared for a new job before being promoted into it, often doing the work before the promotion becomes official; an assistant vice-president may become a high performing vice-president from the first official day in the job because the work was mastered before the promotion. Finally, expectations of potential often influence formal evaluation of managers during that learning period. Such managers are likely to be rated as "doing very well for someone new at the job" or are given a "too early to evaluate" performance rating. Thus, for a specific promotion or movement into a new job, a given manager may skip the learner category, may remain in it for only a short period of time, or may be in the category without public acknowledgement by other organizational members. These possibilities were not seen by the interviewers as challenging the validity of the category, nor were they seen as mitigating the necessity of managing and supporting the development process during the learning period.

Careers over Time

This essentially static model classifies managers at a particular point in time. But the model also can be viewed as a description of how careers progress over time. Individuals typically enter an organization and embark upon their careers as learners. Mastery of the job brings movement into the star category and candidacy for promotion. Subsequent promotions and sustained performance produce passages between the learner and star categories. Individuals gradually or abruptly drop out of competition for the next promotion and move on to the inevitable career plateau—they become solid citizens and remain there as long as their performance holds up. As age, lack of challenge, lack of motivation, or lack of attention begin to undermine performance, they drift toward the deadwood category. This progression traces out a life cycle of growth-stability-decline (Figure 2A) which parallels descriptions of other aspects of human development.

This description of the progress of a managerial career resembles the Peter Principle, a popular but pessimistic description of organizational life [21]. This principle suggests that the typical career is a series of promotions based on effective performance in successively higher positions, culminating with promotion to the individual's "level of incompetence." If organizations were allowed to follow thier preferred procedures, managers would not reach the solid citizen category but would recycle between learner and star until they are "terminally placed" as deadwood (Figure 2B).

Neglecting the Solid Citizen

The solid citizen—the effective plateauee—is performing well in her or his present job, not identified as a star nor as deadwood. Much of an organization's management development efforts are focused on the extremes of the performance continuum. High potential managers are most likely to have access to development programs, and poor performers are likely to be targets for remedial programs or decisive action such as demotion or dismissal.

Comparable attention is not focused on maintaining the performance of the solid citizens who constitute the great bulk of the management group. Organizations need solid citizens to maintain stability, provide continuity, and keep the level of competition for high level jobs within manageable bounds. But interviewees reported a tendency to treat solid citizens passively. They may be denied access to development programs and challenging assignments. Such practices may starve solid citizens of exactly the types of stimulation and opportunity they require to remain effective.

FIGURE 2
THREE VIEWS OF CAREER DYNAMICS

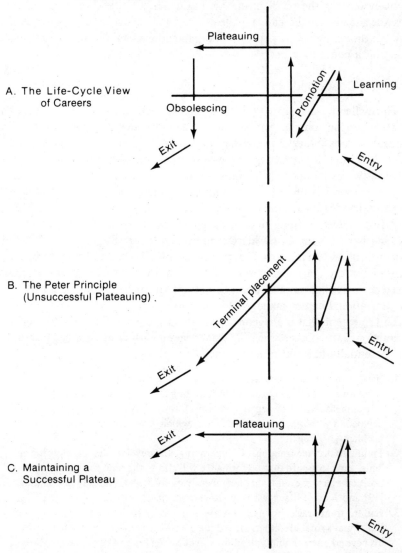

A. The Life-Cycle View of Careers

B. The Peter Principle (Unsuccessful Plateauing)

C. Maintaining a Successful Plateau

WHAT TO DO: TENTATIVE SUGGESTIONS

Although understanding in this area is at an early stage, recent research offers suggestions about what senior executives and their organizations should and should not do to manage the plateauing process more effectively. Three areas of action are: (1) preventing plateauees from becoming ineffective (preventing a problem from arising), (2) integrating the relevant career-related information systems (improving monitoring so emerging problems can be detected and treated early), and (3) managing ineffective plateauees and frustrated managers more effectively (curing the problem once it has arisen). These three areas of action focus specifically on the career plateau. Hall [14] provides a more general yet thorough discussion of ways in which organizations can promote more effective careers on a continuing basis.

Preventing Deadwood

The ineffective plateauee's performance has declined, and he or she may have a negative impact on the performance of subordinates and co-workers. While dismissal is a possibility, it is a distasteful action for many managers. Consideration of obligations incurred through past service, age, and the limited availability of alternative work opportunities mitigate against severe action. Recognition that the organization has played a role in making some managers ineffective contributes to reluctance to use the dismissal route.

Rising concern among middle managers about their career situations and prospects is accompanied by increasing pressures for job security, educational opportunities, and an improved bargaining position with upper management [17]. Potential for these trends to result in organized collective action by middle managers, including unionization [8], provides a further rationale for attention to organizational career management practices.

To the extent that management can avoid practices that lead to ineffective plateauing, painful decisions arising from dealing with deadwood can be reduced. Some potentially harmful practices include:

1. Failure to appraise accurately marginal or poor performance and to initiate corrective action. Long-run problems can be fostered by avoiding the short-run unpleasantness of negative appraisal, thus allowing possibly correctable behavior to become entrenched habit, which later becomes someone else's problem [14, 22].
2. Failure to provide training, skill upgrading, and development of solid citizens. This tends to assure that performance will slip as the requirements of a given position change, even if the incumbent's motivation remains high. Kaufman [17] and Kay [18] suggest ways to combat obsolescence.
3. Failure to appraise, counsel, and develop career paths in the context of an individual's total life situation, and the parallel tendency to promote individuals beyond current ability, leading to ineffectiveness and psychological stress.
4. Failure to monitor the attitudes and aspirations of individual managers. Many organizations depend upon informal observations and interpretations of superiors. Conditions maintaining individual performance vary across individuals as a function of particular goals and values [13].

The authors of this article feel that it is unduly cynical to assume that all plateaued managers are incompetent. The Peter Principle is a special case of plateauing, which leaves little room for healthy, constructive solutions (although some suggested solutions for the individual to use in managing his or her own career do appear in *The Peter Prescription* [20]. A more reasonable assumption is that managers can plateau while still effective and are capable of performing well and adjusting constructively to their career situations. Plateauing indicates only arrival at a presumably permanent position in the organizational hierarchy; it does not necessarily imply cessation of personal growth and development. Many avenues for personal and career development remain available to the plateaued individual [18, 25], and it is the task of senior management to assist individuals in adjusting effectively to their hierarchical situation—to remain in the solid citizen category until they leave the organization (Figure 2C).

TWO KEY ISSUES

The managers interviewed identified two ways in which their organizations made the inevitable plateauing phenomenon a potential organizational problem.

Early Identification and Creation of Plateauees

The judgment that an individual has plateaued is becoming increasingly more explicit and, as a result, probably more permanent and consequential. Interviewers reported that their organizations are developing increasingly sophisticated performance appraisal and succession planning systems which bring managers and particularly their promotability under continual scrutiny.

In addition to assessing current performance, managers are being asked to estimate (1) the extent of the appraisee's potential for promotion, (2) when the appraisee will be ready for promotion, and (3) the appraisee's training and development needs and plans. Performance appraisal, especially in the early years of an individual's career, frequently determines visibility to high level managers and access to development opportunities. Thus, it initiates organizational actions which subsequently confirm the appraisal.

Even more explicit decisions about an individual's long-range career possibilities are made by succession planning processes that attempt to link individual potential to particular positions. The principal concerns of such systems are to (1) identify specific candidates for specific positions, (2) determine when the candidate will be ready, (3) determine the candidate's need for additional skills and experiences, and (4) develop plans for filling these needs.

The succession plan becomes a definitive mechanism for identifying plateauees because it forces a distinction between abstract potential (common in the appraisal process) and potential for a specific position. To the extent that these formal systems become more widely adopted, definitive judgments increasingly will be made *early* in the individual's career. These judgments, whether accurate or not, affect training and development opportunities offered to individuals, and strongly influence eventual career experience. Studies show that early job experiences and events are powerful predictors of future work performance and career mobility [3, 4, 9, 26]. As early organizational judgments increasingly become formalized, these judgments will more nearly become self-fulfilling prophecies. Organizations will have to develop conscious strategies for managing the plateauees that the systems help to create.

Integrating Career Management Procedures

Performance appraisal and succession planning, which make the plateauing judgment explicit and self-confirming, are seldom integrated or cross-referenced within an organization. In many organizations, the several personnel functions, such as development, internal placement, out-placement services, and counseling, are not only vested in different units or individuals but are frequently conducted as if the other activities did not exist. Poor coordination leads to confusion in signals transmitted to individuals and to failure to identify developing problem areas.

The systematic integration of appraisal systems and succession planning would sharpen the organization's manpower planning efforts, facilitating attention to career progress, and increasing possibilities for intraorganizational transfer of individuals. It also would highlight discrepancies between assessment of potential on appraisal forms and designation for promotion in succession plans. Hall [14] suggested potential for improved organizational performance and individual satisfaction through a more explicit integration of the wealth of information buried within personnel systems.

Managing Ineffective or Frustrated Plateauees

There are no easy answers to the critical problem of how to bring the performance of ineffective plateauees to an effective level or how to motivate plateauees frustrated by the absence of advancement. For the ineffective plateauee, promising paths for restoring performance include:

1. Educational programs which upgrade technical skill, allowing the individual to keep pace with the changing job
2. Development programs that allow for emotional and intellectual recharging, although care must be taken to avoid undeliverable promises of advancement or unintentional threats of being phased out [7]
3. Job rotation to provide a change of scene, through new duties, skill demands, or location. This can provide some of the stimulation normally associated with promotion, although careful planning is needed to encourage managers to move from comfortable niches into new challenges. Ironically the same effect can be obtained under certain circumstances through demotion as through lateral transfer [11]

For the frustrated plateauee, the potential and need for job enrichment in place is considerable. Possibilities for growth through education and other special focus activities are limited only by the imagination of senior managers and their willingness to share the excitement and potential of their jobs with subordinates.

CRITICAL QUESTIONS FOR RESEARCH AND POLICY

These suggestions only begin to touch upon the intensity of the challenge to managerial ingenuity presented by plateaued managers. Remaining questions for research and managerial thought include:

1. To what degree is personal and professional stagnation the inevitable consequence of long tenure in a given position?
2. Is it better to tell a manager that he or she has plateaued or to allow the individual to maintain hope of eventual promotion?
3. Are plateaued individuals more effective when they accept their situation realistically or when they continue to aspire?
4. Which career management methods are likely to lead to continued satisfactory performance and to a healthy adjustment to one's career situation?

Relationship to Other Career Models

Further directions for research are suggested by this model's potential to guide extensions of the career models of Schein [25], Hall [14, 15], and Hall and Schneider [16]. Schein has discussed the timing of innovative behavior of managers during their careers. He hypothesizes that managers will be more innovative in the later part of their careers, because they have achieved "organizational tenure," and between "boundary passages" (sometime after a promotion is received and before the next promotion is anticipated). While lacking empirical support, his reasoning is provocative. But conventional wisdom suggests that late career managers are not generally seen as particularly innovative. The distinction between effective and ineffective plateauees, as well as consideration of the timing and level of plateauing, should sharpen an understanding of the conditions under which the innovation hypothesis is likely to hold.

The predictive and explanatory power of Hall's "psychological success" model might be enhanced by contrasting trainees and stars with effective plateauees and ineffective plateauees. Based on the work of Lewin [19] and Argyris [1], its basic components are summarized by Hall and Schneider as follows:

If (1) the individual sets a challenging goal for himself . . . , and (2) he determines his own means of attaining that goal, and (3) the goal is relevant to his self-concept, then he will experience *psychological success* upon attainment of that goal. This sense of personal success will lead to an increase in self-esteem, which in turn will lead to increased future levels of expectation [16, p. 2].

The data used to test their more elaborate version of this basic model did not yield strong confirmation, and led to some revision of the model.

One elaboration that might sharpen the model would be inclusion of the individual's perception of organizational career state as a moderating variable. This would allow a distinction between individuals who direct their efforts towards enhanced organizational performance and those who channel increased motivation stemming from enhanced self-esteem in other directions.

The phenomenon of plateaus in managerial careers presents a challenging problem to organizations. The culture has increasingly emphasized the desirability of fully utilizing one's potential, and somewhere along the way self-actualization has come to be correlated with career success. Aspiring managers have grown up in a society which provides an official view—a conventional wisdom—of the world of work and the nature of proper ambition.

The rhetoric of management thought sustains this imagery. Ambition and desire for promotion are more than just acceptable; they are often essential to being judged as an effective contributor. One manager, in describing a subordinate who turned down an offer to join another company at a higher position and salary, said, "My estimate of his abilities and his work has gone down a lot. I have to question his motivation and ambition." Some respondents doubted that a subordinate who did not desire promotion could really do an outstanding job, and expected such a person to become a problem.

The official description of a managerial career fosters expectations of reasonably steady upward progression in the organization hierarchy and of achieving self-fulfillment through this progression. This expectation is often so pervasive that the termination of upward movement is seen as a sign of failure. Despite this official climate, increasing numbers of managers do reject promotions and transfers; solid citizens are necessary and valuable; and the proportion of plateauees in managerial ranks is likely to increase.

The emphasis on promotion has led many in the managerial and professional ranks to question the quality and value of managerial work. The experience of middle managers in implementing job enrichment programs for their subordinates has led some of them to ask, "What about job enrichment for me?" The need to find ways to enrich managerial jobs is receiving some attention. The challenge to top management is to develop climates that acknowledge the validity of plateauees, and accept and confirm commitments to quality work which do not involve desires or expectations of hierarchical advancement.

REFERENCES FOR ARTICLE

1. ARGYRIS, C. *Integrating the Individual and the Organization.* New York City: John Wiley & Sons, Inc., 1964.
2. BECKHARD, R. "Mutiny in the Executive Ranks." *Innovation,* Vol. 31 (1972), pp. 2–11.
3. BERLEW, D. E., and D. T. HALL. "The Socialization of Managers: Effects of Expectations on Performance." *Administrative Science Quarterly,* Vol. 11, No. 2 (1966), pp. 207–223.
4. BRAY, D. W., R.J. CAMPBELL, AND D. L. GRANT. *Formative Years in Business: A Long-Term AT&T Study of Managerial Lives.* New York City: John Wiley & Sons, Inc., 1974.
5. BYHAM, W. C. "Assessment Centers for Spotting Future Managers." *Harvard Business Review,* Vol. 48, No. 4 (1970), pp. 150–167.
6. CAMPBELL, J. P., et al. *Managerial Behavior, Performance, and Effectiveness.* New York City: McGraw-Hill Book Company, 1970.

7. CONNOR, S. R., and J. S. FIELDEN. "Rx for Managerial 'Shelf Sitters.'" *Harvard Business Review* (November-December 1973), pp. 113–120.
8. DeMARIA, A.T., D. TARNOWIESKI, and R. GURMAN. *Manager Unions?* New York City: American Management Association, 1972.
9. DUNNETTE, M. D., R.D. ARVEY, and P. A. BANAS. "Why Do They Leave?" *Personnel* (May-June 1973), pp. 25–39.
10. FERENCE, T. P., J. A. F. STONER, and E. K. WARREN. "Managing the Career Plateau: Alternatives for the Individual," in process.
11. GOLDNER, F. H. "Demotion in Industrial Management." *American Sociological Review,* Vol. 30, No. 5 (1965).
12. GOLDNER, F. H. "Success vs. Failure: Prior Managerial Perspectives." *Industrial Relations,* Vol. 9, No. 4 (1970), pp. 453–474.
13. GOLDNER, F.H., and R.R. RITTI. "Professionalism as Career Immobility." *American Journal of Sociology,* Vol. 72 (March 1967), pp. 489–502.
14. HALL, D. T. "A Theoretical Model of Career Subidentity Development in Organizational Settings." *Organizational Behavior and Human Performance,* Vol. 6 (1971), pp. 50–76.
15. HALL, D. T. *Careers in Organizations.* Pacific Palisades, Calif.: Goodyear Publishing Co., Inc., 1976.
16. HALL, D. T., and B. SCHNEIDER. *Organizational Climates and Careers: The Work Lives of Priests.* New York City: Seminar Press, 1973.
17. KAUFMAN, H. G. *Obsolescence and Professional Career Development.* New York City: Amacom, 1974.
18. KAY, E. *The Crisis in Middle Management.* New York City: Amacom, 1974.
19. LEWIN, K. "The Psychology of Success and Failure." *Occupations,* Vol. 14 (1936), pp. 926–930.
20. PETER, L. *The Peter Prescription.* New York City: William Morrow & Co., Inc., 1972.
21. PETER, L., and R. HULL. *The Peter Principle.* New York City: William Morrow & Co., Inc., 1969.
22. PORTER, L. W., E. E. LAWLER III, and J. R. HACKMAN. *Behavior in Organizations.* New York City: McGraw-Hill Book Company, 1975.
23. RITTI, R. R., T. P. FERENCE, and F. H. GOLDNER. "Professions and their Plausibility." *Sociology of Work and Occupations,* Vol. 1 (1974), pp. 24–51.
24. REVANS, R. W. *Developing Effective Managers: A New Approach to Business Education.* New York City: Praeger Publishers, Inc., 1971.
25. SCHEIN, E. H. "The Individual, the Organization, and the Career: A Conceptual Scheme." *Journal of Applied Behavioral Science,* Vol. 7 (1971).
26. STONER, J. A. F., J. D. ARAM, and I. M. RUBIN. "Factors Associated with Effective Performance in Overseas Work Assignments." *Personnel Psychology,* Vol. 25 (1973), pp. 303–318.
27. STONER, J. A. F., et al. *Patterns and Plateaus in Managerial Careers. Report to the Ford Foundation* (May, 1974).
28. TARNOWIESKI, D. *The Changing Success Ethic.* New York City: American Management Association, 1973.

50 • THE ANNUAL PERFORMANCE REVIEW DISCUSSION—MAKING IT CONSTRUCTIVE[1]

Herbert H. Meyer[2]

The personnel program in any production or service organization which employs more than a few hundred people would not be considered as completely respectable if it did not include a systematic performance appraisal program. Under such a program the performance of each employee is appraised and carefully documented at least annually. Moreover, such appraisal programs almost always require that the supervisor who appraises must discuss the individual appraisals with the respective employees.

Typically such programs have two primary objectives: (1) to provide an inventory of human resources talent in the organization and (2) to motivate employees. Motivation is accomplished in two ways. First, the performance appraisal is usually tied into the salary administration program; that is, a *merit pay* philosophy is endorsed under which an individual's pay should coincide with demonstrated performance excellence. Secondly, the feedback discussion of the appraisal should provide an effective source of motivation. Each employee is counseled on how performance may be improved.

In theory the performance appraisal program appears to be indisputably sound and logical. Yet the program has proved to be an enigma to both personnel experts and line managers. Both the rating process itself and the feedback interview have presented almost insolvable problems in most appraisal programs. There has already been much discussion of various methods to produce more reliable and valid ratings, particularly when tied to a merit pay program.

Even more problematic in an appraisal program is the feedback discussion. Objective evidence has shown that appraisal interviews seldom have the positive effect attributed to them. Some research actually indicates that such discussions often do more harm than good.[3]

These findings lead us to reexamine the theory on which appraisal interviews are based. As a result, I have come to the conclusion that the annual appraisal interview is *not* a psychologically sound procedure. For one thing, the feedback to the individual is poorly timed. In most appraisal programs this intensive, comprehensive feedback comes but once a year. It is certainly a well-established psychological fact that feedback associated immediately with an act is much more effective than delayed feedback.

An even more serious problem with the appraisal feedback discussion is the fact that it often has a negative side effect on an employee's occupational self-

---

[1]Reprinted with permission, *Personnel Journal,* Costa Mesa, CA, copyright October, 1977.
[2]Herbert H. Meyer, Professor and Director of the Ph.D. program in Industrial/Organizational Psychology at the University of South Florida, Tampa, Florida.
[3]H.H. Meyer, E. Day, and J. R. P. French, Jr., "Split Roles in Performance Appraisal," *Harvard Business Review* (January-February 1965).

esteem. Our research found that employees were more likely to react defensively than constructively to suggestions for improving performance.[4]

Social psychologists have researched the issue of how people handle threats to their self-esteem and found that a number of unconstructive reactions are typically used to cope with such threats.[5] First, the individual may question the measurement criteria used or he may minimize the importance of the activity. Another undesirable response to threats to self-esteem is the tendency to demean the source.

The potential negative effects of threats to self-esteem in appraisal interviews are minimized by the fact that, typically, managers make few discriminations in their ratings. Almost everyone receives an above average rating.

A BETTER WAY

Despite all the problems with appraisal interviews cited here, it does seem that an annual review discussion between supervisor and employee could serve some constructive purposes. Employees do want to know how they are regarded and what the future might hold for them in the organization. The problem is to design a format for accomplishing this discussion which the average manager can use without a great deal of training and which is not demeaning to the person being assessed. We think we have found the solution to this problem.

We started by formulating some specifications for a constructive annual discussion between manager and employees. The first of these, and perhaps the most important, was to minimize the authoritarian character of the interaction. The usual appraisal feedback procedure, where the manager discusses *his* or *her* ratings of a subordinate, is a highly authoritarian process. There is no doubt as to who is the dominant person. Submissive behavior is appropriate for the subordinate. For this reason, the appraisal interview procedure is becoming more and more anachronistic in today's culture. Young people especially are likely to reject authoritarianism. As a solution to this problem, we felt that the discussion must be structured in such a way that the two parties participate more as equals.

Secondly, we felt that if the two parties were to participate as equals, both should prepare for the discussion. The employee, as well as the manager, should think through in advance, and possibly even make notes about, concerns or issues that he or she would like to discuss with the manager in this interview.

A third specification, which follows from the first two, is that the interview format or process should be structured in such a way as to insure two-way communication.

A fourth objective for the new procedure was that threats to the individual's self-esteem should be minimized. If an individual is to be effective on the job, he or she must have high occupational self-esteem. This does not mean that needed

[4]Ibid.
[5]Alvin Sander, "Research on Self-Esteem, Feedback and Threats to Self-Esteem," *Performance Appraisals: Effects on Employees and Their Performance,* edited by A. Zander (Ann Arbor, Mich.: The Foundation for Research in Human Behavior, 1963).

changes in behavior or performance should not be discussed. However, it does mean that discussions of such issues should be problem oriented and not personalized. Unless an individual really is a misfit in the job, it is important that he or she really think that his or her performance is good.

A fifth specification for a constructive annual discussion is that it should not incorporate a "report card" type of rating form. Grades on a form of this kind are not only likely to be threatening to the subordinate, but also to have a demeaning effect. The report card emphasizes the subordinate's dependent status.

A final specification for the procedure is that the manager should not try to cover all issues or aspects of the job in a single interview. A constructive outcome of a discussion of this kind is more likely to result if the manager focuses on just one or two issues or problems. To attempt to cover all aspects of the job, with suggestions for performance improvement or behavior change in a number of areas, is an unrealistic goal for a single interview.

THE DISCUSSION FORMAT

Based on the above specifications, we designed a format for an annual discussion which we thought might be more constructive than the usual appraisal interview. As indicated in the specifications, the first step in the process is to notify the employee that a discussion is scheduled. The employee is invited to prepare by thinking about his or her role in the organization, how individual contribution could be enhanced, and what kinds of plans or aspirations he or she has for the future.

In the discussion itself, the manager will usually start by again reviewing the purpose of the discussion. However, it is important that following this opening statement the actual discussion of issues be started by giving the initiative to the interviewee. Specifically, the manager might start this discussion by asking, "How do you feel things are going on the job? What kinds of concerns do you have?"

We have found that this is the only way to insure that there will be genuine two-way communication. If the manager starts by expressing his or her own point of view about the employee's performance or their working relationship, the interview almost invariably develops in a predominantly one-way communication pattern.

It is only after they have discussed the employee's topics, concerns, and suggestions that the manager's viewpoint should be presented. This might include a general impression of performance. For example, the manager might say "I've been very pleased . . ." or, "I've been somewhat disappointed in the way things have been working out. . . ." Certainly a manager should take this opportunity to commend the employee for significant accomplishments, and especially for improvements that might have been made on the basis of previous discussions or coaching.

The manager can then introduce the discussion of opportunities for growth or improvement in job performance. Many times the most effective way to accomplish this is to ask the employee to take the initiative here. It is much easier to

react to, and perhaps to expand on, plans that someone has for changing performance or behavior than it is to make such suggestion directly. The odds of the
individual's self-esteem being threatened are certainly much less if this approach
is used. In either case, the manager should try to maintain a problem-solving,
rather than a blame-placing approach. The focus should be on future opportunities and plans rather than on past failures.

A natural closing topic of discussion will be what the future might hold for
the individual. However, in many organizations this may not be a relevant topic
for many people. In a very stable organization, for example, there may be little
chance of advancement for many employees. To bring up the topic each year
would probably be more threatening than constructive for such employees. On
the other hand, for the high-performing employee with obvious potential to
advance, a discussion of possible future opportunities and self-development

FIGURE 1
PERFORMANCE REVIEW DISCUSSION

Employee's
Name_____ Date_____

1. Introduction	5. Opportunities for Improvement
Put employee at ease. Purpose: mutual discussion of how things are going.	No more than one or two items. Do not present as shortcomings. Keep it work related.
2. Employee's View	6. Performance Improvement Plans
How does he/she view job and working climate? Any problems? Suggestions for changes, improvement?	Plan should be employee's plan. Supervisor merely tries to help and counsel.
3. Supervisor's View of Employee's Performance	7. Future Opportunities
Summary statement only. Avoid comparisons with others.	Advancement possiblities? Future pay increase possibilities? Warning for poor performer.
4. Behaviors Desirable to Continue	8. Questions
Mention one or two items only.	Any general concerns? Close on constructive, encouraging note.

plans might be very important to the motivation and retention of that individual.

Figure 1 presents an outline which we prepared for the supervisor to be used as a guide to both preparing for and conducting the discussion. The supervisor will find it helpful to make notes in advance relating not only to the topics or issues to be discussed, but also regarding the strategy to be used in introducing each of these topics or issues. Notice that the form does not require scaled ratings of any kind.

The primary purpose of an annual discussion along these lines is not performance feedback and coaching. Performance feedback and coaching must be a day-to-day activity. Effective coaching must be associated immediately and directly with the performance at issue. This annual discussion is designed to open communication channels and to develop a better working relationship between the two parties involved. It is especially valuable in providing a formalized method of insuring upward communication. The manager can learn how employees view the work situation and what their concerns are.

A TEST OF THE PROCEDURE

This approach to the performance review discussion has been used successfully in several organizations with a variety of employees, from assembly line workers to engineers and managers. Invariably both the managers and employees like the procedure much better than the more traditional rating form approach to appraisal.

An ideal opportunity for a more objective test of this discussion procedure arose at a new plant. The personnel staff at that plant had planned to introduce a new appraisal program for hourly employees. Their program conformed to the traditional format—that is, ratings in critical dimensions of the job. Since the plant was composed of two large buildings where similar manufacturing operations were performed, it seemed like an ideal situation for an experiment. Therefore, we decided to introduce the traditional program in one building and the new approach, described here, in the other building. An attempt was made in each case to provide the training that supervisors would need to carry out the respective programs effectively.

After the two programs had been in effect long enough for all employees to have been appraised, a survey was carried out to measure their reactions to the appraisal programs. This survey showed that reactions of employees who experienced the new approach were significantly more favorable than the reactions of employees in the building where the more traditional appraisal program was used. For example, employees in the building where the new approach to appraisal was used were more likely to say that

1. Their supervisor recognized and appreciated their work.
2. They got answers to their own questions.
3. They had an opportunity to participate in the discussion.
4. They had received help in performing their job better.

5. The supervisor's judgments about their work were accurate.
6. The discussion increased their feeling of pride in their work.

Supervisors who used this recommended approach to the performance review discussion also reported, in almost every case, that they like the procedure better than rating programs they had used in the past. Many said that they especially liked the fact that they did not have to assign and discuss numerical grades in various aspects of job performance.

PROVIDING FOR ADMINISTRATIVE NEEDS

Many personnel administrators insist that numerical grades of some kind must be assigned to each of the employees in the organization. They maintain that such grades provide a systematic basis for administrative decisions which need to be made relating to the status or treatment of individuals.

The most common administrative purpose of performance ratings is to implement a merit pay plan. Most organizations use a pay plan at least for professional and managerial personnel which provides for differential increases to individuals depending on their performance ratings. However, there is no reason to believe that a merit pay program could not be administered without necessarily assigning numbers or grades to the performance of individuals. As a matter of fact, in almost any organization there are factors which influence the size of salary increases granted to individuals other than just performance level achieved in the previous year. Decisions regarding amount of salary increase to be granted, and reasons for the size of increase involved, can certainly be communicated to an employee without necessarily attaching a specific number or grade to the employee's performance level. This decision might be communicated in the annual review discussion recommended here, or in a separate discussion, depending on the timing of the increase, the manager's preference, or similar considerations.

Another administrative need for which appraisal information is likely to be generated is to facilitate manpower planning. Here, again, qualitative information rather than qualified grades or classifications can be recorded for this purpose and discussed with the individuals involved. As a matter of fact, experience of personnel specialists has shown that qualitative information in the form of written out performance or behavioral descriptions on appraisal forms usually proves to be of greater value for manpower planning purposes than the grades or ratings assigned to employees.

In most organizations, promotions to higher level positions are rarely based on the performance appraisals which managers record as a part of the annual rating program. In almost every case, more comprehensive information is obtained on the qualifications of candidates relating to the specifications for the open position. The opinions of many people in the organization, other than the individual's immediate manager, are likely to be sought. Moreover, in many organizations today "assessment center" type programs are used to provide more detailed and objective data for making promotional decisions than is typically revealed in the documented annual appraisals.

When we consider an even more critical personnel decision, the decision to demote or terminate an employee, many personnel administrators have insisted that we need systematically recorded annual appraisals to protect the organization against discrimination suits. However, it is very doubtful that a subjective judgment of the supervisor or manager, regardless of how precisely this judgment is categorized, will be accepted in court if the manager is accused of bias. In fact, experience to date has shown that such ratings are not accepted as unbiased in discrimination cases.[6]

To be accepted in a court of law, decisions to demote or terminate an individual will undoubtedly have to be backed up by objective performance evidence. This kind of evidence will also have to be recorded, and should be communicated to the respective individual at the time of occurrence—not on the occasion of the employee's anniversay date when his or her performance review is scheduled. Whether the supervisor judges performance to warrant a "2" or a "4" or "poor" or whatever will be immaterial in court in most situations. On the other hand, specific descriptions of performance failures, preferably backed by objective data, are much more likely to be accepted. This kind of documentation will be necessary to substantiate critical decisions such as terminations, whether or not the organization has a formal program for annual performance review.

Many of the problems that we have had with appraisal programs appear to stem from the fact that we try to achieve too many objectives with a single program. Some of these objectives are incompatible. For example, we may expect the same program to provide the kind of detailed and candid data needed to make hard administrative decisions and, at the same time, expect the manager to use such data in a supportive manner to stimulate improved performance. This often proves to be an impossible task: either the data are distorted so that the message is palatable, or the feedback is so threatening to the individual that the results are more negative than constructive.

Appraisal to be effective must be an *ad hoc* procedure. We must use different approaches to satisfy different objectives.

With the approach described here, we have concluded that an annual review discussion can be constructive if we set relatively modest, although important, objectives for it. Admittedly it does not provide for all appraisal needs. It does appear, however, to serve one important need very well—that of opening communication channels between manager and employee. This is likely to be much more than is accomplished with programs that are designed to serve a much broader range of needs.

[6]Layer, Robert I. "The 'Discrimination' Danger in Performance Appraisal," *The Conference Board Record* (March, 1976).

BIBLIOGRAPHY, CHAPTER 14

Ackerman, Leonard. "Career Development: Preparing Round Pegs for Square Holes." *Training and Development Journal,* Vol. 30, No. 2 (February, 1976), pp. 12-14.

Archer, Frank W. "Charting a Career Course." *Personnel Journal* (April, 1984), pp. 60-64.

Beard, Donald W. "The Effects of Organizational Size and Complexity on Managerial Role Structure: An Exploratory Analysis." *Proceedings of Academy of Management Meetings* (August, 1978), pp. 170-174.

Bray, Douglas W., and A. Howard. "Keeping in Touch with Success." *The Wharton Magazine,* Vol. 3, No. 2 (Winter, 1979), pp. 28-33.

Brown, M. Craig. "Administrative Succession and Organizational Performance: The Succession Effect." *Administrative Science Quarterly,* Vol. 27, No. 1 (March, 1982), pp. 1-16.

Burck, C. G. "A Group Profile of the Fortune 500 Chief Executive." *Fortune,* Vol. 93, No. 5 (May, 1976).

Campbell, Richard T., and Douglas W. Bray. "Assessment Center: An Aid in Management Selection." *Personnel Administration,* Vol. 30, No. 2 (March-April, 1967), pp. 7-13.

Decotiis, Thomas, and A. Petit. "The Performance Appraisal Process: A Model and Some Testable Propositions." *Academy of Management Review,* Vol. 3, No. 3 (July, 1978), pp. 635-646.

Dipboyle, Robert L. "Self-Fulfilling Prophecies in the Selection-Recruitment Interview." *Academy of Management Review,* Vol. 7, No. 4 (1982), pp. 579-586.

Griffin, Ricky W. "Task Design Determinants of Effective Leader Behavior." *Academy of Management Review,* Vol. 4, No. 2 (1979), pp. 215-224.

Haider, Michael L. "Tomorrow's Executive: A Man for All Countries." *Columbia Journal of World Business,* Vol. 1, No. 1 (Winter, 1966), pp. 107-113.

Kipnis, David, *et al.* "Patterns of Managerial Influence: Shotgun Managers, Tacticians, and Bystanders." *Organizational Dynamics* (Winter, 1984), pp. 58-67.

Kotter, John P. "What Effective General Managers Really Do." *Harvard Business Review,* Vol. 60, No. 6 (1982), pp. 156-167.

McGregor, Douglas. *The Professional Manager.* New York: McGraw-Hill Book Co., 1967.

Mintzberg, H. "The Manager's Job: Folklore and Fact." *Harvard Business Review,* Vol. 53, No. 4 (1975), pp. 49-61.

Norton, Steven D. "The Empirical and Content Validity of Assessment Centers vs. Traditional Methods for Predicting Managerial Success." *Academy of Management Review,* Vol. 2, No. 3 (July, 1977), pp. 442-453.

Price, Margaret. "Women: Reaching for the Top." *Industry Week,* Vol. 217, No. 4, (May 16, 1983), pp. 38-42.

Rawls, J. R., D. J. Rawls, and R. Radosevich. "Identifying Strategic Managers." *Business Horizons,* Vol. 18, No. 6 (1975), pp. 74-78.

Shetty, Y. K., and N. S. Perry, Jr. "Are Top Executives Transferable across Companies?" *Business Horizons,* Vol. 19, No. 3 (1976), pp. 23-28.

Tichy, Noel M., Charles J. Fombrun, and Mary Anne Devanna. "Strategic Human Resource Management." *Sloan Management Review,* Vol. 23, No. 2 (Winter, 1982), pp. 47-61.

Tracy, E. J. "The Loneliness of the Master Turnaround Man." *Fortune,* Vol. 93, No. 2 (1976), pp. 118-128.

Tryon, Warren W. "The Test-Trait Fallacy." *American Psychologist*, Vol. 34, No. 5 (May, 1979), pp. 402-406.

Veiga, John F. "Plateaued versus Nonplateaued Managers: Career Patterns, Attitudes and Path Potential." *Academy of Management Journal,* Vol. 24, No. 3, pp. 566-578.

_____ . "Mobility Influences during Managerial Career Stages." *Academy of Management Journal,* Vol. 26, No. 1 (1983), pp. 64-85.

Warren, E. K., T. P. Ference, and J. A. F. Stoner. "Case of the Plateaued Performer." *Harvard Business Review,* Vol. 53, No. 1 (1975).

Chapter 15

Developing
Managers

Since any monitoring or evaluation system of managers is likely to reveal a lack of perfection, it behooves managers to consider in what ways they may improve themselves and their subordinate managers (and, in some cases, the potential managers) through experience or education. It is on the job that most learning about management takes place, approved behavior is reinforced, and inappropriate behaviors are discouraged. Thus, if a person is judged to possess a weakness in some aspect of managing, designing some assignment or series of tasks to aid in overcoming the weakness is often deemed the most appropriate response. On the other hand, there are unresolved issues in development. Should we shore up weaknesses or maximize already existing strengths? Or both? Should we develop basic knowledge or skill in the use of the knowledge? The list of what we do not know probably exceeds that which we do know, and we may not know the difference.

The first article, by Schein, progresses through the development concept to conclude that the manager-subordinate relationship is primary in identifying and in motivating change. Thus, the managerial influence process is central to development.

In the second paper Gregg examines the question of what we can do to get executives who are experiencing problems back on track. Finally, Byham defines how behavior can or cannot be changed. Given the ambiguity of many prescriptions about management, this paper represents a fresh breeze in an otherwise stagnant atmosphere.

51 • MANAGEMENT DEVELOPMENT AS A PROCESS OF INFLUENCE[1]

Edgar H. Schein[2]

The continuing rash of articles on the subject of developing better managers suggests, on the one hand, a continuing concern that existing methods are not providing the talent which is needed at the higher levels of industry and, on the other hand, that we continue to lack clear-cut formulations about the process by which such development occurs. We need more and better managers and we need more and better theories of how to get them.

In the present paper I would like to cast management development as the problem of how an organization can influence the beliefs, attitudes, and values (hereafter simply called attitudes) of an individual for the purpose of "developing" him, i.e. changing him in a direction which the organization regards to be in his own and the organization's best interests. Most of the existing conceptions of the development of human resources are built upon assumptions of how people learn and grow, and some of the more strikingly contrasting theories of management development derive from disagreements about such assumptions.[3] I will attempt to build on a different base: instead of starting with assumptions about learning and growth, I will start with some assumptions from the social psychology of influence and attitude change.

Building on this base can be justified quite readily if we can consider that adequate managerial performance at the higher levels is at least as much a matter of attitudes as it is a matter of knowledge and specific skills, and that the acquisition of such knowledge and skills is itself in part a function of attitudes. Yet we have given far more attention to the psychology which underlies change in the area of knowledge and abilities than we have to the psychology which underlies change in attitudes. We have suprisingly few studies of how a person develops loyalty to a company, commitment to a job, or a professional attitude toward the managerial role; how he comes to have the motives and attitudes which make possible the rendering of decisions concerning large quantities of money, materials, and human resources; how he develops attitudes toward himself, his co-workers, his employees, his customers, and society in general which give us confidence that he has a sense of responsibility and a set of ethics consistent with his responsible position, or at least which permit us to understand his behavior.

It is clear that management is becoming increasingly professionalized, as evidenced by increasing emphasis on undergraduate and graduate education in the field of management. But professionalization is not only a

[1] From *Industrial Management Review* (May, 1961), pp. 59-76. Reprinted by permission of *Industrial Management Review*.
[2] Edgar H. Schein, Associate Professor of Industrial Management, Massachusetts Institute of Technology.
[3] An excellent discussion of two contrasting approaches—engineering vs. the agricultural—deriving from contrasting assumptions about human behavior can be found in McGregor, 1960, Chapter 14.

matter of teaching candidates increasing amounts about a set of relevant subjects and disciplines; it is equally a problem of preparing the candidate for a role which requires a certain set of attitudes. Studies of the medical profession (Merton, Reader, and Kendall, 1957), for example, have turned their attention increasingly to the unravelling of the difficult problem of how the medical student acquires those attitudes and values which enable him to make responsible decisions involving the lives of other people. Similar studies in other professions are sorely needed. When these are undertaken, it is likely to be discovered that much of the training of such attitudes is carried out implicitly and without a clearly formulated rationale. Law schools and medical schools provide various kinds of experiences which insure that the graduate is prepared to fulfill his professional role. Similarly, existing approaches to the development of managers probably provide ample opportunities for the manager to learn the attitudes he will need to fulfill high level jobs. But in this field, particularly, one gets the impression that such opportunities are more the result of intuition or chance than of clearly formulated policies. This is partly because the essential or pivotal aspects of the managerial role have not as yet been clearly delineated, leaving ambiguous both the area of knowledge to be mastered and the attitude to be acquired.

Existing practice in the field of management development involves activities such as: indoctrination and training programs conducted at various points in the manager's career; systematic job rotation involving changes both in the nature of the functions performed (e.g. moving from production into sales), in physical location, and in the individual's superiors; performance appraisal programs including various amounts of testing, general personality assessment, and counseling both within the organization and through the use of outside consultants; apprenticeships, systematic coaching, junior management boards, and special projects to facilitate practice by the young manager in functions he will have to perform later in his career; sponsorship and other comparable activities in which a select group of young managers is groomed systematically for high level jobs (i.e. made into "crown princes"); participation in special conferences and training programs, including professional association meetings, human relations workshops, advanced management programs conducted in business schools or by professional associations like the American Management Association, regular academic courses like the Sloan programs offered at Stanford and MIT, or liberal arts courses like those offered at the University of Pennsylvania, Dartmouth, Northwestern, etc. These and many other specific educational devices, along with elaborate schemes of selection, appraisal, and placement, form the basic paraphernalia of management development.

Most of the methods mentioned above stem from the basic conception that it is the responsibility of the business enterprise, as an institution, to define what kind of behavior and attitude change is to take place and to construct mechanisms by which such change is to occur. Decisions about the kind of activity which might be appropriate for a given manager are usually made by others above him or by specialists hired to make such decisions. Where he is to be rotated, how long he is to remain on a given assignment, or what kind of new training he should undertake, is masterminded by others whose concern is "career development." In a sense, the individual stands alone against the institution where his own career is concerned, because the basic assumption is that the institution knows better than the individual what kind of man it needs or wants in its higher levels of management. The kind of influence model which is relevant, then, is one which considers the whole range of resources available to an organization.

In the remainder of this paper I will attempt to spell out these general themes by first presenting a conceptual model for analyzing influence, then providing some illustrations from a variety of organizational influence situations, and then testing its applicability to the management development situation.

A MODEL OF INFLUENCE AND CHANGE

Most theories of influence or change accept the premise that change does not occur unless the individual is *motivated* and *ready* to change. This statement implies that the individual must perceive some need for a change in himself, must be able to change, and must perceive the influencing agent as one who can facilitate such change in a direction acceptable to the individual. A model of the influence process, then, must account for the development of the motivation to change as well as the actual mechanisms by which the change occurs.

It is usually assumed that pointing out to a person some of his areas of deficiency, or some failure on his part in these areas, is sufficient to induce in him a readiness to change and to accept the influencing agent's guidance or recommendations. This assumption may be tenable if one is dealing with deficiencies in intellectual skills or technical knowledge. The young manager can see, with some help from his superiors, that he needs a greater knowledge of economics, or marketing, or production methods, and can accept the suggestion that spending a year in another department or six weeks at an advanced management course will give him the missing knowledge and/or skills.

However, when we are dealing with attitudes, the suggestion of deficiency or the need for change is much more likely to be perceived as a basic threat to the individual's sense of identity and to his status position vis-à-vis others in the organization. Attitudes are generally organized and integrated around the person's image of himself, and they result in stabilized, characteristic ways of dealing with others. The suggestion of the need for change not only implies some criticism of the person's image of himself, but also threatens the stability of his working relationships because change at this level implies that the expectations which others have about him will be upset, thus requiring the development of new relationships. It is not at all uncommon for training programs in human relations to arouse resistance or to produce, at best, temporary change because the expectations of co-workers operate to keep the individual in his "normal" mold. Management development programs which ignore these psychological resistances to change are likely to be self-defeating, no matter how much attention is given to the actual presentation of the new desired attitudes.

Given these general assumptions about the integration of attitudes in the person, it is appropriate to consider influence as a process which occurs over time and which includes three phases:

1. *Unfreezing*:[4] an alteration of the forces acting on the individual, such that his stable equilibrium is disturbed sufficiently to motivate him and to make him ready to change; this can be accomplished either by increasing the pressure to change or by reducing some of the threats or resistances to change.
2. *Changing*: the presentation of a director of change and the actual process of learning new attitudes. This process occurs basically by one of two mechanisms: (a) *identification*[5]—the person learns new attitudes by identifying with and emulating some other person who holds those attitudes; or (b) *internalization*—the person learns new attitudes by being placed in a situation where new attitudes are demanded of him as a way of solving problems which confront him and which he cannot avoid; he discovers the new attitudes essentially for himself, though the situation may guide him or make it probable that he will discover only those attitudes which the influencing agent wishes him to discover.
3. *Refreezing*: the integration of the changed attitudes into the rest of the personality and/or into ongoing significant emotional relationships.

In proposing this kind of model of influence we are leaving out two important cases—the individual who changes because he is *forced* to change by the agent's direct manipulation of rewards and punishments (what Kelman calls "compliance") and the individual whose strong motivation to rise in the organizational hierarchy makes him eager to accept the attitudes and acquire the skills which he perceives to be necessary for advancement. I will ignore both of these cases for the same reason—they usually do not involve genuine, stable change, but merely involve the adoption of overt behaviors which imply to others that attitudes have changed, even if they have not. In the case of compliance, the individual drops the overt behavior as soon as surveillance by the influence agent is removed. Among the upwardly mobile individuals, there are are those who are willing to be unfrozen and to undergo genuine attitude change (whose case fits the model to be presented below) and those whose overt behavior change is dictated by their changing perception of what the environment will reward, but whose underlying attitudes are never really changed or refrozen.

I do not wish to imply that a general reward-punishment model is incorrect or inappropriate for the analysis of attitude change. My purpose,

[4] These phases of influence are a derivation of the change model developed by Lewin, 1947.
[5] These mechanisms of attitude change are taken from Kelman, 1958.

rather, is to provide a more refined model in terms of which it becomes possible to specify the differential effects of various kinds of rewards and punishments, some of which have far more significance and impact than others. For example, as I will try to show, the rewarding effect of approval from an admired person is very different in its ultimate consequences from the rewarding effect of developing a personal solution to a difficult situation.

The processes of unfreezing, changing, and refreezing can be identified in a variety of different institutions in which they are manifested in varying degree of intensity. The content of what may be taught in the influence process may vary widely from the values of Communism to the religious doctrines of a nun, and the process of influence may vary drastically in its intensity. Nevertheless there is value in taking as our frame of reference a model like that proposed and testing its utility in a variety of different organizational contexts, ranging from Communist "thought reform" centers to business enterprises' management development programs. Because the value system of the business enterprise and its role conception of the manager are not as clear-cut as the values and role prescriptions in various other institutions, one may expect the processes of unfreezing, changing, and refreezing to occur with less intensity and to be less consciously rationalized in the business enterprise. But they are structurally the same as in other organizations. One of the main purposes of this paper, then, will be to try to make salient some features of the influence of the organization on the attitudes of the individual manager by attempting to compare institutions in which the influence process is more drastic and explicit with the more implicit and less drastic methods of the business enterprise.

ILLUSTRATIONS OF ORGANIZATIONAL INFLUENCE

Unfreezing

The concept of unfreezing and the variety of methods by which influence targets can be unfrozen can best be illustrated by considering examples drawn from a broad range of situations. The Chinese Communists in their attempt to inculcate Communist attitudes into their youth or into their prisioners serve as a good prototype of one extreme. First and most important was the removal of the target person from those situations and social relationships which tended to confirm and reinforce the validity of the old attitudes. Thus the targets, be they political prisoners, prisoners of war, university professors, or young students, were isolated from their friends, families, and accustomed work groups and cut off from all media of communication to which they were accustomed. In addition, they were subjected to continuous exhortations (backed by threats of severe punishment) to confess their crimes and adopt new attitudes, and were constantly humiliated in order to discredit their old sense of identity.

The isolation of the target from his normal social and ideological supports reached its height in the case of Western civilians who were placed into group cells with a number of Chinese prisoners who had already confessed and were committed to reforming themselves and their lone Western cell mate. In the prisioner of war camps such extreme social isolation could not be produced, but its counterpart was created by the fomenting of mutual mistrust among the prisoners, by cutting off any supportive mail from home, and by systematically disorganizing the formal and informal social structure of the POW camp (by segregation of officers and noncommissioned officers from the remainder of the group, by the systematic removal of informal leaders or key personalities, and by the prohibition of any group activity not in line with the indoctrination program) (Schein, 1960, 1961).

The Chinese did not hesitate to use physical brutality and threats of death and/or permanent non-repatriation to enforce the view that only by collaboration and attitude could the prisoner hope to survive physically and psychologically. In the case of the civilians in group cells, an additional and greater stress was represented by the social pressure of the cell mates who would harangue, insult, revile, humiliate, and plead with the resistant Westerner twenty-four hours a day for weeks or months on end, exhorting him to admit his guilt, confess his crimes, reform, and adopt Communist values. This combination of physical and social pressures is perhaps a prototype of the use of coercion in the service of unfreezing a target individual in attitude areas to which he is strongly committed.

A somewhat milder, though structurally similar, process can be observed in the training of a nun (Hulme, 1956). The novice enters the convent voluntarily and is presumably ready to change, but the kind of change which must be accomplished encounters strong psychological resistances because, again, it involves deeply held attitudes and habits. Thus the novice must learn to be completely unselfish and, in fact, selfless; she must adapt to a completely communal life; she must give up any source of authority except the absolute authority of God and of those senior to her in the convent; and she must learn to curb her sexual and aggressive impulses. How does the routine of the convent facilitate unfreezing? Again a key element is the removal of the novice from her accustomed routines, sources of confirmation, social supports, and old relationships. She is physically isolated from the outside world, surrounded by others who are undergoing the same training as she, subjected to a highly demanding and fatiguing physical regimen, constantly exhorted toward her new role and punished for an evidence of old behaviors and attitudes, and subjected to a whole range of social pressures ranging from mild disapproval to total humiliation for any failure.

Not only is the novice cut off from her old social identity, but her entry into the convent separates her from many aspects of her physical identity. She is deprived of all means of being beautiful or even feminine; her hair is cut off and she is given institutional garb which emphasizes formlessness and sameness; she loses her old name and chronological age in favor of a new name and age corresponding to length of time in the convent; her living quarters and daily routine emphasize an absolute minimum of physical comfort and signify a total devaluation of anything related to the body. At the same time the threat associated with change is minimized by the tremendous support which the convent offers for change and by the fact that everyone else either already exhibits the appropriate attitudes or is in the process of learning them.

If we look at the process by which a pledge comes to be a fullfledged member of a fraternity, we find in this situation also a set of pressures to give up old associations and habits, a devaluation. of the old self by humiliations ranging from menial, senseless jobs to paddling and hazing, a removal of threat through sharing the training, and support for good performance in the pledge role. The evangelist seeking to convert those who come to hear him attempts to unfreeze his audience by stimulating guilt and by devaluating their former selves as sinful and unworthy. The teacher wishing to induce motivation to learn sometimes points out the deficiencies in the student's knowledge and hopes at the same time to induce some guilt for having those deficiencies.

Some of the elements which all unfreezing situations have in common are the following: (1) the physical removal of the influence target from his accustomed routines, sources of information, and social relationships; (2) the undermining and destruction of all social supports; (3) demeaning and humiliating experience to help the target see his old self as unworthy and thus to become motivated to change; (4) the consistent linking of reward with willingness to change and of punishment with unwillingness to change.

Changing

Once the target has become motivated to change, the actual influence is most likely to occur by one of two processes. The target finds one or more models in his social environment and learns new attitudes by identifying with them and trying to become like them; or the target confronts new situations with an experimental attitude and develops for himself attitudes which remove whatever problem he faces. These two processes—*identification* and *internalization*—probably tend to occur together in most concrete situations, but it is worthwhile, for analytical purposes, to keep them separate.[6]

The student or prisoner of the Chinese Communists took his basic step toward acquiring Communist attitudes when he began to identify with his more advanced fellow student or prisoner. In the group cell it was the discovery by the Western prisoner that his Chinese cell mates were humans like himself, were rational, and yet completely believed in their own and his guilt, which forced him to re-examine his own premises and bases of judgment and led him the first step down the path of acquiring the Communist

[6] Both are facilitated greatly if the influence agent saturates the environment with the new attitudes to be learned.

point of view. In other words, he began to identify with his cell mates and to acquire their point of view as the only solution to getting out of prison and reducing the pressure on him. The environment was, of course, saturated with the Communist point of view, but it is significant that such saturation by itself was not sufficient to induce genuine attitude change. The prisoner kept in isolation and bombarded with propaganda was less likely to acquire Communist attitudes than the one placed into a group cell with more reformed prisoners. Having a personal model was apparently crucial.

In the convent the situation is essentially comparable except that the novice is initially much more disposed toward identifying with older nuns and has a model of appropriate behavior around her all the time in the actions of the others. It is interesting to note also that some nuns are singled out as particularly qualified models and given the appropriate name of "the living rule." It is also a common institution in initiation or indoctrination procedures to attach to the target individual someone who is labelled a "buddy" or "big brother," whose responsibility it is to teach the novice "the ropes" and to communicate the kinds of attitudes expected of him.

In most kinds of training and teaching situations, and even in the sales relationship, it is an acknowledged fact that the process is facilitated greatly if the target can identify with the influence agent. Such identification is facilitated if the social distance and rank difference between agent and target are not too great. The influence agent has to be close enough to the target to be seen as similar to the target, yet must be himself committed to the attitudes he is trying to inculcate. Thus, in the case of the Chinese Communist group cell, the cell mates could be perceived as sharing a common situation with the Western prisoner and this perception facilitated his identification with them. In most buddy systems, the buddy is someone who has himself gone through the training program in the recent past. If the target is likely to mistrust the influence attempts of the organization, as might be the case in a management-sponsored training program for labor or in a therapy program for delinquents in a reformatory, it is even more important that the influence agent be perceived as similar to the target. Otherwise he is dismissed as a "company man" or one who has already sold out, and hence is seen as someone whose message or example is not to be taken seriously.

Internalization, the discovery of attitudes which are the target's own solutions to his perceived dilemmas, can occur at the same time as identification. The individual can use the example of others to guide him in solving his own problems without necessarily identifying with them to the point of complete imitation. His choice of attitude remains ultimately his own in terms of what works for him, given the situation in which he finds himself. Internalization is only possible in an organizational context in which, from the organization's point of view, a number of different kinds of attitudes will be tolerated. If there is a "party line," a company philosophy, or a given way in which people have to feel about things in order to get along, it is hardly an efficient procedure to let trainees discover their own solutions. Manipulating the situation in such a way as to make the official solution the only one which is acceptable can, of course, be attempted, but the hazards of creating real resentment and alienation on the part of the individual when he discovers he really had no choice may outweigh the presumed advantages of letting him think he had a choice.

In the case of the Chinese Communists, the convent, the revival meeting, the fraternity, or the institutional training program, we are dealing with situations where the attitudes to be learned are clearly specified. In this kind of situation, internalization will not occur unless the attitudes to be learned happen to fit uniquely the kind of personal problem the individual has in the situation. For example, a few prisoners of the Communists reacted to the tremendous unfreezing pressures with genuine guilt when they discovered they held certain prejudices and attitudes (e.g. when they realized that they had looked down on lower class Chinese in spite of their manifest acceptance of them). These prisoners were then able to internalize certain portions of the total complex of Communist attitudes, particularly those dealing with unselfishness and working for the greater good of others. The attitudes which the institution demanded of them also solved a personal problem of long standing for them. In the case of the nun, one might hypothesize that internalization of the convent's attitudes will occur to the extent that asceticism offers a genuine solution to the incumbent's personal conflicts.

Internalization is a more common outcome in those influence settings where the direction of change is left more to the individual. The influence which occurs in programs like Alcoholics Anonymous, in psychotherapy or counseling for hospitalization or incarcerated populations, in religious retreats, in human relations training the kind pursued by the National Training Laboratories (1953), and in certain kinds of progressive education programs is more likely to occur through internalization or, at least, to lead ultimately to more internalization.

Refreezing

Refreezing refers to the process by which the newly acquired attitude comes to be integrated into the target's personality and ongoing relationships. If the new attitude has been internalized while being learned, this has automatically facilitiated freezing because it has been fitted naturally into the individual's personality. If it has been learned through identification, it will persist only so long as the target's relationship with the original influence model persists unless new surrogate models are found or social support and reinforcement is obtained for expressions of the new attitude.[7]

[7] In either case the change may be essentially permanent, in that a relationship to a model or surrogate can last indefinitely. It is important to distinguish the two processes, however, because if one were to try to change the attitude, different strategies would be used depending upon how the attitude had been learned.

In the case of the convent such support comes from a whole set of expectations which others have of how the nun should behave, from clearly specified role perscriptions, and from rituals. In the case of individuals influenced by the Chinese Communists, if they remained in Communist China they receive constant support for their new attitudes from superiors and peers; if they returned to the West, the permanence of their attitude change depended on the degree of support they actually received from friends and relations back home, or from groups which they sought out in an attempt to get support. If their friends and relatives did not support Communist attitudes, the repatriates were influenced once again toward their original attitude or toward some new integration of both sets.

The importance of social support for new attitudes was demonstrated dramatically in the recent Billy Graham crusade in New York City. An informal survey of individuals who came forward when Graham called for converts indicated that only those individuals who were subsequently integrated into local churches maintained their faith. Similar kinds of findings have been repeatedly noted with respect to human relations training in industry. Changes which may occur during the training program do not last unless there is some social support for the new attitudes in the "back home" situation.

The kind of model which has been discussed above might best be described by the term "coercive persuasion." The influence of an organization on an individual is coercive in the sense that he is usually forced into situations which are likely to unfreeze him, in which there are many overt and covert pressures to recognize in himself a need for change, and in which the supports for his old attitudes are in varying degrees coercively removed. It is coercive also to the degree that the new attitudes to be learned are relatively rigidly prescribed. The individual either learns them or leaves the organization (if he can). At the same time, the actual process by which new attitudes are learned can best be described as persuasion. In effect, the individual is forced into a situation in which he is likely to be influenced. The organization can be highly coercive in unfreezing its potential influence targets, yet be quite open about the direction of attitude changes it will tolerate. In those cases where the direction of change is itself coerced (as contrasted with letting it occur through identification or internalization), it is highly unlikely that anything is accomplished other than surface behavioral change in the target. And such surface change will be abandoned the moment the coercive force of the change agent is lessened. If behavioral changes are coerced at the same time as other unfreezing operations are undertaken, actual influence can be facilitated if the individual finds himself having to learn attitudes to justify the kinds of behavior he has been forced to exhibit. The salesman may not have an attitude of cynicism toward his customers initially. If, however, he is forced by his boss to behave as if he felt cynical, he might develop real cynicism as a way of justifying his actual behavior.

MANAGEMENT DEVELOPMENT: IS IT COERCIVE PERSUASION?

Do the notions of coercive persuasion developed above fit the management development situation? Does the extent to which they do or do not fit such a model illuminate for us some of the implications of specific management development practices?

Unfreezing

It is reasonable to assume that the majority of managers who are being "developed" are not ready or able to change in the manner in which their organization might desire and therefore must be unfrozen before they can be influenced. They may be eager to change at a conscious motivation level, yet still be psychologically unprepared to give up certain attitudes and values in favor of untried, threatening new ones. I cannot support this assumption empirically, but the likelihood of its being valid is high because of a related fact which is empirically supportable. Most managers do not participate heavily in decisions which affect their careers, nor do they have a large voice in the kind of self-development in which they wish to participate. Rather, it is the man's superior or a staff specialist in career development who makes the key decisions concerning his career (Alfred, 1960). If the individual manager is not trained from the outset to take responsibility for his own career and give a heavy voice in diagnosing his own needs for a change, it is unlikely that he will readily be able to appreciate someone else's diagnosis. It may be unclear to him what basically is wanted of him or, worse, the ambiguity of the demands put upon him combined with his own inability to control his career development is likely to arouse anxiety and insecurity which would cause even greater resistance to genuine self-assessment and attitude change.[8] He becomes preoccupied with promotion in the abstract and attempts to acquire at a surface level the traits which he thinks are necessary for advancement.

If the decisions made by the organization do not seem valid to the manager, or if the unfreezing process turns out to be quite painful to him, to what extent can he leave the situation? His future career, his financial security, and his social status within the business community all stand to suffer if he resists the decisions made for him. Perhaps the most coercive feature is simply the psychological pressure that what he is being asked to do is "for his own ultimate welfare." Elementary loyalty to his organization and to his managerial role demands that he accept with good grace whatever happens to him in the name of his own career development. In this sense, then, I believe that the business organization has coercive forces at

---

[8] An even greater hazard, of course, is that the organization communicates to the manager that he is not expected to take responsibility for his own career at the same time that it is trying to teach him how to be able to take responsibility for important decisions!

its disposal which are used by it in a manner comparable to the uses made by other organizations.

Given the assumption that the manager who is to be developed needs to be unfrozen, and given that the organization has available coercive power to accomplish such unfreezing, what mechanisms does it actually use to unfreeze potential influence targets?

The essential elements to unfreezing are the removal of supports for the old attitudes, the saturation of the environment with the new attitudes to be acquired, a minimizing of threat, a maximizing of support for any change in the right direction. In terms of this model it becomes immediately apparent that training programs or other activities which are conducted in the organization at the place of work for a certain number of hours per day or week are far less likely to unfreeze and subsequently influence the participant than those programs which remove him for varying lengths of time from his regular work situation and normal social relationships.

Are appraisal interviews, used periodically to communicate to the manager his strengths, weaknesses and areas for improvement, likely to unfreeze him? Probably not, because as long as the individual is caught up in his regular routine and is responding, probably quite unconsciously, to a whole set of expectations which others have about his behavior and attitudes, it is virtually impossible for him to hear, at a psychological level, what his deficiencies or areas needing change are. Even if he can appreciate what is being communicated to him at an intellectual level, it is unlikely that he can emotionally accept the need for change, and even if he can accept it emotionally, it is unlikely that he can produce change in himself in an environment which supports all of his old ways of functioning. This statement does not mean that the man's co-workers necessarily approve of the way he is operating or like the attitudes which he is exhibiting. They may want to see him change, but their very expectations concerning how he normally behaves operate as a constraint on him which makes attitude change difficult in that setting.

On the other hand, there are a variety of training activities which are used in management development which approximates more closely the conditions necessary for effective unfreezing. These would include programs offered at special training centers such as those maintained by IBM on Long Island and General Electric at Crotonville, N. Y.; university-sponsored courses in management, liberal arts, and/or the social sciences; and especially, workshops or laboratories in human relations such as those conducted at Arden House, N. Y., by the National Training Laboratories. Programs such as these remove the participant for some length of time from his normal routine, his regular job, and his social relationships (including his family in most cases), thus providing a kind of moratorium during which he can take stock of himself and determine where he is going and where he wants to go.

The almost total isolation from the pressures of daily life in the business world which a mountain chateau such as Arden House provides for a two-week period is supplemented by other unfreezing forces. The de-emphasis on the kind of job or title the participant holds in his company and the informal dress remove some of the symbolic or status supports upon which we all rely. Sharing a room and bath facilities with a roommate requires more than the accustomed exposure of private spheres of life to others. The total involvement of the participant in the laboratory program leaves little room for reflection about the back home situation. The climate of the laboratory communicates tremendous support for any efforts at self-examination and attempts as much as possible to reduce the threats inherent in change by emphasizing the value of experimentation, the low cost and risk of trying a new response in the protected environment of the lab, and the high gains to be derived from finding new behavior patterns and attitudes which might improve back home performance. The content of the material presented in lectures and the kind of learning model which is used in the workshop facilitates self-examination, self-diagnosis based on usable feedback from other participants, and rational planning for change.[9]

The practice of rotating a manager from one kind of assignment to another over a period of years can have some of the same unfreezing effects and thus facilitate attitude change. Certainly his physical move from one setting to another removes many of the supports to his old attitudes, and in his new job the manager will have an opportunity to try new behaviors and become exposed to new attitudes. The practice of providing a moratorium in the form of a training program prior to assuming a new job would appear to maximize the gains from each approach, in that unfreezing would be maximally facilitated and change would most probabaly be lasting if the person did not go back to a situation in which his co-workers, superiors, and subordinates had stable expectations of how he should behave.

Another example of how unfreezing can be facilitated in the organizational context is the practice of temporarily reducing the formal rank and responsibilities of the manager by making him a trainee in a special program, or an apprentice on a special project, or an assistant to a high ranking member of the company. Such temporary lowering of formal rank can reduce the anxiety associated with changing and at the same time serves officially to destroy the old status and identity of the individual because he could not ordinarily return to his old position once he had accepted the path offered by the training program. He would have to move either up or out of the organization to maintain his sense of self-esteem. Of course, if such a training program is perceived by the trainee as an indication of his failing rather than a step toward a higher position, his anxiety about himself would be too high to facilitate effective change on his part. In all of the illustrations of organizational influence we have presented above, change was defined as being a means of gaining status—acceptance into Communist society, status as a non or a fraternity brother, salvation,

---

[9] Although, as I will point out later, such effective unfreezing may lead to change which is not supported to be considered desirable by the "back home" organization.

etc. If participants come to training programs believing they are being punished, they typically do not learn much.

The above discussion is intended to highlight the fact that some management development practices do facilitate the unfreezing of the influence target, but that such unfreezing is by no means automatic. Where programs fail, therefore, one of the first questions we must ask is whether they failed because they did not provide adequate conditions for unfreezing.

Changing

Turning now to the problem of the mechanisms by which changes actually occur, we must confront the question of whether the organization has relatively rigid prescribed goals concerning the direction of attitude change it expects of the young manager, or whether it is concerned with growth in the sense of providing increasing opportunities for the young manager to learn the attitudes appropriate to ever more challenging situations. It is undoubtedly true that most programs would claim growth as their goal, but the degree to which they accomplish it can only be assessed from an examination of their actual practice.

Basically the question is whether the the organization influences attitudes primarily through the mechanism of identification or the mechanism of internalization. If the development programs stimulated psychological relationships between the influence target and a member of the organization who has the desired attitudes, they are thereby facilitating influence by identification but, at the same time, are limiting the alternatives available to the target and possibly the permanence of the change achieved. If they emphasize that the target must develop his own solutions to ever more demanding problems, they are risking that the attitudes learned will be incompatible with other parts of the organization's value system but are producing more permanent change because the solutions found are internalized. From the organization's point of view, therefore, it is crucial to know what kind of influence it is exerting and to assess the results of such influence in terms of the basic goals which the organization may have. If new approaches and new attitudes toward management problems are desired, for example, it is crucial that the conditions for internalization be created. If rapid learning of a given set of attitudes is desired, it is equally crucial that the conditions for identification with the right kind of models be created.

One obvious implication of this distinction is that programs conducted within the organization's orbit by its own influence agents are much more likely to facilitate identification and thereby the transmission of the "party line" or organization philosophy. On the other hand, programs like those conducted at universities or by the National Training Laboratories place much emphasis on the finding of solutions by participants which fit their own particular needs and problems. The emphasis in the human relations courses is on "learning how to learn" from the participant's own interpersonal experiences and how to harness his emotional life and intellectual capacities to the accomplishment of his goals, rather than on specific principles of human relations. The nearest thing to an attitude which the laboratory staff, acting as influence agents, does care to communicate is an attitude of inquiry and experimentation, and to this end the learning of skills of observation, analysis, and diagnosis of interpersonal situations is given strong emphasis. The training group, which is the acknowledged core of the laboratory approach, provides its own unfreezing forces by being unstructured as to the content of discussion. But it is strongly committed to a method of learning by analysis of the member's own experiences in the group, which facilitates the discovery of the value of an attitude of inquiry and experimentation.

Mutual identification of the members of the group with each other and members identifications with the staff play some role in the acquisition of this attitude, but the basic power of the method is that the attitude of inquiry and experimentations *works* in the sense of providing for people valuable new insights about themselves, groups, and organizations. To the extent that it works and solves key problems for the participants, it is internalized and carried back into the home situation. To the extent that it is learned because participants wish to emulate a respected fellow member of staff member, it lasts only so long as the relationship with the model itself, or a surrogate of its, lasts (which may, of course, be a very long time).

The university program in management or liberal arts is more difficult to categorize in terms of an influence model, because within the program there are usually opportunities both for identification (e.g. with inspiring teachers) and internalization. It is a safe guess in either case, however, that the attitudes learned are likely to be in varying degrees out of phase with any given company's philosophy unless the company has learned from previous experience with a given course that the students are taught a point of view consistent with its own philosophy. Of course, universities, as much as laboratories, emphasize the value of a spirit of inquiry and, to the extent that they are successful in teaching this attitude, will be creating potential dissidents or innovators, depending on how the home company views the result.

Apprenticeships, special jobs in the role of "assistant to" somebody, job rotation, junior management boards, and so on stand in sharp contrast to the above methods in the degree to which they facilitate, indeed almost demand, that the young manager learn by watching those who are senior or more competent. It is probably not prescribed that in the process of acquiring knowledge and skills through the example of others he should also acquire their attitudes, but the probability that this will happen is very high if the trainee develops any degree of respect and liking for his teacher and/or supervisor. It makes little difference whether the teacher, coach, or supervisor intends to influence the attitudes of his trainee or not. If a good emotional relationship develops between them, it will facilitate the learning of the knowledge and skills, and will, at the same time, result in some degree of attitudes change. Consequently, such methods do not maximize the probability of new approaches being invented to management problems, nor do they really by themselves facilitate the growth of the manager in the sense of providing opportunities for him to develop solutions which fit his own needs best.

Job rotation, on the other hand, can facilitate growth and innovation provided it is managed in such a way as to insure the exposure of the trainee to a broad range of points of view as he moves from assignment. The practice of shifting the developing manager geographically as well as functionally both facilitates unfreezing and increases the likelihood of his being exposed to new attitudes. This same practice can, of course, be merely a convenient way of indoctrinating the individual by sending him on an assignment, for example, "in order to acquire the sales point of view from Jim down in New York," where higher management knows perfectly well what sort of a view Jim will communicate to his subordinates.

Refreezing

Finally, a few words are in order about the problem of refreezing. Under what conditions will changed attitudes remain stable, and how do existing practices aid or hinder such stabilization? Our illustrations from the non-industrial setting highlighted the importance of social support for any attitudes which were learned through identification. Even the kind of training emphasized in the National Training Laboratories programs, which tends to be more internalized, does not produce stable attitude change unless others in the organization, especially superiors, peers, and subordinates, have undergone similar changes and give each other stimulation and support, because lack of support acts as a new unfreezing force producing new influence (possibly in the direction of the original attitudes).

If the young manager has been influenced primarily in the direction of what is already the company philosophy, he will, of course, obtain strong support and will have little difficulty maintaining his new attitudes. If, on the other hand, management development is supposed to lead to personal growth and organizational innovation, the organization must recognize the reality that new attitudes cannot be carried by isolated individuals. The lament that we no longer have strong individualists who are willing to try something new is a fallacy based on an incorrect diagnosis. Strong individuals have always gained a certain amount of their strength from the support of others, hence the organizational problem is how to create conditions which make possible the nurturing of new ideas, attitudes, and approaches. If organizations seem to lack innovators, it may be that the climate of the organization and its methods of management development do not foster innovation, not that its human resources are inadequate.

An organizational climate in which new attitudes which differ from company philosophy can nevertheless be maintained cannot be achieved merely by an intellectual or even emotional commitment on the part of higher-ranking managers to tolerance of new ideas and attitudes. Genuine support can come only from others who have themselves been influenced, which argues strongly that at least several members of a given department must be given the same training before such training can be expected to have effect. If the superior of the people involved can participate in it as well, this strengthens the group that much more, but it would not follow from my line of reasoning that this is a necessary condition. Only some support is needed, and this support can come as well from peers and subordinates.

From this point of view, the practice of sending more than one manager to any given program at a university of human relations workshop is very sound. The National Training Laboratories have emphasized from the beginning the desirability of having organizations send teams. Some organizations like Esso Standard have created their own laboratories for the training of the entire management complement of a given refinery, and all indications are that such a practice maximizes the possibility not only of the personal growth of the managers, but of the creative growth of the organization as a whole.

CONCLUSION

In the above discussion I have deliberately focused on a model of influence which emphasizes procedure rather than content, interpersonal relations rather than mass media, and attitudes and values rather than knowledge and skills. By placing management development into a context of institutional influence procedures which also include Chinese Communist thought reform, the training of a nun, and other more drastic forms of coercive persuasion, I have tried to highlight aspects of management development which have remained implicit yet which need to be understood. I believe that some aspects of management development are a mild form of coercive persuasion, but I do not believe that coercive persuasion is either morally bad in any *a priori* sense nor inefficient. If we are to develop a sound theory of career development which is capable of including not only many of the formal procedures discussed in this paper; but the multitudes of informal practices, some of which are more and some of which are less coercive than those discussed, we need to suspend moral judgments for the time being and evaluate influence models solely in terms of their capacity to make sense of the data and to make meaningful predictions.

52 • HOW TO SALVAGE PROBLEM EXECUTIVES[1]

Gail Gregg[2]

Everybody knows him: the talented professional—the engineer, marketing expert, planner, financial analyst—whose career speeds ahead until he is promoted to a top managerial job. In his new position of power he becomes autocratic, barking orders at subordinates and challenging his superiors. He might take to drink or to overeating or to letting family problems follow him to the office. Or perhaps he will retreat into himself, becoming so withdrawn he can't assert enough authority to get his new job done.

Not too long ago, many companies would have shaken their heads over such a manager and lamented that the "Peter Principle" had asserted itself once again. A hard-nosed firm might have suggested that the troublesome executive look elsewhere for employment; a more benevolent one might have "outplaced" him through one of the many firms that specialize in pruning problem personnel from corporate ranks.

Today, however, top managements have become increasingly aware that many such executives are failing not because they have exceeded their abilities, as the Peter Principle would have it, but because they lack the interpersonal and managerial skills to be effective at their new jobs.

A number of companies have called on leading human-relations consultancies that offer short-term counseling and special training to salvage problem executives. Firms like BeamPines, Inc. in New York City, Farr Associates, Inc. in Greensboro, North Carolina, and Rohrer, Hibler & Replogle in Chicago promise to refit these executives with a new awareness of themselves, teach them new techniques for dealing with people, and send them back into the workplace as more sensitive, enlightened managers.

From the companies' point of view, such services may in some cases be a last resort. The problem executive has often become so much trouble that he must either change or be fired (rarely is it a "she," since there are still few women in these top-echelon jobs). The companies would thus prefer to pay the relatively small cost of counseling than lose experienced employees and all that has been invested in their careers.

On the other hand, there are observers who are justifiably skeptical that mature adults can be taught, in the "short course," how to get along with and lead other people. A few are skeptical of the new consulting services, among them Eugene Jennings of Michigan State University, author of *Routes to the Executive Suite* and *The Mobile Manager,* who says that many of the consultants act as "confidants" to the problem executives rather than as trained counselors. Jennings, who heads his own consulting firm, remarked in a telephone interview, "It sounds as if outplacement people are out of work and trying to get into counseling."

[1] From *Across the Board,* Vol. XXI, No. 4 (April, 1984), pp. 24–30. Reprinted by permission of The Conference Board and Gail Gregg.
[2] Gail Gregg, freelance writer, New York.

Why are such services needed in the first place? According to many experts, it's because of American companies' traditional sink-or-swim attitude toward newly promoted managers. "The culture of management in this country is very much a Western culture—freewheeling, do it on your own," says Dr. John R. Sauer, New York manager of Rohrer, Hibler & Replogle. "It continues to amaze me in dealing with senior executives that we still haven't developed a good way to teach people to manage."

The idea of providing counseling to managers is not exactly new, however. Such management specialists as Dr. Leonard R. Sayles, of Columbia University's School of Business, stress that the best-run corporations have been providing such guidance for their executives for decades.

What is new is the growing demand for one-shot, short-course, problem-solving services. Dr. James Farr, president of the Greensboro-based Farr Associates, has been offering such intensive counseling for the last 12 years as part of his broad training in leadership development. But he says that in the past several years, he has been marketing that particular service separately because interest in it has grown so much. "Before, it was just something we quietly had available," he said.

Howard Pines, president of BeamPines, suspects that the heightened interest in help programs for problem executives stems from a more humane management approach in the 1980s, and from the economic advantages of "rehabilitation" over outplacement. Pines, a former human-resources director for Standard Brands, and Dr. Jerome Beam, a clinical psychologist, offer an Executive Development Counseling Service, for which they charge a flat fee of $5,000. That's a lot less than what it would cost a company to place a problem executive in a new job, find a replacement for him, and relocate and train the replacement; Beam and Pines estimate that the total cost of all that could be as much as $100,000.

In the three years since they initiated their service, Beam and Pines have counseled more than 75 executives—mostly middle managers such as head actuaries, operations chiefs, comptrollers, or financial analysts. Their clients have included corporate giants such as Time and Nabisco and smaller firms such as New York City's Edison Parking Corporation.

One company that recently gave the BeamPines approach a try was Avon Products. A vice president for the large cosmetics corporation hired the human-relations firm to counsel a "sergeant-type" manager with problems fostering teamwork. "I had an employee who had been quite successful in a lot of ways but had some other problems," the corporate vice president said in an interview. "At the rate he was going, he was not going to stay."

The vice president first investigated a number of leadership seminars and training programs but decided none was "individual" enough to help the manager overcome his particular problems. Instead, the vice president selected one-to-one counseling for his subordinate. "He's not a model," the vice president says of the results of the five-month program. "But he's a much better member of management than he would have been. We clearly have saved him." And while the vice president says he was impressed by the BeamPines program, he hopes he won't be using their services too often. "Good management should correct such problems along the way," he cautions. The vice president asked that he not be named in order to protect the identity of the problem manager.

Once Avon contracted for the counseling program, Beam and Pines interviewed the executive's superiors to get a clear idea of their views of his problems and their goals for him. The consultants then prepared a report for the executive, first stressing the positive aspects of his behavior and then detailing the need for change. That appraisal was presented at a meeting with his boss—where Beam and Pines also got the two to agree about which problems to focus on in the subsequent months of counseling.

After the executive underwent psychological and personality tests, he began about five months of counseling. Because he was based outside New York, he met with Beam and Pines twice a month for a full day; by contrast, New York-area executives meet with the human-resources team every other week for about two-and-a-half hours. The sessions included formal counseling in which Beam explored the client's history with him to understand patterns in his behavior; training in management and communications skills; role-playing and videotaping sessions; and more casual discussions with Beam and Pines over lunch or dinner.

During a typical video session, the manager was asked to conduct a performance review, with Pines posing as an Avon subordinate with whom the manager was distressed. Afterwards, they reviewed the tape—which clearly showed the executive's impatience with his employee. "He did most of the talking," Pines said of the executive. "I never had a chance to say anything, so pretty soon I lost interest in talking."

Armed with such evidence of the executive's negative behavior, Pines and Beam then were able to teach him to modify that behavior—by using words that encourage communication rather than turning it off; by learning ways to solicit information from people; and even by changing his body language and voice intonation. "Lean back in your chair," Pines urged the aggressive manager. "Don't signal with your face or body the impatience you might be feeling inside."

After each session, the counseling team prepared a memo for the manager's boss, discussing his progress. "We establish at the outset that we'll be in touch with the company," Beam says. "But we tell the client that anything personal that he doesn't want us to pass on, we won't."

During the period of counseling, Beam and Pines encouraged the client's boss to act as his mentor, praising him when he succeeded at changing his behavior and urging him to continue working on problems that persisted. "What you're trying to do is get them to go back out in the field and practice their new techniques," Pines said. They also suggested that the boss notify the client's peers that he was "working on his problems" and encourage them to "meet him halfway for a while."

Once the executive completed the program to his and his company's satisfaction, he was invited to return to BeamPines for refresher sessions whenever necessary for the rest of the year. The two consultants also maintain contact with former clients after that to monitor their progress. "We've had individuals get very nice promotions," Beam said, "and most also report an improvement in their relationships with their families."

• • •

One "classic" type of problem manager, according to Beam and Pines, is the tyrannical executive who is a shy and sensitive man at heart and feels that his natural personality traits are inappropriate to his position. In such cases, Beam says, he and Pines try to show clients how to use their personalities to advantage without appearing weak.

Beam cited a highly successful marketing executive who felt that if he showed his sensitive side, his subordinates would take advantage of him and slacken their efforts. After convincing him that his behavior was affecting the performance of his employees, Beam encouraged him to tell them that he had been made aware of his gruff style and was attempting to change. But Beam also advised him to caution them that such a change would not mean he was lowering his work standards. Most employees, Beam believes, react "very positively" to such an honest confession and support their boss as he attempts to improve his behavior.

Another problem is the executive who has risen to his position without receiving any management training along the way and has trouble communicating, both with superiors and subordinates. "The realm of people skills is an enigma to many managers," Beam said. "They've given lip service to it, but they haven't been given an approach." Such executives often have to be taught simple skills such as not interrupting when someone else is talking, doing a better job of explaining tasks, or asking questions instead of dictating.

Other managers have to be persuaded to put aside minor complaints on temporary grievances if they are not compatible with long-term business goals. One executive who was overly concerned about the appearance of his employees had to be taught not to open a department meeting with such comments as, "John, why do you have your tie pulled down like that?" If improving the dress of his subordinates was the focus of the meeting, Pines told him, then the comment was appropriate. If not, Pines continued, "it was not a very productive thing to say."

Still other executives may develop problems because of changes in the corporate environment—a departmental reorganization, for instance, or a personality "mismatch" with a new boss. Or they may have difficulty with their reactions in specific social situations, which they can control once they understand what sets them off. One manufacturing manager who consistently lost his temper at division meetings worked hard at role-playing exercises to learn to control his emotional responses. "We'd challenge him, get under his skin," Pines said of the sessions. "We tried to alert the guy to what would happen and prepare him for that. And then we'd talk about how he could respond in a more positive manner."

Crucial to his program's success, Beam stresses, is the way the firm initially approaches the problem executive about its decision to hire the human-relations firm: He or she must be made to feel it is a supportive gesture rather than a vote of disapproval. "They have to have a willingness to give it a try," Beam said. He and Pines urge the boss to explain that although the company has become unhappy with an executive's performance, it values him enough to spend $5,000 to help him become a better manager. "The individual usually senses he has problems. It usually is very positive to know that the company supports him," Beam says.

Beam admits, however, that it is not always the case that the company wants the executive to improve: It may have waited until the situation had gotten completely out of hand and contracted for counseling as a last resort. "Many people come into the program feeling they've been set up. And sometimes they have been," Beam says.

"If we have a feeling that they [the company] really want the person out of the job, we surface this at the beginning," Beam asserts. At times, he believes, top management may not even be aware that they really want to be rid of the person. Sometimes they have waited too long to help the executive, and their opinions about him may become so fixed that they simply don't believe he can change.

This was the underlying problem in one of the firm's counseling failures. The employee had a personality style, according to Beam, which was too rigid for his wheeler-dealer boss. "It became evident that no matter what the person did, he would not be able to accommodate himself to his boss's expectations," Beam notes, though he believes that the company's decision to seek counseling for the man was not a "conscious setup" to justify dismissal.

Beam acknowledges his firm has had "a couple of failures," involving differences in leadership style between executive and company. "But we have other cases in which the jury is still out." Beam mentioned one client, an older man whose boss didn't really seem to care about salvaging him. His reputation had been so damaged by his behavior, Beam said, that the company acknowledges he is working hard to change his behavior but "doesn't know if it has time to wait for him to accomplish the changes."

• • •

If they really want to keep the problem executive, the companies must, of course, assure him of the counseling's constructive aims. The Pepsi-Cola Company, which has used the Beam Pines program a few times, may recommend the service to a problem executive as part of an annual employee review in which managers meet with their subordinates to discuss their "developmental goals." According to Pepsi-Cola's human-resources director, Dr. Bruce B. Saari, introducing the idea of counseling in this way ensures that the program is not seen as a last-ditch effort. "Everybody has some defensiveness they have to deal with," Saari said. "But in most cases, this kind of developmental opportunity is viewed as a kind of perk. They feel it reflects the company's support for their growth."

James Farr, a former head of the graduate program in psychology at New York University, agrees that company support is essential for such a manager: Before he'll take on a client, he requires that the firm sit down with the executive and explain his value—and his problems—to him. Farr's staff then interviews the client's subordinates, peers, and superiors about his behavior and presents him with the resulting "image study" as a "powerful incentive for change." This report, which Farr describes as "devastatingly negative," is often necessary because many executives deny that they're doing anything wrong or argue that changing their behavior would mean lowering their standards.

Executives coming to Farr Associates then take a battery of psychological tests and attend a five-day workshop designed to "develop awareness in the deeper sense." Half the week is devoted to a self-examination program of "guided fantasies," hypnosis, and Gestalt techniques (which emphasize role-playing attempts to put the client in the skins of his superiors and subordinates). The second half of the week is reserved for training in management techniques such as communication skills, developing teamwork, or managing time effectively. In a guided fantasy, an executive relaxes in a dimly lighted room with soft background music while a leader gives instruction in relaxation technique. Once he is totally relaxed, the client is asked to recall past experiences from both his personal life and career— difficult relationships which he handled badly, for instance. "After a while, he might see a pattern running through," Farr said. Similarly, hypnosis sometimes is used to "help a person get behind his defenses and find out something about himself that is interfering with his effectiveness," Farr said.

A dozen problem executives went through Farr's month-long Executive Job Clinic last year, at a cost of $3,500 each. (For those who want more advanced management training afterwards, the firm offers a nine-month group leadership course which meets twice a month and costs $2,000.) Among the firms that have used Farr's Job Clinic are First Union National Bank of Charlotte, North Carolina, and the Renfro Hosiery Mills Company of Mt. Airy, North Carolina.

Hay Career Consultants of New York offers yet another variation on the theme: the so-called Third-Party Career Crisis Consulting program. According to president Clifford J. Benfield, Hay's service is designed not so much to "save" an executive but to evaluate whether he should remain with the company. "Sometimes you find out it's merely a case of poor communication," Benfield said, and a solution is worked out between "the wobbly peg" and his boss. But 9 times out of 10, the problem executive says, "If I could cut a deal, I'd be out of here in a flash." Then it's up to Hay to make that arrangement with management and place the executive in a new job. The "career-crisis" program costs between $2,000 and $2,500; outplacement fees are extra.

Rohrer, Hibler & Replogle offers counseling to problem executives as part of its broad-ranging psychological consulting services to corporations.

Working on a monthly retainer of $2,500 and up, RHR acts as what John R. Sauer terms a "well-baby clinic" for companies concerned about ongoing evaluation and development of their staffs. The firm currently has 900 clients ranging from two-man partnerships to *Fortune* 500 companies.

Because RHR has an ongoing relationship with the companies it serves and is familiar with their goals and markets, Sauer believes it is more successful at putting executive problems "in context" than one-shot counseling programs. "Quite frequently," he noted, "individual problems are a function of circumstance." In one recent case, RHR was asked to help counsel a bank executive who had become abusive toward her supervisor. The consulting firm discovered that the bank had changed its loan-review requirements without telling branch managers. "All of a sudden, loans were being turned down," Sauer said, "and the executive thought her boss was out to get her." Once the change was explained, "everything was fine."

Management experts warn that companies considering using such a counseling service to rehabilitate a problem executive should not expect a substantial change in the subject's basic personality. As Columbia's Sayles noted, "Most of the data suggest that supervisory style is to a significant extent a function of personality." Even the new MBAs who are exposed to a great deal of human-relations training during their studies "are as autocratic as can be," Sayles warned.

But if a company sets "modest targets" for the executive's improvement and urges him to make certain tangible changes in his behavior, counseling can be a useful investment. Even the most autocratic manager, Sayles continued, can learn communications skills that will improve his performance: Simple notions, obvious to some but not to everyone, can help, such as, "Don't just open your mouth but think about how what you say is going to affect the other person."

That's a conclusion with which both Beam and Farr agree. They stress that their programs are targeted to executives with "adjustment" or "behavioral" problems—not with deep psychological difficulties. "If I sense that an individual has severe personality problems, I urge that he get counseling from someone else," says Beam, adding that he has made such a recommendation for a few of his clients.

Saari of Pepsi-Cola also advises that companies carefully check the professional credentials of firms offering problem-executive programs and contract only with those staffed by licensed psychologists. And he further notes that Pepsi believes a human-relations firm retained for counseling services should not also be used for outplacement: Otherwise, a manager undergoing counseling might worry that outplacement could be the next step.

"No service is any better than the competence of the person doing it," stresses Dr. Harry Levinson, head of the Levinson Institute and professor of organizational diagnosis at the Harvard Medical School. He worries that untrained career counselors may not recognize serious psychological problems in their clients—and may even dissuade them from seeking long-term help. "If I were running a company," Levinson suggests, "I'd find a well-trained clinical psychologist whose competence I had checked out and with whom I could build a continuing relationship—and to whom people could turn with some confidence."

But if handled in the proper way, Saari maintains, intensive counseling for problem executives can be a "very positive experience" for both the company and the client. He concludes: "It's been an effective way to deal with people we have a lot of confidence in and whose success we'd like to ensure."

53 • CHANGING SUPERVISORY AND MANAGERIAL BEHAVIOR[1]

William C. Byham[2]

Can supervisors and managers change their fundamental ways of behaving in areas such as judgment, leadership, sensitivity, initiative, and business creativity? While we would all like to think they can, there is little evidence to back up that hope.

There are very few research studies that actually show behavioral change resulting from training or development. In the 1971 *Annual Review of Psychology*, all the published training programs up to that time were reviewed. Few documented behavioral changes were found.[3]

Since that review, training programs have tended to become more behavioral as programs using job enrichment and behavior modification have been introduced, but still there are very few available documented cases of behavioral change particularly at the supervisory or managerial levels.

Particularly strong evidence against the notion that basic behavioral patterns in supervisors and managers can be changed comes from the *Management Progress Study* conducted by AT&T (American Telephone & Telegraph Co.)[4] They put 124 new college hires through an assessment center when they joined the company, and after eight years reassessed them. No feedback on the assessment results was given to the individuals or to company management. No differences between the two assessments on most assessment center dimensions were found. This was in spite of the telephone company's organized program of development through a variety of work assignments, special projects, and so on.

Surprisingly assessed interpersonal skills of the executives decreased over the eight years. The authors speculate that this loss may result more from a lessening of concern for group harmony as one goes through early adult years than the actual loss of ability. Whatever the reason, these findings are certainly contrary to what most managers would expect to be happening to their management trainees during their formative years . . . and they do not promote the hope that people can change their behavior!

The *Management Progress Study* findings do not mean that people cannot change. What the study actually shows is that individuals, left to their own devices and exposed only to generalized training and development procedures, do not change. The very characteristics that make the *Management Progress Study* such an excellent research study mitigate against behavioral change taking place. One must remember that the participants in the study were given no feedback

[1]Reproduced by special permission from the April-May, 1977, *Training and Development Journal.* Copyright 1977 by the American Society for Training and Development, Inc.

[2]William C. Byham, President of Development Dimensions, Inc., Pittsburgh, Pennsylvania.

[3]J. P. Campbell, "Personnel Training and Development," *Annual Review of Psychology,* Vol. 22, (1971) pp. 565–602.

[4]D. W. Bray, R. J. Campbell, and D. L. Grant, *Formative Years in Business: A Long-Term AT&T Study of Managerial Lives* (New York City: John Wiley & Sons, Inc., 1974).

whatsoever as to their performance in the first assessment center. Therefore, self-development actions were precluded.

More importantly, management was not given any information regarding the individual performance of the participants. Thus, there was no supervisor or organizational response to the findings in the form of changing jobs, developing better learning situations, or attendance at remedial training programs.

What the negative results from the study (or lack of positive results from other studies) show is that we have been going about training in the wrong way. Below I would like to present some reasons why conventional systems and programs have not worked. In Part II of this article I will suggest some ways meaningful behavioral change can be brought about.

PRACTICE DOES NOT MAKE PERFECT

The old saying that practice makes perfect is incomplete. It should read, "Practice with critique makes perfect." Without feedback relative to the success or quality of performance, a person cannot improve. Unfortunately this is exactly the situation in which most supervisors and managers find themselves. This explains why a supervisor can conduct 200 performance reviews and still do it poorly. The supervisor starts out doing a poor job and keeps on repeating the mistakes because no one tells him or her differently.

TENURE DOES NOT MAKE A GOOD SUPERVISOR

It seems clear from the *Management Progress Study* results that people in general don't change their basic skills by just being in a work situation. In the study, the assessed management skills were largely unchanged over the eight years.

EXPERIENCE IS A POOR TEACHER

Although widely assumed to the contrary, I can find no evidence that experience alone changes management skills. Managers may become faster at planning or communicating due to experience, but no evidence shows improvement in quality. In some situations, experience may even cause a decrease in skill, as evidenced by the lessening of assessed interpersonal skills reported in the *Management Progress Study* research and from studies of the interviewing skills of life insurance managers.[5] In the interview studies, it was found that the more experienced the interviewer, the fewer the dimensions about the job applicant that were sought. Interviewers settled into an interviewing rut that resulted in the more experienced interviewer actually obtaining less breadth of information about an applicant than an inexperienced interviewer.

[5]R.E. Carlson, "The Current Status of Judgmental Techniques in Industry," *Symposium on Alternatives to Paper and Pencil Testing* (Pittsburgh: University of Pittsburgh Press, May, 1972), pp. 1–68.

LEARNING BY MISTAKES IS A WASTE OF TIME

An examination of how a supervisor or manager learns new supervisory or managerial behavior reveals that they do so by a very inefficient process. Learning from mistakes implies two happenings: (1) stumbling on the right (or at least a better) method of behavior and (2) knowing that the behavior is better once tried. Both events are unlikely.

Managers very quickly get into habits of dealing with people, problems, challenges, and so on. Many psychologists would speculate that the basic methods are learned early in life and certainly are well defined by the time individuals enter management. At any rate, the odds of a supervisor or manager just happening on a better method are slim. Supervisors usually develop a system and pretty much follow it in spite of differences in situations or people involved.

The possibility of a supervisor recognizing a better method when it occurs is even more unlikely. While some sense of achievement can occur at the conclusion of a discussion with a subordinate, the real reinforcement usually comes later in the form of an employee's better job performance, a successful new product introduction, less absenteeism, or some other index. The reinforcement is too far removed from the stimulus to be an effective reinforcer and, therefore, has little impact.

There is no reason to believe that humans will intuitively recognize the right way when it is shown—particularly when subtle, interpersonal relationships are involved. Many times they will pick the poor way if it seems to work. This situation is often observed while conducting assessor training. In assessor training, it is common to show video tapes of how several people (similar to those who will be assessed) perform in an exercise in order to provide practice in assessment skills.

On seeing the models, the first reaction of the typical assessor-to-be is often to evaluate the participant on tape by his or her success (amount of commitment, money obtained, and so forth, depending on the simulation). A very poor participant who comes out well in the exercise in spite of the participant's lack of skill, rather than as a result of it, is usually seen as an effective model of how the situation should be handled. A great deal of time must be spent in training assessors to watch the participant's behavior, not just the results.

In applying the above observations to on-the-job situations, it can easily be seen how supervisors pick up bad habits and poor skills. A supervisor behaves poorly in handling a problem but accidentally gets positive reinforcement by a success experience. The behavior seems to work. Poor habits or skills are thus encouraged.

TRIAL-AND-ERROR LEARNING IS INEFFICIENT

The success of the many highly organized and controlled training programs has clearly shown the inefficiency of traditional trial-and-error, sink-or-swim training techniques. It is not unusual for an organization to cut training time to one tenth of its previous time by providing detailed learning objectives; by controlling the work experiences so that an individual learns the task once, not ten times; and by accurately determining who is responsible for what phase of the development of the individual. By structuring their training program, the J.C. Penney Co. was able to reduce the training needed to produce a department manager from a college trainee from four years to 13 months.

SYSTEMS CAN'T CHANGE PEOPLE

When top management wants people to change, it often issues a new form or procedure. It is hoped the system and the controls related to it will change the way people will behave. Examples of such control systems designed to make people better are employee selection systems, appraisal forms, and management by objectives (MBO) programs. The intent is to *make* people behave differently by instituting a new control. Meyer, Kay, and French[6] have shown that managers learn how to beat systems and don't change. The current reexamination of MBO systems, in light of many notable failures, provides evidence of the inability of a system to change people. Most of the programs that failed were well conceived and well introduced, but they became inoperative as soon as top management's attention was diverted to other projects. More and more it seems clear that it is not a system that shapes people, but the attention, training, and positive reinforcement that accompanies the system.

I have never seen a system that will make a good manager out of a poor one. A system or procedure may help a good manager do better by providing aids to accomplish a task more efficiently, but it is not changing skills—merely maximizing existing skills.

BOSSES ARE OFTEN POOR MODELS

The success of the interaction modeling programs[7] is a good illustration of the need to provide appropriate models of behavior. A person who has never been the recipient of a good performance-appraisal interview can hardly be expected to know how to conduct one. The same situation holds true for many other significant areas of supervisory or managerial performance.

Providing the appropriate model is increasingly recognized as a necessary component of learning. Children follow adult models in learning how to cope with the world around them, and adults continue to learn from models when faced with new situations where they have no established model. For this reason, chance assignments are probably the leading determinants of supervisory skills. If an individual has worked under good supervisors, he or she is much more likely

[6]J. J. Meyer, E. Kay, and J. R. P. French, Jr., "Split Roles in Performance Appraisal," *Harvard Business Review,* Vol. 43, No. 1 (1965), pp. 123–129.
[7]J. Moses and D. Ritchie, "Assessment Center Used to Evaluate an Interaction Modeling Program," *Assessment and Development Newsletter.* Pittsburgh: Development Dimensions, Inc. (January, 1975).

to know how to successfully handle supervisory tasks than an individual not so exposed. This explains one of the reasons why some managers seem to produce many good new managers and others none. Good managers are good models for future managers.

If we accept the idea that providing a positive model is a very important component of learning, then we must be concerned with the kinds of models we provide for new supervisors and managers. Some of an organization's most important resources are its supervisors and managers who can serve as good models. This resource must be conserved and its use carefully planned.

To be a good model, a manager does not have to be perfect. He or she needs only to be good in a subset of dimensions—as when a young supervisor with good analytical and administrative skills but poor interpersonal skills is placed with a mature manager with good interpersonal skills but, perhaps, with poor analytical skills. In this case, they can learn from each other.

SELF-STUDY ISN'T ENOUGH

While the idea of self-development is as sacred as apple pie and motherhood to most people, the fact is that self-development is extremely difficult at supervisory and low managerial levels in organizations. Most key supervisory and managerial dimensions do not lend themselves to development outside the work area. A few dimensions, such as oral presentation skill, can be improved through attendance at easily accessible programs such as Dale Carnegie or Toastmasters. A few other dimensions can be improved by attendance in college programs or by obtaining positions of responsibility in outside organizations in order to gain leadership experiences. But these examples are rare and only attack specific types of problems within the dimensions.

Very little, if any, relationship has been found between attendance in the usual self-study programs and supervisory skills evaluated in management assessment centers. This results from two factors: (1) most self-study programs concentrate on training individuals on concepts, not skills, and (2) there is usually no tie to on-the-job application in such programs.

Most managers would agree that knowledge of concepts alone does not make a good manager. The AT&T research study establishing the validity of their interaction modeling program substantiates this view. Even though great skill differences were found between the trained and untrained groups, tests of knowledge of managerial concepts showed no difference between groups.[8]

To be effective a self-study program must be tied to the job, and this is usually best achieved through the involvement of the trainee's boss in the plan. For example, it may be slightly beneficial for a supervisor to read a management book, but it is certainly much more beneficial for that supervisor to discuss the book with his or her manager and even more beneficial if the intent of the discussion is focused on an on-the-job application.

[8]W. C. Byham and J. C. Robinson, "Interaction Modeling: A New Concept in Supervisory Training," *Training and Development Journal* (February, 1976).

The above is not meant to say that the motivation of the individual to learn or to develop is unimportant. Surely this is crucial to training and development. What I am saying is that, given the needed motivation, an individual usually must have the benefit of a specific, planned program facilitated by organizational support in order to capitalize on developmental possibilities.

TRAINING ALONE WILL NOT PRODUCE BEHAVIOR CHANGE

One way to differentiate between management development and management training programs is to say that development programs consist of all on-the-job activities and training programs of off-the-job activities. Training programs usually consist of in-house classes, study materials, or programs conducted away from work. Development programs usually include all forms of on-the-job activity which increase skills and knowledge, such as working for a particularly skilled boss, being given a challenging assignment, participating on a task force, or receiving a change in responsibility. While there may be little hard research evidence showing the effectiveness of management training programs, there is *none* showing the effectiveness of management development programs. Yet I strongly believe that management development activities have the *most* potential to produce change and are *an absolutely necessary* ingredient in achieving it.

Management development activities are important in two areas: (1) as a follow-up of skills learned in training and (2) as a source of the training itself.

In the first area there is no substitute for a receptive, reinforcing environment to solidly implant new behavior provided in training programs. The new skills must be met with an accepting, rewarding environment or they will be lost.

The second area (management development activities as producers of new skills) is also very important. Transfer of training is not a problem in developmental efforts, because learning takes place on the job. Development programs provide multiple practice opportunities in, hopefully, a supportive environment, and good programs provide some method of relatively immediate feedback.

I am not saying that all developmental programs work—most do not. I am saying that on-the-job development efforts have relatively more potential to really change behavior than the necessarily short and necessarily somewhat artificial training situations. Both have their place and, for most skills, a combination is required to produce change.

In the second part of this article I will propose some systems to overcome the problems cited above and give an example of a program that has succeeded in bringing about quantifiable behavioral change.

PART II. GENERAL CONCEPTS OF DEVELOPMENT

In the first part of this article I enumerated nine reasons why many of our conventional training and development activities are ineffective in bringing about behavior change in dimensions such as leadership, initiative, planning and organization, judgment, independence, and delegation. The reasons were:

1. Practice does not make perfect.
2. Tenure does not make a good supervisor.
3. Experience is a poor teacher.
4. Learning by mistakes is a waste of time.
5. Trial and error learning is inefficient.
6. Systems can't change people.
7. Bosses are often poor models.
8. Self-study isn't enough.
9. Training alone will not produce behavior change.

Now I would like to take a positive stance and suggest some ways that meaningful behavior change can be brought about. These suggestions have arisen from Development Dimensions' experience in trying to bring about behavioral changes in employees of hundreds of organizations around the world and have come to be known around our office as Byham's Laws of Behavioral Change.

1. ADEQUATE DIAGNOSIS OF TRAINING AND DEVELOPMENT NEEDS IS VITAL

We would not think very highly of an M.D. who prescribed pills to us without asking us anything about where we felt ill or doing some kind of examination. Nor would we think very highly of an individual who tried to cure himself or herself by taking medicine on a random basis. We all would agree that before any medication is administered proper diagnosis of the problem is necessary. Yet this is what is lacking in most management training and development programs. We do not have a good fix on the individuals who are being trained; therefore, even if we have the proper tools, we cannot react appropriately. One can be the best trainer in the world; but, without insight into the needs of the people being trained, it is difficult to achieve effective training. The result of poor diagnosis is that programs very often train the wrong people about the wrong things at the wrong times.

A few years ago I ran a training program for a branch of the United States federal government. When the trainees introduced themselves at the beginning of the program, four out of 12 mentioned that they were retiring within the next three months. Naturally this intrigued me. During a coffee break, I asked my liaison within the department why these people would be trained when obviously they would have little time to apply the learning. The answer was that managers had been sent to the training program on the basis of seniority! Need was not even considered.

On the other side of the spectrum, one often sees people going through training and development programs years before they will ever use the content of the programs. Good examples are the content of many programs which teach supervisors how to be managers rather than supervisors and teach lower level managers how to be top executives rather than lower level managers. There is no opportunity to use the newly developed behavior (if behavior change is achieved) and thus the behavior is lost. One must practice behavioral skills to incorporate them. No training programs can provide enough practice during the program to permanently bring about change. One must go back to the job and use the new skills or they are lost. Skills cannot be stored for later use!

We train people in the wrong things when we train them in skills which are not related to their current jobs or expected future jobs. We put people in programs where they have development needs. Think about the individuals in your last training program and consider how many were wrongly placed. How many would have benefited from a longer program? How many could have been more highly challenged?

We train the wrong people and we waste our training money when we choose individuals who cannot benefit most from the training. An example of this is spending a great deal of money on a first level supervisor who really does not have the basic personal skills to be a first level supervisor or wasting good developmental opportunities within an organization on individuals who do not have higher career potential.

Three kinds of diagnoses are needed:

1. Identification of the specific personal skills or dimensions needed in a job
2. Identification of the specific strengths and weaknesses of trainees relative to the identified critical dimensions
3. Identification of the specific problem situations or tasks most commonly confronted; e.g., absenteeism, orienting a new employee

Many managers have difficulty identifying specific strengths and weaknesses of subordinates. They can't articulate how they want the subordinate to change. Terms like *poor attitude* and *not working hard enough* are used. They lack the opportunity to observe the individual in situations similar to those he or she would face in a higher level job. They need to be taught how to diagnose better on the job and need outside help such as that provided by the assessment center method.[9] The diagnostic information provided from an assessment center, coupled with improved performance information, is a vital first step in the chain to behavior change.

2. THE IMMEDIATE SUPERVISOR IS VITAL IN BRINGING ABOUT BEHAVIORAL CHANGE

An accepting and, hopefully, encouraging on-the-job atmosphere that offers positive reinforcement for trying out new, on-the-job behavior is vitally important to the development and/or permanent transfer of new skills to a job. This was documented as far back as 1948 when researchers at the International Harvester Co. found that, when managers held views counter to those taught to their subordinate supervisors in a training program, the supervisors returning from the training program actually ended up performing in ways opposed to those taught in the training program.[10]

---

[9]W. C. Byham, "The Assessment Center as an Aid in Management Development," *Training and Development Journal* (December, 1971), pp. 10–22.

[10]E. A. Fleishman, "Leadership Climate, Human Relations Training, and Supervisory Behavior," *Personnel Psychology,* Vol. 6 (1953), pp. 205–222.

At best, training programs can provide only a small amount of skill practice. Some provide none. In those that do provide practice, the supervisors and managers who are trained develop some confidence in their ability to effectively use the new behavior, but it is always limited. Once back on the job, this fragile confidence can easily be broken by a few remarks or actions by the immediate superior. When a newly trained supervisor returns to the job and is met with, "Okay, so you have had your vacation, now forget that behavioral science stuff and get back to work," there is little chance that the newly acquired behavior will ever be tried.

In fact, for most supervisors or managers, a neutral environment is not encouraging enough. They return from training with deep doubts. They must be actively encouraged in trying out new behaviors. Possible applications must be pointed out and the subordinate encouraged to use the new skill. For example, a manager might discuss a performance problem involving one of a subordinate supervisor's employees and may suggest the problem as a good application of the newly learned skill.

Negative sanctions associated with failure must be lessened. Experimentation must be encouraged. A manager must let the subordinate supervisor know that perfect use of the new skills is not expected from the beginning, but that in the long run the new methods or techniques will produce positive results.

An even more important role of the immediate supervisor is to reinforce positive behavior when it occurs. The mere use of a new skill or method of dealing with subordinates may not result in sufficient, immediate reinforcement to encourage the supervisor or manager to continue using the skill or method. Reinforcement must come from the boss, and it must be consistent and meaningful.

Only a situation where a supervisor or manager will feel comfortable trying out new skills will allow the new skills to be practiced. During these trials, supervisory behavior must be shaped through positive reinforcement. Often the reinforcement must, at the beginning, encourage less than perfect application of the skills and become more demanding with time. A breakdown anywhere in this sequence prevents change from coming about.

3. MANAGERS MUST BE PROVIDED WITH SUGGESTIONS ON WHAT TO DO TO DEVELOP SUBORDINATES

Managers left to their own devices without some kind of aid are generally very poor in thinking up responses to developmental needs. They may have every motivation in the world to help their subordinates; but aside from commitments to work with the individual, they just don't know what to do.

Creating a list of developmental actions is difficult. What would you prescribe for a person found low on the dimension *judgment, initiative,* or *flexibility?*

We have typically found that supervisors without some form of outside stimulation find it extremely difficult to come up with developmental responses, except for some of the easy dimensions, such as oral communications.

This finding will not surprise many people who are involved in supervisory and management development, but the nature of the assessment center process particularly drives the insight home. By stating a few standard managerial truisms, a manager can sound like he or she knows a good bit about the development of subordinates. But, when faced with the development of specific dimensions, a lack of creativity and originality often shows up. This lack of ideas partially comes from a lack of prior experience with developmental activities, or even the knowledge that certain activities exist.

Another difficulty line managers have in prescribing training and developmental actions results from their lack of total organizational insight; that is, they may not know what is going on in various parts of the organization which would allow a subordinate to get certain experiences. Of course, there are many exceptions to this situation but, in general, we find that supervisors and managers must be aided in suggesting developmental responses.

4. MANAGERS MUST BE TRAINED IN HOW TO DEVELOP SUBORDINATES

Just because a manager knows *what* to do to develop subordinates does not mean that the manager knows *how* to do it.

Just because a person is a manager, there is no reason to think that he or she necessarily is a good teacher or developer. Yet, as noted above, many developmental suggestions require managers to assume this role. Like any other human characteristic, the ability to effectively play the additional roles of tutor or developer is probably normally distributed in the population and the skill seems to be somewhat independent of other achievements of management; that is, an excellent manager in terms of productivity and other characteristics may be either good or poor in the development of subordinates, and, similarly, some managers who are not as good on productivity measures may be excellent at developing their subordinates.

The issues are those of time devoted to the task, the ability to communicate, the ability to articulate concepts and underlying premises, the ability to explain the *why* behind actions and programs, the ability to set up learning situations where the individual will be stretched, the ability to provide positive reinforcement, and the ability to maintain a person's ego during critical portions of the learning curve. These tasks are not easy, and one should not be depressed or disappointed that everyone cannot handle them equally well.

An organization cannot totally rely on placement to put individuals under managers with high skills for developing subordinates. There are just not that many "natural trainers" available in most organizations. Also, key developmental slots may be supervised by people who do not naturally have training skills. A logical response is to train managers in training and development techniques.

5. HIGHER MANAGEMENT MUST BE INVOLVED

Because of the difficulties cited above, I have come to the conclusion that effective development planning must involve, and be the final responsibility of, not the immediate supervisor of the individual being developed, but of the *manager* of the supervisor. This second level manager usually has a much more positive attitude toward employee development. He or she is shielded from the immediate negative effects that might result from implementation of major developmental recommendations, such as the movement of an individual to another department or a major reassignment of work. Yet he or she benefits from having strong backups for positions. The higher level manager wants to be able to replace subordinate managers with good people as needed. The second level manager has a better perspective of total organizational needs and thus sees the greater organizational good that can come from a sound development program.

Let me expand on a few of the reasons immediate supervisors don't develop their subordinates:

1. The lack of on-the-job development which is often observed must partially be due to a lack of motivation on the part of many supervisors to develop their subordinates. This motivation may be recognized or not recognized by the supervisor. There are many reasons why a supervisor does not gain and may actually lose by developing subordinates. Development actions may cause the loss of a valued, highly trained individual, one upon whom the boss leans a great deal. The loss of this individual may trigger a great deal of effort in recruiting and training a replacement and may cause, initially, the boss to step in and resume many areas of activity which had been successfully delegated to the individual.

    Even if an employee is to stay in a department, the fact that he or she may be given special assignments or projects could interfere with productivity. In most organizations, managers are rewarded for performance as measured by productivity, number of rejects, and output of reports—not for the development of their subordinates. Most organizations negatively reinforce developmental activities with their actions, while at the same time lauding them in training programs and top management speeches.

2. Effective development of subordinates takes a great deal of time. Most effective developmental responses require a supervisor to spend a considerable amount of time working with the individual, or critiquing his or her work. For example, it might be suggested that an individual should develop a presentation for a management meeting to broaden his or her horizons in that area and to develop presentation, planning, or other skills. Such a suggestion is usually followed by the suggestion that the plan then be discussed with the person's boss. Such activities are nice, but they take time.

3. Immediate supervisors may not recognize or accept the need for development. If a supervisor thinks a subordinate is strong in all areas, there is little hope that he or she will commit much energy to development. Some supervisors are blinded to the faults or developmental needs of subordinates by good performance in some areas (positive halo) or by an exaggerated fraternal feeling about "their" people.

    A common example of the former is the attitude of some managers that goal achievement is all that counts; the method of achieving a goal is unimportant. These managers do not recognize that even higher attainment may be possible or that a closer examination of the methods applied by the individual in achieving goals might disclose practices that may result in some long-term negative effects. The manager who increases productivity in each unit managed by making severe staff cuts often gets credit for the savings and gets promoted prior to the recognition of the personnel problems that later develop. A salesperson who overpromises to get sales may appear great for a short period of time.

Some research evidence that illustrates management's often inaccurate knowledge of on-the-job behavior comes from the validity study of the AT&T salespersons' assessment center.[11] In that study, a sales effectiveness criterion was carefully developed using judgments of experts who went with the salespeople on calls. This criterion correlated highly with assessment center predictions, but not at all with ratings made by the salespeople's own supervisors. If one accepts the AT&T criterion as accurate (as I do), then one must conclude that the supervisors didn't have a very accurate fix on the behavior and, hence, the development needs of their subordinates.

A lack of accurate observation or objectivity about subordinates is frequently highlighted when a supervisor receives an assessment center report about a subordinate. Overly protective supervisors, or supervisors blinded by a positive halo, will often reject the results and take no developmental action. While no one connected with the use of the assessment center method would suggest that the results be accepted blindly, they should be given some credence. The usual suggestion when assessment center data and job observation data are in conflict is to recheck the job observation data. This can be done by closer observation of performance (not results) or by setting up special situations where a particular dimension might be observed. If the supervisor's judgments are substantiated, they should be followed. Many supervisors will not take the necessary steps to check behavior when faced with negative assessment center results.

4. A few managers are just plain selfish. They don't see what is in it for them, and they are not willing to put out the extra effort. Few managers start out in this category, but their behavior changes as they respond to the organization's negative reinforcement of training activities.

Second level managers must be involved to overcome many of the problems cited above and for several other reasons:

1. Higher level management can create an environment for development by rewarding subordinate supervisors or managers for their contribution toward employee development. Development time can be rewarded and compensated for on an equal status with production time.

2. Higher level management can lessen the negative impact of developmental responses. He or she has the authority to promise the supervisor a skilled person from another department to take the place of the individual who might be leaving for developmental reasons to actually lessen the production requirements of the department in relation to the perceived impact of the personnel change, or to make certain development responsibilities a specific objective for that supervisor for the next year.

3. Higher level management can help the immediate supervisor recognize and accept the need for development. The supervisor can be encouraged to go out and observe behavior in the field.

[11]D. W. Bray, and R. J. Campbell, "Selection of Salesmen by Means of an Assessment Center," *Journal of Applied Psychology,* Vol. 52 (1968), pp. 36–41.

4. Higher level management can actively encourage subordinate managers to develop their subordinates by setting goals and appropriate management controls.

5. Higher level management has the organizational authority to put an individual on a special assignment or task force. This is not usually a prerogative of the immediate supervisor, except when you are dealing with very high levels in the organization.

6. Higher level management feels no threat from the individual, while an immediate supervisor may feel some sense of competition in moving the individual along. There may be a situation where the person might look better than the supervisor by moving up the ladder faster. There is, in any organization, the feeling by some managers that subordinates should suffer as much as they did in order to get to their level in the organization. A higher level manager, by virtue of his or her position, can be more tolerant of "fast movers" and feel less threatened.

7. Higher level management can move individuals so that they will be exposed to better models. The pairing of a boss and subordinate in most organizations is very much a chance occurrence. Usually little attempt is made to match a subordinate to a boss in terms of working style, personal skills, and specialized knowledge. Few organizations attempt to make assignments based on the ability of the manager to be an effective model for a subordinate. Yet the notion of a manager being a model for his subordinate is a major tenet underlying many developmental suggestions. Only a higher level manager can take care of this development need.

6. THE INDIVIDUAL'S NEEDS MUST BE CONSIDERED

The forgotten person in many development-planning decisions is the individual being developed. Does he or she really want to advance? If advancement is desired, what problems will moving cause? Are there unique timing constraints, such as a child who wants to finish high school in the same school or a spouse in the middle of professional training?

Supervisors may think they know this information, but many times they do not. One of the main reasons for including background interviews in assessment centers for first level supervisors is to weed out participants who do not want to be supervisors. Usually one is found out of every 24 people assessed. Why was the person sent? The supervisor never asked the participant. He or she assumed interest or offered attendance in a way that the participant couldn't tactfully turn down. Highly motivated supervisors project their needs and values on outstanding subordinates and assume that the subordinate wants advancement on the organization's terms.

At higher levels there are fewer examples of individuals who, flat out, don't want to be advanced, but many put restrictions on the type of positions in which they would be interested, and on what they will personally go through, or put their families through, to get advanced. These restrictions should be fully understood by higher level management prior to developmental planning.

7. DEVELOPMENT PLANS MUST BE COMMITTED TO WRITING

Managers have many pulls on their time, energy, and attention. While they may be committed to a development plan at the time it is conceived, follow-through action on the plan may falter as time passes. This is particularly true if a job shift is called for.

Employee development plans are as important as profit plans and, like profit plans, should be committed to writing. Unless they are written out and signed by all the managers concerned, no effective follow-up activity can take place.

8. A FOLLOW-UP PROCEDURE MUST BE INSTITUTED

Like most other management programs, an employee development program will collapse unless constantly stimulated. Managers may have the best intentions in the world, but the exigencies of the organization, conflicting pressures, and good old-fashioned procrastination will often distract managers from these good intentions. To be effective, an organization must build into its procedures a follow-up system which monitors the progress of individuals toward the designated development goals and stimulates managers to take the actions to which they are committed.

9. CHANGE IS DIFFICULT AND ONLY RESULTS FROM A MASSIVE, PINPOINTED, COORDINATED EFFORT

Training large numbers of individuals with diverse needs at the same time assures that very few will have their specific needs met. It also assures that little time will be available for individual skill practice and confidence acquisition. Providing training on multiple subjects in one program keeps any one subject from being covered in sufficient depth to result in behavioral change. One or two specific training goals must be defined and all training and development resources must be aimed at those goals.

10. CHEAP, EASY PROGRAMS ARE A WASTE OF TIME

The two old sayings that you can't get something for nothing and a sucker is born every minute are both true when it comes to training programs. Shortening programs or running them in situations where the trainees have their minds on other matters results in a diminished end result. Buying a program that doesn't take managers off the job or can be tacked on at the end of a field management meeting almost assures failure.

There simply is no easy way, no magic elixir, no baptismal font in which managers can be immersed and come up trained. Yet organizations buy programs that overpromise and have no proven effectiveness—often because a program is efficient, i.e., it fits into the time period they have set aside for training.

All these laws can be followed and do result in behavioral change. The proven success of interaction management training programs in bringing about behavioral change is proof that behavior can be changed through a combination of training and development.

BIBLIOGRAPHY, CHAPTER 15

Alhander, G. G. "Planning Management Training for Organizational Development." *Personnel Journal,* Vol. 53, No. 1 (1974), pp. 15-25.

Bailey, Robert E., and Barry T. Jensen. "The Troublesome Transition from Scientist to Manager." *Personnel,* Vol. 42, No. 5 (September-October, 1965), pp. 49-55.

Crotty, P. T. "Continuing Education and the Experienced Manager." *California Management Review,* Vol. 17, No. 1 (1974), pp. 108-123.

Dalton, Dan R., and Idalene F. Kesner. "Inside/Outside Succession and Organizational Size: The Pragmatics of Executive Replacement." *The Academy of Management Journal,* Vol. 26, No. 4 (December, 1983), pp. 736-741.

DeVries, M. F. R. K. "Managers Can Drive Their Subordinates Mad." *Harvard Business Review,* Vol. 57, No. 4 (July-August, 1979), pp. 125-134.

Dill, William R., Wallace B. S. Crowston, and Edwing J. Elton. "Strategies for Self-Education." *Harvard Business Review,* Vol. 43, No. 6 (November-December, 1965), pp. 119-130.

DuBrin, Andrew J. "Management Development: Education, Training or Behavioral Change." *Personnel,* Vol. 49, No. 12 (December, 1970), pp. 1002-1008.

Granick, D., "Why Managers Perform Differently in Different Countries." *Challenge,* Vol. 17, No. 3 (1974), pp. 27-34.

Hand, Herbert, M. D. Richards, and J. W. Slocum, Jr. "Organizational Climate and the Effectiveness of a Human Relations Training Program." *Academy of Management Journal,* Vol. 16, No. 2 (1974), pp. 185-195.

Hein, John. "What Should I Do with My Life? (Or What Should I Have Done with It?)." *Across the Board,* Vol. 19, No. 7, pp. 17-24.

Hunsaker, Phillip L., W. C. Mudgett, and B. E. Wynne. "Assessing and Developing Administrators for Turbulent Environments." *Administration and Society,* Vol. 7, No. 3 (November, 1975), pp. 312-327.

Hunt, David Marshall, and Carol Michael. "Mentorship: A Career Training and Development Tool." *Academy of Management Review,* Vol. 8, No. 3 (1983), pp. 475-485.

Pitts, Robert A. "Unshackle Your Comers." *Harvard Business Review,* Vol. 55, No. 3 (1977), pp. 127-136.

Schmuckler, E. "Management Development: A Joint Venture." *Personnel Journal,* Vol. 55, No. 1 (1976), pp. 30-32.

Shaffer, Paul L. "Evaluation of a Management Development Methodology." *Proceedings of Academy of Management Meetings* (August, 1976), pp. 53-57.

Shaw, Malcolm E., and P. Rutledge. "Assertiveness Training for Managers." *Training and Development Journal,* Vol. 30, No. 9 (September, 1976), pp. 8-14.

Sweet, James. "How Manpower Development Can Support Your Strategic Plan." *Journal of Business Strategy,* Vol. 2, No. 1 (Summer, 1981).

Truskie, Stanley D. "Getting the Most from Management Development Programs." *Personnel Journal* (January, 1982), pp. 66-68.

Waters, James A. "Managerial Skill Development." *Academy of Management Review,* Vol. 5, No. 3 (1980), pp. 449-453.